Territoriality, Citizenship and Peacebuilding

Perspectives on Challenges to Peace in Africa

Published by
Adonis & Abbey Publishers Ltd
United Kingdom
P.O. Box 43418
London
SE11 4XZ
http://www.adonis-abbey.com

Nigeria:
No. 3, Akanu Ibiam Str
Asokoro,
P.O. Box 1056, Abuja.

Year of Publication 2013

British Library Cataloguing-in-Publication Data
A catalogue record for this book is available from the British Library

ISBN: 9781909112261

Territoriality, Citizenship and Peacebuilding
Perspectives on Challenges to Peace in Africa

Kelechi A. Kalu, Ufo Okeke Uzodike, David Kraybill & John Moolakkattu

Adonis & Abbey
Publishers Ltd

TABLE OF CONTENT

INTRODUCTION

PART I -- HISTORICAL PERSPECTIVES

PART II -- CONCEPTUAL AND EMPIRICAL ISSUES

PART III -- CROSS-BORDER ISSUES

PART IV -- INTRA-NATIONAL DISPARITIES, NATURAL RESOURCES AND LAND

Tables

Figures

Appendices

Preface and Acknowledgements

This book arises out of the view that territorial endowments and group identities are important elements in conflict within and between nation states in Africa. It is our contention that peacebuilding efforts must take those two factors into account in building institutions that make strengths out of geographical and group differences rather than permitting those two factors to lead to an erosion of national unity and destruction of civil society.

Territorial endowments, both natural and man-made, affect the balance of power, influence, and wealth among sub-national areas of a nation. The spatial diversity that characterizes territory can be a source of economic growth through increasing regional specialization, or it can lead to contested territorial claims over the resources of the state; and attempts to redefine territorial boundaries are even worse than contested territorial claims.

Group identity, which includes ethnicity but goes beyond it, can become a basis of strong communities of persons with shared values. But on the other hand, it can lead to contested claims among groups in which the rights of citizenship of some are partially or wholly denied.

In 2008, the Center for African Studies at The Ohio State University (Ohio State) submitted a proposal to the Mershon Center for International Security Studies for a conference on "Territorial Origins of African Civil Wars and Institutions for Addressing Territorial Grievances." The proposal was funded and the conference was held January 29-30, 2010 at the University of Kwa Zulu Natal (UKZN) in Pietermaritzburg, South Africa. The conference was jointly organized by the Center for African Studies at Ohio State and the School of Politics at UKZN. The papers presented at the conference included commissioned requests as well as contributions in response to an open call.

The conference created synergies that gave shape to ideas that expanded the original vision of the conference. A number of the papers presented at the UKZN conference went beyond the relationship of territories to the nation state, addressing ways in which the territorial origin of social and cultural groups serves to exclude some individuals from the full rights of citizenship and to give some individuals special rights. This view of territoriality, expanded to

xi

encompass both state-territory relations and state-individual relations, is reflected in the papers presented in this volume.

Financial, material, logistical and research resources for this project were made possible through the support of institutions and individuals that invested in our project from which Territoriality, Citizenship and Peacebuilding emerged. The Mershon Center for International Security Studies at Ohio State played a crucial role through a conference grant awarded to Professor Dave Kraybill (Ohio State) for the project; and the School of Politics at the University of Kwazulu-Natal, Pietermaritzburg, South Africa provided the venue and logistical support for the conference venue that brought researchers/contributors together in January 2010 in Pietermaritzburg.

Various individuals in these institutions supported our project. We acknowledge the financial assistance provided by Professor Nelson Ijumba and the Research Office of the University of KwaZulu-Natal to support the conference. The organizational support provided by many colleagues and postgraduate students, and the administrative assistance provided by Ms. Perdita Peters and Ms. Sisanda Vapi (UKZN) and Ms. Melinda Bogarty (Ohio State) are greatly appreciated. The Conflict Transformation and Peace Studies Programme at UKZN are particularly grateful for the congenial collaborative relationship with the Center for African Studies at The Ohio State University. We would like to express our thanks and appreciation to Professor Richard K. Herrmann, the former Director of the Mershon Center, for his support for and encouragement of the project. We thank the staff of the Mershon Center, especially Ms. Ann Powers and Mr. Kyle McCray for their many contributions to the success of the project. In addition, several individuals associated with The Ohio State University, Anthonia Kalu, Ruthmarie Mitsch, and Gifty Ako-Adounvo read all or some of the chapters in this book for which we gratefully acknowledge their assistance.

The staff at the Center for African Studies at The Ohio State University worked tirelessly to make the conference successful; and for that, we thank Ms. Darby O'Donnell and Ms. Laura Joseph for a well-managed conference. We are also grateful to Laura and Darby for assisting us in the research and preparation of this volume. We thank everyone, including the student assistants, for the many contributions they made to the success of the conference that resulted in the current book.

Finally, we would like to express our appreciation to the contributors for participating in the project. We thank the authors of commissioned papers for researching and writing their papers for the conference, and for contributing to the various lively discussions and exchanges at the conference. We also greatly appreciate the time and effort the contributors invested in writing their papers and incorporating various comments from reviewers and editors on their chapters, which have greatly improved the quality of the chapters and overall strength of the book.

David Kraybill
Morogoro, Tanzania

Kelechi A. Kalu
Columbus, OH, USA

Ufo Okeke Uzodike
Pietermaritzburg, South Africa

John Moolakkattu
Kottayam, Kerala, India

INTRODUCTION

CHAPTER 1

Territorial Origins of African Civil Conflicts: Space, Territoriality, and Institutions

Kelechi A. Kalu, David Kraybill and Laura Joseph

I. Introduction: Issues and Arguments

In early 2010, the Center for African Studies at The Ohio State University and the School of Politics at the University of Kwazulu-Natal (UKZN) jointly organised and held a conference at UKZN's Pietermaritzburg campus. That conference on *Territorial Origins of African Civil Conflicts* was funded by The Ohio State University's Mershon Center for International Security Studies. This book is the result of that conference, which focused on understanding and explaining the sources of territorial origins of African civil conflicts and proffering suggestions for mitigating territorially induced conflicts in Africa.

Civil conflicts in Africa are constant and conceptually problematic. These conflicts range from a few interstate wars, several intrastate conflicts characterized by secessionist movements, irredentism, coups and countercoups, genocide, and wars of liberation to resource-based wars. Although some of the civil conflicts, such as those in the DRC, Northern Uganda, Sudan, and Somalia, are well known, others, like the civil conflicts in Morocco/Western Sahara, Senegal/Casamance, and Nigeria/Jos Plateau and Niger Delta and the several-decades-long conflict involving the Karamajong of Uganda with the Pokot of Kenya over grazing land in the Kenya-Uganda border, are less known. Thus, understanding territorial origins of African civil conflicts based on existing empirical measures that define *war* as those involving at least 1,000 battle deaths will make nonsense of the millions of people's lives that have been wasted in various dimensions of territorially induced conflicts/wars in Africa. Many of these conflicts defy empirical measures but have a persistent impact on the capacity of states to function and of citizens to live normal lives, as the cases of those trapped in ongoing conflicts in the Casamance region of

Senegal, Western Sahara against Morocco, and Northern Uganda demonstrate.

Indeed, as Oliver Furley and Roy May (2006: 3) argue, based on the use of 1,000 battle-related deaths as a definition of war, only three wars-Somalia against Ethiopia (1977-1978), Ethiopia against Eritrea (1998-2002), and Uganda against Tanzania (1978-1979)-qualify as interstate wars in Africa. Thus, while scholarly definitions of interstate conflicts reflect a bias toward major state conflicts whose wars largely reflect territorial battles are not helpful in understanding persistent conflicts in Africa, issues of intrastate wars and opportunistic wars for resource control rather than for the soul of the state continue unabated. As Carl von Clausewitz states, 'war has a chameleon-like character'; it changes its color to a degree in each case, but also has a 'remarkable trinity' of irrational action, rational action and chance' (Quoted in Furley and May 2006: 4). We contend that in the case of Africa, most conflicts are rationally rooted in the territorial contestations that started with the Berlin Conference and remain ineffectively mediated by transparent governance institutions and processes that account for the needs and values of the citizens.

The contemporary history of the African continent is one of conflicts rooted in European states' imposition of arbitrary and illogical boundaries on various nations and ethnonationalities according to European interests and imaginations. While the exercise at the Berlin Conference in 1884-1885 secured exploitation opportunities for Europeans on the continent of Africa without resorting to war with each other, it laid the foundation for new, persistent, and varied forms of conflicts in Africa. Analytically, the varied causes of conflicts in the continent's complexly structured social formations are seen in ethnic terms and include struggles for economic/environmental resources, poor institutions of governance, and issues of identities such as religion, language, and racial differences. The core issue addressed in this volume is how to understand and explain the structural and analytical reasons African civil conflicts have become persistent, especially since the end of the Cold War. For example, the Libyan context of the Arab Spring reveals the dirty politics of racism instrumentalised by the former Gaddafi regime and later by the insurgent 'revolutionaries' and their foreign handlers. The racial dimensions of civil conflicts in Africa range from the apartheid era of exclusionary politics and violence on the basis of race to its variants in the Sudan, Egypt, Mauritania, and several other Arab-dominated states in the continent.

Understanding the structural causes of these conflicts requires in-depth examination of different regions and states. This approach is important because it enables scholars to move away from the idea of Africa as one country and effectively study the civil wars, territorial disagreements, economic, political, and/or ideological conflicts that have gone on far longer in some areas than others in different African countries. Specifically, given poor infrastructure across the sub-Sahara African region and relevant governments' inattention to logistical issues of national development, the likelihood that any given country will be involved in a civil war in Africa is much higher than the likelihood that it will be involved in an international war. Thus far, most of the countries in that region do not have the capacity to wage effective internal or external wars without some form of external intervention either through arms supplies and or hiring of mercenaries and equipment. Indeed, except for the intervention of six nations (Rwanda, Uganda, Angola, Zimbabwe, and Sudan) in the DRC in 1996, empire-imposed arbitrary boundaries in Africa have been quite resilient-with only two successful challenges-in Ethiopia and the resulting independence for Eritrea and in Sudan with the result of political independence for Southern Sudan in 2011.

Based on the foregoing, our project is founded upon a core assumption that Africa's civil conflicts erupt largely because of the nature of state formation in the continent and the slow efforts at nation-building across the continent. Against this backdrop, issues of territoriality, climate change, ethnicity, ideological incongruities, institutional problems, nature of postcolonial state, unreformed governance and economic structures, corruption, and several variables are explored as explanations for the persistent instances of civil conflicts in sub-Saharan Africa. Also, we contend that noticeable inequity in access to land and the resources it provides-the old question of citizenship vs. indigeneity-in most instances intensifies the class relationship evident in subnational regional disparities in many African countries that erupt in armed conflicts. Significant core explanations for the persistent eruption of civil conflicts in Africa

17

reside in the unresolved issues of Africa's redesigned geographic spaces.

II. Territoriality, Space and Civil Conflicts in Africa

Theoretically, in examining the role territory plays in the formation of nationalist thought, Jan Penrose argues that part of our understanding of the connection between territory and nationalism should be based on how the concept of *space* is defined and territorially contextualized in the real world. He conceptualizes *space* as "structures of the real world... [that result from]...slow processes of long duration" (Penrose 2002: 278) as perceived, experienced, and interpreted by human beings. According to Penrose:

> ...Space holds two sources of latent power for human beings. First, it comprises the substance that is fundamental to human life on this planet. Through its constitution of land, water and atmosphere, space encompasses the basic prerequisites of human survival: the food that we eat, the water that we drink, the air that we breathe and the resources for protecting ourselves. The existence of these things reflects the material dimension of space, but the deployment of these qualities (for example, the identification of what constitutes food and its procurement) is relational. This relationship between space and human life in any form means that space is a source of latent material power: the power to sustain human life. Second, space is a source of latent emotional power. When the substantive qualities of space (for example, its physical features) are filtered through human experiences of time and process (the relational dimension of space) they have the capacity to invoke or release an emotional response. For example, where space is perceived as beautiful it moves us; where it is perceived as threatening it frightens us; where it is perceived as powerful we respect it. (278-79)

Penrose also argues that 'space is present whether anyone knows about it or not, but space only becomes a place when it acquires a "perceptual unity"...and...becomes a territory when it is delimited in some way' (279). Thus, "territories are the product of human agency and this agency is usually referred to as 'territoriality" (Ibid). And in debunking the inevitability of human-nature-based conflict deterministic theses on territoriality, Penrose agrees with Robert Sack that territoriality is not an instinctive emergence of space in nature, but a deliberate geographic strategy for controlling space and people. In this context, 'territoriality…[is] the attempt by an individual or group to affect, influence or control people, phenomena and relationships by delimiting and asserting control over a geographic area…called a territory' (quoted in Penrose 2002: 279). And ultimately, 'the *control* of space is an extremely potent component of power relations… [As] there is power in the actual *creation* of territories because the application of territoriality reflects the needs and values of those who design and maintain them' (Penrose 2002: 279-80).

Strategically, Great Britain, Austria-Hungary, Belgium, Denmark, France, Germany, Italy, the Netherlands, Portugal, Russia, Spain, Sweden and Norway, and Turkey (the Ottoman Empire) met in Berlin, Germany in 1884 to discuss, map out, and impose European will on Africa's peoples and its geography. The Berlin Conference had no African representative and therefore the notion of territory and territoriality that emerged from that conference primarily reflects European states' and their peoples' latent power characterized by violence against Africans. In the so-called *General Act of the Berlin Conference on West Africa*, which is the formal title of the treaty, the signatories vowed 'in the name of God almighty', to 'obviate the misunderstanding and disputes which might in future arise from new acts of occupation (prises de possession) on the coast of Africa' (*The Berlin Act*). With potential conflicts between European powers over Africa averted, France, Britain, Belgium, Germany, and other European states took their 'possession' and in the wake, temporarily buried the latent power of relevant indigenous ethnonationalities but hardly the emotional powers of those peoples. In the interim, with sovereignty over African spaces and territories, Europeans imposed their values on Africa; one of the legacies of those values is violent repression of 'others', especially in the context of agitations for control of territorially based scarce resources. Indeed, while European states' sovereign control allowed them to act in Africa with impunity in their various territories, other parties and signatories to the Berlin Conference simply exercised "neutrality" per Article X of the Act, inter alia:

> In order to give a new guarantee of security to trade and industry, and to encourage the maintenance of peace…the High Signatory Parties to the present Act, and those who shall hereafter adopt it, bind themselves to respect the neutrality of the territories, or portions of territories, belonging

to the said countries...so long as the Powers which exercise or shall
exercise the rights of sovereignty or Protectorate over those territories...
shall fulfil [sic] the duties which neutrality requires. (*The Berlin Act*)

Unfortunately, the peace between Europeans, secured by their
partition of Africa, did not last: two major wars over economic
resources, ideology, identity, and territory were to later engulf the
European landscape and weaken the capacity of these states to hold on
to their control of the African States. The consequence was
decolonisation following the end of the Second World War in 1945.
But while the resolution of European wars resulted in the political
independence for Africans, the new custodians of postcolonial states in
Africa left the colonial state and its inherent repressive institutions
intact. Eventually, the unreformed state boundaries, territories, and
spaces yielded battles over issues of territoriality across the continent.
Thus, emotional power derived from memories of 'our space' by many
ethnonationalities, the imposed arbitrary boundaries that mapped out
cartographically problematic lines that forced nations to co-exist with
each other as multi-ethnic,-religious, and-nationalities in megacities
remain in Africa-contested and therefore sources of conflicts.
Analogously, African States are like megacities whose residents come
from all walks of life, nationalities, regions, religions, and other forms
of identifications without productive considerations for community,
which according to Odia Ofeimum,

> ...Is a poetics linked to origins, size, and geography, defined by its parts
> rather than by a fraction of it...For the citiness of a city lies in the
> absorption of its many parts into a common whirlpool. Its core experience
> intimates a civis: a place of civilization where people who may not have the
> same occupation, or accept the same ancestors, and people who may not
> bow to the same deity, can live within a common frame of politics, thus
> entrenching the possibility of shared decision-making as a permanent way
> of life. The city is, in this sense, an ever-ready challenge. (2001:12)

The challenge of citiness for African States is how to construct a
narrative of community, unified by the 'perceptual unity' (Penrose,
279) of space and territory. Overcoming such a challenge requires
transforming the colonial and postcolonial territory in ways that
impose new and uplifting narratives in the space whose memory is of
state violence and abjection of the masses and is emptied of relevant

meaning to the contemporary occupants. Thus, the challenge for postcolonial states in Africa includes finding ways to build viable nations within the states where the citizens can all share in their civic responsibilities with pride and in peace. These challenges, some of which are addressed in the section of the book on postconflict and peacebuilding by necessity require that Africans take control of relevant spaces through nation-building efforts and institutional designs that clearly delineate the nature of power and authority relations such that territoriality in Africa truly reflects 'the needs and values' of citizens in various states and communities, designed and maintained according to their memories of the past and visions for the future.

III. Overview of the Book

The book examines and explains some identified sources of unresolved issues of territoriality and their connections to political violence and sociopolitical and cultural tensions across sub-Saharan Africa. It also offers suggestions on ways scholarly research and policies could help mediate if not mitigate future territorially based conflicts in Africa. For example, within the context of citizenship vs. indigeneity, the book explores the intersections between unresolved issues of territoriality, land ownership, and spates of political violence in various states and regions across sub-Saharan Africa. In some chapters (see for example Agbese, Mbaku, Mhlanga, and Kalu), closer attention is paid to the nature of national policies or lack thereof that aim to mitigate the tensions that arise from uneven national development and its connections to patterns of civil conflicts in seemingly stable states evidenced in the case of Senegal and the Casamance conflict. This is important because the link between uneven national development and armed conflict is scantily explored in the literature, even as it remains a significant issue across sub-Sahara African States. For example, Angola, Burundi, Chad, Côte d'Ivoire, Democratic Republic of Congo, Kenya, Liberia, Nigeria, Rwanda, Sierra Leone, Somalia, Sudan, Uganda, and Zimbabwe have all recently experienced civil wars or armed civil unrest, and all these countries are states with uneven national development.

21

In each of these countries, civil conflict is a territorial phenomenon: that is, armed conflict has arisen as part of the struggle over natural resources concentrated in particular regions or as a result of regional grievances regarding central government decisions, often involving resources for development and these resources are invariably land-based. At the 'conclusion' of each conflict, the general tendency has been for the state in question to establish reconstruction plans aimed at redressing economic deficiencies in the region where the civil conflict occurred. However, reconstruction plans generally do not address regional inequities in other regions where 'the next civil war' might occur. In other words, there have been no serious efforts to deal with the issue of territoriality, for example through efficient institutions of property rights and active citizenship, as mitigating strategies against future territorially based conflicts. There is ample evidence that in conflict-ridden and postconflict African countries, institutions for addressing interregional inequality may be a viable way to reverse political and economic marginalization, and ultimately, perhaps, to reduce social unrest and armed conflict (Kieh and Mukenge 2002). Such an institution has to reflect the values and needs of the people; be comprehensively national; and be perceived to be legitimate from the perspective of the citizens. An institution such as a nationally ratified constitution that privileges citizenship over other primordial identities is more likely to anchor the process and mechanisms for solving problems of territorial sources of conflicts before they erupt.

Uneven economic development affects a state's national security as such territories become vulnerable for economic and criminal-related nonstate and sometimes state actors. Also, an economically lagging region in a country, e.g., Northern Nigeria as well as the Niger Delta region, may serve as a staging ground for an insurgent group from another region of the country or from outside of the state that aims to target the national government or communities in the country for nonpeaceful purposes. As most of these civil conflicts are land-based, a rebel or insurgent activity on international borders can quickly escalate into civil conflicts that transcend state boundaries. For example, in the Great Lakes region of Africa, Rwanda and Uganda each attempted to snuff out rebel groups in economically lagging regions just across their borders in the Democratic Republic of Congo;

22

consequently, Rwanda and Uganda both became involved in the ongoing civil unrest in Congo. In recent decades, cross-border spillovers of rebel activity have also occurred in Sudan and Chad, Somalia and Ethiopia, Eritrea and Ethiopia, Liberia and Côte d'Ivoire, Chad and Cameroun, Angola and Zaire (now Democratic Republic of Congo), and Mozambique and South Africa. In each of these cases, various dimensions of citizens' physical security as well as the states' national security became vulnerable.

A long-standing theory of political and social unrest is that people rebel because of relative deprivation (Gurr 1970). An alternative theory is that rebels are motivated by personal or group gain. Collier and Hoeffler (2004) test these two explanations for civil war: grievance and greed. Using data from a large number of countries over several decades, they reject the grievance hypothesis in favour of the greed hypothesis. In contrast, Østby (2007) argues that horizon inequalities-inequalities among identity groups--have a greater effect on conflict than individual inequalities. Using data from 55 developing countries, including a number of African countries, she finds a statistically significant and positive relationship between inequality and conflict; that is, high levels of inequality are associated with high levels of conflict. Using data from national demographic and health surveys, Østby measures inequality as disparity in socioeconomic well-being. The author also developed estimates of inequality for three identity groups: ethnic, religious, and regional. She concludes that regional inequality has a stronger relationship with civil war than does ethnic or religious group inequality. In other words, the evidence suggests plausible explanatory strength for the relationship between civil conflicts and territorial claims that are often argued away as identity politics.

Regional inequalities may arise from differences in natural resources endowments but may also arise from differences in livelihood opportunities, allocation of central government resources, or ethnic and language discrimination. In Africa, regional differences often appear to have an ethnic dimension, though ethnic tension may be more a consequence than a cause of civil war. According to Nafziger and Auvinen (2002: 159): 'Ethnicity, when implicated in humanitarian emergencies, is created, manifested, combined, and reconstituted in struggles to share benefits from modernization and

23

self-government but is not a source of these struggles.' And as Kalu (2001) has argued, there is nothing inherently conflictual about ethnicity. Instead, when entrepreneurs instrumentalise ethnicity for political, economic, religious, and racial outcomes, ethnicity becomes manifest as part of territorial issues in African conflicts.

Beyond its impact on civil war, inequality matters because of its effect on economic growth. Alesina and Perotti argue that inequality affects political stability, which in turn affects investment. They found support for this hypothesis in a study of 71 countries, including 22 in Africa, over the period 1960-1985. Redressing regional economic inequalities may require fiscal redistribution, implying taxation of more favoured regions, which (depending on one's political ideological position) may be seen as having a dampening effect on investment or merely good public policy aimed at ensuring political stability for all citizens. However, if regional economic inequality increases political instability, inequality may reduce investment by its impact on political stability; or as the case of South Africa demonstrates, such inequality may become a source of serious class tensions without sporadic violence in an otherwise stable state. Thus, there is no simple trade-off between regional equality and investment. According to Alesina and Perotti:

Fiscal redistribution, by increasing the tax burden on capitalists and investors, reduces the propensity to invest. However, the same policies may reduce social tensions and, as a result, create a socio-political climate more conducive to productive activities and capital accumulation. Thus, by this channel fiscal redistribution might actually spur economic growth. Therefore, the net effect of redistributed policies on growth has to weigh the costs of distortionary taxation against the benefits of reduced social tensions. (1996: 1226)

Various policies have been developed to build capacity in different regions and communities to provide for basic needs and to manage common resources in ways that minimise conflict (Mbaku 1999). Among these approaches are fiscal decentralisation, administrative decentralisation, civic engagement, and empowerment of women. If scholars of political economy and society adopt multidisciplinary approaches in their research, they are likely to contribute to mitigation of civil conflicts in ways that will strengthen local voice in national political and economic processes and policies, while at the same time extending the developmental reach of the national government to the local level and indeed bring erratic civil conflicts in Africa to a halt.

Most peace accords in recent African civil wars (Schou and Haug 2005) propose some form of decentralisation. In a federal government, decentralisation is mandated in a national constitution, which provides at least a minimal set of rules for power sharing between the central government and subnational governments. In a unitary government, decentralisation is an executive decision of the central government to move the locus of public service delivery away from the center, relocating it in a dispersed manner throughout the national territory. Service delivery is then carried out by local branches of central government agencies, an approach known as administrative decentralisation. Alternatively, responsibility for service delivery may be assigned to elected local governments, an approach known as political decentralisation. Decentralisation is often justified on the grounds that the locus of expenditure decisions will then be closer to constituents, potentially increasing the transparency of governmental management and service delivery. It is often argued that such relocation of expenditure will improve the efficiency of government decision making and service delivery. On the revenue side, however, decentralisation is fraught with problems. Lagging regions generally lack an economic base sufficient to generate the revenues that would be required to provide governmental services equal to those in more well-off regions (Kimenyi and Meagher 2004). In most countries with decentralised systems of governance, the central government transfers some revenue to subnational governments. In practice, however, the transfers are often meagre and subnational governments lack resources to provide the services they are expected to deliver. Furthermore, intergovernmental transfers are plagued by the 'common pool problem': decentralised subnational governments have an incentive to lobby for revenues levied on other regions rather than on themselves, diminishing some of the presumed efficiency gains from decentralisation (Boadway and Shah 2006). Furthermore, the struggle over allocation of intergovernmental revenue could exacerbate tensions among regions. This book examines several important decentralisation issues/questions that are

25

fundamentally important for any viable effort at civil conflicts mitigation in Africa:

a) Decentralisation as a viable tool for addressing regional grievances.
b) Types and elements of decentralisation that is most likely to allow for fundamental redressing of regional grievances.
c) Appropriate sequencing of decentralisation that will result in reforms in postconflict situations, and
d) The role, if any, for foreign aid in funding decentralisation initiatives. Some of these issues are explored in the chapters by Ayee, Mbaku, and Kalu.

In addition to decentralisation as a means of addressing regional grievances and building strong communities, the book also deals with civic engagement aimed at providing communities or groups of people with material resources, property rights, or political access as a robust way of ensuring that the space occupied by the citizens reflect their values and needs. Civic engagement includes electoral participation, capacity building for local leadership, and the activities of producer associations, women's associations, village savings and credit associations, environmental organisations, cultural organisations, and other community-based entities. Given that women play a vital social and economic role in communities, particular attention is paid to institutions that empower women within the household and the larger community, which are partly examined in the chapters by Isike and Uzodike.

An important issue that is emerging as potential source of civil conflicts in the book that is not directly covered but demands increased scholarly attention is the intersection between climate change and civil conflicts in Africa. Given the theme of this book, it is significant that scholars begin to examine the empirical evidence on how increases in temperature are likely to result in severe weather patterns that might lead to intensified civil conflicts. A study conducted by Stanford, Berkeley, and Harvard scholars found that climate change poses risks of severe civil conflicts in Africa with potentially devastating outcomes for human lives. According to the lead author, Marshall Burke, '[T]ill now we had little quantitative evidence linking' climate change and civil conflicts, adding 'Unfortunately, our study finds that climate change could increase the risk of African civil war by over 50 percent in 2030 relative to 1990, with huge potential costs to human livelihoods" (Quoted in Lobell 2009). Using historical data to examine the relationship between temperature and conflict, the authors project from 20 global climate models that civil conflicts in Africa are likely to increase by about 55% by 2030, resulting in approximately 390,000 battle deaths in future civil wars. According to Burke, 'Our findings provide strong impetus to ramp up investments in African adaptation to climate change, for instance by developing crop varieties less sensitive to extreme heat and promoting insurance plans to help protect farmers from adverse effects of the hotter climate' (Ibid). While policy implications of the study are not in doubt, it is not the fact of increase in temperature per se that necessarily results in conflicts in Africa. Consistent with the theme of the book, Africanist scholars need to pay closer attention to the causal explanations in studies such as Burke's to fully account for the territoriality implication of studies on African civil conflicts. For if changes in temperature lead to conflict, the phenomenon would be global and necessitate a worldwide rather than an Africa-specific study. Even if such causal specificities were empirically found to be plausible, scholars still need to provide deep explanations for why changes in temperature necessarily lead to increased incidences of civil wars in Africa. This understanding is important to avoid attributing generic causes to deep issues that truly provide insights on why civil conflicts are more likely in certain territories and not others. Our suggestion here is the avoidance of situations where, for example, scarcity-induced sources of conflicts are overlooked in favour of climate change explanations. Indeed, rather than climate change, we accept as a proposition that scarce resources may be connected to changes in temperature that reduce food availability or territorial space for cultivation, shelter, and other values that are fundamentally insightful as sources of conflicts.

To be sure, climate change mitigation is essential for African livelihood issues; these are best secured through effective economic, social, and cultural governance structures and processes that are informed by the values and needs of the citizens. For example, mitigating citizens' adverse exposure to the negative impact of climate change largely requires the building institutional structures by an accountable government whose policies in managing territories and territoriality protects citizens against floods, wild fires, and drought that directly impact issues of livelihoods that could initiate conflicts. Indeed, a governing space that is characterised by good governance and reflects the values and needs of the citizens (see Mbaku in this volume) is likely to contain new and empowering narrative vision rather than the often-repeated stories of state violence perpetrated by leaders who are unresponsive to the needs and demands of the people. Accountable governments and institutions in Africa are more likely to have systems in place to study, understand, and develop effective responses and policies that will mitigate the impacts of climate change on the citizens and the sources of their livelihoods. The rest of this chapter provides an overview of the chapters with concluding remarks.

IV. Overview of the Chapters

Generally, the literature on wars and conflict tends to adopt the 1,000 battle-related deaths as empirical definition of conflict. We agree with Bujra (2002) that a conflict, especially in the African context is '...a violent and armed confrontation and struggle between groups, between the state and one or more groups, and between two or more states. In such confrontation and struggle some of those involved are injured and killed. Such a conflict can last anything from six months to over twenty years' (3). But while these conflicts can take different shapes and dimensions, for example, civil wars, religious, ethnical, or ideological contention, genocide, irredentism, natural resource-induced clashes, we argue that whatever form civil conflicts/wars take in Africa, their linkages to broader issues of territoriality provides better insights on their causes and therefore solutions. Therefore, the book is divided into:

1) Historical perspectives.
2) Conceptual and empirical issues
3) Cross-border issues,
4) Intranational disparities, Natural resources and land,
5) Culture, identity, and ethics,

6) Institutions and organizations, and
7) Conclusions: Practical issues, governance and decentralisation.

The section on *historical perspectives* is anchored by chapter 2 on 'Historical origins of African territorial conflicts', by Ufo Uzodike and John Moolakkattu. Examining the historical trajectories of conflicts generally, and specifically African conflicts, the authors argue that similar to European social formation, the ongoing intrastate conflicts in various states and their consequent impacts and 'violations of people' in Africa are part of the process of historical state formation. For Uzodike and Moolakkattu, 'all African civil conflicts-regardless of whether they are civil insurrections against the central state, protests over citizenship issues, xenophobia, or the control of resources-have a territorial dimension to them that has been formed historically.' Given that state formation in Africa did not result from internal adjustments of power and resources, the nature of citizenship-territorially based-demands and partly explains persistent intrastate conflicts within many African States as citizens adapt and adjust to the redesigned territorial spaces on the basis of indigeneity and settler claims, which the authors argue often lead to exclusion of '…people from within the country who are residing in areas where movements of autochthony assume salience.' Conceptually, Uzodike and Moolakkattu argue that 'horizontal inequalities', defined as 'the extent to which a particular group is able to mobilise resources to achieve political visibility and access to power' are more relevant for explaining an aspect of territorial conflicts in Africa, which according to the authors is likely to result in a mobilisation on the basis of 'ancestry and residence in securing full citizenship rights' with implications for general patterns of conflicts in many countries 'for control of resources…[and]…access to the vital commodity-the state itself.'

In chapter 3 on 'Footsteps in history, colonial origins of African conflicts: An insight from the Nigeria/Cameroun border conflict,' Kenneth Chukwuemeka Nwoko presents a rich description of the fundamental issues of space, politics, and territoriality in his examination of the territorial dispute between Nigeria and Cameroon over the Bakassi Penninsula. In exposing the extent of European involvement in African territorial politics, Nwoko argues that the arbitrariness of colonially imposed state boundaries reflect the persistent tensions and conflicts in postcolonial Africa. Based on the case of the dispute over the Bakassi peninsula, Nwoko documents the process and consequences of arbitrarily drawn colonial borders and subsequent transfers of land in the region. He also calls attention to the novel approach of the preventive diplomacy ultimately employed to reconcile judicial outcomes with political initiatives. According to Nwoko, the British ceding of the territory containing the Old Calabar Kingdom to the Germans in 1913 laid the foundation for Cameroon's eventual claim to the peninsula despite Nigeria's insistence on the inhabitants' greater ethnic affiliation to Nigeria. In addition to the peninsula's strategic location, tensions over local fishing rights and later over state interests in hydrocarbon resources resulted in interstate violence in the 1980s and 1990s, leading to intervention by the International Court of Justice (ICJ). The ICJ's 2002 rulings on border demarcations, which largely reflected the coordinates of earlier colonial treaties, favoured Cameroon's administration of the area and were seen as a threat to the security of indigenous Nigerian ethnic groups such as the Efik and Ibibios, as well as to the Nigerian state's interests in oil exploitation. Nigeria's rejection of the ICJ's ruling, citing the invalid basis of these colonial treaties underlying the rulings, threatened to reignite the conflict and exemplifies the dilemma posed by interstate conflicts emanating from intrastate territorial issues throughout the continent. The subsequent formation of an UN-supervised Cameroon-Nigeria Mixed Commission used skillful diplomacy to achieve peaceful transfer and demilitarisation of territory, as well as assurances of protections for the Bakassi Nigerians. Nwoko makes a strong case for applying this model of crisis mitigation to similar tensions throughout the continent, including Nigeria's Delta region, with the implication that while the conflicts spawned by the Berlin Conference demarcations can never be fully resolved, they can at least be successfully attenuated. But while Nigeria handed over the Peninsular to Cameroon in 2006, it is doubtful if the territorial problem has finally been resolved to the satisfaction of the various ethnonationalities that occupy the Bakassi Peninsula.

The *Conceptual and empirical issues* section contains two chapters. In chapter 4 on 'Major conceptual approaches in the analysis of territorial conflicts,' Adekunle Amuwo examines the notion of territory within the context of contemporary globalisation--its discourses, functional realms, and dimensions. He reviews the nature and character of new wars/civil wars and armed conflicts in the post-Cold War era, and critically interrogates the major conceptual approaches in the analysis of territorial conflicts. He argues that since the dawn of the modern state system in 1648, the territorial integrity of states has been prominent for its breaching rather than for the observance of the sovereignty of states in the international system. Based on the number of wars, especially since 1945, Amuwo argues that the multifaceted nature and constancy of interstate and intrastate wars is that 'the post-Cold war era of intrastate wars is also, in one and in the same breadth, an era of accentuated capitalist globalization, decline of bipolar power and resurgence and exacerbation of identity politics.' In the case of Africa, most of the wars (approximately two-thirds) since the end of the Cold War have been civil wars, which are directly tied to the challenge by both separatists and mobilised identity groups' territorial challenges against the state. Granted some of the challenges may not be tied to a desire to wrest the territorial boundaries from the national government, it is significant that most of the challenges-whether resources-or identity-based-are territorial challenges emanating from the unresolved issues of nation-building and questions of citizenship, which Amuwo argues are central to notions of territoriality. Relying more on issues-based theoretical insights and explanations for war than from realist or neorealist perspectives, Amuwo is of the view that contrary to realist viewpoints, states do not dominate the territorial space within their boundaries. States as actors encounter challenges from cultural forces and ethnic nationalities within their borders. And more generally, in spite of existing norms of territorial integrity of states in various international organisations and agreements, issues such as resources and identity politics lead to contestations between the sovereign states and other forces within specified territorial space. Amuwo argues that 'the dominant conceptual and theoretical approaches in the analysis of territorial conflicts in contemporary literature are heterogeneous' and reflect the 'severely contested terrain' that gives insight on 'why territorial conflicts and other forms of intrastate political violence are extremely savage and brutal.' He concludes with two important points. First, most of the conflicts across Africa may qualify as low-intensity conflicts largely because of the weakness of states in Africa, which provides 'opportunity to strike' by those that choose to challenge state authority. Secondly, he argues that while 'war-lordism' and imperialism reinforce each other, imperialism remains a significant explanatory concept and event for understanding territorial conflicts in Africa.

In chapter 5, 'Horizontal inequalities and internal conflict: The impact of regime type and political leadership regulation', Gudrun Østby and Håvard Strand argue that most large-N studies of inequality and civil war conclude that inequality does not increase the risk of conflict. However, such studies tend to rely on measures of vertical (i.e., interindividual) inequality, largely ignoring spatial variations in group welfare. Case studies, on the other hand, suggest that what matters for conflict is 'horizontal inequalities' (HIs), or inequalities that coincide with identity-based cleavages, and show that HIs may enhance both grievances and group cohesion among the relatively deprived, and thus facilitate mobilisation for conflict. Based on quantitative tests, the authors investigate the relationship between socioeconomic horizontal inequalities and civil conflict onset, with a particular focus on interregional inequalities in sub-Saharan Africa and the influence of regime type and political leadership on this relationship. Using demographic and health surveys (DHS) from 73 developing countries in the period 1986-2008, Østby and Strand calculate welfare inequalities between ethnic, religious, and regional groups based on indicators such as household assets and educational levels. Their findings indicate that most of the HI measures are positively associated with conflict, but the effects seem to be most robust when using the regional group identifier; and that the conflict potential of interregional inequalities seems to be particularly strong in sub-Saharan Africa. Furthermore, the authors find that the conflict potential of regional HIs is slightly stronger for democracies than for other regime types, but that 'this result does not hold for the African sample.' The authors argue that 'what rather seems to play an important role in influencing the effect of HI on conflict in Africa is the nature of political leadership.' Also: "For countries with regularly elected leaders, high levels of regional inequality are associated with significantly higher risks of conflict. Countries with long-tenured irregularly installed leaders are more conflict-prone than countries with regularly elected leaders for low and medium levels of regional inequality. For the highest levels of regional inequality, there is no difference resulting from leadership type.' Thus, to the extent that African States can engage in regionally focused policies and strategies that reduce inequalities between and among states, the outcome is likely to be enhanced 'peaceful democratic transitions' and consolidation that in turn will resolve cross-the-board issues.

In chapter 6, 'Strengthening ties among landlocked countries in Eastern Africa: Making Prisoner's Dilemma a strategy of collaboration' in the section on *Cross-border issues*, Abdul Karim Bangura and Hunter Sinclair examine how conflicts may be provoked or prevented based on the strategies adopted by landlocked countries in negotiation with neighbouring coastal countries on whom they are dependent on for international trade. Applying game theoretic insights and in particular the conundrum of Prisoner's Dilemma, the authors explain how Uganda, Kenya, and Tanzania as members of the East African Community weigh the prospects of gains and losses if they collaborate as opposed to 'defecting' purely in their own self-interest. Uganda's reliance on low value-to-cost agricultural commodities (coffee) rather than more valuable ones (Botswana's diamonds) adds to the challenge of negotiating favourable terms and conditions for the movement of goods and services. Despite some of the limitations of the Prisoner's Dilemma construct, Bangura and Sinclair provide useful descriptions of how the East African Community states' collaborations and conflicts have affected their individual and collective prosperity over the last 30 years.

In chapter 7, 'How African civil wars hibernate: The warring communities of Senegal/Guinea Bissau borderlands in the face of the Casamance forgotten civil war and the Bissau-Guinean state failure,' Aboubakr Tandia looks at the dynamics of interstate and intrastate relations that affect irredentist movements, and the impact on the border communities that straddle conflict areas. Tandia traces the Senegalese state's historical pattern of neopatromonialism towards the resource-rich region, and its use of centralisation and military force to suppress the *Mouvement des Forces Démocratique de la Casamance* (MFDC) and its affiliates over the last 60 years. More significantly it describes Senegal's diplomatic alliances with various regimes in neighbouring Guinea-Bissau and its ultimately failed bid to secure anti-MFCD support through military, political, and financial ties to those regimes. Against the backdrop of macro-level interstate maneuvers, as well as the notable lack of wider international visibility regarding the conflict, Tandia draws attention to the plight of local populations in the Senegal-Gambia-Guinea Bissau affected border areas, with the attendant assaults and appeals based on their diverse ethnic and citizenship identities. Displacement and disruption of livelihoods due to warfare, cattle rustling, drug and arms smuggling and other criminal activities increasingly undermine the human security of border communities. Most disturbing, regional militias with their respective agendas exact collaboration from civilians with a 'join us or perish' coercion tactic reminiscent of the RUF in Sierra Leone, with the result that youths of the region are maturing into a culture of defensive or offensive warfare. Tandia concludes his essay with recommendations that stress the importance of linking local with international borderland initiatives.

The section on *Intranational disparities, natural resources, and land* examine intrastate issues in Uganda, Nigeria, Sudan, and Swaziland. In chapter 8, the 'northern problem' in Uganda is the focus of Nsamba Morris's essay on 'Recovering from conflict, dealing with structural imbalances: mplementing the peace re covery and development program (PRDP) in Northern Uganda'. The essay examines the poor track record of previous phases of the PRDP in moving beyond service provision to individual victims of the conflict to more substantive reconciliation and redistribution of wealth and authority to the traditionally marginalised districts of Northern Uganda. Morris describes the legacy of the colonial government's under development of the North, reinforced by National Resistance Movement's (NRM) continued distrust of the regions, which yielded Idi Amin and Milton Obote, and the NRM's subsequent emphasis on PRDP services as benevolences in the interest of vote-garnering and central government consolidation. Morris argues that unfunded mandates and failures to meet PRDP expectations at the district levels, particularly among critical NGO and civil society groups, have also been used by the State to justify a stronger central hand at the expense of vigorous reforms. However, and assuming the existence of political and administrative will, he concludes that the more recent versions of the PDRP have the potential to improve the conditions that provided the initial fodder for the LRA and other irredentist militias.

In chapter 9 on 'Social protection, labor markets and economic reconfiguration of postconflict in Northern Uganda,' Frederik Kisekka-Ntale takes a clearer look at the 'northern problem' in Uganda, complementing Nsamba Morris's chapter 8. Kisekka-Ntale's chapter calls attention to the changes in concentrations and sectors of employment, demographics of workers, and the need for government and NGO sectors to do better analyses to match these to disarmament, demobilisation, and rehabilitation (DDR), vocational, integration, and development programs. The protracted conflict's displacement of agricultural labour continues to have a dampening effect on men's and women's employment in this key economic sector of the region, with attendant conflicts over land as people begin to return to rural areas, and undue reliance on humanitarian assistance and uncoordinated job training schemes. Kisekka-Ntale also makes a strong case for better social protection and employment prospects of child soldiers and other combatants, those maimed and disabled, and others for whom an uncertain economic future could result in a relapse into conflict.

The power and authority of monarchial politics is evident in the case study of 'The monarchy, land contests, and conflict in postcolonial Swaziland' by Hamilton Sipho Simelane in chapter 10. The chapter tells the story of King Mswati III's eviction of two traditional chiefs from their land holdings and how the chiefs and their followers, from local and regional civil society and human rights groups, resisted the monarchial authority. Making use of the historical evolution of the Swazi monarchy and the evolution of the land tenure system from the colonial era to independence, Simelane concludes that the conflict, indeed, is characteristic of historical materialism rather than an issue of center-periphery or traditionalism and modernity in conflict.

Similar to traditional rulers, leaders of modern states have not always been kind to their subjects or citizens whose resources they seek to acquire by consent or force. Thus, resistance politics has remained part of the dance between power and weakness. These issues are manifest in chapters 11 and 12, which examine the contested nature of resource politics in the Niger Delta region of Nigeria as well as the environmental implications of the conflicts between the Federal

35

Government of Nigeria and the various local actors in the region. In chapter 11 on 'MOSOP and rights claims: Reflections on the relative deprivation theory of social movements', David Lishilinimle Imbua uses the theory of relative deprivation to examine the premise and historical development of Ken Saro Wiwa's Movement for the Survival of the Ogoni People (MOSOP). He argues that the largely nonviolent MOSOP developed into a broad-based social movement in response to the visible gap between the promise of the tremendous oil wealth being generated in Nigeria's Rivers State and the deteriorating environmental, economic, and cultural conditions in the region. Imbua argues that the conflict between the Federal Government of Nigeria and MOSOP was not inevitable, but a direct response to the disappointed expectations to the failures of various commissions established to deal with the real and perceived grievances of indigenes of the Niger Delta region whose territorial space yields the oil wealth for Nigeria without concrete returns in terms of development in Niger Delta states. Similarly, Bheki Mngomezulu in chapter 12 on 'Economic inequalities and the Niger Delta crisis in Nigeria: Challenges and prospects' revisits the historical roots of the Niger Delta crisis that started with the forced amalgamation of Northern and Southern Nigeria into a disunited political entity as a premise for the marginalisation of various regions. In recounting the Delta region's experiences of economic, political, and environmental abuse and neglect since oil exports began in 1958, Mngomezulu traces the parallel development of groups in the Delta devoted to redressing regional inequities. In particular, he draws attention to the increased militancy of 'ethnic nationalists' and youth militias in the Delta, and the capacity for harm to Nigeria's economic and political stability without a constructive, locally focused policy of development in lieu of the current policies of military responses to what is clearly a political issue of resource politics and development.

The section on *Culture, identity and ethics* examines issues of citizenship, indigeneity, and land as sources of conflicts and their resolutions. In chapter 13, Pita Ogaba Agbese's essay on 'Violence, citizenship and the settler/indigene imbroglio in Nigeria" grapples with the concepts of citizenship and indigeneity as a source of conflict with regard to land and other resources. He calls attention to inherent tensions in Nigeria's 1999 constitution, which 'promotes an equal basket of rights' to all citizens, yet gives latitude to local favouritism for different regions' 'indigenous' populations, under the guise of recognising diversity and preventing the predominance of any one ethnicity. Aside from the inherent inequities and resentments that emerge from the subordination of settlers' rights to those of indigenes, the lack of consistent criteria for determining one's ancestral ties to a region and subsequent privileges as an indigene further complicates dynamics between the two groups. Agbese explores how the political economy of various regions in Nigeria influences one's status as an indigene or a settler in ways that do not always reflect chronological migration trends. He points out that it is the division of land and material goods and appointments on the basis of indigeneity that is at the root of violence in Jos and elsewhere, despite their usual depiction as Muslim-Christian conflicts. Agbese furthermore argues that the vast expansion of state and local governments since independence-from a federation of three regions to one of 36 states and 774 local governments-has exacerbated indigene-settler competitions over resources. Corruption and leverage of local conflicts for political ends also serve to fuel the conflict. According to Agbese, the federal government's failure to acknowledge and deter indigene/settler-based violence is likely to continue, due to the many interests who capitalise on the dichotomous distinctions of indigeneity.

While Agbese privileges constitutional mechanisms for dealing with problems emanating from citizenship and indigeneity politics, other views advocate for traditional spirituality and conflict resolution systems to regain central place in resolving contemporary incidences of territorial conflict. In chapter 14 on "Age-long land conflicts in Nigeria: A case for traditional peacemaking mechanisms," Gbenda Joseph Sarwuan documents the history of cooperation and conflict alleviation involving the Mbaduku-Udam and the Ife-Modakeke communities, as well as numerous examples of traditional justice and conflict resolution strategies among the Yoruba, the Igbo, and other societies. Gbenda critiques Western-derived judicial and legal institutions, geared towards punishment rather than reconciliation as ineffectual and subject to the self-interest of youths and elites who lack knowledge or commitment to the well-being of communities in conflict. He argues that traditional justice and peacemaking bodies should be reinstated at authoritative levels that carry more weight in

37

resolving conflicts based on traditional rituals, oracles, and other aspects of spirituality to ground stakeholders in their mutual history of cordiality and interdependence.

The section on *Institutions and organizations* is anchored by John Mukum Mbaku's chapter 15 on "Constitutionalism and the territorial origins of African civil conflicts." He traces the origins of civil conflicts in the continent to the nature of colonial politics and administration, especially in British West Africa. Mbaku argues that the brutal nature of colonial administration destroyed traditional forms and methods of resource allocations, conflict resolution, and governance by replacing African methods with European forms of governance of colonial territories. The use of brutal force by European colonial administrations in annexing African lands made it difficult for Africans to mount effective resistance against colonial police forces established to help Europeans bring more African lands under its control. Mbaku argues that the strategies used by Europeans in recruiting and establishing the police force-intentionally staffing the police with nonindigenes, primarily training the police in military tactics and denying institutional autonomy for the police from the political administration-sowed the seed of police disrespect for law and order that was carried over to postindependence Africa. Consequently, bloody conflicts in postindependence Africa are connected to the failure of decolonisation and nation-building to engage Africans in their own governance through constitution-making. Contemporary institutions of governance have changed very little in terms of their capacities to function in service of the people. Mbaku argues that indeed, post-Cold War institutional reforms have largely been opportunistic and have failed to enfranchise the citizens to effectively participate in their own governance. He concludes that what is needed to bring African civil conflicts to a halt is a democratic constitution-making approach that finally reflects the values and cultural norms familiar to Africans. Such a participatory form of governance and institutional reforms will enable the citizens to reverse the legacies of autocratic, noninclusive and wicked laws. Participatory constitution and institutional reforms will enable the various ethnic nationalities to build an inclusive political culture that benefits from the best experiences of every group, enable the collective to craft and adopt laws and institutions that are capable of resolving civil conflicts, promote efficient and socially equitable allocation of resources, and provide a platform for peaceful coexistence of the citizens.

In chapter 16, Charles Nyuykonge, on 'Postconflict reconstruction and the resurgence of supposedly resolved territorial conflicts: Examining the DRC peace process', questions why conflicts so often resurge even after the successful conclusion of negotiations and elections meant to mark the resolution of hostilities. Using theoretical constructs of Liberalism and Realism, Nyuykonge examines the peacekeeping activities of the United Nations in the series of interstate and intrastate conflicts in the DRC since 1996. Beyond the resource and other causes of the initial conflict, Nyuykonge argues that lack of indigenes' involvement in the peacebuilding process predisposes it to usurpation by nonindigenous interests and structures incapable of sustaining peace. One of his most compelling observations is the complexity of identity among political, military, entrepreneurial, and civil society stakeholders in the peace process, and the subsequent difficulty of crafting strategies that accurately reflect and capitalise on them. The ultimate loss of credibility by the United Nations Organization Mission in the Democratic Republic of the Congo (MONUC) in Eastern DRC is seen as being grounded in its fundamental failure to reconcile the competing indigenous and external actors in the conflict.

While Mbaku's chapter deals with the intersecting historical issues, national constitution-making and participatory politics and African civil conflicts, Nyuykonge examines issues of international peacekeeping operations over a time span of the conflicts in the DRC. In chapter 17, 'towards an indigenous theory of conflict resolution: reinventing women's roles as traditional peace builders in neo-colonial Africa', Chris Isike and Ufo Uzodike examine the influence of gender in peacebuilding and conflict avoidance. Isike and Uzodike draw on studies that establish women's personality and human capacities-including moral imagination based on transcendence and creativity-as more conducive to holistic peacebuilding than their male counterparts'. The chapter makes reference to numerous precolonial African societies (Somali, Igbo, Mungo) in which women maintained spheres of influence over conflict, conflict avoidance, and postconflict reconciliation practices based in some cases (Igbo) on the dual-gender character of traditional political institutions. Even as it decries the

39

erosion of such systems and the defeminisation of women's distinct spiritual and moral authority as a result of colonial and other influences, the chapter goes on to describe African women's impact on conflict mitigation in modern conflicts such as Liberia, the DRC, and Burundi. The chapter's overall implication is that women's peace activism is most effective when grounded in distinctly identified feminine values and their interrelationships with the masculine.

V. Conclusions: Practical Issues, Governance, and Decentralisation

Authors of the various chapters briefly discussed above offer several explanations for the persistence of civil conflicts in various African States. Chapters 18-21 conclude the book with suggestions for practical strategies for mitigating civil conflicts in Africa-ranging from constitutional reengineering and decentralisation of political authorities to the remapping of Africa's geopolitical boundaries to enhance the capacities of African States to govern their territories with effective public policy autonomy that will ensure the authority of the institutions, economic production, and reallocation decisions to reflect the values and aspirations of the citizens. In chapter 18 on 'The "Northern Problem" and national belonging in Zimbabwe: Finding common grounds in a new system of governance', Brilliant Mhlanga's argument is focused on Zimbabwe as a case study with depth and continental application. Mhlanga's chapter expands on the idea espoused by Sabelo Ndlovu-Gatsheni that every country in Africa is home to one or more groups perceived to be marginalised vis-à-vis a more dominant group (irrespective of the regions' actual geographic location in the country). This presents challenges to weak central governments who fear the loss of control they associate with decentralisation and devolution of authority to regions, regardless of the potential economic and democratisation gains for the state as a whole in the long run. In the Zimbabwean context, the centralisation of authority in dominant Mashonaland over energy, foreign exchange, teacher training, and industry, and the lack of devolution of control in these sectors to Matabeleland regional authorities are explored as examples of such counterproductivity. Mhlanga takes issue with the negative divisive role typically ascribed to ethnicity, often through the rubric of tribalism. He recommends that ethnicity must be positively 'harnessed' in concert with a thoughtful, incremental process of decentralisation characterised by nonelite regional constituencies and by a central government that can override its short-term insecurities with regards to devolution of power.

Joseph Ayee's chapter 19 on 'Decentralization and conflict in Africa: A paradox?' takes the discussion about decentralisation of power and authority a step further by articulating its practical governance implications, especially in the context of administrative, political, economic, and fiscal decentralizations. Ayee argues that while decentralisation is a strategy for conflict resolution, it at the same time promotes and exacerbates conflicts because implementation of decentralisation leads to winners and losers in the political process. Furthermore, he argues that decentralisation has not been very successful in several African countries because of postcolonial governments' tendencies of centralising authority, lack of political commitment to decentralisation, absence of competent bureaucrats at various levels of government, and the failure of postindependence leaders to articulate the costs and benefits of decentralisation to their constituents. For Ayee, one of the problems with poor implementation of decentralisation in Africa stems from opportunistic behaviour by politicians who use it as a tool for personal primitive accumulation. When it works, decentralisation is a strategy that forces national elites to redistribute their powers in favour of subnational political elites and units and should lead to changes in political and administrative structures with the attendant conflicts such processes generate. He concludes that although decentralisation is bound to result in winners and losers in political and administrative structures, 'decentralisation reform is inevitably complex because of the many different factors and interests involved and, in particular, because of decentralisation's highly political nature.' But, it is one practical strategy for bringing the government closer to the people, ensure good governance, and help resolve territorial/civil conflicts at their source.

In chapter 20 on "Territorial origins of African civil conflicts: Consolidation and decentralisation toward practical solutions,' Kelechi Kalu argues that at the root of African civil conflicts and other political violence in various African States is the absence of strong indigenous elites whose interests lie in cultivating existing indigenous forms of cultures, languages, and forms of conflict management in building nationalism and citizenship in support of the government and the territorial spaces referred to as 'states' in Africa. He proposes institutional reforms that:

1) Significantly improve state capacity through geographic remapping of Africa's geopolitical landscape.
2) Provide Africans with a significant level of policy autonomy and with focused attention on agricultural/farm policies as the basis for industrialisation.
3) Create an enabling institutional environment for more enhanced participation by all constituencies in national development. And
4) Provide the facilities and the wherewithal for African States to participate fully, effectively, and gainfully in both the global economy and international affairs.

Perhaps, and more important, institutional reforms that enhance the ability of these countries to impact the global political economy should include clear guidelines for mitigating territorial origins of African civil conflicts. Kalu provides suggestions for practical solutions, including economic and political consolidation at the continental level. One of the strategies for ending civil conflicts in Africa he suggests is a remapping of contemporary Africa's geopolitical boundaries as a way to decentralise political, administrative, and fiscal authorities and bring the government closer to the people. In conclusion, Kalu argues that reconstructing and reconstituting existing African States on a platform that creates internally strong, productive, and viable states in the continent with policy autonomy and capabilities to effectively discharge their domestic and international responsibilities on behalf of the citizens are necessary for political stability, sustainable peaceful coexistence and prosperous states in Africa.

Policies that support regional inequalities, religious and ethnic differences and disparities, uneven economic development, and inattention to potential threats from climate change and other natural disasters are likely to continue to trigger civil conflicts in many African States. Ultimately, a major source of civil conflicts in Africa remains the unreformed state institutions and structures and lack of effective bureaucratic capacities that tend to result in policy makers and their followers privileging individual and group identities over collective state interests in resolving public goods problems.

Chapter 21, 'Conclusion: Towards territoriality, peacebuilding and conflict transformation', is the last chapter in the book. Within the contexts of state capacity, human insecurity, and regional capacity, Ufo Okeke Uzodike and John Moolakkattu argue that enhancing state capacity in Africa is a starting point for conflict resolution and peacebuilding in Africa. As well, strengthening state capacity is likely to enhance the project of nation-building, increasing human security and economic development in Africa. What the contributors to this book have attempted to do with reasonable success is to show how understanding and explaining the intersections between territoriality, space, and identity sources of civil conflicts in Africa will clarify and suggest possible solutions to these conflicts. A major weakness of the volume is the absence of effective female voices in both explaining and proffering solutions to sources of African civil conflicts. We therefore urge that in subsequent projects, persistent efforts be made to ensure that female Africanists/scholars are effective participants in identifying, thinking through, and making suggestions for resolving sources of African civil conflicts. Suggested solutions to African civil conflicts will tend to have more positive effects on women and children when they are considered viable participants in ongoing discussions for peacebuilding in Africa.

References

Alesina, Alberto and Roberto Perotti. 1996. 'Income distribution, political instability, and investment'. *European Economic Review* 40 (6): 1203-28.

Berlin Act.*General Act of the Berlin Conference on West-African History, 26 February 1885*, http://africanhistory. about.com.

Boadway, Robin W. and Anwar Shah. 2006. *Intergovernmental fiscal transfers: Principles and practices.*Washington, DC: World Bank.

Bujra, Abdulla. 2002. 'African conflicts: Their causes and the political and social environment'.*DPMF Occasional Paper* No. 4. Addis Ababa, Ethiopia: Development Policy-Management Forum.

Collier, Paul and Anke Hoeffler. 2004. 'Greed and grievance in civil war'. *Oxford Economic Papers* 56 (4): 563-95.

Fearon, James D. and David D. Laitin. 2003. 'Ethnicity, insurgency, and civil war'. *American Political Science Review* 97 (1): 75-90.

Furley, Oliver and Roy May. 2006. *Ending Africa's wars: Progressing to peace*. Burlington, VT: Ashgate Publishing.

Gurr, Ted Robert. 1970. *Why men rebel*. Princeton, NJ: Princeton University Press.

Hegre, Håvard, Ranveig Gissinger, and Nils Petter Gleditsch. 2003. 'Globalization and internal Conflict'. In: *Globalization and armed conflict*, edited by Gerald Schneider, Katherine Barbieri, and Nils Petter Gleditsch, pp. 251-76. Lanham, MD: Oxford: Rowman & Littlefield.

Kalu, Kelechi. 2004. *Agenda setting and public policy in Africa*. Aldershot, England: Ashgate Publishing.

———. 2001. 'Ethnicity and political economy of Africa: A conceptual analysis.' In: *The Issue of Political Ethnicity in Africa*, edited by E. Ike Udogu, pp. 35-58. Aldershot, England: Ashgate Publishing.

Kieh, George Klay and Ida Rousseau Mukenge (Eds.). 2002. *Zones of conflict in Africa: Theories and cases*. Westport, Connecticut: Praeger Publishers.

Kimenyi, Mwangi S. and Patrick Meagher (Eds.). 2004. *Devolution and development: Governance prospects in decentralizing States*. Aldershot, England: Ashgate Publishing.

Lobell, David. 2009. 'Global warming increases risk of civil war in Africa'. http://news.stanford.edu/news/2009/november23/climate-civil-wars-112309.html (accessed September 2011).

Mbaku, John M. 1999. 'Preparing the Third World for the new century' *Journal of Third World Studies* 16 (3): 1-10.

Nafziger, Wayne and Juha Auvinen. 2002. 'Economic development, inequality, war, and state violence'. *World Development* 30 (2): 153-63.

Ofeimun, Odia. 2001. 'Imagination and the city.' *Glendora: A Quarterly Review on the Arts* 3 (2): 11-15 and 137-41.

Østby, Gudrun. 2007. 'Horizontal inequalities, political environment, and civil conflict: Evidence from 55 developing countries, 1986-2003.' World Bank Policy Research Working Paper No. 4193. http://ssrn.com/abstract=979665.

Penrose, Jan. 2002. 'Nations, states and homelands: territory and territoriality in nationalist thought.' *Nations and Nationalism* 8 (3): 277-97.

Sack, Robert David. 1986. *Human territoriality: Its theory and history.* Cambridge: Cambridge University Press.

Schou, Arild and Marit Haug. 2005. 'Decentralisation in conflict and post-conflict situations.' Norwegian Institute for Urban and Regional Research, Oslo, Norway.

PART I

HISTORICAL PERSPECTIVES

CHAPTER 2

Territorial Underpinnings of African Civil Conflicts:
A Historical Overview

Ufo Uzodike and John Moolakkattu

Introduction

Over the years, many historians and conflict analysts have attempted to trace the origins of African civil conflicts. In some ways, the introduction of a territorial dimension serves to complicate matters with respect to untangling causal factors. Africa has witnessed the least number of interstate wars and secessionist insurrections of prolonged duration compared to what we see in postcolonial societies elsewhere. Leaving aside a few conflicts like the Ethiopian and Eritrean conflict and the conflict between Chad and Libya, most recent conflicts in the region are of an intrastate nature. This makes the notion of territoriality seemingly not a major consideration in conflicts. However, territoriality is embedded in every event in that it takes place in a geographical space, in certain regions and not in others. In that sense, civil conflicts also have a territorial dimension to them because they are claims over space and citizenship rights, which have physical, discursive, and imaginary elements to them. The conflicts are not often spread all over the individual countries as such; rather, they are located in territories from which individuals and resources can be marshalled and logistics of campaigns, whether armed or civilian, can be planned and fine-tuned. The overthrow of regimes by insurgents from the rural periphery or from the borderlands of a neighbouring state has been a common feature in many civil conflicts in Africa. Chad (1990), Liberia (1990), Ethiopia (1991), Somalia (1991), Rwanda (1994), and the two Congos (1997) are some of the cases in point.

Bearing all that in mind, we intend in this paper to look at the origins of civil conflicts with some territorial import. In many ways, this is an attempt to find geographical markers of civil conflicts within a historical frame. Further, given the putative weakness of the international diplomacy of African countries, it is largely around the capacity (or otherwise) of handling civil conflicts that many countries in Africa are not only better known in the international arena but also around which they construct their external identity.

Some scholars argue that territory can be a factor in the causation of civil war because groups fight for control of the region they perceive to be theirs. Thus, territory has a (perceived or real) value for groups and, as a consequence, constitutes the very reason people fight (Toft 2003). Is territory a motivation for conflict? Or, do groups fight because their spatial arrangement makes it possible for them to fight better? Clearly, these are moot questions for consideration. The recent obsession with explanations of conflicts in terms of theories and concepts based on ethnicity and rational choice tends, seemingly, to have marginalised the historical. The recent focus on horizontal inequalities does not foreclose with respect to generated disaggregated data that space also includes historical data.

Thus, this paper will focus primarily on tendencies rather than on specific events and conflicts. Illustrations provided are aimed merely at clarifying such tendencies rather than detailing the historical events underlying particular conflicts. Civil war is usually defined as 'armed combat taking place within the boundaries of a recognized sovereign entity between parties subject to a common authority at the outset of the hostilities' (Kalyvas 2006: 17). If we accept this definition, we can see that Africa has many destructive and deadly civil wars on the continent that are comparable to interstate wars. Therefore, peace in Africa is possible by focusing on intrastate rather than interstate dimensions of peace, a sphere in which Africa's record has been quite exemplary.

With the above in mind, this paper will briefly touch upon the colonial legacy and the differing implications of British and French colonialism for civil conflicts on the continent and then proceed to discuss the different tendencies in civil conflicts in terms of their territorial underpinnings. These interrelated tendencies have been problematised in terms of the artificiality and fuzziness of borders, creation of hierarchies and a regime of privileges, uneven development, citizenship questions, decentralisation, and identity construction in a liberal economic environment. Needless to say, many of these tendencies are not only mutually reinforcing but also closely interrelated.

Colonial Legacy

Colonialism is routinely cited as a factor responsible for sowing the seeds of civil conflict in many African States. But the colonial experience is not the same in all the countries. Besides the dominant British and French colonialist legacies, we also have Belgian, German, Italian, Spanish, Dutch, and Portuguese legacies. Lonsdale (1981) notes the variation in the political experience of Africa that took place along three lines: nature of the colonial regime; political character of the nationalist movement; and structure and dynamics of indigenous societies. Other factors that need to be taken into account include size (geography and population), time of independence (for example, Liberia, 1848; DRC and Côte d'Ivoire, 1960), and sectors of economic importance (for example, agriculture or mining).

It is true that the colonial era had sown the seeds of disintegration by crafting mutually exclusive identities. This was aimed at preventing any unified form of resistance to colonialism. The British were particularly known for their *divide and rule policy* and the stirring of ethnic consciousness, which allowed them to govern with minimal force and cost to themselves. While some of these categories were built on racial origins, others hinged on whether a person was a native or a settler in a specific territory. Further, colonialism created divisions of labour to suit the political and economic interests of the colonial administration. In colonial Uganda, for example, the relatively underdeveloped northerners were recruited into the military while those from the South found themselves in the administration. Such a division of labour was either maintained or reinforced after independence with those who were worse off trying to change the situation, often unsuccessfully. The system of preferential treatment of certain groups and the stratification to create a natural hierarchy of races affected a number of groups. In order to reap profits, colonialism also promoted immigration, bringing people from other parts of the world or from regions within the country to work on plantations and in industries. The Indian migrations to Uganda, South Africa, Burma, and Fiji, and to Assam within India itself, are cases in point. The presence of such migrant population and their relative success compared to that of the natives has been a source of tension in postcolonial states.

The European powers left behind weak states with very little capacity to govern the country as a whole. However, blaming all that has happened in the independent African States on colonialism is in many ways deterministic and does not recognise adequately the power of agency in emancipation. Also, the failure of post-colonial African leaders to balance effectively their need for political survival with the goal of nation-building is equally an important contributory factor to Africa's problems after independence (Okeke Uzodike 1999).

French and British Colonialism

There were differences between French and British colonialism as far as their conflict potential is concerned: 'By allowing traditional institutions to remain, the British did not force all subjects of a given colony to integrate into a single centralized system of formal bureaucratic control, as was the French practice. In fact, the British system encouraged the opposite: it maintained control by cultivating factional rivalries among the different ethnic communities within a colony' (Blanton et al. 2001: 480). In contrast, the French followed an assimilationist model into which the elites were integrated. Following independence, the assimilated elites were able to capture control of the state machinery. Since assimilation was an uneven process, the unassimilated groups found themselves lacking in resources be it to access power or to mobilise against the ruling elite. The centralised system of bureaucratic authority in the French colonies undermined local authorities and social institutions, leaving the subordinate groups with no leadership or mobilisable resources to take on these elites. Since the bureaucracy controlled not only national politics but also the local machinery of government, it could easily detect and repress dissidence before it could pose a challenge to the regime, leaving out any scope for unarmed civilian insurrection (Blanton et al. 2001: 480).

Unlike the French case, the British indirect style 'left intact traditional patterns of social organization that facilitated the mobilization of aggrieved minorities for collective action' (Blanton et al. 2001: 481). In other words, 'the distinctive colonial styles had generalizable differences in the mobilization structures of the African polities, and these differences are a significant determinant of the frequency and severity of ethnic conflict' (Blanton et al. 2001: 481).

Scholars like Mamdani (1996) cite also the emergence of regional despotisms of local chiefs under colonial tutelage, which was exploitative and repressive, a feature that was more prevalent in the British colonies.

Artificial Borders

One legacy of colonialism was the artificial states that it created, which did not take into consideration the nature of precolonial settlement patterns and their natural boundaries. They were instead created to suit the interests of the European powers following the Berlin Conference (1885/86). There are more straight lines demarcating country boundaries in Africa than anywhere else in the world. The demarcation of territories was done in a rather mechanical manner without cognisance of the physical and cultural specificities of the peoples in the colonies. For example, Nigeria of the colonial period was an amalgamation of approximately 300 autonomous groups with separate linguistic claims. According to Ali Mazrui, 'Europe is . . . the illegitimate parent of the national consciousness of Nigerians, Kenyans and Ivorians' (2008: 7). He also notes: 'The political boundaries created by colonial powers in Africa enclosed groups with no traditions of shared authority or shared systems of settling disputes. These groups did not necessarily have the time to become congenial' (37). Further, he aptly argues that 'if colonialism forced into the same political entity people who would otherwise have lived apart, it also separated people who otherwise would have lived together' (37). In Lord Salisbury's words, the Europeans 'have been engaged in drawing lines upon maps where no white man's foot ever trod; we have been giving away mountains and rivers and lakes to each other, only hindered by the small impediment that we never knew exactly where the mountains and rivers and lakes were' (quoted in Ajala 1983: 180). It is clear that African boundaries did not reckon with historical antecedents, preferring instead to follow rivers, watersheds and straight lines. For example, the nomadic ethnic groups and herders like the Masai found their living space divided into Kenya and Tanzania by the straight-line boundary from a point near Mount Kilimanjaro to Lake Victoria (Ajala 1983:181). This anomaly had serious ramifications for intragroup and interstate relations in the immediate

51

postcolonial epoch in several African countries and within regions. For instance, although Ghana initially wanted a readjustment of its boundary with Togo to allow the Ewe-speaking Togolese to be located within Ghana, it had also agreed by 1960 to adhere to the existing boundaries. The then Nigerian Prime Minister, Sir Abubakar Tafawa Balewa, asserted the Nigerian stand during a foreign affairs debate in the House of Representatives on 20 August 1960:

> On the problem of boundaries, our view is that although in the past some of these were created artificially by the European powers, which even went so far as to split some communities into three parts, each administered by a different colonial power, nevertheless those boundaries should be respected and, in the interest of peace, must remain the recognised boundaries until such time as the peoples concerned decide of their own free will to merge into one unit. (Quoted in Ajala 1983: 183)

He then went on to declare that Nigeria would 'discourage any attempts to influence such communities by force or through undue pressure to change, since such interference could only result in unrest and in harm to the overall plan for the future of this great continent' (183).

Africans could only be spectators in this boundary delimitation exercise. One could blame the colonialists for their failure to re-draw the boundaries along more rational lines at the time of decolonisation. Instead, the boundaries inherited by postcolonial African governments were largely the net results of European colonial interests. For instance, the division of Hausaland between Nigeria and Niger was solely the result of a treaty between the British and French by which the latter renounced their fishing rights off the coast of Newfoundland (Miles 1994: 68). Chad was forced to have within its boundaries northerners and southerners, the former known for their earlier slave raids on the South. In Angola, the BaCongo represent about 15% of the population and live mainly in the northern provinces of Cabinda, Zaïre, and Uíge. They have traditionally regarded Kinshasa, not Luanda, as their cultural, economic, and political centre. Cabinda separatists claim that, unlike mainland Angola, their region was never a Portuguese colony. It was, rather, a protectorate, subject to only 90 years of colonial rule, in contrast to the many longer years experienced by coastal Angola. Between 1885 and 1956, the Cabinda province held semi-autonomous status under the Portuguese. This ended when the Portuguese reneged on this arrangement and merged the province with the rest of Angola in 1956. This situation angered the Cabindans because they were not consulted beforehand, subsequently leading them to rebel in 1961. As Clapham argues:

> In colonial Africa, the congruence of territorial boundaries and indigenous peoples was often taken to extremes, but rarely raised immediate political conflicts because there was no indigenous basis of statehood to clash with the territorial demarcation. The state was as artificial as its frontiers, and no one was inherently excluded from the state because no one was represented by it. (1995: 73-74)

Thus, the rebellion by the Cabindans is illustrative of the effect of artificial borders. Nevertheless, Clapham notes that during the early colonial era African kings and chiefs ruled over people, not territories (73-74). This made it impractical for the British officers to draw up maps with the precise boundaries of the territories. Kingdoms and chiefdoms were defined by the number of subchiefs and villages over which they had control, a practice which continued well into the 1950s when local and district councils were first created in Ghana on the basis of the existing chiefdoms (Lentz 2002).

For Mbembe and some other scholars, the idea that all African borders are arbitrary is debatable. Rather, they contend that the borders evolved in particular historical circumstances. As Mbembe argues:

> Far from being simple products of colonialism, current boundaries thus reflect commercial, religious, and military realities, the rivalries, power relationships, and alliances that prevailed among the various imperial powers and between them and Africans through the centuries preceding colonization proper. From this point of view, their constitution depends on a relatively long-term social and cultural process. Before the conquest, they represented spaces of encounter, negotiation, and opportunity for Europeans and Africans. At the time of conquest, their main function was to mark the spatial limits that separated colonial possessions from one another, taking into account not ambitions but the actual occupation of the land. Later on, physical control over the territory led to the creation of devices of discipline and command, modeled on those of chiefdoms where these did not exist. (2000: 265)

Fluidity of Borders

In the typical European formation of states, boundaries are clear cut and well defined. In Africa, however, boundaries are not rigid territorial markers. The clear-cut lines on an African map are not operationalisable in practice, in that they are imperceptible (Griffiths 1996: 68). As noted previously, African polities were often based more on controlling people than land, what Mbembe has referred to as 'itinerant territoriality' (2000: 263). Naturally, most of the administrative efforts were concentrated on populous towns and villages, leaving the remote regions to fend for themselves. In this sense, formal boundaries were the contributions of colonialism. While porosity has its own political and economic implications, the contested nature of the borders itself has not led to wars over territory. If porosity is going to be reduced in the future, it might increase the salience of borders in conflicts. Given that in the precolonial era,

> ...The costs attached to extending power usually exceeded potential benefits, the population of remote areas had considerable freedom from such governmental demands as taxes, military conscription, or forced labor. The periphery could function as a frontier to exploit at times of land scarcity or drought, as a place for escaping dissidents and clandestine activities or as a source of slaves and other resources. (Silberfein and Conteh 2006: 344)

This notion of fuzzy borders on the continent tends to reinforce attachment to the nation rather than promote fissiparous tendencies. Borders often provided safe havens for those groups in conflict with their government, and support of their kin living across the borders. In this way, the ease with which they are accommodated across the border and allowed to train themselves for further combat is another factor fuelling intrastate and interstate conflicts. For example, for those living in the border areas such as Goma in eastern DRC, the fluid border is such a daily part of their lives that, for all practical purposes, it does not seem to exist as such. At the same time, a parallel dynamic of identity formation that strongly stresses the national scale is observed. During political crises and wars, reference to national identity is widely used as strategy of inclusion and exclusion. Both of these processes are visible in Goma (Vlassenroot and Büscher 2009).

Interestingly, the borders are maintained by the borderlanders rather than the central state. Lentz writes:

> Because the colonial state and, later, the postcolonial regimes never had the personnel or infrastructure to actually enforce the new border "top-down," the reality of the border, its permeability or capacity to divide, depended to a large extent on how the borderlanders dealt with it "from below." With respect to political allegiance-more specifically, the colonial institution of chieftaincy-the local population soon adopted the border as an important resource, capable of protecting them from criminal prosecution and the imposition of taxes and forced labor. Instead of controlling the movement of the population-as the colonial regimes intended-the borders thus became incentives for additional mobility. In terms of strategies of land use and kin as well as ritual networks, however, the border was more or less ignored, at least until quite recently. (2003: 285)

Most precolonial African societies had low population density and technology. For many, there was neither the need or capacity, nor a general interest in projecting power over large territories. Political authority and property rights extended over people more than land, with a few exceptions such as Ethiopia. The concept of territorial delimitation of political control was by and large culturally alien (Herbst 1999). For instance, although entities such as Baganda, Ashanti, and Zulu were powerful kingdoms, or historically so, the same lack of territorial delimitation applied in these cases as well.

The gross imperfections in the way the continent was divided into states notwithstanding, the colonial boundaries were accepted as the basis of state territorial delimitation by the Organisation of African Unity. Often, pan-Africanism was propped up to surmount the boundary issues and whenever boundary-related disputes emerged they were generally resolved without war. The United Nations' principle of territorial integrity and the general tendency to resist new forms of African imperialism also made borders sacrosanct. While interstate contestation of borders did not take place, the salience of such border areas for conflict has increased with the general decline in the capacity of the state.

African governments focus on a narrow base of urban interests where the elites are located and tend to neglect the rural areas. Government policies generally cater to the urban space and interests, elements through which the state is known to the outside world. Also, this strategy not only allows ruling elites to continue with their clientelist networks but also to make governance manageable while boosting the capacity of the political regime to survive (Bates 1981). However, such a situation also makes it possible for many enclaves to exist far away from the main cities with little or no control by the central government. It is extremely costly for the central state to penetrate effectively such far-flung regions and extend functions of the state such as the collection of taxes. Often, however, the political opportunity structure extant does not provide enough incentives to the insurgents to pursue the goal of a separate state for the very same reasons. Thus, most of the civil conflicts have tended to target the central government either with the intention of gaining access to the allocation of resources-a monopolistic function of the state-or to replace the existing government with a new one in which the conflicting parties have a significant say. Insofar as political power has often been used to gain economic advantages during the postcolonial era, inequality has changed little in the 40 years since political independence. This is despite the official focus on development and poverty alleviation by donors and governments alike (van de Walle 2009). Marxists would not find it difficult to see that class relations in weak states such as the ones found in Africa are transformed from relations of production to relations of power (Sklar 1979: 537).

Privilege and Creation of Racial Hierarchies

Colonialism led to the favouring of certain ethnic groups or local rulers, which also led to bifurcation and the loss of communal lands previously held by particular cultural groups. A land/boundary dispute in the Grasslands of Bamenda, Cameroon, is a case in point (Mbah 2009). Borders came to the fore on previously borderless stretches of land. With the advent of independence, these contested borders were left unchanged and proved to be a source of significant number of conflicts. Boundary issues notwithstanding, the dawn of colonialism also resulted in various uneven administrative arrangements. Village-groups or ethnic clusters that collaborated with the colonial authorities were rewarded, often based on colonial perceptions that a particular group was superior to another on the grounds of being more 'intelligent', 'talented', or 'friendly'. This resulted in administrative arrangements that benefited the favoured ethnic groups or tribes-causing conflict among and between those colonised (Mbah 2009). While some groups were usually denied access to goods and services, other groups enjoyed privileged access. Indeed, certain forms of inequity may be a result of historical developments and hence socially accepted. However, if it suddenly becomes more difficult for certain groups to gain access to social and economic benefits; political entrepreneurs may exploit the situation to secure support from these groups against the ostensibly more privileged ones.

In Newbury's (1983) studies of both Zanzibar and Rwanda, she claims that a secondary form of colonialism built on racial superiority seemed to have existed, with Arabs and Tutsis filling that role, respectively. This putative racial superiority of the Arabs was also asserted with respect to Sudan, and in Mauritania where black Africans were enslaved by Arabs. In Rwanda, the distinctions between the various groups were historically racialised into hierarchies, with the Europeans at the top, the Tutsis in the middle, the Hutus at the bottom, and the Twa on the periphery. Because the Tutsis were considered to be racially closer to the Europeans (whites), a history was created to depict the Tutsis as a separate Hamitic people migrating into the region from the north to conquer the Bantu-speaking Hutu. Under the Belgian colonial rule and administration, ethnic identities were fixed, supported by seemingly scientific proof (such as skull size and nose measurements). The Belgians also arbitrarily replaced Hutu rulers with Tutsi rulers on occasions. In addition, new sources of power and privilege emerged under colonial rule, accruing exclusively to the white rulers and their designated Tutsis (White 2009: 473-74).

In those regions where the domination of certain groups was more pronounced, it was a source of resentment. Nevertheless, while political entrepreneurs make electoral gains banking on such sentiments, they generally have not led to large-scale violence (Höhn 2009). This is despite the experiences of Rwanda and Burundi.

Ethnicity, Secessionism, and Irredentism

Cases of secession in Africa are few, although there are some prominent ones, such as the Biafran revolt led by the Igbo, who constituted the majority in the oil-rich southeastern part of

Nigeria. The revolt of Katanga (Zaïre/DRC) may have been driven or encouraged by economic considerations-specifically its vast copper resources. Although both the Katangan and the Biafran cases suggest that richer regions of the respective countries tried to secede from poorer regions, such assessments may actually mask more complex social and political contexts and intrigues of the two insurgencies. Indeed, the Katangan revolt was controversial from the start because it was seen as less organic and more artificial-aimed at creating a Belgian puppet state catering to Belgian interests and antagonistic to the nationalistic Lumumba regime rather than a true reflection of the will of the majority of people of the province. A similar economic rationale can be found in European cases such as the Basque of Spain. Movements for autonomy are still found in places like Senegal (in Casamance), in Cameroon (in the anglophone provinces), in Angola (in the enclave of Cabinda), in Namibia (in the Caprivi Strip), and in the Comoros (on the island of Anjouan). For the most part, however, they have remained as sporadic conflicts of very low-intensity.

The most serious ongoing irredentist conflict in the postcolonial period is that of claims made by the state of Somalia on ethnic Somali territories in Kenya, Ethiopia, and Djibouti. The fact that the Somali state, not merely its citizens, pursued irredentist policies is what makes the movement politically salient. However, this is an exception and at least does not appear to be an issue now when the very integrity of the existing state of Somalia itself is threatened by civil war.

One of the ways by which the potential of ethnic groups for conflict is comprehended is to map them and examine their vulnerability, an initiative undertaken by Robert Gurr's 'minorities at risk' project. According to Young, identifying a 'minority at risk' in much of Africa is far more problematic because the state as 'nation' has a territorial personality and contains a multiplicity of identity groups (2002: 556). While Young thinks that identity politics could provide in part the key to deciphering disorder in states like Rwanda, Burundi, and Sudan, civil wars have also strengthened national attachments in many cases. For example, all contending parties involved in long-running civil wars in countries such as Liberia, Sierra Leone, Angola, or Congo-Kinshasa have made definitive commitment to the territorial unity and integrity of the countries concerned (Young 2002: 556).

As already noted, territorially formed states in most parts of Africa are a European invention. Although all traditional African States had notional territories, they were often quite fluid, and we do not have evidence of wars being waged for possession of territory in the far-flung regions where many states did not have effective control anyway. Mozaffar and Scarritt elaborate:

> The introduction of the modern state with its territorial basis of political authority in Africa under colonialism established the initial conditions for encouraging the occasional territorial demands by ethnonationalists as well as militating against their success. The exigencies of colonial rule established administrative divisions and invested potential ethnic groups with authority in them, thus creating a historical basis for territorial autonomy demands after independence. These demands, however, clashed with the juridical sovereignty of the state, also a colonial innovation in Africa. (2000: 248)

There is communal contention in Africa at the expense of territorial autonomy demands (Mozaffar and Scarritt 2000: 249). Mozaffar and Scarritt add: '[C]ompared to ethnonationalists globally, territorial autonomy demands by African ethnonationalists that combine putative cultural differences and past political autonomy are extremely rare. Autonomy demands are not those of natural primordial communities; but are last resort actions against perceived political repression' (2000: 244). This applies also to notions of autonomous rule within well defined borders. Mozaffar and Scarritt explain:

> African ethnic groups also cannot lay claim to a history of autonomous rule based on control over a well defined territory. The concept of territoriality as a basis of rule is a colonial innovation introduced in Africa with the concept of the modern state. This is not to suggest that territory was not an important basis of political organisation before the onset of colonial rule. However, the significance of territory for organising people and circumscribing the physical boundaries of political authority varied according to the power capabilities of different types of polities in pre-colonial Africa. But nowhere did territory take on the juridical meaning commonly attached to it in the modern state. (2000: 237)

Generally, when ethnic groups are dispersed but sufficiently territorially concentrated in more than one state, demands of irredentism are likely to arise. Barring the case of the Somalis in

Ethiopia and Kenya, such claims are not widely seen in the rest of sub-Saharan Africa.

Uneven Development

Normally uneven development and regional inequalities emerge either due to resource distribution or due to differential levels of early modernisation that have allowed some groups a head start in seizing the opportunities that emerged in the independent country. Colonialism itself was a highly uneven process. Consider for example the south of Ghana compared to the north. The south is a hub of agriculture, unlike the north where there is only single cropping. The south, which is rich in resources, including gold, was the area of focus of British investment and the north was kept as a reservoir for the provision of cheap labour for gold mining and cocoa cultivation in the south, and a source for recruitment for the police and army. Unlike the northern regions, the Ewe-dominated Volta Region was set apart by early missionary activity which created a pool of educated classes who could find gainful employment in educational and armed services. Although postcolonial leaders such as Kwame Nkrumah had sought to develop the north through proactive public policies, the region continued to lag behind its southern counterparts (Langer 2009: 537). Using earnings from resources drawn from the south, the state attempted to trigger development in the north by setting up state-owned enterprises. As with many such interventions in other parts of Africa, these frequently proved to be highlyinefficient, unviable, and inadequate tools for bridging existing regional disparities. The renouncement of the import substitution approach and the adoption of market principles only increased regional inequalities with most investments going to the south (Langer 2009: 538). Although the north-south disparity remains real, no mobilisation along regional lines has occurred so far, and the mobilisation plank with potential for political tensions still continues to be ethnic, between the Ewes and Akans (mainly the Ashantis). Hence we do not have evidence that suggests that horizontal inequalities will lead to conflict if we take Ghana as a case study. This is due to factors like the existence of ethnic groups of small size that compete among themselves rather than forge a common identity. Although the Muslim religion has a major

60

presence in the north, it has not reached the critical mass capable of mobilising a northern identity along religious lines. This may be the net result of the commitment and concerted efforts by the southern elites, through Ghana's central governments, to reduce regional inequalities and actively seek the political inclusion of northern elites (Langer 2009: 545).

Colonial development was not only fundamentally skewed and intended to serve the interests of the colonial powers but was also inherently disparity-promoting. This is equally true for unbridled capitalist development. Regional disparities in development can be seen in many countries in sub-Saharan Africa. Normally between the North and South of many countries, this is often reflected in the regions in terms of different ethnic groups. While some divisions have been a continuation of the colonial legacy, new regional disparities can (and sometimes do) emerge in the postcolonial era through deliberate policies of dominant political elites. Alex Waal explicates the two hypotheses emerging from these two frameworks:

> The stronger version of this hypothesis is that there exists a deliberate and consistent conspiracy by administrative, military and commercial elite to exploit the provinces. The country's wars are a logical continuation of historic processes of asset stripping and proletarianisation of the rural populace which began in the nineteenth century and which has continued during war and peace alike. War is but a continuation of primary accumulation and displacement through other means.
> …The weaker version argues that extreme centre-periphery inequalities are the logical outcome of the historic imbalance of power and wealth in the country, inherited from colonial times. There is no conspiracy as such, but rather the operation of merchant capital according to its own iron laws, which mean that those who already have accumulated capital will continue to do so, at the expense of those who have only their labour to rely on, lacking even recognised title to their own lands. (Waal 2007: 5)

In Uganda, conflicts in the colonial state were exacerbated by the partition of the country into economic zones. For example, while a large portion of the territory south of Lake Kyoga was designated as cash-crop-growing and industrial zones, the territory north of the Lake was designated as a labour reserve. This partition, which was not dictated by development potentials, led to economic disparities between the south and the north. The fragmentation of the society was compounded by the economic-cum-administrative policy that left the civil service largely in the hands of the Baganda and the army largely in the hands of the Acholi and other northern ethnic groups. These policies also widened the gulf between the south and north in socio-political terms. This was further sustained by the administrative policy that relied on the Baganda as colonial agents in other parts of the country. Since gaining independence in 1962, Ugandan politics have been marked by continued ethnic and regional divisions, mainly the North-South divide. In addition, armed rebellion was widely accepted as the sole and legitimate means to express political grievances and attain political power. As Kisekka-Ntale (2007) argues, the use of Buganda as the model to create modern-day Uganda made Buganda, in large measure, a super and/or treaty state, with some form of 'favoured position in Uganda.' This made the Baganda as a people and as a Kingdom, together with many of their Bantu allies in the south, feel privileged and advanced compared to their Nilotic counterparts. To a great extent, this served to exacerbate the ethnic rifts in the country. Kisekka- Ntale adds:

> In the north and north eastern regions are the Nilotics of the Acholi, Langi, Kakawa and Itesots, among others. In the south we find the Bantu tribes like the Baganda, Banyoro, Banyakore and Basoga, among others. We also find that the climate in the south is more favourable, with more forests, rivers and lakes compared to the north. As a result, plantation agriculture was rooted in the south with coffee and cotton, and sugarcane as the leading cash crops. Mineral resources such as copper, tin, limestone, phosphates, oil and others are also located in the south. In short, the south became the base for the colonial administration and industrialisation-and hence the economic backbone for this British colony. The north, on the other hand, was established as a labour reserve with many of the northern tribes imported into the south to work as labourers on the coffee, cotton and sugar plantations, particularly in Buganda. The north being a labour pool also provided the much needed recruits for the military that constituted part of the regiments for the King's African Rifles (KAR). (2007: 428)

Some kind of forced territorialisation was implemented in apartheid South Africa with the creation of the homelands, both for administrative convenience of the white state as well as for the marginalisation of the ethnic groups from the mainstream. It was a mechanism that sought to create non-white states with which the African could identify, although it was also a case of marginalisation of the blacks to the relatively poor and densely populated areas that could also alternate as labour reserves for the South African economy. This type of forced migration created a three-tier political and territorial structure with the whites arrogating privileges to themselves and occupying the best available lands. This also found reflection in the demarcation of urban spaces. The apartheid state created a divided sense of territory and denied citizenship or accorded a second-class one to the indigenous people. Dismantling it would therefore require the creation of a unity of territory and government, a factor that prompted the constitution drafters of postapartheid South Africa to recognise land rights as a key element of full citizenship and state sovereignty (James 2009).

Citizenship

Territoriality is also linked to questions of citizenship. For many ethnic groups, this is more a group concept than one of individual identity and rights, and it is intimately linked up with affinities with one's kinsmen residing in different countries. Jackson points out that in the last couple of decades the laws regulating citizenship and nationality have become more restrictive in African countries (2007: 481). Mass expulsions in Uganda, Nigeria, and Ghana can also be seen as a process of building the nation by excluding groups based on ethnic and nationalist criteria (Whitaker 2005: 118). In 2008, migrants from the DR Congo were brutally expelled by the Angolan state agencies (Neocosmos 2008). These examples of internal ethnic clashes, tensions, or scapegoating with locally resident foreigners such as occurred in Côte d'Ivoire (with people from Burkina Faso and Mali), in Nigeria (with Ghanaian and other foreigners), and in Kenya (with Somalis) are noteworthy. In all such cases, there was an exclusion of 'strangers' who have been living in the respective countries for decades. Mostly, land titles and the land issues were at the centre of such conflicts. In Liberia, where a conflict between the Loma and Mandingo emerged in the 1990s, the latter were seen as foreigners and what initially emerged as a local conflict gradually developed into a national conflict and civil war.

Why has territory become increasingly central in Africa? One could say that invoking territorial and citizenship questions is one way of political mobilisation in the absence of a programmatic politics. Hence, with the expansion of electoral democracy both at the national and local levels, territory, citizenship, and land questions assume great importance, particularly questions like who can vote and who can hold office. What emerges is a form of citizenship in which some act as hosts and the others as guests with any rights granted to the guests being seen as not an entitlement, but a patronising concession, which could be withdrawn by the host at pleasure. The control of resources is another factor that has served to increase the importance of territory; ditto for factors such as the depletion of resources such as land, water, and tree cover with population expansion. In Côte d'Ivoire, a failed coup in 2002 split northerners and southerners, with the north being dominated by those whose citizenship was challenged by the south, the claimants of a true Ivorian identity. Distinctions between 'early' indigenes and 'later' settlers is a common current in many parts of Africa, though the political currency of 'indigenousness' has lately become strong and the institutions of the state are going to the extent of determining who arrived first. As Adejunmobi aptly notes: 'Africans today, and especially the poor who make up the majority, are living through and confronting an unparalleled sense of insecurity about physical space. Whether they live in the city or in a rural area, many Africans cannot be certain that they will have the right tomorrow to call "home" the place that they call it today' (2009: 81). Citing the Ivorian example, she adds: 'The most violent confrontations in Africa are battles over foreign bodies in local *territory*' (85).

Under Mobutu's government in 1972, citizenship was granted to all migrants living in the Congo before 1950. In 1981, however, his government introduced a bill-aimed primarily against the Banyarwanda-which tried to redefine citizenship more rigorously. Now citizenship should be granted only to those who could trace their ancestry-living 'on the soil'-to the period before the Berlin conference (1885). Although the bill was not implemented, it led to violent attacks and counterattacks in 1992 and 1993 between Banyarwanda and other groups with the associated extensive blazing and looting of villages and crops and thousands of deaths.

Strangers were welcomed in Africa when land was in abundance. This is no longer the case with land scarcity and increases in land value. The stranger is interestingly defined as not only the foreigner but also the internal migrant. The crisis in eastern Congo is often presented as an 'international conspiracy' and a modern 'resource war', given the pillage and plunder of coltan and cassiterite, which overlooks its historical aspect. In fact, the conflict in North Kivu is 'deeply entrenched in history, in the complex web of uncertainties concerning citizenship and land rights that have become an integral part of peoples' livelihoods (Bøås 2008), particularly the Banyarwanda. The politics of defining citizenships in various Acts of the DRC is a reminder of how the questions of nativity are central even though the state may not have the means to effectively enforce the rules governing them. Social distance and xenophobia against foreigners from other African countries is high. This 'othering' is related to a new form of nationalism. The old nationalism, which was an overarching entity at the time of independence, discouraged ethnic parochialism by focusing on an external enemy in the form of the former colonial power. In the new nationalism, the concern is with more intimate enemies. Questions concerning autochthony in the form of the politics of place, belonging, identity, and contested citizenship are currently among the most crucial and controversial in African politics, and laws regulating citizenship and nationality have become restrictive in a number of countries in the last couple of decades, particularly with regard to minority and/or immigrant identity groups (Jackson 2007: 481).

Take the case of Côte d'Ivoire, a country that is dependent on cocoa production. The contemporary political economic and geographical stratification of cocoa production in the country is the result of labour migration from the north to the cocoa-producing areas of the south, and a shift in the location of production from southeast to southwest. The consequence is that land issues in southern Côte d'Ivoire are structured by an autochthon-migrant dichotomy. The 1998 land law excludes not only foreigners from land ownership but also fellow citizens belonging to northern groups from land rights and land registration in the southern cocoa-producing areas, as the law uses autochthony as the source of legitimate entitlement. Land, land rights questions, and contested citizenship issues are therefore burning issues in the country just as they are in Liberia and in eastern Congo (Bøås 2009: 31). The plantation economy 'provided the context in which the colonial state was to "produce" ethnic identity, giving rise to a territorialized and ethnicized definition of citizenship and national identity. It was precisely through the processes of the "ethnographer state" that the opportunities for social mobility and for assimilation-or on the contrary, the possibility of exclusion, violent coercion, or death-were determined' (Marshall-Fratani, 2006: 14).

In countries like Uganda and the Democratic Republic of the Congo, where the ownership and control of land (the main means of livelihood) is still vested in native authorities, 'non-natives' are not only often denied access to land but also the right to have their own native authorities, as recognizing this right would imply recognizing them as 'indigenes' and subsequently granting them access to land. In other words, the criterion for inclusion as 'local citizens' is not residency, but 'indigenity.' In most cases, the local or state laws sanction this arrangement. In Nigeria, for example, until recently, 'indigenity', and not residency, was a criterion for qualification to run in local elections (Adejumobi 2001: 161). Elaborating on the Nigerian situation Ostien says:

> In effect Nigeria is tending in some respects towards disaggregation into its constituent ethnic and subethnic groups. Those formerly somewhat vague and fluid clusters are increasingly precisely and immutably defined as indigenes of particular LGAs: those who trace their patrilocal ancestry back to that place, no matter where they were born or have resided. Some powers of sovereignty are moving, not towards the Nigerian nation run democratically by its citizens without regard to ethnicity or place of origin, but towards many little principalities run by their indigenes to suit themselves. Non-indigenes-though Nigerians-resident within those enclaves is denied not only access to resources, but also basic rights purportedly guaranteed under the constitution, beginning with basic civil and political rights. (2009: 3)

Herbst (1999) says that African States, though weak, are known for their capabilities to define citizenship. Given the large number of refugees and the existence of several conflicts with potential to produce even more refugees, the citizenship question is of vital importance to the stability of the continent. In this context, it may be noted that countries like Tanzania with less restrictive citizenship laws 'have experienced less political violence and have scored some notable successes in uniting their populations' (Herbst (1999: 277). Echoing the same sentiment, Whitehouse notes: 'African States may lack the power and strict border policing of states found in other regions of the world, but modern concepts of nationhood and citizenship nevertheless remain central to the process of defining identity in the region. As in many societies around the world, immigrants in Africa today are scapegoated for local problems. The inclusive rhetoric of pan-Africanism, while continuing to infuse official discourse, often holds little sway in the face of this exclusionary tendency' (2009: 41).

Decentralisation

Often decentralization is seen as a way out to meet the identity needs of ethnic and minority groups. Uganda's decentralisation programme has helped to prevent a repeat of the type of conflicts such as that of the Buganda kingdom that attempted to secede from the country in the sixties. The uniform way in which decentralisation has been implemented across the whole country has helped to counter the accusations of regional bias that exists at the national level. But in the Ugandan case it has only transferred conflict to the local, primarily district, level with political elites vying to capture that political space. This is because, instead of diffusing power among the five tiers, the powers tended to be concentrated in the 80 districts. Decentralisation in other African countries, like Kenya, Nigeria, and Zimbabwe, has also been undertaken by the ruling parties primarily as a means to extend their political power into the countryside in order to win elections rather than to extend democracy to the local level (Green 2008).

What is striking about the Third Schedule of the Ugandan constitution is the way it defines indigeneity in Uganda as based on ethnic membership rather than geographic residence. Thus, according to the constitution, one is not an indigenous Ugandan unless one's ethnic group is listed in the Third Schedule, thereby creating the pressure for inclusion in the list. While the Third Schedule is not the basis for the creation of new districts, those ethnic groups recognised in the constitution have a greater claim to their own districts (Green 2008).

One of the clear lessons from Uganda is that the decentralisation of power to the highest level of local government without further decentralisation of power to lower levels of local government is a recipe for conflict. The same problem exists in southern Sudan, where the concentration of power in the Government of Southern Sudan has excluded non-Dinka Equatorians, which has led to violent local ethnic conflict (Branch and Mampilly 2005).

Decentralisation always involves the definition of new boundaries of districts and similar geographical spaces at the local level. In Ghana, for example, the number of districts was increased under Rawlings in 1985 from 65 to 110. This led to many conflicts over the exact boundaries. The problems that emerged not only included ethnicity but also issues such as the first settler versus the late settler, land ownership rights, and claims of chiefs; all had to be balanced in the definition of boundaries. A joint Nandom-Lambussie district was suggested when Nandom did not have the qualifying population size (50000) to have a separate district. The Sisalas did not want this because of fear of domination by the Dagaras. Instead they were keener on being merged with the distant Dagaba from Jirapa district, who were seen as more friendly. These are not a new type of conflicts. They are the direct result of the focus on native rule during the British period. While a member of the same ethnic group, even if a late comer, is seen as part of the group, this is not conceded for settlers who may have been living there for nearly a century and with whom marriage relations might have taken place in the course of time. The idea that specific political rights emerge from being the first-comer who owned property was the British model of native authorities, which is invoked by the Sisala to contest the claims of the Dagara farmers who, given their access to patronage and education from the Catholic Church, had an advantage (Lentz 2002).

Xenophobia

Xenophobia and the scapegoating of immigrants is not a new problem in sub-Saharan Africa. In fact, such phenomena predate political independence in the region. From Gabon in 1953 to Côte d'Ivoire in 1958, conflicts between hosts and immigrants set the stage for periodic violence and expulsions during the postcolonial era (Whitehouse 2009). Comparing postelection violence in Kenya with xenophobic attacks in South Africa, Loren B. Landau and Jean Pierre Misago note appositely:

> In it we find remarkable similarities rooted in colonially imposed ideas of territory and its relation to political and economic privilege. These have allowed discourses of indigeneity to be mobilised to exclude competitors from national or sub-national economic and political resources. In such environments, there are irreconcilable conflicts between conceptions of national or universal rights (economic, social, and political) and beliefs that such rights are inextricably tied to someone's territorial origins and physical location. Where such understandings are linked to sub-national space, ethnic conflict ensues. Where they accept, naturalise and reify national boundaries, the result will be xenophobia. In both cases, such perspectives on rights lead to varying degrees of social and institutional exclusion. (2009: 100)

In the Case of South Africa:

> The goal was not control over the central state nor was the violence coordinated by anyone other than local gangsters and politicians. Even as the attackers evoked the nation in expelling outsiders from their communities, the violence was not about establishing a national political culture or protecting the nation-state. Rather, it helped to reinforce a territorialised heterodoxy composing multiple systems of rights and systems of rule, each attempting to make exclusive claim to territory and the resources held within. At times this meant claiming resources provided by the central state-particularly houses or local offices-but not the central state itself. Indeed, the success of the violence will ultimately reduce the central state's ability to integrate and regulate the territory it ostensibly controls. (Landau and Misago 2009: 101)

Whereas the Kenyan violence was about controlling the state, the South African xenophobic attacks were a further reflection of a political culture that is territorialized, but anti-state in nature. The attacks not only had ethnic components, but also simultaneously drew on discourses of nation and the right to space. Landau and Misago say that the 'South African case demonstrates that we must look at more than control over the state. Where space is seen as belonging to a group or subgroup, it is not the state over which people necessarily fight-even if they ostensibly mobilise on the basis of nationality-but for semi-autonomous control over sub-national territory' (2009: 107).

Take Zimbabwe where also the nativist-versus-settler notion gained ground: citizenship was re-defined in the context of repudiation of the earlier policy of reconciliation. In particular, the white commercial farmers who owned large tracks of land were quickly re-defined as *amabhunu* (Boers, a reference to white settlers in South Africa) rather than citizens, and Mugabe declared that 'our party must strike fear into the heart of the white man. They must tremble.' Citizenship became re-defined in nativist terms that excluded white races as Mugabe proclaimed 'Zimbabwe for Zimbabweans' ideology (Ndlovu-Gatsheni 2009: 71).

Religious and Other Conflicts

Despite an earlier history of living together in relative harmony, Muslim-Christian hostility has been increasing in Nigeria since about 1980, especially in the north, where there have been several severe episodes of murders since the early 1980s (Howard 1995/96 : 43-44). However, these religious conflicts have not been accompanied by secessionist demands. They are internal in nature, and religion is not the prime factor, but an additional one; contestations over space and resources along ethnic lines constitute the prime factor. Sharia is popular among the migrants and it provides them with a divine mission to assume supremacy over the local non-Muslim population and to shape public institutions to conform to their interpretation of the will of God. The 'indigenes', however, have little interest in a religious confrontation, but tend to use the settler-versus-indigene ploy instead. In other words, the religious conflict is nothing but a disguised settler-versus-indigene conflict, and it is merely the fact that the indigenes happened to be Christians in the middle belt of Nigeria that a religious colour is attributed to the conflict. Elsewhere, this could be between groups that are Christians or Muslims against Muslims. There are also several cases of farmer-herder conflicts in many parts of Africa, and this is often attributed to resource scarcity and the expansion of agriculture, land degradation, and desertification (Benjaminsen et al. 2009; Turner 1999; Moritz 2006).

Neoliberalism and Identity Construction

What impact does neoliberalism have in all these situations? Whereas the old redistributive central state claimed to subscribe to a certain degree of developmentalism (even if very minimal), it is no longer the case in many states, where due to a new form of territorial politics, the state no longer has the capacity to address the problems at hand given the liberalisation of the economy and the consequent weakening of the developmentalist claims of the state. Open economies are more likely to increase group contestations in the years to come as resources become scarcer and the effects of structural adjustment asphyxiates further the capacity of people and the state to mediate among competing claims.

How are identities constructed in the age of globalisation? Some identities, like the youth rebellion, are not necessarily associated with any territorial claims. Hence, the civil wars of Liberia and Senegal may not be based on territorial claims only. In Nigeria, for example, unlike the south where 'majority' groups are distinguished from minority groups on the basis of ethnicity, majority-minority distinctions in the north have been more religious than ethnic (Osaghae and Suberu 2005). Barring Lesotho, no other sub-Saharan African country is mono-ethnic. Ethiopia is perhaps one country that tried to create roughly ethnic federal units since 1991 with the constitution going as far as to provide for the right to self-determination. However, it does not actually devolve powers. Uganda has also multiplied the number of its districts several-fold, possibly to achieve congruity between ethnicity and territoriality. However, such congruity still seems elusive. Africa has a large number of ethnic groups, often of very small size. Arguably, no single ethnic group in any of the sub-Saharan countries is so dominant and unified that it is able to dominate the state without contestation. Many of them are territorially dispersed. These are key structural impediments to the creation of territorially autonomous units. Further, historically, there has only been a nebulous continuity between territoriality and political organisation in African States. Indeed, Mozzafar and Scarrit argue: 'In the absence of supportive historical and structural conditions for territorial autonomy, the political struggle for power and resources centred on the state has been the principal determinant of

71

ethnopolitical identity construction and the resulting ethnopolitical conflicts in contemporary Africa' (2000: 242).

Conclusion

This paper has shown that all African civil conflicts-regardless of whether they are civil insurrections against the central state, protests over citizenship issues, xenophobia, or the control of resources-have a territorial dimension to them that has been formed historically. Citizenship is constructed by developing a sense of belonging to a group within a territorial confine, both physical and imaginary. Far from changing the external contours of the state, borders are continually created internally, around categories of autochthony such as the settler and the indigene, the early and late settler, the citizen and the stranger. Often such categories tend to exclude people from within the country who are residing in areas where movements of autochthony assume salience.

Indeed, while horizontal inequalities do contribute to conflict potential, mobilisation towards that end is still a long way off in the African context. However, there is another aspect of horizontal inequality-the extent to which a particular group is able to mobilise resources to achieve political visibility and access to power-which appears to be more crucial in the African situation. This is because of the primacy of the state as the biggest source of power, resource accumulation and patronage in Africa, with groups vying with one another to access them (Throup 1995). In this way, differential access to power reflected in the attitudes of the elites of the underprivileged groups is more likely to be a cause of conflict. This is because citizens in many African countries have learned through years of neglect not to expect economic and developmental resources from the state unless they are adequately connected to those in high offices. In this way, inequalities resulting from differential treatment by office holders are often seen as normal. Clearly, then, inequalities in Africa cannot be isolated from the issue of access to power resources. Thus, studies such as Oztby's (2008), which focus on economic and social inequalities among groups while neglecting the links between them and political inequalities, underestimate seriously the role of the latter in creating tensions and triggering conflict. In the earlier era, African civil conflicts were seen as a form of barbarism, a Hobbesian state of nature, and early commentators used the word 'tribalism' to denote them. Many African countries lack the economic, institutional, and propaganda resources necessary to promote national unity. Often, they are plagued by the continued existence of precolonial social stratification, including instances of quasi-feudal social relations between some ethnic groups. They are also burdened by the colonial policy of privileging particular groups, ethnic or otherwise. As is to be expected in new states, political regimes are rarely democratic; personalist dictatorships and military regimes abound (Howard, 1995/96: 52)

Is ethnicity then more used instrumentally to gain control or a foothold over the central state? State building is a historical process that is preceded by birth pangs of a prolonged duration at different stages during which violations of people take place. It cannot be compressed into a short-term framework. African civil conflicts are therefore manifestations of these birth pangs, many of which Europe underwent in its evolution into nation-states. African rulers have little to fear from their external environment given the general agreement on the principle that existing territorial boundaries are inviolable. However, there is a flip side to it: they also have little incentive to exert any effort to establish internal sovereignty (Thies, 2009: 630).

African civil conflicts have shown a general tendency to downplay the civilian element and focus on their more coercive and military aspects. This explains the reasons some of the rebels are able to sustain themselves even without considerable popular support. In other words, mass mobilisation of an aggrieved group is not seen as essential for the emergence and durability of a civil conflict. For example, the Lord's Resistance Army has been active in the north of Uganda now for several years without much mass support.

When uneven development is accompanied by ethnic difference with varying degrees of access to political power, the territorial question becomes a point of contention for mobilisation. In sum, then, civil conflicts in the region are usually built around power and identity, control of resources, and issues of citizenship; often, these are played out around a territorial template that is both imagined and real. This template opens up space for expression of conflicts; yet the conflict itself is played out within a controlled frame that recognises the inviolability of borders and unity and territorial integrity of the nation-state.

This historical survey suggests that secession or the creation of ethno-nationalist states is a last resort rather than a primary goal of the contesting groups within states. Nonetheless, conflicts can continue within the territorial confines of the state with the aim of carving out social and territorial space by invoking notions such as ethnicity, citizenship, and nativity. The contestation between ancestry and residence in securing full citizenship rights is going to be a general pattern of conflicts in many countries. This is not only for control of resources, but also for having access to the vital commodity-the state itself. The question is one of who can participate in the political community that will come to represent the state which allocates resources (Mamdani 2002).

Perhaps, effective decentralisation and accommodation by the central state through imaginative public policies that also address questions such as power sharing and power diffusion can moderate some of these conflicts. It would also be interesting to explore why some anglophone countries like Kenya (barring the recent events), Tanzania, Zambia, and Botswana have been relatively free from conflict. Is it because of the nature of the nationalist movements in these states or because of the policies of the governments that succeeded the colonial ones? The extent to which nationalism was spurred by some kind of an overarching nationalist ideology cutting across the ethnic divisions and the early efforts to retain it in that fashion in the immediate aftermath of colonial era could be factors explaining the relative stability of these states. Obviously, these are important questions for further examination.

References

Adejunmobi, Moradewun, 2009. 'Urgent tasks for African scholars in the Humanities'. *Transition* 101: 80-93.

Adejumobi, Said. 2001. 'Citizenship, rights, and the problem of conflicts and civil wars in Africa'. *Human Rights Quarterly* 23 (1): 148-70.

Ajala, Adekunle. 1983. 'The nature of African boundaries'. *Africa Spectrum* 18 (2): 177-89.

Bates, Robert H. 1981. *Markets and states in tropical Africa.* Berkeley: University of California Press.

Benjaminsen, Tor A., Faustin P. Maganga, and Jumanne Moshi Abdallah. 2009. 'The Kilosa killings: political ecology of a farmer-herder conflict in Tanzania'.*Development and Change* 40 (3): 423-45.

Blanton, Robert, T. David Mason, and Brian Athow. 2001. 'Colonial style and post-colonial ethnic conflict in Africa'. *Journal of Peace Research* 38 (4): 473-91.

Bøås, Morten. 2008.'"Just another day"-The North Kivu security predicament after the 2006 Congolese elections'. *African Security* 1(1): 53-68.

———. 2009. '"New" nationalism and autochthony-tales of origin as political cleavage'. *Africa Spectrum* 44 (1): 19-38.

Branch, Adam, and Zachariah Cherian Mampilly. 2005. 'Winning the war, but losing the peace? The dilemma of SPLM/A civil administration and the tasks ahead'. *Journal of Modern African Studies* 43 (1): 1-20.

Clapham, Christopher. 1995. 'The Horn of Africa: A conflict zone'. In: *Conflict in Africa*, edited by Oliver Furley, pp. 72-91. London: L.B. Tauris Publishers.de Waal, Alex. 2007. 'Sudan: What kind of state? What kind of crisis?' Occasional paper 2, Crisis States Research Centre, London School of Economics.

Green, Elliott D. 2008. 'Decentralization and conflict in Uganda'. *Conflict, Security and Development* 8 (4): 427-50.

Griffiths, I. 1996. 'Permeable boundaries in Africa.' In: *African boundaries: Barriers, conduits and opportunities*, edited by P. Nugent and A. I. Asiwaju, 68-83. London: Pinter.

Herbst, Jeffrey, 1999. 'The role of citizenship laws in multiethnic societies: Evidence from Africa'. In: *State, conflict and democracy in Africa*, edited by Richard Joseph, 267-83. Boulder, CO: Lynne Rienner.

Höhn, Judy Smith. 2009. *A strategic conflict assessment of Zambia.* ISS Monograph 159, ISS Pretoria. http://www. iss.co.za.

Howard, Rhoda E. 1995/96. 'Civil conflict in sub-Saharan Africa: Internally generated causes'. *International Journal* 51 (1): 27-53.

Human Rights and Peace Centre, 2003. 'The hidden war: The Forgotten People War in Acholiland and its ramifications for peace and security in Uganda.' http://www.huripec.ac.ug/Hidden_War.pdf.

Jackson, St. 2007. 'Of "doubtful nationality": Political manipulation of citizenship in the D.R. Congo'. *Citizenship Studies* 11 (5): 481-500.

James, Deborah. 2009. 'Burial sites, informal rights and lost kingdoms: contesting land claims in Mpumalanga, South Africa'. *Africa* 79 (2): 228-51.

Kalyvas, Stathis N. 2006. *The logic of violence in civil war*. Cambridge: Cambridge University Press.

Kisekka-Ntale, Fredrick. 2007. 'Roots of the conflict in Northern Uganda'. *Journal of Scoial, Political, and Economic Studies*.http: //find articles .com /p/articles/mi_7631/is_200712/ai _n32251341/.

Landau, Loren B., and Jean Pierre Misago. 2009. 'Who to blame and what's to gain? Reflections on space, state, and violence in Kenya and South Africa'. *Africa Spectrum* 44 (1): 99-110.

Langer, Arnim, 2009. 'Living with diversity: The peaceful management of horizontal inequalities in Ghana'. *Journal of International Development* 21: 534-46.

Lentz, Carola. 2003. '"This is Ghanaian territory!" Land conflicts on a West African border'. *American Ethnologist* 30 (2): 273-89.

Lonsdale, John. 1981. 'States and social processes in Africa: A historiographical survey'. *African Studies Review* 24 (2-3): 139-224.

Mamdani, Mahmood. 1996. *Citizen and subject: Contemporary Africa and the legacy of late colonialism*, Princeton: Princeton University Press.

———. 2002. 'African States, citizenship and war: A case-study'. *International Affairs* 78: 493-506.

Mbah, Emmanuel M. 2009. 'Disruptive colonial boundaries and attempts to resolve land/boundary disputes in the Grasslands of Bamenda, Cameroon'. *African Journal of Conflict Resolution* 9 (3): 11-32.

Marshall-Fratani, Ruth. 2006. '"The war of "who is who": Autochthony, nationalism, and citizenship in the Ivoirian crises. *African Studies Review* 49 (2): 9-43.

Mbembe, Achille. 2000. 'At the edge of the world: Boundaries, territoriality, and sovereignty in Africa'. *Public Culture* 12 (1): 259-84.

Merera, Gudina. 2007. 'Ethnicity, democratisation and decentralization in Ethiopia: The case of Oromia'. *EASSRR* 23 (1): 81-106.

Mazrui, Ali. 2008. 'Conflict in Africa: an overview'. In: *The roots of African conflicts: The causes and costs*, edited by Alfred G Nhema and Paul Tiambe Zeleza, 36-50. Oxford: James Currey.

Miles, William F.S. 1994. *Hausaland divided: colonialism and independence in Nigeria and Niger*. Ithaca: Cornell University Press.

Moradi, Alexander. 2008. 'Confronting colonial legacies-lessons from human development in Ghana and Kenya, 1880-2000'. *Journal of International Development* 20: 1107-21.

Moritz, Mark. 2006. 'The politics of permanent conflict: farmer-herder conflicts in Northern Cameroon'. *Canadian Journal of African Studies / Revue Canadienne des Études Africaines* 40 (1): 101-26.

Mozaffar, Shaheen, and James R. Scarritt. 2000. 'Why territorial autonomy is not a viable option for managing ethnic conflict in African plural societies'. In: *Identity and territorial autonomy in plural societies*, edited by William Safran and Ramón Maíz, 230-55. London: Frank Cass.

Ndlovu-Gatsheni, Sabelo J. 2009. 'Africa for Africans or Africa for "natives" only? "New nationalism" and nativism in Zimbabwe and South Africa'. *Africa Spectrum* 44 (1): 61-78.

Neocosmos, Michael. 2008. *from foreign natives to native foreigners: Explaining enophobia in South Africa.* Dakar: CODESRIA.

Newbury, Catherine. 1983. 'Colonialism, ethnicity and rural ethnic protest: Rwanda and Zanzibar in comparative perspective'. *Comparative Politics* 15 (3): 253-80.

Okeke Uzodike, Ufo. 1999. 'Development in the new world order: Repositioning Africa for the twenty-first century'. In: *Preparing Africa for the Twenty-First Century: Strategies for peaceful coexistence and sustainable development*, edited by John Mukum Mbaku, 61-97. Aldershot, UK: Ashgate.

Osaghae, Eghosa E., and Rotimi T. Suberu. 2005. 'A history of identities, violence, and stability in Nigeria'. Working Paper 6.

Oxford: Centre for Research on Inequality, Human Security and Ethnicity. http://www.crise.ox.ac.uk/pubs/workingpa per6.pdf.

Østby, Gudrun. 2008. 'Polarization, horizontal inequalities and violent civil conflict'. *Journal of Peace Research* 45 (2): 143-62.

Ostien Philip. 2009. 'Jonah Jang and the Jasawa: ethno-religious conflict in Jos, Nigeria'.

Muslim-Christian Relations in Africa. http://www.sharia-in-africa.net/pages/publications.php (accessed on 25 January 2010).

Silberfein, Marilyn, and Al-Hassan Conteh. 2006. 'Boundaries and conflict in the Mano River region of West Africa'. *Conflict Management and Peace Science* 23: 343

Thies, Cameron G. 2009. 'National design and state building in sub-Saharan Africa'. *World Politics* 61(4): 623-69.

Throup, David. 1995. 'The colonial legacy'. In: *Conflict in Africa*, edited by Oliver Furley, 237-74. London. L.B Tauris Publishers.

Toft, Monica Duffy. 2003. *The geography of ethnic violence: Identity, interests, and the indivisibility of territory.* Princeton, NJ: Princeton University Press.

Turner M. D. 1999. 'No space for participation: pastoralist narratives And the etiology of park-herder conflict in southeastern Niger'. *Land Degradation and Development* 10: 345-63.

White, Kenneth R. 'Scourge of racism: Genocide in Rwanda'. *Journal of Black Studies* 39 (3): 471-81.

Whitehouse, Bruce. 2009. 'Discrimination, despoliation and irreconcilable difference: host-immigrant tensions in Brazzaville, Congo'. *Africa Spectrum* 44 (1): 39-59.

Van de Walle, Nicolas 2009. 'The institutional origins of inequality in sub-Saharan'. *Africa Annual Review of Political Science* 12: 307-27.

Vlassenroot, Koen, and Karen Büscher. 2009. 'The city as frontier: Urban development and identity processes in Goma'. Crisis States Working Paper 61. London: London School of Economics and Political Science.

Young, Crawford. 2002. 'Deciphering disorder in Africa: Is identity the key?' *World Politics* 54: 532-57.

CHAPTER 3

Footsteps in History, Colonial Origins of African Conflicts: An Insight from the Nigeria/Cameroon Border Conflict

Kenneth Chukwuemeka Nwoko

Introduction

In Africa, border conflicts have been a recurring decimal in the postindependent era. However, many scholars have argued that the border disputes of today are traceable to the ill-defined, or ill-delimited and ill-demarcated, artificial boundaries of the colonial period. Undoubtedly, apart from concretising the claims of defended area or territory (Ardrey 1966), no serious importance was attached to actual demarcation of boundaries. Consequently, the attempt to do the latter in the postcolonial period has led to conflicts because the definition or limitations on paper do not correspond with the features on ground. In other words, the attempt at demarcating, especially in the face of discoveries of resources of high economic value along these borders, has brought about escalation of disputes between countries sharing borders. In some cases, the disputes assumed territorial form, such as in the case of Senegal/Guinea Bissau dispute arising from counterclaims of the hydrocarbon deposits along their common border in 1990, the dispute in central Africa between Gabon and Equatorial Guinea in 1974 over the hydrocarbon deposits in the maritime region of Cocisco Bay; Libya's dispute with Chad over the rich uranium deposits at the Anouzou strip in 1973; and the Cameroonian/Nigerian dispute over the ownership of Bakassi Peninsula. Others took the form of disputes over access to resources, for instance, the Mauritanian dispute with Senegal over access to the Senegambia River Basin (United Nations 15-16) as well as the dispute in the Nile Valley over access to the Nile River by Sudan, Ethiopia, and Kenya against Egypt. In all these cases, the crisis management capability, effective regional integration, and the peace and security of Africa were challenged.

Nigerian shares its boundary with three coastal countries, namely, Cameroon, Benin, and Equatorial Guinea, and two low landlocked countries, Niger and Chad (Asiwaju 2003: 295). These five proximate countries share some level of cultural, geographic, and historical homogeneity with Nigeria. Hence, the imposed boundaries hindered the perpetuation of this contiguity. However, the dispute between Nigeria and Cameroon over the Bakassi Peninsula was seen as a spectacular one. Asiwaju sees it as being more related to economics than politics (Asiwaju 2003: 296), because this 'troublesome coastal and maritime extension of the Nigeria-Cameroon border is seen as the economic underbelly of the two states' (Asiwaju 2003: 296). Consequently, the dispute was one that required an extraordinary and sensitive handling to ensure that mutual satisfaction was derived by the disputant parties not only because the dispute was resource-provoked, and transborder-located, but because the settlement would not simply entail the drawing and redrawing of boundary lines to 'separate and divide the inherently inseparable and indivisible' (Asiwaju 2003: 296).

Colonial Origins of the Conflict

The Nigerian/ Cameroon conflict was a boundary and territorial dispute, with the Bakassi Peninsula being the most contested area (Baye 2010: 16) Before the Berlin Conference in 1885, Bakassi existed under the ancient kingdom of Calabar. The local people of the Bakassi Peninsula owed allegiance to the Obong of Calabar. By signing the Treaty of Protection on 10 September 1884, the Obong of Calabar and the local chiefs of Efike and Ibibio placed the peninsula under the status of a British protectorate. Through a series of treaties, the territory was ceded by the British to Germany in 1913. Later it was placed under the mandate of the League of Nations and the Trusteeship of the United Nations in 1919 at the end of the First World War (Baye 2010: 18-19). It was allegedly ceded by plebiscite to independent Cameroon in 1961.

The Berlin Conference of 26 June 1885 necessitated that the German government conclude with the colonial powers and establish agreements with contiguous territories for the purpose of delimitation of the areas subject to their sovereignty. Consequently, Germany and Britain defined their territorial spheres of influence in Africa on 15 November 1893. Further agreements were reached between Great Britain and Germany with regard to their territories in Nigeria and Cameroon, including the London agreements of 11 March 1913 entitled '(1) the Settlement of the Frontier between Nigeria and the Cameroons, from Yola to the sea, and (2) the Regulation of Navigation on the Cross River' as well as the Anglo-German Protocol signed in Obukun on 12 April 1913, demarcating the Anglo-German boundary between Nigeria and Cameroon from Yola to the Cross River (Baye 2010: 19). By these agreements, the frontier between Nigeria and Cameroon was demarcated from Yola in the north, running southward along the Thalweg of River Akpayafe to the sea. Britain's territory comprised a strip bordering Nigeria from the sea to Lake Chad, with its population that was administered from Lagos. Though this territory involved an expanse strip of land, the most contentious was the Bakassi area, obviously because of the discovery of oil in this region.

On 10 September 1884, the treaty of protection was signed between Britain and the Old Calabar kings, chiefs, and local people. The protectorate included Bakassi, the very issue of contention between Nigeria and Cameroon ('Statement of the 23 October 2002 by the Federal Government of Nigeria on the Judgment of the International Court of Justice at The Hague (Cameroon vs. Nigeria with Equatorial Guinea intervening' in Asiwaju 2009: 127). This treaty, while recognising the people's title to sovereignty over the Bakassi, did not empower the British to alienate any part of the protectorate signed into their protection by the kings, chiefs, and people of Old Calabar, whose possession and title to the area were believed to be superior to any other form of title. However, by the Anglo-German treaty of 1913, the British allegedly ceded the territory that technically still belonged to the people of Old Calabar to the Germans without the consent of the former, who had the original title to their ancestral home (Ibid.128). While this conflict became manifest in the postcolonial period, its seed was sown by the reckless, selfish, and exploitative interest of the colonialists who arbitrarily partitioned the continent among themselves without any consideration of parameters like history, demographic realities on the ground, ethnicity, language, and sociocultural affinities (Ngang 04/07: 6). According to Baye, 'the Germans were interested in getting assurance that Britain would not seek to expand eastwards. The British were interested in uninterrupted and secure sea route access to Calabar, a key trading port. Since the Germans already had the option of using the Douala port, they conceded the 'navigable portion' of the offshore border to Britain. In exchange, Britain conceded the Bakassi Peninsula proper to Germany' (Baye 2010: 19-20). This was done without any regard and respect for the rights of the people of Old Calabar or their kings and chiefs. To back this view further, Lord Robert Salisbury, British Prime Minister at the time of partitioning and well known for his successes in expanding British influence in Africa, commented in 1890 thus: 'We have been engaged in drawing lines upon maps where no white man's feet have ever trod; we have been giving away mountains and rivers and lakes to each other, only hindered by the small impediment that we never knew exactly where the mountains and rivers and lakes were' (quoted in Asiwaju 1984, Ajibola 1994).

The agreement between the United Kingdom and Germany signed in London on 11 March 1913, as well as others such as the Anglo-German Protocol signed in Obukun of 12 April 1913 and the Thomson Marchand Declaration of 1929-1930, became the substructure upon which the Cameroonian claims of sovereignty over the territory were laid. Indeed, the victory of the Allied powers in the First World War sealed this colonial arbitrariness as Germany renounced in favour of the principal allied powers all her rights over her colonial possessions including Cameroon (Barkindo 1985: 37). The League of Nations mandate and trusteeship system under which the German territories in Cameroon and Nigeria, including the ceded territories, were placed gave the administering powers to France and the United Kingdom by June 1919, and consequently in 1922, the mandate came into effect. The boundaries between British- and French-mandated Cameroon were defined by the Franco-British Declaration of 10 July 1919; consequently, Bakassi and other areas known as 'British Cameroons' were placed under British mandate and administered conterminous with Nigeria but not merged. In 1946 after World War II, Britain divided the Cameroons into Northern Cameroon and Southern Cameroon. These agreements and declarations were ratified and incorporated in an Exchange of Notes on 9 January 1931 between the French Ambassador in London and the British Foreign Minister. In those correspondences, maps from that period show the Bakassi Peninsula within 'British Cameroons' (Omoigui 2006).

Although Southern Cameroon was distinct from the Eastern Region and the Calabar Province, the United Nations requested the

Trusteeship council to delineate Cameroon. Consequently, by 1960 when Nigeria attained independence, Bakassi was clearly part of Cameroon. A year after, on 11 and 12 February 1961, a plebiscite was held in Southern Cameroon. Though the ICJ based its decision on the results of the plebiscite, which was believed to have indicated that the majority of the population of Southern Cameroon exercised their rights to self-determination to join Northern Cameroon, the Nigerian position voided this argument on the grounds that the Southern Cameroons plebiscite order of 1960 did not mention any polling station with any name of a Bakassi village, coupled with the fact that Nigerians did not participate in the referendum ('Statement of the 23 October 2002...' in Asiwaju 2009: 128). However, from the Tafawa Balewa administration up to the end of the Nigeria Civil War, Bakassi was administered as part of Cameroon.

In the series of adjudications, in order to lay claims, Nigeria relied on the precedent set by the ICJ in the Advisory Opinion on Western Sahara where the local rulers' possession and title took precedence over any other forms of claim or title (Ibid. 127) She also relied, among others, on the principle of the right to self-determination to strengthen her position of claims to the territories involved, presupposing that the Efik, Ibibio, and Efike of the area had ethnic affiliation with Nigeria but not Cameroon.

The focus of this work is not to apportion ownership of the territory to either Nigeria or Cameroon, but to expose the colonial origins of the conflict and tension that the boundaries between the two nations generated in the postcolonial period. It is obvious that the colonial boundaries were established and callously delimited according to the terms of the mandate, but in total disregard of the indigenes of those territories, thus splitting people of the same ethnic stock across two different countries and making them minorities in the same. It is evident also that the exploitative considerations of the colonialists that led to the arbitrary drawing and redrawing of boundaries were their primary concerns both in the scramble and partition of Africa generally and in the administering of the peoples of these territories.

The Crisis and Issues at Stake

The territories ceded by Britain to the Germans included the southern end of the Nigeria/Cameroon border, referred to as the Bakassi Peninsula. The *casus bellum*, however, was the discovery of hydrocarbon resources, fishery, as well as the strategic location of this coastal and maritime area. The contested Bakassi Peninsula is an area of some 1000 km of mangrove swamps and half-submerged islands mostly occupied by fisher settlers (Anene 1970: 56). These contentious stakes were heightened by the interplay of conflicting and conjugal interests in the dispute. It should be noted that within both disputant states the harnessing of the hydrocarbons resources in this estuary was primarily the responsibility of the states either by direct exploitation or the concessionary of the prospecting and production rights to the foreign capitalists oil companies. On the other hand, other maritime activities such as fishing, interstate water transportation, smuggling, etc., were operated as early as the precolonial days by the local inhabitants, on the Nigerian side, the kings and chiefs of Old Calabar who were originally vested with the title to sovereignty over the Bakassi (The treaty of protection of 10 September 1884). However, their interest was subsumed in that of Nigeria as the sovereign state during the period of this conflict. Furthermore, the Peninsula, and its adjoining Cross River estuaries located in the strategic part of Calabar, Nigeria, the Export Processing Zone, and the eastern Navel Command Headquarters. As early as the 1980s, relations between Nigeria and Cameroon had been strained consequent upon the disputes on the border between the adjoining coastal regions of both states. Although the plebiscite held in 1961 and the consequent transfer of Northern Cameroon to Nigeria had been challenged by the Cameroonian authorities since President Ahmadou Ahidjo of Cameroon was in power, the tension generated by the dispute was minimal since the latter refrained from further territorial claims (Degenhardt 1982: 97). This did not suggest at anytime that the *casus bellum*, the western Cameroonian border with Nigeria, in particular, the Bakassi Peninsula, was pacified. In fact, in another direct vote of 1961, 30 percent of the valid votes rejected the incorporation of the inhabitants' territory into the Cameroon. However, it should be noted that the Bakassi Peninsula now on the Cameroonian side of the border and to the western side of Rio del Ray River was inhabited by Nigerians even before the former British Cameroon was united with that of French Cameroon in the year 1961; hence they sought protection from the authorities of the now Cross River State of Nigeria (Degenhardt 1982: 7). This was Nigeria's cardinal argument at the International Court of Justice. In 1975, agreement was signed at Marouna in Cameroon by the then Nigerian head of state General Yakubu Gowon and President Ahidjo of Cameroon, leaving the access channel to the point of Calabar in Nigeria's territorial waters, providing that the fishing activities of the 'Nigerian fishermen in a two-kilometer wide strip should not affect the territorial waters issue' (Degenhardt, 1982: 97). However, this agreement was never ratified by the succeeding Nigerian military administration, due to what it considered 'defective parts' (Degenhardt 1982: 97). Nevertheless on 16 May 1981, Cameroonian gendarmes attacked and killed five Nigerian soldiers on patrol duties, while three were seriously injured at Ikang, a border customs post near Calabar (Okon 1989: 300) well within the Nigerian territory from the Cameroon border by the Akpa Yafi River (Ate, Akate, or Agpa Yafe River). In addition to this incident, Prof. Ishaya Audu (1979-1983) protested the incessant harassment of Nigerians living in the border areas as well as Cameroonian incursions into Nigerian villages and added in a protest letter that the Nigerian Government reserved the right to take any action deemed appropriate to safeguard and protect the lives and properties of her citizens and that the Nigerian government would refer the matter to the then Organisation of African Unity (OAU) (Okon, 1989: 30). On 22 May, President Ahidjo ordered an inquiry into the incident and subsequently the Cameroonian Government came out with the claim that the incident occurred on the Rio del Ray River, in the Cameroonian territory, 20 miles near the east of the border. Nevertheless, in response to the protest note by the Nigerian Government, the Cameroonians came out with a working document piece for a bilateral cooperation in the border region of the two countries. This move was however rejected owing to what the National Security Council of Nigeria termed the failure of the proposal to address the protest content. The strained relations between these two neighbouring states were further exacerbated by the damage or the criticism and propagandas alleging the preparedness of both states for any eventuality. In fact, it was claimed in the Nigerian press that Cameroon was mobilising for a possible military confrontation with Nigeria. On the Nigerian side, the then Defence Minister Alhaji, Akanbi Oniyangi, however, did not foreclose the possibility of military exchanges with Cameroon. Attempts at settling the crisis under the aegis of the Organisation of African Unity failed following the inability of the continental body to place the issue on its agenda of the Assembly of Heads of State and Government held in Nairobi, Kenya, during 24-28 June 1981. Further meditational efforts by the former late Ivoirian President Houphet-Boigny, Gnassingbe Eyadema of Togo and Seym Kountche of Niger moved President Ahidjo on 20 July 1981 to announce a compensation package for the families of the five Nigerian deceased soldiers, as well as an 'unreserved' apology to the government of Nigeria.

Further diplomatic overtures and cessation of hostilities led to talks between the leaders of both states in Lagos. And on 13 January1992 in a joint communiqué issued at the end of the talks, Presidents Shagari and Ahidjo regretted the escalation of tensions between the two sister countries and affirmed their resolve to engage in joint commission to strengthen their bilateral cooperation.

Position of the Disputants at ICJ

The events that led to the International Court of Justices ruling on 10 October 2002 in the Cameroon/Nigeria border case was the renewed border violence between the two countries in the 1990s. The government of Cameroon had, on 29 March 1994, filed an application instituting proceedings against Nigeria concerning a dispute described as 'relat(ing) essentially to the question of sovereignty over the Bakassi Peninsula.' It further stated that the 'delimitation (of the maritime boundary between the two states) has remained a partial one (that) despite many attempts to complete it, the two parties have been unable to do so.' Hence, it was its desire that the ICJ 'in order to avoid further incidents between the two countries…determine the course of the maritime boundary between the two states beyond the line fixed in 1975.'

Moreover, to found the Court's jurisdiction, the application relied on the declarations by the two parties pledging to accept the court's jurisdiction as contained in Article 36, paragraph 2, of the statute of the Court (ICJ Press Release 2002/26). On 6 June 1994, further application was made by Cameroon 'for the purpose of extending the subject of the dispute' to a further dispute described as 'relat[ing] essentially to the question of sovereignty over a part of the territory of Cameroon in the area of Lake Chad.' In addition, Cameroon also requested that the Court 'specify definitively' the frontier between the two states from Lake Chad to the sea and asked it to join the two applications and 'examine the whole in a single case' (ICJ Press Release 2002/26). As a sequel to this, the Nigerian Government expressed no objection to the additional applications being treated as an amendment to the initial application in order that the Court could take it as one case and examine as such. Consequently, by an order of 16 June 1994, the Court obliged the procedure and fixed the time limits for filing of written proceedings (ICJ Press Release 2002/26).

However, Nigeria filed preliminary objectives to the jurisdiction of the Court as well as the application's admissibility on 13 December 1995 well within the time limit fixed for the filing of its countermemories, which could suspend the proceedings based on the merit (ICJ Rep. 1998: 312). On 11 June 1998, the ICJ delivered judgment on the preliminary objections raised by Nigeria. It ruled that it had jurisdiction to adjudicate upon the merits of the dispute and that the requests made by Cameroon were admissible. Similarly, the Court rejected seven of the preliminary objections raised by Nigeria and treated the eighth as lacking the exclusive preliminary character and suspended ruling on it until the judgment be rendered on the merits. The summary of Cameroon's Application was:

a) That sovereignty over the Peninsula of Bakassi was Cameroonian; by virtue of International Law and that, that peninsula was an integral part of the territory of Cameroon

b) That the Federal Republic of Nigerian had violated and was violating the fundamental principle of respect for frontiers inherited from colonization (*utipossidetis juris*).

c) That by using force against the Republic of Cameroon, the Federal Republic of Nigeria had violated and was violating its obligations under International Treaty Law and Customary International law.

87

d) That the Federal Republic of Nigeria, by military force occupied the Cameroon Peninsula of Bakassi and consequently violated and was violating the obligations in combat upon it by virtue of Treaty Law and Customary International Law. (Oyewo, 2005: 187)

In the adjudication of the case, before it filed by Cameroon, the ICJ relied on specific instruments namely;

i.   A Treaty of protection concluded on 10 September 1884 between Great Britain and the kings and chiefs of Old Calabar
ii. Two agreements concluded between the British Government and Germany dated respectively 11th March and 12 April 1913, which placed Bakassi Peninsula in German territory
iii. A declaration (Yaoundé I Declaration) adopted on 14 August 1970, by a joint boundary commission: established by the two countries
iv. A second declaration (Yaoundé 11 Declaration) adopted on 4 April 1971, whereby the Heads of State of the two countries agreed to regard as their maritime boundary 'as far as the 3-nautical-mile limit" (a line running from a point) to a point 12, which they had drawn and signed on British Admiralty Chart No.3433 annexed to the declaration
v.   An agreement signed on 1 June 1975 at Marouna (Cameroon) by the Heads of State of Cameroon and Nigeria, for the partial delimitation of the maritime boundary between the two states. (Oyewo 2005: 187-88)

ICJ's Ruling

After entertaining arguments from both countries, the Court ruled concerning the boundary in the end the sovereignty over the boundary, inter alia:

II (A) by fifteen votes to one; decided that the land boundary between the Republic of Cameroon and the Federal Republic of Nigeria is delimited, from Lake Chad to the Bakassi peninsula, by the following instruments:

i.   from the point where the River Ebeyi bi-furcated as far as Tamnyar Peak by paragraph 2 to 60 of the Thomson-Marchaud Declaration of 1929-1930, as incorporated in the Henderson-Fleurian Exchange of Notes of 1931;…

ii. from Tamnyar Peak to Pillar 64 referred to in Article XII of the Anglo-German Agreement in 12 April 1913, by the British Order in Council of 2 August 1946;

iii. from pillar 64 to the Bakassi Peninsula by Anglo-German Agreements of 11 March and 12 April 1913;

(B) Unanimously, decided that the aforesaid instruments were to be interpreted in the manner set out in paragraphs 91, 96, 102, 114, 119, 124, 129, 134, 139, 146, 152, 155, 150, 168, 179, 184 and 189 of the present judgment;

III (A) by thirteen votes to three decided that the boundary between the Republic of Cameroon and the Federal Republic of Nigerian in Bakassi was delimited by Articles XVII to XX of the Anglo-German Agreement of 11 March 1913;

A. By thirteen votes to three, decided that sovereignty over the Bakassi Peninsula lay with the Republic of Cameroon;

B. By thirteen votes to three decided that the boundary between the Republic of Cameroon and the Federal Republic of Nigeria in Bakassi followed the Thalweg of the Akpakorum (Akwayafe) River, dividing the Mangrove Island near Ikang in the way shown on map TSGS 2240, as far as the straight line joining Bakassi point and King point…(ICJ year 2002, 10 October General list No 94: 147-48)

The Court also delineated that up to point A below, the Nigeria/Cameroon Maritime boundary took the following course: Starting from the point of intersection of the centre of the Navigable Channel of the Akwayafe River with the straight line joining Kassi point and King point as referred to in point III (C) above, the boundary followed the 'compromise line' drawn jointly at Yaoundé on 4 April 1971 by the Heads of State of Cameroon and Nigeria on British Admiralty chart 3433 (Yaoundé 11Declaration) and passing through

12 numbered points, whose coordinates were as follows (ICJ year 2002, 10 October General list No 94: 149):

	Longitude	Latitude
Point 1:	8°30'44"E	4°40'28"N
Point 2:	8°30'00"E	4°40'00"N
Point 3:	8°28'50"E	4°39'00"N
Point 4:	8°27'52"E	4°38'00"N
Point 5:	8°27'09"E	4°37'00"N
Point 6:	8°26'36"E	4°36'00"N
Point 7:	8°26'03"E	4°35'00"N
Point 8:	8°25'42"E	4°34'18"N
Point 9:	8°25'35"E	4°44'00"N
Point 10:	8°25'08"E	4°33'00"N
Point 11:	8°24'47"E	4°32'00"N
Point 12:	8°24'38"E	4°31'20"N

From point 12 the boundary followed the line adopted in the declaration signed by the heads of state of Cameroon and Nigeria at Marona on 1 June 1975 (Marona Declaration), as corrected by the exchange of letters between the said heads of state of 12 June and 12 July 1975, that line passes through points A to G, whose coordinates were as follows:

	Longitude	Latitude
Point A:	8°24' 24" E	4°31' 30"N
Point A1:	8°24' 24" E	4°31' 20"N

Point A:	$8^0 24$' 10" E	$4^0 26$' 32" N
Point A:	$8^0 23$' 42" E	4^0 23' 28" N
Point A:	$8^0 22$' 41" E	4^0 20' 00" N
Point A:	$8^0 22$' 17"E	4^0 19' 32" N
Point A:	$8^0 22$' 19"E	4^0 18' 46" N
Point A:	$8^0 22$' 19" E	4^0 17' 00" N

(C) The Court also unanimously decided that from point G, the boundary line between the maritime areas between the two countries followed 'a Loxodrome having an azimuth of 270^0 as far as the equidistance line passing through the midpoint of the line jointing West point and East point; the boundary meets this equidistance line at a point X, with co-ordinates 8^0 21' 20" longitude east and 4^0 17' 00" latitude North' (ICJ year 2002, 10 October General list No 94: 149).

The Court also unanimously decided that from point X, with the boundary between maritime area of the two states follows a Loxodrome having an azimuth of 187^0 52' 27"; and by fourteen votes to two, that Nigeria is under an obligation 'expeditiously and without condition' to withdraw its administration and its military and police forces from the territories under Cameroon pursuant to points I and III of the operative paragraph (ICJ year 2002, 10 October General list No 94: 150).

Furthermore, the Court unanimously decided that Cameroon had the same obligation in the Nigeria territories pursuant to point 11 of the operative paragraph and vice-versa. And finally, the Court took note of the commitment by Cameroon pledging the continuous protection of Nigerians in the peninsula and Lake Chad areas as well as unanimously rejecting all other submissions by Cameroon as to the state responsibility of Nigeria and Nigeria's counterclaims.

Reactions to the ICJ's Judgment

As expected, reactions to the ruling of the ICJ was diverse, and this was not unconnected with the varying interest of the stakeholders in the case, as well as the dissenting opinions of some of the members of the 16-man Bench, especially on the ruling which decided that "the boundary between the Republic of Cameroon and Nigeria in the Bakassi Peninsula is delimited by Articles XVIII to XX of the Anglo-German Agreement of 11 March 1913" as well as the ruling which decided "that Sovereignty over the Bakassi peninsula lies with the Republic of Cameroon." In the above, the dissenting opinions were those of judges Koroma, Rezek and Judge ad hoc Ajibola (ICJ year 2002, 10 October General list No 94: 145). By this decision, many believed that the fact that the ICJ relied on 'Cameroon's conventional titles' was clear evidence that it gave precedence to contemporary Western constructions of the notions of boundaries and sovereignty to the detriment of the historical consolidation argument especially as canvassed by Nigeria (Sama and Johnson-Ross 2005-2006: 111).

The second phase of the reaction was the one from the Government of the Federal Republic of Nigeria, in particular the allegation that the ruling was politically motivated because of the presence of the English and German judges who themselves were citizens of the colonial governments blamed for the dispute arising from the arbitrary boundary creations in Africa. Similarly, the physical presence of the French President of the Court whose country was the colonial master of one of the parties was seen as influential to the outcome of the judgment. Therefore for the simple reason that these judges acted as judges in their own cause, rendered their judgment null and void. In her protest, the Government of the Federal Republic of Nigeria maintained that it 'does not accept that a protectorate treaty made without jurisdiction should take precedence over a community title rights and ownership existing from time immemorial' (Nigerian Information service center, 7 November 2002. See also *Guardian*, Thursday, 24 October 2002: 1-2). The government of Nigeria believed that Germany could not have transferred to Cameroon what it did not derive from Britain, since the right to title ownership lay with kings and chiefs of Old Calabar.

The most pronounced of the reactions was that by the indigenes of the Bakassi Peninsula who were Nigerians of mainly Efik ethnic group. They had settled there right before the former British Cameroon was united with the former French Cameroon in 1961. Many of them were fishermen and traders, and some were smugglers. They totally rejected the ruling and urged the Government of Nigeria to use the last resort, war, to enforce their sovereignty, for failure of which they threatened to enforce their right to self-determination by declaring themselves independent *(Daily Times,* Monday, 14 October 2002: 1, 2). This view was generally supported by other Nigerians who believed that the clamour for self-determination was a continuation of the historical consolidation argument. According to them:

> We are in support of the declaration of the Republic of Bakassi. The United Nations should realize that we have the right to decide where we want to be and the right to self-determination. We are Nigerians and here in our ancestral home. You can see some of the graves here dating back to the 19th century. How can you force a strange culture and government on us? We appreciate what the Nigerian government is doing but let it be on record that they have betrayed us and we will fight for our survival and self-determination. *(The Guardian,* 18 August 2006)

Perceived Implication of the ICJ's Ruling

While the ICJ's judgment shall perhaps stand as precedence in subsequent adjudications in the international Court, to both countries involved it had socioeconomic and sociopolitical implications. Firstly, the sociopolitical implication is that Nigerian indigenes in Bakassi would have to face challenges arising from their evacuation from their ancestral homeland, consequently losing both their cultural connection as well as their source of livelihood and resources (Nicholas, and Baroni 2010:207). Similarly, the judgment could imply the withdrawal of the oil companies from the territory and the forfeiture of their investments and assets to Cameroon, of course posing adverse economic implications for Nigeria. To the Cameroonians, the exploration and exploitation of the huge oil deposits in the Peninsula meant the expansion of the economy; direct foreign investment in the oil sector, job creation, and increase in the revenue that would have direct impact on economic growth and development. Sociopolitically, while the decision made the Nigerian government seem weak and unable to protect the interest of its citizens, it was a boost for the government of Cameroon, considered unpopular with the Cameroonians. For Nigeria, cooperating with the decision could be a diplomatic instrument to gain the respect of the international community, a prelude to gaining acceptance as a member of the United Nations' Security Council (Nicholas and Baroni 2010: 207).

Approaches to Solving the Problem

Over time, experience had demonstrated states' willingness to employ a variety of mechanisms to contain, contend, and adjudicate crises with one another in the international system. International Crisis Behavior (ICB) data on crises in contemporary times point to the fact that the majority of crisis situations had witnessed actors resorting to violence or the threat of the use of violence either exclusively or in conjunction with other techniques to manage their crises (Wilkenfeld et al. 2005). Others employed a variety of nonviolent approaches, ranging from negotiation, adjudication and arbitration, and mediation to nonviolent military actions, in search of their goals within a crisis (Wilkenfeld et al. 2005). To avoid the former scenario or any further confrontations that might have arisen from the ICJ's decision, the then Secretary General of the United Nations, Mr. Kofi Anan, adopted the latter by inviting the presidents of Nigeria and Cameroon to a meeting in Paris, France, on 5 September 2002, to 'work out modalities for the implementation of the anticipated decision.' To the number one diplomat, there had to be a political solution to facilitate the implementation of the ICJ's judgment since he anticipated that the latter might not be acceptable to one party, despite the declaration of both parties pledging to accept the jurisdiction of the Court under Article 36, paragraph 2 of the statute of the ICJ at The Hague. The result of this diplomatic overture was the establishment of the Cameroon-Nigeria Mixed Commission, under the supervisor of the United Nations.

The United Nations, apart from diplomatic overtures and mediations, also advanced some financial incentives to ensure that both countries obeyed the ICJ's ruling (Oyewo 2005: 129). The Commission's mandate covered the following:

i. The demarcation of the land boundary between the two countries; withdrawal of civil administration, military and police forces and transfer of authority in relevant areas along the boundary;

ii. The eventual demilitarization of the Bakassi Peninsula;

iii. The need to protect the rights of the affected populations in both countries: the development of projects to promote joint economic ventures and cross-border cooperation and,

iv. The reactivation of the Lake Chad Basin Commission. (Oyewo 2005: 129)

The Commission, pursuant to the achievements made, set up subsidiary organs with technocrats and experts from the United Nations and the two countries. Indeed, huge progress was recorded in the implementation of the first two mandates of the Commission. In fact, by the end of 2003, the transfer of the authority in the Lake Chad area was accomplished; however, it was the actual handing-over of the contentious Bakassi Peninsula area to Cameroon by Nigeria that witnessed a snail's speed.

Nonetheless, by the sheer diplomatic astuteness of the Mixed Commission, the political flexibility of the two countries, and the spirit of compromise, the Commission achieved the partial handing-over of the Bakassi Peninsula by the Nigerian government to the government of the Republic of Cameroon in September 2006, at least on paper. More important, the Commission was able to persuade the parties to find the process acceptable. This led to the Green Tree Agreement, which culminated in the 14 August 2008 total hand-over of the said territory to the Cameroonian government by Nigeria. Nevertheless, at the 13th session of the Commission in Yaoundé in 2005, the government of Nigerian complained about the plight of Nigerians living in Cameroon, a situation that had continued to the present period and that could have made Nigeria renege on the Green Tree Agreement.

In the posthandover period, debates in Nigeria heightened on the wisdom of ceding a Nigerian territory and its people. Indeed, this contentious debate was heightened by the perceived illegality that was observed by the Nigerian legislature in the planned execution of the Green Tree Agreement by Nigeria's executive. Part of the legislature's argument was that considering the issues involved in the conflict and the aftermath of the ICJ ruling, it was unconstitutional for any international agreement entered into by the country to be binding without full ratification of such agreements by the country's legislature (Price 2005), a condition that is routine in international law. In fact, one of the undoings of the defunct League of Nations was the non-membership and non-commitment of the United States of America to its aims and objective as a result of the non-ratification of the organisation's Charter by the US Congress. However, this misconception of the Green Tree Agreement by the legislature was clarified by the then Nigeria's Attorney General and Minister of Justice, who emphasized that the Green Tree Agreement was never a treaty, but a paper agreement entered into willingly by the two state parties involved and the Mixed Commission as a witness party, which would serve as a vehicle for the execution of the ICJ ruling. Consequently, the root of the agreement was the ICJ ruling and it therefore needed no ratification by Nigeria's legislature since the Green Tree Agreement was not a treaty and had no substance without the ICJ ruling (Aondoukaa, 08/08/08).

There was also another side of the debate, especially from the military, that the country was not under any obligation to abide by the decision of the ICJ or that of the Mixed Commission, in particular when the country had little to gain but everything to lose, citing instances from the practices of the superpowers, especially the United States, in international politics. A particular interest of the Nigerian military that had influenced its objection to the ceding of the Bakassi territory to Cameroon seemed to be strategic. For it, the expected control of the Bakassi estuary by Cameroon would make the Nigerian Eastern Naval Command lose navigable waters and make it impossible for the Nigerian eastern border to be navigated and effectively patrolled.

Conclusion and Suggestions

The establishment of the Mixed Commission, the marrying of judicial outcome with political initiative, was a novel approach in preventive diplomacy and a model for peaceful settlement of conflicts between states in the face of recurrent border dispute in Africa, especially those resulting from transborder resources of high economic value. To assuage the fears and apprehensions of the Bakassi inhabitants whose land had been transferred to the Cameroon, the present writer suggests that dual citizenship be accorded the Bakassi Nigerians now on the side of Cameroon. In the same vein, confidence-building measures should be adopted to ensure a lasting solution of the dispute and consolidation of peace in the peninsula.

The judgment of the ICJ and the reactions that trailed it further confirmed that a purely legalistic solution to the dispute and to all border disputes in Africa stands little chance of being accepted, if not by one government or the other, then by the people in the area (Yagba 1995: 30). Hence, having so many potential Bakassi situations in Africa, it is the opinion of this writer that there should be an instituted framework that would be comprehensive in nature for transborder cooperation capable of provoking cooperation at the grassroots level, 'that is at the level of territorial communities and authorities across the border land localities' (Yagba 1995: 26). This institutional framework should adopt the Nigerian/Cameroon Mixed Commission, *mutatis mutandis* (in view of its observed limitations) as a model for resolving future crisis. This suggestion hinges on the fact that the model has proven to prevent crisis escalation and to offer, rather, a quick resolution to conflicts. It also, to a large extent, enjoyed the confidence of the crisis actors, who demonstrated their satisfaction, though not totally, with the outcome of the crisis resolution. However, the Commission was not able to remove the tension arising from the crisis; thus, to that end, it is advisable that all domestic procedures especially recognised in international law for the formalisation and affirmation of treaties and agreement entered into by states should be fully exhausted to avert inherent contradictions in domestic politics of the states involved.

This recommendation is more direct to the Nigerian government, which may wish to avert a future alliance with those considered militants or antisocial elements in the Niger-Delta region of the country from taking advantage of the plight of the Bakassi people and calling for self-determination to infiltrate the area and make themselves relevant, a situation that may be too difficult for the Nigerian state to handle alongside the extant Niger-Delta issue.

Similarly, to prevent future problems in Africa as a result of the transborder location of resources of high economic values, this writer suggests the adoption of future orientation towards international cooperation; mutual confidence-building, and preventive diplomacy (Utton 1987: 1). To bring about these processes, the problem-solving approach must be employed. This, however, involves a thorough investigation and consequent identification of the needs to be met or founded and legitimate grievance to be redness; and the selection of the option mutually acceptable to the parties in the conflict (Asiwaju, 2003:296)

It is also plausible to note that just as the issue of legitimacy arising from colonial transfers of territories should be upheld, at least as a working piece in the settlement of post colonial territorial claims and disputes in Africa, the more overriding consideration of self determination should also be uppermost at least to assuage the fears of domination of the people who might lose their ancestral homeland in such decision, and rendered minorities in their new country. The Bakassi people in this instance have not been adequately considered and consulted either in the ICJ ruling or even in the high politics of the contending states. Indeed, the principle of self-determination enshrined in the UN article seems to be invoked only when certain situations do not benefit the super powers who themselves only choose and comply with international legal frameworks that suit them. It may not be out of place for adequate compensation to be paid to the Bakassi people who have been dislodged from their ancestral homes and maltreated and manhandled by the Cameroonian military, and whose means of survival, especially fishing, have been unsettled.

All these processes would have to involve the Second Track/Citizens' Diplomacy (Davies and Kaufman 2002), which John Davies and Edy Kaufman broadly defined as 'facilitated dialogue to address conflict issues between unofficial representatives or equivalent opinion leaders from communities in conflict.' It is an essential complement to official (first track) diplomacy for responding to the enormous challenge that these complex conflicts pose to building a sustainable and dynamic peace, thus providing a functional instrument for peace and conflict resolution for a long time to come, especially in Africa.

Figure 1: Map of Bakassi Area

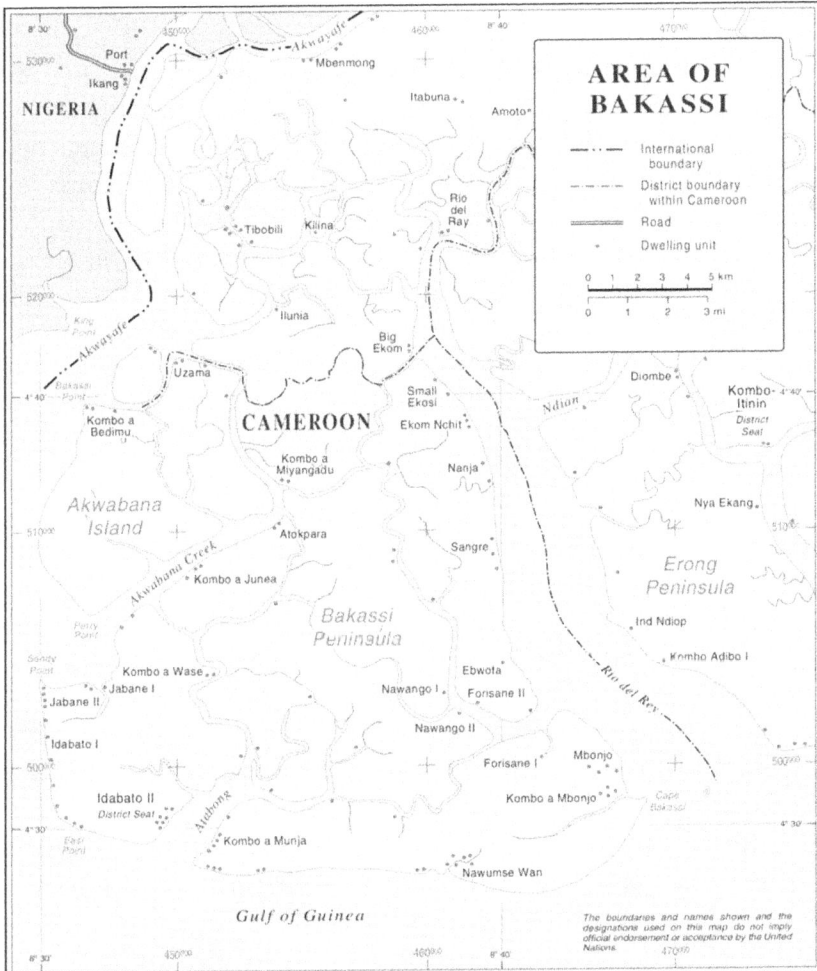

Map N0-4247 UNITED NATIONS
May 2006

Source: UN Department of Peacekeeping Operations Map No. 4247, May 2005

Bibliography

Ajibola, B. 1994. ICJReports. http://www.Nuigalway.ie/human_rights/ Docs/Publications/Castellino%20Abstract.html

Akpan, Anietie. 2006. 'Emotions, worries as Nigeria hands over Bakassi Peninsula to Cameroun'. *The Guardian* http://www .guardiannewsngr .com/weekend/ article01/180806 (accessed 1 April 2007).

Anene, J.C. 1970. *The International boundaries of Nigeria, the framework of an emergent African nation.* London: Longman.

Aondoukaa, Michael (SAN). 2008. (Nigeria's Attorney General and Minister of Justice, 2007-2010). Interview on *Focus Nigeria*, an AIT television programme, 9.00 am, 8 August 2008.

Ardrey, R. 1966. *The territorial imperative: a personal inquiry into the animal origin of property and nations.* New York: Dell Publishing Inc.

Asiwaju, A.I. 2003. *Boundaries and Africa integration, essays in comparative history and policy analysis.* Lagos: Panaf Publishing Inc.

Barkindo, B.M. 1985. 'The Mandara astride the Nigeria-Cameroon Boundary'. In: *Partitioned Africans: Ethnic relations across Africa's international boundaries 1884-1984,* edited by A. I. Asiwaju, pp. 29-49. London: C. Hurst and Company.

Baye, F.M. 2010. 'Implications of the Bakassi conflict resolution for Cameroon'. *African Journal on Conflict Resolution* 10 (1): 9-34.

Daily Times Newspaper Publication of Monday, 14 October 2002, front page and page 2, for the report of the reaction of the Bakassi indigenes against the ICJ's ruling.

Davis, J. and K. Edward. 2002. *Second Track/Citizens' Diplomacy*: Concepts and Techniques for Conflict. Transformation .Lanham, MD: Rowman and Littlefield Publishers, Inc.

Degenhardt, H.W. 1982. 'Cameroon-Nigeria', in *Border and Territorial Disputes*, edited by J. Alan Day. London: Longman.

ICJ year 2002, 10 October General list No. 94, Case concerning the land and Maritime Boundary between Cameroon and Nigeria (Cameroon v Nigeria: Equatorial Guinea Intervening).http:// www.IcjCij.Org/icjwww/Idocket/icnjudgment/icn_ijudgement_20 021010.PDF, Pis 147-148 (accessed on 4 October 2006).

Guardian Newspaper, Thursday, 24 October 2002.

International Court of Justice Press Release 2002/26 bis, 'Land and maritime boundary between Cameroon and Nigeria (Cameroon v

Nigeria: Equatorial Guinea intervening), Summary of the judgment of 10 October 2002.http://WWW.icj-cij.Org/icj WWW/ ipresscom /ipress2002 /ipresscom 2002-26bis_Cn_20021010.htmlI/I/ 1999. (Accessed on 4 October 2006).

Land and Maritime Boundary between Cameroon and Nigeria (Cameroon v Nigeria: Equatorial Guinea intervening) Preliminary objections, judgment, 1998 1CJ Report.

Nicholas, K. T. and S. Baroni. 2010. 'The Cameroon and Nigeria negotiation process over the contested oil rich Bakassi Peninsula'. *Journal of Alternative Perspectives in the Social Sciences* 2 (1): 198-210.

Nigeria's reaction to the judgment of the International Court of Justice in the case concerning the land and Maritime Boundary between Cameroon and Nigeria (Cameroon V Nigeria: Equatorial Guinea Intervening) as published by the Nigerian Information service center, 7 November 2002.

Okon, E.J.L. 1989. 'Potentials of Nigerian boundary corridors as sources of international economic conflict'. In: *Borderlands in Africa. A multidisciplinary and comparative focus on Nigeria and West Africa,* edited by A. I. Asiwaju P.O. Adeniyi. Lagos: University of Lagos Press.

Omoigui, N. 2006. 'The Bakassi story'. http://www.omoigui.com (accessed 18 October).

Oyewo, O. 2005. 'The lingering Bakassi boundary crisis: The way forward'. *Contemporary Issues in Boundaries and Governance in Nigeria,* edited by R.T. Akinyele. Nigeria Lagos: Friedrich Ebert Stiftung.

Price, F. 2005. The Bakassi Peninsula: The border dispute between Nigeria and Cameroon ICE

Case Studies, No. 163, November. www. american. Edu /ted /ice /Nigeria Cameroon .htm.

Sama M.C and D. Johnson-Ross. 2005-2006. 'Reclaiming the Bakassi Kingdom: The anglophone Cameroon-Nigeria border'. *Afrika Zamani* 13 and 14: 103-22.

'Statement of the 23 October 2002 by the Federal Government of Nigeria on the Judgment of the International Court of Justice at The Hague (Cameroon vs. Nigeria with Equatorial Guinea intervening)'. 2009. In: *Peaceful resolution of African boundary conflict, imperatives for multidisciplinary and international research collaboration on the Bakassi Peninsula dispute settlement,* edited by A.I. Asiwaju. Nigeria, Imeko: African Regional institute.

The treaty of protection between Great Britain and the Kings and Chiefs of Old Calabar, 10 September 1884.

United Nations, workshop on the Role of Border Problems in African Peace and Security,2007.

Utton, A.E. 1987. 'The emerging need to focus on trans-boundary resources'. Transboundary Resource *Report* 1 (1):1

Wilkenfeld, J., K. Young, D. Quinn, and V. Asal. 2005. *Mediating international crises.* Oxford: Routledge.

Yagba, T.A.T. 1995. 'The legal regime of African boundaries: An analysis of the Bakassi Peninsula dispute'. Paper presented at the Nigerian Institute of Advanced Legal Studies (NIALS), Lagos Staff Seminar Series 25 August.

PART II

CONCEPTUAL AND EMPIRICAL ISSUES

CHAPTER 4

Major Conceptual Approaches in the Analysis of Territorial Conflicts

Adekunle Amuwo

Introduction and Problématique

While the state's territorial integrity has been a major defining norm of interstate relations since the end of the First World War, this crucial normative edifice was not robust enough to prevent the outbreak, between 1648 and 1945, of over 90 wars involving territorial issues, and about 40 between 1946 and 2000. There were also, between 1945 and 1999, no fewer than 25 interstate wars, a number that was a far cry from 127 intrastate (or civil wars) during the same period (Quinn et al. 2005: 2). What this seems to suggest is that territorial integrity at the national level (or intrastate boundary) has tended, across the globe, to be honored more in its breach than in its observance (Hensel et al. 2006: 4-5). By the same token, about 115 armed conflicts took place across the globe between 1989 and 2001; in 2001 alone, there were no fewer than 34 conflicts in 28 states, including four new ones in Macedonia, Central African Republic (CAR), Guinea-Conakry, and the U.S. invasion of Iraq and Afghanistan consequent upon the events of September 11, 2001 (Gleditsch et. al. 2002: 616).

In view of these extremely cold conflict statistics, it has been argued that "internal conflict has been the dominant form of conflict throughout most of the post-World War II period and certainly since the late 1950s" (Gleditsch et.al. 2002: 623). To the extent that territorial disputes constitute a core of the internal conflicts during the period in question, Forsberg describes them as potentially 'the most threatening phenomena (sic) in the post-Cold War world, supplanting the traditional notion of war as expansionism and territorial disagreements between states' (1996: 433). For Mitchell and Prins, between 1648 and 1989, 'territorial disputes have resulted in more wars across the entire time period than any other single issue' (1999: 171). Even before the formal end of the Cold War, intrastate conflict had already been identified as a major threat to both national and regional peace and stability (Ellingsen 2000: 244). A major theoretical explanation for this multifaceted phenomenon is that the post-Cold War era of intrastate wars is also, in one and the same breath, an era of accentuated capitalist globalization, decline of bipolar power, and resurgence and exacerbation of identity politics (Newman 2004: 175). In the case of Africa, not only did several countries experience separatist conflicts between 1970 and 2001 (Buhaug and Rod 2006: 328), but about two-thirds of the conflicts that took place on the continent in the 1990s were civil wars (Ross 2003).

Yet, the norm of the state's territorial integrity was enshrined in various international and regional organizations and multilateral agreements, including notably the United Nations, the Conference on Security and Cooperation in Europe (CSCE)-the forerunner of the OSCE-and the now defunct Organisation of African Unity (OAU). The CSCE/OSCE affirmed two major elements of the territorial integrity norm in the 1990s, namely, that international borders should not be changed by the use of force (including wars of aggression and secession) and that governments should defend this integrity through the intermediary of an enfranchised citizenry and inclusive governance (Talbott 2000: 157). In a similar vein, Article 2 of the OAU Charter stipulated, for instance, that one of the purposes of the organization was to defend the sovereignty, territorial integrity, and independence of African states. Additionally, Article 3 promised the adherence of the pan-African body to the principle of 'Respect for the Sovereignty and territorial integrity of each state and for its inalienable right to independent existence' (Quinn et al. 2005: 6, 9).

Germane to the major argument of this chapter is a mélange of theoretical approaches, including insights from realist/neorealist perspectives on world politics as well as issue-based theoretical framework. This chapter is anchored more on the latter than on the former. The realist and neorealist perspectives have tended to perceive international relations, respectively, as "a struggle for power" and as "a struggle for security in an anarchic interstate system" (Hensel 2001: 82). Critics who adjudge these perspectives as not rigorous enough have argued that world politics is more about issues. An issues-based approach conceptualizes foreign policy decisions and interactions of major actors (states and non-states alike) as the product of severe contestations over different types of issues. Thus, for Hensel, paraphrasing Mansbach and Vasquez, politics can only be meaningfully understood as 'the quest for value satisfaction, where values are abstract and intangible ends such as wealth, physical security, freedom/autonomy, peace, order, status, or justice' (2001: 82). Territorial or intrastate actors pursue exactly the realization of these objectives and the contestation and disputation are no less severe than at the interstate level. As I show below, the territory is far from being dominated by the state; there are equally a legion of sociopolitical and cultural forces, including ethnic nationalities, competing for space and the resources under the soil (Jeffrey 2006: 837).

Territorial conflicts have ensued, since the second half of the twentieth century, as a result of contested politics and sovereignty: where domestic politics has largely been conducted as a zero-sum game, the protection and enhancement of the rights of the dominant ethno-national, political, racial, cultural group or class has been at the expense of the needs of their minority/dominated/less dominant counterparts and compatriots. Much of the time, all that minority ethnicities are asking for is a legally sanctioned and politically relevant space under the sun for the maintenance and enhancement of their group identity. Many of these conflicts have been categorized as civil wars or new wars. These notably include revolutions, rebellions, secessionist movements, and ethnic revolts (Forsberg 1992). Their occurrence has often been a function of contested sovereignty with its recurrence consequent upon dual sovereignty. In the latter scenario, there is an apparent balance of force, power, and terror between the central government and the rebel movement.

The major *problématique*, or thesis, of this chapter is that the contemporary literature on territory is a severely contested terrain, which perhaps explains why territorial conflicts and other forms of intrastate political violence are extremely savage and brutal. This also explains why the dominant conceptual and theoretical approaches in the analysis of territorial conflicts in contemporary literature are heterogeneous. They are, to that extent-and not unlike the territory-'a pluralized space that is complex, flexible and discontinuous' (Luke 1996: 504). Unless these approaches are taken together holistically, each of them captures no more than a severely limited portion of the reality on the ground.

The chapter is divided into four sections. The first section explicates the notion of territory within the context of contemporary globalization, in terms of its discourses, functional realms, and dimensions. The second reviews the nature and character of new wars/civil wars and armed conflicts in the post-Cold War era, while the third critically interrogates the major conceptual approaches in the analysis of territorial conflicts. The fourth is the conclusion.

I. Explicating Territory

Territory has generally been described as a fundamental feature of a nation-state's sociopolitical life in several respects. For one, territory, from a realist theoretical perspective, is what basically defines a sovereign entity; it is a complete misnomer to talk about a state without a given physical space, a homeland, and a more or less defined border or boundary, one that, as it were, separates it from its neighbors and circumscribes both its authority and legitimacy. In a related manner, power-no less than government-is organized territorially (Keating 2000: 1-2). For another, territory is not only a fundamental power base; it equally constitutes a salient organizing framework and principle for substantive politics. The latter is multifaceted and variegated; the state is the basis for hegemony construction and deconstruction; articulation and de-articulation of the system of representation and participation; construction of identity symbols, spaces, and myths for collective representation and solidarity; distribution of power and resources; definition of reference groups for public policy and the articulation of socioeconomic issues (Keating 2000: 2, 9; Forsberg 1996: 435). There is thus a strong linkage between territory, sovereignty, and identity, such that "territory is a basic source of identity both for states and for people who live in them" (Forsberg 1996: 438)

Territory is also about daily behavior and practices at the local and micro-levels of the territorial scale (Newman n.d: 4). It is arguably at the level of the perpetual sociopolitical construction and reconstruction of territory-with the result that territories are continually being made, de-made, and re-made, and boundaries becoming, not unexpectedly, rather "unstable and fluctuating" (Keating 2000: 8)-that territory has acquired its reputation (not to say notoriety) as something more than a mere geographic expression. Some pertinent analysts (e.g., Forsberg 1996) have described it as a conceptual and notional category with 'political, social, psychological, economic, and cultural perspectives' (438). Thus, as a product of history, territory is something that is

108

constantly constructed and reconstructed by human agency, violently or otherwise. In the words of David Knight, 'territory is not; it becomes, for territory itself is passive, and it is human belief and actions that give territory meaning' (cited in Forsberg 1996: 438).

Two mutually exclusive discourses of territory in the post Cold War era-the contemporary phase of capitalist globalization- come into bold relief here. The first discourse, apparently borrowing from the controversial Fukuyama thesis of 'the end of history' has tended to celebrate the so-called 'end of territory' and a de-territorialized and borderless world. In view of the harsh reality evinced in particular by the hard boundaries of EU member-states and the United States against labor (but certainly not against capital) from much of the Global South, the notions of de-territorialization and a borderless world have been rejected by some analysts in favor of re-territorialization as an on-going concern as well as the changing configurations of power in territories (Newman n.d: 4). Thus, the argument that whereas the territorial compartmentalization of humanity has been historically challenged by both globalism and regionalism; not only is the compartmentalization 'a major abiding and resolute phenomenon of our time,' but political authority remains, for all practical purposes, 'solidly territory-bound' (Duchacek 1986: 206, 208).

More recently, Jeffrey (2006) has concurred by saying that 'despite frequent claims of "de-territorialization," 15 years of state rollback, increasingly globalized markets and harmonized economic landscapes have not reduced the importance of territorial control and border-making' (830). Territory, in short, has not ceased to define the spatial realities of sovereignty, yet the major counter-narrative to the de-territorialization discourse is not so much about fixed and rigidly bordered spaces as it is about a dynamic category that is in a perpetual state of reconfiguration (Newman n.d: 3, 4, 6). As I show below, manifold territorial conflicts in several polities across the globe in the post-Cold War era have fundamentally circumscribed the realist notion of an ordered global system of sovereign states with incontrovertible territorial integrity. Thus, in place of centered sovereignty, there are 'unstated souvrantees(or sovereignties)-decentred power centers, illegitimate law-making bodies, unruly rule-setting agencies'; the territorial battle is between unfixed 'souvran' (sovereign) authorities and fixed 'sovereign' rule (Luke 1996: 495, 500, 505).

There are other aspects of territory that are relevant to our analysis and therefore merit attention. One, there is hardly any consensus in the literature over the significance of territory. For some, territory is arguably 'the most salient of all possible issues' insofar as it is a highly coveted prize due to its 'tangible contents such as strategic military terrain, deposits of valuable resources (such as oil or precious metals), warm water ports, or control over important trade routes' (Hensel 2001: 85). For others, on the contrary, regardless of its primacy as a source of contention amongst state and non-state groups, territory is far from being the most dominant issue in the aftermath of the Cold War (Mitchell and Prins 1999: 179). Two, territories vary in the concentration of value, symbolism, and significance and, by virtue of this, in the degree of attractiveness. On this score, Hensel has argued that 'a claim to a territory that includes a substantial population and resources, has an economic or military strategic location, or is at least partially anchored on ethnic and/or religious bases is considered to be more salient than a claim lacking these characteristics because leaders should be more reluctant to give up a source of partially valuable resources, substantial population, or ethnic/religious kinsmen' (2001: 94). Three, territories are organized in three major functional ways: control exercised over the distribution of resources; maintenance of law, order and authority; as well as legitimization of public order through the intermediary of societal cohesion and integration (Newman n.d: 2).

Four, territorial behavior is exhibited in three main ways: territorial scale (from the macro (central) through meso (state/provincial/local) to micro (grassroots/individual/commune) levels); the tangible/concrete and symbolic/intangible properties of territory in terms of affective and emotional attachment and belonging to specific places and spaces; and the use to which borders and boundaries are put in territorial organization (Newman n.d: 4). On the notion of territorial scale, it is important to underline the saliency of a local geography of armed conflict or civil war (Buhaug and Rod 2006: 331) as well as tendency to pay little more than a nodding attention to the interior. This is often done at great peril to a probable resolution of the conflict, since sparsely populated hinterlands have generally been more favorable to rural guerilla warfare (Buhaug and Rod 2006: 316). It has been argued, for instance, that local tensions principally accounted for the civil war in the Democratic Republic of Congo beginning from the

1990s. Thus, while a peace deal was signed in 2002 and 'democratic' elections were held in 2006, 'the conflict was lasting (sic) because the peace settlement focused on the national and regional levels leaving the sub-national dimension unaddressed' (*Observatoire de l'Afrique* 2008: 9). Similarly, there is a fundamental difference between tangible and non-tangible/symbolic properties of territories over which belligerents dispute and fight and, more importantly, the consequences of the differentiation for the contestation for territorial control and hegemony. Whereas the tangible can be quantified (in form of, say, economic resources or strategic assets), the symbolic is the direct opposite. Thus, while the one lends itself to a less onerous resolution 'through a process of quantification, bartering and exchange, resulting in the contraction or expansion of state territory,' the other is more difficult to resolve by virtue of its intangibility. This is largely due to the fact that 'historical and homeland spaces are so tied up with the formation of national identities that the symbolic components of territorial conflict remain indivisible' (Newman n.d: 21)

Five, while the state is, by far, the most significant organization and interest group from the point of view of maintenance of law and order and the provisioning of public and social goods, there are non-state territorial institutions and interest groups that act as 'rights and duties bearing communities'. This is with a view to protecting not so much individual rights and liberties as the 'collective dignity and collective political and economic rights of territorial communities' (Duchacek 1986: 198). The corollary of this state-society dichotomy at the organizational/conceptual level is the structuration of territorial politics into two unequal parts. The state or central government is said to be imbued with 'high politics' and lower-level governments and private groups with 'low politics'. Now, while the dividing line between the two seemingly irreconcilable levels of government is sometimes blurred, the dichotomy is such that national territories are often sliced into what Duchacek refers to as 'fragmented citizenship and multiple communal identities territorially distributed' (1986: 219).

In Africa, the elites who inherited the evacuated structures of colonial hegemony and their subsequent successors did little to mitigate the colonially inspired unitary form of territorial power arrangement-any more than they reversed lopsided federal systems of political governance in countries such as Nigeria and the Sudan. The result has been the reproduction and, in some cases, exacerbation of

111

the colonial construction and division of African people into master and subject races and ethnicities. The dual colonial process of hierarchically constructed races that were governed by law with rights and responsibilities and horizontally constructed ethnicities that were governed by tradition was paralleled after juridical independence by a political process of bifurcated citizenship of indigenes and settlers. It was an unambiguous recipe for tension and conflict not only between central and lower-level governments, but, more significantly, between 'majority' and 'minority' political ethno-nationalities with all the consequences Africans have witnessed in the past half-century or so, not least secessionist and rebel movements. As recently summarized by Aiyede (2009: 262) in an analysis anchored on the Nigerian federal system, conflict ensues when some groups (mainly 'minority') in the process of trying to preserve their cultural identity and traditional institutions are resisted by the central government and other groups (mainly 'majority'), with reasons for the resistance being the need for collective national identity as well as struggles for resources and political power to reverse discriminatory policies.

II. On Territorial Conflicts

What the foregoing suggests is that post-Cold War territorial conflicts are nothing but a narrative of two opposing logics between identity groups and central governments that compete for hegemony and domination (Luke 1996: 491). Territorial claims are no more than unresolved territorial disputes that have historically been left to fester for a very long time. They are also complex political struggles to the extent that they are largely based on what Jeffrey calls 'historically, culturally and spatially mediated differences' (2006: 843). Territorial conflicts, moreover, involve attempts, with varying degrees of success, to dissolve territoriality and undermine state sovereignty; there is the risk, over time, that violence and conflict may become at once trivialized and de-territorialized (Luke 1996: 493-94). In more or less democratic and more or less authoritarian states, the most victimized regions/provinces and groups and non-state traditional actors and institutions tend to resort to self-help with a view to recovering what they consider-rightly or wrongly-as their social rights and entitlements, including the right to contested space (Boege 2006: 3; Cohen and Frank 2009: 948; Adejumobi 2001).

Two preliminary remarks are in order here. One, there is the view that while the notion of 'new wars' underlines the oft-overlooked relationship between security and development, they hardly represent a paradigm shift insofar as they appear to have many things in common with traditional or old interstate wars. Newman contends that 'all of the factors that characterize new wars have been present to varying degrees, throughout the last 100 years. The actors, objectives, spatial context, human impact, political economy, and social structure of conflict have not changed to the extent argued in the new wars literature' (2004: 179). Second, what has happened to the post-Cold War promise-and hope-of global 'democratic and peace dividend'? It would appear, in relation to Africa, that the incomplete nature of the post-Cold War democratic process, partly due to the value dissonance between the state and society, provides an environment conducive for the emergence and cultivation of political violence (Jeffrey 2006: 831).

Intrastate or territorial conflicts are caused by several factors: state failure, bad governance, poor economic performance, and social grievances. Others are seemingly non-ideological factors such as religious intolerance, ethnic discrimination, wealth inequalities, as well as access to contrabands and peripheral havens (Lichbach et.al. 2003: 10; Buhaug and Rod 2006; Mason 2003: 33). There are two other important explicatory factors of conflict. The first is the collapse of public authority, a phenomenon that tends to blur 'the distinction between public and private combatants, and between combatants and civilians' (Newman 2004: 175). The other is the role of stakes and values in conflict situations, with the former being, on occasion, more significant than the latter (Holsti 1991: 18). New wars have also been characterized by a dramatic increase in the number of civilian casualties and forced human displacement; increasing and deliberate targeting of civilians; and ethnic homogenization. The notion of new wars equally underlines the nonconventional dimensions of war, in particular the territorialization, regionalization, privatization, commercialization of conflicts, and proliferation of conflict parties. Belligerents tend to fight less over state-related issues such as seizure of power and more over access to lucrative natural resources and primary commodities; civil wars are not only 'loot-seeking,' they also are 'justice-seeking' (Soysa and Wagner 2006; Collier and Hoeffler 2004; Le Billion 2001; Englebert and Ron 2004).

In addition, the political economy of new wars throws up a legion of uncommon actors involved in unusual business (or business-*not*-as-usual). These actors, operating within an extremely dynamic and unpredictable context, consist of, amongst others, warlords, private military companies, insurgency groups, ethnic parties, mafia-like criminal networks, mercenaries, regular armies, and international aid organizations. There is little doubt that these complex national and transnational networks and groups pay little attention to notions of state, sovereignty, borders, and territorial integrity (Boege 2006; Tilly 2004:10; Newman 2004: 175; Kalyvas 2008: 1045). In this respect, Luke (1996) raises the important point about day and night control of different swathes of the national territory, respectively, by central and provincial governments. Thus, while the former controls much of the urban ecology during the day, 'after sundown, and throughout most of the interior, no one has supreme power, even though many criminals, renegade military commanders, guerilla movements and village chiefs wield some controlling influence in the narrow locales where they are operating at the time' (492).

This suggests that civil wars fought, as they are, within the boundaries of recognized nation-states 'between parties subject to a common authority at the outset of the hostilities' (Kalyvas 2007: 417) often take place in the countryside with traditionally rugged, rough, forested, and sparsely populated rural terrains where rebels and guerillas find it relatively easy to operate (Buhaug and Rod 2006: 317, 328; Kalyvas 2007: 422). It is at this level that the difference between territorial and governmental conflicts comes into sharp focus. While territorial wars are essentially conflicts over the autonomy question, their locale is often tucked away in the most disadvantaged peripheral regions. On the contrary, governmental conflict is, to a large extent, an urban-based phenomenon close to important sites of strategic mineral and oil resources and other key primary commodities (Buhaug and Rod 2006: 325, 327, 332). The scenario is often more complex, however: the exploitation and export of actual resources (oil, diamond, copper, and other minerals) is dominated and controlled by agents of the government (e.g., transnational corporations, TNCs). The government rarely exploits these resources-that job is, as it was during the colonial period, handled by western TNCs and, in recent years, Chinese state agencies.

Perhaps a final element of analysis here (before the more substantive third section) is the international dimension of territorial conflicts in Africa, in particular the problematic nature of external interventions. Two main sets of actors are involved at this level. The first set of actors is made up the global powers-that-be, with the United States leading a pack of Western and Eastern powers, whose overarching Africa foreign policies are meant to maximize their national, geo-strategic and politico-cultural interests at all costs and whose intervention through international aid in African conflicts often has mixed results. The second set of actors consists of transnational social forces and groups, which not only defy territories and borders in their global outreach to foster and intensify capitalist accumulation, but also maximize space for development purposes; however development is understood (Robinson 2002). To all intents and purposes, therefore, conflicts in Africa have always been a function of the interests of a combination of transnational capital/class/state/social forces and the governments of global hegemonic states in search of lucrative but cheap primary commodities and resources on the continent. Clearly, a combination of easy and profitable access to resources, manipulation of local ethnicities and identities for commercial purposes by foreign powers and economic support by external patrons (Le Billion 2001: 574, 578; Jeffrey 2006: 838; Soysa and Wagner 2006) has often sustained secessionist conflicts and rebel movements in Africa.

III. Major Conceptual Approaches

This section adumbrates the major conceptual approaches in the analysis of territorial conflicts in developing political economies, amongst which many African countries are chief. As separate conceptual or theoretical models, each of them can, at best, offer only a partial explanation of conflict situations, especially in the post-Cold War era-an era that has seemingly thrown up a new political economy of self-reliance and dependence on internal resources, both material and political. This explains the often frantic and frenetic drive for the appropriation and control of both productive and extractive resources (especially the latter) by rebel and guerilla movements. While an increasingly influential section of the contemporary literature on new wars has cautioned against an excessively deterministic analysis of civil or territorial wars anchored on materialist explanations of conflicts, the rational-actor model of political violence-the organizing framework of this conceptual approach-continues to be dominant. This approach is based on the 'new institutional economics' or the 'new political economy' that subscribes to a major tenet of rational choice theory according to which 'social behavior (and hence outcomes) is explicated by the interplay of individuals pursuing their own best interests and preferences on the basis of rational choices and available information' (Robinson 2002: 1058). In a fundamental sense, greed hypothesis is rooted in rational choice economics (Stewart 2002: 343). In the same vein, materialist explanations stipulate that 'natural resources invite loot-seeking behavior, which supplies the motive and finance for violence' (Soysa and Wagner 2006: 2)

The scholarly critique against the rationalist approach is two-fold. One, objectives of war practitioners are hardly reducible to material factors; rationality is not limited to calculations of greed and profit making, nor is it the exclusive preserve of insurgents. Rational strategic and economic reasons or, for that matter, inordinate ambition and desire to have control over primary commodities and lootable natural resources are but one path to violence. Other paths include ethnic mobilization and genocide, and genuine normative, power-political, ideological, and identity grievances. Men-and women-are concerned not only about their economic or material welfare (tangible demands), but also about intangible grievances such as who they are, their dignity and how public authorities treat them and the groups to which they belong. Power struggles can be the result of disagreement over territory much in the same way they can be over normative questions. Another way of putting the foregoing is to say that the dichotomy between 'greed model' and 'grievances model' is too simplistic to the extent that both are intertwined-'resource curse' may, for instance, be as potent an explicatory schema as 'poverty' (Kaufman 2009: 660; Newman 2004: 176, 183; Englebert and Ron 2004: 77; Sambanis 2004; Forsberg 1996: 436). Two, 'methodological individualism,' the core unit of analysis privileged by proponents of the rational-choice model of analysis, while relevant, appears not wholly suited to a comprehensive understanding of conflict situations in Africa where societies are largely run as communitarian and moralistic entities. In Africa, the significance of groups (generally organized on the basis of race, geography, gender, religion, ethnicity, etc.) and social movements, in contradistinction to atomized, if rational, individuals, can hardly be over-emphasized (Walder 2009).[1]

In what follows, our implicit argument is that political explanations of conflict situations should be privileged above economic factors insofar as 'resources are unlikely to trigger civil war in a stable political environment' (Englebert and Ron 2004: 64). In concluding their analysis of the effects of oil wealth on armed conflict in Congo (Brazzaville), Englebert and Ron (2004) argue that the interface between primary commodities and domestic politics is crucial in understanding both the cause and the prolongation of territorial conflicts. For them, 'if a country has a stable political system, authoritarian or otherwise, it is unlikely to experience civil war, regardless of resource availability and distribution' (75). Expressed differently, theories of rebel motivation should encompass both greed/desire for economic gain by potential rebels and political grievance, the latter is regarded as an umbrella category under which is hidden 'a wide range of perceived injustices' (Englebert and Ron 2004: 63). Conflicts should, moreover, be regarded as being spurred not only by resource scarcity ('need') or resource abundance ('greed'), but, more holistically, as a sociopolitical phenomenon and a 'historical product' that is 'inseparable from the social construction and political economy of resources' (Le Billion 2001: 575).

Finally, virtually all the major conceptual approaches are socially constructed and, by virtue of that, cannot be deemed to constitute sufficient explicatory schemas for conflict, even though they may be useful as necessary explanatory factors. On the specific linkage between natural resources and armed conflict in Africa (one that has spiraled into so-called 'resource curse' on the continent), it has been argued that 'the role played by diamond extraction and revenues in contemporary African conflicts is neither unique nor a recent phenomena (sic), but is inscribed in the long succession of extraction of resources, bringing together networks of local elites, trans-border commercial agents, and global markets to export slaves, rubber, timber, coffee, minerals, petroleum or diamonds' (Le Billion 2001: 566). In the same vein, ethnicity as a potent structural factor in the understanding of armed conflicts in ethnically-segmented societies merely predisposes ethnic combatants to war; it does not fully explain why some ethnic disputes turn violent and others do not (Stewart 2002: 344; Jeffrey 2006: 832).

Rational-Actor Approach

This approach is generally applied to mineral/natural-resource-rich and primary commodity-dependent states, the main proposition being that economic opportunities constitute a major motivation for conflict. Governments in such countries, moreover, are more susceptible than their resource-poor counterparts to conflict through a combination of several factors. These vary from state weakness through reduced growth and corruption to poor accountability and increased poverty. Further, many a resource-dependent government hardly provides adequate public goods for the majority of the population largely due to a rather tenuous or fragile relationship between the state and the citizenry. Because the latter hardly pay any meaningful tax--except for public servants whose tax contributions are deducted at source--they are hard put to it to demand effective social service delivery and transparent and accountable governance from public authorities. Resource-linked corruption further saps the capacity of central governments to exercise effective control over their territorial integrity, let alone provide law and order in extractive regions. The lack of appropriation of national wealth seems to push disgruntled identity groups in resource-rich areas to seek self-determination by organizing rebel movements (Ross 2003; Sambanis 2004; Fearon 1994; Fearon and Laitin, 2003; Collier and Hoeffler 1998, 2004). In other words, irredentist movements--such as in Angola's Cabinda exclave and Nigeria's Niger Delta region--arise when resource-rich communities feel that they do not get a fair share of the revenues obtained from the exploitation and sale of oil and other mineral resources, but are forced to bear all the costs (especially environmental) of exploitation.

The rational-actor analytical framework has at least four related theories embedded in it. The first is the structural theory of violence that postulates a largely negative impact of exogenous factors over indigenous power and resource relations. These theories stipulate that the vulnerability of poor, primary commodity-dependent countries stems from their incorporation as junior partners into the extremely asymmetrical and exploitative global capitalist system. The tripartite alliance of unequal trade, labor-unfriendly foreign direct investment (FDI), and transnational corporations (TNCs) exploit the economy, cheap labor, and natural resources, and by so doing, sow seeds of violence. Oil and mineral-extracting TNCs appear to go further by hiring or constituting local armies or militias for their own protection and exacerbating conflicts by directly or indirectly funding rebels. The distinct possibility of a permanent praetorian state always looms large within that context. Two caveats are in order here. One, poor local institutions in many poor countries tend to enhance the ability of local elites to 'cooperate' with their foreign benefactors and principals (the TNCs) to exploit, almost without mercy, national resources. The point is that major oil companies have not been able to behave with the same type of impunity in some oil-rich countries because of the existence of different sets of institutions--those that have effectively prevented political and other elites from engaging in opportunistic arrangements with the TNCs. Two, property rights play a key role in many conflict situations. There is the distinct possibility that conflict is generated by the fact that property rights in environmental and/or natural resources in many African countries are hardly well specified, let alone rigorously and robustly enforced. The main issue is the failure of many African countries to specify property rights for their environmental resources. The 'open-access' approach, which exists in virtually all these countries, where ownership is established only through capture (with the central government having the wherewithal to be the first to capture), provides opportunities for conflict and destructive mobilization.[2]

The second adjunct theory is the political ecology of war, or what Le Billion refers to as 'the geography and political economy of natural resources' (2001: 561). Four elements of the geography of resources--equally related to property rights--can be underlined. These are:

a) The proximate or distant location of resources such that 'the higher the availability of valuable resources at the periphery of control, the greater the likelihood of prolonged conflict';

b) The respective geographical location of both extractive and productive industries;

c) Fragmentation or the spatial distribution of the people across economic activities; and

d) Peripheralization of economic networks the further they are from the seat of power and its potential impact on conflict (Le Billion 2001: 570-71).

Similarly, there is emphasis on two major hypotheses. The first is that the scarcity of renewable resources engenders conflicts: people will not only fight one other to secure access to resources capable of assuring their survival, 'the more scarce the resource, the more bitter the fight'. The second is the direct opposite of the first, namely, abundant non-renewable resources (such as oil, diamond, timber, gems, etc.) have the potential to cause conflicts. This is due to the fact that as primary commodities, they are 'easily and heavily taxable and are, therefore, attractive to both the ruling elites and their competitors' (Le Billion 2001: 564).

The third embedded theory is that of the supply of arms to private military organizations. The main hypothesis, following Paul Collier et al. is that 'if rebels can secure enough human resources for the battle against authorities, and if they can escape the persecution of state authorities, civil war is likely to occur' (cited in Lichbach et al. 2003: 7). Diamond-fuelled conflicts in Angola, Liberia, and Sierra-Leone (and not in other diamond-rich countries such as Botswana and South Africa, where property rights are much better defined and more clearly specified--and the National Question and interethnic contestation are not as vexed as in many other African countries) in the 1990s, which were veritable politico-economic civil wars, provoked the suggestion that loot was at their root. Fourth and lastly, the private motivation or greed hypothesis postulates that war is a profitable venture from the - perspective of unemployed/underemployed/unemployable urban, semi -urban and rural youth, with both sundry licit and illicit trading and networking permissible (Buhaug and Rod 2006: 320; Stewart 2002: 343; Ukeje 2007).

The rational-actor model is encapsulated in several key arguments. One, violent conflicts are mainly driven by economic motives or agendas. Collier's oft-quoted argument (or broad generalization) on greed best surmises the proposition: 'the true cause of much civil war is not the loud discourse of grievance, but the silent force of greed' (2000: 101). It should perhaps be added that Collier's definition of 'greed' is akin to the profit-maximization that drives much capitalist exploitation. While the objective of combatants at the outset may be to wrestle political power, as the armed conflict progresses and proves profitable, the continuation of violence, rather than military victory, becomes the goal of rebels (Collier 2000: 91; Newman 2004: 177-78).

120

For David Keene, 'wartime political economy may benefit governments and rebels, and as a result some parties may be more anxious to prolong a war than to win it' (cited in Englebert and Ron 2004: 63). Two, the importance of primary commodities in understanding the outbreak of civil wars can only be underestimated by the political and policy elite at the peril of the all-round health of the nation-state. These commodities are valorized in two major senses: on the one hand, they require neither much manufacturing nor significant marketing expertise; and, on the other, they are easily preyed on by rebels when they are transported through so-called geographical 'choke points,' that is, areas of extraction and/or transportation routes and sold for much-needed foreign exchange (Englebert and Ron 2004: 63; Buhaug and Rod 2006: 320). Three-and related to the foregoing-there is an apparent interplay between territory and resources, that is to say, between 'physically accessible and geographically dispersed' spaces and places and 'widely dispersed subsoil minerals'. The point here is that the more proximate the commodities, the more heightened the possibility of armed rebellion. By the same token, combatants, to the extent of their rationality, display and market their martial skills only for the appropriation of territories that are simultaneously densely populated and have proven economic worth (Le Billion 2001: 566; Englebert and Ron 2004: 76; Buhaug and Rod 2006: 320, 328, 330).

Four, armed conflict is a function of opportunities for looting by rebels. On this score, it can be argued that the provision of institutional arrangements that offer all ethno-national/regional and other groups within the country equal opportunity to participate in, and benefit from, the dividends of post-independence economic growth and development may contribute to reducing or minimizing engagement in such violence. After all, what the 'rebels' seek to achieve is little more than primitive accumulation. Insofar as what Le Billion refers to as the 'economy of proximity' and 'economy of networks' (2001: 569) are woven around extracted mineral resources, they tend to make up for lack of infrastructural power by central governments and guerilla movements. Finally, the rational-actor approach differentiates between two different, if related, phenomena: natural resources that cause conflicts; and natural resources that fuel or prolong conflicts (Alao and Olonisakin 2000: 25). In other words, conflicts are more likely to be provoked by present, clear, and definite grievances, but could be prolonged and exacerbated by economic considerations. Goran Hyden avers that whereas African conflicts are often fought over resources, 'they are usually triggered off by competitive politics associated with election systems' (cited in Agbu 2006: 3). Related to this is that both greed and grievance often get enmeshed in the real world of conflict and violence; with key external interests at stake, the dynamics of contemporary international political economy of oil and other strategic minerals is that political grievances easily metamorphose into economic-driven warfare.

Identity/Ethnicity

By all accounts, most of the civil wars since the second half of the twentieth century are conflicts fought over people's identity, which essentially is based on ethnic and religious differences. While ethnic identities have historically been used for socialization, mobilization, and collective action, nowhere has a systematic and unambiguous link been established between ethnicity and conflict. Some of the time, poverty can easily tie ethnicity and conflict together in materialist or class analysis. The linkages between identity, resources, and violence are, at best, tenuous and fragile because several factors are at play in a conflict situation and it is not always possible to isolate the ethnic factor and determine its approximate role in causing and fueling civil wars (Le Billion 2001: 568). Nobody would ever know for sure the personal agendas of warlords and militia heads who claim to fight in the name of their ethnic group--a point already alluded to above. How much of individual self-aggrandizement and group interests are involved in conflicts over both the tangible and the intangible? While there is no direct correlation or one-to-one relationship between ethnic identity and political support for ethnic organizations and ethnic-based militia/guerilla movement, it has been argued that 'the distinction between ethnic and non-ethnic civil war is based on a micro-foundation that posits a clear link between identity and behavior . . . this micro-foundation violates constructivist insight' (Kalyvas 2008: 1044). Precisely because ethnic issues are about crucially important affective ties, some analysts are of the considered opinion that ethnic issues are, at least in some contexts, more important than resource issues (Forsberg 1992: 470-71).

The major reason for the absence of a convincing linkage between ethnicity and conflict in, say, Africa is the fact that ethnicity has been a socially constructed or invented category since the colonial times. To the extent that the postcolonial state has preserved the status quo, ethnicity, and, in consequence, the definition of the people and their territorial borders, are constantly in a state of flux and subject to the meanings and symbolism attached to them by domestic and transnational powers-that-be (Kaufman 2009: 658). Identity shift and, on occasion, ethnic defection have been the major defining characteristics of the constructivist approaches in the study of ethnicity (Kalyvas 2008; Ellingson 2000: 232). The flip side is that whereas civil wars shape ethnic identities by hardening them, conflict situations engender fundamental changes driven by sundry demands and incentives (Kalyvas 2008: 1046, 1063). In short, whereas ethnicity is an ascriptive and constructive identity covering 'color, appearance, language, religion, some other indicator of common origin or some combination thereof', it is not formed once and for all time, but rather over time. Multi-ethnicity factors also include shared history, beliefs and homeland.

A section of the contemporary literature on ethnicity suggests that, subject to the degree and extent of ethnic fragmentation, the ethnic factor comes into play in several ways. The first is the presence of a dominant ethno-national group that is large and politically homogenous enough to institutionalize 'differentiated and unequal status of citizenship' and political discrimination (Adejumobi 2001: 148) vis-à-vis less dominant and minority groups. The broad generalization formulated at this level of analysis is that 'the larger the dominant group, the greater the likelihood of domestic conflict' (Ellingson 2000: 232). Two, a crude combination of ethno-nationalism, clan politics, and social exclusion is capable of engendering not only armed conflict, but also calls by ethnic minorities for what Ghoukassian refers to as 'territorial re-distribution along ethno-national loyalties' (2008: 154). This is, however, a rather complex political process; an ethnically homogenous society is capable of fragmenting and disintegrating much in the same way that minority ethno-nationalities that are hegemonic in their home region can also be responsible for the outbreak of violent conflicts (Buhaug and Rod, 2001: 321).

In consequence of the foregoing, ethno-territorial conflicts are a function of several concrete factors on the ground. These include: the seeming determination of ethnic leaders, according to the theory of indivisible territory, to defend their peculiar territorial or spatial turf by all possible means, including the deployment of force; and non-protection of rights of ethnic/racial/political minorities particularly in polities that have yet to cultivate adequate political sagacity and democratic acumen necessary to manage heterogeneity and diversity in ethnically segmented and culturally pluralistic societies, in particular those in the hinterlands (Talbott 2000: 159; Newman n.d: 11). Others are: the undue politicization of domestic disputes and spaces that, ultimately, result into violence; as well as the politically insensitive act of treating ethnic groups as if they are unitary actors (Jeffrey 2006: 839; Kalyvas 2008: 1063).

Power Politics

Power politics is traditionally cast in relational terms, as 'the consequences of one actor using its power advantage over another' (Cohen and Frank 2009: 949). Implicated in power politics are relations of coercion, domination, hegemony, elite manipulations-as well as the politics of resistance. In territorial terms, power politics involves attempts, in the real world, by majority groups and ruling elites to construct power hegemonies over minority groups and non-ruling elites and concerted efforts at resistance by the latter. The end justifies the means for resistance politics, which explains why no stones are left unturned in an attempt to vitiate the essence of power politics which, for dominant groups, is 'the private appropriation of space, the monopolization of space, or the exclusion of others from space' (Keating 2000: 6). Since the state is the 'primary territorialization of power'-as well as the most important territorial organization-power politics can also be explicated as the competition to wrest power with a view to controlling the state and, more significantly, exploiting its immense resources, including strategic resources and primary commodities. To realize this goal would entail, on the part of dominated groups and classes, the putting in place of mechanisms capable of compromising the sovereignty and autonomy of the state as presently constituted (Newman 2004: 176; Jeffrey 2006: 836-37). To all intents and purposes, therefore, power politics comes into sharp focus as 'the critical factor which determines to what extent territorial intangibility is used as a social construction in the perpetuation, or resolution, of conflict' (Newman n.d: 1).

The power politics approach has a number of important elements. One, territorial space and resources are dominated by some groups at the expense of others; where dominated groups are so much hedged in and so-called democratic artifacts such as power-sharing arrangements/agreements are inadequate to guarantee minority groups neither the political rights nor the physical safety they desire, political violence may be the only way out. Thus, the importance of the observation by Ellingsen that 'power-sharing by itself is not enough. It must also be in the political or ethno-national leaders' interest to share power' (2000: 246). Expressed differently, there are important linkages between power relations, conflict, and territorial characteristics. The main explicatory variables include the following: the nature of power relations between majority and minority groups, as well as their leaders; the extent and intensity of power-sharing and power imposition; and what other contentious/intervening variables get out of hand, such that attachment to territories and their resources produces conflicts some of the time and does not some other time (Newman n.d: 4-5, 10). Two, the argument that the explanation of territorial conflict through the lenses of power politics is about the intersection between inherency and contingency, that is to say, 'the interaction between diverse aspects of political economy context and contentious politics'. While inherency denotes 'prior lower-level conflicts', contingency refers to those structural factors that give impetus to low-intensity conflict; how processes of repression and dissent not only get transformed into civil wars but also 'transform democratic opposition movements into revolutionary insurgencies' (Lichbach et al. 2003: 5; Mason 2003: 33).

Three, and finally, there are equally important linkages between resource rents, patron-client networks, and power relations. It is perhaps at this level, more than anywhere else, that the concept of interest defined in terms of power (Forsberg, 1996: 434) reaches its concrete apogee. No soft power is at play here; on the contrary, when minority groups and the political opposition are dealt a severe blow by the failure or inability of ruling elites in resource-rich countries to diversify the economy, it is hard power that is on display. This is because economic diversification, when it produces alternative platforms of economic power, tends to strengthen political competition against the ruling elites. Le Billion's (2001) insight on this score is particularly illuminating. Resource rents shape politics through the creation of clientelist networks that, except in oil-rich micro-states (Gulf states, for example), are as closed as possible. The tight control of the resource sector by the ruling elites forecloses primitive and wealth accumulation outside the official patron-client network. Privatization and deregulation policies that have favored the largely foreign private sector further reinforce the hegemonic political position of the ruling elites at the expense of the political opposition. The consequence is that 'as the wealth power gap between the ruling and the ruled increases, so does the frustration of marginalized groups seeing political change as the only avenue for satisfying their greed and aspirations or expressing their grievances. In the absence of widespread political consensus…violence becomes for these groups the main, if not the only, route to power' (Le Billion 2001: 567).[3]

Unequal Development and Horizontal Inequalities

Whereas some scholars of contentious politics and civil war claim that inequality does not constitute a cogent or viable explanatory schema for armed combat, preferring rather to prioritize the resources and opportunities available to political entrepreneurs (Fearon and Laitin 2003; Collier 2000: Collier and Hoeffler 2004), there is ample scholarly literature to the contrary. With two sides to it-horizontal and vertical, which, respectively, measure welfare differences between groups and individuals-inequality, following Robinson, is perhaps best explicated as 'the permanent consequence of the capitalist social relations' (2002: 1067). A conflict being largely a group affair, emphasis in the literature is not so much on vertical inequalities as on horizontal inequalities, the latter are understood as systematic inequalities, using indices such as political access and economic opportunities, between culturally formed groups, such as ethnic, religious, or regional groups. They are, by the same token, inequalities that coincide with identity cleavages and are capable of worsening group grievances (Ostby 2006; Stewart 2002: 343). Generally rooted in historical circumstances, such as colonial policies, which-as already remarked-created a hierarchy or ethnicities favorable to the colonial administration, historical inequalities have been exacerbated during the postcolonial period by, amongst other things, exclusivist politico-economic policies of the ruling elites and, since the mid-1980s, by market-friendly but people-hurting economic policies regrouped under the IMF/World Bank-stipulated structural adjustment programs (SAPs).[4]

Inspired by group motivation hypothesis, historical inequalities are perceived as an aggregate of accumulated resentments and ambitions inspired by group differences. Historical and vertical inequalities find common expression in the war process; while group motivations flag off conflict, private ambitions prolong them, as the examples of the Sudan, Sierra-Leone and Liberia copiously demonstrated in the 1990s (Stewart 2002: 343).These inequalities are essentially welfare in nature and their non-provision to some segments of the national population generally reflects a failure of the social contract between the state and the citizenry. The inequalities are calculated amongst different groups using several indicators including household assets and educational levels (Ostby 2006). For all practical purposes, therefore, rebellion movements are under-girded by what Jeffrey refers to as 'complex historical dynamics' (2006: 833). Thus, the argument that 'horizontal inequalities are most likely to lead to conflicts where they are substantial, consistent and increasing over time' (Stewart 2002: 343). In the same vein, changes in inequality over a period of time are critical in explaining the geographical expansion and escalation of conflict (Macours 2006: 3).

There is, further, a dynamic relationship between socioeconomic historical inequalities at the mass level and political historical inequalities at the elite level. Political elites who are excluded from the mainstream political economy have strong incentives to mobilize their supporters for violence along decidedly group lines, much in the same way that widespread socioeconomic inequalities amongst victimized masses lend them to easy mobilization by ethnic champions. The argument, however, is that, from the point of view of mass mobilization for conflict, political historical inequalities amongst the elites are more critical than socioeconomic historical inequalities amongst the masses (Ostby 2006: 10).

Decentralization and Regional Grievances

This approach seems to correspond to the model of justice-seeking wars, according to which 'groups form on the basis of ousting a grievance-causing government (political system) and ending injustice'. Insofar as justice is a public good that, paradoxically, is often conspicuous by its absence in many a putative neoliberal democracy, it is suggested that movements devoted to its realization often face enormous collective action problem (Soysa and Wagner 2006: 8).[5] A slice of the problem in question stems from the lack of direct correlation between grievances/deprivation and conflict: whereas political entrepreneurs are needed to begin conflict, successful mobilization of a defined victimized group willing and able to seize upon its sense of discrimination and grievance is a *sine qua non* for the continuation of conflict (Macours 2006: 2).

The central thesis of grievance-or what can also be referred to as the political-ideological explanation of conflict-is that conflicts are at once a political project and a political struggle. Social, political, and economic deprivation, income and asset inequality, political repression, lack of political tolerance or exclusionary politics have been the main causes of political violence. Political grievances have generally revolved around four main issues, namely, identity, participation, distribution, and legitimacy. A major grievance of many ethnic nationalities (both majority and minority, aside from those in power) is the almost total absence of human development and human security for their own people. Preoccupation with human development has tended to focus attention, following Michel Foucault, on *bio-politics*. The latter is concerned with the biological wellbeing of a population, particularly disease control and prevention, adequate food and water supply, sanitation, shelter, and education (Amuwo 2009). Ethno-nationalities and other social groups often have either of the following two policy stances as far as welfare-enhancing benefits are concerned. The first is that the government should do no more than provide them with an enabling policy-institutional environment within which they can create the wealth they need to meet their social obligations. This position seemed to have been reinforced by the orthodox market reforms of the 1980s and 1990s that, among other things, occasioned the rolling back of the state. The second is that these groups want the government not only to guarantee these benefits to them but, perhaps more important, also supply them with all these welfare-enhancing benefits. Both stances are far from being mutually exclusive--and nothing, in theory, stops a government--any government--from playing both roles, even though, in practice, many neo-Structural Adjustment regimes in Africa may be in a position of *'neither nor'*.

Decentralization consists, *inter alia*, of granting both legally and constitutionally sanctioned citizenship and group rights to ethno-nationalities and regions. These rights include greater autonomy, higher degree of self-determination, recognition of communal identities and sensitivities in such areas as language and education, as well as the transfer of power by the central government to local authorities (Talbott 2000: 156). Regional grievances constitute a bold response to the failure of the central government to initiate and sustain genuine and wide-ranging decentralization reforms not only territorially, but, perhaps more significantly, over the sharing of national power, wealth, and resources. Collective grievances emanate from members of disadvantaged groups and regions that have been antagonized and frustrated by the state's inadequate or unfair responses to their particularistic regional demands-including attacks on them to prevent them from demanding for more resources and political power (Ostby 2006: 6). Separatist movements are, thus, a function of perceived unfair appropriation by central governments and richer regions of the wealth and resources that belong to rebel regions (Ross 2003: 15-16). When grievances persist and the central government appears incapable of dealing with them fairly and justly, there is a strong temptation on the part of the aggrieved to abandon nonviolent collective action.

There are important local-central linkages here: as articulated by Mason, 'whether local activists succeed in mobilizing a following will be determined primarily by local conditions. Whether local movements remain non-violent or transform into revolutionary movements depends in large part on how the state responds to non-violent opposition movements' (2003: 26). There is also the important consideration about the extent to which post-Cold War 'democratic infrastructure' (much of which is neoliberal, top-down, donor-driven, labor-hurting, and market-regarding.

While there may be nothing intrinsically wrong with 'market-regarding' infrastructure, many an African state hardly responds positively and productively to market-regarding institutions because it is anything but a capitalist and market society and people-unfriendly) How much positive impact would a seeming politically inclusive proportional electoral system have in a polity where majority of the population, across well-known social cleavages, are systematically denied the *means to live* by an actually existing capitalist production and accumulation system even though the national constitution generously accords them the *right to life*? According to Ross, 'governments that are less than fully democratic are less able to resolve the grievances of their citizens, and hence may be more prone to outbreaks of violent conflict' (2003: 14).[6]

Relative Deprivation and Poverty

Relative deprivation and poverty may be regarded as two sides of the same coin and are, by that singular fact, not mutually exclusive. Landlessness and poverty were, for instance, listed as elements of relative deprivation by Nepal's Maoist Party in its 1998 publication *Political economic rationale of People's War* (Macours 2006: 2). Relative deprivation has been explicated in two related senses: it is, on the one hand, a growing gap between *expected need satisfaction* and *actual need satisfaction*, and, on the other, 'a subjective characteristic that occurs when a person does not receive what he (sic) thinks he has the right to receive' (Ellingsen 2000: 230). One of the earliest formulations of the group anchorage in the relationship between relative deprivation and conflict comes from veteran scholar Ted Gurr. For him, 'the greater the deprivation an individual perceives relative to his (sic) expectations, the greater his discontent, the more widespread and intense is discontent among members of a society, the more likely and severe is civil strife' (1970: 596).[7]

Poverty, on its part, can be understood in several ways. One, it is a material state when a bad economic predicament begins to worsen (Ross 2003: 6). Two, it is fostered by-and is perhaps the result of-'economic discrimination, income inequality, and scarce and unequal access to various resources' (Ellingsen 2000: 245), as well as repression and state breakdown (Lichbach et al. 2003: 28; Mason 2003: 33). Three, rising levels of poverty are worsened by a decline in state services (Stewart 2002: 343). The reciprocal relations between poverty and conflict are furnished by the Green War hypothesis, which states that environmental degradation is not only a source of poverty, but also a cause of conflict. This hypothesis also draws a strong linkage between environmental poverty, resource riches and conflict (Stewart 2002: 344).[8]

IV. Concluding Remarks

Two points merit emphasis in closing. One, while low-intensity internal wars are an on-going social concern in virtually all unequal and unjust societies, isolated from the others, none of the major conceptual approaches adumbrated in this chapter can satisfactorily explain conflict situations. By virtue of being essentially politicized, constructed, and reconstructed conceptual and explicatory schemas, what each of them does is to *predispose* change agents towards rebellion-as well as help to mobilize foot-troops towards the attainment of their objectives. They do not explain why political violence takes place at a particular point in time, and not another. The critical intervening variable in this respect is opportunity-that is to say, opportune time to strike-which is itself contingent on the balance of power, interest, and terror in any given conflict-latent polity (Ellingsen 2000: 230).

Two, the saliency of the external factor--or imperialism, *tout court*--in understanding Africa's territorial conflicts can hardly be over-emphasized. To be sure, it has become increasingly unfashionable in the post-Cold War era of so-called 'end of history' to privilege the use of radical historiography/political economy in explaining sociopolitical phenomena (because of the formal triumph of capitalism/neo-liberalism and its productive and social relations over their socialist homologues), yet imperialism and sub-imperialism remain core defining features of interstate relations at the global level. And these relations also continue to have deep-seated domestic resonance and impact. In a similar vein, war-lordism and imperialism reinforce each other. Thus, while sundry internal actors abound both in the foreground and background of territorial conflicts, largely invisible but powerful transnational forces and actors are actively at work contributing to causing and prolonging conflicts on the African continent. These forces need to be thoroughly interrogated and brought to bear, both conceptually and empirically, in the analysis of the continent's territorial conflicts.

Acknowledgment

The author gratefully acknowledges the critical insights and comments of a peer reviewer on the original version of this chapter.

Notes

1. To be sure, 'methodological individualism' and other such approaches based on rational choice have been used to study conflict situations in Africa and other societies that are organized along 'communitarian and moralistic' lines. The approach has also proved useful in analyzing the behavior of leading lights of the opportunistic African political elite who, while maximizing their self-interest, manage to convince their ethno-national/regional entity that their 'fight' is the group's fight and drags the group into what are no more than personal attempts at primitive accumulation. There is little doubt that many post-independence conflicts in Africa have been of this type. Except for individuals such as Mandela, Lumumba, and Nyerere, very few post-independence African political leaders have exhibited self-interested characteristics (the most common example of which is obsession with *primitive accumulation*). Not only the usual suspects--Mobutu, Bongo, Biya, Bokassa--but also the great pan-Africanist Kwame Nkrumah all exhibited self-interested behaviors while in office. As far as the People's Republic of China (PRC) is concerned, whereas the communist political leadership sought, between 1949 and 1978, to promote collectivism and wipe out any vestiges of individualism supposedly imbibed by the people through the agency of Western missionaries during the pre-communist era, today, individualism is adjudged as the most important motivator behind the PRC's emergence as an economic superpower. Finally, the importance of many individualism-based theories goes beyond an analysis of the behavior of the individual. Public choice theory has been shown, for instance, to offer societies-communitarian or otherwise--effective ways to improve their understanding of how to deal with their *collective choice* problems. The main emphasis is on:

    a) How rules are designed (that is, how to compact an effective and viable constitution); and
    b) How the rules so selected function to regulate sociopolitical interaction in the post-constitutional society.

2. In Cameroon--to cite only this example--ownership of oil resources was not defined until French, American, Italian, and UK companies discovered viable (that is, marketable) reserves of oil. The central government in Yaoundé, which had previously been totally absent from the region (had

provided absolutely no social services), and several ethnic groups began to make claims to ownership of the resources. The central government, with its comparative advantage in the employment of coercion, won the struggle and now has absolute control over exploitation and allocation, with, of course, the help of various transnational companies. The ethnic groups--which claim ownership, by virtue of the fact that these resources are located on land that they have occupied for ages (and who will eventually have to bear the environmental costs of exploitation)--now threaten to go to war to reclaim their 'stolen' birth right.

3. As earlier alluded to, most of the violence comes primarily from resource-rich groups that, in essence, hold 'beneficiary' title to resources (the 'legal' title is held by the central or national government)-by virtue of the fact that the resources are located on their ancestral lands-but who do not get any benefits from the exploitation of these resources. A new property rights scheme that vests both legal and beneficiary titles in the relevant groups and allows the government only the right to levy taxes on the net revenues generated would most probably transfer the struggle to the central government where the revenues so extracted are located. In addition, such an approach would ensure sustainable exploitation since it would be to the benefit of the owners of the resources to choose only those exploitation methods that are sustainable.

4. SAPs failed miserably in Africa and imposed on the people, especially the historically marginalized and deprived individuals and groups, most of the costs of implementation, while at the same time, enhancing the ability of center elites to enrich themselves. This phenomenon was due to two major factors. One SAPs we are nothing but foreign impositions. Two, virtually all African economies lacked the institutional arrangements capable of making certain the SAPs were not implemented in an arbitrary and capricious manner.

5. The justice in question here is simultaneously procedural and substantive. On the first score, the groups seek to create political and economic societies in which every individual and/or group has the opportunity to participate fully and effectively in wealth creation. On the second, the groups are concerned to create societies that guarantee certain outcomes and, hence, a given level of 'social benefits' to individuals and groups.

6. The major problem with most post-Cold War democratic infrastructure in Africa is not so much their neoliberal or market-regarding linkages, as that these laws and institutions are external impositions-little or no effort has been made to engage the African countries in people-driven, inclusive, participatory, and bottom-up constitution-making processes; to create institutional arrangements that reflect the values, cultures, customs, aspirations, world-view, and concerns for the environment, of the relevant key social actors/role players in each country. As a result of this failure, most of the laws and institutions that now govern sociopolitical interaction in the majority of African countries are not locally focused and, to that extent, do not reflect 'realities on the ground'-they remain, as were

colonial institutional arrangements, alien impositions. There is no room for counterfactual hypothesis here: African people, if given the opportunity and the facilities to participate fully and effectively in rules selection and the construction of political and economic institutions, may, in the end, choose institutions that are neo-liberal and market-centred or they may not. Right now, it is premature for us to imagine that Africans are incapable of relating gainfully to neoliberal policies or market-centred mechanisms when Africans have really never been granted the opportunity to choose for themselves what types of institutional arrangements they want to regulate their political and economic relationships.

7. The discontent arises not so much from the gap between perceived levels of deprivation and personal expectations as from the failure of the system to provide the individual with the opportunities to fill or narrow the gap. For, if the economic and political system provides all individuals-- especially the poor and the poorest of the poor--with the viable and reasonable opportunities to bridge the gap, such individuals are unlikely to engage in violent mobilization. Witness: many poor Haitians, offered the opportunity to join opposition groups determined to use violence to change the government, have instead opted to migrate to the US (Florida in particular), where they can significantly improve their economic positions by engaging in productive activities within an economy, which, unlike the one in Haiti, offers them opportunities to work, invest, increase their human capital through education, and even become citizens with the opportunity to participate in molding the political system.

8. One of the most pertinent contributors to poverty in Africa is the absence of institutional arrangementsthat enhance the ability of individuals and groups to create wealth. Africans are very entrepreneurial and should the government provide necessary laws and institutions, they would be able to create the wealth that they need to meet their social obligations. Unfortunately, most institutional arrangements in these countries, virtually all of which trace their origins to opportunistic colonial impositions, actually stunt the creation of wealth. It is often said that during the civil war in Nigeria, the absence of government intervention in economic activities created a level of entrepreneurship in Biafra that the country has yet to experience. Thus, despite the war and the severe shortages of raw materials, entrepreneurs in Biafra manufactured and flooded Cameroon markets with incredibly sophisticated goods, which earned a lot of the money used to purchase military equipment for the war effort.

References

Adejumobi, Said. 2001. 'Citizenship, rights, and the problem of conflicts and civil wars in Africa'. *Human Rights Quarterly* 23: 148-70.

Agbu, Osita. 2006. *West Africa's trouble spots and the imperative for peacekeeping*. Dakar: CODESRIA.

Aiyede, Emmanuel R. 2009. 'The political economy of fiscal federalism and the dilemma of constructing a developmental state in Nigeria'. *International Political Science Review* 30 (3): 249-69.

Alao, Abiodun and Funmi Olonisakin. 2000. 'Economic fragility and political fluidity: explaining natural resources and conflicts'. *International Peacekeeping* 7 (4): 23-36.

Amuwo, Adekunle. 2009. 'Globalization and the role of the international community in resource conflicts in Africa'. *Africa Development* 34: 227-66.

Boege, Volker. 2006. *Traditional approaches to conflict transformation--potentials and limits*. Berlin: Berghof Research Center for Constructive Conflict Management.

Buhaug, Halvard and Jan K. Rod. 2006. 'Local determinants of African civil wars, 1970-2001'. *Political Geography* 25: 315-35.

Cohen, Shaul and David Frank. 2009. 'Innovative approaches to territorial disputes: using principles of riparian conflict management'. *Annals of the Association of American Geographers* 99 (5): 948-55.

Collier, Paul. 2000. 'Doing well out of war: an economic perspective'. In: *Greed and grievance: economic agendas in civil wars,* ed. by Mats Berdal and David Malone, pp. 91-112. Boulder and London: Lynne Rienner Publishers.

Collier, Paul and Anke Hoeffler. 2004. 'Greed and grievance in civil war'. *Oxford Economics Papers* 56 (4): 653-95.

———. 1998. 'On economic causes of civil war'. *Oxford Economics Papers* 50: 563-73.

Duchacek, Ivo D. 1986. *The territorial dimension of politics: within, among and across nations*. Boulder and London: Westview Press.

Ellingsen, Tanja. 2000. 'Colorful community or ethnic witches' brew? Multiethnicity and domestic conflict during and after the Cold War'. *The Journal of Conflict Resolution* 44 (2): 228-49.

Englebert, Pierre and James Ron. 2004. 'Primary commodities and war: Congo-Brazzaville's ambivalent resource curse'. *Comparative Politics* 37 (1): 61-81.

Fearon, James D. 1994. 'Rationalist explanations for war'. *International Organizations* 49: 379-414.

Fearon, James D. and David D. Laitin. 2003. 'Ethnicity, insurgency, and civil war'. *American Political Science Review* 97 (1): 75-90.

Forsberg, Tuomas. 1996. 'Explaining territorial disputes: from power politics to normative reasons'. *Journal of Peace Research* 33 (4): 433-49.

————. 1992. 'Territorial changes and international conflict'. *Journal of Peace Research* 29 (4): 465-71.

Ghoukassian, Khatchik D. 2008. 'Instability in the new imperial periphery: a conceptual perspective of the 'turbulent frontiers' in the Caucasus and Central Asia'. *Caucasian Review of International Affairs* 2 (3): 146-55.

Gleditsch, Nils P., Peter Wallensteen, Mikael Eriksson, Margareta Sollenberg, and Havard Strand. 2002. 'Armed conflict 1946-2001: a new dataset'. *Journal of Peace Research* 39 (5): 615-37.

Gurr, Ted R. 1970. *Why men rebel*. Princeton, NJ: Princeton University Press.

Hensel, Paul R. 2001. 'Contentious issues and world politics: the management of territorial claims in the Americas, 1816-1992'. *International Studies Quarterly* 45 (1): 81-109.

Hensel, Paul R, Michael E. Allison, and Ahmed Khanani. 2006. 'Territorial integrity treaties and armed conflict over territory'. Earlier version of paper presented at the 2006 Shambaugh Conference on 'Building Synergies: Institutions & Cooperation in World Politics', University of Iowa, and 13 October. http://www.paulhensel.org/Research/cmps07/pdf (accessed on 12 September).

Holsti, Kalevi J. 1991. *Peace and war: armed conflicts and international order, 1648-1989*. Cambridge: Cambridge University Press.

Jeffrey, Alex. 2006. 'Writing territorial conflict'. *Review of International Political Economy* 13 (5): 830-45.

Kalyvas, Stathis N. 2008. 'Ethnic defection in civil war'. *Comparative Political Studies* 41 (8):1043-68.

———. 2007. 'Civil wars'. Chapter 18 in *The Oxford Handbook of Comparative Politics*, edited by Carles Boix and Susan C. Stokes. Oxford: Oxford University Press.

Kaufman, Robert R. 2009. 'Inequality and redistribution: some continuing puzzles'. *Political Science* (PS) 42: 657-60.

Keating, Michael. 2000. *The new regionalism in Europe: territorial restructuring and political change.* Glasgow: Edward Edgar Publishers.

Le Billion, Philippe. 2001. 'The political ecology of war: natural resources and armed conflicts'. *Political Geography* 20: 561-84.

Lichbach, Mark I., Christian Davenport, and David A. Armstrong II. 2003. 'Contingency, inherency, and the onset of civil war.' http://www.bsos.umd.edu/gvpt/davenport/dcawcp/pa per/ContingencyInherencyandOnset.pdf (accessed on 8 December 2009).

Luke, Timothy W. 1996. 'Govern mentality and contragovern-mentality: rethinking sovereignty and territoriality after the Cold War'. *Political Geography* 15 (6/7): 491-507.

Macours, Karen. 2006. 'Relative deprivation and civil conflict in Nepal'. SAIS-Johns Hopkins University, 15 March. http: //www .csae .ox. ac.uk/conferences/2006-eoi-rpi/papers/grpg/ macours. Pdf (accessed on 17 December 2009).

Mason, T. David. 2003. 'Globalization, democratization and the prospects for Civil War in the new millennium'. *International Studies Review* 5 (4): 19-35.

Mitchell, Sara M. and Brandon C. Prins. 1999. 'Beyond territorial contiguity: issues at stake in democratic militarized interstate disputes'. *International Studies Quarterly* 43 (1): 169-83.

Newman, David. n.d. 'The resilience of territorial conflict in an era of globalization'. http://ibcperu.nuxit.net/doc/isis/7630. pdf (accessed on 8 December 2009).

Newman, Edward. 2004. 'The "new wars" debate: a historical perspective is needed'. *Security Dialogue* 35 (2): 173-89.

Observatoire de l'Afrique. 2008. 'Fragile statehood in Africa: a useful paradigm for action? Conference Report', 12-13 May, Didimala Lodge, South Africa, August.

Ostby, Gudrun. 2006. 'Horizontal inequalities, political environment and civil conflict: evidence from 55 developing countries'. Working Paper No. 28, August, Centre for Research on Inequality,

Human Security & Ethnicity (CRISE), Queen Elizabeth House, University of Oxford.

Quinn, Jason M, T. David Mason, and Mehmet Gurses. 2005. 'Sustaining the peace: determinants of civil war recurrence'. University of Texas, Denton, 23 December. http: //www .cas. unt.edu/~ ./mg003 /Sustainingthe peace-11.pdf (accessed on 10 December 2009).

Robinson, William I. 2002. 'Remapping development in light of globalization: from a territorial to a social cartography'. *Third World Quarterly* 23 (6): 1047-71.

Ross, Michael. 2003. 'Natural resources and civil war: an overview'. Submitted for review to World Bank Research Observer, 15 August. http://www.ssnet.ucla.edu/polisci/faculty/ros s/WBpaper.pdf (accessed on 9 December 2009).

Sambanis, Nicholas. 2004. 'Using case studies to expand economic models of civil war'. *Perspectives on Politics* 2 (2): 259-79.

Soysa, Indra de and Angelika Wagner. 2006. 'Global market, local mayhem? Foreign investment, trade openness, state capacity and civil war, 1989-2000'. Department of Political and Cultural Change, Center for Development Research (ZEF), University of - Bonn, Germany. http://www.idrc.ca/uploads/users/10588052011de soysa_Wagner.pdf (accessed on 17 December 2009).

Stewart, Frances. 2002. 'Root causes of violent conflict in developing countries'. *Business and Management Journal* (BMJ) 324 (9): 342-45.

Talbott, Strobe. 2000. 'Self-determination in an interdependent world'. *Foreign Policy* 118: 152-65.

Tilly, Charles. 2004. 'Terror, terrorism, terrorists'. *Sociological Theory* 22 (1): 5-13.

Ukeje, Charles. 2007. 'Globalizations and conflict management: reflections on the security challenges facing West Africa'. *Globalizations* 4 (3): 355-68.

Walder, Andrew G. 2009. 'Political sociology and social movements'. *Annual Review of Sociology* 35: 393-412.

CHAPTER 5

Horizontal Inequalities and Internal Conflict: The Impact of Regime Type and Political Leadership Regulation[1]

Gudrun Østby & Håvard Strand

1. Introduction

Since the end of World War II, a total of 240 armed conflicts have been active in 151 locations around the world. In 2008, 36 conflicts were active in various locations around the world (Harbom and Wallensteen 2009). Although the number of conflicts has gone down since the Cold War, the last decade saw an increase in armed conflicts. The biggest increase occurred in Africa, from seven conflicts in 2005 (lower than any time since the 1970s) to twelve in 2008. In 2008, conflicts were taking place in Algeria, Burundi, Chad, DRC, Djibouti, Eritrea, Ethiopia, Mali, Niger, Somalia, and Sudan, according to the PRIO/Uppsala *Armed Conflict Dataset* (see Gleditsch et al. 2002). Only through understanding the motives of belligerents can the international community hope to influence their actions in ways that are conducive to peace in Africa.

Socioeconomic status has long been thought to be associated with engagement in violent conflict. More than thirty years ago, Lipton (1977) argued that spatial inequality in poverty between urban and rural areas is an overriding source of conflict in poor countries, particularly in Africa. Yet, there is still at best insufficient understanding of the relationship between regional inequalities and civil conflict. Recently, geographical variations of inequality within countries have begun to attract considerable interest among policy-makers (see, e.g., UNDP 2005; World Bank 2006). Despite popular concerns, there have been remarkably scarce systematic documentation and analyses of spatial and regional inequalities and their consequences, with the notable exception of a WIDER-UNU project on inequality and development (Kanbur and Venables 2005).

Inequality is among the grievance factors largely dismissed by recent large-N country-level studies of civil war (e.g., Collier and

Hoeffler 2004; Fearon and Laitin 2003). However, such studies typically address economic inequality between individuals while ignoring geographical variations in socioeconomic welfare. We argue that such conclusions may be premature because of the neglect of the group aspect of inequality. Civil wars are group conflicts-not confrontations between individuals randomly fighting each other (Duclos et al. 2004). Hence, the focus should be on inequality between identity groups, not between individuals. In line with this, a number of case studies suggest that what matters for conflict is so-called 'horizontal inequalities'-systematic inequalities that coincide with ethnic, religious, or regional cleavages (see Stewart 2000, 2002).[2] In brief, the argument is that inequalities coinciding with cultural cleavages may enhance group grievances and thus facilitate mobilization for conflict.

In a series of case studies, Stewart (2002) found that various dimensions of HIs provoked some kind of conflict, ranging from a high level of criminality in Brazil to civil war in Uganda. In order to test whether these findings can be generalised beyond the particular case studies, there is a need for large-N investigations. Drawing on national survey data, Østby (2008a) provided quantitative evidence that Stewart's findings held when socioeconomic inequalities between ethnic groups were tested systematically across 36 developing countries. Brown (2005) reports statistical evidence for a positive effect on conflict of horizontal inequalities between religious groups, while Østby, Nordås and Rød (2009) found that regional inequalities are associated with a higher conflict risk in African regions.

An important issue that has not been sufficiently addressed in the quantitative literature is whether horizontal inequalities are especially conflict-provoking under certain political conditions. To our knowledge, there has also been little systematic theorisation of the role of political institutions in ameliorating (or exacerbating) the conflict potential of horizontal inequalities. This paper examines the independent and interactive effects of socioeconomic horizontal inequalities and regime type, political rights and civil liberties, and political leadership, with a particular focus on sub-Saharan Africa.[3] We put forth specific hypotheses as to how the political environment interacts with socioeconomic horizontal inequalities. For instance, we expect that horizontal inequalities may be particularly explosive in democratic regimes because the relatively deprived groups have both a strong motive and an opportunity for violent mobilisation. In order to test these hypotheses, we conduct a large-N analysis of civil conflict in up to 67 developing countries (out of which 33 are located in sub-Saharan Africa) in the period 1986-2008.

The paper is organised as follows: Section 2 provides a theoretical framework for the relationship between horizontal inequalities and conflict. We discuss three different group identifiers relevant to horizontal inequalities: ethnicity, religion, and regional affinity, and argue that the latter may be particularly relevant in the African context. Section 3 discusses the possible impact of regime type, political rights and civil liberties, and characteristics of political leadership with regard to the relationship between socioeconomic horizontal inequalities and conflict. Section 4 presents the data and research design, demonstrating how national survey data provide an invaluable source of generating objective measures of horizontal inequality. Section 5 provides the results from the empirical tests. The results show that horizontal inequalities matter for civil conflict, especially along ethnic and regional cleavages in Africa. For the global sample, the HI-conflict link seems to be particularly strong in democratic regimes, but this finding does not hold for the African subsample. Rather, what seems to play an important role in influencing the effect of HI on conflict in African countries is the nature and duration of political leadership. For countries with regularly elected leaders, high levels of regional inequality are associated with significantly higher risks of conflict. Countries with long-tenured irregularly installed leaders are more conflict-prone than countries with regularly elected leaders for all levels of regional inequality. This implies that a reduction of regionally based inequalities could contribute to peaceful democratic transitions.

2. Horizontal Inequalities and Civil Conflict

Stewart (2002:1) defines horizontal inequalities as 'systematic inequalities between culturally formed groups', such as ethnic, religious, or regional groups. Systematic, socioeconomic inequalities between identity groups often have their origin in historical circumstances, such as colonial policies, which privileged some groups over others. Sometimes, however, horizontal inequalities are not caused by deliberate agency at all but simply become evident

141

through social processes, such as when traditional peoples on the periphery of modernizing societies are drawn into closer contact with more powerful and technologically proficient groups (Gurr 2000). An initial advantage often leads to long-term cumulative advantages, as resources and education allow the more privileged groups to secure further advantages. Likewise, group deprivation tends to be reproduced over time, as in South Africa-even after apartheid (see, e.g., World Bank 2006:1).[4]

A shared cultural identity may be a powerful organising principle for a group. First of all, a shared identity overcomes the collective action problem (Olson 1965) whereby people are unable to cooperate because of mutual suspicions. However, there is reason to believe that a shared identity is not a sufficient factor to produce conflict. In line with this, Murshed and Gates (2005) argue that some well-defined grievances are required for identity-based conflict.

Given that groups are the central units in conflicts, the question, then, is how they are mobilised. Stewart (2000) argues that different identity bases have been the source of group differentiation and mobilisation in various parts of the world: In Central Africa, ethnicity has been the major basis of group categorization; in Central America, group identification and organisation has developed along social class lines, with some overlapping ethnic dimensions; and in the Balkans and Northern Ireland, religion has been the primary feature of categorisation. However, regional location is also a source of group differentiation, which often coincides with ethnic or linguistic cleavages, as for example in Uganda (Minority Rights Group International 1997) and Zambia (Posner 2004). The question of regional, or spatial, inequality has become increasingly important over recent years, and has begun to attract significant interest among scholars and policy-makers. In most developing countries, there is a sense that regional inequalities within countries in terms of economic activities and social indicators are rising (Kanbur and Venables 2005). Moreover, data on group inequalities are far more accessible for regional than ethnic or religious groups, since questions concerning ethnic affiliation are often dropped or at least not published in national surveys and censuses. However, regional groups may also be important in their own right: In a natural field experiment among the Chewa and Tumbuka groups in Zambia, Posner found that regional cohesion seemed to be stronger than the claims of ethnic affiliation.[5]

Whether or not a cleavage matters would seem to depend not at all on the material from which it is built. That material can be as sturdy as the traits, customs, norms, and practices that a professional ethnographer might identify or as flimsy as an arbitrary boundary drawn by an uninformed colonial officer (2004: 543).

Why should horizontal inequalities be relevant for conflict? The most obvious answer to this question relates to the effect of collective grievances. Members of disadvantaged groups are likely to feel frustration and antagonism, especially when their relative deprivation is the result of actual exploitation and discrimination, which is apparently often the case (e.g., in Senegal and Uganda). Indeed, Horowitz (2000) holds that in most cases conflicts are initiated by the less privileged groups. Despite the intuitive logic of this argument, one cannot, however, assume that it is only resentment on the part of the disadvantaged groups that may cause political instability. When people in rich regions perceive the central government's policies as unfair and authoritarian, they may see greater autonomy, or even secession, as a better alternative than the status quo. As Aristotle said, 'Inferiors revolt in order that they may be equal, and equals that they may be superior' (quoted in Sigelman and Simpson 1977: 106). For example, privileged groups that are geographically concentrated may demand independence. In line with this logic, the initiative for conflict may come from the richest and most privileged groups as well as the poorest and most deprived groups.

Both types of reactions point to the conclusion that a society of high horizontal inequalities has a higher risk of civil war than societies without such inequalities. It is easier to maintain group cohesiveness and motivation for rebellion if the elite can draw on ethnic, religious, or regional differences to construct a well-defined identity group with a common enemy.

However, what may matter more than the identity bases between which the cleavage is created is whether the groups are systematically different in terms of economic and social welfare. This leads to our first hypothesis:

H1: Countries with severe socioeconomic horizontal inequalities are particularly likely to experience civil conflicts, *ceteris paribus.*

As indicated above, inequality can be multidimensional (economic, social, or political) and can be based on various group-identifiers, such as gender (Caprioli 2005; Melander 2005); ethnicity and religion (e.g., Gurr 1994; Stewart 2002); urban-rural groups (Gurr 1994; Lipton 1977; Sahn and Stifel 2003); or subnational regions (Østby et al. 2009). According to many scholars, in most African countries, the predominant social cleavage is ethnic and/or regional identity (Erdmann 2004; Scarritt and Mozzafar 1999; Stewart 2002). Although regional belonging is just one of many social identities, such geographical affiliation can be among the most salient and promote the greatest degree of conflict (Herb and Kaplan 1999). First, regional identity often stems from a shared history and overlapping regional and cultural cleavages. Particularly in Africa, subnational regions frequently correspond to ethnic group demarcations, with each region being dominated by a particular ethnic group (Stewart 2002). Regional affiliations may be enforced by regional institutions and parties, or primarily as a set of cultural relations between a specific group and a particular place, i.e., a social community. Second, regional boundaries often structure the distribution of state patronage, welfare, and political influence. For example, inequalities between coastal and hinterland regions may sharpen as new economic activities are spatially concentrated (Kanbur and Venables 2005), or the state might choose to favor regions that are dominated by its ethnic kin. Hence, regional boundaries may suddenly form gaps between the haves and the have-nots, which may in turn reinforce geographical identities (Erdmann 2004). This gives subnational regions added political and economic relevance. Regions can be important as both cultural commonalities and socioeconomic and political realities can reinforce or even construct regions as relevant identity units. Regional inequality and limited economic integration can exacerbate regional competition for the bounties of the state and may even foster conflict.

Several African examples illustrate that regional inequalities might be the outcome of state processes of distribution, which can create a sense of commonality and spur aggression. In Kenya regions are ethnically distinct, have political relevance in the aligning of parliamentary constituencies with ethnic boundaries, and differ systematically in terms of infrastructure and educational attainment (Alwy and Schech 2004). In Cameroon there is a similar logic of regional consciousness based on the ethnic representation of the regions and ethno-regional communities becoming 'conduits in regional quests, thirsting for access to state resources' (Fonchingong 2005: 368). In Nigeria, regions rely on the federal state's distribution of oil revenues for a majority of their income. When oil rents are assigned exclusively to subnational governments, they tend to produce extreme regional inequalities. However, due to extensive revenue reallocation, the oil-producing regions have become increasingly cut off from the oil rents over time. Hence, tensions have mounted in the oil-rich Niger Delta regions based on a sense of injustice by not being allowed to keep the share of the revenues they feel entitled to (Davis et al. 2003).

Based on the discussion above, we expect that horizontal inequalities related to ethnic and/or regional affiliation should be particularly conflict-provoking in Africa:

H2: Horizontal inequalities along ethnic and regional lines have higher conflict potential in sub-Saharan African than elsewhere, *ceteris paribus*.

3. Mediating Effects of the Political Environment on the HI-Conflict Nexus

Rogowski and MacRac (2004), among others, have demonstrated that political institutions tend to co-vary with socioeconomic inequality in society. For example, societies with clientelistic politics are often associated with extreme economic inequality, [6] and democracies are characterised by greater economic equality between rich and poor than autocracies. The bulk of studies on inequality and institutions focus on inequality between individuals. One could expect, however, that the findings presented above also hold for the relationship between institutions and group-based inequalities. Alternatively, one could argue that requirements for plurality would force coalitions of identity groups and hence mitigate horizontal inequalities.[7] However, establishing a causal link between horizontal inequalities and political institutions is beyond the scope of this paper. Rather, its focus lies in investigating how the political environment in a country may influence the relationship between horizontal inequalities and civil conflict onset.

The Impact of Regime Type

According to Rothchild (1983:172), 'group disparities and unequal exchange are, in and of themselves, insufficient to explain the course of interethnic conflict'. In line with this, Stewart argues that the sheer existence of objective horizontal inequalities may not spur conflict 'if there is a strong state which suppresses it or if ideological elements are such that the inequalities are not widely perceived' (2000:11). If this is actually the case, the emergence of violent group mobilisation in countries with sharp horizontal inequalities may depend on the characteristics of the political regime.

The relationship between regime type and civil conflict has been widely studied. Hegre et al. (2001) have demonstrated an inverse U-shaped relation between the level of democracy and the incidence of civil war over time, concluding that semidemocracies are indeed the most prone to civil strife. At both extremes, in autocracies and democracies, civil wars are rare-and even rarer under a democracy than under an autocracy. However, in a semidemocracy, they argue, the combination of both grievances and the opportunity to rebel is at its peak. In a democracy, grievances are generally less common and more moderate while there are plenty of possibilities to express these grievances and to secure change through channels other than violence. In an autocracy, on the other hand, grievances are likely to be great and frequent, but state repression may prevent them from being openly expressed. In a semidemocracy, both grievances and opportunities for violent conflict exist. This suggests that violent opposition is more likely in regime types that fall between autocracy and well-functioning democracy.

The first interaction we investigate in this paper is that between horizontal inequalities and regime type. Regime characteristics may provide incentives for deprived groups to riot against the government, as autocratic regimes are likely to have a very restricted recruitment process both for political and economic positions (Goldstone 2001). Autocracies have a tendency to exacerbate inequality (Rogowski and MacRae 2004). Consequently, one could reason that when horizontal inequalities are pervasive, autocracies are likely to be more at risk of conflict than democracies. This paper turns this reasoning upside-down, arguing rather that it is democratic regimes that suffer from the most serious effects of horizontal inequalities. The rationale for this is elaborated below.

The theory of democratic peace makes a heroic assumption: that democracies are actually responsive and do address group grievances. Intuitively, this makes perfect sense. Democracies are by definition expected to be more responsive than autocracies, if for no other reason than that they usually entertain a free press, which makes it harder to ignore petitions from below, and because governments can be voted out. However, the fact that it is more responsive than an ideal autocracy is not sufficient reason to argue that a democracy is able to avoid all potential conflicts. If, for various reasons, a democracy is unable to satisfy basic needs universally and ensure a certain level of group equity, a whole set of new dynamics may appear. The opportunity to rebel is still present, but it is now combined with the presence of strong group grievances, or motives. In other words, in a country with both a suppressive regime and persistent horizontal inequalities, there will be very little opportunity to mobilise, although grievances among the disadvantaged groups are likely to be very strong indeed. In a democracy with sharp horizontal inequalities, on the other hand, opportunities and grievances are both present. A democracy, however, is expected to host moderate inequalities and consequently less severe grievances between identity groups. This is due to the existence of multiple peaceful channels through which relatively deprived groups may express and voice their grievances and try to influence the process of redistribution through democratic means. However, if this effort does not reduce the growing gap between the expected and the actual outcome for the relatively disadvantaged groups, it may cause frustration and facilitate the mobilisation of people to engage in conflict. This argument was originally expressed by Davies (1962) as the J-curve of need satisfaction and revolution. In line with this reasoning, one should expect the most conflict-prone societies to be democracies with sharp horizontal inequalities. Hence, we propose the following hypothesis:

H3: The positive effect of socioeconomic horizontal inequalities on civil conflict onset is stronger for democracies than for semidemocracies and autocracies, *ceteris paribus*.

147

The Impact of Political Leadership Regulation

There exists one key difference between democracies and nondemocratic regimes: In democracies, we expect political leaders to change fairly frequently and undramatically. In contrast, the transition of power is a major problem in nondemocratic systems (Weber 1965) and one that can cause armed conflict. Keeping in mind that the best predictor of a change of leadership is the duration of the tenure (Bienen and van de Walle, 1989), one can approach the difference between political institutions and armed conflict from a different angle.

We have previously argued that the theoretically more responsive regimes should be more vulnerable to large horizontal inequalities than the less responsive ones. However, there is reason to believe that democratic rulers in developing countries seldom are as responsive as the theory dictates, both for a lack of will and means. But what about the responsiveness of autocrats? To some extent, the fact that a leader is able to grab and hold onto power without the support of a traditional political system should imply that he is either responsive or capable of managing social unrest in other ways.[8] Horizontal inequities are not likely to be a major cause of armed conflict these regimes.

However, in regimes where the question of leadership is regulated within political institutions, there are fewer uncertainties regarding succession, but perhaps more avenues to pursue for those interested in the top office. This institutionalised uncertainty is linked to the main theoretical statement in this paper. Horizontal inequalities are more likely to contribute to conflict in countries where acquiring and retaining executive power is more dependent on addressing them. This provides the basis of the fourth and last hypothesis:

> H4: The positive effect of socioeconomic horizontal inequalities on civil conflict onset is only present when the executive recruitment process is institutionalised, *ceteris paribus*.

4. Data and Research Design

A statistical analysis of onsets of civil conflicts in developing countries serves as the empirical test of the outlined hypotheses. The sample includes all developing countries where at least one demographic and health survey (DHS) had been conducted during the period 1986-2008, and for which the relevant data were available. After being aggregated to the national level, the total number of observations in the dataset used for the present analysis adds up to 1,618 country-years for the full sample, and 779 for sub-Saharan Africa. However, when consecutive years of conflict are removed from the analysis, a maximum of 1,256 country-years (full sample), or 634 (sub-Saharan Africa), remains.

The Dependent Variable: Conflict Onset

We are interested in explaining why conflicts start in the first place. To do this we use conflict data from the Uppsala/PRIO Armed Conflict Dataset (ACD), which includes all known armed conflicts between the government of a country and an organised opposition group where at least 25 persons are killed in battle-related situations per year (Gleditsch et al. 2002).

We define the onset of a new conflict whenever a conflict is recorded as active in a given year, but not in either of the two preceding years. Each observation of the dependent variable refers to a country in a particular year (e.g., Liberia, 1990). We disregard from the sample all years where a country is engaged in active conflict. In the end, our dependent variable is a binary variable that reports the value 1 for every instance of conflict onset within a particular calendar year for a particular country. Accordingly, we code the dependent variable to 0 for each calendar year and each country where conflict could have started, but did not.

The Core Variables: Socioeconomic Horizontal Inequalities

DHS is an ongoing research project that provides data on the population, health, and nutrition of women and children in developing countries, funded primarily by USAID and administered by Macro International Inc. In each country where DHS is implemented, a sample of households is selected throughout the entire country and then interviewed using a questionnaire to collect data on household characteristics. Women between the ages of 15 and 49 are interviewed using a women's questionnaire to collect information mainly on background characteristics, children's and women's health, and other issues, such as household assets and education level.

149

The DHS data provides a rich set of large, representative surveys with nearly identical questionnaires, hence presenting an excellent opportunity for generating objective measures of inequalities across identity groups. However, a challenge is that the DHS surveys generally lack information on income or consumption expenditures. We overcome the absence of such data by using the information collected on respondent and household characteristics. More specifically, we use two different indicators of socioeconomic welfare to calculate inequality measures and evaluate hypotheses: a household asset index and a variable counting the years of education for each respondent.

First, we construct a household asset index, generated on the basis of the following variables from the DHS: v119-v125 (dummies for whether or not each household has electricity, a radio, a television, a refrigerator, a bicycle, a motorcycle and/or a car). Our second indicator, schooling inequality, is based on variable v133 (years of education completed). We measure horizontal inequalities in household assets and educational level using three group identifiers from the DHS surveys: ethnicity (v131), religion (v130), and region of residence (v101) First, we calculate the socioeconomic differences (HIs) between the two largest ethnic groups in each country. Second, we do the same for the two largest religious groups.[9] finally; we examine horizontal inequality as ratios of welfare scores between the region in which the capital is located and the rest of the country. This measure is calculated on the basis of a formula introduced by Østby (2008a)

$$HI = 1 - \left(\exp\left(-\left| \ln\left(\sum_{i=1}^{M} \frac{A_{i1}/A_{i2}}{M} \right) \right| \right) \right)$$

where M is the maximum number of household assets; $A1$ refers to mean asset score of group 1 (e.g. the capital region); and $A2$ is the corresponding mean score of group 2 (e.g. the rest of the country).[10] This provides a continuous variable potentially ranging from 0 (the lowest level of asset inequality between capital region and the rest of the country) to 1 (the highest level of such inequality). The measure of educational inequality is generated along the same lines.

The DHS data used to generate the HI measures for this study amount to 177 national surveys in 73 countries. With an average number of more than 11,000 respondents per survey, this implies an immense amount of data. The total number of respondents that form the basis of the analyses in this paper is 2,016,932 individuals. Appendix A1 provides a complete list of the surveys (countries and survey years) used in this analysis to generate the HI variables. For countries where multiple surveys have been undertaken, we use linear interpolation to estimate inequalities for the intervening years. For series in which 2008 data are not available, we copy the results from the survey closest in time to the subsequent years, within the period 1986-2008, to increase the sample size. This could introduce endogeneity (i.e., HI could result from former conflict instead of vice versa), and it would of course be preferable to have yearly data on group inequalities for each country. However, as stated earlier, group inequalities tend to be quite stable over time, which is also evident from the data for some of the countries that have had several surveys during the period 1986-2008. As an illustrating example of the relatively stable level of HIs, Figures 1 and 2 depict the level of inequality in terms of average household assets and years of education for the capital region and the rest of the country in Kenya and Zimbabwe, respectively, for various survey years. In both countries the level of inequality has remained relatively stable over the entire period.

Figure 1. Regional horizontal inequalities in Kenya, various years

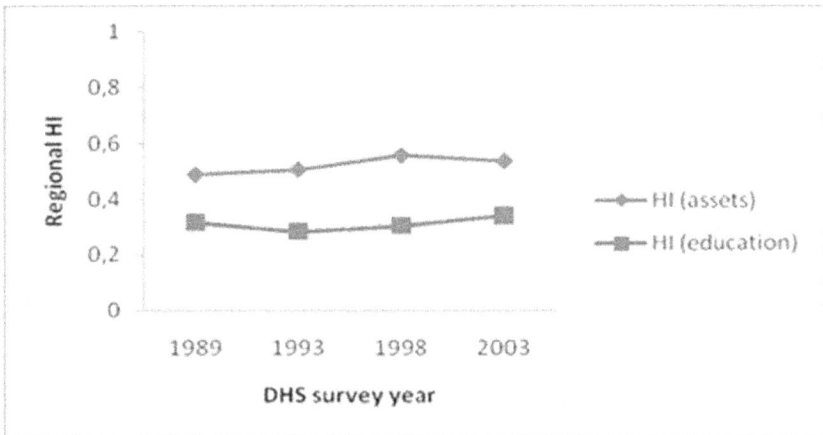

Source: Author's calculations based on Kenya DHS surveys
1989, 1993, 1998, and 2003.

151

Figure 2. Regional horizontal inequalities in Zimbabwe, various years

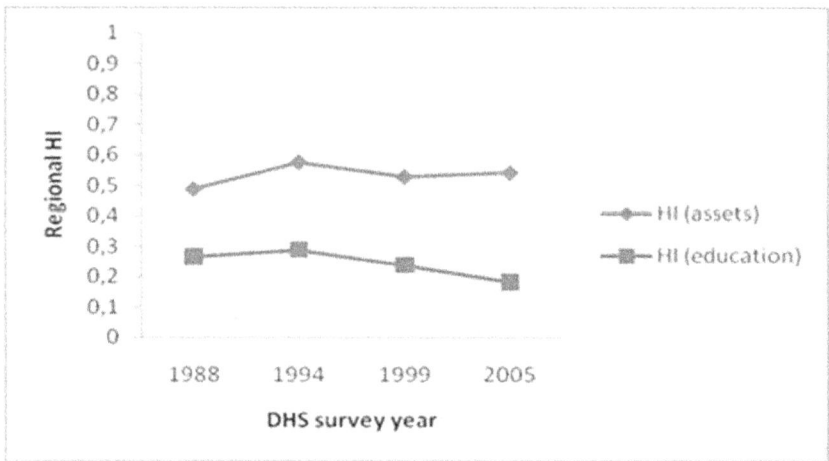

Source: Author's calculations based on Zimbabwe DHS surveys 1988, 1994, 1999, and 2005.

The Political Regime Type

We use data on regime type from the Polity IV data (Marshall and Jaggers 2003). Like Jaggers and Gurr (1995), we compute one single regime indicator, subtracting the score of autocracy from that of democracy, ranging from-10 (most autocratic) to 10 (most democratic). In order to test the curvilinear relationship between regime type and civil conflict we include a squared term for regime type. Finally, in order to assess whether horizontal inequalities are more dangerous in certain regime types, we split the polity term into three categories: democracies (6 to 10), semidemocracies (-5 to 5), and autocracies (-10 to -6), following Ellingsen (2000) and others. We include the dummies for semidemocracies and autocracies in the analysis, with democracies as the reference category. In order to test Hypothesis 3, we include interaction terms multiplying regime type and regional HIs.

Many observers note that there have been discrepancies between the ideal functioning of formal democratic institutions (input) and the actual politics and practice (output) in African politics (Knutsen 2009). Therefore, one should use measures that capture the functioning of institutions, and not only their formal-constitutional existence, when investigating the effects from democracy in Africa. One such data source is the Freedom House Comparative Survey of Freedom (Freedom House, annual), which has rated countries in terms of political rights and civil liberties since 1972-73. The surveys are coded across two dimensions-political rights and civil liberties-on a 7-point scale, whereby countries coded 1 were countries coded most free and those coded 7 were least free. As an alternative test of Hypothesis 3, we include interaction terms between these two scales and our regional HI measures.

Political Leadership Regulation

To identify the duration of the tenure of irregular leaders, we rely on the *Archigos* database developed by Goemans et al. (2009), which identifies the term in office of a country's effective leader and whether this leader's inauguration was regulated or not. However, we want to single out the durable irregular regimes to compare these with the regular regimes. The variable 'lnten', which is the log of the number of days a leader has been in office (tenure) in a given country-year, is therefore multiplied by the 'irregular' dummy, resulting in a variable measuring the tenure of an irregular executive. In order to test our Hypothesis 4, we include interaction terms between the duration of irregular leaders and our regional HI measures.

The mere fact that a leader has reached the political summit through irregular means suggests that there is a high probability of observing conflict in association with such changes. In order to gauge the effect of the institutions that surround an executive, it is more interesting to compare the regulated offices with the long-tenured irregular leaders.

The Control Variables and Statistical Model

Achen's (2002) 'Rule of Three' states that every analysis with more than three variables on the right-hand side will invariably be invalidated by serious problems of multicollinearity. We do not adhere to this rule, but believe that it is wise to keep the control variables at a minimum, especially given the limited sample size under study.

As noted by Hegre and Sambanis (2006), three core variables are almost always included in models of civil war onset: the natural log of per capita GDP; the natural log of population; and the length of peacetime until the outbreak of a war (i.e., the time since the last conflict). We include these three controls, of which the first is particularly relevant due to potential problems of spuriousness, given that inequality may be related to the actual level of economic development in a society. Data on population size are from the WDI (World Bank 2009). The variable is log-transformed. To proxy economic development we use log-transformed GDP per capita measured in constant 1995 US$, also from the WDI (World Bank 2009). The variable is lagged by one year. Following Hegre et al. (2001), we control for proximity to previous conflict through a decay function, ranging from 0 (no recent conflict) to 1 (ongoing conflict). The statistical tests were conducted using STATA, version 10.0 (StataCorp. 2003), and all models were estimated by logit regressions with robust standard errors clustered by countries. Appendices A2 and A3 provide summary statistics for all the variables used in the analysis.

5. Results

The findings from the empirical tests of theoretical propositions are presented in the tables and figures in this section. All models include the base variables, i.e., the terms for population size, GDP per capita, and controls for conflict history. To these we add various terms for horizontal inequalities and interactions of these with the terms for political regime type and political leadership in order to evaluate Hypotheses 1-4.

The Conflict Potential of Various HI Measures

Figures 3 and 4 below report the effects of socioeconomic horizontal inequalities (measured in terms of household assets and education years) with regard to conflict onset. We test the impact of HIs between ethnic, religious, and regional groups, respectively. Figure 3 compares the effect for the sub Saharan Africa sample with the global sample (of which SSA is a part). Figure 4 compares the effects for sub-Saharan Africa with the rest of the DHS countries (non-SSA countries).

Figure 3: Six horizontal inequality measures compared, global vs. SSA sample

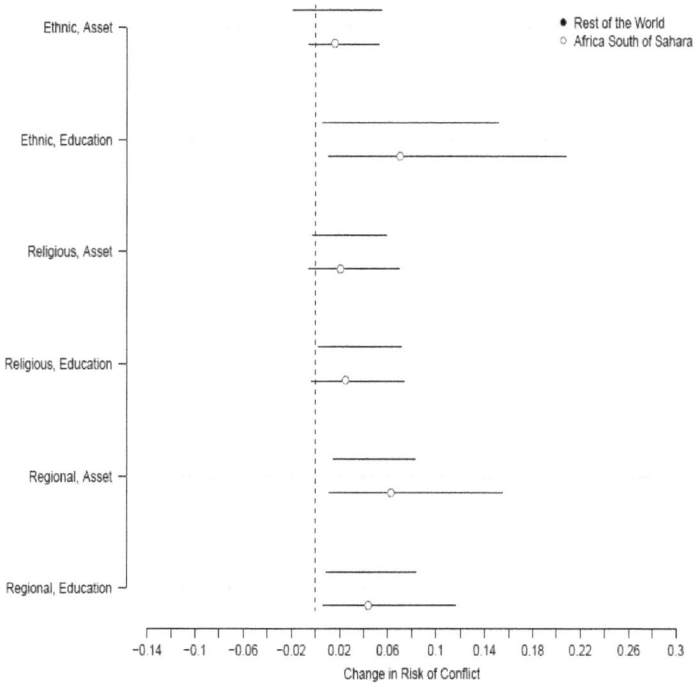

Note:

The dots in this figure should be interpreted as the expected increase in the annual probability of conflict, computed as the average of 1000 simulations based on the regression results presented in Appendix B1. The lines represent the 95% confidence interval of these estimates (see Tomz et al. 2003). Control variables are economic development, population size, and conflict history.

Figure 3 summarises the results from twelve regression models with six different measures of horizontal inequalities and two different samples (see Appendix B1 for full regression model output). We look at two dimensions of inequality (household assets and education) that are both calculated for three different group identifiers (ethnic, religious, and regional groups). The six measures are applied to both the global sample of countries with DHS surveys and Africa South of Sahara (SSA), and all models include control variables: economic development, population size, and conflict history.

The dots in Figure 3 indicate the effect of horizontal inequality on the probability of conflict onset. The figures on the x-axis tell us how much the *estimated* probability of conflict onset increases (or decreases) if we take a fairly average country and increase horizontal inequality from a very low to a very high level (5th and 95th percentile on the corresponding HI measure). For instance, we can see that using the variable measuring horizontal inequality based on a regional comparison of asset levels, the global sample reports that a typical country is about 0.065, or 6.5 percentage points, more likely to experience a conflict, whereas the sample for Africa South of Sahara reports that the effect is about 0.105, or 10.5 percentage points. While 10.5 percentage points per year might not appear all that alarming, this figure corresponds to a difference of 65 percentage points per decade!

The horizontal lines indicate the uncertainty of this estimate. When the dot and the corresponding horizontal line both are entirely to the right of the vertical dotted line (which represents 0 or no effect), we label the finding statistically significant, meaning that we are quite certain that there is an effect present, even if we remain uncertain as to how strong this effect is.

Figure 3 reveals that three of the HI measures stand out as particularly strong and significant for the global sample: Ethnic inequality in terms of education and both of the measures of regional divides (i.e., inequality in terms of both household assets and education between the capital region and other regions). Religious divides do not appear to be very important (although both effects are significant at the 10 and 5 percent level of significance, respectively, as can also be seen in Appendix B1), whereas ethnically based asset inequality is positive, but the effect is not statistically significant. Both asset and education yield strong and substantially important effects for regional inequality, which also is estimated on the largest number of cases.[11] hence, for the reminder of the paper, we base the analyses on these regional measures.

The first hypothesis, that countries with severe socioeconomic horizontal inequalities are particularly likely to experience civil conflicts, is supported by the available data. While the uncertainty regarding the estimates for ethnic- and religious-based asset inequality is larger than the accepted level of 95%, the overall impression from Figure 3 is that horizontal inequality is strongly linked with armed conflict.

Table 1 shows the full regression output for the models that include the two regional inequality measures (asset and education) and all the control variables.

Table 1. Logit regression of civil war onset and horizontal inequality, (all DHS countries vs. SSA), 1986–2008

	1	2	3	4
	Global	SSA	Global	SSA
Regional HI (Assets)	2.388***	3.790**		
	-0.842	-1.75		
Regional HI (Education)			1.603***	1.957**
			-0.611	-0.89
Population (ln)	0.163	-0.228	0.13	-0.185
	-0.138	-0.151	-0.14	-0.124
GDP pc (ln, $_{t-1}$)	-0.213	-0.509	-0.286*	-0.592
	-0.167	-0.337	-0.17	-0.364
Conflict Prox.	1.099***	0.753	1.170***	0.921*
	-0.389	-0.498	-0.397	-0.489
Constant	-5.239**	1.983	-4.019	2.565
	-2.599	-2.891	-2.643	-2.793
LL	-243.56	-140.15	-244.97	-142.05
Pseudo R²	0.0789	0.1085	0.0736	0.0964
# Conflicts	68	43	68	43

# Countries	67	33	67	33
N	1256	634	1256	634

Note: Logit regression coefficients, robust standard errors are in parentheses. *p < 0.10; **p ≤ 0.05; ***p ≤ 0.01.

As for the control variables, the results are inconsistent. We fail to find the positive relationship between population size and conflict reported by most other studies of civil war (see, e.g., Collier and Hoeffler 2004; Fearon and Laitin 2003). Similarly, the term for GDP pc yields inconclusive results, and the negative effect is only significant at the ten percent level for the global sample in Model 3. However, these results are perhaps not so surprising, given that the sample is restricted to low- and medium-income countries. Finally, the term for conflict history has the expected positive sign in all models, but is only borderline significant for the SSA sample. Despite the potential sample size effects, it is interesting to note that the regional inequality measures overall perform much better than any of the 'usual suspects' across both the samples.

Are HIs Particularly Salient in Africa?

Figure 3 above indicated that horizontal inequality systematically is more important in the SSA sample than in the global sample, across all group identifiers and dimensions of inequality. This is worth a closer look. Figure 4 differs from Figure 3 in that sub-Saharan Africa is now compared to all *other* DHS countries, and not the global sample (of which it is a part). These comparisons reveal a number of interesting differences.

Figure 4: Six horizontal inequality measures compared, non-SSA vs. SSA sample

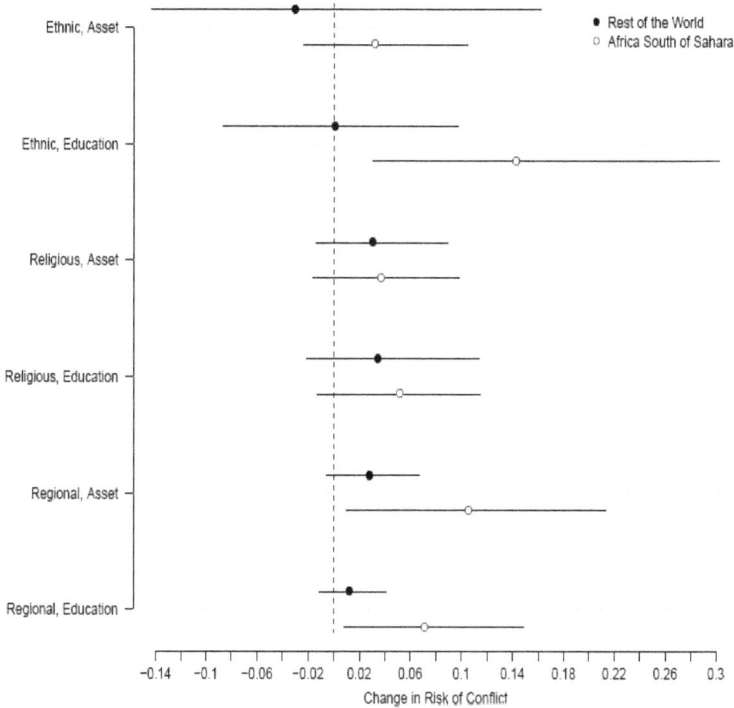

Note:

The dots in this figure should be interpreted as the expected increase in the annual probability of conflict, computed as the average of 1,000 simulations based on the regression results presented in Appendix B1. The lines represent the 95% confidence interval of these estimates (see Tomz et al. 2003). Control variables are economic development, population size, and conflict history.

According to Figure 4, there are virtually no differences in the way that religious divides fuel conflict in Africa compared with the rest of the world. Indeed, while there are good examples of how inequality along religious divides has contributed to conflict, these patterns do not seem to be generalisable within this sample of cases. The conflict potential of ethnic differences in terms of assets seems to be stronger for African countries than for other developing countries, but the effects are not statistically significant. However, when it comes to the effect of ethnic differences in education and regionally based horizontal inequalities along both dimensions of education and assets,

159

the differences between SSA and other developing countries is dramatic. Whereas none of these variables have significant effects on conflict risk in the other DHS countries, the positive effects are very strong and significant for the African countries. The strongest effect is the one for ethnic differences in education. This term contributes to a 14-percentage-point difference in the annual risk of conflict between equal and unequal countries (and this estimate most likely is between 1 and 21 percentage points). In contrast, the effect of the same variable for other countries is 0. The two measures of regional inequality have less statistical uncertainty, and both terms show very strong effects for the SSA subsample, whereas the effects are weak and insignificant for other developing countries. An African country that has high HI in terms of regional asset inequality has an annual conflict risk that is about 11 percentage points higher than an African country with low regional asset inequality. The corresponding figure for education is 7 percentage points. These effects are quite substantial and yield strong support for the second hypothesis, stating that horizontal inequalities along ethnic and regional lines have higher conflict potential in sub-Saharan Africa than elsewhere. The policy implication is that reducing ethnic and regional HIs is particularly important in Africa.

Is the Conflict Potential of HIs Affected by Regime Type?

Can we expect the effect of horizontal inequalities to be contingent on regime type as indicated by the third hypothesis? This assumption is tested in Table 2. In line with previous studies (e.g., Hegre et al. 2001), most of the models show that semidemocracies are particularly at risk of civil conflict onset, more so than full-fledged democratic and autocratic regimes. Furthermore, the positive effect of regional inequalities is robust to the inclusion of dummies for autocracy and semidemocracy, but there is only a slight negative interaction effect with inequality in terms of education and semidemocracies, and this only applies for the full sample of countries, and is only significant at the ten percent significance level, as shown in Model 3, Table 2. More specifically, the positive effect of regional education inequality is does not exist in semidemocracies, whereas the effect for autocracies is not significantly different from the effect for democracies. This provides some support for the third hypothesis, stating that the conflict potential of horizontal inequalities should be particularly strong in democratic

160

regimes. We found similar effects in a previous, related study with a smaller sample (see Østby 2008b), and this finding also corroborates Acemoglu and Robinson (2006), who argue that the risk of conflict is likely to be high if civil society is well developed, inequality is substantial and the people find it easy to organise. For the asset indicator and the African sample, however, this result is not significant.

Table 2. Logit regression of civil war onset, regional inequalities and regime type (polity), 1986–2003

	1 Global	2 SSA	3 Global	4 SSA
Regional HI (Assets)[c]	2.285**	3.810**		
	(0.902)	(1.735)		
Regional HI (Education)[c]			1.890***	2.117**
			(0.578)	(0.915)
Semidemocracy[c] t-1	0.830**	1.181*	0.926**	1.042
(ref.c.: Democracy)	(0.385)	(0.706)	(0.398)	(0.696)
Autocracy[c] t-1	0.561	0.088	0.766*	0.474
(ref.c.: Democracy)	(0.468)	(0.907)	(0.448)	(0.829)
Regional HI (Assets)*Semidemocracy	-2.298	-3.817		
	(2.013)	(3.560)		
Regional HI (Assets)*Autocracy	-0.213	-0.001		
	(2.047)	(3.558)		
Regional HI (Education)*Semidemocracy			-2.589*	-2.336
			(1.449)	(2.218)
Regional HI			-1.466	-0.784

(Education)*Autocracy				
			(1.458)	(2.260)
Population (ln)	0.169	-0.236*	0.135	-0.194*
	(0.134)	(0.130)	(0.140)	(0.117)
GDP per capita (ln) $_{t-1}$	-0.205	-0.565*	-0.233	-0.681*
	(0.165)	(0.312)	(0.176)	(0.355)
Conflict Prox.	1.165***	0.764	1.203***	0.907*
	(0.383)	(0.536)	(0.392)	(0.493)
Constant	-4.702*	4.056	-3.988	4.020*
	(2.430)	(2.657)	(2.593)	(2.432)
LL	-239.54	-138.34	-240.12	-140.52
Pseudo R^2	0.0926	0.1196	0.0904	0.1058
# Conflicts	68	43	68	43
# Countries	67	33	67	33
N	1248	633	1248	633

Note: Logit regression coefficients, robust standard errors are in parentheses. *$p <$ 0.10; **$p \leq 0.05$; ***$p \leq 0.01$. [c]centred term.

As argued in the research design section, there is reason to believe that there could be discrepancies between the ideal functioning of formal democratic institutions (input) and the actual politics and practice (output) in African politics (Knutsen 2009). Hence, we reran the models on the African sample replacing the regime dummies with scales for civil liberties and political rights from Freedom House Comparative Survey of Freedom (Freedom House annual), measures that arguably better capture the functioning of institutions, and not only their formal-constitutional existence. None of the terms yielded any significant effects, nor did the interaction terms (results are reported in Appendix B3). In conclusion then, Hypothesis 3 seems to get some support for the global sample, but not for the African sample.

What about Political Leadership?

Could it be that actual political leadership is more critical for the HI-conflict nexus than actual institutions in Africa? This possibility is investigated in Table 3, which includes interaction terms between the two kinds of interregional horizontal inequality and the institutionalisation of the recruitment process of the executive. The controls include terms for political rights and civil liberties.

Table 3 shows that the term for irregular leadership tenure has a separate positive effect on conflict risk, which implies that conflict outbreak is more likely in countries with well-established irregular leaders in Africa. The term for political rights is negative and significant in Model 1, which implies that the less political rights, the higher the risk of conflict onset in Africa. When we control for political rights and irregular leadership tenure, we find no effect from regional asset inequality (Model 1). The interaction between irregular leadership tenure and regional asset inequality does not have a significant effect, but the picture is different with regard to regional inequality in terms of educational opportunities, which can be seen in Model 2. Here the term for regional education inequality is still positive and significant and there is also an interaction effect between this term and political leadership. This relationship is graphed in Figure 5.

Table 3. Logit regression of civil war onset, regional inequalities and political leadership, sub-Saharan Africa 1986-2003

	1 SSA	2 SSA
Regional HI (Assets)[c]	3.075	
	(2.167)	
Regional HI (Education)[c]		2.220*
		(1.198)
Irregular executive tenure[c]	0.147**	0.157***
	(0.058)	(0.052)

Regional HI (Assets)* Irregular executive tenure	-0.276	
	(0.413)	
Regional HI (Education)* Irregular executive tenure		-0.389*
		(0.232)
Political Rights ^{c} $_{t-1}$	-0.331**	-0.265
	(0.166)	(0.184)
Civil Liberties ^{c} $_{t-1}$	0.312	0.348*
	(0.214)	(0.208)
Population (ln)	-0.273	-0.214*
	(0.187)	(0.124)
GDP per capita (ln) $_{t-1}$	-0.381	-0.357
	(0.327)	(0.333)
Conflict Prox.	0.963*	0.958*
	(0.516)	(0.505)
Constant	3.578	2.012
	(3.498)	(2.889)
LL	-115.15	-114.7
Pseudo R²	0.1195	0.1230
# Conflicts	36	36
# Countries	33	33
N	519	519

Note: Logit regression coefficients, robust standard errors are in parentheses. *p < 0.10; **p ≤ 0.05; ***p ≤ 0.01. ^{c}centered term.

Figure 5: Civil conflict risk as a function of regional inequality and political leadership, South Saharan Africa, 1986-2008.

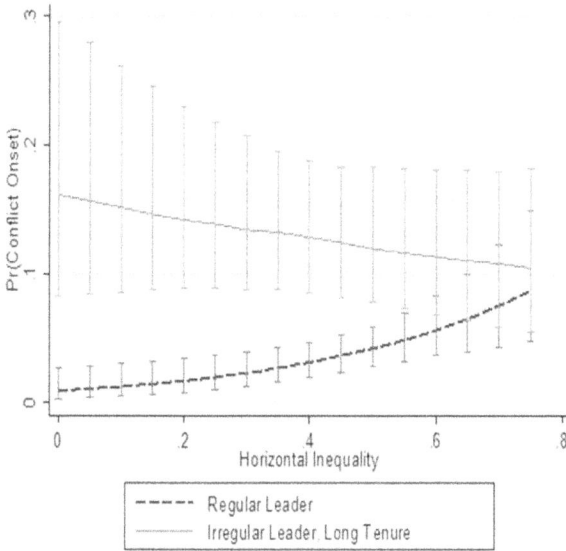

Note:

The figure is based on Model 2, Table 3. All control variables are held constant at the median. 'Inequality' refers to regional inequality in terms of education. The figure is created using the CLARIFY software (see Tomz et al. 2003).

Figure 5 portrays the estimated annual probabilities of armed conflict onset as a function of regional inequality in terms of education, comparing regular leaders with well-established irregular leaders. The vertical bars represent the uncertainty in probability estimates, and when these vertical bars overlap, we are not in a position to make any claims regarding the statistical significance of the effects. Thus, there are no effects of leadership installation procedures when regional education inequality is high (above .6). However, there is a very clear and important effect when inequality is low. Regularly installed leaders are much less prone to conflict when horizontal inequality is low than are their irregular counterparts.

If we focus on the two lines by themselves, we see that the rather large vertical bars surrounding the estimates for the long-tenured irregular leaders does not support any claim that inequality is significantly affecting the hazard of conflict for this category. While there is a tendency for the upper line to slope downwards as inequality goes up, the uncertainties associated with this effect are very large, and therefore no conclusion can be drawn. The uncertainty estimate for the lower line is much smaller, and it appears that the estimated risk of conflict for a country with a regularly installed leader and high horizontal inequality is significantly larger than for that of a similar country with low inequality.

In sum, what Figure 5 reveals is that regularly elected leaders with low horizontal inequality are much less at risk of conflict than both regularly elected leaders facing high inequality and all long-tenured irregularly installed leaders. In other words, the positive effect of HIs is strong and significant for regularly elected leaders only, which supports the fourth hypothesis presented in the theory section. This finding has the important policy implication that regional inequality can be particularly explosive with regard to regime change, and that a reduction of regionally based inequalities could contribute to peaceful democratic transitions in Africa.

6. Concluding Remarks

This paper has investigated the relationship between socioeconomic horizontal inequalities and civil conflict onset, with a particular focus on interregional inequalities in sub-Saharan Africa and the influence of various political factors on this relationship. For the global sample consisting of 67 developing countries, socioeconomic horizontal inequalities seem to be positively related to conflict for all three kinds of group identifiers suggested here (ethnic, religious, and regional groups). However, when we split this sample into African countries vs. other countries, it becomes clear that the effect of horizontal inequalities in general is salient in sub-Saharan Africa, but not so much so in other developing countries around the world. Furthermore, inequalities along regional divides seem to be most robustly and strongly associated with a heightened conflict risk.

Furthermore, for the global sample we found some evidence that the relationship between regional (educational) HIs and conflict is affected by regime type. In fact, horizontal inequalities seem to be particularly conflict provoking in democratic regimes. This is of course not to say that democracy as such breeds conflict. Nevertheless, countries with sharp socioeconomic HIs, despite democratic rule, may be particularly at risk of conflict. This result does not hold for the African sample of countries, however. For this sample of countries, we rather find that what influences the HI-conflict relationship is the nature of political leadership. Countries with regularly elected leaders and low regional inequality are much less at risk of conflict than countries with regularly elected leaders facing high regional inequality and all long-tenured irregularly installed leaders. This implies that a reduction of regionally based inequalities could contribute to peaceful democratic transitions in Africa. In sum, these results provide some support for each of the four hypotheses posited in this paper, but the estimates are sensitive to what indicator of inequality is used, and whether the sample analysed includes all countries or only African countries.

The analyses presented herein highlight the value of bringing survey data tools into the study of political violence. First, national household surveys provide a source of data that would be difficult to find elsewhere. Figures for horizontal inequalities can be politically sensitive, and national governments are likely to report biased data, if any. Second, survey data are descriptive rather than evaluative. That is, researchers do not need to rely on their personal judgment as the source of scores on horizontal inequality.

Despite some interesting findings, several factors call for caution when interpreting the results reported here. First, the sample is limited to developing countries that have hosted DHS in the period 1986-2008, which calls into question the degree to which the results can be generalised. Also, within this sample the intra-and extrapolations of inequality values could be problematic. However, this should not be too serious a problem, since horizontal inequalities seem to remain quite stable over time, as noted above.[12] Second, there is always a potential problem of producing misleading findings due to poor operationalisation of certain variables. Generating summary measures of horizontal inequalities at the national level is a challenging task. There is a need to define the relevant groups, calculate their respective mean welfare scores, and then measure inequalities based on these scores. Most empirical work on group differences, including the tests presented here, uses simple measures of differences in performance between the major groups in society, aggregating these for cross-country comparisons. The advantage of such an approach is that the measure is simple and makes sense intuitively. However, it is potentially problematic, since it may ignore certain politically relevant groups in society. Hence, one could argue that whenever possible, horizontal inequalities should, if possible, be measured and analysed at the subnational level. A handful of quantitative case studies of particular countries have done exactly this (see, e.g., Hegre, Østby and Raleigh 2009; Mancini 2005; Murshed and Gates 2005; Østby et al. 2011), but this of course requires disaggregation of the dependent variable and preferably the other independent variables (see also Østby et al. 2009 for a preliminary disaggregated analysis of inter-and intraregional inequalities and civil conflict in selected African countries, based on national survey data).[13] Despite the advantage of disaggregated studies of conflict, political variables such as regime type and electoral system (which are important indicators in this chapter) are by definition country-level variables. Testing the combined effects of subnational and national variables could be carried out in a multilevel model (see, e.g., Goldstein 1995).

The main policy implication that can be drawn from the results reported in this paper is the importance of addressing horizontal inequalities, particularly in Africa. Political institutions are not sufficient to ensure peace. The findings of this chapter support the conclusion of Stewart and O'Sullivan (1998) drawn from case studies: The combination of two factors seems to be of utmost importance in mitigating conflict. The first factor is the establishment of politically inclusive government that incorporates representatives from all the major identity groups at the political level. The second factor is the realisation of a social system that spreads the benefits of progress widely, providing socioeconomic growth among all the significant regional, religious and ethnic groups in society. In other words, what seems to be required in order to ensure peace in developing countries is the combination of politically and economically inclusive government.

Notes

1. This chapter builds on an earlier version published as Østby (2008b). We thank Palgrave Macmillan for permission to reprint parts of this material here.

168

2. Stewart (2002) found that horizontal inequalities (HIs) have provoked some kind of conflict, ranging from severe criminality in Brazil to civil war in Uganda. See Østby (2008a) for a critique of these studies.
3. Throughout this paper we will use the terms Africa and sub-Saharan Africa interchangeably.
4. Without analyzing each country in depth it is hard to tell whether group inequalities predate repression or not. Furthermore, objective measures of group inequalities do not necessarily perfectly reflect people's perceptions of such inequalities. There have been some recent efforts of collecting such perception data at both the Centre for the Research on Inequality, Ethnicity and Human Security (CRISE) at Oxford University, as well as at the Peace Research Institute, Oslo (PRIO).
5. Nevertheless, some of the worst forms of ethnic attack have been nonregional, such as the conflict between Hutus and Tutsis in Rwanda.
6. It might also be the case that clientelism is very widespread in early stages of development.
7. One should also note a possible reverse causality, implying that political inequalities might lead to economic inequalities.
8. Indeed, having a political enemy in the shape of a rebel organisation can in many cases prolong a political career.
9. The group sizes are based on weighted measures of ethnic and religious groups (see Rutstein and Rojas 2003) for details on DHS weighting procedures.
10. The capital is coded based on the CIA World Factbook, various editions.
11. The reason for the differences in N is differences in availability of data. All the DHS surveys include questions regarding regional affiliation, but several surveys exclude questions about ethnic and religious affiliations.
12. We reran all the models without allowing for any backward extrapolation of the inequality values. Most of the results remained similar, though some effects dropped below significance (results not reported here). This procedure radically decreases the sample to less than half and the number of conflicts drops to very low figures in many of the models.
13. A next important step would be to gather micro-level data about people's actual perceptions of horizontal inequalities. Some preliminary work by researchers at CRISE, Oxford University and the Peace Research Institute in Oslo has already undertaken some preliminary perception surveys for a selection of countries for this purpose.

References

Acemoglu, Daron and James A. Robinson. 2006. *Economic origins of dictatorship and democracy: economic and political origins.* Cambridge: Cambridge University Press.

Achen, Christopher H. 2002. 'Toward a new political methodology: microfoundations and ART'. *Annual Review of Political Science* 5: 423-50.

Alwy, Alwiya and Susanne Schech. 2004. 'Ethnic inequalities in education in Kenya'. *International Education Journal* 5 (2): 266-74.

Bienen, Henry and Nicholas Van De Walle. 1989. 'Time and power in Africa'. *American Political Science Review* 83 (1): 19-34.

Brown, Graham. 2005. 'Horizontal inequality or polarization? Inter-group Eeonomic disparity and its relationship with conflict'. Paper presented at the IGCC conference 'Disaggregating the Study of Civil War and Transnational Violence', San Diego, CA, USA, 7-8 March.

Buhaug, Halvard and Scott Gates. 2002. 'The geography of civil war'. *Journal of Peace Research* 39 (4): 417-33.

Caprioli, Mary. 2005. 'Primed for violence: the role of gender inequality in predicting internal conflict'. *International Studies Quarterly* 49 (2): 161-78.

CIA. Annual. *The world factbook.* Washington, DC: Central Intelligence Agency.

Collier, Paul and Anke Hoeffler. 2004. 'Greed and grievance in civil war'. *Oxford Economic Papers* 56 (4): 563–95.

Davenport, Christian. 2003. *Minorities at risk: dataset user's manual.* College Park, MD: CIDCM, University of Maryland.

Davies, James C. 1962. 'Towards a theory of revolution'. *American Sociological Review* 27 (1): 5-19.

Davis, Jeffrey M., Rolando Ossowski, and Annalisa Fedelino. 2003. *Fiscal policy formulation and implementation in oil-producing countries.* Washington, DC: International Monetary Fund.

Demographic and Health Surveys. 1996. *DHS sampling manual.* http://www.measuredhs.com/pubs/pdf/DHSM4/DHS_III_Sampling_Manual.pdf

Duclos, Jean-Yves, Joan Esteban, and Debraj Ray, 2004. 'Polarization: concepts, measurement, estimation'.*Econome-trica* 72 (6): 1737-72.

Ellingsen, Tanja. 2000. 'Colorful community or ethnic witches' brew? Multiethnicity and domestic conflict during and after the Cold War'. *Journal of Conflict Resolution* 44 (2): 228-49.

Erdmann, Gero. 2004. 'Party research: Western European bias and the "African Labyrinth"'. *Democratization* 11 (3): 63-87.

Fearon, James D. and David D. Laitin. 2003. 'Ethnicity, insurgency, and civil war'. *American Political Science Review* 97 (1): 75-90.

Fonchingong, Charles C. 2005. 'Exploring the politics of identity and ethnicity in state reconstruction in Cameroon'. *Social Identities* 11 (4): 363-80.

Freedom House, annual, 1973-2009. *Freedom in the world.* New York: Freedom House Press http://www.freedomhouse.org.

Gleditsch, Nils Petter, Peter Wallensteen, Michael Eriksson, Margareta Sollenberg, and Håvard Strand. 2002. 'Armed conflict 1946-2001: a new dataset'. *Journal of Peace Research* 39 (5): 615-37.

Gleditsch, Kristian S. and Michael D. Ward. 1999. 'Interstate system membership: a revised list of the independent states since 1816'. *International Interactions* 25: 393-413.

Goemans, Henk E.; Kristian Skrede Gleditsch, and Giacomo Chiozza. 2009. 'Introducing Archigos: a dataset of political leaders'. *Journal of Peace Research* 46 (2): 269-83.

Goldstein, Harvey. 1995. *Multilevel statistical models.* New York: Halstead Press.

Goldstone, Jack A. 2001. 'Demography, environment, and security'. *Environmental Conflict*, edited by Paul F. Diehl and Nils Petter Gleditsch, pp. PAGES, Boulder, CO: Westview (84-108).

Gurr, Ted Robert. 1994. 'Peoples against states: ethnopolitical conflict and the changing world system'. *International Studies Quarterly* 38 (3): 347-77.

Gurr, Ted Robert. 2000. *Peoples versus states: minorities at risk in the new century.* Washington, DC: United States Institute of Peace Press.

Harbom, Lotta and Peter Wallensteen. 2009. 'Armed conflicts, 1946-2008'. *Journal of Peace Research* 46 (4): 577-87.

171

Hegre, Håvard and Nicholas Sambanis. 2006. 'Sensitivity analysis of empirical results on civil war onset'. *Journal of Conflict Resolution* 50 (4): 508-35.

Hegre, Håvard, Tanja Ellingsen, Scott Gates, and Nils Petter Gleditsch. 2001. 'Toward a democratic civil peace? Democracy, political change, and civil war, 1816-1992'. *American Political Science Review* 95 (1): 17-33.

Hegre, Håvard; Gudrun Østby, and Clionadh Raleigh, 2009. 'Economic deprivation and civil war events: a disaggregated study of Liberia'. *Journal of Conflict Resolution* 53 (4): 598-623.

Herb, Guntram H. and David H. Kaplan, eds. 1999. *Nested identities: nationalism, territory, and scale.* Oxford and Lanham, MD: Rowman and Littlefield.

Horowitz, Donald L. [1985] 2000. *Ethnic groups in conflict.* 2nd ed. Los Angeles, CA: University of California Press.

Jaggers, Keith and Ted Robert Gurr. 1995. 'Tracking democracy's third wave with the Polity III data'. *Journal of Peace Research* 32 (4): 469-82.

Kanbur, Ravi and Anthony J. Venables, eds. 2005. *Spatial inequality and development.* Oxford: Oxford University Press.

Knutsen, Carl-Henrik, 2009. 'Africa's growth tragedy revisited: weak states, strong rulers'. GARNET Working Paper No. 71/09. www.garneteu.org/fileadmin/documents/working_papers/71 09.pdf

Lipton, Michael. 1977. *Why poor people stay poor: urban bias in world development.* Cambridge, MA: Harvard University Press.

Mancini, Luca. 2005. 'Horizontal inequality and communal violence: evidence from Indonesian districts'. CRISE Working Paper No. 22. Oxford: Centre for Research on Inequality, Human Security and Ethnicity, Queen Elizabeth House.

Marshall, Monty G. and Keith Jaggers. 2003. *Polity IV Project: political regime characteristics and transitions, 1800-2001.* College Park, MD: CIDCM, University of Maryland.

Melander, Erik. 2005. 'Gender equality and intrastate armed ronflict'. *International Studies Quarterly* 49 (4): 695-714.

Murshed, Mansoob S. and Scott Gates. 2005. 'Spatial-horizontal inequality and the Maoist insurgency in Nepal'. *Review of Development Economics* 9 (1): 121-34.

Olson, Mancur. 1965. *The logic of collective action.* Cambridge, MA: Harvard University Press.

Østby, Gudrun, 2008a. 'Polarization, horizontal inequalities and violent civil conflict'. *Journal of Peace Research* 45 (2): 143-62.

Østby, Gudrun, 2008b. 'Inequalities, political environment and civil conflict: Evidence from 55 developing countries', in Frances Stewart, ed., *Horizontal inequalities and conflict: Understanding group violence in multiethnic societies.* Basingstoke: Palgrave Macmillan (136-157).

Østby, Gudrun, Ragnhild Nordås, and Jan Ketil Rød. 2009. 'Regional inequalities and civil conflict in 21 sub-Saharan African countries, 1986-2004'. *International Studies Quarterly* 53 (2): 301-24.

Østby, Gudrun, Henrik Urdal, S. Mansoob Murshed, Zulfan Tadjoeddin, and Håvard Strand. 2011. 'Population pressure, inequality and political violence: A disaggregated study of Indonesian provinces, 1990-2003'. *Journal of Development Studies* 47 (3): 377-98.

Polity IV.n.d. Polity IV Project webpage: http:// www .cidcm .umd. edu /inscr /polity/ (accessed on 26 March 2005).

Posner, Daniel N. 2004. 'The political salience of cultural difference: why Chewas and Tumbukas are allies in Zambia and adversaries in Malawi'. *American Political Science Review* 98 (4): 529-45.

Rogowski, Ronald and Duncan C. MacRae. 2004. 'Inequality and institutions: what theory, history and (some) data tell us'. Paper presented at the APSA Conference, Chicago, IL, USA, September 2-5.

Rothchild, Donald. 1983. 'Collective demands for improved distributions'. *State Versus Ethnic Claims: African Policy Dilemmas*, edited by Donald Rothchild and Victor A. Olorunsola. Boulder, CO: Westview Press (172-98).

Rutstein, Shea Oscar and Guillermo Rojas. 2003. *Guide to DHS Statistics.* Calverton, MD: Demographic and Health Surveys, ORC Macro.

Sahn, David E. and David C. Stifel. 2003. 'Urban-rural inequality in African living Standards'. *Journal of African Economies* 12 (4): 564-97.

Scarritt, James R. and Shaheen Mozaffar. 1999. 'The specification of ethnic cleavages and ethnopolitical groups for the analysis of democratic competition in contemporary Africa'. *Nationalism and Ethnic Politics* 5 (1): 82-117.

Sigelman, Lee and Miles Simpson. 1977. 'A cross-national test of the linkage between economic inequality and political violence'. *Journal of Conflict Resolution* 21 (1): 105-28.

StataCorp. 2003. Stata statistical software: release 10.0 (1) (user's guide). College Station, TX: Stata Corporation.

Stewart, Frances. 2000, 'Crisis prevention: tackling horizontal inequalities'. *Oxford Development Studies* 28 (3): 245-62.

Stewart, Frances. 2002. 'Horizontal inequalities: a neglected dimension of development'. Queen Elizabeth House Working Paper No. 81. Oxford: Queen Elizabeth House.

Stewart, Frances, Graham Brown, and Luca Mancini. 2005. 'Why horizontal inequalities matter: some implications for measurement'. CRISE Working Paper No. 19. Oxford: Centre for Research on Inequality, Human Security and Ethnicity, Queen Elizabeth House.

Stewart, Frances and Meghan O'Sullivan. 1998. 'Democracy, conflict and development-three cases'. Queen Elizabeth House Working Paper No. 15. Oxford: Queen Elizabeth House.

Tomz, Michael, Jason Wittenberg, and Gary King. 2003. *CLARIFY: software for interpreting and presenting statistical results.* Stanford University, University of Wisconsin, and Harvard University.

UNDP. 2005. *Human development report 2005. International cooperation at a crossroads: aid, trade and security in an unequal world.* New York: United Nations Development Programme.

Weber, Max. [1919] 1965. *Politics as a vocation.* Philadelphia, PA: Fortress Press.

World Bank. 2006. *World development report 2006. Equity and development.* Washington, DC: World Bank.

World Bank. 2009. *World development indicators 2009.*

Washington, DC: Development Data Center, International Bank for Reconstruction and Development/the World Bank.

Appendix A1. DHS surveys used to generate HI variables

Country Code	Country Name	Year	DHS survey
41	Haiti	1994	HTIR31FL
41	Haiti	2000	HTIR42FL
41	Haiti	2005	HTIR52FL
42	Dominican Republic	1986	DRIR01FL
42	Dominican Republic	1991	DRIR21FL
42	Dominican Republic	1996	DRIR32FL
42	Dominican Republic	1999	DRIR41FL
42	Dominican Republic	2002	DRIR4AFL
42	Dominican Republic	2007	DRIR52FL
52	Trinidad and Tobago	1987	TTIR01FL
70	Mexico	1987	MXIR00FL
90	Guatemala	1987	GUIR01FL
90	Guatemala	1995	GUIR34FL
91	Honduras	2005	HNIR51FL
93	Nicaragua	1998	NCIR31FL
93	Nicaragua	2001	NCIR41FL
100	Colombia	1986	COIR01FL
100	Colombia	1990	coir22fl
100	Colombia	1995	COIR31FL
100	Colombia	2000	COIR41FL
100	Colombia	2005	COIR51FL

110	Guyana	2005		GYIR50FL
130	Ecuador	1987		ECIR01FL
135	Peru	1986		PEIR01FL
135	Peru	1991		PEIR21FL
135	Peru	1996		PEIR31FL
135	Peru	2000		PEIR41FL
135	Peru	2004		PEIR50FL
140	Brazil	1986		BRIR01FL
140	Brazil	1991		BRIR21FL
140	Brazil	1996		BRIR31FL
145	Bolivia	1989		BOIR01FL
145	Bolivia	1994		BOIR31FL
145	Bolivia	1998		BOIR3BFL
145	Bolivia	2003		BOIR41FL
150	Paraguay	1990		PYIR21FL
359	Moldova	2005		MBIR52FL
369	Ukraine	2007		UAIR51FL
371	Armenia	2000		AMIR42FL
371	Armenia	2005		AMIR53FL
373	Azerbaijan	2006		azir51fl
432	Mali	1987		MLIR01FL
432	Mali	1995		MLIR32FL
432	Mali	2001		MLIR41FL

432	Mali	2006	MLIR52FL
433	Senegal	1986	SNIR02FL
433	Senegal	1992	SNIR21FL
433	Senegal	1997	SNIR32FL
433	Senegal	2005	SNIR4HFL
434	Benin	1996	BJIR31FL
434	Benin	2001	BJIR41FL
434	Benin	2006	BJIR50FL
436	Niger	1992	NIIR22FL
436	Niger	1998	NIIR31FL
436	Niger	2006	NIIR51FL
437	Cote D'Ivoire	1994	CIIR35FL
437	Cote D'Ivoire	1998	CIIR3AFL
438	Guinea	1999	GNIR41FL
438	Guinea	2005	gnir52fl
439	Burkina Faso (Upper Volta)	1993	BFIR21FL
439	Burkina Faso (Upper Volta)	1998	BFIR31FL
439	Burkina Faso (Upper Volta)	2003	BFIR43FL
450	Liberia	1986	LBIR01FL
450	Liberia	2007	LBIR51FL
452	Ghana	1988	GHIR02FL
452	Ghana	1993	GHIR31FL
452	Ghana	1998	GHIR41FL

452	Ghana	2003		GHIR4AFL
452	Ghana	2008		GHIR5HFL
461	Togo	1988		TGIR01FL
461	Togo	1998		TGIR31FL
471	Cameroon	1991		CMIR22FL
471	Cameroon	1998		CMIR31FL
471	Cameroon	2004		CMIR44FL
475	Nigeria	1990		NGIR21FL
475	Nigeria	1999		NGIR41FL
475	Nigeria	2003		NGIR4BFL
475	Nigeria	2008		NGIR51FL
481	Gabon	2000		GAIR41FL
482	Central African Republic	1994		CFIR31FL
483	Chad	1996		TDIR31FL
483	Chad	2004		TDIR41FL
484	Congo	2005		CGIR50FL
490	Congo, Democratic Republic of (Zaire)	2007		cdir50fl
500	Uganda	1988		UGIR01FL
500	Uganda	1995		UGIR33FL
500	Uganda	2000		UGIR41FL
500	Uganda	2006		UGIR51FL
501	Kenya	1989		KEIR03FL
501	Kenya	1993		KEIR33FL

178

501	Kenya	1998	KEIR3AFL
501	Kenya	2003	KEIR41FL
510	Tanzania/Tanganyika	1991	TZIR21FL
510	Tanzania/Tanganyika	1996	TZIR3AFL
510	Tanzania/Tanganyika	2003	TZIR41FL
510	Tanzania/Tanganyika	2004	TZIR4IFL
510	Tanzania/Tanganyika	2007	TZIR50FL
516	Burundi	1987	BUIR01FL
517	Rwanda	1992	RWIR21FL
517	Rwanda	2000	RWIR41FL
517	Rwanda	2005	RWIR52FL
530	Ethiopia	2000	ETIR41FL
530	Ethiopia	2005	ETIR50FL
541	Mozambique	1997	MZIR31FL
541	Mozambique	2003	MZIR41FL
551	Zambia	1992	ZMIR21FL
551	Zambia	1996	ZMIR31FL
551	Zambia	2001	ZMIR42FL
551	Zambia	2007	zmir50fl
552	Zimbabwe (Rhodesia)	1988	ZWIR01FL
552	Zimbabwe (Rhodesia)	1994	ZWIR31FL
552	Zimbabwe (Rhodesia)	1999	ZWIR41FL
552	Zimbabwe (Rhodesia)	2005	ZWIR51FL

553	Malawi	1992	MWIR22FL
553	Malawi	2000	MWIR41FL
553	Malawi	2004	MWIR4CFL
560	South Africa	1998	ZAIR31FL
565	Namibia	1992	NMIR21FL
565	Namibia	2000	NMIR41FL
565	Namibia	2006	nmir51fl
570	Lesotho	2004	LSIR41FL
572	Swaziland	2006	szir51fl
580	Madagascar (Malagasy)	1992	MDIR21FL
580	Madagascar (Malagasy)	1997	MDIR31FL
580	Madagascar (Malagasy)	2003	MDIR41FL
581	Comoros	1996	KMIR32FL
600	Morocco	1987	MAIR01FL
600	Morocco	1992	MAIR21FL
600	Morocco	2003	MAIR43FL
616	Tunisia	1988	TNIR02FL
625	Sudan	1989	SDIR02FL
640	Turkey/Ottoman Empire	1993	TRIR31FL
640	Turkey/Ottoman Empire	1998	TRIR41FL
640	Turkey/Ottoman Empire	2003	TRIR4HFL
651	Egypt	1988	EGIR01FL
651	Egypt	1992	EGIR21FL

651		Egypt	1995	EGIR33FL
651		Egypt	2000	EGIR41FL
651		Egypt	2005	egir51fl
651		Egypt	2008	EGIR5AFL
663		Jordan	1990	JOIR21FL
663		Jordan	1997	JOIR31FL
663		Jordan	2002	JOIR42FL
663		Jordan	2007	JOIR51FL
678		Yemen (Arab Republic of Yemen)	1991	YEIR21FL
703		Kyrgyz Republic	1997	KYIR31FL
704		Uzbekistan	1996	UZIR31FL
705		Kazakhstan	1995	KKIR31FL
705		Kazakhstan	1999	KKIR41FL
750		India	1992	IAIR22FL
750		India	1998	IAIR42FL
750		India	2005	IAIR51FL
770		Pakistan	1990	PKIR21FL
770		Pakistan	2006	pkir52fl
771		Bangladesh	1993	BDIR31FL
771		Bangladesh	1996	BDIR3AFL
771		Bangladesh	1999	BDIR41FL
771		Bangladesh	2004	BDIR4JFL
771		Bangladesh	2007	BDIR50FL

780		Sri Lanka (Ceylon)	1987		LKIR02FL
790		Nepal	1996		NPIR31FL
790		Nepal	2001		NPIR41FL
790		Nepal	2006		NPIR51FL
800		Thailand	1987		THIR01FL
811		Cambodia (Kampuchea)	2000		KHIR42FL
811		Cambodia (Kampuchea)	2005		KHIR51FL
816		Vietnam, Democratic Republic of	1997		VNIR31FL
816		Vietnam, Democratic Republic of	2002		VNIR41FL
840		Philippines	1993		PHIR31FL
840		Philippines	1998		PHIR3AFL
840		Philippines	2003		PHIR41FL
850		Indonesia	1987		IDIR01FL
850		Indonesia	1991		IDIR21FL
850		Indonesia	1994		IDIR31FL
850		Indonesia	1997		IDIR3AFL
850		Indonesia	2002		IDIR41FL
850		Indonesia	2007		IDIR51FL

Note:

Surveys in SSA marked with bold; surveys from country-years censored from the analyses due to ongoing civil conflict highlighted in grey. Country code and-name stem from Gleditsch & Ward (1999). An updated version of these data is available at http:// private www. Essex .ac.uk /~ksg/ statelist. html.

Appendix A2. Descriptive statistics, global sample

Variable	Obs	Mean	Std. Dev.	Min	Max
Conflict onset	1266	.054	.226	0	1
Ethnic HI (Assets)	1025	.204	.16	.00015	.710
Ethnic HI (Education)	1025	.307	.235	.0017	.835
Religious HI (Assets)	1214	.139	.117	.0013	.490
Religious HI (Education)	1214	.243	.215	.00037	.858
Regional HI (Assets)	1618	.329	.210	.0161	.801
Regional HI (Education)	1618	.343	.236	.0014	.850
Population (ln)	1618	16.391	1.420	12.853	20.841
GDP pc (ln, $_{t-1}$)	1600	6.438	1.010	4.131	9.274
Conflict Prox.	1618	.308	.433	2.17e-19	1
Semidemocracy	1610	.324	.468	0	1
Autocracy	1610	.255	.436	0	1
Political Rights	1606	4.405	1.743	1	7
Civil Liberties	1606	4.367	1.292	1	7
Irregular Executive Tenure	1330	2.186	3.535	0	9.531

Appendix A3. Descriptive statistics, SSA sample

Variable	Obs	Mean	Std. Dev.	Min	Max
Conflict onset	639	.067	.251	0	1
Ethnic HI (Assets)	618	.208	.170	.0042	.710
Ethnic HI (Education)	618	.298	.226	.0017	.835

Religious HI (Assets)	664	.176	.133	.0020	.490
Religious HI (Education)	664	.322	.249	.00037	.858
Regional HI (Assets)	779	.4478	.186	.0238	.801
Regional HI (Education)	779	.453	.238	.015	.850
Population (ln)	779	16.000030	1.216	12.853	18.813
GDP pc (ln, $_{t-1}$)	774	5.893	.877	4.131	8.542
Conflict Prox.	779	.280	.417	3.55e-15	1
Semidemocracy	778	.378	.485	0	1
Autocracy	778	.330	.471	0	1
Political Rights	779	4.987	1.648	1	7
Civil Liberties	779	4.724	1.272	2	7
Irregular Executive Tenure	643	3.359	3.945	0	9.531

Appendix B1. Logit regression of civil war onset and various horizontal inequality measures (All DHS ctrs. vs. SSA), 1986-2008

	1	2	3	4	5	6	7	8	9	10	11	12
	Global	SSA	Global	SSA	Global	SSA	Global	SSA	Global	SSA	Global	SSA
Ethnic HI (Assets)	0.597	1.153										
	-1.034	-1.142										
Ethnic HI (Education)			1.962**	2.656***								
			-0.932	-1.012								
Religious HI (Assets)					1.938*	1.675						
					-1.143	-1.265						
Religious HI							1.523**	1.402*				

184

(Education)												
							-0.676	-0.803				
Regional HI (Assets)									2.388***	3.790**		
									-0.842	-1.75		
Regional HI (Education)											1.603***	1.957**
											-0.611	-0.89
Population (ln)	-0.028	-0.23	-0.148	-0.374*	0.038	-0.203	0.068	-0.143	0.163	-0.228	0.13	-0.185
	-0.155	-0.183	-0.166	-0.214	-0.159	-0.164	-0.165	-0.162	-0.138	-0.151	-0.14	-0.124
GDP pc (ln, $_{t-1}$)	-0.545***	-0.772**	-0.477**	-0.734**	-0.353	-0.705**	-0.244	-0.578	-0.213	-0.509	-0.286*	-0.592
	-0.206	-0.328	-0.21	-0.372	-0.218	-0.347	-0.209	-0.367	-0.167	-0.337	-0.17	-0.364
Conflict Prox.	1.109**	1.036*	0.955**	0.7	1.337***	1.247*	1.267***	1.121*	1.099***	0.753	1.170***	0.921*
	-0.454	-0.54	-0.409	-0.496	-0.496	-0.645	-0.486	-0.612	-0.389	-0.498	-0.397	-0.489
Constant	0.732	5.184	1.778	6.686**	-1.831	4.094	-3.13	2.209	-5.239**	1.983	-4.019	2.565
	-2.799	-3.397	2.701	-3.224	-3.506	-3.746	-3.346	-3.252	-2.599	-2.891	-2.643	-2.793
LL	-175.21	-124.3	-171.37	-119.54	-182.51	-117.26	-181.05	-116.25	-243.56	-140.15	-244.97	-142.05
Pseudo R²	0.0589	0.0824	0.0796	0.1175	0.0606	0.0756	0.0681	0.0836	0.0789	0.1085	0.0736	0.0964
# Conflicts	50	38	50	38	50	34	50	34	68	43	68	43
# Countries	43	27	43	27	50	28	50	28	67	33	67	33
N	787	513	787	513	921	539	921	539	1256	634	1256	634

Note: Robust standard errors are in parentheses. Statistical significance: *p < 0.10; **p ≤ 0.05; ***p ≤ 0.01.

Gudrun Østby & Håvard Strand

Appendix B2. Logit regression of civil war onset and various horizontal inequality measures (non-SSA vs. SSA), 1986-2008

	1 Non SSA	2 SSA	3 Non SSA	4 SSA	5 Non SSA	6 SSA	7 Non SSA	8 SSA	9 Non SSA	10 SSA	11 Non SSA	12 SSA
Ethnic HI (Assets)	-2.993	1.153										
	(3.504)	(1.142)										
Ethnic HI (Education)			-0.058	2.656***								
			(1.629)	(1.012)								
Religious HI (Assets)					4.014	1.675						
					(2.901)	(1.265)						
Religious HI (Education)							3.290	1.402*				
							(2.637)	(0.803)				
Regional HI (Assets)									2.295*	3.790**		
									(1.362)	(1.750)		
Regional HI (Education)											0.890	1.957**
											(0.930)	(0.890)
Population (ln)	0.363	-0.230	0.214	-0.374*	0.194	-0.203	0.210	-0.143	0.453**	-0.228	0.369*	-0.185
	(0.275)	(0.183)	(0.225)	(0.214)	(0.186)	(0.164)	(0.213)	(0.162)	(0.217)	(0.151)	(0.193)	(0.124)
GDP pc (ln, $_{t-1}$)	-0.249	-0.772**	-0.144	-0.734**	-0.092	-0.705**	-0.020	-0.578	-0.109	-0.509	-0.136	-0.592
	(0.427)	(0.328)	(0.316)	(0.372)	(0.289)	(0.347)	(0.280)	(0.367)	(0.243)	(0.337)	(0.240)	(0.364)
Conflict Prox.	0.432	1.036*	0.623	0.700	1.025*	1.247*	1.297*	1.121*	1.048*	0.753	1.236**	0.921*

	(1.061)	(0.540)	(0.954)	(0.496)	(0.616)	(0.645)	(0.741)	(0.612)	(0.618)	(0.498)	(0.611)	(0.489)
Constant	-7.040*	5.184	-5.725	6.686**	-6.301	4.094	-7.231	2.209	10.705***	1.983	-8.864**	2.565
	(4.131)	(3.397)	(3.896)	(3.224)	(3.897)	(3.746)	(4.729)	(3.252)	(3.866)	(2.891)	(3.567)	(2.793)
LL	-47.59	-124.30	-48.32	-119.54	-63.19	-117.26	-63.07	-116.25	-97.56	-140.15	-98.69	-142.05
Pseudo R²	0.0341	0.0824	0.0193	0.1175	0.0486	0.0756	0.0505	0.0836	0.0695	0.1085	0.0587	0.0964
# Conflicts	12	38	12	38	16	34	16	34	25	43	25	43
# Countries	16	27	16	27	22	28	22	28	34	33	34	33
N	274	513	274	513	382	539	382	539	622	634	622	634

Note: Robust standard errors are in parentheses. Statistical significance: *p < 0.10; **p ≤ 0.05; ***p ≤ 0.

Appendix B3. Logit regression of civil war onset, HIs and regime type (FH), sub-Saharan Africa 1986-2003

	1 SSA	2 SSA	3 SSA	4 SSA
Regional HI (Assets)^c	3.703**		3.158*	
	(1.811)		(1.719)	
Regional HI (Education)^c		2.041**		1.934**
		(0.938)		(0.925)
Political Rights$^c_{t-1}$	-0.009	0.084		
	(0.101)	(0.112)		
Civil Liberties$^c_{t-1}$			0.024	0.148
			(0.154)	(0.153)
Regional HI (Assets)* Political Rights	0.126			
	(0.707)			
Regional HI (Education)* Political		-0.140		

187

Rights				
		(0.497)		
Regional HI (Assets)* Civil Liberties			1.116	
			(0.765)	
Regional HI (Education)* Civil Liberties				0.223
				(0.648)
Population (ln)	-0.228	-0.180	-0.223	-0.165
	(0.154)	(0.119)	(0.143)	(0.120)
GDP per capita (ln) $_{t-1}$	-0.508	-0.574	-0.492	-0.527
	(0.336)	(0.355)	(0.323)	(0.336)
Conflict Prox.	0.752	0.886*	0.749	0.866*
	(0.485)	(0.472)	(0.485)	(0.456)
Constant	3.686	3.229	3.435	2.721
	(3.085)	(2.682)	(2.983)	(2.665)
LL	-140.14	-141.81	-139.33	-141.26
Pseudo R^2	0.1086	0.0980	0.1138	0.1015
# Conflicts	43	43	43	43
# Countries	33	33	33	33
N	634	634	634	634

Note: Robust standard errors are in parentheses. Statistical significance: *p < 0.10; **p ≤ 0.05; ***p ≤ 0.01. ^{c}centred term.

PART III

CROSS-BORDER ISSUES

CHAPTER 6

Strengthening Ties Among Landlocked Countries In Eastern Africa: Making Prisoner's Dilemma A Strategy of Collaboration

Abdul Karim Bangura, and Hunter Sinclair

Introduction

The arbitrary lines drawn by colonisers at the Berlin conference in 1885 still have a tremendous impact on the millions of Africans living in countries that have no direct access to the sea. More than a third of the world's landlocked nations are in Africa, and three of these landlocked nations (Burundi, Rwanda, and Uganda) are located in eastern Africa. One of the key ways that landlocked countries have ensured access to the sea and favourable terms of trade with their seaborne neighbours has been their possession of vital commodities like oil (as is the case with Niger). Unfortunately, in East Africa, no extremely valuable commodity exists in significant amounts, and the export economies of these countries largely consist of primary commodities that have low value-to-cost ratios.

This article explores ways in which landlocked nations can build trade and other interdependencies with their seaborne neighbours without possessing oil or other precious commodities. It focuses on Uganda's relations with Tanzania and Kenya and addresses possible areas of expansion in regional trade cooperation through the formation of the East African Community (EAC), which has recently expanded to include Burundi and Rwanda.

Thus, the major research question probed in this article is the following: What alternative strategy can landlocked countries such as Uganda employ to expand their trade relations? To explore this question, the *Prisoner's Dilemma* (PD) Theory (discussed in the third section of this article) is used.

At the outset, however, it should be noted that relations between landlocked developing countries and littoral countries have been said to differ from the set-up of the PD model. It is argued that in its classic form, PD is based on absence of communication between the actors, which is different from the actual communication engaged in by states and their diplomats. Robert Keohane (1982, 1984, and 1989), for example, has argued that in decentralised cooperation theory, international cooperation can take place in an institutionless void. This is because, according to him, policies to cooperate are decided upon by states through international bargaining and enforced through the repeated PD. Keohane then points the way to an explicit focus on institutions, not just cooperation, but on the international features that make cooperation possible by eliminating some of the impediments to it.

A realist perspective on regime theory has also been advanced by scholars like Joseph Greico (1988, 1990), utilizing hybrid theories that take a realist-based approach to Keohane's fundamentally liberal theory. Realists do not say that cooperation never happens; it is just that it is not the norm. Greico argues that states are positional in character. Therefore, states prefer that the relative achievements of jointly produced gains do not advantage partners, and their concerns about relative gains may constrain their willingness to cooperate. Conventional presentations of PD do not depict Realism's specification of the relative gains element of the structure of state preferences, or Realism's analysis of the capacity of state concerns about relative gains to impede cooperation. By distinguishing between game payoffs and state utility, Greico believes that an Amended PD model can depict both the relative-gains element of state preferences and the relative-gains preference of cooperation. The Amended PD, then, facilitates analysis of an important systematic constraint on international cooperation identified by Realist political theory, contributes to an understanding of international institutions, and draws attention to a number of potentially interesting research problems concerning international collaboration.

Literature Review

The economic and political impact of being landlocked is a widely discussed issue. Therefore, trade relations in Eastern Africa have been discussed primarily in the context of greater landlocked nation issues. The literature review that follows adopts a thematic approach to discuss a sample of sources on this topic. This review first discusses the various problems facing landlocked developing countries (LLDCs) throughout the world and goes on to address problems specifically facing the countries of East Africa. Finally, the review addresses the implications of the recent implementation of the EAC.

In *Geography against Development* (2006), Anwarul Chowdhury and Sandagdorj Erdenebileg seek to address the various ways in which being geographically landlocked impacts development and international trade. They focus on the need for infrastructural development in landlocked countries as well as in the transit countries upon which they are dependent. The authors see increased trade as the main engine for economic development. In *The challenges facing landlocked developing countries* (2004), Faye, McArthur, Snow, and Sachs take a similar view. While they emphasise the importance of regional cooperation in building infrastructure, their main focus is on the different dimensions of dependence and ways to overcome these constraints. In addition to recommending infrastructural improvements, Faye et al. emphasise the need for administrative cooperation and a shift towards industries less impacted by restrictive transportation costs.

Another way of addressing the problems of landlocked countries was taken up by Vratislav Pěchota in "The right of access to the sea" (1973). Pěchota's focus is on the theory and legal rights ensuring landlocked nations' access to the sea. He encourages landlocked nations to unite as a single interest group and pressure the United Nations and other international governing bodies to improve their legal guarantees in terms of trade and access to ports. In contrast to Pěchota's arguments, in *Access to the sea for developing land-locked states* (1970), Martin Glassner posits that shared interests and economic growth should be the driving factors ensuring landlocked countries' access to the sea, instead of natural or necessary rights arguments. He proposes this in the context of a generalised study of the geographic, economic, political, and historical factors impacting landlocked nations, particularly Afghanistan, Bolivia, and Uganda.

Of the studies that focus on the specific problems of African landlocked countries, and not simply landlocked developing countries (LLDCs) in general, *Land-locked countries of Africa* (1973) by Zdenek Cervenka and *Regional integration in Africa* (2002) by Jorge Braga de Macedo and Omar Kabbaj are exemplary. Cervenka's work attempts a broad analysis of the problems facing LLDCs in Africa, but focuses predominantly on southern Africa and specifically on the legal, economic, and political factors that affect these countries.

Regional integration in Africa focuses on regional integration in Africa as a means by which overall African economic integration can be achieved. De Macedo and Kabbaj base their analysis on recent integration efforts in Latin America and strongly advocate investments in infrastructure and strengthening capital markets. The authors also encourage governance reforms and stress the importance of globalization's effects on Africa in more than purely economic terms.

As noted earlier, most studies focusing on trade issues for LLDCs take a global or continental approach. To read beyond the broad analyses of the issues facing trade in eastern Africa, it is important to turn to works that do not focus purely on economic issues. One such work is A.B.K. Kasozi's *Social origins of violence in Uganda, 1964-1985* (1994). While the book's main goal is to examine the causes of the high levels of violence prevalent in Uganda since independence, significant space is also given to the ways in which Kenya and Uganda exert significant influence on each other economically and politically. While specific works addressing trade and transit issues in East Africa are hard to find, Yashpal Tandon's "The transit problems of Uganda within the East African community" (1973) provides this focus. Tandon focuses on the higher cost of trade for LLDCs due to distance as well as the further costs incurred through tariffs, taxes, and transfer fees. Tandon takes an extensive look at the historic trade relations between Kenya and Uganda and also discusses Tanzania's trade relations with these countries. The emphasis of his work is on ways in which Uganda can both break away from dependency on its coastal neighbours and ways in which Uganda can increase its coastal neighbor's dependence upon trade with Uganda.

Finding literature on the rise, fall, and rebirth of the EAC is far easier than locating works addressing trade relations among the member countries. One such work focusing on the rise and fall of the EAC is Jakaya Kikwete's "Regional alternatives and national options" (2002). During its first incarnation, the EAC was seen as an exemplary effort at economic integration and many are hopeful that it will again be an example for efforts at integration. Kikwete analyses the EAC's collapse to try and understand ways to avoid another collapse and to provide a model that other economic unions can follow, without repeating past mistakes. Other viewpoints on the EAC are provided by David Tarimo's *East African community: Is it really working?* (2006) and Leslie Stein's *the growth of East African exports and their effect on economic development* (1979). Stein's book is insightful and comprehensive, but ultimately not that helpful because it only addresses the first EAC's impact on Eastern Africa prior to and not after its collapse in 1977. Stein's review covers the period from 1959 to 1971 and seeks to understand if dependency theory is valid in Africa, based on an analysis of interregional and international trade. Tarimo's account addresses the current state of the second EAC and weighs its positive and negative impacts upon each member nation. Tarimo seeks to dispel misunderstandings about the EAC's impact and also look to the future impact of current policy decisions.

Theoretical Framework and Research Methodology

The theoretical framework that guides this article is based on the *Prisoner's Dilemma* (PD) Theory. In its classic rendering, PD is a non-zero-sum game in which two players can choose to either betray (defect) or cooperate with the other player. If both players cooperate, a mutually beneficial outcome is achieved, while if one player defects and the other cooperate, the defector receives the best available outcome and the cooperating player receives the worst possible outcome. While both players would benefit most by both choosing to cooperate, the 'rational' decision for each player is to defect, which leads to a Pareto suboptimal solution for both actors (Rapoport 1974: 17).

The following anecdote will help to explain the basic premise of PD: Manja Sam Zoker and Karmor Jaia Kallon have been arrested for setting fire to Rev. Alfred SamForay's Masankay oil farm because he did not support their party's candidate during the 2008 Sierra Leonean election, and they are placed in separate isolation cells. Both care much more about their personal freedom than about the welfare of their accomplice. Attorney John L. Musa, a clever prosecutor, makes the following offer to Manja Zoker and Karmor Kallon: 'You may choose to confess or remain silent. If you confess and your accomplice remains silent, I will drop all charges against you and use your testimony to ensure that your accomplice does serious time. Likewise, if your accomplice confesses while you remain silent, he will go free while you do the time. If you both confess, I get two convictions; but I will see to it that you both get early parole. If you both remain silent, I will have to settle for token sentences on lesser charges. If you wish to confess, you must leave a note with the jailer, Baba Mzuri Yaya Fanusie, before my return tomorrow morning.'

The 'dilemma' faced by Manja Zoker and Karmor Kallon is that whatever the other does, each is better off confessing than remaining silent. But the outcome obtained when both confess is worse for each of them than the outcome they would have obtained had both remained silent. A common view is that the puzzle illustrates a conflict between individual and group rationality. A group whose members pursue rational self-interest may all end up worse off than a group whose members act contrary to rational self-interest. More generally, if the payoffs are not assumed to represent self-interest, a group whose members rationally pursue any goals may all meet less success than if they had not rationally pursued their goals individually. A closely related view is that the PD game and its multiplayer-generalisations model are familiar situations in which it is difficult to get rational, selfish agents to cooperate for their common good. Much of the contemporary literature has focused on identifying conditions under which players would or should make the 'cooperative' move corresponding to remaining silent. A slightly different interpretation takes the game to represent a choice between selfish behaviour and socially desirable altruism. The move corresponding to confession benefits the actor, no matter what the other does, while the move corresponding to silence benefits the other player no matter what that player does. Benefiting oneself is not always wrong, of course, and benefiting others at the expense of oneself is not always morally required, but in the PD game both players prefer the outcome with the altruistic moves to that with the selfish moves.

Of course, the theory has evolved since Merrill Flood and Melvin Dresher postulated it in 1950, as part of the Rand Corporation's investigations into game theory (which Rand pursued because of its possible applications to global nuclear strategy) and Albert Tucker sought to make Flood and Dresher's ideas more accessible to an audience of Stanford psychologists. A variety of more precise characterisations of PD, beginning with the simplest and moving to the most complex, include Systematic 2x2 PD with Ordinal Payoffs, Assymmetry, Multiple Moves, Multiple Players, Single Person Interpretations, Cardinal Payoffs, the PD with Replicas and Causal Decision Theory, the Stag Hunt and the PD, Asynchronous Moves, Transparency, Finite Iteration, the Centipede and the Finite PD,

Infinite Iteration, Iteration with Error, Evolution, Spatial PDs, PDs and Social Networks, and Group Selection and the Haystack PD. Discussion of these characterisations of PD is beyond the scope of this essay. The interested reader will be well served by consulting the *Stanford encyclopedia of philosophy* (2007) and other works on the subject cited in its bibliography.

The theory is useful because it can be used to try to understand individual state actions in their relations with their neighbours. According to PD Theory, the rational decision for any state would be to always pursue its own national interests at the expense of its neighbours. Nonetheless, real states must continually interact with one another; and when the game is iterated in this manner, defecting states must face real consequences for defecting. Therefore, when iterated PD is played in real life, states quickly learn the importance of encouraging mutual cooperation with their neighbours.

The recognition of this need for building mutual cooperation is why PD is so important to this study. Landlocked countries, like Uganda, are in a particularly vulnerable position in PD situations because they are much more severely impacted by a defection from their coastal neighbours. Due to their severe dependence on their neighbours for access to trade, landlocked countries must almost always choose to cooperate and, therefore, must work even harder to build incentives for their neighbours to cooperate. Only by building trust through a reciprocal approach to cooperation and by finding ways to make their coastal neighbours dependent on their goodwill can landlocked countries make PD a game of mutual cooperation.

The PD model, while quite useful, has been shown by some scholars to be limited and they have offered more complex games. Robert Axelrod (1984), for example, demonstrated almost three decades ago that 'group' victory illustrates one of the important limitations of the PD in representing social reality: that is, it does not include any natural equivalent for friendship or alliances. And almost two decades ago, Youssef Cohen (1994) showed that in a PD situation, both prisoners have freedom of action. Their choices are determined by what they think is in their own best interests. Cohen demonstrated that in the case of Latin American political elites operating in a nascent democratic environment, this is rarely the case. The limits on action by political elites are largely defined by what their constituents will accept. While personal charisma or persuasiveness may increase

197

the range of decisions political elites may take, ultimately they can only lead where their constituents are willing to follow. When they push for too much compromise, or argue for greater patience, they find themselves without a following. As Cohen notes in his two case studies, there will almost always be an alternative actor willing to promise the population what they wish to hear.

From the late-1980s to the mid-1990s, Axelrod's tit-for-tat model was touted as the most robust basic strategy. In more recent competitions, however, tit-for-tat was not the most effective strategy, even under the game-theory definition of effectiveness. Tit-for-tat would have been the most effective strategy if the average performance of competing teams were compared. The team that recently won over a pure tit-for-tat team outperformed it with some of its algorithms because it submitted multiple algorithms that would recognize each other and assume a master and slave relationship: that is, one algorithm would 'sacrifice' itself and obtain a very poor result for the other algorithm to be able to outperform tit-for-tat on an individual basis, but not as a pair or group. The advantage of tit-for-tat therefore pertains only to a Hobbesian world of so-called rational solutions, with perfect communication, not to a world in which humans are inherently social.

For example, the University of Southampton's strategies were in the first three places, despite having fewer wins and many more losses than the GRIM (or grim-trigger) strategy. It should be noted that in a PD tournament, the aim of the game is not to 'win' matches-that can easily be achieved by frequent defection. It should also be pointed out that even without implicit collusion between software strategies, exploited by the Southampton team, tit-for-tat is not always the absolute winner of any given tournament; it would be more precise to say that its long run results over a series of tournaments outperform its rivals. In any one event, a given strategy can be slightly better adjusted to the competition than tit-for-tat, albeit tit-for-tat is more robust. The same applies for the tit-for-tat with forgiveness variant and other optimal strategies: on any given day, they might not 'win' against a specific mix of counter strategies (http://www.prisoners-dilemma.com/results /cec04/ ipd_cec04_full_run.html). Another odd case is 'play forever' PD. The game is repeated infinitely many times and the player's score is the average, suitably computed (Le and Boyd 2007).

The methodological approach used in this study is a qualitative historical analysis. Decision making is an extremely complicated process impacted by innumerable factors. Due to the complexity of the inputs affecting state decisions and the nonnumerical nature of these data, a qualitative approach is essential and is required to compile and analyze the factors causing states to cooperate at the temporary expense of their own national interests. Furthermore, qualitative historical analyses are superior in their ability to use historical documents 'in service of theory development and testing' (Thies 2002: 352). Only by analysing multiple documents is it possible to obtain the various viewpoints necessary to acquire a more complete picture of the many factors impacting decision making. Finally, decision making is an easily observable phenomenon that is often impacted by identifiable variables, but these variables are often impossible to operationalise and put into numerical form, which further lends support for a qualitative approach.

This article hypothesises that it will be in the best interests of seaborne states to defect, or cut off landlocked states' trade, unless landlocked states can provide incentives for collaboration and build seaborne states' dependence upon them. A particularly illustrative case is Uganda, which has no available outlet to the sea and has recently entered into an economic community with its two seaborne neighbours. Thus, landlocked countries such as Uganda are able to increase the likelihood of cooperative outcomes with their coastal neighbours, even though PD game theory claims that actors should always choose to not cooperate when it is not in their national interest. The unit of analysis used in this study is the individual state because it is the interaction between different states that is the focus of the article. While this article is concerned with the motivations behind decision making, the level of analysis is macro because the focus is on states themselves and not on individual actors within states. The technique used to collect data was document analysis of books, academic journals, and Internet publications, as well as interviews with experts on the subject (all of whom, interestingly, wanted to remain anonymous). The factors that shaped the choice of this data collection technique are the abundance of material, time constraints, and the cost of utilising an alternative data collection technique.

Data Analysis

The world's landlocked countries are some of the poorest states in the world, and the direct link between poverty and being landlocked is a frequently studied phenomenon. Despite this growing awareness and the numerous policy suggestions offered to combat this problem, there are few positive examples of landlocked countries escaping debilitating poverty and trade problems. Of the landlocked countries that have achieved reasonable economic growth and development, most have only been able to do so through exploitation of a valuable and essential resource like oil (as is the case with Kazakhstan and Turkmenistan) or a lightweight and valuable resource like diamonds, as has been the case with Botswana (Faye et al., 2004: 40). The reason that Uganda was chosen as the focal point for this study on landlocked countries' ability to pressure positive collaboration from their coastal neighbours is because Uganda has been able to keep its inflation rate down and achieve some of the fastest Gross Domestic Product (GDP) and economic growth rates in East Africa, and been able to do all this while still relying on a single primary commodity (coffee) for more than 50% of its foreign export earnings (Africa-business.com). It is believed that if a landlocked country with an economy still strongly rooted and dependent on primary commodity exports can find ways to ensure its neighbours' collaboration, then other landlocked countries will be able to emulate Uganda's success.

The data collected for this study are analysed synchronically or thematically. The following subsections address the ways in which landlocked countries, in particular Uganda, are vulnerable to defection from their neighbours; the ways in which Uganda has been able to influence collaborative outcomes, particularly through economic unions (like the EAC); and finally, areas in which collaboration and interdependence can be increased and Uganda's success can be copied.

Landlocked Helplessness and the Devastating Results of Coastal Defection

a) Following the breakup of the Mali Federation in 1960, Senegal and Mali severed ties for three years and Senegal placed an embargo on Malian trade (Nationsencyclopedia.com). Senegal tore up the rail lines near the border, confiscated all the

200

rolling stock and thus effectively shut down the route that had previously carried 80% of Mali's foreign trade. Mali had to spend large amounts of capital to reroute its trade to Abidjan by the construction of a road link to the Ivory Coast's rail line (Hodder et al. 1998: 18-19). Later in 1985, Nigeria refused food shipments destined for Chad on the grounds of alleged congestion in the Nigerian transport system, although the decision was probably directly influenced by concurrent border disputes (Hodder et al. 1998: 21). An even more malicious and consequential intervention in the flow of trade occurred in 1979, when the Kenyan government facilitated the collapse of Idi Amin's government by preventing the importation of military supplies and petroleum, which left Amin's tanks helpless against the invading Tanzanian Army (Hodder et al. 1998: 21). All three of these examples show the ways in which transit states are able to exert tremendous influence over the politics, economies, and lives of those in the countries that depend upon them for access to international trade. Faye and his coauthors (2004) list the key dimensions in which landlocked countries are dependent on their neighbours. These scholars posit that landlocked countries are most dependent on:

a) Their neighbours' internal peace and stability,
b) Their neighbours' transit infrastructure, and
c) Their political relations with their neighbours (2004: 40-43).

Analysing LLDCs' dependence along these dimensions, and particularly Uganda's dependence upon Kenya and Tanzania in these areas, reveals the significant challenges that LLDCs must overcome to elicit positive outcomes from their transit countries.

As the economies of most LLDCs depend upon their ability to quickly, efficiently, and cheaply transport primary commodities to markets overseas, the impact of transit infrastructure is of paramount importance to their economic development and political stability. Most landlocked countries have never possessed great transit infrastructures; and even where adequate infrastructure once existed, deterioration has occurred due to overuse and a lack of maintenance funds. Uganda was once said to possess the best transit system in Africa; but due to deterioration and lack of repairs, the country lost 75% of its initial investment in the road network. When Yoweri Museveni came to power and civil order was restored in 1986, only 10% of the roads were said to still be in 'good' condition (Snow et al. 2003: 44). Furthermore, landlocked countries face high transit costs due to their distance from the sea. However, distance is not the only cause of high transit costs for LLDCs. Areas of China, India, and Russia are further away from the coast than many landlocked countries, yet the cost of trade is comparatively less because they do not have to pay the levies, tariffs, and transfer taxes that arise as a direct result of being landlocked and forced to transition through a neighbouring country. In East Africa, for example, the administrative costs of transit alone account for as much as 20% of the cost for transporting freight (Faye et al. 2004: 24).

While distance, administrative costs, and poor internal transit structures constrain LLDCs' trade competitiveness, a more important factor (that landlocked countries are almost powerless to combat) is the often intentional or self-interested failure of transit countries to invest in infrastructure benefiting their neighbours. Chowdhury and Erdenebileg found that when there was an absence of trade agreements between trading countries, there was a decisive underinvestment 'in those forms of infrastructure in which the investments will have spillover effects on other countries' (2006: 46). Burundi, in particular, suffers from this problem. Despite possessing a relatively well-maintained transit infrastructure, Burundi's investments are relatively worthless because of the severe disrepair of the shortest route to the sea along Tanzania's Central Corridor. Because of her neighbour's poorly maintained infrastructure, the majority of Burundian trade still travels through Rwanda and Uganda, and finally to Kenya before going overseas (Faye et al. 2004: 44). Even along Uganda, Rwanda, and Burundi's main trade route through Kenya, known as the 'Northern Corridor', it still takes an average of 14 to 21 days for goods to travel from Kampala to Mombasa by rail (Faye et al. 2004: 48). The time that it takes for a container to travel from Mombasa to Kampala is twice as long as the time that it takes for that same container to travel from London to Mombasa (globalsecurity.org, 2003). While this amazing disparity in speed of transit is not entirely due to Kenya's underdeveloped infrastructure, mutual investments in infrastructure and trade agreements that would encourage countries to engage in construction with spillover effects would greatly impact the price of Ugandan exports and bolster its growing economy.

As noted earlier, even when adequate infrastructures are in place, LLDCs must depend on friendly or at least peaceable relations with their neighbours to use these routes. For example, despite the fact that 80% of Rwanda's exports now travel through Uganda, prior to the Rwandan Patriotic Front (RPF) coming to power in Rwanda in 1994, Rwanda was unable to easily import or export goods along this route - (Africa.upenn.edu/NEH). Even when landlocked countries have real complaints against their coastal neighbours, these complaints often go unvoiced due to fears of repercussions in terms of a loss in trade concessions. Landlocked countries must also back the governments of the countries upon which they are dependent for trade, which explains why Uganda's President Museveni was the sole international leader who continued to fully support Kenya's President Mwai Kibaki during the postelection violence in Kenya in 2007-2008 (*The Economist,* 2008). Tensions between countries can even impact countries that retain friendly relations with both powers as evidenced in the severe impact on Burundi when Ugandan and Rwandan relations soured over events in the Democratic Republic of the Congo (Faye et al. 2004: 57). Another way in which coastal countries are able to influence decision making in their landlocked neighbours is through LLDCs' frequent inability to decide their own trade conditions. For example, before the EAC, Tanzania could risk angering Kenyan manufacturing interests by raising tariffs, because they would still be able to freely engage in international trade. On the other hand, Uganda and other landlocked nations are unable to risk angering their key transit partners who have the power to raise trade barriers to the point that LLDCs would be unable to competitively trade internationally.

One final and very important way in which LLDCs are forced to be dependent is their reliance upon peace and stability within their neighbouring transit partners. Well-maintained transit systems and good political relations are rendered worthless when violence and unrest disrupt trade routes within a transit country. The landlocked nations of Eastern Africa primarily export tea and coffee, which are both commodities that can ruin quickly and have high demand elasticities. Both of these factors mean that any lengthy disruption of trade (such as that which occurred in 2007-2008 in Kenya) has disastrous effects for these countries' economies, which are so dependent upon the revenue made from the export of these two commodities. For example, approximately 90% of foreign currency earnings in Rwanda and Burundi are derived from tea and coffee (Africa.upenn.edu/NEH). One of the revealing and vivid examples of internal strife impacting the economies of landlocked countries occurred in 2007-2008 following the 2007 election in Kenya. When the election results announced victory for the incumbent Kibaki, they were denounced as fraudulent by the opposition and widespread rioting and violence occurred. The rail line to Kigali was cut, roads were blockaded, truckers were assaulted, and massive oil shortages affected Uganda (Anonymous 1, personal communication, 16 April 2008). It has been reported that the crisis in Kenya cost Uganda over $500 000 in lost revenues. Furthermore, due to their inability to import raw materials and other inputs, several factories were forced to close, which caused hundreds of layoffs (*International Herald Tribune*, 2008). The whole crisis was estimated to have cost the Ugandan Government over $25 million dollars (1/100th of its yearly budget) due to lost customs duties (Glauser 2008: 1).

It would have been profitable to provide international trade data that indicate the volume of trade by the landlocked East African countries when they cooperated with ocean-front neighbours, as a result of friendly regimes in power, compared to periods when they did not cooperate. Unfortunately, such data are hard to get. While trade data between East African countries and the European Union member states and the United States are easily available, those among the East African states themselves are sporadic and unreliable. Besides, a significant amount of the trade among those states is informal (USAID 2009; Okuttah 2010). Even more important is the fact that the informal trade across the borders is most often vital to rural livelihoods and the customs union is unlikely to significantly impact the barriers that this faces. In addition, taxes are still being fixed separately by the member countries (Booth et al. 2007).

Nonetheless, anecdotal evidence exists to suggest that the volume of trade between Uganda, a landlocked country, increased when it cooperated with Kenya and Tanzania, its ocean-front neighbours, as a result of friendly regimes in power, compared to periods when they did not cooperate. For example, trade between Uganda and the other two countries declined as mistrust among the leaders mounted after Uganda's Idi Amin took power by force in 1971 and ruled until he himself was deposed in 1979 with the help of Tanzania's Julius Nyerere. Furthermore, the East African region has had its fair share of disputes and disagreements. The main bone of contention has been the long-held perception by Uganda and Tanzania that Kenya's economy, mainly the manufacturing sector, was more competitive than theirs despite the fact that it has been declining over the past few years under pressure from imports from the Middle East and inadequate infrastructure. Kenya exports approximately three-fifths of its goods to Uganda and Tanzania and had been facing tariffs of between 10 and 20 percent before the establishment of the EAC. However, the EAC is expected to present a good investment platform for both domestic and foreign investors due to their economies of scale. Benefits should also accrue to Uganda and Tanzania, who have, of late, reaped immensely from food commodity supply fluctuations in Kenya (http://www.africa-business.com/features/eac.html).

b) Landlocked Countries' Ability to Force Cooperation

While the outlook for landlocked countries' ability to influence their coastal neighbours' decisions may look bleak at this point, LLDCs are not without options and means with which to exert power over their neighbours. Among these means of exerting influence, there are ways to both threaten and incentivise coastal countries to concede to landlocked countries' demands. Furthermore, there are many ways in which landlocked countries are able to strengthen their bargaining position by decreasing their dependence upon their coastal neighbours for access to trade and as trading partners. Finally, landlocked countries must insist on making their trading partners realise that collaboration is not a zero-sum game and can benefit both countries. Countries controlling access to the sea must be made to realise that there are definite incentives for collaboration and definite consequences for choosing to defect.

One of the most obvious ways that landlocked countries can influence the decisions of coastal countries is through their function as key markets for the goods produced in the transit countries. While LLDCs depend upon transit countries to gain access to world markets, transit countries often depend upon their landlocked trading partners as destinations for their manufactured goods and agricultural products. Coastal countries have cheaper access to the inputs needed for manufacturing, and it is therefore much more likely for coastal countries to serve as manufacturing suppliers for landlocked countries. In few areas is this more apparent than in eastern Africa. Under the British, Kenya was designated to engage in industry, while Uganda's economy was structured around agricultural production. Upon the division of the British's protectorate in East Africa, Kenya already had a marked advantage in industrial production and has widened this gap since independence. Although the products that Uganda imports from Kenya are unlikely to be sold overseas, they are ideal for the underindustrialized landlocked countries of central and eastern Africa (Tandon 1973: 85). Kenya became further dependent on Uganda as a market for its goods when Kenya's manufacturing sectors expanded greatly to meet the rising demand that followed Idi Amin's expulsion of Asians in 1971. In addition to needing access to Ugandan markets for the expansion and continued success of its industries, Kenya relies on Ugandan as the cheapest and shortest route to access markets in Burundi, Rwanda, eastern Congo, and southern Sudan (Kasozi 1994: 38). While Uganda's economy would certainly also be damaged by severing trade with Kenya, Uganda does possess a powerful bargaining position in being able to threaten to limit or cut off trade. The two countries' economies have become so intertwined that a break in relations would have severe implications for them and their neighbours. Therefore, each country's economic decisions must be carefully weighed against their potential impact on its neighbour's interests.

As a corollary to the discussion on Uganda's ability to influence Kenya through withholding or limiting trade, landlocked countries with more than one route to international markets possess a powerful bargaining tool in their ability to reroute trade away from one country to the next. Uganda is one such country with multiple routes and the option of transporting goods through Tanzania, Kenya and, in extreme cases, through Lake Tanganyika and Lake Nyasa to Mozambique. Kenya has developed a very large and influential transport industry due to the great volume of goods that pass through Kenya from eastern and central African countries. The importance of Ugandan trade to Kenya was obvious in 1987 when war almost resulted from Uganda's decision to save money by switching from truck transport to an increased use of rail lines. In 1986-1987 alone, the Museveni government saved \$56 million, but the increased use of the rail lines enraged Kenyan trucking interests so much that the governments had to engage in high-level meetings to reduce tensions between the two countries (Kasozi 1994: 39-40). It is remarkable that Ugandan trade's influence on Kenya is so great that a mere shift in the means of transportation (and not the transport country) can lead to internal and international conflict and arouse serious concern. Even more influential upon Kenyan decision making is Uganda's ability to shift trade to the so-called 'Central Corridor' to the port of Dar es Salaam in Tanzania. Uganda has been able to greatly reduce its transit dependency on Kenya in recent years by further developing and increasing the share of traffic along the lake/rail route through Tanzania (Chowdhury and Erdenebileg 2006: 53). Uganda is still; however, highly dependent upon the route through Kenya for transit, and the recent disruption of trade through Kenya has served as a powerful impetus for measures to increase trade share distribution to Tanzanian routes (Anonymous 2, personal communication, 17 April 2008).

Finally, landlocked nations like Uganda are able to reduce their transit dependence by increasing air freight capacities. Transport by air is obviously very expensive, but it can be made cost effective in industries such as diamonds and other light-weight and high-cost products/commodities or with commodities that are time dependent and spoil quickly. This method of transit independence has been used to great effect in Botswana's rapidly expanding economy, and Uganda has recently taken serious measures at Entebbe Airport to increase the competitiveness and capacity of its air freight enterprises (Africa-business.com).

Permanent Forced Collaborative Outcomes?

One of the most powerful ways for landlocked countries to influence their coastal transit partners has been through entering binding trade unions or communities with them. In Africa especially, there has been a recent proliferation of economic communities, as both landlocked countries and coastal states have come to the realisation that increased regional integration provides the most promising and effective means for escaping poverty. Many of the issues confronting East Africa, in particular, are not merely national issues, but are, instead, regional issues. To deal with such issues as trade imbalances, increased global economic competition, HIV/AIDS prevention, and refugee issues, the nations of eastern Africa decided to overcome national interests and vowed to cooperate regionally through the re-creation of the EAC, which originally died in 1977 (Kikwete 2002: 154). By deciding to integrate economically, Kenya and Tanzania have essentially agreed to permanently choose to collaborate on economic decision making with Uganda, Rwanda, and Burundi. Furthermore, Kenya has decided that economic integration is so important that it must permit its partners unrestricted access to its internal markets, while its partners remain protected by tariffs for an additional five years.

In other words, Kenya has essentially agreed to suffer defection for five years because of the incentives provided by unrestricted access to neighboring markets and other benefits of union (Tarimo 2006: 1). Even when Ugandan tariff barriers were scheduled to come down in 2010, Kenya and Tanzania decided to permanently collaborate with their landlocked neighbours on economic decisions. Finally, and most important, one of the explicitly stated goals of the EAC's formation treaty calls for the ultimate political federation of the member nations. Political differences were the essential causes for the dissolution of the initial EAC and there is much hope that with political integration such an outcome can be avoided. Many are hopeful that the landlocked countries of eastern Africa have finally found a way to permanently avoid the consequences of being landlocked, by literally no longer being landlocked through political unions with coastal states (Anonymous 1, personal communication, 16 April 2008).

Of course, some scholars may argue that side payments are not necessarily a form of defection. In this case, Kenya's granting Tanzania and Uganda five years of unrestricted access to its market can be viewed not as a defection suffered by Kenya but rather as a foregoing by Kenya of the immediate benefits for future returns. We are, however, inclined to accept the former perspective given the evidence provided by David Tarimo and the other observers cited above.

Conclusion

Following the postelectoral crises in Kenya in 2007-2008, Ugandan lawmaker Nandla Mafaba said: 'When Kenya sneezes, Uganda catches a cold' (*International Herald Tribune* 2008). While there is much optimism that Uganda may have found a way to permanently influence collaborative outcomes in its relations with Kenya and Tanzania, recent events have shown that, even within an economic union, events in neighboring countries still have a profound impact on the domestic economy and domestic decision making of Uganda. In addition, there is always the danger of serious defection on the part of Kenya or Tanzania in the form of withdrawing from the EAC, as happened in 1977.

This article has explored the ways in which landlocked countries like Uganda are both influenced by their direct trading partners and the ways in which they are able to exert influence. Furthermore, this article has explored ways in which permanent cooperation among trading partners may ultimately be achieved. It is our hope that other landlocked developing countries can emulate Uganda's success in encouraging or forcing cooperative outcomes with their transit partners (in terms of trade) and achieve significant economic progress.

References

Africa Business Pages. 'The East African Community: East African countries of Kenya, Uganda and Tanzania establish the East African Community (EAC) to boost regional trade and commerce'. http://www.africa business.com/features/eac.html (accessed on 30 June 2010).

Anonymous. http://www.globalsecurity.org/military/facility/mombass a.htm (accessed 21 March 2008).

Anonymous. *Mali: History*. http://www.nationsencyclopedia.com/Afri ca/Mali-HISTORY.html (accessed 16 April 2008).

Anonymous. *Business Opportunities in Uganda*. http: //www.africa-business.com/features/uganda_dubai.html (accessed 21 March 2008).

Associated Press. 2008. Ugandan economy hit by Kenyan violence. *International Herald Tribune*. http://www.iht.com /articles/ap/200 8/02/01/africa/AF-GEN-Uganda-Kenya Violence .php (accessed 21 March 2008).

Axelrod, Robert. 1984. *The evolution of cooperation*. New York, New York: Basic Books.

Booth, David et al. 2007. "East African integration: How can it contribute to East African development?" In: *Overseas*

Development Institute (ODI) Briefing. London, England: ODI Publications.

Cervenka, Zdeněk (Ed.). 1973. *Land-locked countries of Africa*. Uppsala, Sweden: The Scandinavian Institute of African Studies.

Chowdhury, Anwarul K. and Sandagdorj Erdenebileg. 2006. *Geography against development: A case for landlocked developing countries*. New York, New York: United Nations.

Cohen, Youssef. 1994. *Radicals, reformers, and reactionaries: The Prisoner's Dilemma and the collapse of democracy in Latin America*. Chicago, Illinois: The University of Chicago Press.

De Macedo, Jorge Braga and Omar Kabbaj (Eds.). 2002. *Regional integration in Africa*. New York, New York: OECD Publishing.

Faye, Michael L., John W. McArthur, Thomas Snow, and Jeffrey Sachs. 2004. 'The challenges facing landlocked developing countries'. *Journal of Human Development* 5 (1): 31-68.

Greico, Joseph M. 1990. *Cooperation among nation states: Europe, America and non-tariff barriers to trade*. Ithaca, New York: Cornell University Press.

———. 1988. 'Realist theory and the problem of international cooperation: Analysis with an Amended Prisoner's Dilemma model'. *The Journal of Politics* 50 (3): 600-624.

Glassner, Martin Ira. 1970. *Access to the sea for developing land-locked states*. The Hague, the Netherlands: Martinus Nijhoff.

Glauser, Wendy. 2008. 'Kenya violence hurts trade flows in Uganda, throughout East Africa'. *World Politics Review*. http:// www. World politics review.com/article.aspx?id=1583 (accessed 20 March 2008).

Hodder, Dick, Sarah Lloyd, and Keith McLachlan. 1998. *Land-locked states of Africa and Asia*. London, England: Routledge.

Kasozi, Abdu Basajjabaka Kawalya. 1994. *Social origins of violence in Uganda 1964-1985*. Montreal, Canada: McGill-Queen's University Press.

Keohane, Robert O. 1989. *International relations and state power: Essays in international relations theory*. Boulder, Colorado: Westview Press.

———. 1984. *after hegemony: Cooperation and discord in the world political economy*. Princeton, New Jersey: Princeton University Press.

————. 1982. 'The demand for regimes'. *International Organization* 36 (2): 325-55.

Kikwete, Jakaya. 2002. 'Regional alternatives and national options'. In: *Regional Integration in Africa*, edited by J. B. De Macedo and O. Kabbaj. New York, New York: OECD Publishing.

Le, Stephen and Robert Boyd. 2007. 'Evolutionary dynamics of the continuous iterated Prisoner's Dilemma'. *Journal of Theoretical Biology* 245 (2): 258–67.

Marhoum, Abdelaziz and David A. Samper. 2002. 'Rwanda: Economy'. *East Africa living encyclopedia.* African Studies Center, University of Pennsylvania. http://www.africa.upenn.edu/NEH/rweconomy.htm (accessed 2 April 2, 2008).

Okuttah, Mark. East Africa: 'EAC eyes trade growth with cyber laws'. *Business Daily* (Nairobi). http:// allafrica. Com /stories /orintable /201006240090 .html (accessed on 30 June 2010).

Pěchota, Vratislav. 1973. 'The right of access to the sea'. In: *Land-locked countries of Africa*, edited by Z. Cervenka. Uppsala, Sweden: The Scandinavian Institute of African Studies.

Rapoport, Anatol. 1974. *Game theory as a theory of conflict resolution.* Boston, Massachusetts: D. Reidel Publishing Company.

Snow, Thomas, Michael Faye, John W. McArthur, and Jeffrey Sachs. 2003. *Human development report 2003.* New York, New York: United Nations.

Stanford enclopedia ofpPhilosophy. 2007. 'Prisoner's dilemma'. http://plato.stanford.edu/entries/prisoner-dilemma (accessed on 11 November 2009).

Stein, Leslie. 1979. *The growth of East African exports and their effect on economic development.* London, England: Croom Helm.

Tarimo, David. 2006. 'East African community: Is it really working?' *The Monitor.* Distributed by AllAfrica Global Media (allAfrica.com).

Tandon, Yash. 1973. 'The transit problems of Uganda within the East African community'. In: *Land-locked countries of Africa*, edited by Z. Cervenka. Uppsala, Sweden: The Scandinavian Institute of African Studies.

The Economist. 7 February 2008. 'Kenya's tragedy: Stop this descent into hell'. 85 (66): 53-55.

Thies, Cameron G. 2002. 'A pragmatic guide to qualitative historical analysis in the study of international relations'. *International Studies Perspectives* 3 (4): 351-.

United States Agency for International Development (USAID). 2009. *Cross border trade in East African countries: Shared issues and priorities for reform.* Washington, DC: Government Printing-Office

CHAPTER 7

How African Civil wars Hibernate: Conflict and State Failure in the Borderlands of the Casamance and Guinea-Bissau

Aboubakr Tandia

Introduction

During the last five years, new developments around and within the Casamance conflict have brought it back to the attention of the local media and put it at the heart of the agenda of civil society organisations that have been dedicated to ending it. A rarer thing to see, there is a growing popular mobilisation[1] of the southern region of Senegal demanding peace. Yet, the Casamance conflict, probably more than other centres of tension, remains largely unknown. What focuses our attention here, the borderland dynamics of the conflict, remains underconsidered so far, even though the eastward displacement of the conflict and the territorial changes and their likely important effects on the ground should provoke the opposite.

The study of African civil wars has been suffering from two important biases. Because the focus was often the macro-level aspects of conflicts, the main objective was not only to document the conditions and utility of intervention, but also to justify nonintervention and to reinforce intergovernmental strategies of conflict management. This scholarly tendency was manifested in two ways. On the one hand, quantitative methods oversimplified the picture with the famous 'rates' and 'indexes' of violence and threshold of fatality or destruction, leaving what some called 'low intensity conflicts' to ignorance or lack of consideration.[2] On the other hand, intellectual activism exaggerated civil society organisations' and their sponsors' capacity to end conflicts, thus neglecting the territorialities of violence and its root causes. The tendency has been to look at conflicts as threats to state order, while states have been denied effectiveness or even existence in some contexts.

The Casamance conflict has been captured in such a paradigmatic prism for 28 years now. It has always been analysed in relation to state-making in Senegal and in the neighbouring countries of Guinea Bissau and the Gambia (Faye 1992: 190-212; Marut 2001: 11-20). As a result, the focus has been on bilateral relationships between Senegal and its neighbours (external geopolitics including state-rebellion encounters) and the various networks that have developed to bind local clients and patrons in national politics (internal geopolitics). The deafening silence over ordinary people as vulnerable victims, and yet local actors, is tantamount to the paucity of concern about the territorial dynamics[3] of the conflict that are curiously attributes of a state.

This paper deviates from this commonplace perspective that has minimised if not dismissed the borderland politics and territoriality of the conflict. Instead, it tries to reconcile the traditional approach with a borderland approach, in a combined spatial and political perspective, - to show how (inter) governmental or international and state-rebellion dynamics of the conflict are best revealed in and impact on the (inter)local borderland landscape straddling Senegal and Guinea-Bissau.[4] Actually, it is at this micro-level that the conflict can be called a 'civil war',[5] especially as many nationally labeled wars, notably in the African context, have transnational elements (Buhl 2009: 1-33) and often cross state borders, which is an important feature of 'new' or post-Cold War conflicts (Andersen, Barten, and Jensen 2009: 3). Borderland studies have also shown how borders have been used by rebel groups and other criminal groups to wage and internationalise wars (see Bakewell 2009; Scorgie 2009; Titeca and Mereike 2009) as a way to put pressure on intervening parties or destabilise neighbouring countries. In West Africa, we know how the Casamance war and other localised conflicts transformed the region into a regional war complex during the 1990s (see Ero and Ferme 2002; Adebayo 2005; Osita 2006).

Drawing from the background above, this paper basically argues that the causes, manifestations, and aggravating effects of the Casamance conflict mainly appear in the territorial peripheries of neighbouring states, influencing in one way or another the life of border communities. In this vein, how border dynamics of wariness relate to local politics and cross-border relationships is an important aspect of our analysis, as well as how they definitely foster the hibernation of the conflict. However, considering how the national-level political dynamics impact on the borderland war system is a first step to understanding the emergence of popular political and arms-based borderland power structures on the ruins of traditional and formal political and social structures.

Looking at the Casamance conflict through the lens of borderland geopolitics, as long as a borderland war complex can be talked of, entails a deducible secondary concern for this paper. As shown from studies of the Mano River and the Great Lakes conflict types (Raeymaekers 2007; Abdullah 2005a: 1-9; Richards and Vlassenroot 2002: 13-26), border approaches to conflicts recall the view that if wars raise issues of state-making in Africa, it is because African states did not engender their borders but were engendered by them (Asiwaju 1984). As a matter of fact, borders also frame wars, just as they shape states and politics in many instances. Mindful of spatial and popular idioms and characteristics of wars and borders as sociopolitical realities, such a perspective addresses the need to probe the question of why and, most importantly, how wars like the Casamance conflict still endure, prolonged and yet often forgotten (Sonko 2004: 35-38).

The first part of this paper will give a background picture of the Casamance conflict and its interconnections with the post-civil war situation in Guinea-Bissau. Recalling the root causes of the conflict helps evaluate the extent to which borders are still affected by their persistence. The second part will be concerned with the failure of the Senegalese government and its neighbours, in their occasional impulses of solidarity, to solve the conflict. The last part of the paper pays attention to how these factors intermingle with local borderland politics to the point of provoking and keeping the conflict going on in the margins.

The Casamance Conflict and the Post-Civil War in Guinea-Bissau: Ingredients of a Borderland War-System

Even though it is intended here to review the classical macro-geopolitical treatment of the conflict, we need to present the background of the conflict and the relationships it has developed with the political context in Guinea-Bissau, effects that are important aspects of the construction of a borderland war-system.

Back to the Root Causes of the Casamance Conflict

Many arguments have been put forth to explain the conflict in the south of Senegal that erupted in 1982 after the government violently repressed a march of women following youth street protests that took place within the framework of school strikes. An ethnic argument was first made to explain the conflict, given the irredentist or separatist tone of the rebel group, the Mouvement des Forces Démocratiques de la Casamance (MFDC). However, given the political origin of the movement and the multiethnic construct of the region, the ethnic hypothesis seems highly implausible. The MFDC was a political party created in 1947 as a regional party of the natural landscape of Casamance. Even though most leaders of the rebellion are from the Jola ethnic group, this party was created by local elites in the central part of the region inhabited by the Mandingos, notably the ancient department of Sédhiou which has become an administrative region in 2008[6] for interesting reasons that we will come back to later. After the regional party MFDC was dissolved, the early leaders of the rebellion took its name, which was tolerated by colonial powers and in the early postindependence era of the Senghor regime. Ethnically the Casamance region is not as homogenous as it may appear in the official name it has been given since colonisation. Many ethnic groups[7] are scattered in the region up to Guinea-Bissau and Guinea-Conakry. These ethnic groups constitute the communities of precolonial Gabu and the Fouladou kingdoms that were defeated by colonial powers (Renner 1984: 78-81; Barry 1992: 294-98). This state of affairs is reflected spatially through the discontinuity of the territory of Casamance, which lends credence to the reality of borderland communities that have been partitioned throughout the three countries[8] and in the Gambia (Hargreaves 1984: 19-28; Renner 1984: 75-78). Other explanations have been given in addition to the ethnic argument that was based mainly on the Jola origin of many leaders and army troops of the MFDC.

Class struggle, urban/rural cleavages, and failure of the Senegalese democratic model are the other factors that altogether point to the conflict as a 'centre-periphery problem', labeling it a direct product of statecraft in Senegal. Four fifths of the Casamance region is delineated by international boundaries. The ethnic diversity that resulted from this developed into a social way of living that is largely different from that of the northern Sudanese-Sahel part of Senegal. It is on these social and cultural differences that class formations were constructed through time, from colonisation to the postcolonial order in the favour of northern populations brought into Casamance by colonial rule and postcolonial labour migration and administrative conscription. Actually, the recruitment of the Casamance bureaucracy from the northerners, mainly Wolof people, only translated the 'Wolofisation' of the Casamance and the Senegalese political or state order, known as the 'Islamo-Wolof' model of state building (Diop 1992). Partly inherent to the one-party rule at the time, the many power abuses and ill-treatments of the local people as 'bushmen' or rural people, and the compulsory purchases that were frequently practiced by local administrators built on these class divides and nurtured the feeling of marginalisation and exclusion of the Casamance people from nation-building. This explains why the MFDC has always referred to historical identity markers such as the Portuguese presence before the French and the immemorial ties and the resemblances the people of Casamance have with those of Guinea-Bissau. The state-building enterprise was only limited to controlling the urban centers such as Ziguinchor, Bignona, and Sédhiou. Consequently, only these areas were endowed with basic infrastructures for the sake of administrative authority in the area. This also built another cleavage between urban areas occupied by local administrators coming from the north and rural areas occupied by autochthons, most of whom were peasants. While it is difficult to isolate one of these factors as the most important cause of the Casamance irredentism, all of them undoubtedly refer to the faulty lines of state-building in Senegal ranging from colonial rule to postcolonial hegemonic projects, which many authors do not contend (Faye 1992; Diaw and Diouf 1998: 259-86; Diallo 2008: 23-87).

All aforementioned factors have had a significant impact on the root causes of the conflict and its prolongation (Marut 2001: 12-15). For sure, all actually refer to and persist through the territorial character of the conflict, which is the exclusion or marginalisation of the Casamance region as a political and sociocultural space inscribed in its own historicity.

The Territorial Characters of the Casamance Conflict

The Casamance region was the last to surrender to colonial hegemony and as such received less attention in the process of state-making, at least politically. This attitude was inherited from the colonisers by the postindependence regime of Senghor under which a special status was assigned to the region, the rather pejorative and menial role of providing resources to the country, and serving as a haven to civil servants and other privileged and influential social groups and networks.This has been summarised in the literature as the multidimensional marginalisation of the Casamance region and people (see Diop and Diouf 1992; Marut 1995; Ngaïdé 2002; Lambert 2002; Sonko 2004). Actually, all those forms of marginalisation reflect the devalued territoriality the State and central elites allocated to the region in the sense that territory and territorialisation are inherently endowed categories of a state formation process.

As the last bastion of anticolonial struggle, the Casamance region and its peoples could not but react negatively to the reduced political role it had been given in national politics in Senegal after independence was gained. That region and its people have a long tradition of political participation and struggle, as exemplified in the former partisan vocation of the MFDC as a regional party already born in 1947. This political exclusion of the region has been accentuated in national party politics where regional leaders only played the role of local clients and wards for central decision-makers mainly of northern descent.

Political marginalisation was based on other patterns of exclusion ranging from economic to sociocultural forms that are actually brought to reality more by how they are represented than by their likelihood. The region has long been functioning as a natural reserve full of resources to sustain the Senegalese economy and State clientelism (Fanchette 2002: 322-37; Faye 1992: 190-91). In the framework of an economy of extraversion, it was especially providing rice as a basic commodity to satisfy the food demands of urban centers of the north, while at the same time facing the competition of the low-cost importations of trade networks animated by religious centers in the north. This is related to a social marginalisation of a population that was seen as rural and constituting the unwavering labour force for northern regions (Lambert 2002). The cultural exclusion of the region was based on the religious particularity of the region where are concentrated most of the Pagans of the country, included in the 5% Non-Muslim believers along with Christians. The importance of paganism and the attachment of the population to its traditions are seen as signs of backwardness (Sonko 2004: 36; Marut 1995: 6-7; Faye 1992: 194-95).

All these levels of exclusion of the Casamance region stem from a territorial marginalisation that dates up to the colonial perception of the region as a hostile, savage, and obscurantist territory. Through the course of state building, national leaders have been framing the popular perceptions of the region as 'la région naturelle de Casamance', meaning the wetland, the lungs of the national economy, the bush lived in by *niaks*, or forest people, the inexhaustible labour force, and the retarded mentality (Faye 1992: 194). Such a territorial ascription was manifested through the endless and stubborn efforts of the Senegalese government to mention, in the school curricula[9] as well as in official records, the particularity of the region as the granary of the country (Marut 1995: 7). This was coextensive with a social and cultural territorialisation that defined the Casamance identity as multiethnic in order to negate the regional identity convoked by the rebel movement in its political discourse. The reference to the Guinean affinities of the territory, both in geographical and historical terms, was also meant to mark the particularity of the region. But this process of naming and drawing the Casamance map in the national landscape was betrayed by the natural divide constituted by the Gambian enclave in the course of colonisation (Marut 1995: 7; Renner, 1984: 75-78). This can also be observed through the spontaneous solidarity developed by the different Casamance ethnic groups in the face of frustrations and deprivations suffered in the national fate within the Senegalese state (see Darbon 1988). The endeavours of the local peoples to safeguard and exalt their traditions added to the difficulties of the nationalist territorial strategy to thwart the rebellion's instrumentation of these spatial and social identitary representations through political mobilisation. That is why both the rebellion and the national government utilise the language of territory to name and draw the identitary and physical maps as well as the frustrations and lamentations of the Casamance region in the conflict (Marut 1995: 2-7; Sonko 2004: 35-36). But as we will see later, both actors in the long run failed at manipulating the territorial representations of the region, which has become one of the main obstacles to the settlement of the conflict.

The situation in Guinea-Bissau also reflects the territorial character of the Casamance conflict. From a historical perspective borders are also expressions and products of histories (see Donnan and Wilson, 1999) constructed by way of strong social and cultural ties among ethnic groups that live astride them. The geopolitical configuration of the conflict reflects an intermingling of internal and external territories and social spaces (Marut 1995; Tandia 2007a, 2009b). If the territorial representations constructed and manipulated by the rebel movement and the Senegalese government constitute important stakes, it is because they refer to the transboundary range of the Casamance identity. It is also because the local area of the conflict is far more different in scale from the global regional area that is named by the rebellion and populations who feel shackled by bonds dating back to the ancient kingdoms of Gabu and Fouladou. This is exemplified in the constant fear of the Senegalese government that the so-called 3B axis (Banjul, Bignona, and Bissau) emerges on the ruins of these precolonial entities (Faye 1994: 198-99). This explains why the Casamance conflict has always strained the relationships between Senegal and its Bissau Guinean and Gambian neighbours with which border disputes and localised conflicts erupted in 1997 for the former, and in 2003 and 2005 for the latter (Tandia 2007a). So given that the external territorialities of the conflict determine the strategies of actors, the situation in Guinea-Bissau and the Gambia may obviously have some implications on the Casamance conflict and vice-versa. Therefore, the borderlands straddling Senegal and Guinea-Bissau seem rather to be closer to alienation, despite the many sociocultural and economic patterns of their 'interdependence' and 'coexistence' (Cassarino 2006; Tandia 2009b). The patterns of interactions among peoples are being undermined by the chaotic situation in Guinea-Bissau opportunely exploited by the MFDC rebellion and the Senegalese government.

The Effects of State Failure in Guinea-Bissau

The *longue durée* of the anecdotic situation in Guinea-Bissau has been extensively documented, namely in official and civil society grey literature[10] as a state failure scenario. Scholarly treatment has also been informative in the historicity of the instability of the country since independence (see Forest 2003; Chabal 2002). Many authors view repercussions only as coming from the Casamance conflict to ignite the political situation in Guinea-Bissau (Faye 1995; Dumont 2009). But contrary to that view, the recent civil war of 1998-1999 in this country and its aftermath appeared as an additional evidence of the important impact the Guinea-Bissau anarchistic context has on and relates to the Casamance conflict.

From the encouraging processes of late 2009 and early 2010 of calm electoral politics[11] Guinea-Bissau has resumed in instability and uncertainty mirrored in up to six coups since 2008 and the exile of regular civil government of Prime Minister Carlos Gomez since the last 12 April coup following President Bacai Sanha's death in January in 9 January. The situation in Guinea-Bissau will keep on influencing the Casamance ordeal as it always did (Diop and Diouf 1990), all the more than the current transition is taking place in a context of power struggles among army factions and between the military and the main wings of the historical PAIGC, both sharpened by the stakes of political succession and the prospects of the narco-economy that feeds many barons of the military.

The identitary and territorial rhetoric of the rebellion mingles with the solidarity impulses of the Bissau-Guinean army to disrupt intergovernmental relationships between Senegal and its neighbor as a strategy to shield the narco-economy it has been building since 2005. As a result, the effects of the conflict go beyond the mere geopolitics of the warring networks and actors. As far as borderland wariness is concerned, we can consider some levels at which the state failure situation can affect the borderland governmentality, meaning attitudes directed towards politics of cross-border management.

Undoubtedly, the easy way in which the recent civil war in Guinea-Bissau erupted shows how it reflects the historical trajectory of the State that has been punctuated for a huge part of the postindependence period by government collapse, strong militarisation of politics, ethnicisation of a tramp military and survival of weaponry from liberation wars (Ferreira 2004: 45-56). To date, the porosity of the border and the dense human and commercial traffic, greatly criminalised, has set up a historicity and territoriality of violence on the borderland. Historicity of violence from liberation wars fuels the circulation of light weapons, drug trafficking and farming, and popular violence in response to insecurity originating from criminal activities such as arms trafficking, cattle rustling, path cutting, and armed robbery (Crisis Group 2008, 2009).

The whole criminal and insecure environment has two fundamental and concomitant effects. On the one hand, the rebellion takes advantage of the insecure and porous borders to raise funds and establish logistics for its war, which, on the other hand, forces populations to wander constantly throughout the borderland in search of security and minimal conditions for a peaceful life among parents or neighbours who deign to show hospitability. This criminal tendency has been uncontrollable whenever the networks of the rebellion in the Bissau-Guinean military has waned or disappeared. This has been the case, for instance, since the assassination of the Guinean Brigadier Ansoumane Mane who was deemed to be a supporter of the Casamance rebellion and a promoter of the reinvention of the Gabu kingdom in the form of a state straddling the south of Senegal and Guinea-Bissau (Crisis Group 2009; Foucher 2003; Dykman 2003). The proliferation and wanton use of landmines since 1997 and light weapons has risen to be the most important factor driving the increasing waves of refugees and internally displaced communities into the Senegalese side, and sometimes up to Gambia (IDMC 2008).

As a consequence of the anarchistic situation and the stagnation of both the Casamance and Guinean messes, the divisions and the scattering of the rebellion and nonidentified armed groups extend the war eastward and northward (Foucher 2003: 102-03), worsening the already worrisome humanitarian picture. The way both conflicts evolved through time and are managed explains a lot why and how the Casamance conflict is impacting on, and hibernates, in the borderlands.

The Manifestations of the Casamance 'Forgotten Civil War'

The title of a 'forgotten civil war' is neither a gratuitous assumption nor a purely theoretical view. As West Africa's longest civil conflict, the Casamance war is virtually unknown to the outside world (Evans, 2002; Sonko, 2004) just as it is not well understood by most Senegalese citizens themselves. It is hardly possible to have even one fifth of the Senegalese depict the root causes of the conflict and why it is everlasting. Most of the time, people would simply blame the ethnic group of the Jola as being hostile to the Northerners or fire on the government for tolerating the rebellion. But as some well-advised observers have emphasised (Evans 2002; Harsch 2005), even though the conflict has never reached the scale of many other conflicts in the region, it is ignored in the sense that it is hidden to the local public and jealously shielded from international curiosity. While the patterns of the internal management of the conflict are the main elements that work for it, international indifference is also a blamable factor.

The Faulty Patterns of the Management of the Conflict

The least we can say about the management of the conflict is that it has been following two main principles for the Senegalese government, and their prevalence since independence suggests that the political elites and the administrative and political direction of the Senegalese State share the same views and doctrines about this conflict: a threat to national cohesion that has to be erased by any means, including a deterioration strategy. Centralisation and a military solution are the main markers of the Senegalese management policy, but relative changes had been noted after the advent of the new liberal regime of President Abdoulaye Wade.

The culture of centralisation that so far has developed at a governmental level was 'presidentialised' by the late regime of Wade, while his successor Macky Sall has not made any significant move towards any changes from that status quo, despite his voiced will to count on Presidet Yaya Jammeh as the "key to the resolution of the Casamance conflict"[12] when he visited him in April 2012. The rare occasions when the conflict is evoked over national boundaries coincide with problems between Senegal and neighbouring countries. For example, under the socialist government, the Gambian regime of Dawda Kaïraba Diawara was targeted for severe public criticism from President Abdou Diouf of Senegal in 1990; the Gambian president presumably disclosed the casualties suffered by the Senegalese government and hundreds of refugees that were rescued in Gambia after rebel attacks near the southern borders of Gambia. In 2005, the local radio broadcasting station Sud FM lost its license in Gambia under pressure from the Senegalese government, because it had broadcast an inflammatory interview with Salif Sadio, one of the radical leaders of the armed wing of the Casamance rebellion.

Between 2000 and 2003, the new Senegalese regime opted for a presidential management of the conflict for many reasons. As the newly elected president who promised to resolve the conflict in 100 days, he believed that it was possible to end it if he wanted to break off from the methods of Abdou Diouf: 'We got bogged a lot in this case. Many intermediaries, well remunerated, have profited from the gullibility of my predecessor, just like others are exploiting the misery of the Third world. […] When I came to power I decided to put aside all the intermediaries. It is a national problem and I don't allow foreigners to interfere in it'[13]. As it appears from these words of the Senegalese President Abdoulaye Wade, centralization was meant to respond to the implication of neighbouring countries in the conflict, as much as the relationships between Senegal and its neighbours have always been characterized by suspicion in coexistence (Faye, 1994:199-206).

Already noted under the reign of Diouf (see Faye 1994; Diop and Diouf 1992; Havard 2003), the influence of neighbouring countries is also taken seriously as the President talked about securing the borders and reequipping the military[14]. The centralization option of the Senegalese Presidency from 2000 was not only directed towards neighbouring countries. Civil society actors have been kept out of the process, notably the Collectif des Cadres Casamançais.[15] The media also was systematically refused to be fluent on the conflict, as the dismissal of the French reporter of Radio France Internationale (RFI) Sophie Malibeaux in February 2005 seemed to ascertain. If many of the interveners come from President Wade's partisans and supporters, religious leaders, businessmen, notabilities and civil society organisations are more and more involving themselves[16]. Civil society organizations have been specially addressing issues of displacement, mine bombing and basic services delivery so that their import is recognized in the few successes of current social and economic reconstruction programs initiated by the government.

The military option is also a constant position of the Senegalese government toward the Casamance conflict. The army has never left the region since it was deployed in the early days of the conflict, despite promises to do so in the various agreements with rebellion for which it is a core demand. Military response has even grown whenever the army suffered surprising attacks. For example in May 1990 it opened a new stage in the conflict when the MFDC issued a declaration of an "armed struggle" in which they meant to gain independence in a guerilla war as declared its leaders (Marut 2001:12-15). The agreements that such a strategy forced the rebellion to sign hardly helped to enforce some short truces. Since as the rebellion's political wing is torn apart by divisions, while its armed wing *Atika* ('Warrior' in Jola) is now factionalized[17] and in search of significant allies after the death of many leaders and combatants, the presence of the military and a military option resembles more and more an inconsistency. However, the many recent attacks on the military and on national symbols such as the new university of Ziguinchor show that the armed conflict is not yet over, not to mention the regional environment[18]. The supports some groups in the influential military of Guinea-Bissau have been bringing to the Casamance rebellion are important explanations of the prevalence of the military option.

Centralization and militarization are not the only channels through which the Senegalese government used to handle the conflict. Through national politics of state-making and electoral competition, successive regimes managed to control the Casamance region (Faye 1994; Marut 1995, 2001) and keep the conflict far lower from the normal standards of open gravity. As one civil society organization leader declared[19], 'there is a link between the failure of the political system, bad governance and the Casamance conflict'. In previous studies bad governance through neopatrimonial politics proved to be an important characteristic and instrument of the liberal regime of Senegal (Tandia, 2009a), and has a lot influenced the eruption and prolongation of the conflict. Neopatrimonial politics has especially impeded the unprecedented strategy of social and economic reconstruction program that was devised to reduce frustrations and marginalization the Casamançais have been condemning.

In many regards, the Casamance conflict reflects the relationships the successive regimes in Senegal have often had with the southern part of the country. The neopatrimonial[20] basis of the management of the conflict derives from the general framework of the attempts of different regimes and statesmen, including colonial rulers, to control and subjugate the region (Diop and Diouf 1990; Faye, 1992; Marut 2001). The implementation of neopatrimonial politics in the State-Casamance relationships was and is still based on a messianic conception of politics. Not only has the conflict been approached and managed in this way, but the designation and mandating of a "Mister

Casamance"[21] since the hardest times of the conflict has been drawing from a neopatrimonial framework of control and assimilation of the southern part of Senegal. According to Faye, neopatrimonial politics in Casamance mainly aimed at a close control of populations (Faye 2005:191). First, local administrations and governments in the 1990's and up to now are identified as political actors of the presidential regime (ministers, members of parliament, mayors, etc.). They are charged with diffusing the discourse of national integration. Second, religious notabilities and traditional leaders were used for a close control of populations and served as local representatives of the powerful party-state which satellizes social organizations such as labour unions and grassroots organizations. For these procedures to succeed no means were saved to promote a moral and material fulfillment of civil servants, repress opposition parties and organizations that do not support the government's policy, ensure the vigor of financial networks that feed the political clients (Faye 1994:191-192). The Parti Socialiste (PS) of Abdou Diouf succeeded by these means to stay in power for 40 years, and to monopolize the local governments of Casamance.

The fragmentation of the local political life as a result of the neopatrimonial strategy has allowed the new regime of Wade to rule the incumbent socialists in 2002 from the local scene.[22] Administrative control is ensured by many changes at the head of decentralized divisions of the State and by the election of the regime's partisans as local councilors. At the territorial level, the former subdivision of Sédhiou, in the western part occupied by the Mandigo people, has been erected as a region in 2008 from a splitting of the Kolda region.[23] This change implying new local elected to represent the ruling party, Parti Démocratique Sénégalais (PDS), in the region is meant at the same time to split the territorial identity of Casamance as a whole. Now the spatial identity coincides with the Mandingo ethnic identity of Sédhiou. Seemingly, the goal of the Senegalese government is to confine and ascribe the Jola ethnic group to the western region of Ziguinchor or the 'Jola land'. Neopatrimonial politics is not restrained to local political and administrative representation and meshing. It has also to do with the management of the conflict at different levels. A first stage is at the level of the relationships with the rebel group of the MFDC and the intermediaries in the process of negotiation. A second one is the reconstruction policy program newly conceded and implemented under the liberal regime of Wade.

The rebel group of the MFDC has been rather divided since it entered into a guerilla war of liberation in 1990 which it always requested to include in any peace talk as a precondition for dialogue. This division mingled with a parallel recession of its popular support while the conflict started to exhaust the Casamançais. The regime of Diouf played on this default to privilege the political wing and the less radical leaders of the movement, aiming thus to divide the rebellion. This strategy proved to be successful if we consider that it has reduced the capacity and political support of the rebel group, but lived the conflict more destructive. The forefront leaders like the remnant Abbot Diamacoune, first moral and political authority of the MFDC, were settled down to a comfortable life, while military leaders were obliged to flee in the bush and in neighbouring countries as arrest warrants were released against them[24]. The intermediaries ranging from local religious and traditional notabilities to political and business leaders profited as well from the privileges dedicated to silencing the conflict (Foucher 2003: 104-05).

As mentioned earlier, there are at least four groups to take into account today as the MFDC has been fractionalized. If the new liberal regime declared in the first years to keep aside intermediaries, it has allowed local politicians and influent notabilities to engage in negotiations with the MFDC. While the civil society organizations and some local councilors' call for a unification of the movements as a preliminary stage to bring the MFDC to the table of negotiation. As President Wade's first move was to block the rents political leaders of the MFDC had been gaining since the reign of Diouf, the latter multiplied initiatives to restore its ancient profitable ties. In 2001, after he resorted to President Chirac of France to call on Wade, Abbot Diamacoune publicly evoked the resource issue, claiming that he no more received the support of the Senegalese government to face his important duties[25]. The Government is not the sole advocate and promoter of this rent-seeking strategy. Civil society[26] and intermediary groupings also feed the rebel leaders. Recently, the Collectif des Cadres Casamançais[27] has been recognized a mandatory to propose a policy plan for the conflict. Wade even makes use of leaders of local grassroots' organizations[28] to win the trust of the Casamance populations, or else attract some fringes of the rebellion. As a result, the factions in the MFDC are not only tearing apart, but are also beset with intestinal wars to capture the rent; many rebel leaders have been auto-declared themselves at the head of some factions, each trying to claim legitimacy for its own (Foucher, 2003). Undoubtedly, this rather nuclearized environment has important implications for the economic and social levels of the conflict resolution policy named the *Programme de Relance des Activités Economiques et Sociales de la Casamance*[29] (PRAESC) devised in 2001 and implemented later on in 2004.

When it was set up in 2004, the PRAESC was meant to address the social and economic damages the conflict had caused for 22 years of conflict in many domains.[30] However, as clientelist party politics developed and came to the fore of stakes in the local landscape (Tandia 2009b; Fanchette, 2002: 328-337), the reconstruction program became an instrument of local political struggles. It even suffered the rivalry or duplicity of other local strategies mushrooming from local associations. For example, the Convention pour la Paix Definitive en Casamance nearly succeeded in burying this program by promoting the resort to local social cultures for the settlement of the conflict (Foucher 2003). Led by a certain Malamine Kourouma, this group has mobilized traditionalist women associations around a purgatory procession held in October 2002 to get rebel combatants from so-called evil oaths that keep them in the bush and join the peace initiatives. A Mandingo and local leader of the ruling party PDS, Kourouma is facing many other adversaries in this game[31]. As a result of the local rivalries that fall out of the neopatrimonial politics, many assassinations[32] remained unsettled since 2004 and the political and military leaders of the MFDC more than ever have become rivals.

If the new regime of President Wade profited from many advantages, such as a propitious international and local political environment for a long time, it unfortunately borrowed the undermining techniques of the former party-state PS: the old Senghorian instruments such as cooptation and coercion, neopatrimonialism and populism have hardly prevented the radicalization and hierarchisation of the MFDC (Foucher 2003:110-13). In effect, the rebellion split into many rival factions trapped in local party politics while its prominent figures are dying. Basically, the Casamance conflict seems to have evolved but keeps the same records of many unimplemented peace agreements, civil society rhetoric and rent politics of power and economic accumulation. Both the state and the MFDC have failed to get the conflict out of its 27 years exploitation and prolongation, and the international interveners at regional or further levels do not seem to have done better.

Inadequacies and Insufficiencies of International Interventions

The nature of international intervention in the Casamance conflict has proved to be a cause of its ignorance and oblivion. Actually, the lack of international resonance is due to insufficient and inadequate engagement from the international community, at least from main interveners that could be legitimately called on. No doubt that as a sovereign state Senegal has anticipated any genuine involvement of foreign actors by the only fact of refusing interference in the management of the conflict. However, no significant effort has been shown to break this diplomatic firewall, not to mention the political possibilities yet offered by new conceptions of intervention and responsibility in current international discourses of civilian protection and human security. As a matter of fact, the Casamance conflict lacks a foreign government or organization acting as a guarantor to a concrete peace process (Harsch 2005). Neighbouring countries have been partaking in the settlement of the conflict but displayed much more ambiguity, namely the Gambia (Marut 2000; Havard 2003; Tandia 2007b). Even though he does not miss opportunities to voice his solidarity and willingness to help through a pacific negotiation and settlement process, President Jammeh of Gambia has been rather undetermined.[33]

Concerning Guinea-Bissau, political leaders and the military seldom share opinions about the Casamance conflict. The military has been most of the time supporting the MFDC as exemplified by the role of late Brigadier Ansoumane Mane in the conflict (Marut 2001: 2-11; Foucher 2003:106-07; Ferreira 2004: 46-47; Crisis Group 2008: 10-14). After his early neutrality that bred suspicion from Senegalese former socialist regime, President Vieira resolved to combat the rebellion until the death of Mane[34] in 2000 and other MFDC leaders during the following years. Under the Yala Regime, the MFDC was again declared an enemy of Guinea-Bissau[35] and was combated and repelled towards its borderline rear bases (Marut 2008:2-3). Senegal and Guinea-Bissau had been trying a strategy of encirclement until

March 2009 when President Vieira and General Tagmé Na Waï were assassinated. Having said that, it would be erroneous to see the disposal of Bissau only as a spontaneously philanthropic attitude. As I will show later, Dakar had to make significant concessions to win that cooperation.

In comparison with the Sierra Leone and Liberian civil wars, which of course reached larger scales of violence and destruction (Abdullah 2005b), but lasted much less time, international intervention has been lacking from the United Nations (UN) and France on the Casamance question. The Casamance has not received support from concerted military efforts as seen elsewhere from the Economic Community of West African States (ECOWAS) and the UN (Adebayo 2005; Evans 2002). Besides its specialist agencies, mainly active in humanitarian issues like mine depollution and displacement, the UN action in the conflict has been limited to occasional calls for dialogue. The former colonial power, France, has also been reluctant, as the French government seems to regard the conflict as an embarrassment in its bilateral relations with Senegal (Evans 2002). Even when the journalist of Radio France International was expelled from Senegal in 2005 for her fluency about the conflict, no reaction was ever recorded (Tandia 2007a). Yet the MFDC was unsuccessful when it had sought mediation from France and the UN, probably as a sign of the insurgency's keenness to make its case to the outside world. This seems rather strange as France has been offering asylum to MFDC leader Nkrumah Sané for many years now. Interestingly, one can question such hospitality as some rebel leaders are yearning for more significant public engagement that can foster a peaceful and definite settlement of the conflict.

As the management of the conflict is influenced by the situation in neighbouring Guinea-Bissau, the shortcomings of international intervention in that country obviously condemn the Senegalese conflict. In Guinea-Bissau, militarisation of politics is the core challenge for international peacemaking policy, which instead focuses on economic sanctions that only encourage the military to emerge as the sole political force and a big wheel of the interminable transition (Crisis Group 2009: 15). As was exemplified by the Mano River conflicts, international sanctions in the context of state failure only exacerbate the socioeconomic situation of overwhelmed livelihoods of rural communities while encouraging predatory governance. Despite the presence of no fewer than fourteen organisations and countries in the reform processes, alternatives clearly coming from interveners are still lacking, while civil society activism lingers after more sustained donor funding (Crisis Group 2008: 23-24). Obviously, the financial costs of enriching the military[36] and senior political leaders cannot be reduced as long as the military can jeopardize the political process in Guinea-Bissau. At the level of humanitarian relief, the impacts of many programs have been limited by poor support from donors, with only around 30 percent of its appeals funded as of May 2008 (IDMC 2008: 7). As a result, organisations like the Gesellschaft für Technische Zusammenarbeit (GTZ), the United States Aid Agency for Development (USAID), and the World Food Program (WFP) are subcontracting their missions to local NGOs as they face problems in accessing border areas (USAID, 2006: 56). Rebel attacks and mine bombing also impede the action of international NGOs and agencies, as when a delegate of the Red Cross was killed in a mine accident in September 2006 in Casamance. This situation of chaos and despair retards domestic ownership of the dynamics of conflict resolution as a crucial stage in conflict settlement, a situation that is of more concern in Guinea-Bissau where the main obstacle remains the lack of coordination between the main interveners, the European Union and the United Nations (Crisis Group 2009: 12-14).

Senegal's Interventionism in Guinea-Bissau

What appeared heretofore as interdependence between two neighbouring countries that are bound to cooperate[37] has evolved into a more complex situation where Senegal not only bargains but is trying to take control of the course of national politics.[38] As we are used to seeing in relationships between African countries and their former colonial settlers, mainly in francophone Africa, intervention was often meant to preserve foreign interests of interveners and save incumbent regimes from political protest or unrest, as the latter objective depended on this condition. Senegal has been bargaining with a Bissau-Guinean State where regimes are keen to hold on to power. The most known regime was President Vieira's twenty-year reign based on the maintenance of a tramp and ethnicised military. Therefore, the interventions of Dakar in Guinea-Bissau had to sustain the local regimes, from which a neutrality or collaboration was expected to encircle the irredentism of the MFDC. As the destabilising incursions of the rebel group multiplied in a context of increased internal instability, Bissau-Guinean leaders resolved to play the Dakar game, with other add-ons in mind. So Dakar is obsessed[39] by the Casamance separatist movement, so that its disputes over oil fields with neighbouring Guinea-Bissau have lost credibility in its agenda. As such, it has to engage in political stability in Guinea-Bissau, and sometimes let the situation deteriorate so as to put pressure on Bissau authorities and get them meet its demands about the MFDC. Such is the deal between Dakar and Bissau on the Casamance war, despite the huge threat it poses to the fragile peace in Guinea-Bissau.

In 1998, on the basis of mutual agreements on defense signed with the country in 1976, Senegal intervened in Guinea-Bissau where president Vieira was being overthrown in a coup. Senegal was expecting to double the score: saving President Vieira as a way of rewarding his mediation and military support in the Casamance conflict, while at the same time neutralising some combatants of the MFDC. But this intervention just added stains on the reputation of the ECOWAS, already tested in Liberia and Sierra Leone (Tandia 2007a; Adebayo 2005), for it did not succeed in overturning Vieira's failure, much less break the solidarity networks of the MFDC in the Bissau-Guinean army (Foucher 2003: 107; Marut 2008: 3-4). A one-year violent civil war followed, costing economic sanctions to Bissau-Guineans and a scattering of the MFDC northward and eastward, with obviously terrible consequences. A fringe of the military, identified with the Jola ethnic group of Casamance and Guinea-Bissau, was led by Mane, himself a Jola, in another coup in 2000. However, military intervention is not the only pattern of the Senegalese strategy in 'bargaining' interference. Financial support and economic negotiations are part of the machinery: in 1995, as he needed a rapprochement, President Diouf conceded 15 percent of the possible benefits to Guinea-Bissau from the so far unexploited oil of the Dome Flore that was still litigious between the two countries. In 2003, President Wade took the share of Guinea-Bissau to 20 percent, while some billets of the military in Guinea-Bissau are being taken up by Senegal. In November 2002, as he was facing severe cash flow hardships, President Coumba Yalla halted in Dakar in his tours of friendly countries (Foucher 2003: 107).

If Senegalese interventionism had been successful, the one-year civil war would not have been followed by various coups in 2001 and 2003, fragilising the current 22-year transition in Guinea-Bissau, nor would the assassination of Brigadier Mane, as a Jola supporting the MFDC and willing a joint attack of Senegal with the MFDC, be mourned by Guinean populations and religious leaders (Ferreira 2004). On the contrary, growing anti-Senegalese feeling is recorded since the intervention of 1998, and recently, the celebrations of late President Vieira's assassination as a sort of revenge to Brigadier Ansoumane Mane's killing in November 2000. Obviously, Senegal and Guinea-Bissau have failed in their interstate attempts to territorialize this conflict and the local regional dynamics through which it is daily manifested.

In Senegal, aside from the erratic effects of neopatrimonial politics in hindering political participation of the Casamance populations, the strategy of confinement of the rebellion from Guinea-Bissau has actually complicated the prospects of the conflict. As it is based on the centre/periphery distribution and exchange of emoluments and militarisation, this strategy reveals the constant objective of Senegal to break the MFDC in distant political and armed wings in order to wear it down. While populations feel that the lines of marginalisation of the Casamance region and identity have sharpened, the MFDC has imploded into many rival factions led by illegitimate leaders that hoard electoral and economic rents from the situation and blockade the conflict in a no peace/no war situation.[40] As a result, the conflict that was initially confined to the Ziguinchor region spread into western parts of Kolda as of 1995. What if the MFDC was just wandering, taking all the border spaces as possible pathways to survival?

How the Civil War Hibernates In the Borderlands between Senegal and Guinea-Bissau

The borderland manifestations and effects of the conflict stem exactly from this picture of the conflict where armed rebels are doing more harm and maintain the conflict in the field, to the detriment of local communities, but are given less consideration. Roughly, we can conceive of the hibernation of the conflict in the borderlands as the consequences of its deterioration and its spatial development towards the eastern part of Casamance on the borderlands of Senegal and

Guinea-Bissau. Quite likewise, the reproduction of the Casamance conflict as a manifestation and inscription of its consequences in the borderland space is fuelled by local politics of cross-border governmentality, that is, the attitudes towards politics and communal life (natural resources, transboundary criminality, socioeconomic dynamics, and community relations). It is useful to briefly sketch out the process in which the Casamance conflict is throwing its sparks on borderlands through the growing violence of the MFDC in these areas.

The Increased Violence of the MFDC on Borders

The consequences of the division of the MFDC at which the Senegalese government has been partly working are thoroughly exemplified through the new tactics of the rebellion. As its legitimacy and mobilisation capacity have been drastically reduced by the logic of fragmentation between factions, the MFDC is seeking to scare the local population and force them to collaborate.[41] Recalling the strategies of the Revolutionary United Front in Sierra Leone (RUF) and the National Patriotic Front of Liberia (NPFL) in Liberia (Abdullah 2005b), growing repression from the MFDC is operated through mine bombing, wanton civilian attack, and transboundary criminality.

Violence of the MFDC not only is growing in intensity but is given new functions. First, the MFDC seemingly wants to mobilise by force the populations of Casamance whose attention it has failed in the long run to grab. So violence against civilians makes more sense to the conflict, which thus takes on a civil character. The rebellion has moved from attacks on military targets to violence with an impact on those same people, for example by restricting access to farming land and undertaking armed robberies[42]. Disturbing security incidents involving kidnappings and mutilations have been reported along the border with Guinea-Bissau, where MFDC rebels have started to use violence to prevent villagers from accessing their land and homes. In March 2008, some villagers were reportedly kidnapped close to new rebel bases (IRIN 2008). Second, as a consequence, violence is meant to breed a war economy, since the MFDC needs to supplement the shortage of resources for its survival.

Criminalisation of the Conflict and War Economy

Issues of criminalisation in civil wars have gained prominence and depth in Africa. Criminalisation refers to militarisation of politics and state-making as a whole (see Bayart, Ellis, and Hiboux 2000) but should be limited to the construction and sustenance of war economies (Raeymaekers 2007), as many wars evolve at the level of both politics and accumulation. In the case of the Casamance conflict, criminalisation can refer not only to the maintenance of a war economy by the MFDC and other parallel armed groups that profit from the war system, but also to the politicians and intermediaries who live off the conflict by engaging in the process of management and in the local party politics. Thus, we will specifically focus on the territorial aspect of criminalisation as it is also consistent with the military pattern that proves to be most important.

Criminalisation of conflict yields another issue about violence in civil wars. If the logic of political violence remains, as separatism is still in the agenda of the MFDC, criminalisation towards a war economy introduces criminal violence, which interacts with and serves banditry and brutality as civilians are blamed in the attacks for their lack of enthusiasm in the rebellion's cause (Bangura 2005: 13-40). The attack against civilians is a new pattern of the rebellion's behaviour since the onset of the conflict. Either they collaborate or they leave their homes and land for rebels to establish new bases. The rebels are currently displacing civilians by armed force[43] and aim to scatter their bases throughout the whole region of Casamance; many are asked to move to Guinea-Bissau[44] without their harvests and goods that probably end up as rebel food. However, even though the MFDC is trying on a new use of violence, the RUF-like 'join us or perish', it is rather more a movement that lives with the conflict, because only a few factions now keep on believing in the sacred cause of independence; criminalisation has always been the most common pattern of the rebellion, let alone military clashes with the Senegalese army. But definitely, this war economy is not only dedicated to personal accumulation and greed of leaders and combatants, but also to gathering war expenditures. Thus, has it been specialised in drug trafficking (marijuana on the rear bases on the Gambian borders, and cocaine throughout the Senegal/Guinea-Bissau borders) originally on the littoral in Ziguinchor and more and more towards Kolda region in the eastern parts of Casamance (Foucher 2003, Marut 2008; Tandia 2009b). The MFDC has also been involved in the smuggling of arms for decades now, in an environment where the stock of arms left by the Liberation wars is recycled in the party politics of an unending transition in Guinea-Bissau (Lehtinen 2000; Marut 2001: 2-5).

Borderlands between Enclavement, Scarcity, and Wariness

The borderland space we are studying is the transboundary territory straddling the four 'communautés rurales' of the Kolda division (degraded green colors) and the neighbouring Bissau-Guinean area of Citato-Cuntima and Contuboël in the Regùlado of Gabu. This area is the political territory of the ancient Gabu kingdom that reached the republic of Guinea and the Futa Jallon. On the Senegalese side, the Fula territory is called the Fouladou, while the name of Gabu prevails in Guinea-Bissau. This territory is still marked by the liberation wars in Guinea Bissau and the long-lasting Casamance 'war' (Faye 1994; Crisis Group 2008; Tandia 2009b). It also stretches toward the central part of Guinea-Bissau, which relativises the ethnic homogeneity of the community formed by the Fula people, called the Fulas of Gabu (Borshik 2008). Indeed, the ethnic homogeneity is disrupted by the sedentary type of migration flows of central Senegalese farmers, and western and central Bissau-Guinean Balanta people fleeing political instability and poverty. The same can be said of Mandingo and Fula communities that cross the border, which does not come without causing problems. Poverty and insecurity are guised in the insecurity system formed by land mines, cattle rustling, fraudulent trading, and growing armed robbery (Tandia 2009b), which yields insecurity dilemmas where dynamics are just cooking the Casamance conflict as community violence and conflict for survival mingle with frustrations sustained by the situation in Casamance.

Borderland Insecurity Dilemmas: Transboundary Criminality, Extreme Poverty and Conflicts

The prolongations of the Casamance civil war in time are replicated spatially on borderlands. The overall scenario of scarcity, chaos, and wariness indeed unfolds some factors that interact as insecurity dilemmas for borderlanders: transboundary criminality (cattle rustling, path-cutting), poverty, and conflicts. As we intend to highlight, these ordeals nurture the conflict in low-intensity conflictuality. Yet, this apparent landscape of precariousness constitutes a serious threat that sustains the Casamance war on borderlands, as not inconsiderable frustrations greatly resemble the rebellion's complaints against the Senegalese State.

An overview of the borderlands makes them appear to be nests of insecurity related to the importance of armed groups. This environment explains why armed groups[45] are able to commit their crimes[46] in total impunity. In the communauté rurale of Tankanto Escale (see Map), 896 inhabitants of frontier villages found refuge in Senegal in 1999 before returning in 2001. More than 1 000 cows were stolen between 2004 and 2005, and surveillance has lapsed as herdsmen are getting rare. Populations are scared to speak out since their assailants are still armed.

Cattle-rustling is an important insecurity problem as much as it is closely related to conflicts that arise between farmers and herdsmen. Managing rural spaces of farming and herding is more of a thorny issue in so far as the displaced from battlefields and landmine-polluted areas lose their instruments for farming and herding. The 'border effect' between territories of Senegal and Guinea-Bissau is manifested through criminality. 'It is more common to see Bissau-Guineans rustle their Senegalese counterparts, which fosters tensions and community violence'.[47] The conflicts as such are generated by the decrease in the size of the livestock as cattle are used for farming. The livestock destroy rice fields since there are fewer herdsmen to get them to graze, a situation that fuels conflicts that often degenerate, as no particular solutions are available in the short term. Since prejudices are often poorly compensated following unattended complaints and legal suits, they do not relieve the rancor amongst families and villages. Moreover, this situation forestalls traditional mechanisms of conflict resolution, which are even avoided since the populations are dissuaded by systematic arms wearing, a local pattern of territoriality and history of violence deriving from the liberation war in Guinea Bissau and the Casamance conflict.

Borderlanders are also affected by a situation of extreme poverty worsened by the lack of social infrastructures and the enclavement from main roads and local markets. Without cattle and instruments for farming, populations have witnessed aggravated living conditions, which accentuates sanitation and nutrition problems, since sanitary districts are inaccessible, mainly when they are located near rear bases of the rebellion: 'We all know the problems we have here, they are rebels and mines. But our daily lot is hunger, everybody is hungry here'[48]. To survive, some take the risk of making connections with the rebels, or else join armed groups in cattle rustling, path-cutting, or other crimes. Obviously, this situation has been ripe for the destruction of the borderland economy.

As the war in Casamance and instability in Guinea-Bissau generated migration flows of displaced communities, there has been a tendency toward the increase of population densities on the borderland. The displaced are likely to engage in criminality, as they come with bare hands and are sometimes hardly welcome in places where poverty and cattle rustling are raging. For example, migrants who become herdsmen in their host families are often involved in cattle-rustling, which by way of consequence exposes them to suspicion if not violence. Besides displaced people of the war, migrants that are involved in cross-border trade (*bana-bana*[49]) or farmers coming from the northern and central parts of Senegal (the Northerners) also practise farming and herding. They manage to get land to cultivate, many of them in the forest, as long as they can be connected to local trustees led by religious and traditional chieftaincies in the northern villages of Kolda (Tandia 2009b).

The issue of land access[50] in a context of poverty and poor employment opportunities is related to the whole problem of natural resources management. In this regard, not only do displacements and migrations create demographic and security problems, but they also arouse the suspicions and frustrations among local communities, given that new settlers amidst local trustees and administrations favour them in some domains, such as forestry, with access to land (Fanchette 2002: 337-46; Tandia 2007b, 2009b).

Frustrations are interesting indicators of the manifestation and hibernation of the Casamance war and related chaos in neighbouring Guinea-Bissau. They are indeed numerous and concern many aspects of this particular life of peoples who are living in the prism of wariness. What is more, it is expressed in the form of grievances: 'Those who help cattle rustlers are many. Government itself is a participant by way of its inaction. Government is the first to blame and the police as well. Cattle rustlers operate in total impunity and are freed as you take them to the police'[51]. At another level, populations find it hard to turn the wheel of justice and get through the administrative procedures for the security of their fellows, goods, and herd: 'Even though our silence condemns any attempts of the gendarmerie, there are problems that are due to the slowness and complicity of administrative services [...] The guys from the slaughterhouse seem to play the acolytes of cattle rustlers. They don't help identify cattle rustlers'[52].

Among the Senegalese Fulas of Fouladou in Upper Casamance, a commonplace phrase to hear is the following: 'They [the Northerners] are taking away our resources'. A farmer complaining about migrants and local politics said this to us: 'we happen to ask ourselves whether we should not have done like our Jola brothers in Low Casamance'[53], referring obviously to the current irredentism against the Senegalese State. More than frustrations, the literature and empirical treatments of some memorable civil wars have pinpointed the youth or generational issue as important in the waging and prolongation of conflicts.

The Heirs of the Conflict: 'Youth of the War' Vs. 'Youth at War'

The youth question is of particular interest in the viewpoint of the borderland dynamics of the Casamance war, but also as it relates to the issue of the role of violence in survival strategies and socialisation in contexts of state crisis. In Sierra Leone and other wars, the youth have been central in the warfare machineries where the patterns of their recruitment, socialisation, and relation to politics are impressing (Bangura 2005: 13-40; Abdullah 2005b). As for the transboundary criminality issue we have encountered in the case of the Casamance, we can recall the body of work that also has highlighted the determinants of their engagement in careers of banditry and their relationships with their communities as well as their view and practise of politics (Saïbou 2006:2). The Casamance conflict contributes to those issues of war prolongation and politics of socialization and revolt among the youth at least on two levels. As modalities of violence embrace the logics of accumulation and survival, youth engagement raises the question of whose engagement among youngsters, why, and for what aims. What are the implications for the use and the functions of violence as far as the prospects of conflictuality are concerned? What are the dynamics in the field that contribute to these youth politics of violence and survival at the edges of civil war? To what extent social structures can suggest a youth reacting to a sociohistorical determination?

The least one can do is to consider the hypothesis of the youth inheriting the conflict as they appear as actors who reproduce it in their plans for survival. Furthermore, reproducing the conflict is likely to continue to create doubts, in as much as they embody the repression of frustrations in a form of local politics. What is happening on borderlands is that youth see and react to wariness as a consequence of violence, but in two different and even more competing ways.

What is commonly known from African civil wars is youth that are deemed to be seeking revenge against the state, or blaming governmental regimes, for their proneness to failure and indifference. In Sierra Leone, exaggerated analyses depicted a 'lumpen youth' (Richards 1996), born to kill, just because their prospects were limited to the time they spent with warlords. The conflict was then seen as a way for them to erase failed states. But as Bangura noted, not only has the defection of the Revolutionary United Front youth impacted on its late failure, but there also were two distinguishable categories of youth: the 'youth in peace' and the 'youth in war' (Bangura 2005:34). The former are those who have been disappointed by the RUF, with which they have been associated from the beginning, while the latter refer to the youth that were prepared to become gladiators in the insurgent army.

In the case of the Casamance, violence is not only breeding violence, but 'youth in peace' engage in cross-border initiatives of security governance that aim to pacify the borderlands in the (post)war context. Actually these 'youth in peace' are at war against the wariness resulting from the Casamance conflict. Thus, to violence in the war economy and transboundary criminality, involving 'youth in war' or 'youth of the war' (that is made of war, made by the Casamance war), is opposed violence for peace throughout mechanisms of cross-border security governance. Such new instruments of community peacemaking are called the forums and vigilante groups that are arising on the borderland to discuss security issues, prevent and settle conflicts, and promote cross-border integration (Tandia 2009a, 2007a).

The agency approach to the youth response to its sociohistorical and territorial environment of wariness enables to not negate the resistance of societal and communal mechanisms of unwariness. In the same way, the effects of the conflict are also not exaggerated. Therefore if the 'youth of the war' translate their deprivation (lack of schooling and employment, poverty), migrate in urban centers, or engage in banditry and survival accumulation, or else blame local governments, it is because they take for granted the bankruptcy of sociocultural and political dynamics that pour changes upon them. They may not be wrong in this sense, as it is obvious that survival is the only chance offered when schooling, sanitation, and employment are luxuries, when parents and families have nothing to give, and there are only irregular wages for migrants who are willing to watch a livestock that they will stealthily sell later. Cultural dynamics of change also foster a logic of violent youth as the youth question the gerontocracy of adults who accuse them of laziness and criminality, a situation that increases the assets of bellicosity in the sense that it evolves in a polarisation where the other cleavage is the civil youth, or 'youth in peace' (Bangura 2005). The youth at war for peace stand as a counterpart only by playing a role in policing the border and by fighting the criminal activities of survival in which the 'lumpen' youth is involved. Though traditional mechanisms of social regulation are rather ineffective in mobilizing people, the 'youth at war' try hard to rebuild those social structures as a means of thwarting wariness and overlapping insecurity dilemmas. Nevertheless, the fact remains that violence is so pervasive that survival violence and rebel war economy will have more to gain in the polarisation against violence for peace, and will do so for a long time ahead.

Conclusion

I have tried in this paper to look at the Casamance conflict from a renewed perspective that of the border issue, in both the literature of civil wars and in the empirical dynamics of the conflict on borderlands. Of course, I have maintained the classical geopolitical readings that start from the classical state and intergovernmental framework of realism in international relations. This was a necessary move as we specifically intended to highlight the ways in which the classical configuration of the conflict, in theory as well as in practice, could be mapped on the reduced perimeter of borderlands. Furthermore, as in the classical view, geopolitics is still an important configuration in the sense that the borderland micro-level underpins

241

the manifestations of macro-geopolitics on the local peripheries in terms of the territorial character and prolongation of the Casamance conflict. This is revealed in the discontinuity of borderland security dilemmas and the way that, by being reproduced, the latter maintains the conflict in hibernation. State dynamics did not also disappear in this micro-level 'borderising' of the Casamance conflict. The border effect of war prolongation and periterritorialisation has determined many instances where the Casamance conflict follows the same logic as in the classical macro-geopolitical reading. From the failures of interstate plans and local politics to the borderland insecurity complex of dilemmas, frustrations proved to be quite the same. Reaction to state failure and to an unending conflict equates to responding to different forms of violence. Just as warring parties are pressured by grassroots peacemakers at the national and international levels, on borderlands youth in peace counterattack and mobilise against the wariness resulting from the conflict, which is only perceptible at the micro-level of borderland geopolitics. However, chances are that violence against civilians and civil mobilisation for peace prevails again for some more time.

As we have seen, the damages on borderlands and to borderlanders are greater and more complicated than they seem to be at the level of interstate politics. Likewise, the chances are slimmer for borderlanders to avert the prolongation of the conflict, as they are not involved in the official peace process. The resolution of community hardships instead depends on the betterment of the peace processes in the Casamance and Guinea-Bissau.

If the Casamance conflict is to be resolved, it will be mingled with the next-door situation in Guinea-Bissau. As a border perspective is possible and even more informative on the territorial developments of civil wars, and then what we have tried to demonstrate, two levels of policy, can be sketched out. At the level of intergovernmental relations, a regional approach has to be displayed, as time has proven that Senegal is unable to move alone, unlike Guinea-Bissau. To that end, the negotiations that have been being recalled and pushed on with no advancement have to be regionalised. This implies crossing borders and authorizes a linking of borderland local initiatives to international initiatives. That is because cross border governmentalities of peace building and security governance have been mushrooming successfully to mitigate the throes of conflictuality in the borderlands and in many conflicts in West Africa (Cisse 2007; Tandia 2009b).

Bibliography

Abdullah, I. 2005a. *Between democracy and terror: The Sierra Leone civil war*. Dakar: CODESRIA.

————. 2005b. 'Bush path to destruction: The origin and character of the RUF/SL. In: *Between democracy and terror: The Sierra Leone civil war*, edited by I. Abdullah, pp. 41-64. Dakar: CODESRIA.

Adebayo, A. 2005. *Liberia's civil wa: Nigeria, ECOMOG and regional security in West Africa*. Boulder, Colorado: Lynne Rienner Publishers.

Akpan F. 2008. 'Road map to failed states: The nexus between bad governance and failed states'. *Pakistan Journal of Social Sciences* 5 (9): 945-52.

Asiwaju, A.I. 1984. *Partitioned Africans: Ethnic relations across Africa's international boundaries 1884-1984*. Lagos, Nigeria and London, England: University of Lagos Press and C. Hurst and Company.

Bangura, Y. 2005. 'The political and cultural dynamics of the Sierra Leone civil war'. In: *Between democracy and terror: The Sierra Leone civil war*, edited by I. Abdullah, pp. 13-41. Dakar: CODESRIA.

Andersen, D., U. Barten, and P.S. Jensen. 2009. 'Challenges to civil war research. Introduction to the special issue on civil war and conflicts'. *JEMIE* 8 (1): 19. http://www.ecmi.de/jemie/do wnload/1-2009-Intro-Andersen-Barten-Jensen.pdf.

Bakewell, O. 2009. 'The changing face of the Zambia/Angola border'. African Border Research Network Conference *How Is Africa Transforming Border Studies*, University of the Witwatersrand, School of Social Sciences, 10-12 September.

Barry, B. 1988. 'La Grande Sénégambie au XXeme siècle'. IN: Diop, M-C. (ed.) *Le Sénégal et ses voisins*, edited by M-C. Diop, pp. 293-98. Dakar: Sociétés-Espaces-Temps.

Bayart, J-F., S. Ellis and B. Hiboux. 2000. *The criminalization of the State*. London: James Currey.

Beneduce, R., L.Jourdan, T. Raemaeykers, and K. Vlassenroot. 2006. 'Violence with a purpose: exploring the functions and meaning of violence in the Democratic Republic of Congo'. *Intervention* 4 (1):3246. http://www.cerisciencespo.com/themes/re imaginingpeace/.../congo_violence. Pdf.

Borschik, A.-K. 2008. 'Chieftaincy in Gabu: The meaning of borders in 'traditional' rule'. Seminar paper, Aegis African Studies in Europe, Cortona Summer School 2008, Borders and Border-Crossings in Africa, 16-22 June.

Bridges, R. C. 1974. *Senegambia* .Aberdeen, Scotland: University of Aberdeen Press.

Buhl, K. O. 2009. 'Legalization of civil wars: The legal institutionalization of non-international armed conflicts. *JEMIE* 8 (1): 1-33. Http: //www .ecmi. de /jemie/download/1-2009-Buhl.pdf.

Chabal, P. 2002. *A history of postcoloniallLusophone Africa*. London: Hurst.

Cisse, P. 2007. Communautés Bobofing du Mali et du Burkina Faso. Concept de frontière et pratique des espaces transfrontaliers au sud-est de Sikasso, Mali. In: *Stratégies de populations et stratégies de développement. Convergences ou divergences?*, pp. 29-53. Conference Proceedings, Dakar-Cheikh Anta Diop University IPDSR.

Darbon, D. 1988. *L'administration et le paysan en Casamance*. Paris: Pedone.

Diallo, B. 2009. *La crise casamançaise: problématique et voies de solutions*. Paris: L'Harmattan.

Diop, M-C. 1992. *Senegal: Essays in statecraft*. Dakar: CODESRIA.

Diop, M-C. and M. Diouf. 1992. *Le Sénégal sous Abdou Diouf*. Paris: Karthala.

Diaw, A. and M. Diouf. 1998. 'Ethnic group versus nation: Identity discourses in Senegal'. In *Ethnic Conflicts in Africa*, edited by O. Nnoli, pp... 259-86. Dakar: CODESRIA.

Dumont, G F. 2009. 'Le Sénégal: Une géopolitique exceptionnelle en Afrique'. *Géostratégiques* 25 (October): 107-133.

Dykman, A. 2000. 'The reintegration of the Casamance region into the Senegalese society'. *SAIS Studies on Senegal*. Washington, DC, Johns Hopkins University, Summer.

Ero, C. and M. Ferme. 2002. 'Liberia, Sierra Leone et Guinée: Une guerre sans frontières?' *Politique Africaine* 88 (Décembre): 5-12.

Evans, M. 2002. 'The Casamance Conflict: Out of sight, out of mind?' *Humanitarian Exchange Magazine* 20 (March):http://www.odihpn.org/humanitarian-exchange-magazine/issue-20/the-casamance-conflict-out-of-sight-out-of-mind.

Fanchette, S. 2002. 'La Haute Casamance à l'heure de la régionalisation. Enjeux fonciers et territoriaux'. IN: *La société sénégalaise entre le local et le global,* edited by M-C. Diop, pp. 307-55. Paris: Karthala.

Faye, O. 1994. 'La crise casamançaise et les relations avec la Gambie et la Guinée-Bissau (1980-1992)'. In: *Le Sénégal et ses voisins,* edited by M-C. Diop, pp. 190-212. Dakar: Sociétés-Espaces-Temps.

Ferreira, P. M. 2004. 'Guinea-Bissau: Between conflict and democracy'. *African Security Review* 13 (4): 45-56.

Foucher, V. 2003. 'Pas d'alternance en Casamance? Le nouveau pouvoir sénégalais face à la revendication casamançaise'. *Politique Africaine* 91 (Octobre): 101-19.

Forrest, J. 2003. *Lineages of state fragility, rural civil society in Guinea-Bissau.* Oxford: Oxford University Press.

———. 1987. 'Guinea Bissau since independence: A decade of domestic power struggles'. *The Journal of Modern African Studies* 25 (1): 97-100.

Hargreaves, J.D. 1984. 'The making of the boundaries: Focus on West Africa. In: *Partitioned Africans. Ethnic Relations across Africa's International Boundaries 1884-1984,* edited by A.I. Asiwaju, pp. 19-28. Nigeria/London: University of Lagos Press/C. Hurst and Company.

Harsch, E. 2005. 'Peace pact raises hope in Senegal'. *Africa Renewal* 19 (1): 14.

Havard, J-F. 2004. 'De la victoire du "Sopi" à la tentation du "Nopi" ? Gouvernement de l'alternance et liberté d'expression des médias au Sénégal'. *Politique Africaine* 96 (décembre): 22-38.

Hughes, A.1992. 'L'effondrement de la Confédération de la Sénégambie'. In *Le Sénégal et ses voisins,* edited by M-C. Diop, pp. 33-59. Dakar: Sociétés-Espaces-Temps.

International Crisis Group. 2009. *Guinea-Bissau: In need of a state.* Africa Report 142, 2 July.

———. 2008. *Guinea Bissau: Beyond the rule of the gun.* Africa Briefing 61, 25 June.

Internal Displacement Monitoring Center (IDMC). 2008. *IDP's remain vulnerable as obstacles to return and reintegration persist.* Norwegian Refugee Council, June.

Integrated Regional Information Networks (IRIN). 2008. *Senegal: Rebels act on kidnap threats in Casamance*, 20 March.

Lambert, A. 1994. 'Les commerçants et l'intégration régionale'. In: *Le Senegal et ses voisins*, edited by M-C. Diop, pp. 81-94. Dakar: Sociétés-Espaces-Temps.

Lehtinen, T. 2000. 'The military-civilian crisis in Guinea Bissau'. http://www.conflicttransform.net/Guinea.pdf.

Marut, J-C. 2001. *Guinée-Bissau et Casamance: stabilisation et instabilité.* WRITENET 15/2000, UNHCR, 21 June.

———. 1995. 'Les représentations territoriales comme enjeux de pouvoir: la différence casamançaise'. Conference Paper, *Le territoire: lien ou frontière?*, Paris, 2-4 October.

Ngaïdè, A. 2002. *Identités ethniques et territorialisation en Casamance. Histoire croisée d'une périphérie turbulente.* Paris: Karthala.

Newman, D. 2009. 'Contemporary research agendas in border studies: An overview'. Paper at the African Borderland Research Network Conference, *How Is Africa Transforming Border Studies?* School of Social Sciences, University of the Witwatersrand, Johannesburg, South Africa, 10-14 September.

Osita, O. 2006. *West Africa's trouble spots: The imperative for peace-building.* Monograph Series. Dakar: CODESRIA.

Raeymaekers, T. 2007. 'The power of protection: Governance and transborder trade on the Congo-Ugandan frontier'. Doctoral thesis, Ghent University.

Renner, F. A. 1984. 'Ethnic affinity: Partition and political integration in Senegambia'. In: *Partitioned Africans. Ethnic Relations across Africa's International Boundaries 1884-1984*, edited by A.I. Asiwaju, pp. 71-86. Lagos, Nigeria/London: University of Lagos Press/C. Hurst and Company.

Richards, P. 1996. *Fighting for the rainforest: War, youth and resources in Sierra Leone.* London: James Currey.

Richards, P. and K. Vlassenroot. 2002. 'Les guerres africaines de type Mano: Pour une analyse sociale'. *Politique Africaine* 88 (Décembre): 13-26.

Saïbou, I. 2006. 'Les jeunes patrons du crime organisé et de la contestation politique du Cameroun, de la Centrafrique et du Tchad'. International Conference, *Youth and the Global South: Religion, Politics and the Making of Youth in Africa, Asia and the Middle East*. Dakar, Sénégal, 13-15 October.

Sall, E. 1992. *Sénégambie: territoires, frontières, espaces et réseaux sociaux*. Bordeaux: Centre d'Etudes d'Afrique Noire, Documents et Travaux 36.

Sall, E. and Sallah, H. 1992. 'Senegal and the Gambia: The politics of integration'. In: *Le Sénégal et ses voisins*, edited by M-C. Diop, pp. 117-41. Dakar: Sociétés-Espaces-Temps.

Schomerus, M. and K. Titeca. 2009. '"We see ourselves as unlucky because of the kind of border we have": Militarized peace along the Sudan/Uganda/DRC border'. African Border Research Network Conference, *How Is Africa Transforming Border Studies*, University of the Witwatersrand, School of Social Sciences, and 10-12 September.

Scorgie, L. 2009. 'Peacekeeping in the borderlands: Confronting networks of conflict in Central Africa, from genocide in Rwanda to conflict in the Congo'. African Border Research Network Conference, *How Is Africa Transforming Border Studies*, University of the Witwatersrand, School of Social Sciences, and 10-12 September.

Sonko, B. 2004. 'Le conflit en Casamance: une guerre civile oubliée'. *Bulletin du CODESRIA* 3-4: 35-38.

Tandia, A., 2009a. 'Migration, mondialisation et sécurité : les facteurs et enjeux de la sécuritisation de la politique d'émigration du Sénégal'. International symposium, *Migrations et Mondialisation*, IPDSR, Université Cheikh Anta Diop, Dakar, 18-20 November.

———. 2009b. 'Borders and borderland identity in Western Senegambia: A comparative perspective of cross-border governance in the neighbourhoods of Senegal, Gambia and Guinea Bissau'. Paper presented at the African Borderland Research Network Conference, *How Is Africa Transforming Border Studies?* School of Social Sciences, University of the Witwatersrand, Johannesburg, South Africa, 10-14 September.

———. 2007a. 'Intégration régionale et politique de sécurité en Afrique: le cas de la CEDEAO'. Master of Litt., Faculté des sciences juridiques et politiques, Université Cheikh Anta Diop de Dakar.

———. 2007b. 'Diplomatie locale et sécurité transfrontalière: quelle pertinence pour la gouvernance sécuritaire régionale de la CEDEAO ?' Seminar Paper, Governance Institute, *Security Governance in Africa*, Dakar, CODESRIA, August 2007.

Notes

[1] See *Agence de Presse Sénégalaise* (2009)19 October. www.aps.sn; *Sud Quotidien* (2009) 12 May; *Walfadjri* (2009) 22 September.

[2] This was one of the most important observations about quantitative approaches to civil war and conflict at a workshop that gathered many authorities of the field at the Human Security Center of Norway in August 2003. See Human Security Center (2003) Mapping and Explaining Civil War: What to do about Contested Datasets and Findings?, Workshop Report, Oslo, Norway, 18-19 August.

[3] One exceptionally comprehensive study that pays attention to the territorial aspects of the Casamance conflict along with the ethnic identities is the work by Ngaïde, A. (2002) *Identités ethniques et territorialisation en Casamance. Histoire croisée d'une périphérie turbulente* (Paris: Karthala).

[4] The same can be noted on the Senegal-Gambia borderland at their southern borders.

[5] The issue of defining and explaining 'new civil wars' whose main feature is to go beyond State territories and engage ethnic groups straddinge national borders has been the concern of the special issue of the *Journal of Ethnopolitics and Minority Issues in Europe*, No 8, 2009.

[6] The new region, which is an ancient department (a lower administrative division) of Kolda, was created by Law No. 2008-14 of 18 March 2008, modifying Law No. 72-02 of 1 February 1972 territorial Administration.

[7] From the national census of 1988 it appears that the main ethnic groups are Jola (35%), Mandingo (20%), and Fula (30%). This act was passed by the National Assembly on 11 March 2008. Minority ethnic groups represent 15% of the Casamance population and are Balanta, Manjago, Papel, Bagnuk, Badiaranke, Koniagi, Kokoli, and so forth.

[8] This explains the resort of many scholars (historians, namely) and successive political leaders to the term 'Senegambia' in analysing and advocating regional integration and pacific coexistence between the four countries (see Bridges 1974; Barry 1988; Sall 1991; Barry 1992; Hughes 1992; Sall and Sallah 1992).

[9] A textbook of geography used in primary school is the means for a manipulation by government of natural and administrative limits of the Casamance region. It is Thiam, I. D. Mangane, S. and Sow, S. (1989) *Géographie du Sénégal* (Dakar: NEA-EDICEF,).

[10] See International Crisis Group, *Guinea Bissau: In need of a state*, Report 142, July 2008.

[11] There might be some reason to welcome the return to a pacified political order in Guinea Bissau after the 26 June 2009 electoral victory of President Bacaï Sanha over Coumba Yala who had defeated him in 2000. The recognition of the results by Yalla and the renewed promises of the international community to address the military question are important incentives to greater hope, as the necessity was again reminded by March and June killings in 2008. However, the fact that these assassinations that took away former President Vieira (knowing the support he gave to the Senegalese Government in the Casamance conflict) are not yet punished continues to sustain skepticism.

[12] « En visite en Gambie : Macky Sall implique Yaya Jammeh dans le dossier casamançais », *Le Soleil*, Monday 16 April 2012. Accessed online on Tuesday 17 April 2012. http://www.lesoleil.sn/index.php?option=com_content&view=article&id=14239:en-visite-en-gambie-macky-sall-implique-yaya-jammeh-dans-le-dossier-casamancais-&catid=78:a-la-une

[13] Interview of President Wade, *L'Intelligent/Jeune Afrique*, 23 May 2000.

[14] His saying that Senegal is sitting in a powder store provoked reactions in Gambia and Guinea Bissau as well.

[15] This group is an association created in the late 1990s by cadres from the Casamance region that settled in Dakar and close to the former President Abdou Diouf. Now many of its leaders have joined the new ruling party PDS, which came to power in March 2000, in particular, an architect named Pierre Goudiaby Atepa.

[16] *Walfadjri* 22 September 2009.

[17] Those factions are the Front Nord of Kamougué Diatta, which ceased fire in 1991 and controls the North of Bignona, the moderate Front Sud in the southwest of the region of Léopold Sagna, and the Radical Front Sud of Salif Sadio in the south and southwest of Ziguinchor who is pursuing the combats.

[18] We refer here to the renewed transition in Guinea-Bissau against the backdrop of March and June 2009 assassinations that are not yet cleared up, as well as the political crisis in neighbouring Guinea Conakry and the growing weakness and unpopularity of the regime of President Jammeh in Gambia.

[19] Mouhamed Mbodj is the coordinator of the Forum Civil, a local branch of Transparency International. According to him, the Casamance conflict results from a bad governance of the Senegalese State since independence, a style of ruling based on favouritism towards the northern ethnic groups and regions, while little was done to provoke the transformation of the peripheral areas including the Casamance region. Instead of making the conflict appear as a national question, the Government is still presenting it as regional problem. See Interview with Mouhamed Mbodj, *Walfadjri* 29 December 2009.

[20] Reacting to Paul Richards's analysis of the Sierra Leone civil war as a 'crisis of patrimonialism' (Richards 1996), Yusuf Bangura insisted on the necessity of not reducing it to resource depletion and patron-client modalities that attracted the attention of most civil war scholars (Bangura 2005: 25). Historical and political processes of state-making should instead be considered. In that respect, by neopatrimonial politics we refer here to the governance styles that were displayed by

the different regimes in Senegal in building, not the State itself, but their regime or power throughout instruments such as partisan representation, resource allocation and local administration. Of course, we also refer to the various political and economic procedures used by governors to control power resources and populations at the same time within the region of Casamance. Those procedures, no doubt, implied the construction and maintenance of patron-client relationships and a personal hoarding of public properties of the State through a clientelism that tied local and central centers of power.

[21] This problem of messianic management seems to be a constantly faced issue in the management of the conflict as says Mouhamed Mbodj: 'We have elected three presidents, but we still wrestle with our main problems. Simply because we have not shifted from the messianic model which have been being implemented since independence. Such a model does not exist in any country in the world and has not been successful in neither. Ruling a country is a very complex matter. I think initiatives should be returned back to citizens and no more to a messiah. We did it with Wade, with Diouf and With Senghor. The results have been disastrous. Actually the "saviour" does not exist. Today all the candidatures that have been recorded proceed from a messianic perspective: "elect me and I will get you rid of your problems!" This is the discourse we always hear from politicians. We think that it does not work and it will never work'. Nevertheless, all political leaders still make promises to resolve the conflict and allude to the enclavement and economic backwardness of the Casamance region as they most of the time promise maritime or airline shuttles. Many press articles about the attitude of political leaders are available at www.aps.sn.

[22] After 40 years in office, the former socialist mayor of Ziguinchor Andre Sonko has now been replaced by Abdoulaye Baldé, Secretary of State between 2002 and 2009 and Minister of Armed Forces (since 2009).

[23] Redrawing the map of Casamance into three administrative regions occupied each by one of the three main ethnic groups of natural region helps the regime to isolate the rebellion and link its separatist identity to the Jola ethnic group. Moreover, the regional identity of Casamance is split apart, as the Casamance word has been erased from official discourse, school curricula, and political discourse (Dyman 2003; Marut 1995). Local traditional leaders and religious leaders have paid allegiance to the new regime during the last presidential elections of 2007. As a matter of fact, they share with local elected leaders a considerable grasp on issues such as land management, policy making, and community representation, and have access to environmental resources such as forestry. Local elites also have informal exemption on trade throughout borders (Tandia 2009b).

[24] For instance, Mamadou Nkrumah Sané had been in exile in Paris since 1991 at the onset of the guerilla war of the MFDC. But a presidential amnesty was voted on 6 July 2004 and dedicated to getting back all rebel leaders whose return and unity is deemed to be a condition for better negotiations after the failure of all past agreements and in a context of the spell of violence.

[25] *Le Soleil*, 4 October 2001.

[26] Civil society organisations like the Rencontre Africaine des Droits de l'Homme (RADDHO) and the Collectif des Cadres Casamançais released public appeals to the Government. See Comité des Cadres Casamançais (2000), 'Note sur la situation du Front Nord du MFDC'. Dakar, multigr. 18 Novembre.

[27] This group was created during the socialist reign of Diouf and has been refigured by Pierre Goudiaby Atépa, an architect and political defector from the incumbent socialist regime and former local big man of President Diouf who has joined the PDS after the political alternation of 2000.

[28] Youba Sambou, a Jola leader of the Association pour la promotion rurale de l'arrondissement de Nyassa (Apran), was elected Minister of Armed Forces in 2000. As a recent member of the ruling party since 1995, he was meant to serve as an interlocutor of Wade near the rebel leaders. Since 2000, all ministers of the Armed Forces have been from Casamance. Recently, in December 2009, Abdoulaye Baldé, former Secretary of State and mayor of Ziguinchor, replaced Bécaye Diop, who is a PDS leader and Mayor of Kolda at the same time.

[29] Programme for the Revival of Economic and Social Activities (PRAESC) in Casamance.

[30] Aside from issues of poverty and humanitarian challenges, it had to reset economic activities such as tourism, agriculture, herding, etc., and build infrastructures for service delivery, mainly in rural areas that are mostly affected (see PRAESC 2001)

[31] One of his direct adversaries in party politics and the Casamance conflict agenda is Adama Sonko, another local PDS leader who left the former ruling party PS after the political turnover in 2000. Malamine Kourouma has been quite imposed on the latter as Mayor of the subdivision (department) of Goudomp, a local council in Sédhiou, the new region in the Mandingo land of the central part of Casamance. See Map 1.

[32] In December 2007, the president of the Regional Council of Ziguinchor was assassinated in the frame of what appears so far as partisan rivalries for the control of the town; which crystallises all efforts and resources yielded by the management of the Casamance conflict. So far no direction has been indicated by the Government and the investigations are yet to deliver the culprits (Tandia 2007a).

[33] Sometimes incendiary in his opinions about the conflict and President Wade's pan-African mood, his Jola belongingness and repeated decisions on border-crossing that resulted in diplomatic crises depreciate the sincerity of his engagement (Tandia 2007b). This is corroborated by the Gambian Human Rights activist Muhamed Lamin Sylla, according to whom the calls for peace in the Casamance conflict coming from Jammeh are not to be taken seriously, as his connections with the MFDC date back to his military life. Muhamed Lamin Sylla also made reference to the funding and armed support of Jammeh to the MFDC. Interview of Muhamed Sylla on Radio France International on Wednesday 21 October 2009. Available at: [http://www.rfi.fr/actufr/articles/118/article_85840.asp], (28 November 2009).

[34] President Vieira first expressed his hostility to the presence of the MFDC in Guinea Bissau as he realized that Salif Sadio was supporting General Ansumane Mane in an aborted coup attempt in 2000.

[35] *Agence France-Presse*, Ziguinchor, 14 December 2000.

[36] Following from the International Crisis Group report, legitimate fears of the military about the security sector reform process are related to the issue of their financial treatment as many of them are supposed to retire. The reform has also to face the ethnic issue in the military and politics, as the Balanta might feel evicted in the course of restructuring (Crisis Group 2009: 13)

[37] The groundwork for cooperation between the two countries was set in the 1970 when President Senghor of Senegal was helping the PAIGC struggle for independence. Many factors explain why relationships between Senegal and Guinea-Bissau or Gambia are in a constant dialectics of suspicion and cooperation. First a dispute over oil fields discovered on their borders in 1978 brings the two neighbours to communicate and negotiate, as much as Guinea-Bissau is still contesting the settlement decisions of the International Court of Justice released in 1998 and 2002 in favour of Senegal. Second, Senegal has been suspecting some fringes of the political elites of Guinea Bissau of supporting the rebellion of the MFDC, notably in the military. Third, the mixed borderland geopolitics of the Casamance conflict and the repercussions from and in neighbouring Guinea Bissau force cooperation upon the two countries.

[38] This is at now proven by the public avowal of late Brigadier Ansumane Mane to support the Casamance irredentism that took the different regimes of Vieira and Yalla (2000-2003) to fight Mane and declare the MFDC as an enemy of the Guinea Bissau State (Crisis Group, 2009; Foucher, 2003).

[39] This obsession certainly explains why in 1994 the Senegalese army nearly took the capital city of Guinea Bissau, where President Vieira was suspected of willingly sustaining MFDC rear bases, following murderous and ravaging assaults against the army in Casamance.

[40] *Le Quotidien* 6 October 2009.

[41] The border strategies of the MFDC might also be explained by the interfactional clashes as rivalries have grown in the rebellion. The insurgents are also trying to survive the financial shortages induced by the capture of an exhausting rent on behalf of the few political leaders that happen to position themselves in the clientelist networks of the management processes.

[42] Chatam House (2004) *Sénégal: Mouvement des Forces Démocratiques de la Casamance (MFDC)* December.

[43] More than 500 people belonging to 79 families were moved from villages of Sanou in the Kolda region frontier areas to the Bissau-Guinean village of Bégène in 4 February 2010 by the rebel groups. On 5-6 February they pillaged the village of Mahmouda Chérif located in the communauté rurale of Katabal where they raped the wife of one of the local Muslim religious chiefs. It is in this village also that one of the special counselors of the President Wade on the Casamance conflict Cherif Samseddine Aïdara was killed in 2007 by the rebels. See *Agence France presse*, 4 February; www.nettali.net (8 February).

[44] The civilian attacks and displacements might not be a consciously organized strategy of the rebellion given its fractionalization even though it is thereby reorganizing by occupying the ground. Factions might be trying to find strongholds

for each one in order to remobilise. The frequency of displacements from Senegal side to Guinea-Bissau may also indicate that rebels groups are operating a retrieval strategy from an unstable Guinea-Bissau. In other words, this is not good news for the conflict managers neither for borderland communities as they might choose to fight back or join the rebellion just to save their harvests and livelihood means, inasmuch as the army seems to be powerless in the face of this new spell of rebel violence.

[45] These gangs are of two types: they are one the one hand organised armed groups connected with international networks collaborating with mercenaries from Liberia and Sierra Leone. These gangs constitute the armed wing of the MFDC. The second type comprises youngsters of neighbouring villages of the borderland who do not hesitate to attack their own families or neighbours as they are driven by survival in a context where schooling or employment are a luxury.

[46] The violence perpetrated by these bandits began to intensify in 1999 when, for example, the village of Saré Yoba on the Senegalese side was burnt.

[47] Moussa Baldé, Mayor of Salikegne, Interviewed by author. Salikegne (Kolda), 19 May 2010.

[48] Sabali Kontan, Driver at the coach station of Salikegne, Interviewed by author in Salikegne (Kolda), 19 May 2010

[49] They are traders who are very implicated in the cross-border trade. They shuttle between urban trading centers and borderland markets known as the *loumo* (a Fula word meaning weekly market). They are involved in cattle rustling, as they buy the livestock cheap and resell them in those *loumo* or in bigger markets of northern urban centers in Kolda, Gambia, or on the northern bank of Gambia. As they have wives among local communities, they tend to make their way in other local activities such as farming, forestry, and herding.

[50] Land has become a cause of conflicts and intense speculation as the borderland population increases, whereas mine bombing, transboundary criminality, and rebel attacks have made important surfaces unusable.

[51] Moussa Sow, Mayor of Salikegne, Interviewed by author in Salikegne (Kolda), 19 May 2010

[52] Moussa Sow, Op.cit.

[53] Sabali Kontan, Interviewed by author in Salikegne (Kolda), 19 May 2010.

PART IV

INTRA-NATIONAL DISPARITIES NATURAL RESOURCES AND LAND

CHAPTER 8

Recovering from Conflict, Dealing With Structural Imbalances: Implementing the Peace Recovery and Development Programme (PRDP) in Northern

Nsamba A Morris

1. Introduction

The conflict in northern Uganda that started in the early 1980s displaced more than 1.8 million persons into squalid camps for the Internally Displaced People (IDPs),[1] affected the international and national image of the ruling National Resistance Movement (NRM) government. Whereas it can be argued that rebel movements are a threat to political elites and the state, the conflict in northern Uganda appears to differ from that thinking. The immediate casualties of the conflict are the people living in northern Uganda, the army officers, and the lord's Resistance Army (LRA). The beneficiaries from the conflict appear to be the political elites in Kampala who use it to justify their lavish expenditure on defence, and the maintenance of a large army.[2] There is growing a body of literature especially from political scientists who argue that conflicts serve or help political elites to maintain and consolidate their power.[3] Just as conflicts help to advance the interests of the political elites, postconflict recovery and reconstruction is blended with their political concerns.

This paper aims to expand the discussion of the northern Uganda recovery process, in particular the Peace Recovery and Development Plan (PRDP). The PRDP is the recovery programme designed for northern Uganda. It was launched by the president in October 2007 and based on four strategic pillars: a) consolidate state authority (including the cessation of armed hostilities, the establishment of law and order, improvement of the functionality of judicial and legal services, and strengthening of local government capacity); b) rebuild and empower communities (including the improvement of the conditions of people in IDP camps, the return of IDPs to their homes, and community rehabilitation and development); c) revitalise the economy (including re-activation of the productive sectors, infrastructural development and management of land and

257

environmental and natural resources), and lastly d) peacebuilding and reconciliation (access to the media, provision of counseling services, and reinforcement of mechanisms for intra/intercommunal conflicts and socioeconomic integration of ex-combatants).[4]

The paper examines the extent to which PRDP helps the political elites not just to retain power but to widen their support base for the forthcoming 2011 elections. It is argued that the delay in fully funding the PRDP is a political manoeuvre geared at turning the north into an NRM stronghold. Secondly, the failure of the recovery programme to focus on structural and systematic causes of the conflict, in particular socioeconomic inequalities between the north and south and within areas in the north raises, concerns about the intention of the programme. And lastly, the paper examines power relations between the districts and central government over the recovery process.

Reconceptualising the Causes of the Conflict in Northern Uganda: The North-South Economic Differentiation and the Conflict in Northern Uganda

The conflict in northern Uganda between the LRA and the government of Uganda is rooted in a history of colonial and postcolonial structural and systematic marginalisation of northern Uganda, ethnic politicisation and polarisation, and institutional weaknesses.[5] The political causes[6] have been well highlighted in literature but there is a conscious and unconscious attempt to minimise economic causes of the conflict, in particular how they restructure socioeconomic and political relations. Greed has been advanced as one of the causes of the conflicts in developing world generally.[7] The conflict in Sierra Leone is mostly used to justify greed as an economic rationale for conflict in the developing world. Although the decision to go to war is complex and involves a number of interrelated drivers as such to suggest that greed alone can lead to war without interrogating in particular how it plays out is to undermine communal demands. In the case of northern Uganda, the National Resistance Army/Movement (NRA/M) government initially explained the conflict as caused by greed by a few northerners who were interested in maintaining power. While this view may have offered a simple explanation of the cause of the conflict, greed would be used to explain the cause, since northern Uganda is not a mineral-producing area.

With the failure of the greed theory, attention was turned to the political and civil causes of the conflict.[8] This explanation is underpinned by a political and civil rights approach, which places such rights over socioeconomic rights.[9] While it is true that conflicts do arise out of the denial of political and civil rights, the technology of denial of rights is not confined to political rights; it extends to socioeconomic rights as well. However, it is important to note that the literature that underlines economic causes of conflict only highlights, for example, the Gross National Product per capita[10]--without questioning the institutional apparatus that structures and defines how the GNP or income is shared or accumulated. In essence, conclusions are drawn that low-income countries are highly at risk of conflict.

It is important to mention that socioeconomic rights are rooted within the systemic and structural apparatus of the state and society, and that they cannot easily be addressed in any postconflict situation. During the colonial era, the northern part of the country was put under military authority until 1921 because it was considered a disturbed hostile area.[11] Therefore, colonial development in Uganda was mainly concentrated in the southern part, effectively turning the north into a labour reserve for the blossoming industrial and plantation establishments in the south. The chairman of Gulu District, Mr. Norbert Mao, concludes that the problem of northern Uganda is about social differentiations and inequalities that the British colonial state passed on to the postindependence state in Uganda.[12]

This systematic and structural marginalisation of the north turned the north into a plundering ground for slave-capturing caravans from the centralised kingdoms of the south,[13] effectively de-populating the north.[14] The growth of the cash crop sector in the south attracted infrastructural development, creating conditions for the attraction of capital investment. Without major infrastructural development, the north could not attract such investment capital. The growth of capital in the south also meant that the service sector, in particular education, was mostly concentrated in the south, leading to a north-south migration pattern. Second, because fewer persons moved to the south to benefit from education, few were absorbed into the public service. This created discrepancies in the composition of the public service in Uganda, favouring the south. These discrepancies were later to be the basis for vertical and horizontal tensions and conflicts in independent Uganda, in particular during the Africanisation of the public service. The vertical tensions and conflicts pitted the north and south, and horizontal tensions and conflicts created conflictual classes-educated and uneducated-within and among northern Uganda communities.

This north-south divide has been the hallmark of the relation between the different postindependence governments and northern Uganda. The existence of economic discrepancies between the south and north is regarded by many northerners not just as an inevitable consequence of decades of conflict but as evidence that the postindependence governments have purposely failed to redistribute development so as to keep the north out of poverty.[15] However, during an interview with *The Drum* magazine in 1985, Mr. Museveni described the problem of Uganda as 'the leadership that has been mainly from the north'.[16]

As such, the conflict in the north represented two sides of the same coin. To President Museveni, the Acholi and Langi communities who had been involved in the plundering of Uganda were fighting for the control of the national government, which had stopped this looting.[17] The political views about the conflict in northern Uganda are partly informed by how the NRA won over the north in 1986. When the NRA captured power in Uganda in 1986, the centre of political organisation and power shifted back from the north to the south. The NRA thought of the Uganda National Liberation Army (UNLA) as a political force, without realising its political bankruptcy[18]. As such the intention of the NRA was to dismantle and disengage populations in northern Uganda-using forced displacement, surveillance, para-militarisation, intimidation, arrest, torture and murder.[19] This limited the political options available to the people in northern Uganda, in particular in Acholiland.

Government military interventions have undermined political mobilisation and organisation in Acholiland that is capable of addressing socioeconomic marginalisation. The fear of political organisation has meant limited institutional capacity building capable of driving the region's economic development. As such, most of the infrastructural developments, in particular roads, have aimed at opening security corridors rather than acting as a basis for easy transportation and movement of goods and services. In addition, whereas the PRDP, just like other reconstruction programmes that have been implemented in the north, might offer a semblance of services, the failure to redefine how those services are offered beyond individuals might trigger new sources of conflict. Without politically effective leadership, in particular at the community level, economic needs have been neglected. Government investment has focused on individuals rather than communities, keeping in place structural and systematic marginalisation.[20]

Righting or Cementing Wrongs: Reconstruction and Rehabilitation Programmes in Northern Uganda

Since 1992, the government of Uganda has implemented several reconstruction and rehabilitation plans in northern Uganda. These plans have included the Northern Uganda Reconstruction Programme (NURP-I) launched in 1992 and implemented until 1998. This reconstruction programme focused on infrastructural facilities like health centres, roads, schools, and the provision of water.[21] During the implementation of NUPI-I, the government was less interested in addressing the economic imbalances that caused social injustices leading up to the conflict in northern Uganda. The conflict was still termed a northern problem, and since the government enjoyed international and national support, the northern conflict was of little interest to them. But it continued to serve the purpose of justifying expenditures in the ministry of defence. In fact, NUPI-I was intended to facilitate the movement of the army in the pacification of the north rather than addressing the root causes of the conflict. Hence the first reconstruction did not attempt to undo the south-north divide; if anything, it only buttressed it. This was unconsciously and consciously done in particular through several military operations and the forced encampment of the population, which effectively reduced the options available to the people in northern Uganda.

Encampment and militarisation undermined mobilisation to challenge both government and rebel actions. In terms of reconstruction, the camps offered an opportunity to the government to offer controlled services to a closed population. Such services were denied to the rebels as a military strategy, but the population was also made dependent on the government military as camps became centres of military surveillance.[22] Without proper reconstruction programmes, some populations moved from the camps, becoming urban IDPs in towns like Mbale, Jinja, Entebbe, and Kampala. But the national policy on IDPs in Uganda does not recognise urban IDPs,[23] and those who moved to cities have been bereft of all reconstruction and relief programmes. They have been left to the gutters of poverty and town life. Because NURP-I was based on challenging political mobilisation in the north against the government or in support of the LRA, it did not achieve much, since it excluded local community and political leaders.

With the failure of NURP-I, the government, together with donors, put together NURP-II. The main component of NURP-II was the Northern Uganda Social Action Fund (NUSAF), implemented in 18 districts (in the north and northeast) with the intention of bringing communities into the transition process from conflict to peace.[24] NUSAF was designed according to the Community-Driven Development Approach so as to promote community empowerment and ownership in the context of decentralization.[25] This was done in the wake of the Structural Adjustment Programmes (SAPs), and as a result, the implementation process of NUSAF was much influenced by the SAPs. Emphasis was put on individual rather than community interests, effectively disregarding social capital within the communities of northern Uganda. While NUPI-I was state-driven, NUPI-II combined a number of approaches, sometime involving nongovernmental organisations (NGOs) and community-based organisations. The logic was to monetise the recovery process and also to integrate the victims of the conflict into the monetary economy and thereby create a market for the private sector. The notion of a minimalist state amidst postconflict recovery processes is questionable. To push for this kind of argument in a postconflict situation is to put populations recovering from conflict at the mercy of private profiteers interested in profits. This economics is guided by political rather than economic considerations, which demand that the state redistribute wealth, and causes equity and equality.

Peace Recovery and Development Plan: Recovery Programme as Usual or a New Wind of Change

The PRDP is based on the four strategic pillars mentioned earlier, but of most importance are pillars one-consolidation of state authority-- and three--revitalisation of the economy. The crucial question is to what extent the PRDP addresses the economic imbalance between the north and the south and how well it re-establishes state authority in northern Uganda. PRDP planning was based on simple technical thinking that the development gap between the north and south of Uganda[26] would be solved by the facilitation of development in northern Uganda--simply put, filling the development gap between the north and south. Uncertainty surrounds the PRDP, with some political leaders and government technocrats describing it as having a strong reparation potential for northern Uganda. In fact, the state minister in charge of northern Uganda described it as a Marshall Plan, and the permanent secretary in the prime minister's office described it as an affirmative action programme for the north. But government documents and the PRDP document itself do not term it reparations or liken it to a reparations programme. While this may appear to be politics at play, it is important to examine how the plan intends to revitalise the north, in particular the extent to which it differs from the earlier programmes that only helped the government to further its legitimacy claims in northern Uganda without offering economic equity and equality between the north and south.

Revitalisation of the Economy in Northern Uganda under the PRDP

If earlier programmes helped the government to further its legitimacy claims in northern Uganda, in particular through the re-establishment of state institutions, the PRDP is no exception.[27] In this section I want to examine how the PRDP helps rebuild the conflict-affected areas in a manner that offers not just individual but institutional recovery and insures socioeconomic and political justice. Strategic pillar two of the PRDP is rebuilding and empowering communities, which includes provision of health, education, livelihood, and basic social services; these are short-term programmes that only help affected communities to comfortably settle back into their homes. The question remains: what happens after resettlement? Long-term strategic objective three reads: economic intervention is the revitalisation of the economy in northern Uganda. Under this strategic objective, the PRDP envisages the following programmes: infrastructural rehabilitation, in particular roads, and energy (construction of a hydropower dam), environment and resource management, specifically wood coverage and wetlands, and lastly a production enhancement programming covering agriculture, livestock, and fisheries.[28] Who are the intended beneficiaries of the short-term and long-term developments? To what extent can the PRDP offer infrastructural development in northern Uganda capable of attracting investment, and can it redistribute wealth between the north and south and within the region?

Categorising Beneficiaries in Reparations and Development Projects

According to the Agreement on Accountability and Reconciliation of the Juba Peace talks, victims are defined as persons who individually or collectively suffered harm as a result of crimes and human rights violations committed during the conflict. The conflict is defined as the conflict between parties in the north and northeast, including its impacts on neighbouring countries. Clause 8.1 of the Agreement acknowledges the importance of addressing the suffering of the victims of the conflict, and in particular the vulnerable groups. This redress includes reparations, compensations, restitution, guarantees of nonrecurrence, and other symbolic measures, such as apologies, memorials, and commemorations. The PRDP emphasises the provision of basic services including health, education, water, and sanitation to vulnerable citizens.[29] Two conclusions can be drawn from the above. First, the problem of northern and northeast Uganda is defined as only caused by the conflict whose solution is provision of services to those affected by the conflict. As such, historical and systematic marginalisation is dropped from the agenda, limiting government responsibility and accountability to redistribute resources and wealth. In addition, emphasis on individual restitutions rather than community[30] reparations offers the government the opportunity to avoid focusing on issues of accountability in Uganda as a whole. Restitutions restore the status quo without addressing the structural problems of systemic marginalization; they focus on what an individual lost and not on how the state apparatus or development projects have been distributed and organised.

Second, the categorisation of persons as victims, vulnerable, and perpetrators is problematic in itself as it is embedded in an exclusionist postconflict politics. Like the focus on reparations and restitution, this categorisation narrows the focus of PRDP to specific individuals. For the moment let me focus on the category 'vulnerable'. Those considered to be vulnerable are always women, children, and the elderly. This categorisation is based on the logic that in society, women, children, and the elderly occupy the lower ranks of a hierarchy. Although it may be true that these groups occupy the lower ranks in society, the effects of structural marginalisation and conflicts are so deep and far reaching that it is difficult to single out the most affected groups. For example, colonial and postcolonial marginalisation deprived both men and women of wealth and development. In addition, the LRA recruited mostly boys who grew up in captivity. Attempts at recovery that exclude such individuals on the basis that they are men might provide a basis for further violence.

But this categorisation has its political reasons that are intended to maintain the status quo in society.[31] If restitutions and reparations were to be offered to all persons without categorisation, may lead to a development of a political in northern Uganda. In addition, this categorisation is based mostly on human rights violation and abuse.[32] Peace processes that negotiate and shape the postconflict environment also put much emphasis on political and civil rights.[33] In Uganda, the debate about who are victims, perpetuators, and vulnerable has overshadowed the debate on redistribution of wealth and development between north and south Uganda. Under this shadowing, the state has managed to pay reparations and restitutions to individuals and specific groups, limiting the development of a powerful challenge to its interests in the north by fragmenting society along the three categories mentioned above.

The problem of northern Uganda is about structural and systemic marginalisation, and the categorisation of society as victims, perpetrators, and vulnerable groups does not offer a good recipe for dealing with systemic and structural marginalisation. Failure to address the structural weaknesses may create an opportunity for a relapse into conflict and violence. In addition, the categorisation of members of society into the different groups not only increases competition over resources, but distorts gender and power relations in society, giving rise to violence as groups struggle for their 'rightful' space in society.[34]

Categorisation along gender lines is based on a patriarchal logic that views women and children as the weaker category and men as the powerful muscular beings. But the kinds of victims of social injustices are so numerous that they include men as well. There is a systematic, yet conscious and unconscious disempowerment of one of the genders, as well as distortion of gender relations within communities. The reconstruction of gender relations has produced violence in the family. Any effective form of reparations or development effort in northern Uganda has to take into account the historical differences between the north and south. This includes the education system, which is strong in the south and offers the provision of development that is capable of attracting investment. Development may not work if it is aimed only at re-establishing its authority.

2. Implementation of the PRDP at the District Level

The PRDP set up a national and local structure for the implementation of the recovery programme. At the national level, political responsibility is in the office of the State Minister for Northern Uganda Rehabilitation, who oversees and coordinates all national programmes in northern Uganda.[35] The technical daily management is in the office of the Permanent Secretary Office of the Prime Minister. The framework further establishes the Northern Uganda Rehabilitation Policy Committee (NURPC), chaired by the State Minister for Northern Uganda Rehabilitation. The central responsibilities of the committee are: advocating and mobilising resources; ensuring the coherence and consistency of PRDP programmes with national policies; reviewing on-going interventions; and advising on broad government policy changes in the northern Uganda.[36] The NURPC is, in a sense, the think tank of the recovery programme. But it is interesting that one of its roles is to ensure that the PRDP is consistent with national programmes. Hence, the PRDP is a mix of on-going projects and new unfunded interventions. This makes the PRDP neither a new initiative nor a plan for the required additional interventions.[37] At best, it is a framework that is intended to guide government and donor interventions.

Using districts as avenues for implementation, the PRDP offers hope that the programme may benefit people in northern Uganda; yet it casts doubt about the capacity of districts to implement such a programme as well as about the seemingly conflicting programme implementation structures of the PRDP and the districts. In this section the paper examines the capacity of districts to implement the PRDP, in particular how the PRDP will affect or be affected by the district structure. The second set of questions of this section revolves around: who is in charge at the district level? What kind of power and capacities do they have?

At the district level the chief administrative officer (CAO) is technically responsible for the implementation.[38] This includes developing implementation plans, and overseeing and managing the PRDP. The district technical planning committees (DTPCs) rather than the district councils are responsible for developing strategies, the identification of key activities, and the supervision of partners.[39] However, the use of district structures raises questions about their ability to marshal the needed capacities. How do the PRDP and decentralisation structures intersect, when the former emphasises a top-down system of decision-making and the latter claims inefficiency of down-top decision-making? Considering this contradiction, why is the government committed to using decentralised district structures to implement PRDP? To answer these questions, I start by examining the link between the structure of the PRDP and the local governance structures in Uganda.

While the structure of local government is fairly decentralised, thus offering avenues for the communities to make claims on the state at the local level, PRDP implementation structure is centralised. In addition, local government structures demand significant community participation in the planning and design of programmes and projects, while PRDP organisation only involves communities at the later stage of monitoring. PRDP structure puts emphasis on central government and sectoral planning over community participation; effectively turning districts into conduits in the implementation process with limited power. This is partly intended to keep the recovery programme under the control of the central government rather than the local government. But it creates tensions between the central and local interests and priorities. While some of the local governments and communities are interested in righting historical and structural marginalisation and differentiation, the central government appears to have limited interest in attempts to craft the transition process in a manner that begins to lay the foundation to address the structural challenges. Part of the government hesitation may be a result of the expensive nature of structural transformation processes. It is also true that such processes call for concerted political interest and often take time. t is important to look at the capacities districts have for implementing the PRDP.

3. Capacities of Districts

The capacity to integrate and execute PRDP activities appears to be adequate at the national but not at the district level. At the district level there is a significant lack of institutional, human, and financial resources.[40] While block grants for service delivery are sent to districts, the districts lack resources to meet the management costs of delivering the services.[41] Appendix one shows the human resource and wage gaps in the PRDP districts.

In the recovery process, the districts are to coordinate and implement all services delivered. The human resource and wage gaps faced by the PRDP districts are enormous partly due to the conflict, which made it impossible for the districts to attract and retain qualified staff. While the conflict in northern Uganda made the problem even worse, the failure to attract and retain qualified staff is not confined to PRDP districts only. This is a general problem affecting most of the districts in Uganda. It can be argued that the human resource gap can be filled relatively easily, but the wage gap will be much harder to bridge. In addition, filling the human resource gap is dependent on other institutional capacities, for instance, the district service boards. Yet, a number of districts lack the space to host such structures.[42] Why is government interested in using such apparently ineffective structures in the recovery process?

4. Politics of Districtising the PRDP

The relationship between national and local politics in Uganda is very interesting in so far as it allows national and local political elites to use state structures at both the national and local levels to retain political power. The PRDP recognises that there is on-going conflict in the Lango and Acholi subregions and underlines the need for peace and reconciliation. But peace and reconciliation are defined to include increased access to information by the population, enhanced counselling services, establishment of mechanisms for intra/inter-communal and national conflict resolution, strengthened local governance and informal leadership structures, and reinforced socioeconomic reintegration of ex-combatants.[43] Under SO4, peace is defined in terms of strengthening rather than creating legitimacy for state institutions. It is therefore no wonder that funding under SO4 has focused on state consolidation rather than reconciliation or integration of combatants. The problem of northern Uganda is explained as poorly functioning state institutions and lack of social services. At the local level, emphasis is thus placed on making the district apparatus implement the PRDP, and with limited if any regard to the legitimacy of those institutions.

PRDP is oriented around service provision, which is a technical solution when seen in contrast to more political solutions embodied in reconciliation, democracy, establishment of civil society rights, and other comprehensive rights-based approaches. While it is true that social services are needed in northern Uganda, considering the years of neglect and the effects of the conflict, sustaining peace will need more than technical solutions. It requires political solutions. If technical solutions are concerned with provision of services, political solutions are concerned with how those services are provided, who gets them, and by what means. Simply put, politics is about the institutions, in particular to what extent are they responsive, accountable, to whom are they accountable, how representative are, and lastly whose interests do they represent?

Literature on decentralisation more often than not assumes that the transfer of power to democratically elected local leaders is always a rational planned process that automatically creates responsive institutions at the local level.[44] But the decision whether to decentralise, how much power to decentralize, or which institutions to create at the local level are sometime taken by default or as a result of internal and external pressure. Decentralisation then becomes an outcome of unplanned processes.[45]

In the case of Uganda, decentralisation of power was an outcome of internal and external processes[46]--internal in the sense that decentralisation was seen and used as a vehicle for offering security and external because it fit within the World Bank programmatic approach to governance reforms of the 1990s. It is at this level that the difference between the technical and political solutions becomes very clear. The political intention of decentralisation in Uganda was to manage local security and challenges to the central government,[47] yet the economic rationale offered by the World Bank was to offer social services.[48] In essence, districts serve two intentions, and although these are sometimes mutually complimentary, there is room for conflict.

In the implementation of the PRDP, political solutions could challenge the power of the central government. This shifts the debate away from meaningfully challenging the role of the government forces, before, after, and during the conflict, and so obscures issues of accountability. It is also important to note that northern Uganda has been politically 'unfriendly' to the ruling NRM since 1986; thus, in reconceptualising the recovery process as reconstruction, the ruling political elites are able to use the programme to present themselves as a caring regime. As such, the recovery programme is couched as something the government gives to the people rather than as the right to which they are entitled.

The use of NGOs, self-help groups, and districts as channels of distribution is intended to insulate the state from any backlash during the process of recovery. It creates a sense of responsibility among the victim communities, the districts, and NGOs, as it expands the degree of governability beyond the state. Expansion of the actors in the recovery programmes beyond the state creates a sense of ownership and responsibility among the victim communities. This is because some NGOs and districts are led by victims and local politicians, respectively. While this creates an opportunity for the victims to actively engage in the recovery process, it also offers the central state the opportunity to blame others if they do not deliver on the promised recovery and reconstruction programmes, or to selectively cooperate and co-opt some of the groups involved. This is all intended to control access, and to determine how funds for the recovery are used. It is this form of control that limits activism and localises recovery processes in Uganda. This means that recovery processes are not seen as a right or an entitlement by the affected communities, but rather one of the many reconstruction programmes that government is offering to the country.

This occurs even within the civil society groups working on issues of transitional justice. Presently, there is a northern Uganda transitional justice working group. This group was formed after heated debates about a national vs. a local working group. Most of the civil society organisations in northern Uganda viewed the problem as a northern question. By forming this group, the national-minded groups were effectively thrown off the board of Transitional Justice Initiatives in northern Uganda, as local civil society groups took it as their moral obligation to focus on local issues. These divisions are exploited by the central government, but it is also true that the central government is key in creating those divisions. Using these divisions, some of the political elites are able to consolidate their political power within the north without addressing state legitimacy, which is an underlying structural problem in Uganda.[49]

The use of districts is explained by the fact that these local institutions offer the central government a way to distance itself from criticism. Because the districts are nearer to the people rather than the central government, a perception is generated that the districts are autonomous from the central government. With the district taking the centre stage in the implementation of the recovery programme rather than planning and monitoring, the central government can afford to underfund the process or dictate the agenda of recovery. When districts fail, the central government argues that local politicians are frustrating the recovery process, without explaining why the local governments are not delivering. This argument is based on the reality that district leaders in northern Uganda are mostly from opposition political parties.[50] Thus, the recovery programme is turned into an avenue to trade political abuse between the opposition and the ruling NRM.

It also appears that the NRM is trying to use the recovery programmes to win political capital in the northern and eastern Uganda before the 2011 elections. This is evident in how new districts have recently been created in northern and eastern Uganda. The new districts being created are put under the leadership of NRM cadres. Examples of such districts include Amuru, Bukwa, Oyam and Dokolo. In addition, full funding of the PRDP has been extended to the 2009/10 financial year. There are worries that this is intended to be used as a political platform to canvass for votes. In a recent cabinet reshuffle, the president is quoted to have said, 'I am looking to 2011 elections in naming this cabinet by rewarding areas that voted overwhelmingly for NRM and sidelining those that did not'. He added, 'If you give me 20 percent of your votes and another area gives me 90 percent votes then I will consider the region with the higher votes'.[51] This statement was delivered in Arua District in the northwest Uganda. This is one of the regions where the NRM has had limited political support since 1986. Hence, the PRDP may be one of the instruments to aid the ruling political elites in garnering political support. In Gulu and Amuru District, the beneficiaries of the agricultural mechanisation are mostly NRM cadres, creating fears that funding and implementation of the programmes is likely to be used as a source of rewards for the patrimonial regime in Uganda.

There are different strategies that the national political elites, and in particular the president, has employed in the management of, and determination of funds disbursed during the recovery process. The creation of new districts is one of them. For instance, 17 out of the current 40 PRDP districts were created in the aftermath of creation of the Technical Committee on Post Conflict Recovery Plan for Northern Uganda. Since 2005 the region has witnessed the creation of another 16 new districts. While the justification for the creation of these districts is improvement in the delivery of services, the reality is different. Districts created in Acholi (Amuru) and Lango (Amolatar, Dokolo, and Oyam) very much reflect the desire by the ruling national and local elites to politically capture northern Uganda. Because of the desire to establish a political presence in the north, demands for a political settlement of the northern Uganda Question, which would necessarily involve government taking political responsibility for the failure to protect the population in northern Uganda, are deliberately brushed aside as petty. When the Acholi Parliamentary Group (APG) raised concern about the coverage of the recovery plan, the minister for northern Uganda responded by claiming that the parliamentarians are interested in politics not development.[52]

If it is true that some of the politicians in northern Uganda are fighting not to lose political capital to the ruling government, it is worthwhile for the government to look into some of the issues raised about the PRDP. The argument that local concerns are petty and that local leaders should focus on owning the recovery programme and devote all their efforts to development is misleading and contemptuous. Branding concerns as mere politics shifts attention from what the situation is in northern Uganda to a politics of labelling and counter labelling. The government appears to be interested in having the recovery in place rather than how it relates to the real problems of northern Uganda. For example, in 2005, the government initiated a voluntary return to villages after the northern region began experiencing relative peace, but many people still prefer to stay in the camps or transit centres. They are not sure that the government and the LRA will finally sign the peace agreement.[53] While one of the reasons for not returning to villages mentioned by the people still in the camps is the lack of social services, the most important factor that still causes a lot of fear is the continued presence of the LRA. And as I have said before, that is not an issue the districts can deal with.

5. Conclusion

The PRDP offers some hope to the people of northern Uganda in so far as it attempts to coordinate reconstruction programmes. But some of the programmes, especially national programmes, focus on technical service provision rather than reconciliation, peacebuilding, or redistribution of wealth in a manner that addresses a legacy of decades of marginalisation and differentiation between the north and south, and within the north. These are vital political issues that need to be addressed in the postconflict situation. Streamlining such political processes into the existing programmes appears to be difficult, as districts do not have the capacity to address some of these national problems. In addition, the use of the PRDP in a particularised and individualised manner limits beneficiaries to individuals and specific groups that may cause a relapse into conflict, based on competition over resources. Thus, the government through the PRDP needs to forget its own political interests and focus on solutions that offer a platform for reconciliation, development, and redistribution of wealth. While some of these are long-term solutions, the PRDP offers an opportunity to start thinking and working towards their achievement.

Both central and local governments together with communities should jointly identify projects to implement, and agree on the monitoring and supervision functions, rather than having the central government ministries plan and districts only implement. The creation of synergy between these three constituencies rather than competition is imperative in dealing with structural differentiation and marginalisation. While some central and local government politicians may be interested in using the recovery programme for political gains, the current structural set-up at the district and central government level (if well used) can salvage the situation. But this approach calls for the political and administrative will to religiously implement the programme.

Bibliography

_____. 2003. A Hidden War: Forgotten people: Causes and effects of war in northern Uganda and its ramification for peace and security in Uganda. Kampala. Human Rights and Peace Centre

Branch A. 2005. 'Political violence and the peasantry in northern Uganda'. *African Studies Quarterly* 8 (2): PAGES.

Ahikire, J. 2002. 'Decentralisation in Uganda today: Institutions and possible outcomes in the context of human rights'. ICHRP Working Paper.

Suhrke A, Wimpelmann T and Dawes M. 2007. *Peace Processes and State-Building: Economic and Institutional Provisions in Peace Agreements*, Berlin. Chr. Michelsen Institute.

Avery, William P. and David P. Rapkin. 1986. 'World markets and political instability within less developed countries'. *Cooperation and Conflict* 21 (2): 99-117.

Barber J. 1968. *Imperial Frontier*. Nairobi: East African Publishing House.

Beattie J. 1971. *The Nyoro State*. Oxford: Oxford University Press.

Claussen J, Lotsberg R, Nkutu A, and Nordby E. 2008. Appraisal of the Peace Recovery and Development Plan for Northern Uganda. Final Consultancy Report to NORD

Collier, Paul. 2000. *Economic causes of conflict and their implications for olicy makers*. Washington DC: The World Bank

Collier, P and Hoeffler A. 1999. *Justice-seeking and loot-seeking in civil war*. Washington, DC: The World Bank

Ddungu, E. 1999. 'Popular forms and the question of democracy: The case of resistance councils in Uganda'. In: *Uganda: Studies in Living Conditions, Popular Movements and Constitutionalism*, edited by M. Mamdani and J. Oloka-Onyango Vienna: JEP Book Series.

Drum (East). 1985. October.

Hauge W and Tanja E. 1998. 'Beyond environmental scarcity: Causal pathways to conflict'. *Journal of Peace Research* 35 (3): 299-317.

ICG. 2004. 'Northern Uganda: Understanding and solving the conflict'. African Report 77.

International Council on Human Rights Policy. 2002. *Local rule: Decentralisation and human rights*. Versoix Switzerland: International Council on Human Rights Policy.

Pham J Peter, (2007) 'Making sense of a senseless war'. *Human Rights and Human Welfare* 7: 35-51

Herbst J, "Economic Incentives, Natural Resources, and Conflict in Africa," *Journal of African Economies* Vol. 9, no. 3, 2000;

Ballentine K and Nitzschke H, 2005 *the Political Economy of Civil War and Conflict Transformation*: Berghof Center for Constructive Conflict Management

Komakech L and Muyombya L. 2008. Review of past Development programs in Northern Uganda: Lessons and Implications for the Implementation of the PRDP. A paper presented at a PRDP training workshop for District leaders in Northern Uganda on February 21st 2008,

Leggett I .2001. *Uganda: The Background, the Issues, the People*: An Oxfam County Profile. Kampala. Fountain Publishers.

Mamdani M. 2001. *When Victims Become Killers: Colonialism, Nativism and the Genocide in Rwanda*, Princeton, and Princeton University Press

Mamdani M. 2001. *Politics of Class Formation in Uganda*: Kampala, Fountain Publishers.

Rama M. 2008. "Dilemmas of Expanding Transitional Justice or Forging the Nexus between Transitional Justice and Development" In *International Journal of Transitional Justice,* Vol.2, No: 3, pp.253-265

Mao N., "The northern question is about social differentiations and inequalities", *The New Vision* 24th February 2009

Miller Z "Effects of Invisibility" In *International Journal of Transitional Justice* Vol. 2, Issue 3 pp.266-291

Museveni Y.K (1997) *Sowing the Mustard Seed: The Struggle for Democracy in Uganda*, London: Macmillian

Nannyonjo J. 2005. *Conflict, Poverty and Human Development in Northern Uganda*, UNU WIDER Research, No 2005

Cooper N. 2003. "State Collapse as Business: The Role of Conflict Trade and the Emerging Control Agenda," In Jennifer Milliken (ed). *Sate Failure, Collapse and Reconstruction:* Malden, MA: Blackwell,

Nsamba, A. M. 2009. *Breeding Fragmentation? Issues in the Policy and Practice of Decentralisation in Uganda,* Beyond Juba Project: Issues Paper, No. 1

Paige A. *Identities in Transition: Developing Better Transitional Justice Initiatives in Divided Societies,* ICTJ, November, 2009

Refugee Law Project. 2008. *Uganda's Urban IDPs Risk being Left out Government's Return Plans,* Refugee Law Project Special Bulletin

Republic of Uganda. 2007. *Peace, Recovery and Development Plan for Northern Uganda (RPDP), 2007-2010.* Office of the Prime Minister, Kampala

Sida .2007. *Uganda Strategic Conflict Analysis*, Department for Africa

Uganda Debt Network policy Review Newsletter, Vol 4 Issue 3 2004

UN, (2008), *Rule of Law Tools for Post-Conflict States: Reparations Programmes,* Geneva, UN

Reno W. 1998. *Warlord Politics and African States:* Boulder, CO: Lynne Rienner

Lomo Z. and Hovil L. 2004. *Behind the Violence: Causes, Consequences and the Search for Solutions to the War in Northern Uganda*, Working Paper No 11.

---

[1] _____ (2003) A Hidden War: Forgotten People: Causes and Effects of War in northern Uganda and its ramification for peace and security in Uganda.

[2] ICG (2004) Northern Uganda: Understanding and Solving the Conflict, African Report, No 77

[3] Karen Ballentine and Heiko Nitzschke, (2005) *The Political Economy of Civil War and Conflict Transformation*: Berghof Center for Constructive Conflict Management; Neil Cooper, "State Collapse as Business: The Role of Conflict Trade and the Emerging Control Agenda," in Jennifer Milliken (ed). (2003) *Sate Failure, Collapse and Reconstruction*: Malden, MA: Blackwell, (2003); Jeffrey Herbst, "Economic Incentives, Natural Resources, and Conflict in Africa," *Journal of African Economies* 9, no. 3, 2000; J. Peter Pham, "Making Sense of a Senseless War," *Human Rights and Human Welfare* 7, 2007; William Reno, (1998) *Warlord Politics and African States:* Boulder, CO: Lynne Rienner

[4] Republic of Uganda (2007) *Peace, Recovery and Development Plan for Northern Uganda (RPDP), 2007-2010*. Office of the Prime Minister, Kampala

[5] Nannyonjo (2005) *Conflict, Poverty and Human Development in Northern Uganda*, UNU WIDER Research, No 2005/47 pp.1

[6] See for instance RLP (2004) *Behind the Violence: Causes, Consequences and the Search for Solution to the War in Northern Uganda*, RLP Working paper No. 11

[7] Collier, Paul, (2000) *Economic Causes of Conflict and their Implications for Policy Makers*, Washington DC: The World Bank

[8] Zachary Lomo and Lucy Hovil, (2004), *Behind the Violence: Causes, Consequences and the Search for Solutions to the War in Northern Uganda*, Working Paper No 11.

[9] Mani Rama (2008) "Dilemmas of Expanding Transitional Justice or Forging the Nexus between Transitional Justice and Development" In *International Journal of Transitional Justice,* Vol.2,No:3, pp.253-265

[10] Hauge, Wenche, and Tanja Ellingsen (1998) "Beyond Environmental Scarcity: Causal Pathways to Conflict", In *Journal of Peace Research*, 35, 3, 299-317; Avery, William P, and David P. Rapkin (1986) "World Markets and Political Instability within Less Developed Countries" In *Cooperation and Conflict*, 21, 2, 99-117; Collier, Paul, and Anke Hoeffler (1999) *Justice-Seeking and Loot-Seeking in Civil War*, Washington, DC: The World Bank

[11] Barber J (1968) Imperial Frontier, Nairobi: East African Publishing House,

[12] Mao Norbert, "The northern question is about social differentiations and inequalities", The New Vision 24th February 2009

[13] Beattie (1971) *the Nyoro State*. Oxford University Press

[14] Leggett (2001) *Uganda: The Background, the Issues, the People*: An Oxfam County Profile. Fountain Publishers, Kampala; Mamdani (2001) Politics of Class Formation in Uganda: Fountain Publishers, Kampala

[15] Sida (2007) *Uganda Strategic Conflict Analysis*, Department for Africa

[16] Drum (East), October 1985, p.9Zzswaa

[17] Museveni Y.K (1997) *Sowing the Mustard Seed: The Struggle for Democracy in Uganda*, London: Macmillian

[18] Adam Branch (2005) "Political Violence and the Peasantry in Northern Uganda" In *African Studies Quarterly*: Volume 8, Issue 2, Spring, 2005

[19] ibid

[20] Miller Z "Effects of Invisibility" In *International Journal of Transitional Justice* Vol. 2, Issue 3 pp.266-291

[21]Komakech and Muyombya, (2008) Review of past Development programs in Northern Uganda: Lessons and Implications for the Implementation of the PRDP

[22]Adam Branch (2005) "Political Violence and the Peasantry in Northern Uganda" In *African Studies Quarterly*: Volume 8, Issue 2, Spring, 2005

[23] Refugee Law Project (2008) *Uganda's Urban IDPs Risk being Left out Government's Return Plans,* Refugee Law Project Special Bulletin

[24]Komakech and Muyombya, (2008) *Review of past Development programs in Northern Uganda: Lessons and Implications for the Implementation of the PRDP*

[25]Uganda Debt Network policy Review Newsletter, Vol 4 Issue 3 2004

[26]Ibid; see also Dolan Chris (2008) is the PRDP a Three Legged Table? Key note address delivered at Scandinavian International NGOs operating in Northern Uganda

[27] Chris Dolan, 2008

[28] Republic of Uganda (2007) *Peace, Recovery and Development Plan for Northern Uganda (RPDP), 2007-2010.* Office of the Prime Minister, Kampala

[29] Ibid, p27

[30] See Miller, 2008

[31] Ibid

[32] Paige Arthur, *Identities in Transition: Developing Better Transitional Justice Initiatives in Divided Societies,* ICTJ, November, 2009;see also UN, (2008), *Rule of Law Tools for Post-Conflict States: Reparations Programmes,* Geneva, UN

[33] Astri Suhike, et al (2007) *Peace Processes and State-Building: Economic and Institutional Provisions in Peace Agreements,* CMI

[34] See Mahmood Mamdani (2001) *When Victims Become Killers: Colonialism, Nativism and the Genocide in Rwanda,* Princeton, Princeton University Press

[35]Uganda, 2007

[36]ibid

[37]Claussen et al (2008) *Appraisal of the Peace Recovery and Development Plan for Northern Uganda,* Final Consultancy Report to NORD

[38]Ibid (pg81)

[39]Republic of Uganda (2007) *Peace, Recovery and Development Plan for Northern Uganda (RPDP), 2007-2010.* Office of the Prime Minister, Kampala, Pg 84

[40]Claussen et al (2008) *Appraisal of the Peace Recovery and Development Plan for Northern Uganda,* Final Consultancy Report to NORD

[41]Republic of Uganda (2007) *Peace, Recovery and Development Plan for Northern Uganda (RPDP), 2007-2010.* Office of the Prime Minister, Kampala, pg.35

[42]Office of the Prime Minister (OPM) Report on Joint Monitoring Committee

[43]Republic of Uganda (2007) *Peace, Recovery and Development Plan for Northern Uganda (RPDP), 2007-2010.* Office of the Prime Minister, Kampala

[44] International Council on Human Rights Policy (2002) Local Rule: Decentralisation and Human Rights, Versoix: International Council on Human Rights Policy

[45] ibid

[46] Nsamba, (2009) *Breeding Fragmentation? Issues in the Policy and Practice of Decentralisation in Uganda,* Beyond Juba Project: Issues Paper, No. 1

[47] Ddungu, E. (1994) "Popular Forms and the Question of Democracy: The Case of Resistance Councils in Uganda" In M. Mamdani & J. Oloka Onyango (eds.) *Uganda: Studies in Living Conditions, Popular Movements and Constitutionalism,* JEP Book Series, Vienna

[48] Ahikire, (2002) *Decentralisation in Uganda today: Institutions and Possible Outcomes in the Context of Human Rights,* ICHRP Working Paper

[49] Dolan Chris, 2008

[50] Interview with sub-county chairperson in Gulu District on February, 15 2008

[51] The Daily Monitor News Paper, February 17th 2009

[52] The Daily Monitor October 2 2008

[53] Daily Monitor November 18 2008

CHAPTER 9

Social Protection, Labour Markets, and Economic Reconfiguration of Postconflict in Northern Uganda[1]

Frederik Kisekka-Ntale

Introduction

One of the main issues on the agenda of postconflict rehabilitation is the socioeconomic reintegration of former combatants and the creation of socioeconomic opportunities for the population. Although labour market issues are rarely the main element in peacebuilding processes, tasks associated with employment opportunities are important issues when government and international actors design policies to alleviate conflict and consolidate peace. Studies such as those by ILO and UNDP[2] assert that employment in postconflict societies not only is important for reducing poverty and vulnerability, but also substantially contributes to confidence and peacebuilding, especially among ex-war combatants and displaced communities.

The concept of social protection is problematic. Scholars and practitioners in this field use it variedly. For instance, in the realm of physical disasters, it means restoring physical and institutional structures to their pre-disaster levels. Sometimes it is used in reference to rehabilitation and reconstruction with distinction made between rehabilitation and reconstruction, the former referring to crisis affected households, the latter to physical and social infrastructures. Such a varied conceptualisation of the term social protection presents limitations in case of war-torn societies. Nonetheless, Holzmann and Jørgensen (2000) agree that the main idea behind social protection measures is that all individuals, households, and communities are vulnerable to multiple risks from different sources, whether they are natural (such as earthquakes, flooding, and illness) or man-made (such as unemployment, environmental degradation, and war). These shocks hit individuals, communities, and regions mostly in an unpredictable manner or cannot be prevented, and therefore they cause and deepen poverty (2000: 3).

The causes of civil war are mostly political; civil wars signify failed political systems that could not perform essential government functions, thereby generating political insurgencies. The need therefore is not to go back to pre-crisis conditions but to move in a different direction. In this case, social protection in war-torn societies then involves redefining, reorienting, and reconciling relationships between political authority and the citizenry, revisiting the relationships between the different social and ethnic groups, creating a civil society in its broadest sense, promoting psychosocial healing and reconciliation, and reforming economic policies and institutions that foster entrepreneurship and individual initiative (Paris 2004). Paris further argues that where institutions are lacking in governing political and economic competition, violence could result. The solution, which he calls 'institutionalization before liberalization' (IBL), is for peacebuilders to focus on constructing institutions that can provide political stability and effective administration prior to initiating political and economic competition. The key elements of this strategy are: wait until conditions are ripe for elections, design electoral systems that reward moderation, promote good civil society, control hate speech, and adopt conflict-reducing economic policies, the common denominator being to rebuild effective state institutions (2004: 188-207).

As Kumar (1997) points out, due to the widespread destruction of many critical economic, political and even social institutions, undertaking social protection programmes is in most cases a long process; it may take several years, perhaps decades before societies shattered by civil wars are able to effectively rebuild themselves and their governments to the point where they are able to perform the essential functions expected of them. In that regard, the most critical element in rebuilding war-torn societies is undertaking policies and programs designed to promote employment, the efficient operation of labor markets and the protection of workers. This is premised on the notion that work is the poor's main source of earning. Ghossa (2003) points out that understanding labour markets is essential to reduce poverty and ensure inclusive labor absorption and efficient development patterns. Improving labour market operations is also an important element of strategies to develop human capital, address gender discrimination, and enhance welfare and productivity.

Northern Uganda has been engulfed in an armed insurgency for the last twenty-three years. Before then, the subregion had a vibrant agricultural-based economy with a population close to two million people. The insurgency caused displacements that left thousands of people living in internally displaced people's camps (IDPs). Although the actual death toll caused by this conflict has never been computed, it was estimated to be at 146 people per week in 2006.[3] In this conflict, the northern tribes and to some extent eastern Luo-speaking tribes, which are historically acephalous and perceived to be politically and economically marginalized (from colonial times to postindependence times), have been engaged in a protracted conflict with the central government forces, which are dominated by several of their historically centralised and politically dominant southern counterparts: the Baganda, Banyakole, and Batoro, Bakiga and Banyoro. Due to intense peace efforts, the insurgency has tremendously subsided and the displaced people are voluntarily returning to their home areas, including ex-war combatants. However, many of the returnees, including ex-war combatants and other youths, are faced with fundamental challenges, particularly unemployment and underemployment; yet these returns have political and security ramifications in addition to socioeconomic challenges.

In this article, I argue that although there have been several social protection programmes aimed at reducing vulnerability, there has been a limited focus on employment and labour markets despite its relevancy in peace building processes. With specific reference to northern Uganda, this article seeks to analyze, the policies and instruments of reintegration in postconflict situation in relation to reducing marginalization and fostering the economic reconfiguration of the region into country's wider political economy in the medium and long term. In so doing, the paper also makes an analysis of the nature of vulnerability defined within a broader realm. In that regard, social protection consists of policies and programmes designed to reduce poverty and vulnerability by promoting efficient labour markets, diminishing people's exposure to risks, and enhancing their capacity to protect themselves against hazards and interruption/loss of income (Jorgensen and van Domelen 2000).

Social protection as an agenda for primarily reducing vulnerability and risk of low-income households with regard to basic consumption and social services has become an important building block of the development discourse. However, it remains a term that is unfamiliar to many and has a range of definitions both in the literature and among policy makers that are responsible for implementing social protection programmes. Accordingly, the ILO posits that in order for social protection to achieve its objectives, including reducing vulnerability, especially in the realm of postconflict situations, it must be approached in several dimensions and through several phases (ILO 2007). These dimensions include access to essential goods and services, prevention of and protection against various risks, and promotion of potentials and opportunities in order to break vicious cycles and pervasive tendencies. The phases are: before, during, and after working years. With this in mind, it is evident that in the context of postconflict northern Uganda, the definitions and boundaries of social protection are far from agreed upon and that different sets of stakeholders perceive social protection in different ways. It is these differences that in part account for the failure to meet the essential needs and aspirations of the people and to effectively accommodate and reconcile the demands of competing groups within the framework of economic growth, political stability, and the fuller reconfiguration of this subregion into the wider political economy.

Embedding Social Protection in Postwar Societies: Some Theoretical Considerations

The World Bank postulates that development and international financial institutions have a critical role to play, along with political, peacekeeping and humanitarian assistance agencies, in making post-conflict reconstruction and development a success. But they must become involved at an early stage in order to prepare the groundwork for viable development plans and the reintegration of displaced populations. During postconflict situations, there is tension between the need for income security, and the apparent nonaffordability of providing it, which breeds further conflict. For that reason development agencies also have a role to play in the prevention of conflicts by seeking to remedy the economic inequities underlying conflict (Holzman and Jogensen 2000).

Labour markets issues as an integral part of social protection have been studied in relation to postconflict transitions. As Cramer (2006) indicates, it is necessary to study the relation between labour markets, war, and war-to-peace transitions in developing countries at the levels of labour supply, labour demand, wages and employment regulation, and as a core concern. What is more, consolidating peace following violent conflict has little chance of success unless jobs are created and the economy is quickly stabilised and brought onto a path of investment and growth with low inflation (Castillo and Phelps 2007).

The United Nations reckons that if economic reconstruction fails in terms of promoting dynamism and inclusion, countries in the transition to peace have an even chance of reverting to war (Evans 2009). Armed conflicts can produce changes in the local economies, or wars can accelerate processes of economic transformation in developing countries. Some of these changes could be identified in the land and labour markets (Wood 2008). Cramer (2006) further points out that war to peace transitions are characterised by processes of primitive accumulation-including forced displacement-resulting from the wars. Such processes usually cause transitional shift to 'capitalism' as victims and other opportunists exploit wartime survival techniques. Cramer argues that this is due to fact that postwar economies attract resources that in most cases stimulate reconstruction activities. In turn this creates a labour market and wage labourers; and leads to a market for goods produced in the post war economy. In fact, as if to expand the famous dictum by Carl von Clausewitz, Keen, cited in Ballentine and Nitzschke (2005), described many of the conflict dynamics as 'the continuation of economics by other means'. Indeed, where there is 'more to war than winning', those benefiting from violence may have a vested economic interest in conflict continuation (see Ballentine and Nitzschke, 2005: 3).

During reconstruction time, negative effects resulting from the war are sometimes very difficult to reverse. For example, war causes forced displacement of a lot of the population affecting the labour participation at local level, creating pressures to urban labour markets (Ballentine and Nitzschke 2005). This sometimes results from failure to access land during postwar times (Sebina-Zziwa et al. 2008; Bruck 2001). This makes postwar reconstruction and poverty alleviation much slower than expected. In war and war to peace transitions, labour markets play complex and varied roles, and one of the main issues is to avoid the risks to return to war (Cramer 2006; Suhrke and Strand 2005). As an example, almost eighteen years after the end of the war in Mozambique, postwar reconstruction and poverty alleviation in northern Mozambique is still an on-going process. In this regard the supply of labour is affected during the war by factors such as the recruitment or the creation of employments in war economies. (Cowen and Coyne 2005)

Employment could be taken as a part of the set of policies designed to stabilise and consolidate peace. Workers could have perspectives to keep their employments created during the war, some of them related with war economies-in legal and illegal activities (Ballentine and Nitzschke 2005). For instance, the influx of new weapons, and the availability of those from older conflict, is one of the most serious issues that may affect the transition process. It is clear from the conflicts on the continent over the last decade that automatic weapons have upgraded conflicts and increased the scale of their lethality (Wannenburg 2005). Thus, it is necessary to point out that there is a possibility of transformation of war into other forms of violence, facilitated by the existence of 'violence specialists' and the trade of small arms. This contributes to the risks of returning to war (Surhke 2004). Therefore social protection policies in the postconflict situation can be designed only to benefit ex-combatants, neglecting the demands of other sectors of population; or they could benefit a nonproductive 'rentier class' (beneficiaries of the war become beneficiaries with peace), perpetuating unequal and unregulated labour relations. In that regard, social protection policies related with war economies may not support the peace; hence, national as well as humanitarian intervention must create new formal employment opportunities to replace informal jobs created during the war. But note must be taken that a growth of the formal sector does not necessarily produce a reduction of informal employment. Other relevant theoretical issues for peace building and the transformation of war economies into peace economies include appreciating issues of risk and vulnerability. This is key to understanding the dynamics perpetuating poverty. Poverty is more than inadequate consumption or inadequate education and health, but rather the degree of fear for the unknown and uncertainty regarding the future. Vulnerability affects everyone but is greater for the poor who face large risks from shocks to their income-earning capacity due to natural and man-made disasters, crime and violence, unemployment, old age, exclusion and discrimination, gender inequality, etc. In short, the poor need to feel empowered with skills and voices to overcome their fear of isolation and governments need to be able to respond to risks through a series of market and nonmarket mechanisms that do not adversely affect long-term development. Hence social protection programs to assist vulnerable individuals, households and communities must encompass all forms of public action, government and nongovernment, that are designed to transfer resources to eligible vulnerable and deprived persons such as war victims, orphans and disabled persons, whose vulnerability requires some form of entitlement (Landau 1998).

Political Economy of the Conflict in Northern Uganda

British colonial rule in Uganda left a typically complex legacy regarding longer-term prospects for economic and political development. Allen (2006) notes with concern that the British administrative policies in northern Uganda in contrast to the rest of the country were the recipe for the chaos created in the postcolonial period. For the north was characterised as a military and labour recruiting ground. This led to a deliberate division of the country into productive and nonproductive regions. Labour from the north was essential for carrying out essential services in the central producing districts. The denial to northern Uganda of such bounties of social advancement as the colonial administration chose to bestow upon the protectorate, made that region distinctively backward even by Ugandan standards, and the full cost of that neglect had to be paid, not by the colonial officials, but by Ugandans themselves (Atkinson 1994). Moreover, the postcolonial repressive regimes led by mainly northerners only served to escalate the north-south divide of the country. It is little wonder therefore that when the southern-led NRM government captured power in 1986, various factions in the north would seek to regain power. Movements like the Holy Spirit movement of Alice Lakwena, Odongo Latek's Uganda People's Democratic Army (UPDA), and the infamous Lord's Resistance Army (LRA) sprouted. These mobilised popular support by appealing to ethnic anxieties about revenge, although they later squandered it by turning on the population through mass killings and abductions (Kisekka-Ntale 2007).

Although significant inroads were made particularly in the early years of the NRM to integrate the country and reduce the north-south divide, stark divisions continued, especially in the progressive years of the regime until today. The NRM years have seen an exacerbation in the disparity of development indicators between the north and south, symptomatic of neglect that resulted in further rebellion. Although relative calm has returned to the region, the north is in a dire state and vulnerability of the population has been on its worst scale over the years. From 1979-2004, about 7million people, i.e., about one-third of Uganda's population have been affected by civil conflict and cattle rustling. The LRA war that has lasted over 21 years in northern Uganda has resulted in the displacement of over 1.4 million people and led to the deterioration of rural infrastructure and local government service delivery. The north has the largest proportion of people living in poverty, estimated at 61%, almost twice the national poverty level of 31% (Dolan 2005).

As a result, the north remains one of the poorest regions in Uganda, with some of the lowest human development indicators in the country. The 2005/6 national household survey reveals that the north has the largest proportion of people living with poverty. The gap between the north and national poverty levels has widened from 17 percentage points in 1992 to 30 percentage points in 2005/2006, with poverty in the north falling less than in any other region. By the end of 2005, an estimated 1.6 million people had been forced out of their homes in northern and eastern Uganda to live in internally displaced people's camps for fear of being attacked or abducted by LRA rebels (Branch 2005). In financial terms, the cost of the conflict to the national economy has been estimated at over 1.3bnUS dollars between1986 and 2002, more than 3% of the country's GDP. Moreover, parts of the region have been affected by cattle rustlers.

For nearly two decades, the international community ignored the plight of the people in northern Uganda to increasingly grave repercussions. In late 2003, the north found itself re-designated as an area with one of the worst humanitarian crises following the visit of the UN under secretary for humanitarian affairs, Jan Engelaad.[4] Since then there has been an influx of humanitarian agencies, many of whom describe their activities as 'protection oriented'. This reflects increased international awareness of the rights dimensions of external intervention. Dolan (2006) has aptly described this as 'social torture'. He is at pains to explain that there is no war in northern Uganda. Rather, the situation there is one of 'social torture' in which the Acholi people have for decades been subject to systemic anguish through their enforced dependency on a protection system that is itself a primary source of violations. Such violations-of rights to a livelihood, to education, and to healthcare and to physical and psychological well-being, among others-have subordinated a population that might otherwise represent a threat to Museveni's hegemony, and have provided populations on the verge of dissent with a powerful warning.

Hickey (2007) adds that the lack of a social contract between the government of Uganda and the citizens in northern Uganda arguably informs the tendency to deal with the high levels of chronic poverty in that region through piecemeal social funds that are further diluted by the politics of patronage. He argues that the greatest problem with the Ugandan government when it comes to the problem of IDPs is 'denial'. Despite the high number of IDPs, in some cases, they blame the IDPs for their predicament, accusing them of complicity in their own suffering. This is why the national IDP policy came more than 10 years after the government first began forcefully herding people into the camps in northern Uganda. Ninety-seven percent of all war-related deaths are attributed to the inhuman conditions in the camps.

Postconflict in Northern Uganda and the Question of Vulnerability

In the aftermath of prolonged civil conflicts, governments are usually faced with three urgent problems; first, they are plagued with a critical shortage of trained personnel because of the systematic killing of the intelligentsia, emigration of the educated, and decay of existing educational and training institutions and facilities. Therefore governments find it difficult to operate in economic, social, and even internal security sectors. Second, and somewhat paradoxically, there is a plethora of superfluous departments, agencies and parastatal organizations-created or reinforced during the conflict to regulate

287

production, trade, and civil supplies and to exercise political control over people. Such bloated bureaucracies are not only a severe drain on the precious resources of the government but also inhibit economic growth.

The second issue is that problem areas have surfaced in international assistance programmes for institutional capacity building. First is the limited relevance and high cost of training and technical assistance. There exists a widespread impression that highly paid expatriate expats lack an in-depth understanding of the local political and social landscape and often develop training activities that are not pertinent to the existing realities. This problem has not been unique to war torn societies. Rather, it has been common to most of the international assistance programmes. But the problem is compounded in transition societies because of the intense pressure to solve urgent problems caused by personnel shortages. Second, international assistance programmes have occasionally aggravated labour shortages in the public sector. For instance, skilled and professional employees are lured away from the government to take up better paying jobs in international agencies and organizations. Many professionals even preferred semi skilled jobs because of huge salary differentials (USAID 2008).

International efforts to promote human rights have also been frequently criticized. Often host governments perceive human rights monitoring as an unwarranted intrusion in their internal affairs. In a few cases, government officials in war-torn societies have accused international actors of imposing western standards that are inappropriate given their traditions and political circumstances- a criticism that is usually a smoke screen to hide their authoritarian impulses and failure to curb human rights abuses. A more valid criticism is that international interventions have focused more on strengthening formal legal mechanisms than on promoting respect for human rights through rehabilitation efforts (Dolan 2006). The latter approach includes such activities as instilling a culture of peace and tolerance through educational curricula and building a cross-ethnic component into rehabilitation projects.

While it is true to affirm that democracy is a key instrument to peace and that democracies are more at peace with each other, in ethnically divided societies, such as Uganda, societies' application of the winner takes it all model of democracy has tended to stroke rather than prevent conflict. Thus governments have to deal with the difficult problems of widespread inefficiency and a conspicuous lack of transparency that are compounded during wars. In northern Uganda, the international community has provided modest, though multifaceted assistance to address these problems. Donor agencies have funded salary support initiatives for public employees, supported training of government employees and undertaken technical assistance projects to improve performance of key government ministries and organisations. Donor agencies have also devised and implemented projects to induce the educated overseas Diaspora to return and help in the reconstruction process.

Many international agencies have preferred to build institutional capacities at the local rather than the national level because it is widely believed that local governments tend to be more efficient because they understand local problems better and can find innovative solutions. They are also more responsive because of their proximity to people. This is further rooted in the notion that power and resources are distributed and shared in local public space among local governments, including civil society groups, donors and nongovernmental organisations in order to effectively deliver on services. In essence it is important to point out that such efforts are tailored to empower the elected local leaders such as councilors in planning, overseeing service delivery, and their involvement in the public financial management processes. The above parameters are premised on the thinking that elected local leaders seek to best represent the interests of the local citizens, their involvement in local planning processes helps to reflect the local preferences in these processes.

Reconfiguration of Northern Uganda in the National Political Economy

It is apparent that building a peace economy, where different groups have access to decent work opportunities and a share in economic growth, is an essential ingredient for consolidating peace in the long run. While there is an emerging awareness that a country's economy is often intertwined with its conflicts, and that conflict affected and fragile regions cannot simply be subjected to economic development as usual, it is less clear what alternative approaches are required and how these can feed into the bigger picture of long-term peace and economic development, than focusing purely on economic growth as the end goal. Despite efforts to the contrary, many of the interventions continue to be informed by the existing aid, trade and investment paradigms, rather than an understanding of the political economy of each conflict in context (Le Billon 2000). The question therefore remains, how and under what conditions can interventions designed to stimulate economic development contribute to building a peace economy, and avoid exacerbating the conflict in turn?

In this subsection, we therefore seek to analyse the policies and instruments of reintegration in postconflict Northern Uganda in relation to reducing marginalisation and fostering the economic reconfiguration of the region into the country's wider political economy in the medium and long term. One of the core challenges for the government of Uganda is the restoration of security, dealing with the consequences of conflict and improving regional equity. In this regard, accelerating poverty reduction and development is essential in order to keep pace with other regions. To that effect, a number of programmes have been implemented by the government with the support of the international community. These include but are not limited to; the Northern Uganda Rehabilitation Programme (NURP), the Northern Uganda Social Action Fund (NUSAF), and the Peace Recovery and Development Plan (PRDP). NURP1 lasted six years and was implemented in a top-down approach by the central government and did not connect development to peace building or psychosocial support to communities. Additionally, the original NURP 1 budget was around 600 million US dollars but only USD 93.6 million was actually spent. In response to some of these shortcomings, NURP 1 was reorganised as NURP11 in 1999 with the stated intention of incorporating a more bottom-up demand-responsive approach. As part of the Government of Uganda's broader Northern Uganda Reconstruction Program, the project empowered communities in the 18 (now 29) districts of northern Uganda by enhancing their capacity to systematically identify, prioritise, and plan for their needs within their own value systems and, ultimately, to improve economic livelihoods and social cohesion.

During the last six years, there has been significant progress made in enhancing the capacities of the communities in northern Uganda by making local governments more accountable to the communities. The most significant initiative of NURP11 was the World Bank-funded Northern Uganda Social Action Fund (NUSAF 1), also a CDD project, which started in 2003 and closed in March 2009. The Northern Uganda Social Action Fund, a World Bank project in Uganda aimed at eradicating poverty in northern Uganda, covered 18 districts (now 29) spanning over the greater northern region. This included the districts of Pallisa, Nakapiripirit, Gulu, Lira, Pader, Kumi, Moroto, Kitgum, Soroti, Katakwi, Kaberamaido, Yumbe, Moyo, Nebbi, Adjumani, Kotido Arua, and Apac. The targeted beneficiary region has a population of about 6.3million people as per the 2002 census.

The project was funded to the tune of 135.5 million US dollars. Therefore, the approximate per capita allocation for the project was 19.6 dollars, which simply means that each person in the targeted area was expected to have a share of 350 000 Uganda shillings ($175). NUSAF was established with the following objectives: to eradicate poverty, promote sustainable development, and create conditions for higher levels of investment in agriculture and rural development. It was established to complement efforts of other projects under the broad second northern Uganda rehabilitation programme whose aim is to tackle poverty and regional inequalities.

The design of NUSAF was based on community-driven development, meaning it is supposed to be promoting community empowerment and ownership in the context of decentralised development. The Fund was based on the premise that many rural poor in northern Uganda are small farmers with the barest survival means, a situation that has been worsened by the prolonged LRA insurgency. It was therefore expected that if NUSAF was to be a vehicle for poverty eradication, then the strategy had to enhance access of the extreme poor to become productive and generate incomes to enable them afford their basic survival needs such as food, shelter, and clothing, thus breaking out of the poverty trap. The second strategy of NUSAF was to promote broadbased agricultural and rural development through community development initiatives.

NUSAF included five components:

a) Community development initiatives with a range of targeted project options covering education, health, sanitation, water supply, economic infrastructure, agriculture,and the environment;
b) Community reconciliation/ conflict management;
c) Vulnerable group support;
d) Institutional development; and
e) The Northern Uganda Youth Rehabilitation Fund.

Under NUSAF 1, over 3 million people, or 47 percent of the population in northern Uganda, were supported to gain access to improved social services; 67 000 households (336 200 people) got access to safe drinking water and close to 4 000 households (19 075 people) got access to improved sanitation facilities. Although NUSAF registered significant contributions, extreme poverty, vulnerability, and service delivery challenges still remained. This prompted the government in 2006 to launch the Peace Recovery and Development Plan (PRDP) to consolidate the gains of NUSAF1 and also implement lessons learnt. PRDP is a combination of many things. It is a plan of action adopted in the conflict context of the North, to strengthen coordination, supervision, and monitoring of both nationally and internationally supported activities in order to achieve a common set of results. The common objective of the PRDP is stabilisation in order to achieve peace, development, and recovery in northern Uganda. This is to be done through four core objectives:

a) Consolidation of state authority;
b) Rebuilding and empowering of communities;
c) Revitalization of the northern economy; and
d) Peacebuilding and reconciliation.

As a framework, PRDP provides for a combination of political/security and economic interventions that to a greater or lesser degree apply to all the subregions. More so, it recognises that due to the insecurity, conflict, and underdevelopment, the poverty targets for the PEAP were not realistic for northern Uganda. A special effort is required therefore, which includes security/political as well as development objectives in order to create conditions whereby the north is brought up to the same standards as those of the rest of the country. The PRDP hands the responsibility of implementation solely to the Coordination and Management Unit (CMU) in the Office of the Prime Minister (OPM). Due to the lack of funds, the CMU had to be implemented in financial year 2009/2010. OPM officials had to conduct the PRDP activities alongside their daily workloads. More so, the PRDP monitoring committee is comprised of civil society representatives and district leaders that have to meet regularly to monitor the activities of the project have always postponed their meetings.

Related to the above is the government's reluctance to follow through on its promise to increase overall funding levels approved under the medium-term expenditure framework. The MTEF limits government spending nationally in favour of macroeconomic stability. Without an increase in MTEF ceiling, the government must move money from other sectors or districts to finance the PRDP. Government was reluctant, at least in part, because the political cost of moving money from non-PRDP districts would be high. Key local government-elected officials in Gulu have also opined that the PRDP was not incorporated in the district development plans. Some district officials were also not clear on the scope and purpose of the plan; to quote one leader, 'This document has been highly popularized'. In some districts, leaders looked at it as a disaster preparedness plan that could also address cases like floods (Beyond Juba, briefing note no. 2 2008). Since no meaningful consultations were conducted prior to the inclusion of the hydroelectric projects, local communities have expressed fear that the government will use it as a ploy to grab land from the people. Since its launch, the PRDP has achieved little because of insufficient funding, incoherent project selection, and widespread confusion among sectors, local communities, and districts about how implementation is supposed to proceed.

Linking the Economy and Peace Building

Over the last decade, important research and policy initiatives have led to better understanding of the economic aspects of violent conflicts. They show, for example, that misuse of public resources, elite control of economic activities or horizontal inequalities in a country's economic base can all fuel grievances and even cause violent conflict to break out (Cooper 2002). Likewise, economies that are vulnerable to shocks and dependent on few sectors and imports are more vulnerable to instability and conflict. Through 2008, a renewed sense of possibility emerged regarding the rebuilding of the economy in northern Uganda, with government, development partners, and the private sector all planning either to make the most of the opportunities that may present themselves in the north's postsettlement economy or to contribute to peace through revised programmatic interventions (IA 2009). In this subsection we are particularly concerned with the economic dimensions of the rebuilding process in northern Uganda and what it means on the delivery of peace dividends as well as addressing the structural and economic imbalances to deliver meaningful reconstruction of the region.

The attention and interest of various stakeholders in rebuilding the economy of northern Uganda as a part of peace and recovery presents critically important opportunities for change and building sustainable peace in the region, following years of economic breakdown and underdevelopment during the decades of conflict. Here it is imperative to analyse the process of economic recovery within the context of a larger peacebuilding process. The question of who has access to economic opportunities and who does not has profound impacts for long-term prospects for peace. It must be factored into the 'peace economy'. However, note must be taken in regard to the common tendency to regard development programmes as essentially technical exercises (Cassen 1994).

As pointed out by (Keen 1998) such technocratic approaches overlook the power relationships and political dynamics that are especially important when the context is shaped by long-term conflict. Indeed, evidence provided by Fischer (2001) demonstrates that power asymmetries must be considered and the relationship of destruction transformed into one that manages conflict constructively. Conflict transformation further requires that the antagonists agree upon and create the political, economic, and social structures that will engender positive peace with social justice over the longer term. It is clear that these kinds of outcomes require more complex and coordinated third-party activities than the field of conflict resolution has been able to develop and implement so far (2001: 3). In this regard many questions need to be addressed here: how strategic are these plans, given the challenges that persist, put in a peacebuilding perspective? Are the opportunities to address root causes, immediate consequences, and ongoing threats of war being seized? What are the unforeseen risks of re-emergence of conflict?

An Analysis of Labour Markets in Northern Uganda

Work is the poor's main source of earning. Understanding labour markets is essential to reduce poverty and ensure inclusive labor absorption and efficient development patterns. Improving labour market operations is also an important element of strategies to develop human capital, address gender discrimination, and enhance welfare and productivity. Labour market programmes take the form of both passive and active (Fretwell and Goldberg 1994). Active labour market programmes include: direct employment generation--promoting small and medium enterprises, public works, labour exchanges or employment services--job brokerage, counseling--linking supply with demand for labour, skills development programmes--training and retraining of labour. On the other side, passive labour market policies include: unemployment insurance and income support (Fretwell et al. 1998).

In the case of northern Uganda, there is a heavy presence of passive labour market programmes. This is best illustrated by the now familiar 'safety net and 'trampoline' metaphors for the passive approaches. Not only are trampolines more politically attractive but ALMPs also have a theoretical rationale in models of the labour market that incorporate asymmetric information and market failures associated with investments in human capital. It also makes sense at a conceptual level that these programs (specifically retraining) would have heightened importance as technological change increases both skill requirements and the pace of obsolescence. However, as the experience of the past 10 years or so has demonstrated, actually implementing an active labour market policy poses many challenges including the unemployability of earnings of participants in the entire economy.

The ability to work is the only asset of many of the worlds poor. Work can provide individuals with income to meet material needs, reduce social isolation, and impart a sense of dignity and self-worth. By creating opportunities for such work, efficient labour markets directly contribute to poverty reduction. Sound labour market policies and programs help workers manage risks associated with unemployment, lost income, and poor working conditions. Furthermore, in allocating labour to its most efficient use in the economy and encouraging employment and human capital investment, well-functioning labour markets can contribute to economic growth and development standards

Analysis of the labour markets in northern Uganda is very important especially for the rehabilitation and rebuilding of the northern region. Human resource is crucial in the rebuilding and development of this region. The role played by and labour markets in spurring development and reconstruction needs no recount. The northern Uganda is facing big challenges of the labour markets because there are so many young people who cannot find employment and employment opportunities are becoming fewer and fewer (IOM 2009). The nature of the labour force is also a big challenge as it is composed of people who have passed through the trauma of war (former abductees, ex-combatants, PLWDs, women, and youth) and others who have missed the opportunities for skills development. What is more challenging is that investment level is still very low due to several bottlenecks like land availability, attitude, and absence of requisite infrastructure.

Poverty is closely linked with the inadequacy of productive employment opportunities. Through employment, people earn incomes that help them purchase commodities necessary to meet their basic needs. Northern Uganda has been the scene of a mass population movement out of traditional villages and into highly congested, disease-ridden, and poorly managed displacement camps. This movement, prompted by the violent conflict between the LRA and the government army, the Uganda People's Defense Forces (UPDF), has left the countryside of northern Uganda barren. Raids, population movement, and access restrictions have destroyed the livestock and agriculture on which the traditional economy was based. People's ability to earn adequate incomes to pay for education, health care, and household necessities and to expand business activities has become severely constrained. As a result, the population has become reliant on donor aid. As stated earlier, the northern Uganda economy was largely based on agriculture. With large-scale displacement spanning over a decade, this is no longer the case, and until recently, production has been very low. Statistics show the large-scale effect the conflict has had on crop cultivation. Regarding the effect of the conflict on economic activities, complete stoppage of cultivation was rated at 81%, while grievous harm and theft of livestock followed with a rating of 12.5% (IA 2008). Although agriculture is still the main occupation for most people, the character of involvement is different from before the war and reflects a collapsed rural economy. There are more people selling agricultural labour (14.2%) compared to before the conflict (3.5%), as demonstrated in the table below.

Table 1. Status of Labour as June 2008

Changes in occupations/employment	Gender of respondent			
	Male (%)		Female (%)	
	current	Before conflict	Current	Before conflict
Agriculture (crops)	47	49.4	36.7	54.4
Agriculture (livestock)	5.2	20.1	1.2	21.6
Self-employed (trading/brewing)	16.1	12.8	29.5	16.4
Not working (dependent)	13.0	7.7	13.8	4.4
Agriculture (sale of labour)	12.7	4.8	15.5	2.3
Employed (salaried)	1.8	0.7	1.9	0.6
Self-employed (t/port	4.1	2.7	1.2	0.3

/vocations)				
Total	100	100	100	100

Source: *Investing in Peace, Issue 1 2008*

Gender disaggregation between men and women involved in the sale of agricultural labour points to more men 4.8% selling labour, compared to 2.8% for women before the conflict. However, after the conflict, more women 15.5% are involved in sale of agricultural labour compared to 12.7% men engaged in the practice. The role of livestock as a source of livelihood has drastically declined as the numbers dwindled. Livestock as an income option in rural agrarian economies represents a level of growth and transformation that translates into lesser income vulnerability. Sale of agricultural labour, on the other hand, represents a hand-to-mouth situation or a weak base from which to move economically. This is against the backdrop of more than doubled unemployment, 13.5% from 5%, (IA 2008), and again the rate is higher among women than men, which points to the gendered nature of the conflict.

The conflict has also led to the emergence of new productive enterprise and adoption of emergency coping strategies. Petty trade and boda-boda (motor cycle taxis) are prominent. However, such strategies are yet to overtake agriculture as the major source of livelihood. It is important to note that the population in northern Uganda is mainly youth. The 2007 Northern Uganda Livelihood Study notes that 'the population of northern Uganda is a young population. The median age for women is 14 years and 13 for men. The majority of the young population has no experience or many memories of rural life'. Accordingly, recovery, reconstruction, and stabilisation need to be cognizant of the residual conflict dynamics of Northern Uganda. Amongst the 900 000 people that have returned home or closer to their home communities, there are high densities of ex-combatants and other stressor groups, young people all looking, competing, and sometimes fighting for the same few jobs. This means that perceived fairness of development practitioners will be a determining factor in re-integration and stability in the region.

298

More so, the disability-poverty nexus is another issue that should be taken into serious consideration when looking at labour, economic reconfiguration and the whole framework of rehabilitation. Seventy-two percent of all the disabled persons in northern Uganda are living under conditions of chronic poverty (Annan 2008). The most recent approximation of disability prevalence rates in Uganda sits at 7.1%, or approximately 2.1 million people, but the consensus is that this percentage ration is far higher in the north because of the detrimental effects of the war. Systematic mutilation and chopping off of limbs, ears, noses, and lips was a common practice of the LRA at the height of the insurgency. A study carried out by the international organisation for migration in may 2009 in Amuru, Gulu Kitgum, and Pader noted that over 32% of producers and business people were not in favour of employing physically disabled people. Unfortunately, vulnerable populations receive supply-driven, one-off support without consideration of market demand or systemic constrictions on economic activity. Hundreds of formerly abducted children, for instance, have received training in three particular skills (tailoring, carpentry, and brick-making), but the dumping of all these semiskilled labourers into already contracted markets risks reducing economic opportunities for existing workers.

It is imperative to point out that while some trained graduates are able to use the skills they have learnt to earn an income, many continue to seek NGO support after their courses have finished. There is a lot of disconnect between training programmes for the youth and subsequent employment or income generation across the region. Even after training and receiving a starter kit (in the case of tailoring, a sewing machine), many have found themselves unable to formulate viable businesses because of the market saturation, capital access difficulties and personal conflict-related vulnerabilities such as trauma. The resultant effect is that there is a high number of trained but unemployed youth, many of whom are ex-combatants and or former abductees. This is not only a socioeconomic hazard, but a security one too. Others who have never been abducted present themselves to NGOs as falling into this category in order to receive assistance, further exemplifying the problem with vulnerability targeting. This is a coping mechanism developed in conscious response to an aid environment that reduces people's incentive to be productive: benefits are seen to accrue from weakness and vulnerability, as defined by NGO programmes, rather than from hard work.

To mitigate the above effects, price guarantees, market-oriented inputs, and access to market information are particularly important to farmers who are otherwise cut off from the market and forced to rely upon middle-men, who often purchase at below-market prices. Farmers working in groups should be able to stimulate old systems of community support and what is known locally as *kalulu*, or labour exchanges (working as rotational groups on plots of land belonging to individual members of the group). However, land fights and other related disputes are cropping up on a more frequent basis. These are particularly acute in Acholiland, where large-scale returnees have got under way, as long-term displacement has erased traditional land boundaries and weakened traditional structures of land negotiation and adjudication. (Ssebina-Ziwa et al. 2008).

Central attention ought to be given to small-scale interventions that can grow over time through market linkages. Building such links helps to support the regeneration of the economy and motivates individuals to become more productive. The assumption is that certain skills and resources are required for an economy to function: access to credit, the ability to manage earned income, a tradable or marketable skill, demand for such skills or products, and supportive government regulations. This strategy must be implemented through village savings and loan schemes (VSLSs), opening up land for agricultural production in cooperation with the military, the government and local landowners, providing business training and linking farmers with guaranteed markets in the private sector. All of these activities must target the community at large, be demand-driven, and propose alternatives to traditional emergency-style economic support. In essence, gaining sustainable employment and a reliable income must be at the forefront of the northern Uganda rehabilitation efforts. Training must support, not surpass, this goal.

Labour Markets, Ex-War Combatants, and Reconfiguration in Northern Uganda

This treatment focuses on the demobilization of troops, their initial reinsertion into civilian life, and their long-term reintegration as productive members of the society. Issues pertaining to assembly and discharge, reinsertion, and reintegration are discussed herein. The process of disarmament, demobilisation, and reintegration (DDR) of former combatants plays a critical role in war-to-peace transitions. The processes have become an important part of peacekeeping operations and postconflict reconstruction activities. Their success or failure can affect the long-term peace prospects for postconflict areas. As witnessed in the outset of DDR programmes in the Nicaraguan experience, political choices that do not take into account a proper integration of ex-combatants can lead to resumption of hostilities. Under the new government elected in 1990, the 'contras' were marginalised by a new ruling business class. The soldiers who were dismissed from the Sandista army without any concrete offer of integration reorganised themselves into new armed groups and joined the war again[5].

DDR programmes therefore must take the issue of ex-combatants at the forefront of their agenda. DDR can be viewed as a five-stage process of weapons surrender, assembly, discharge, short-to medium-term reinsertion and long-term integration. It is important to note that these processes may not occur in a linear fashion, depending on the specific needs of each peace process. From a normative perspective, reintegration is viewed as any form of assistance given to ex-combatants to enable them settle into civil society. Consequently, reintegration is economic, political and social in nature. It must therefore include medium to long-term programmes, including cash compensation, training, or income generation to enhance the potential for economic and social integration of ex-combatants and their families into society. Reintegration must feed into the wider social and economic development framework of the region. Successful reintegration depends largely on how much short-term concerns about security and political instability are not only addressed but also effectively reconciled with the long-terms social and economic development reconstruction strategies. Notwithstanding the increased importance of DDR, there are big challenges for implementing the program.

Existing DDR Efforts in Northern Uganda

In Uganda, understanding abduction experiences is important in order to understand reintegration. This is because, numerically, virtually all LRA recruits were forcible ones, especially those abducted after 1995. The abduction focused mainly on youths aged 9-15 and this mainly happened as a result of a demographic boom in the populations of young adolescents at that age. More so, the LRA reasoned that youths that age were more likely to be indoctrinated and fear escape. Given that the majority of the LRA recruits were forced abductees, the disarmament and reintegration measures so far have been somewhat incidental to the post conflict process so far. Efforts have mainly focused on the 'R' (reintegration) in DDR, mainly because most returnees headed straight to the villages or into IDP camps without necessarily reporting to the authorities first. Even for those who report, the main focus is put on interrogating them about LRA Intel and then handing them over to an NGO reception center. The reception centers offer the principal instrument of reintegration. These are run alternately by international and local NGOs, which receive formerly abducted youth upon return. Communities and families have also sought to aid reintegration, often through Christian cleansing ceremonies.

Traditional cleansing ceremonies are also performed by elders to cleanse the youth of *Cen*, or evil spirits, and elders appease the spirits through cleansing ceremonies. The collective understanding of *Cen* is that it is spread from one person to another, polluting a family or community. This has serious social implications for a youth with emotional problems like nightmares, since the family may be frightened of mixing with him or her.

The government role in reintegration has been modest, although expanding. From a legal perspective, the government has given amnesty to the former rebels, through the Amnesty Commission, with the exemption of the top LRA leadership. By 1995, the Amnesty Commission started giving out reinsertion packages to returnees, including former abductees. These included substantial cash payments and household items. With financial support and technical assistance from the World Bank through the Multicountry Demobilisation and Reintegration Programme (MDRP) by August 2006, the Amnesty

Commission had provided reintegration support to over 20 000 returnees. It is important to note that the integration of ex-combatants in communities cannot happen without taking into concern the need of those communities too (Kumar1997). The government in this case implemented the Northern Uganda Social Action Fund, NUSAF as a multisectoral initiative to uplift the communities of northern Uganda from chronic poverty.

Under NUSAF, communities were able to apply for funding for community initiatives. These included vocational training, agricultural extension, and micro-enterprise development. It is important to note that NUSAF had the largest provision of a youth reintegration component aimed at promoting employment among vulnerable youth. However, just as was witnessed in postwar Mozambique, training in vocational skills has not yielded employment (Nicole-Ball 1997) and many semiskilled youth have remained unemployed, which raises another question of frustration, which is a recipe for instability.

The main objective of reintegration is to restore ex-combatants to the lives they had before they joined the war, but due to continuing security concerns, this has not been possible since the ex-combatants, who are mostly children, are taken into IDP camps rather than being returned to their home villages. This therefore raises concerns over whether the aims and objectives of reintegration are being addressed at all. Effective DDR programmes must provide specific programmes for the most vulnerable groups of ex-combatants. Child soldiers are one such a group, especially in poor countries, where they are usually enrolled in armed groups involved in internal conflict. However, child soldiers are often neglected and are not able to benefit from DDR programmes that do not take their special vulnerability into account. Child soldiers, having grown up within an armed group and having been exposed to atrocities since a very young age, are often the most difficult ex-combatants to reintegrate into society. Lessons learned from past DDR experiences suggest that child soldiers are best served when they are separated from other ex-combatants, so that their special needs can be addressed and so they can avoid abuse by military authorities, who may force them to enroll in new military forces. In the case of northern Uganda, the issue of children poses an ideological dilemma, since most of the ex-combatants are mainly children of 10-17 years; the question thus arises of whether they must be treated merely as ex-combatants, and therefore be reintegrated as such, or as children, so as to receive child focused interventions.

Moreover, interventions especially in the economic arena have often generalised and made unrealistic assumptions. In northern Uganda, the ex-combatants received pangas and seeds as part of the reintegration package; since the region's major economic activity is agriculture. The policy, however, was misguided because most ex-combatants who are actually child soldiers have very little or no experience in agriculture. Many of them ended up selling or simply eating the seeds. As a result, this produced household diseconomies of scale and consequently, new individual and collective vulnerabilities (Simonetta, Guistozzi, 2006). The Afghan experience offers a more realistic approach, where ex-combatants were given the option of choosing reintegration packages depending on their needs. In conclusion, DDR requires strong technical and political inputs and an appreciation of the political environment where it is undertaken. In particular it is essential to assess whether the necessary conditions are present. Ideally, the political and social context should be assessed to determine when and how to give the necessary assistance. The success of any integration process depends highly on whether the intended beneficiaries view it as meaningful or not.

Concluding Remarks

This paper attempted to analyse social protection and economic reconfiguration in postconflict northern Uganda. It also tried to present a picture of how the economy and labour markets have changed or reconfigured during and after the conflict and how this affects the economy and economic structures of the region. Finally postconflict rehabilitation processes and policies were traced. Some conclusions emerged from this analysis: On the causes of the civil war, it could be claimed that it was a result of several factors, including but not limited to: grievances suffered by the northern tribes, the feeling of marginalisation under the southerners-led NRM government; the colonial legacy of mainly recruiting northerners into the armed forces and therefore ignoring production; and the seeking of political power by groups like the Holy Spirit Movement and Lord's Resistance Army. These factors created and prolonged the war until 2006. With respect to economic reconfiguration and labour markets, we can observe:

I.   The emergence of war generals profiteering from the conflict and loss of control of the government over most of the resources in the region. This affected mainly the agricultural sector and reduced government revenues.

II.   Regarding the rural economy, trends included labour shortage. Land-shortage claims are brewing especially in Acholiland, mainly because of the return of ex-combatants and internally displaced persons to their home villages. Moreover, there is an important diversification in rural employment, with new activities especially in retail trade, vocational skills, and services such as transport. The demographic characteristics of the population have also changed a lot with mainly youth and children remaining. This trend has led to greater poverty, unemployment, and informality in urban areas. It has also increased demand on public infrastructure and education to adapt the population and labour force to new economic structure.

III.   As Ballentine and Nitschke (2005) note, relevant to peacebuilding is the transformation of war economies to peace economies. In this sense, one of the goals is to change the structure of incentives of ex-combatants. The causes of war could be related to structural factors such as inequality, poverty, and historical and political factors. Therefore, the transformation of war economies should include both tackling the structural causes of violence and introducing policies to change the war economy structure.

On Social Protection, We Can Note That:

i.   There has been an influx of international and local nongovernmental organisations trying to either exploit or address the challenges of people in the postwar era. Many children-, youth-, and women-focused NGOs have moved into the area, many claiming to focus on protection and postwar rehabilitation.

ii. The government has also implemented a number of policies mainly funded by international organisations in a bid to address the regional imbalances between the north and the rest of the country, especially to reduce poverty and vulnerability.

References

Annan, J, C. Blattman, K. Carlson, and D. Muzuranan. 2008. *The state of female youth in Northern Uganda*. SWAY-Uganda available at http://chrisblattman.com/documents/policy/sway/SWAY.Phase2.FinalReport.pdf.

Allen, T. 2006. 'Northern Uganda Revisited: A review article'. *Africa* 76 (3): 427-36.

Atkinson, R.R. 1994. *The roots of Ethnicity: The origins of the Acholi of Uganda before 1800*. Kampala: Kampala Fountain Publishers.

Ball, N. 1997. 'Demobilizing and reintegrating soldiers: Lessons from Africa'. In: *Rebuilding Societies*, edited by K. Kumar, pp. 85-105. Boulder, Colorado: Lynne Rienner Publishers.

Ball, N. and L. van de Goor. 2006. *Disarmament, demobilization and reintegration. Mapping issues, dilemmas and guiding principles*. Clengendeal, The Netherlands.

Ballentine, K. and H. Nitzschke. 2005. 'The political economy of civil war and conflict transformation'. Berghof Research Center for Constructive Conflict Management. http://www.berghof-handbook.net

———. 2005. 'Why they fight: An alternative view on the political economy of civil war and conflict transformation'. Berghof Research Center for Constructive Conflict Management. http://www.berghof-handbook.net

Blattermann C., J. Annan and R. Horton. 2006. 'The state of the youth and youth protection in northern Uganda. Findings from a survey of affected youths'. UNICEF, Uganda.

Blattermann C., and J. Annan. 2008. 'Child combatants in northern Uganda: Reintegration myths and realities'. In: *Security and post-conflict reconstruction, dealing with fighters in the aftermath of war*, edited by R.Muggah, pp. 103-26. London: Routledge.

Branch, A. 2005. 'Neither peace nor justice: Political violence and the peasantry in northern Uganda, 1986-1998'. *African Studies Quarterly* 8 (2): 1-31.

Brück, T. 'Determinants of rural poverty in post-war Mozambique: Evidence from a household survey and implications for government and donor policy (March 2001)'. Queen Elizabeth - House Working Paper 67. http://ssrn.com/abstract=267680 or doi:10.2139/ssrn.267680.

Cassen R. 1994. *Does aid work?* Oxford: Oxford University Press.

Castillo. G, and E. S. Phelps. 2007. *The right way to rebuild Georgia: A window on Russia*. Project Syndicate Ideas.

Cooper, N. 2002. 'State collapse as business: The role of conflict trade and the emerging control agenda'. *Development and Change* 33 (5): 935-55.

Cornwall, R. 1999. 'The collapse of the African state'. In: *Peace, profit or plunder? The privatisation of security in war-torn African societies,* edited by Jakkie Cilliers and Peggy Mason. Pretoria: Institute for Security Studies.

Cowen, T., and C. J. Coyne. 2005. 'Postwar reconstruction: Some insights from public choice and institutional economics'. *Constitutional Political Economy* 16: 31-48.

Cramer, C. 2002. [Homo economicus goes to war: Methodological individualism, rational choice and the political economy of war'.*World Development* 30 (11): 1845-64.

Cramer, C. 2006. *Civil war is not a stupid thing: Violence in developing countries*. London: C Hurst & Co Publishers Ltd.

Dolan C. 2005. 'Understanding war and its continuation: A Case of northern Uganda'. Unpublished dissertation. University of London.

Dolan, C., and L. Hill. 2006. 'Humanitarian protection in Uganda: A Trojan horse?' HPG Background paper, ODI.

Evans, M. 2009. 'Post-war reconstruction, international policy transfer and the World Bank: The case of community-driven development'. Paper presented at the annual meeting of the ISA's 50th Annual Convention 'Exploring the Past, Anticipating the Future'. New York, New York, 15 February 2009.

Fischer, R. 2001. 'Methods of third party intervention'. Berghof Research Center for Constructive Conflict Management. http://www.berghof-handbook.net.

Fretwell, D. and S. Goldberg. 1994. 'Developing effective employment services in "Equity, Efficiency and Adjustment in Labor Markets"'. World Bank. Discussion Paper 208.

Fretwell, D., J. Benus, and C. J. O'Leary. 1998. *Evaluating the impact of active labor programs: Results of cross country studies in Europe and Central Asia.* World Bank. SP Discussion Paper - no. 9915.

Ghossa, L. 2003. 'From Humanitarian Protection to social Protection'. In: *Jobs after war: a critical challenge in the peace and reconstruction puzzle*, edited by Eugenia Date-Bah. Geneva: ILO Publications.

GoU. 2007. *Peace recovery and development plan for northern Uganda'. PRDP 2007-2010.* Office of the Prime Minister.

Holzman, R. and S. Jogensen. 2000. 'Social risk management: A new framework for social protection and beyond'. World Bank discussion paper.

ILO. 2007. 'Defining institutions and policies for equitable and flexible labour markets'. Technical paper, Asian Employment Forum: Growth Employment and Decent Work, Beijing, 13-15 August.

International Alert. 2008. *Building a Peace Economy in Northern Uganda.* Issue Number 1

International Organization of Migration. 2009. *Labour market analysis in northern Uganda.* Kampala: IOM Publications.

Jorgensen, S. and J. van Domelen. 2000. 'Helping the poor manage risk better: The role of social funds'. In: Shielding the poor-social protection in the developing world, edited by N. Lustig. Brookings.

Keen, D. 1998. *The economic functions of violence in civil wars.* Adelphi Paper 320. Oxford: Oxford University Press.

Kisekka-Ntale, F. 2007. 'Roots of the conflict in northern Uganda'. *International Journal of Politics and Economics Studies* 32 (4): 421-52.

Kumar, Krishna. 1997. *Rebuilding Societies after Civil War. Critical roles for international assistance*. Boulder, CO: Lynee Rienner Publishers.

Lamwaka C. 2002. "The Peace process in northern Uganda 1986-1998", in L. Okello (ed.), *Protracted Conflict, Elusive Peace: Initiatives to End the Violence in Northern Uganda*. London: *Conciliation Resources and Kacoke Madit.*

Landau, L. 1998. 'Rebuilding the Mozambique economy: Country assistance review'. Washington, DC: World Bank Operations Evaluation Department.

Le Billon, P. 2000. 'The political economy of war: What relief agencies need to know'. Humanitarian Policy Network Paper 33. London: ODI.

Paris, Roland. 2004. *at war's end: Building peace after civil conflict.* Cambridge: Cambridge University Press.

Paul. D. 2007. "Fulfilling the forgotten promise. The protection of civilians in northern Uganda". *InterAction*, January 2006: 34-51.

Rupesighe, Kumar. 1989. *Conflict resolution in Uganda*. OSLO: IPRI.

Sebina-Zziwa, A. et al. 2008. *Emerging Land Related Disputes in Northern Uganda*. Kampala: Makerere Institite of Social Research.

Suhrke, A. and A, Strand. 2005. 'The logic of conflictual peacebuilding'. In: *After the conflict: Reconstruction and development in the aftermath of war*, edited by Sultan Barakat. Pp. 141054... London: I.B. Tauris.

UNDP. 2007. 'The Uganda human development report'. United Nations Development Programme. Uganda Country Office, Kampala, Uganda.

USAID. 2008. 'Value chains: Towards integrating conflict sensitive approaches'. The 2004 Human Development Report. United - Nations. http://cfapp2.undp.org/hdr/ statistics/data/rc_select.cfmi (Accessed 1 July 2010).

---

[1] Fredrick Kisekka-Ntale, PhD, is a Research Fellow at the Makerere University Institute of Social Research (MISR), Makerere University. fkisekka@misr.mak.ac.u g or kisekkantale@yahoo.com.

[2] The UNDP and the ILO agreed to step up their collaboration in the framework of UN reform. To that effect a joint meeting was held on 18 and 19 January 2007 between ILO Director-General Juan Somavía and UNDP Administrator Kemal

Dervis and the regional directors of both institutions. Both executive heads agreed that closer collaboration could only reinforce the role of each institution in giving effect to the July 2006 ECOSOC Ministerial Declaration calling on the whole multilateral system to mainstream full and productive employment and decent work for all in their policies, programmes and activities. The meeting, held at UNDP New York on 18 and 19 January 2007, agreed to a ten-point programme of work for the 2007-08 periods. This included, among others, postconflict employment creation, income generation and reintegration.

[3] A report released by the Civil Society Organizations for Peace in Northern Uganda (CSOPNU) in 2006 revealed that the death rate was three times that of Iraq's during the onset of war in 2003. The report titled 'Counting the cost: 20 years of war in northern Uganda' observed that the death rate for northern Uganda was at 146 deaths per week, which is 0.17 violent deaths per 10 000 people per day. In Iraq, the death toll was estimated to be 0.052 per 10 000 people per day in 2003.

[4] Former United Nations Under Secretary for Humanitarian Affairs Jan Egeland visited northern Uganda in 2003 and spent a night in one of the Internally Displaced Peoples' Camps. He made these remarks after a fact-finding mission regarding the situation in northern Uganda.

[5] Scenarios similar to Sandista have been elucidated at length by Ball (1997) in her study of demobilising and reintegrating soldiers in Africa.

CHAPTER 10

The Monarchy, Land Contests, and Conflict
In Post-Colonial Swaziland

Hamilton Sipho Simelane

Introduction

Conflicts have been a common occurrence in Africa irrespective of the historical period under review. The magnitude of armed conflict increased in the 1950s and the 1980s, but declined sharply after the Cold War ended in 1991 (Vlassenroot and Huggins 2005). For most of the 1990s, conflicts have oscillated between escalation and de-escalation. Even a casual view indicates that there has been an upsurge in the occurrence of conflicts from the last years of the twentieth century into the first decade of the twenty-first century. The costs of conflict are huge not only in terms of loss of human life, but also in terms of a negative effect on the economies of the affected countries or regions, such that there is a suggested strong correlation between conflict and poverty (Mazrui and Tidy 1984; Prosser 1988).

The study of conflict in Africa cannot be divorced from the study of economic development because the continent has experienced different forms of conflicts; all with devastating effects on production and reproduction processes of the society's concerned (Chazan et al. 1988). These conflicts and the dislocations accompanying them have motivated both regional and international communities to create management institutions and structures and also deal with postconflict restructuring. Much as conflict is endemic in Africa, it is certainly not unique to Africa. The spatial distribution of conflicts includes regions in Latin America and South East Asia, and South Asia. Just as the occurrence of conflicts is experienced in most regions of the world, the issue of their origins and causes remains a contested terrain.

If origins and causes of conflicts are contested, the same can be said about conceptualising conflicts. J.H. McEnery has argued that a conflict 'is a necessary element in all human contact and that it is a requirement for creative progress as well as a cause of destructive disruption' (McEnery 1985: 37). This is a provocative conceptualisation, considering the lives lost and the destitution that

311

have occurred as a result of conflict in human history. A more nuanced conceptualization is provided by Jackson, who views conflict as a social construct that derives from existing perceptions (Jackson 1989). A conflict is a socially constructed reality reinforced and maintained by a variety of institutions and socio-political mechanisms. Conflicts develop because of perceptions of incompatibility of values and goals. Such perceptions are driven by a process of conflict articulation in order for that conflict to develop and assume a particular form.

Theoretically, there has been tension between event and process theories in the analysis of conflict. According to event theory, conflict is an occurrence at a specific time synonymous with an eruption without an element of cumulative causation. On the other hand, process theory recognises the interrelationship of developments that cumulatively result in conflict. The strength of this theory is that it provides a broader framework for understanding the dynamics that result in conflict. It also provides more space for realising that even after a resolution has been agreed upon, tension will not be immediately eliminated.

A study of conflict is further made complex by challenges concerning why conflicts occur. Again here, there is a huge variation on the explanatory tools employed. These range from macropolitics and economics of deprivation to levels of poverty at the micro-level. While several scholars have explained the occurrence of conflicts in terms of ethnicity, inequality, regionalism, subnationalism, and others, historicism has dominated the explanations. This derives from a conscious belief that history determines social events and that there is an organic succession of developments that culminate in conflict. Probably borrowing from this theory, Edith Natukunda-Togboa in her analysis of the conflict in northern Uganda points out that the 'roots of conflict are traced to colonial distortions that created a potentially explosive north-south divide' (Natukunda-Togboa 2008: 66). Coming from the same theoretical approach, Anand Mohan in a discussion of the Kashmir conflict argues that history provides the best explanation for understanding why the conflict occurred (Mohan 1992). The same approach is adopted by Robert Miller in his analysis of the conflict in Cambodia (Miller 1990). While historicism is employed in this paper as an analytical tool to understand the origins of conflict, we remain alert to the fact that too much belief in historical determinism can be problematic.

The analysis of conflict in Swaziland is informed by the above conceptual and theoretical approaches. The paper analyses a conflict that took place in 2000 involving a decision made by King Mswati III and the regional chiefs of kaMkhweli and Macetjeni chiefdoms located in the central eastern part of the country. The paper conceptualises the conflict as a constructed process based on a desire by the monarchy to maintain effective political control over the two chiefdoms through land. It argues that this conflict was a struggle for land as a resource and as an instrument of political control, constructed by the Swazi monarchy. Because of the nature of the governance system in Swaziland, the conflict was not between the central government and local government, nor was it a struggle between traditionalism and modernity. It was about power and control of land as a means of production.

Consequently, the conceptual framework of the paper revolves around a political economy approach that creates a discourse on dialectic between materialistic and superstructure construction of conflict. Central to this political economy approach is the concept of historical materialism. This is an approach to social scientific enquiry that highlights the fact that human developments should be analysed in terms of the patterns of production and general economic activity. Accordingly, members of society engage in conflict because they are in specific relations of production that condition the manner in which they relate to resources such as land. The materialist thesis is useful in understanding why the Swazi king was resolute to dispossess chiefs of their territories, and why the chiefs and their subjects were resolute in defending their territories. Historical materialism focuses our attention to the fact that a territorial conflict analysed outside of its materialist context fails to bring out peoples' struggles for production and reproduction.

The Political Economy of Land Control in Swaziland

One of the major questions that can be asked on our analysis of the conflict in Swaziland is: why the centrality of land? The answer to this question is simple and it is that the relationship between land and conflict has long been recognised because access to land, either as a productive resource, speculative investment, or a source of collateral for credit has been one of the currencies of power (Vlassenroot and Huggins 2005). Internationally, it has been observed that land dispossession is a common cause of population displacement and violent conflict (Deininger 2003). According to USAID, land tenure insecurity is one of the major causes of conflict (USAID 2004).

The Macetjeni and kaMkhweli conflict cannot be understood without an analysis of the historical dynamics of land ownership in Swaziland. Land ownership was at the centre of the conflict, and it is one of the most contested resources in the history of Swaziland. The struggle for land in Swaziland began during the formation of the Swazi state and continued during the second half of the nineteenth century when Western imperialism unleashed both British and Afrikaner settlers who acquired numerous land concessions during the reign of King Mbandzenil (Mashasha 1977; Scutt 1966). This resulted in the existence of concessionary land occupied by white settlers who were desirous of developing themselves as capitalist farmers, and land occupied by indigenous Swazi who continued to pursue precapitalist forms of production (Bonner 1983). Land ownership and occupation during the last two decades of the century became complex issues that resulted in serious tensions between the white settlers and the indigenous population. What complicated the issues was that the concessions overlapped and sometimes went three or four times deep. It was only at the end of the first decade of the twentieth century that attempts were made to disentangle what had come to be called the land question in Swaziland. This happened after the British had declared Swaziland their protectorate on the strength of their victory in the Anglo-Boer War of 1899-1902.

In 1907, the British established the Concessions Partition Proclamation, which paved the way for a process of clarifying the land question by evaluating all the available claims on land. Through this proclamation George Grey was appointed as Special Commissioner. When Grey completed his work in 1909, Swaziland was divided into land owned by the British crown known as Crown Land (CL), Individual Tenure Farms (TF) owned by white settlers under a freehold system and land left for occupation by the Swazi population designated as Swazi Nation Land (SNL). According to this division, about two-thirds of the land in the country was allocated to white settlers and the British crown, with only one-third remaining for Swazi occupation (Hailey 1953; Crush 1980; and Youe 1986). This left more than 20 000 Swazi peasants landless, while the rest were congested in thirty-two reserves created by the partition process. This form of primitive accumulation created a lot of tension between the white settlers and the colonial government, on the one hand, and the indigenous Swazi, on the other, who felt that they had been robbed of their land. The Swazi continued to protest against the partition and the British were forced to revise the partition structure at different times during the colonial period (Simelane 1991). The struggle for land between the settlers and the Swazi continued even after independence. It was the control of Swazi Nation Land (besides tradition) that gave power to the monarchy and to chiefs.

The contest for land between the Swazi and the settlers was based on the value of land as a resource for self-reproduction and accumulation. The Swazi side of the struggle was not always centred on peasants in the rural areas, but included traditional chiefs who were political heads in all Swazi-occupied areas. Swazi traditional chieftaincy derives its strength from its control of all Swazi Nation Land. Some scholars have noted that 'the allocation of land, the settlement of land disputes, and related questions are under the authority of the king's appointed chiefs' (Libby 1987: 156-57). From precolonial times to the independence era, chiefs enjoyed the power to allocate homestead and arable cropland to individual Swazi homesteads and the economic fortunes of households revolve around access to land. As a prerequisite for obtaining land, each individual household head must swear allegiance to the king and his chief. The power to allocate homestead land was inextricably interwoven with the exercise of political control over their subjects. Chiefs have the power to evict any subject who for any reason has been deemed not required in the area. Such power has created a lot of consternation in both the colonial and postcolonial periods when some subjects were evicted because they were too progressive for the chief's liking. The centrality of land in Swazi politics has produced hierarchies of control from the household to the national level.

The struggle for land also contained and still contains a very important economic aspect relevant to all agrarian economies. Throughout the colonial period, and for most parts of the postcolonial period, economic production hinged on access and control over land. Household heads nominally controlled family landholdings and the produce from the land (Booth 1986). Economic affluence was partly judged by agricultural surpluses that integrated households into exchange systems culminating into higher levels of accumulation. Even for chiefs, control over land meant control of the produce of the land, which came in a variety of ways. This became a basis for the appropriation of surplus, as relations were defined by the performance of certain obligatory services. The performance of these services was based on some kind of politico-legal compulsion enshrined in Swazi tradition. The forms of surplus extraction included some kind of labour rent, or *corvée* (reminiscent of feudalism), which came in the form of obligations for all subjects to till, hoe, and harvest the king's or chief's fields on command. Subjects were, and still are, also required to perform other chores in the king's or chief's place.

Another form of surplus extraction was, and still is, some kind of rent in kind, or what under feudalism was called *quit rent*, comprising different forms of tribute payment. This came in the form of different tributes of farm produce. The monopoly of control over land as a dominant mode of production combined with the imposition of different forms of obligatory services ensured the exploitation of the subjects and accumulation by the king and chiefs. The relations produce a very unstable social formation in which there is a huge potential for conflict between the subjects and chiefs, subjects and king, and chiefs and king.

The attainment of political independence changed the composition of the contenders over land, but the substance of the contest remained the same. The majority of the white settlers did not leave with the proconsuls at independence, so their land interests were still valid. Major changes occurred on the Swazi side of the contest through fragmentation and emergence of conflicting interests. The monarchy and chiefs were still there, but colonialism, which had united their interests, was no longer there, so their interests over land control tended to diverge. A new player came into the picture in the form of the petit bourgeoisie that desired to accumulate land as a means to capital accumulation (Simelane 1992). However, the kaMkhweli and Macetjeni conflict was between the monarchy and the regional chiefs of the territories with no involvement of the petit bourgeoisie except as secret supporters of one contender or the other. As it has been shown above, the contest that resulted in the conflict is long-drawn, as it derives from the desire of the monarchy and regional chiefs to control land as a dominant source of wealth and power. Most important, in the Macetjeni and kaMkhweli case, the monarchy was tampering with a well-established system of land allocation whereby 'for centuries land has been obtained not by ownership but by use and allegiance to the king through his chiefs' (*Mail and Guardian*, 27 Oct.-2 Nov. 2000). However, from early in the colonial period, Swazi peasants demonstrated their hunger for land and willingness to struggle for accessing it. For instance, a few years after independence, it was reported that Swazi peasants were invading private farms and occupying them by force (Simelane 1997). The matter became so serious that it was progressing to anarchy and King Sobhuza II was forced to warn peasants against such action:

> Makhosini has reported to me that in some areas the Swazi have entered into private farms by force. Some have refused to move out. They claim that they are now independent and they should have their land back. He tells me that the Cabinet is not sure what to do. On the issue of land it is not for individuals to stubbornly decide whenever they want and say they will take the land or they will not move. The land issue is for all of us to discuss. The people who are taking land by force have been deceived by others. You can do this and claim you have succeeded when in fact you have put yourself into big trouble. (King Sobhuza II, 1976)

Macetjeni and Kamkhweli Conflict

Swaziland is a potentially very unstable small country, as it has numerous dynamics that can result in an open conflict at any time. For instance, the country is made up of numerous clans and the larger ones are already asserting their autonomy from the dominating Dlamini clan. Also, the problem of uneven development between the four regions of the country has produced cracks in the unity of the country. The less-developed regions such as Shiselweni have become very critical of resource allocation by the central government. The region continues to be a migrant-sending region to the central region, which is at the same time the seat of power for the monarchy and traditional leadership. Poverty continues to be a source of tension, as it is estimated that about 70% of the Swazi population lives below the poverty line (*Swazi Observer*, 7 July 2009). It is also estimated that about 10% of the Swazi population consumes above 50% of the national income. Swaziland is therefore a country of huge inequalities that could be a source of conflict. However, the major open conflict that has taken place in the country has been the result of a struggle over land. This conflict hit at the heart of royal absolutism in Swaziland. As Nomthetho Simelane stated, 'There is a lot of empathy for the monarch in this country, even among the progressives. But if monarchical powers are used to control resources to the extent of deciding who gets what, then the whole institution has degenerated' (quoted in *Daily Mail and Guardian*, 10 Nov. 2000).

Macetjeni and kaMkhweli are adjacent chiefdoms located in the central-eastern part of the country. From the time of King Sobhuza II, the chiefs of the areas enjoyed power to distribute land to households already resident and also to individuals who followed the tradition *kukhonta* system. The chief's also exercised political power over all residents of the chiefdoms as allowed and dictated by Swazi law and custom. The positions of the chiefs and their authority in these territories were recognised by king Sobhuza II, as they were installed as chiefs in accordance with Swazi law and custom. Their power to distribute land amongst their followers gave them an opportunity to play an important role in the processes of economic reproduction and accumulation. For both political and economic reasons, the chiefs safeguarded the relative autonomy of their chiefdoms. As custodians of the land in the chiefdoms, they had to guard against encroachment from neighbouring chiefdoms. This is especially the case because the boundaries of the chiefdoms have not been clearly demarcated.

The conflict that eventually erupted in these two chiefdoms came when King Mswati III made a ruling that Chief Mtfuso Dlamini of kaMkhweli and Chief Mliba Fakudze of Macetjeni should relinquish their authority over their chiefdoms, and hand over chieftaincy to his elder half-brother Prince Maguga. According to Mswati III, before his father, King Sobhuza II, died in 1982, he had signed a document declaring that Mtfuso and Mliba were not the rightful chiefs of the two areas, and that instead his elder son Maguga was the rightful chief of both Macetjeni and kaMkweli. The royal version of the story is that both Macetjeni and kaMkweli were given to Maguga's mother from the Mngomezulu clan of Ngwavuma in northern Zululand as *liphakelo* (inheritance). As Lamngomezulu's heir, Maguga was said to be the rightful chief of the area. King Mswati III argued that he was implementing a decision made by his father, King Sobhuza II. It became a source of concern for many that this matter was not publicly raised by King Sobhuza during his lifetime. Second, the issue of double chieftaincy had not occurred before in recorded Swazi history. The matter became a serious national issue, as King Mswati III's action was interpreted by some as a deliberate attempt to transfer land and power to the royal family and therefore strengthen monarchical control over rural communities. The action was seen as hegemonistic territorialism, with most regional chiefs feeling vulnerable to possibilities of extended land grabbing by the monarchy. Some civil society groups argued that this was part of a larger agenda by the monarchy to centralise both political and economic power at the expense of regional chiefs and rural communities.

King Mswati III's decision met with resistance from the two chiefs. They argued that they were installed as chiefs in accordance with Swazi law and custom. According to statements by the chiefs, at no point were they ever told that they were under the authority of Prince Maguga. For about ten years, the conflict was at a tension stage whereby the two chiefs were refusing to give up control over the two territories and accept Prince Maguga as chief. It must be noted that the resistance of the two chiefs was no indication of a shift from traditionalism. It was a conflict within the traditionalist camp over land as a means of production. The two chiefs were supported by the majority of their subjects, but there were some who felt that Prince Maguga should be accepted as chief of the two areas because the instruction came from the king. For many residents of the two territories, the king's decision was tantamount to deprivation and a compromise of the economic interests of the communities concerned. That view arose from the concern that if Prince Maguga were to take over the territories, he would allocate land to his supporters and displace those who had been occupying and utilizing the land for generations. For them, resistance was an attempt to preserve their pieces of land from which they produced different commodities for domestic consumption and for sale to the wider market. The economic aspects of the conflict were made more serious by the fact that the two chiefdoms are located in one of the best cotton producing belts in the central-eastern part of the country. Most of the farmers in these areas therefore are cash crop producers to whom access to land was principal and disruption of such access, as threatened by a Maguga take over, would culminate in numerous economic and social dislocations.

As the tension between the monarchy and the two regional chiefs continued, the two territories became economically and politically unstable. It was the common people who carried the brunt of the tension, as they found it difficult to bring the land under the plough because their future in the chiefdoms was not certain. Both chiefdoms experienced widespread economic difficulties, since most families were affected by food shortages while many fields lay fallow. At the same time, Prince Maguga was telling the residents of the chiefdoms that their salvation was in accepting him as chief of the two areas.

The final crunch came in July 2000, when King Mswati III instructed his brother, the Minister of Home Affairs, Prince Sobandla to evict Chief Mliba Fakudze, his brother Madeli Fakudze, and their dependents from Macetjeni. The minister was also instructed to evict Chief Mtfuso Dlamini and his dependents from kaMkhwel. Chief Mliba was ordered to go and settle at Sihlutse in the Shiselweni region, while his brother Madeli was ordered to go and settle at Lundiyaneni under chief Makutwane (*Times of Swaziland SUNDAY,* 6 Aug. 2000). Chief Mtfuso was ordered to go and settle at Ngcoseni. The people who were evicted were directed to go to settle in territories they had no connection to and they were required to be subjects of the chiefs of the areas. When the eviction order was issued, the chiefs and their subjects declared that they were not going to comply.

When the monarchy intensified pressure for the chiefs to leave the territories, Chief Mliba of Macetjeni in collaboration with chief Mtfuso of kaMkweli applied to the Swaziland High Court for a stay of execution of the order and a High Court order was issued stating that the two chiefs should be allowed to see King Mswati III before they were removed from their areas. This appears to have been a very naïve judgment because the eviction order had been signed by the king. While the High Court Order was effective, the monarchy decided to send a royal delegation to Macetjeni and kaMkweli to convince the two chiefs and their dependents to leave their chiefdoms. The delegation was accompanied by police and army personnel. The chiefs were interrogated as to why they were refusing to comply with the eviction order. The chiefs and residents were accused of disturbing peace in the area through their action of being 'thickheaded' (*Times of Swaziland*, 13 Sept. 2000). Chief Mliba responded by saying that 'they would not leave the area until they met the King as per the High Court Order' (*Times of Swaziland*, 13 Sept. 2000). At this point, the conflict was approaching boiling point as threats of violence were becoming commonplace. For instance, the Swaziland Association of Students (SAS) issued a threat to burn down Prince Maguga's home at Macetjeni (*Times of Swaziland*, 14 Sept. 2000). The main result of such threats was the militarisation of both Macetjeni and kaMkweli territories. Police and army camps were established in the territories and the peace that characterised the two chiefdoms before the build up of tension was gone.

The country was thrown into a rule of law crisis when King Mswati III overturned the interim High Court Order. The Attorney General told Chief Justice Stanley Sapire:

> I have today, that is Thursday 5 October, 2000, consulted with His Majesty, King Mswati III, and the King of Swaziland. His Majesty confirmed to me that he, in his capacity as Ngwenyama considered the application of each of the applicants for the review of the removal orders, which are subject of the application and has, after due consideration of all the circumstances, come to the conclusion that he can not set aside such removal orders. His Majesty impressed upon me that in considering the applicant's said application for review of the removal orders he acted with due regard to and in accordance with Swazi law and custom. (Quoted in *Swazi News*, 7 Oct. 2000)

After this pronouncement it became clear that the monarchy was gearing for a violent attack of Macetjeni and kaMkweli and the people would be forcefully removed. Government trucks were assembled at Matsapha Police Training College and Government bulldozers were driven to the two territories to demolish homes (*Times of Swaziland*, 14 Oct. 2000). Police officers, soldiers, and prison warders who were on leave were called back to assist in the attack against the two territories (Ibid.). The intensive military preparations were in anticipation of armed resistance from the residents of the chiefdoms. The attack was affected just before midnight in both territories as the police and the army invaded the chiefdoms forcefully evicting over two hundred families from Macetjeni and an almost equal number from kaMkweli. The people were bundled into army vehicles and dumped in different parts of the country in the middle of the night. However, the police and the army failed to capture the chiefs of the two territories.

This was a period of human displacement of a magnitude never seen in the history of postcolonial Swaziland. More than 400 people became refugees as the monarchy through Prince Maguga removed them from the land of their birthright. The condition of these refugees was very desperate, as indicated by one of them: 'If death is something to be wished, it is now that I want it. The king should have ordered us to be killed than let me suffer like this. I have been treated worse than a dog by the police and one of them would not permit me to eat' (quoted in *Times of Swaziland*, 21 Oct. 2000).

For fear of their lives the two chiefs went into hiding. For some days there was confusion concerning their whereabouts. It was after some days that it was learnt that they had skipped the country into South Africa as refugees. They took their families with them together with some of their supporters. It was revealed that they were in Secunda in South Africa in the second home of Prince Alfred Maseko of Mpumalanga. Both chiefs applied for asylum in South Africa (*Times of Swaziland*, 19 Oct. 2000).

The eviction was a traumatic experience for the people of Macetjeni and kaMkhweli. The residents were treated as objects with no rights and they were degraded to the level of wild animals. Those who were not bundled into army or police trucks fled into forests staying there for some days to allow the tide of violence to subside. This trauma was well portrayed by the experience of Lindiwe Fakudze, who was forced to give birth to a baby girl in the forest four days after the invasion of Macetjeni by the police and soldiers (*Times of Swaziland*, 4 Dec. 2000).

Children of Macetjeni and kaMkhweli were some of the most negatively affected victims of the conflict. The Save the Children Fund (SCF) and Baphalali Swaziland Red Cross estimated that about eighty schoolgoing children were affected by the evictions (*Times of Swaziland*, 19 Jan. 2001). These were children who were uprooted toward the end of the 2000 school year and could not continue with their education. They were rounded up together with their parents and dumped in different parts of the country (*Times of Swaziland,* 17 Oct. 2000). This included children who were due to write their final national examinations at the end of the year. Some of the children did not sit for their final examinations because of intimidation. According to one report:

> The most affected students are those who attend school at the heart of the chieftaincy disputes. At Gilgali Primary school situated between the homesteads of chief Mliba and Prince Maguga, there are 27 students one of them being a daughter of the former. At the High School there were only two students affected. KaMkhweli primary schools situated next to chief Mtfuso's residence is another hard hit institution as 13 were 'packed' with their parents. (Ibid.)

These children were traumatised, and rumour circulated to the effect that the police and soldiers would not allow them to sit for their examinations (*Times of Swaziland,* 23 Jan. 2001). When the following school year was about to begin, it was discovered that these students had no support system to continue with their education because their parents were not in a position to pay for their education. At Ngcoseni, where some of the refugees were dumped, about 33 children needed money to go back to school. These children were under the guidance of some adults who were not gainfully employed (*Times of Swaziland,* 19 Jan. 2001). The children became the responsibility of NGOs such as the Red Cross and SCF. The NGOs were not able to provide for all the students, due to limited funds. A member of one NGO reported:

> We have not been able to raise any money for the students. Right now, they have been admitted in some schools but there is no money to pay for them. The teachers understand the situation. They have allowed the students in while we try to raise the money. We had not anticipated that we would come across some problems; we have started raising the money earlier. (*Times of Swaziland,* 31 Jan. 2001)

While NGOs were busy trying to put resources together to make sure that the young victims of eviction went to school, the Swazi state completely neglected these children. Some commentators called these students the 'victims of state thuggery' (*Times of Swaziland,* 31 Feb. 2001).

Child destitution was a characteristic feature of the height of Macetjeni and kaMkhweli conflict. Immediately after the evictions, social and economic dislocations that affected children negatively were manifested. In Macetjeni, over 20 children were destitute (*Times of Swaziland*, 23 Oct. 2001). Some of the children began to drift into the city of Manzini, increasing the ranks of the destitute. They moved into townships such as Ngwane Park in Manzini after they were forced out of their homes (*Times of Swaziland*, 3 Feb. 2001). According to reports:

> Eight of the children who were displaced during the joint armed forces operation in Macetjeni have been identified and are staying in certain homes in the city. The children are so traumatized that they are afraid of anyone trying to reach them. Efforts…to interview them were unsuccessful because they locked themselves inside their houses and refused to open to any one. They also refused to talk through the closed doors (*Times of Swaziland SUNDAY*, 26 Nov. 2000).

Even in the areas where the children were dumped together with their parents, they lived under difficult conditions characterised by deprivation. They could not get adequate food in the camps and there was no clothing for them. There was no proper accommodation and they continued to live in tents provided by some NGOs. There were also no prospects for school for these children as they were completely isolated; having not yet integrated into the communities they were forced to live in. In an attempted to mobilise help for the destitute children in the camps, one commentator said, 'We believe it is not the children's fault to be where they are. And as people who believe in peace and justice we therefore appeal to all those who believe in such a cause to join hands by making these children's lives pleasant as they would have been in their original homes' (quoted in *Times of Swaziland*, 4 Jan. 2001).

Child destitution was complicated by dislocations in agricultural production. Both Macetjeni and kaMkhweli are agriculture-based economies whose reproduction is dependent on putting land under the plough. At the time of the evictions, many households could not engage in agricultural production. Most households were reduced to beggars as against food producers. The situation became even worse when the NGOs that took the responsibility to support them became thin on funds. For a full season before the evictions, some households were already experiencing acute food shortages because they could not plough their fields because of the move by the monarchy to take over their fields through Prince Maguga (Ibid.). Those who remained with some children of evicted families could not bring the fields of the evictees under the plough because the state had ruled that those fields should not be brought under the plough. These families were overwhelmed by the number of children they had to take care of.

Eviction and Protest

The eviction of the chiefs of Macetjeni and kaMkhweli and a large number of their subjects shook all segments of the Swazi population. One commentator said, 'The kingdom of Swaziland has been wracked by an unprecedented bout of public protest after the eviction of two chiefs that cuts to the heart of a social compact that ties Swazis together' (*Mail and Guardian*, 27 Oct.-2 Nov. 2000). This was the first conflict of its magnitude to occur since the country achieved its independence from the British in 1968. It was also the first time that the police and the army were used to mete out high-scale brutality against citizens who were not armed. Surprisingly, the international community had very little to say about this conflict and its aftermath. However, inside Swaziland voices of protest came from numerous and diverse social formations. By this time the conflict was a configuration of different forces. For instance, those interested in the democratic transformation of the country took advantage of the conflict to protest against the governance system. Because of the involvement of such groups, the conflict assumed the shape of traditionalism versus forces of change and transformation. However, this was misleading because the actual protagonists were all traditionalists.

Organised labour was at the forefront of the protests against the eviction and police and army brutality. The Swaziland National Association of Teachers (SNAT), the Swaziland Federation of Trade Unions (SFTU), and other organisations came out to condemn the evictions and the violence perpetrated by the armed forces. The first action of protest by organised labour was a decision to march and deliver a petition to the prime minister and the king (*Times of Swaziland*, 19 Oct. 2000). The petition was complaining about the violence against the people of Macetjeni and kaMkhweli and the dislocation caused by the eviction. In the petition to the king, organized labour

325

[a]dvised the king that such actions [evictions] were infringing the rights of the people of this country and in breach of the United Nations declaration on human rights to which Swaziland is signatory. They also warned the King that such actions would result in a civil war in the country and should be addressed as a matter of urgency. (*Times of Swaziland*, 19 Oct. 2000)

There were over 1 000 marchers to deliver the petition, but they were met with brutality from the country's armed forces. They were beaten and teargassed, and rubber bullets were used against them (*Times of Swaziland*, 25 Oct. 2000). At least fourteen teachers and students were injured in the confrontation (*Times of Swaziland*, 23 Oct. 2000). After this use of violence against the marchers, the teachers association resolved to organise another mass march to deliver the petition to the king. This time the state responded by banning the march and threatened further brutality against those who would participate. The state moved further to ban all mass gatherings in the country especially those called by the Swaziland National Association of Teachers and the Swaziland Federation of Trade Unions. This was an attempt to frustrate the protests against the Macetjeni and kaMkhweli evictions. The Swaziland Federation of Labour (SFL) came out criticizing state action. Its secretary-general said:

Indeed it would have been better if there was a court order in this regard rather than an administrative order which has all the hallmarks of interfering in the affairs of these organizations as they meet to discuss matters of interest to their constituencies. A court order would atleast have had the possibility of being the outcome of a test by an imperial body. As the protests ring wide and loud we wait to hear what explanations will be brought forth to explain the action. (*Times of Swaziland*, 30 Oct. 2000)

The SFTU called the banning of meetings "a barbaric act" (Ibid.). Its secretary-general, Jan Sithole, said:

It is unfortunate that the erosion of human rights in this country is happening in spite of the fact that Swaziland has ratified the UN charter for human rights, the African charter for people's rights, the Windhoek Declaration and several human rights related conventions. It is true that as long as we are ruled by decree we become incongruent with social justice and the laws are the 1973 decree, the 1998 Swaziland Administration Order, the non-Bailable Offences law and the 1996 law that establishes the fattening ranches of SNCSC, and the Constitutional Review Commission (CRC). (Ibid.)

On the other end, SNAT was contemplating taking legal action against the Government of Swaziland. At this point, tension engulfed the whole country as the possibility of a civil war appeared on the horizon.

Frustrated by the different forms of repression that were imposed by the state, SNAT decided to hold its mass meeting in Nelspruit, Mpumalanga, South Africa. Although this mass meeting was initiated by SNAT, other organisations, such as the nurses association, civil servants, and other workers, joined forces with SNAT. The mass meeting was hosted by the Congress of South African Trade Unions (COSATU). Although most of the presentations in the meeting degenerated to political rhetoric, a major resolution was that the Swazi state should be pushed to reinstate the evicted people.

University and college students were also fully involved in the protests against the evictions. Over 2 000 students from the University of Swaziland and William Pitcher College took to the streets in protest against the evictions. They resolved to march to the king's palace to deliver a petition calling upon the king to reverse the eviction order and allow the evicted people of Macetjeni and kaMkweli to return to their homes. They condemned Prince Maguga as being power-hungry and declared, 'Evictors are killers' (*Times of Swaziland*, 20 Oct. 2000). They demanded to deliver the petition directly to the king and be addressed by him. This did not happen and the students were given an ultimatum by the armed forces to disperse within 15 minutes and they complied. However, the students continued with their protests in their campuses and refused to go to class. Amidst continued protests and non-class attendance, the University of Swaziland was closed indefinitely on 22 October 2000, and William Pitcher College suffered the same fate (*Times of Swaziland*, 23 Oct. 2000). The closure of the institutions killed student protests and their voice was not heard again in the protests. The leadership of the institutions was used by the state to quell student protest over the Macetjeni and kaMkhweli evictions.

The most interesting protest against the eviction came from women of Macetjeni. They requested an appointment with Prince Maguga for 29 November 2000 to offer him gifts (*Times of Swaziland*, 28 Nov. 2000). One of the women who spoke to the media before the gifts were offered stated, 'We will be meeting Prince Maguga on Wednesday to present him with some gifts in appreciation of what he has done to us. I can not disclose the gifts to you now but I want to tell you that all eMakhosikati (wives to chiefs) from the Fakudze household will go there and present the gifts to him' (Ibid.). The women argued that their presentation of gifts to Prince Maguga was in accordance with Swazi tradition, which allows an individual to thank a chief even if what he has done is not acceptable.

The women made sure that both the print and electronic media were there. Prince Maguga appears to have gladly allowed the women to come to his place, probably because he thought they had come to their 'senses' and were accepting his authority. On the day of the gifts, about 50 women assembled at the gate of Prince Maguga's house, but they were prevented by the police from entering the premises. While at the gate, the women lifted their skirts and dresses to their shoulders, all with no underwear except one, and they showed their bare buttocks and private parts (*The Swazi News*, 2 Dec. 2000). When they were questioned, they said they came to present Prince Maguga with bad luck (*kumhlolela*) following his failure to adhere to people's call and that they do not want him as their chief (*Times of Swaziland*, 7 Dec. 2000). This action provoked different reactions from different segments of the Swazi population. For some, such action was an embarrassment to King Mswati III and the whole nation in the international community. They called upon the state to discipline the women together with their husbands, who allowed them to engage in such action. The women were subjected to police interrogation, but it became very difficult to press charges, as the women argued that they were using tradition to protest against the take-over of their land by Prince Maguga.

The interrogation of the women and the subjection to threats by police was actually hypocritical on the part of the monarchy. This was not the first time for women to individually or collectively bare their buttocks in protest against certain actions by national leaders. In the nineteenth century, one of the king's wives, Somnjalose Simelane, climbed to the top of a traditional house and raised her dress to her chest, baring her buttocks and private parts in protest against the actions of the then king (Matsebula 1972). In the 1960s when the British were delaying the granting of independence to the Swazi, women went to the offices of the colonial government to bare their buttocks and private parts before colonial officials. Even then, it was known to be a sign of protest by women who had no strength to fight their enemies except to expose their bodies in disgust. They were showing their dissatisfaction with the decision made by the king to use Maguga to take over their land. The baring of buttocks was a sign of rejection.

While protest by organised labour spread throughout the country, it failed to bring about change in Macetjeni and kaMkhweli. The monarchy was not moved and stuck to its guns in terms of the evictions. Protest by organised labour had a lot of promise, but fell short of bringing about justice and reverse land-grabbing by King Mswati III through Prince Maguga. The residents of these areas were forced to accept Maguga as chief and those who were refugees in South Africa were allowed to return only if they accepted Prince Maguga as chief. Prince Maguga was imposed as chief of Macetjeni and kaMkhweli in spite of all the protests, but did not live long to enjoy the fruits of primitive accumulation.

Conclusion

Swaziland is one of the countries in Southern Africa that has numerous preconditions for conflict. However, for most of the postcolonial period the country has experienced relative peace and stability. It is important to note that such peace and stability has always and still is superficial because very little has been done to manage possible sources of conflict. Conflicts that have occurred in Swaziland after independence have not caught the attention of the international community, possibly because they were small in scale and did not result in high loss of life. This paper has shown that Swaziland is not free of conflict and that the lives of a large number of people have been disturbed resulting in numerous dislocation as a result of conflict.

The colonial and postcolonial history of the country has shown that territoriality based on chiefly, clan, or individual ownership of land has been a source of tension in different parts of the country. Such tension and eventual conflict has not been simply an issue of territorial aggrandizement but a materialistic concern over land as a means of production. Land has been contested by different groups and classes at different times. The conflict between the monarchy and the chiefs and residents of Macetjeni and kaMkhweli shows the extent to which the

Swazi monarchy can go to concentrate land as a resource and a source of power in the hands of members of the royal family. It also shows the extent to which regional chiefs and their subjects can go to protect the land that has ensured their reproduction from generation to generation. To the residents of Macetjeni and kaMkhweli, the conflict was a struggle for economic survival.

The paper has shown that the Macetjeni and kaMkhweli conflict had a very significant political element. This arises from the fact that in Swaziland, land is also a political tool used to control the subject population. Through power over allocation of homestead land and fields for agricultural purposes, both the king and chiefs exercise political control over the rural population. Land is held by the king in trust for the Swazi nation and this gives the king and chiefs the power of coercion over those who occupy the land.

The Macetjeni and kaMkhweli conflict did not result in deaths directly from the violence perpetrated by the monarchy. Few lives were lost as a result of the dislocations that resulted from the conflict. The paper has shown that the conflict, especially the eviction of the chiefs and their supporters, resulted in unprecedented trauma that completely changed the lives of those involved. It resulted in both internal and external refugees as some people were dumped in different parts of the country away from their traditional homes, while others fled the country to seek refuge in neigbouring South Africa. This was the first time such dislocations had taken place in post-colonial Swaziland.

After the evictions the whole country was filled with conflict as different segments of the Swazi population were engaged in protest. Labour organisations, student groups, and other civil organisations stood up in protest in favour of the evicted. This was a major development in the political history of Swaziland, as the country was on the brink of a civil war. However, in spite of all the protests, King Mswati III refused to reverse the evictions, and he eventually won the day. His refusal to hear the voices of protest has much to do with the fact that Swaziland is an absolute monarchy: what the king wants, the king gets.

One of the most significant aspects of the Swaziland conflict is that no genuine resolution mechanism was put in place. The residents of Macetjeni and kaMkhweli were forced to accept Prince Maguga as chief of both areas and the concerns of the residents were not addressed. Those who fled to South Africa were allowed to come back only if they accepted Maguga as their chief. Technically therefore, the Macetjeni and kaMkwheli conflict remains a simmering volcano that may erupt at any time. The situation becomes bleak if the lessons from this conflict are considered. The conflict highlighted the vulnerability of regional chiefs as far their control over land is concerned. It also highlighted the vulnerability of Swazi rural dwellers in terms of land ownership and occupancy. As long as the system of land tenure gives sweeping powers to the king, as long as the king enjoy unquestionable powers of dispossessing and the rural dwellers have no rights over land, then the future of 70% of the Swazi population remains on the balance.

The Swaziland case discussed above depicts the country's specific dynamics of land control and distribution and their relevance to the generation of conflict, but also relates to regional and continental issues relating land. The issue of land control remains a crucial theme in the processes of production and reproduction and is bound to be a source of conflict for many countries. This is particularly the case because the majority of African countries have predominantly agriculture base economies. It appears that the strategics to minimise conflict over land should be accompanied by comprehensive land reform and redistribution that does not give some groups or individuals power over others.

References

Bonner, Philip. 1983. *Kings, commoners and concessionaires: The evolution and dissolution of the nineteenth century Swazi state.* Johannesburg: Ravan Press.

Booth, Alan. 1986. 'Homestead and migrant labour in colonial Swaziland'. In: *Historical perspectives on the political economy of Swaziland: Selected articles*, edited by John Daniel and Michael Stephen. SSRU, University of Swaziland.

Chazan, Naomi, Robert Mortimer, John Ravenhill, and Donald Rothchild. 1988.

Politics and society in contemporary Africa. Boulder, Colorado: Lynne Rienner.

Crush, Jonathan. 1980. 'The colonial division of space: The significance of the Swaziland Land Partition'. *The International Journal of African Historical Studies* 13: 71-87.

Dininger, K. 2003. *Land policies for growth and poverty.* Washington, DC: World Bank/Oxford University Press.

Hailey, Lord. 1953. *Native administration in the British African Territories, Part V, The High Commission Territories, Basutoland, the Bechuanaland Protectorate, and Swaziland.* London: HMSO.

Jackson, William D. 1989. 'The construction of conflicts'. *Conflict* Vol. 9.

Lewis, D. 2004. "Challenges to sustainable peace: Land disputes following conflict;. Paper presented at a symposium on land administration in postconflict areas, 29-30 April, Geneva.

Libby, Ronald T. 1982. *The politics of economic power in Southern Africa.* Princeton: Princeton University Press.

King Sobhuza II. 1997. Speech to the Swazi Nation. Swaziland.

Mazrui, A.A. and M. Tidy. 1984. *Nationalism and new states in Africa.* London: Heinemann.

Mahon, Anand. 1992. 'The historical roots of the Cashmir conflict'. *Studies in Conflict and Terrorism* Vol. 15, Issue 4: 283-308.

Mashasha, Francis J. 1977. *The road to colonialism: Concessions and collapse of Swazi independence, 1875-1926.* Oxford: Oxford University Press.

Matsebula, J.S.M. 1972. *A history of Swaziland.* London: Macmillan.

McEnery, J.H. 1985. 'Toward a new concept of conflict evaluation'. *Conflict:* 6 (1): 37-72.

Miller, R.H. 1990. 'Historical sources of conflict in South-East Asia: Cambodia at the vortex'. *Conflict: International Journal* 10: PAGES?

Natukunda-Togboa, E. 2008. 'From the language of conflict to that of peace-building: The role of discourse in the conflict in northern Uganda'. *Africa Peace and Conflict Journal*, 1:1 (December): 65-80.

Prosser, Gifford and W.M. Roger Lewis, eds. 1988. *Decolonization and African independence: Transfer of power, 1960-1980.* New York: Yale University Press.

Scutt, J.F. 1966. *The story of Swaziland.* London: HMSO.

Simelane, Hamilton Sipho (1997). "The State, Sovereignty and Swaziland, s Future in the New Regionalism in Southern Africa". Paper presented at a Conference on Sovereignty, States and Southern Africa's Future-Towards New Answers to Old Questions, Maseru Lesotho, and 16-17 October, 1997.

Simelane, Hamilton Sipho. 1991. 'Landlessness and imperial response in Swaziland'.*Journal of Southern African Studies* Vol. 17, No. 4 (December): 717-741.

Simelane, Hamilton Sipho. 1992. 'The post-colonial state, class and the land question in Swaziland'. *Journal of Contepmorary Africa Studies* 11: 22-50.

USAID, Office for Conflict Management and Migration. 2004. *Land and conflict: A toolkit for intervention.* Washington, DC: USAID.

Vlassenroot, Koen and Chris Huggins. 2005. 'Land, migration and conflict in eastern DRC'. In: *From the ground up: Land rights, conflict and peace in sub-Saharan Africa,* edited by Chris Huggins and Jenny Clover. Pretoria: Institute for Security Studies.

Youe, C.P. 1986. 'Imperial land policy in Swaziland and the African response'. In: *Historical perspective on the political economy of Swaziland: Selected articles,* edited by John Daniel and Michael Stephen. SSRU, University of Swaziland.

NEWSPAPERS

Mail and Guardian
Mail and Guardian, 27 Nov. to 4 Nov. 2000.
Daily Mail & Guardian, 10 Nov. 2000.

Times of Swaziland
Times of Swaziland, 6 Aug. 2000.
Times of Swaziland, 13 Sept. 2000.
Times of Swaziland, 14 Sept. 2000.
Times of Swaziland, 14 Oct. 2000.
Times of Swaziland, 17 Oct. 2000.
Times of Swaziland, 19 Oct. 2000.
Times of Swaziland, 20 Oct. 2000.
Times of Swaziland, 21 Oct. 2000.
Times of Swaziland, 23 Oct. 2000.

Times of Swaziland, 25 Oct. 2000.
Times of Swaziland, 28 Oct. 2000.
Times of Swaziland, 30 Oct. 2000.
Times of Swaziland, 26 Nov. 2000.
Times of Swaziland, 4 December 2000.
Times of Swaziland, 7 Oct. 2000.
Times of Swaziland, 4 Jan. 2001.
Times of Swaziland, 19 Jan. 2001.
Times of Swaziland, 23 Jan. 2001.
Times of Swaziland, 3 Feb. 2001.
Times of Swaziland, 23 Oct. 2001.
Swazi News
Swazi News, 7 Oct. 2000.
Swazi News, 2 Dec. 2000.

CHAPTER 11

MOSOP and Rights Claims: Reflections on the Relative Deprivation Theory of Social Movements

David Lishilinimle Imbua

Introduction

With a population of over 500 000 inhabiting a total land area of 404 square miles in southeastern Nigeria, Ogoni is one of the most densely populated rural communities in the world. A community of farmers and fishermen, Ogoni was once considered the food basket of Rivers State of Nigeria. The land was considered sacred, and any act that polluted it was viewed as an abomination and promptly visited with appropriate sanctions. The Ogoni people saw themselves as custodians of the land, including the rivers and streams and all that dwelt in it. As a result of this, they went out of their way to protect and safeguard all these resources, knowing that their own survival, indeed, very existence, depended on the well-being of their environment (Okonta and Douglas 2001: 99-100).

The above situation changed following the advent of Shell in Nigeria, which in collaboration with its joint venture partners, the Nigerian National Petroleum Corporation (NNPC), Agip, and Elf, 'began to dig deep into the heart of Ogoni, tearing up farmlands and belching forth gas flames which pumped carbon monoxide and other dangerous gas into the lungs of my people.' (Saro-Wiwa 1996: 40). Ogoni activists saw environmental degradation, endemic poverty, primitive education and health facilities, and lack of electricity and running water in Ogoniland as an attempt at killing the goose that lays the golden egg. This development was against the people's expectation when Shell opened its first oil well in Ogoni near the village of Kegbara Dere in 1958. In one of his published accounts before his hanging on 10 November 1995, Ken Saro-Wiwa laments: 'In this most sophisticated and unconventional war, no bones are broken, no blood is spilled and no one is maimed. Yet, men, women, and children die; flora and fauna perish, the air and water are poisoned and finally, the land dies' (1995:148).

Indeed, Nnimmo Bassey captures the picture rather graphically, stating that 'nothing is allowed to stand in Shell's way: not trees, not swamps, not beast, not man.' Trapped between a vicious global corporation and a visionless government, the Ogoni at first took to the path of nonviolent protest in a bid to protect what little remained of their endangered environment and source of livelihood. It was the resolve to resist the insidious impact of Shell's oil exploration and production on the Ogoni that culminated in the formation of the Movement for the Survival of the Ogoni People (MOSOP).

Founded in August 1992 by the Ogoni people to campaign against ecological devastation and economic exploitation, MOSOP has the mandate to campaign nonviolently to promote development in the region; protect the cultural rights and practices of the Ogoni people; and seek appropriate rights to self-determination for the Ogoni people. With its motto as 'Freedom, Peace and Justice', MOSOP cut across clans, class, age, and traditional and Western beliefs. In Karl Maier's assessment, it represented the most cogent opposition force to a corrupt military dictatorship and uncaring transnational oil company. In his *in the shadow of a saint*, Ken Wiwa posits that 'everyone was getting involved in the movement-professionals, traditional rulers and priests, even unemployed and unemployable youths. Every Ogoni was in MOSOP because MOSOP was in every Ogoni, as the saying went' (Wiwa 2002: 22).

MOSOP initiated its effort with the Ogoni Bill of Rights, which was adopted on 26 August 1990 at the village of Bori, the traditional capital of the Ogoni people. The Ogoni Bill of Rights lists the concerns of the Ogoni people: oil-related suffering, governmental neglect, lack of social services, and political marginalisation. It was wide-ranging in its condemnation of Shell and the Nigerian establishment, declaring that 'the ethnic politics of successive federal and state governments are gradually pushing the Ogoni people to slavery and possible extinction.' A key claim of the 'Ogoni Bill of Rights' is that the Ogoni people have the inalienable right to use a fair proportion of Ogoni economic resource for Ogoni development. In their desire to revert what constituted abuse of rights, the Ogonis demanded autonomy, the right to control resources, direct representation 'as a right in all Nigerian institutions', promotion of Ogoni culture, and protection from environmental degradation.

MOSOP argued in its manifesto that the federal government of Nigeria had denied the Ogoni this right by giving Shell Petroleum Company license to exploit oil and gas in their area. The situation in which the Ogonis received much of the harm but few of the benefits from oil exploitation was not only excruciating, but resurrected memories of a lost era in which their land, streams, and mangrove swamps provided them sustenance. Saro-Wiwa told his people that Ogoni was so far down in the well and only shouting loudly could they be heard by those on the surface of the soil (Saro-Wiwa 1995: 76). MOSOP was therefore formed to execute the shouting and save Ogoni from a harsh plan of obliteration from the face of the earth.

This paper examines the various claims to, and demands for, rights by MOSOP as a social movement in the Niger Delta region of Nigeria. We do this with the consciousness that claims to rights are fundamental to the logic and coherence of social movements. We shall elaborate on the rights-social movement nexus by supporting the claim by relative deprivation theorists that 'where expectation does not meet attainment, the tendency is for people to confront those they hold responsible for frustrating their ambitions.' Before we examine MOSOP and rights claims, it is necessary to go back to history in order to understand where we are coming from. To this end, we begin by looking at MOSOP from a historical perspective.

MOSOP: Historical Insights

One recurrent phenomenon in the checkered history of the contemporary Niger Delta region of Nigeria is the unrelenting attempts by the people of the region to resist ecological vandalisation and economic exploitation. MOSOP emerged after 26 years of the fall of the Isaac Boro Movement, which aspired to create a state of the Niger Delta people in order to address the human and infrastructural development problems of the area. MOSOP was formed to demand for greater revenues from the oil pumped from the land of Ogoni, political autonomy, and an environment cleanup. The movement raised unsettling questions about the final destination of the hundreds of billions of dollars Nigeria had earned in oil revenues since becoming a world-class oil exporter (Maier2000: 76). As a revolutionary movement, MOSOP started on the premise of intellectual warfare through constructive criticism and dialogue by way of demands and protest against the exploitation of Ogoni land by Shell and the Nigeria government, which was described as 'sick and wicked' (Maier 2000: 77).

Saro-Wiwa, who initiated the idea of MOSOP, declared unequivocally that 'the Ogoni took stock of their condition and found that in spite of the stupendous oil and gas wealth of their land they were extremely poor, had no social amenities, that unemployment was running at over seventy per cent, and that they were powerless, as an ethnic minority in a collection of 100 million people, to do anything to alleviate their condition.' Maier argues that despite the proximity of the refinery, most gas stations in Ogoniland are usually closed for lack of fuel, and motorists have to drive into Port Harcourt to buy gasoline on the black market at five times the official price (2000: 79). Worse, their environment was completely devastated by decades of reckless oil exploitation or ecological warfare by Shell (Okonta and Douglas 2001: 147-48). It is in the light of this that Karl Maier argues in his fascinating study, *this house has fallen*, that 'Eleme's heartbeat could be seen in the giant flame, as big as a house, erupting from a flow station to the north of the road. The flame which, burns twenty-four hours a day, was a constant reminder that the resources of this area were being drained away' (2000: 79).

MOSOP, in its agitations for rights, threatened to disrupt the operations of the oil companies if they failed to come to terms with their demands. Its primary targets were the Nigerian Government and the oil company Royal Dutch Shell. Beginning in December 1992, the conflict between the Ogoni and the oil companies escalated to a level of greater seriousness and intensity on both sides than hitherto. Both parties began launching acts of violence against each other. MOSOP issued an ultimatum to the Oil companies (Shell, Chevron, and the Nigerian National Petroleum Corporation), demanding $10 billion in accumulated royalties, damages and compensation, and 'immediate stoppage of environmental degradation'. The ultimatum also demanded negotiations for mutual agreement on all future drillings. Over time, the activities of MOSOP gradually shifted from mere agitation to the use of violence in pushing for its cause, and in response to repression by the government. By mid 1994, bloody clashes between government troops stationed in Ogoni land and

MOSOP began to be recorded. Evidence at our disposal indicates that by June 1994, at least 30 villages had been touched as a result of violence in the area, and over 600 people detained by the government (Ihediwa 2008: 1213).

However, government acts of repression have failed to muzzle MOSOP, courtesy of the astute determination of the people to help bring about progress and social change in the region. Right from the onset, Saro-Wiwa urged his fellow Ogoni to study, conscientising and educating them about what MOSOP was really about-a movement for social and ecological justice, informed by the finest traditions of African participatory democracy and powered by the philosophy of nonviolence. Saro Wiwa boldly stated: 'MOSOP was intent on breaking new ground in the struggle for democracy and political, economic, social and environmental rights in Africa. We believe that mass-based, disciplined organizations can successfully re-vitalize moribund societies and that relying upon their ancient values, mores and cultures, such societies can successfully re-establish themselves as self-reliant communities and at the same time successfully and peacefully challenge tyrannical governments' (quoted in Okonta and Douglas 2001: 149-50).

It is clear from the foregoing that Saro-Wiwa's ultimate goal was a restructured Nigeria, functioning as a proper federation of equal ethnic groups and nations irrespective of size, with each being free to control its resources and environment and also to exercise its political right to rule itself according to its genius. This position was informed by the thought that if managed by their own people, the Ogoni resources would bring about peace, progress, and the good life to its inhabitants.

The failure of government to respond positively to the agitations of MOSOP made the organisation confrontational in its approach. This was what led to the emergence of various militant and intellectual factions from within MOSOP, including the militant National Youth Council of Ogoni People (NYCOP), the Federation of Ogoni Women Association (FOWA), Council of Traditional Rulers Association (COTRA), Ogoni Teachers Union (OTU), League of Ogoni People (LOOP), and Council of Ogoni Churches (COC). As MOSOP developed into different groups, hostilities increased phenomenally in the area by way of roadblocks, stoppage of oil companies from operation, boycott of any government programmes and activities, kidnapping, etc., which eventually led to the 'Ogoni Revolution', which witnessed the controversial killing of four prominent Ogoni leaders in 1994 (Sayeregha 2008: 496). The government attributed the killings to the leadership of MOSOP. Saro-Wiwa was arrested along with fourteen officials of MOSOP and charged with the murder of the four Ogoni prominent chiefs. The sequence of events that followed this incidence culminated in the trial and sentence to death of Saro-Wiwa by hanging. Wiwa's death did not mark the end of MOSOP. The movement is still vibrant in making its claims to rights. We will come to this issue later.

MOSOP and Resource Mobilisation

It is clear from the foregoing that there is a link between the frustrations or grievances of a collectivity of actors and the growth of Social Movements. Recently, a number of social scientists have begun to articulate an approach to social movements, here called the resource mobilisation approach, which begins to take seriously many of the questions that have concerned social movements' leaders and practical theorists. Social movements need organisations first and foremost. Organisations can acquire and then deploy resources to achieve their well-defined goals. Some versions of this theory see social movements operate similar to capitalist enterprises that make efficient use of available resources. These resources may include, but not limited to the following: material (money and physical capital); moral (solidarity, support for the movement's goals); social-organisation (organisational strategies, social networks, block recruitment; human (volunteers, staff, leaders) etc. A look, however briefly, at the aggregation of resources by MOSOP is crucial to the understanding and appreciation of the movement's activity.

Social movements are primarily based upon aggrieved populations that provide the necessary resources and labour. MOSOP is not an exception to this assertion. As we argued earlier, every Ogoni was in MOSOP and they were ready to make any sacrifice of resources that could restore their individual and collective pride. We read in Ken Wiwa's *in the shadow of the saint* that 'no one could opt out. The struggle was defining our people, giving Ogoni a renewed sense of purpose' (2002: 22). Impressed by the great amount of human resources made by the Ogoni, Ken Saro-Wiwa was compelled to declare without mincing words that 'the vast majority of the Ogoni have accepted the MOSOP idea and adversity has taught them to be courageous. It's wonderful that they have withstood all the brutality for so long and are still holding out' (Wiwa 2002: 133). MOSOP depended heavily upon volunteer labour and resources from its members. Without this determination and commitment, no planned action would have been possible. The significance of this grassroots support becomes obvious when we realize that 'at one level the resource mobilization task is primarily that of converting adherents into constituents and maintaining constituent involvement' (McCarthy and Zald, 1977: 155).

The readiness of the Ogoni to make MOSOP a successful social movement got the needed inspiration from Ken Saro-Wiwa's organiSational genius. A consummate publicist who had honed his craft writing novels, newspaper articles, and best-selling soap operas for the government-owned television network, Saro-Wiwa, in collaboration with other MOSOP leaders, had quietly embarked on a mass mobilisation of Ogoni men, women, and children shortly after the movement was launched (Okonta and Douglas 2001: 149). Okonta and Douglas assert further that such simple but ingenious innovations as the 'One Naira Ogoni Survival Fund', whereby all Ogoni people, young and old, were asked to contribute a token sum as an indication of commitment to the cause, and the formation of such pan-Ogoni organisations as the National Youth Council of Ogoni People (NYCOP), The Federation of Ogoni Women's Association (FOWA), the Conference of Ogoni Traditional Rulers (COTRA), the Council of Ogoni Churches (COC), the Ogoni Teachers Union (OTU), the National Union of Ogoni Students (NUOS), Ogoni Student Union (OSU), Ogoni Central Union (OCU), and the Council of Ogoni Professionals (COP), for which MOSOP served as an umbrella, ensured that the movement had a truly democratic, grassroots base (149). With this great skill in grassroots mobilisation, a great company of men, women, and children came to see MOSOP as 'a movement for social and ecological justice, informed by the finest traditions of African participatory democracy and powered by the philosophy of non-violence.'

It is important to mention at this point that the Ogoni are not the only people whose expectations have outgrown the actual material situation in the Niger-Delta in particular and Nigeria in general. The leadership of MOSOP was thus able to mobilise and got the sympathy and support of non-Ogoni Nigerians, majority of whose source of livelihood had equally been despoiled by oil companies. The movement strongly established reasons why Niger-Deltans should fight for change. It was through this same process that Ken Saro-Wiwa made the struggle a national one. Saro-Wiwa found sympathetic ears particularly among Nigerian journalists working in the independent press, where he was considered a member of the house. His talent for publicity was given free rein, and in a matter of months, MOSOP and the travails of the Ogoni people became a subject of debate all over the country. It is instructive to note that *The Guardian* newspaper published in its editorial of 18 July 1994 that 'for several weeks now exceedingly perturbing reports have been coming out of Ogoniland. Tales of military siege, tales of uniformed persons rampaging at night in the villages behind the veil of a delicate news blackout and in the confidence that the nation has far bigger worries at the moment.' It is not in doubt that most Nigerians came to see the Ogoni experience with the oil companies and the Nigerian government as a tragic story of exploitation, degradation, and underdevelopment. To such people, MOSOP was seen as a struggle for the soul of Nigeria and its future. Most Niger Deltans and other Nigerians deemed it unfortunate and annoying that after almost five decades of sending oil to refineries on America's East Coast as well as points in Europe and Asia the vast majority of local people of the region were living in abject poverty. Through the campaign programmes of Ken-Saro Wiwa, it was revealed that more gas was flared in Nigeria than anywhere else in the world. The flares were said to have contributed more greenhouse gasses than of sub-Saharan Africa combined. Even more disturbing was the revelation that the flares contained a cocktail of toxins that affected the health and livelihood of communities even beyond Ogoniland and the Niger Delta.

It is interesting to note that Ken Saro-Wiwa took his campaign to the international community. This was a novel experience in the Nigerian context. To all intents and purposes the international campaign can be reasonably adjudged a success in terms of the creation of international awareness about the Ogoni condition. In his capacity as spokesman of MOSOP, Saro-Wiwa traveled to The Hague in July 1992, where he registered the movement with the unrepresented Nations and Peoples Organization (UNPO). He also brought the suffering of his people to the attention of the United Nations Working Group on Indigenous Peoples in Geneva, and made useful contacts with international environment groups and business organizations such as the London-based Body Shop International, whose founder and chief executive, Anita Roddick, had long been involved in such campaigns as MOSOP was pushing in Nigeria. Saro-Wiwa also took MOSOP's message to the United Nations in New York, USA. The movement was accorded the much needed international attention after presenting its case. Thereafter, the MOSOP leader returned to Nigeria with endorsements from international environmental groups, such as Green Peace, to mobilise his people against degradation and underdevelopment.

The point we have tried to make in this necessarily sketchy section is that MOSOP's reputation as a novel phenomenon in Nigeria is more or less a tribute to its leaders' ability to mobilise available resources to accomplish the movement's aims. The awards that came to MOSOP and its leaders from both within and outside Nigeria translated into effective resource mobilisation.

Rights Claims and the Ogoni Uprising

It is clear from our discussion so far that MOSOP evolved as a right and justice-seeking social movement. In 1990, the Ogoni people formally organised themselves into a powerful bargaining group. They issued a series of demands in the form of a bill of rights. The bill contains twenty points and it is reproduced here verbatim as appendix 1 for the benefit of those who are yet to access it.

Copies of the bill were submitted to all appropriate quarters and published in several dailies. After two years of fruitless waiting for the Nigerian Government and multinational companies to come up with policies to address the issues raised in the bill, Saro-Wiwa's Movement for the Survival of the Ogoni People (MOSOP) was formed to reinforce the aims and objectives of the Ogoni Bill of Rights. Dr. Garrick Barrillee Leton and Ken Saro-Wiwa were president and public affairs officer, respectively. Acting on behalf of the Ogoni people, MOSOP issued, on 3 November 1992, a 30-day ultimatum to all the oil companies operating in Ogoni land-Shell, Chevron, and the NNPC--to pay back rents and royalties and also compensation for land devastated by oil exploration and production activities or quit (Okonta and Douglas, 2001: 148). The memorandum, addressed to Shell, contained the following demands:

a) $6 billion as unpaid royalties;
b) Immediate stoppage of environmental devastation of Ogoni land with particular reference to gas flaring at Yorla, Korokoro, and Bumu;
c) Burying of all high-pressure oil pipelines currently exposed in Ogoni;
d) Payment of $4 billion, being reparation for damages and compensation for environmental pollution; and
e) Dialogue between representatives of the community, Shell, and the Federal Government.

The three companies, like the government two years previously, ignored the demand. On 4 January 1993, 300 000 Ogoni men, women, and children took to the streets and staged a peaceful protest against Shell's ecological war and the government's continued denial of the Ogoni's right to self-determination and a fair share of their natural resources.The Ogoni people, Leton said in his speech at the rallies:

> [Have] woken up to find our lands devastated by agents of death called oil companies. Our atmosphere has been polluted, our lands degraded, our trees poisoned, so much so that our flora and fauna have virtually disappeared. We are asking for the restoration of our environment, we are asking for the basic necessities of life- water, electricity, and education; but above all we are asking for the right to self-determination so that we can be responsible for our resources and environment. (Kertzmann 1997: 5)

On his part, Saro Wiwa used the occasion to declare Shell persona non grata in Ogoniland, and called on other minority groups in the Delta to 'rise up now and fight for your rights' (Maier 2000: 94).

The demonstration was timed to coincide with the start of the United Nations Year of Indigenous Peoples. During the march, Saro-Wiwa declared that the Ogoni people in Rivers State publicly reassessed the bill of rights that they presented to President Babangida and the Nigerian Nation in October 1990. The bill reasserted Ogoni right to self-determination, and although this Bill of Rights was acknowledged by the presidency, nothing was done to effect the changes the Ogoni people wanted (Sayeregha 2008: 496).

MOSOP made a claim to the control and use of Ogoni economic resources for Ogoni development, adequate and direct representation as a right for Ogoni people in all Nigerian National institutions, and the right to protect the Ogoni environment and ecology from further degradation. Any action that negated any of these claims was seen and treated as an infringement on the inalienable rights of the people. Dispossessed of their traditional means of livelihood, an army of unemployed Ogoni youths, angry with a society that had cheated them were ready to fight for the realisation of the demands of the bill of rights. They were not to be deterred by any action of government in the struggle since government actions, as Dr. Olua Kamalu, a MOSOP vice president argued, were a deliberate arrangement to stop the Ogoni people demanding for their rights (Maier 2000: 101). The various rights claims made by MOSOP are best understood through an examination of the Relative Deprivation Theory of Social Movements, and to this we now turn attention.

The Relative Deprivation Theory of Social Movement: Some Reflections

The concept of social movement has been variously defined. As a type of group action, social movements are large informal groupings of individual and/or organisations focused on specific political or social issues; in other words, on carrying out, resisting, or undoing a social change. In his widely accepted definition, Sidney Tarrow defines a social movement as collective challenges (to elites, authorities, other groups or cultural codes) by people with common purposes and solidarity in sustained interaction with elites, opponents, and authorities. They are different from political parties and interest groups. Sociologists have developed several theories related to social movements. Some of the better known are: collective behaviour/collective action theory (1950s), relative deprivation theory (1960s), value-added theory (1960s), resource mobilisation (1970s), frame analysis theory (1980s), new social movement theory (1980s), and political process theory (1980s). Of all these theories, the relative deprivation theory which was widely employed in the social movement literature of the late 1960s and early 1970s is the most fulfilling in the understanding of the rights claims by MOSOP. The theory is still relevant in spite of the growing popularity of some never approaches.

Relative Deprivation Theory contends that social movements have their foundations among people who feel deprived of some good(s) or resource(s). Denton Morrison, one of the proponents of this theory, argues that individuals who are lacking some goods, services, or comfort are more likely to organise a social movement to improve (or defend) their conditions (1978: 202). The main assumption of this theory is that all humans have basic human needs that they seek to fulfill, and that the denial of these needs by other groups or individuals could affect them immediately or later, thereby leading to conflict. It is often emphasised that where expectation does not meet attainment, the tendency is for people to confront those they hold responsible for their suffering and lack. Ted Robert Gurr's relative deprivation thesis emphasises that 'the greater the discrepancy, however marginal, between what is sought and what seem attainable, the greater will be the chances that anger and violence will result' (Gurr 1970: 24).

In his *The Old Regime and the French Revolution (1955)*, Alexis de Tocqueville brought the 'rising expectations' argument into currency by noting that the strongholds of the French Revolution were precisely those regions in which the greatest improvements in the standard of living had occurred and by observing that any relaxation of an oppressive regime engenders expectations in the populace that further reforms are on the way. He opined that failure to deliver reforms renders the situation increasing intolerable to members of affected groups and pushed revolutionary fervour to the point of explosion. There could be no other explanation for the emergence of MOSOP that would be as fulfilling as the perception that achievements have failed to keep space with the general expectations of the people of Ogoni. They considered their communities to be in disadvantageous position, relative to some other groups who are in some case, non-oil-producing communities. This becomes understandable when it is realised that the central issue in relative deprivation is a perceived discrepancy between expectations and reality.

There is widespread agreement that the Ogoni are getting less than they deserve. The Ogoni Bill of Rights, which remains the torch light of the struggle of Niger Delta communities aptly, captures the people's feeling of deprivation as hereunder reflected:

> …the Ogoni languages of Gokana and Khana are underdeveloped and are about to disappear, whereas other Nigerian languages are being forced on us…(T) He Shell Petroleum Development Company of Nigeria Limited does not employ Ogoni people at a meaningful or any level at all, in defiance of the Federal government's regulations…(T) He search for oil has caused severe land and food shortages in Ogoni one of the most densely populated areas of African…Ogoni people lack education, health and other social facilities…it is intolerable that one of the richest areas of Nigeria should wallow in abject poverty and destitution (see *Bill of Rights*)

No one should therefore be surprised that the above tale of deprivation produces a fertile ground for the striving of MOSOP. If the oil companies and governments are surprised at the agitation of MOSOP, it is like beating a child and being surprised that he is crying. On this, Stephen A. Faleti argues that 'a situation where the legitimate desires of an individual is denied either directly or by the direct consequence of the way society is structured, the feeling of disappointment may lead such a person to express his anger through violence that will be directed at those he holds responsible or people who are directly or indirectly related to them' (Faleti, 2012: 48).

The discovery of oil brought much hope and joy to Ogoni communities. It was expected to be an opportunity for them to have access to such basic facilities as electricity, good roads, pipe-borne water, hospitals, health care centres, well-equipped schools, etc. Besides, the oil companies would also provide employment for their sons and daughters. Ogoni communities are grieved that the measures taken by the Federal Government and the oil companies to accumulate wealth are largely at the expense of the fulfillment of the expectations of the oil producing communities' socioeconomic well-being. The Ogoni consistently argue that the immense wealth that oil represents is only seeing by them; they do not touch it. Karl Maier lends credence to this claim by arguing that the Niger Delta stands as a monument to the failure of modern African nation-states to care for its people (Maier 2000: 112). He further argues that 'almost the only time the delta people saw any impact of the oil was when it was spilled into the water in which they fished and bathed' (113). Our experience with the claims of the Ogoni tallies with Burton's assertion that human needs for survival, protection, autonomy, etc. are irrepressible and not easy to give up. The actions of MOSOP aim at the restoration of the inalienable rights of the Ogoni people as a distinct ethnic community in Nigeria.

Indeed, the Ogonis feel short-changed and in line with relative deprivation theory, they have taken the law into their hands in an attempt to be their own saviours. The relative deprivation theory agrees with its cousin, the frustration-aggression theory that aggression is not just undertaken as a natural reaction or instinct as realists and biological theorists assume. It is agreed in some quarters that apart from the pervasive disillusionment with the government and oil companies, the people would not have done most of what is today associated with them. The confession from one of the delta youths who told Karl Maier that 'two years ago he would never have imagined that they would be taking hostage and behaving like crazy men' is instructive. The people resorted to hostage taking as their preferred means of venting their anger in what they considered to be years of neglect and repression by the Nigerian state (2000: 112).

We should state that though the relative deprivation theory offers useful perspective to our understanding of MOSOP as a social movement, it is not without shortcomings. Scholars have identified some significant problems with the theory. The important one to us is that since most people feel deprived at one level or another almost all the time, the theory has a hard time explaining why the groups that form social movement do so when other people who are also deprived do not. It is on the basis of this that some scholars see relative deprivation as an insufficient cause of social movements. Indeed, relative deprivation theorists (except perhaps Gurr 1970; Sears and McConathay 1970) generally give little attention to the emergence of relative deprivation itself, that is, to how a sizeable proportion of a population comes to share a perception of illegitimate status or privilege discrepancies. Joan Gurney and Kathleen Tierney argue on the basis of this that 'to state that RD arises when people perceive that their expectations are not being met and that those expectations may be based upon past experiences, future hopes, or the experiences of another group is merely description, not explanation' (1982: 38).

Commenting on this with a special focus on MOSOP, Osaghae claims that grievances of the Ogoni people do not tell us why they decided to fight for their rights when several other oil-producing minorities even fared worse in terms of oil and environmental deprivations (1995: 325-44). Osaghae attributes part of the blame to the inability of various commissions to achieve the aim for which they were established. He called this 'the apparent failure of extant strategies to bring about desired ends'. There is no doubt that they are local corrupt collaborators or predators whose activities ensured that oil remains a curse rather than a blessing to the people. Whatever the source of deprivation-oil companies, the federal government or its agents-it is clear that environmental devastation and cannibalistic exploitation of resources predicate the emergence of MOSOP as a social movement and should be addressed. There is no doubt that humans would fight naturally over things they cherish. The use of force has not stopped people from fighting for their rights anywhere in the world.

MOSOP has provided the Ogoni people with the vehicle to express themselves and agitate for a better world. On the issue of citizenship, the movement uses a language that suggests that they have no voice in the management of the affairs of the country and that they are being treated as 'colonized subjects', a group of inferiors, outsiders, and second-class subjects. MOSOP is more or less a voice calling for an end to alienation, marginalisation, and abandonment.

Like Toyin Falola suggests, MOSOP represents far more than its portrayal as a nuisance that prevents the flow of oil to the Western markets and diminishes the revenue returns to the government by attacking oil installations and kidnapping oil company workers. For many years, the strategy of MOSOP's agitation was nonviolence. In the 1990s, peaceful protests were met with state violence. On 10 November 1995, the federal government ordered the execution of Ken Saro-Wiwa and nine other key members of MOSOP. The brutalising and barbaric regime of General Abacha and the execution of Ken Saro-Wiwa and the other Ogoni protesters was a major turning point (Osaghae 1995: 325-44).

Viewed from the perspective of the Relative Deprivation Theory of Social Movement, it was improper for the state to take military action on a social movement campaigning for equity, social justice, development, democracy, environmental protection, human rights, and much more. Violent attacks should rather be directed at the conditions that necessitated the formation and continuous existence of MOSOP as a social movement. We again agree with Toyin Falola that 'for a society to move forward, it must be able to accommodate and learn from social movements and all assortments of agitations by interest groups' (Falola, 2008: 29). There is a consensus among Relative Deprivation theorists that 'to resolve a conflict situation, or to even prevent it from occurring, the needs have to be met with appropriate satisfiers, those things that were denied them in the first instance.' It is advisable for government and oil companies to seek ways of negotiating with the Ogonis through constructive dialogue. The feeling that giving in to MOSOP's demands or entering into negotiation with them is a sign of weakness should be discarded. Sometimes, the mere fact that the state or oil companies are showing some concern is enough to make people believe that something is being done. Constant negotiation is likely to build more friendship and confidence than force.

We should also be bold to say that MOSOP should resist the attempt to be violent in its agitation. It was Diigbo who had survived seven attempts on his life while he administered day-to-day affairs of MOSOP that said in February 2002 at the Indigenous Peoples Global Conference, held at the United Nations, New York that 'Ogoni was boxed in, stuck with nonviolence and had no resources to weather the violent storm instigated by Shell and the government. We risked instant extermination, if we, the Ogoni people had dared to resort to violence. We were barricaded by excessive violence. Violence tempted us to respond and watched over us to dare. Let me admit that we were incapable of violent self-defence, so we dared, but without recourse to violence' (http://en.wikipedia.org/wiki/ movement). It follows that no matter how aggrieved the 'militants' in the Niger Delta region think they are by systemic injustice and the antecedent 'violence' of iniquitous treatment, no normal rational person can commend them for kidnapping a three-year-old baby for ransom. Instead, 'such conduct usually attracts universal condemnation as inhuman' (Etuk 2008:8). We should always draw the well-known distinction between spheres of morality and those of legality. When actors throw morality to the winds and pursue their actions in exclusion of the interest of those of other units, it could lead to the abduction of persons who are innocent and helpless. At its beginning, MOSOP took the path of nonviolent protest. While still in detention in Port Harcourt in 1995, Saro-Wiwa penned the now world-famous hymn to nonviolent struggles, 'Ogoni star':

Dance your anger and your joy
Dance the military guns to silence
Dance the dump liars to the dump
Dance oppression and injustice to death
Dance the end of Shell's ecological war of 30 years
Dance my people, for we have seen tomorrow and there is an Ogoni star in the sky (quoted in Okonta and Douglas 2001: 227)

It is now common knowledge that Saro-Wiwa emphasised his preference for nonviolent struggle even in his last days. This informed the content of the letter he wrote to his friend, William Boyd, shortly before he was hanged in November 1995. He wrote:

'... [T]he most important thing for me is that I've used my talents as a writer to enable the Ogoni people to confront their tormentors. I was not able to do it as a politician or a businessman. My writing did it...' (1995: 148).

Of course, MOSOP gained national and international support because of its nonviolent approach to rights claims. In November 1994, MOSOP and its leader were awarded the Right Livelihood Award (also known as the Alternative Noble Peace Prize) for exemplary and selfless courage and in striving nonviolently for the civil, economic, and environmental rights of his people. Two other awards were to follow: the Goldman Award, which is the world's premier environmental prize--given to Ken Saro Wiwa for leading the peaceful movement for the environmental rights of the Ogoni people, and the Hellman/Hammett Award of the Free Expression Project of Human Rights Watch (Okonta and Douglas 2001: 204). Back home in Nigeria, MOSOP was described as the struggle for the soul of Nigeria and its future. The late Nigerian scholar Claude Ake made this clear in the following words:

MOSOP and Ogoni land must survive and flourish for the sake of us all. For better for worse, MOSOP and Ogoni land are the conscience of this country. They have risen above our slave culture of silence. They have found courage to be free and they have evolved a political consciousness which denies power to rogues, hypocrites, fools and bullies. For better for worse, Ogoni land carries our hopes. Battered and bleeding, it struggles on to realize our promise and to restore our dignity. If it falters, we die. (Quoted in Okonto and Douglas 2001: 16)

It is important to stress that the people of Ogoni, under the leadership of the Movement for the Survival of the Ogoni people hoped to achieve autonomy, economic and social improvement, environmental protection, and the payment of reparation for damaged environment by oil companies through a nonviolent approach, incorporating traditional techniques or nonviolence with new ones dictated by the specific circumstances of the Ogoni condition as well as the Nigerian situation (Ikalama 2009: 9-10). Ikalama states further that the struggle largely remained nonviolent to the extent that no single law-enforcement or state security personnel or those of the oil companies were hurt throughout the most active phase of the struggle. This was in spite of extreme provocation and repression by these agencies and despite the fact that Ogoni youth had ample opportunities to retaliate with reciprocal violence (10). Like Mohandas Gandhi and Martin Luther King, Jr., Ken Saro-Wiwa succeeded in immortalising his name as a proponent of nonviolent struggle.

Perhaps one of the great challenges to draw from MOSOP and Ken-Saro Wiwa's leadership is the use of nonviolence strategies in their struggle. The adoption of violent measures has always proved to cause more problems than solved. As recent developments have shown, violence measures often result in the loss of lives and property belonging to the government, investors, and the local people who undisputedly are Niger Deltans. We must once again emphasise the practice of rejecting violence in favour of peaceful tactics as a means of achieving set goals in the struggle for justice and equity.

Let us be challenged by the recent out-of-court settlement in the United States where Shell has agreed to pay $15.5m (£9.6m) in settlement of a legal action in which it was accused of having collaborated in the execution of Ken Saro-Wiwa and eight other leaders of Ogoni. The settlement, reached on the eve of the trial in a federal court in New York, is said to be one of the largest payouts agreed by a multinational corporation charged with human rights violations. Jennie Green, a lawyer with the Centre for Constitutional

Rights who initiated the lawsuit in 1996, said: 'This was one of the first cases to charge a multinational corporation with human rights violations, and this settlement confirms that multinational corporations can no longer act with the impunity they once enjoyed.' On his part, Anthony Dicaprio, a lead lawyer representing the Ogoni side, was optimistic that it would 'encourage companies to seriously consider the social and environment impact their operations may have on a community or face the possibility of a suit.'

Conclusion

In this paper, we have examined MOSOP as a social movement agitating for the rights of the Ogoni people. Official neglect, economic strangulation, environmental damage, and abject poverty amidst unimaginable wealth account for the formation of the movement. MOSOP is still in existence because the rights that it was formed to fight for are yet to be realised. The evidence available to us supports Victor Ojakorotu's assertion that any attempt aimed at addressing the crisis is a call for finding solutions to the fundamental issues that form the bedrock of the crisis in the oil-bearing region. Rather than using mere cosmetic attempts, government and oil companies should give priority attention to the demands of the people. The resources meant for the development of the area should be properly channeled so that they do not end up in private pockets. Relative Deprivation theorists are optimistic that once their needs are catered for, the Ogonis would see government and oil companies in their land as partners rather than parasites and predators.

We conclude with the words of Falola that 'in spite of the failure of many previous movements and the cynicism that is now ingrained in our characterization of movements and leaders ...social movements are important...when historical grudges are allowed to deepen; social movements can become intertwined with nationalism, and the oppressed look forward to becoming the oppressors' (Falola 2008: 29, 34). Fighting for rights is an almost undeniable phenomenon of individuals and communities around the world. The Relative Deprivation theory is unmistakable in its assertion that 'the greater the discrepancy, however marginal, between what is sought and what seem attainable, the greater will be the chances that anger and violence will result.' There is the need to always be conscious of Shehu Usman

Dan Fodio's immutable words that 'a kingdom can endure with unbelief, but it cannot endure with injustice.'

References

Ahmadu, Olusola F. 2008. 'A theoretical consideration of the Niger Delta crises: Who's solution, the people or the government. *Proceedings from the International Conference on the Nigerian State, Oil industry and the Niger Delta.* Port Harcourt: Harley Publications, 993-1001.

Etuk, Udo. 2008. 'Moral personhood'. Paper presented at the 2008 Nigerian Philosophical Association Conference, at the University of Calabar, 8-11 October, 2008.

Faleti Stephen A. "Theories of Social Conflict." In *Introduction to Peace and Conflict Studies in Africa: A Reader*, Shedrack Gaya Best (ed.), Ibadan: Spectrum Books Ltd., 35-60.

Falola, Toyin. 2008. 'From Sokoto to the Niger Delta: Social movements and alternative imaginations of the nation'. Text of the 2008 K. O. Dike Memorial Lecture, delivered at the 53rd Congress of the Historical Society of Nigeria held at Gombe State University, 13-15 October 2008.

Gurney, Joan N. and Kathleen J. Tierney. 1982. 'Relative deprivation and social movements: A critical look at twenty years of theory and research'. *The Sociological Quarterly* 23 (1): 33-47.

Gurr, Rober T. 1970. *Why men rebel.* Princeton: Princeton University Press.

Ihediwa, Nkemjika C. 2008. 'Interrogating protest movements in Nigeria: A comparative discourse of MASSOP and other protest movements in the Niger Delta'. Proceedings from the International Conference on the Nigerian State…, 2008.

Ikalama, Charles. 1997. 'Models of nonviolent civil disobedience in the Niger Delta'. Available Online: chimaubanicentre.org/ebook /ikalama%20final%20copy.doc.

Kretzmann, Steve. 1997. 'Hired guns'. *These Times Magazine,* 3-16 February, 3-6.

Maier, Karl. 2000. *This house has fallen: Nigeria in crisis.* London: Penguin Books.

McCarthy, John D. and Mayer N. Zald. 'Resource mobilization and social movements: A partial theory'. JSTOR: *American Journal of*

Sociology, Vol. 82, No. 6, (May 1977:1212-1241). http://www.jstor.org/stable/2777934. Accessed 15/02/2009.

Morrison, Denton E. 'Some notes toward theory on relative deprivation, social movements and social change'. In: *Collective Behaviour and Social Movements*, edited by Louis E. Genevie. Itasca: Peacock, 1978, 202-209.

Okonta, Ike and Douglas Oronto. 2001. *Where ventures feast: Forty years of Shell in the Niger Delta.* Ibadan: Kraft Books Limited.

Osaghae Eghosa E. 1995. 'The Ogoni uprising: Oil politics, minority agitation and the future of the Nigerian State'. *African Affairs* 94 (376): 325-44.

Saro-Wiwa, Ken. 1996. 'My story'. *Liberty Quarterly Journal of the Civil Liberties Organisation*, Vol. 7, No. 2, 1996: 39-43.

--- . 1995. *A month and a day-A detention diary.* Ibadan: Spectrum Books Ltd.

Sayeregha, Famous S. 2008. 'Petroleum prospecting, state violence and hostage-taking in Nigeria: A study of the Niger Delta region, 1966-2007'" In *Proceedings from the International Conference on the Nigerian State, Oil industry and the Niger Delta.* Port Harcourt: Harley Publications, 483-507.

Wiwu, Ken, Jr. 2002. *In the shadow of a saint A son's journey to understand his father's legacy.* Vermont: Steerforth Press.

Appendix 1

OGONI BILL OF RIGHTS PRESENTED TO THE GOVERNMENT AND PEOPLE OF NIGERIA NOVEMBER 1990

We, the people of Ogoni (Babbe, Gokana, Ken Khana, Nyo Khan and Tai) numbering about 500,000, being a separate and distinct ethnic nationality within the Federal Republic of Nigeria, wish to draw the attention of the Government and people of Nigeria to the under mentioned facts:

1. That the Ogoni people, before the advent of British colonialism, were not conquered or colonized by any other ethnic group in present day Nigeria.
2. That British colonisation forced us into the administrative division of Opobo from 1908 to 1947.
3. That we protested against this forced union until the Ogoni Native Authority was created in 1947 and placed under the then Rivers Province.

4. That in 1951 we were forcibly included in the Eastern Region of Nigeria where we suffered utter neglect.
5. That we protested against this neglect by voting against the party in power in the Region in 1957, and against the forced union by testimony before the Willink Commission of Inquiry into Minority Fears in 1958.
6. That this protest led to the inclusion of our nationality in Rivers State in 1967, which State consists of several ethnic nationalities with differing cultures, languages and aspirations.
7. That oil was struck and produced in commercial quantities on our land in 1958 at K. Dere (Bomu oilfield).
8. That oil has been mined on our land since 1958 to this day from the following oilfields:

    a) Bomu
    b) Bodo West
    c) Tai
    d) Korokoro
    e) Yorla
    f) Lubara Creek and
    g) Afam by Shell Petroleum Development Company (Nigeria) Limited.

9. That in over 30 years of oil mining, the Ogoni nationality have provided the Nigerian nation with a total revenue estimated at over 40 billion Naira (N40 billion) or 30 billion dollars.
10. That in return for the above contribution, the Ogoni people have received NOTHING.
11. That today, the Ogoni people have:

    a) No representation whatsoever in ALL institutions of the Federal Government of Nigeria.
    b) No pipe-borne water.
    c) No electricity.
    d) No job opportunities for the citizens in Federal, State, public sector or private sector companies.
    e) No social or economic project of the Federal Government.

12. That the Ogoni languages of Gokana and Khana are undeveloped and are about to disappear, whereas other Nigerian languages are being forced on us.
13. That the ethnic policies of successive Federal and State Governments are gradually pushing the Ogoni people to slavery and possible extinction.
14. That the Shell Petroleum Development Company of Nigeria Limited does not employ Ogoni people at a meaningful or any level at all, in defiance of the Federal government's regulations.

15. That the search for oil has caused severe land and food shortages in Ogoni - one of the most densely populated areas of Africa (average: 1,500 per square mile; national average: 300 per square mile.)
16. That neglectful environmental pollution laws and sub-standard inspection techniques of the Federal authorities have led to the complete degradation of the Ogoni environment, turning our homeland into an ecological disaster.
17. That the Ogoni people lack education, health and other social facilities.
18. That it is intolerable that one of the richest areas of Nigeria should wallow in abject poverty and destitution.
19. That successive Federal administrators have trampled on every minority right enshrined in the Nigerian constitution to the detriment of the Ogoni and have by administrative structuring and other noxious acts transferred Ogoni wealth exclusively to other parts of the Republic.
20. That the Ogoni people wish to manage their own affairs.

Now therefore, while reaffirming our wish to remain a part of the Federal Republic of Nigeria, we make demand upon the Republic as follows:

That the Ogoni people be granted POLITICAL AUTONOMY to participate in the affairs of the Republic as a distinct and separate unit by whatever name called, provided that this Autonomy guarantees the following:

a) Political control of Ogoni affairs by Ogoni people.
b) The right to the control and use of a fair proportion of OGONI economic resources for Ogoni development.
c) Adequate and direct representation as of right in all Nigerian national institutions.
d) The use and development of Ogoni Languages in Ogoni territory.
e) The full development of Ogoni Culture.
f) The right to religious freedom.
g) The right to protect the OGONI environment and ecology from further degradation.

We make the above demand in the knowledge that it does not deny any other ethnic group in the Nigerian Federation of their rights and that it can only conduce to peace, justice and fairplay and hence stability and progress in the Nigerian nation.

We make the above demand in the belief that, as Obafemi Awolowo has written:

"In a true Federation, each ethnic group no matter how small is entitled to the same treatment as any other ethnic group, no matter how large."

357

We demand these rights as equal members of the Nigerian Federation who contribute and have contributed to the growth of the Federation and have a right to expect full returns from that Federation.

Adopted by general acclaim of the Ogoni people on the 26th day of August, 1990, at Bori, Rivers State.

Signed on behalf of the Ogoni people by:

BABBE
1. HRH Mark Tsaro-Igbara, Gbenemene Babbe
2. HRH F.M.K. Noryaa, Menebua Ka-Babbe
3. Chief M.A.N. Tornwe III, JP
4. Prince J.S. Sangha
5. Dr. Israel K. Kue
6. Chief A.M.N. Gua

GOKANA
1. HRH James P. Bagia, Gberesako XI, Gbenemene Gokana
2. HRH C. A. Mitee, JP, Menebua Numuu
3. Chief E.N. Kobani, JP, Tonsimene Gokana
4. Dr. B.N. Birabi
5. Chief Kemte Gidaom, JP
6. Chief S.N. Orage

KEN-KHANA
1. HRH M.H.S. Eguro, Gbenemene Ken Khana
2. HRH C.B.S. Nwikina, Emah III, Menebua Bom
3. Mr. M.C. Daanwii
4. Chief T.N. Nwieke
5. Mr. Ken Saro-Wiwa
6. Mr. Simeon Idemyor

NYO-KHANA
1. HRH W.Z.P. Nzidee, Gbenemen Baa 1 of Nyo-Khana
2. Dr. G.B. Leton, JP
3. Mr. Lekue Lah-Laolo
4. Mr. L. E. Mwara
5. Chief E. A. Apenu
6. Pastor M.P. Maeba

TAI

1. HRH B.A. Mballey, Gbenemene Tai
2. HRH G.N.K. Gininwa, Menebua Tua Tua
3. Chief J.S. Agbara
4. Chief D.J.K. Kumbe
5. Chief Fred Gwezia
6. HRH A. Demor-Kaani, Menebua Nonw

CHAPTER 12

Economic Inequalities and the Niger Delta Crisis in Nigeria: Challenges and Prospects

Bheki R. Mngomezulu

Introduction

Nigeria is irrefutably a very fascinating country in Africa for many reasons. First and foremost, it is Africa's most populous nation with an estimated population of 152 million people who live in a geographical space of 923 768 square kilometres (*Arise*, July 2010) Second, Nigeria has been ruled by military governments more than any other country on the African continent. Third, the country is one of the top supplies of oil to the global markets. The question then becomes: is Nigeria headed toward the right direction in terms of nation-building and state development? This is one of the key questions scholars from different fields continue to wrestle with in their indefatigable efforts to understand Nigeria. Austine Ikelegbe began his chapter titled 'the construction of a Leviathan: State building, identity formation and political stability in Nigeria' by very emphatically and unapologetically stating, 'The Nigerian state is failing. Its post-independence hope of greatness and of 'giant-hood' in Africa is faltering' (Ikelegbe 2005: 71).

It is a fact that the concepts 'failed/failing state' and 'collapsed/collapsing state' are complex and relative and need a conceptual explanation for them to make any political sense and to be usable. However, even without this detail and problematisation of the concepts, Ikelegbe's submission alludes to the real fact that things have not gone well in Nigeria since the country got its independence from Britain in 1960. The most intriguing question is why? Is it due to human or natural factors or both? Certainly, no simplistic answer would suffice in this regard because the question itself is very complex. However, a close analysis of Nigeria's sociopolitical and economic history will bring us closer to understanding at least some of the causes of this decline. Such an analysis would be incomplete without bringing the Niger Delta area into the equation. Any problem that emerges in the Niger Delta becomes a national problem. This is due to the fact that it is here that Nigeria's oil is extracted to generate money that boosts the national economy and allows the government to implement its national infrastructural programmes.

As a general norm across the world, politics and economy are inextricably interwoven and interdependent. From a theoretical point of view, a country with economic instability is more likely to face political unrests compared to that which is economically stable. Similarly, political upheavals in a country have a direct negative impact on the national economy. Not only do skilled individuals relocate or emigrate as a result of the unstable political and economic conditions, current and prospective investors feel uncomfortable to invest in such a country. They reduce their investment or totally pull out of that country and invest elsewhere to maximise their profit while reducing the risk of losing financial, material, and human resources. To escape from this dilemma, the political leadership demonstrates astuteness in dealing with any crisis whenever it irrupts. If the government of the day fails to provide good leadership, the problem spills over and its negative impact is prolonged indefinitely with all its ramifications.

The Niger Delta crisis in Nigeria fits this synopsis perfectly. As argued below, the problems experienced in this region have both economic and political derivations. Failure by both the government and private oil companies to address the genuine demands of the people of the Niger Delta prompts the local youths to find their own response to the endemic problems. Accusation and counter accusation between the federal government and the militants results in all parties becoming losers. This makes it impossible for the country to perform at its maximum potential economically and politically. Thus, at a macro-level the Niger Delta situation grossly affects Nigeria's national economy and delays or completely halts various national projects. The amount of crude oil that reaches the international markets is far less than what it would have been had the political and economic situation in the Niger Delta been stable. It is on these grounds therefore that this article espouses the view that the Niger Delta holds the key to Nigeria's economic and political stability. Unless the intricacies involved in the Niger Delta crisis are clearly spelt out, wrong assumptions will continue to be made about the people of that area. This article is an attempt to make a contribution in this regard by providing a chronological analysis of the Niger Delta crisis.

The Niger Delta

The primary aim of this article is to provide the broader context within which the Niger Delta crisis should be interpreted. It begins by discussing the historical background to the problem, which began soon after independence in 1960 (EPU Research Papers 2007: 9-10). Secondly, through various examples it demonstrates the role played by different stakeholders in causing and sustaining the crisis. Thirdly and lastly, the article makes recommendations on how the Niger Delta crisis could at least be minimised in spite of its complex nature. Agency in this article is not confined to a single locale; an attempt is made to identify different role-players in the sustenance of the Niger Delta crisis. In the conclusion, the article stresses the need for a unified response by all the constituencies directly and indirectly linked to the crisis-both as groups and as individuals.

Historical Background

There is general consensus in the literature that what eventually became known as Nigeria was a product of the colonial project of creating a nation for administrative convenience (Fawole and Ukeje 2005; Eteng 1998; Fage 1997). In the year 1900, Britain assumed control of Northern Nigeria and made it a British Protectorate. Lord Frederick John Dealtry Lugard became the first governor of Northern Nigeria from 1900 to 1906. At the same time, Eastern Nigeria came under the jurisdiction of the British Colonial Office. In 1906, the Lagos Protectorate in the south-west and the Protectorate of Southern Nigeria in the south-east were amalgamated and became the self-supporting colony of Southern Nigeria (Oliver 2005). Meanwhile, the north remained largely cut off from the world markets. Its communication network only happened through the Niger and Benue Rivers. This reduced the region's chance for economic activity.

Having spent some time in Nigeria, Lord Lugard came to the realisation that the modernisation of Northern Nigeria could only be made possible if there was a political amalgamation of the north and the south. In his view, these would then have to be linked by railways with the cost in part to boost economic activity. This dream was realised a few years later. Lord Lugard returned to Nigeria in 1912. Two years after that, he became the governor-general of the now amalgamated Nigeria-a position he held until 1919. Unfortunately, by this time the differences between north and south had already hardened too much to be easily eliminated (Oliver 2005). Therefore, it is fair to state that from the very start, Nigeria was never a united political entity; geographical divisions were already evident. These would crystallise in later years, thus making it difficult to forge a united nation. The Niger Delta crisis draws from this history of identity politics in Nigeria.

Oil Production in Nigeria

The search for mineral oil in Nigeria began in 1937. But it was not until 1958 that the first export of oil actually began. Shell played an instrumental role in this regard. Port Harcourt, Nigeria's second largest port and the capital of Rivers State, supplied Nigeria's first full cargo of crude oil to Britain. Later, the area's oil refinery became the largest in tropical Africa. Over time, Nigeria became the world's eighth (and recently sixth) largest producer of crude oil. This oil and its subsequent dominance of the Nigerian economy in the 1970s was a giant stride forward. It changed the country from its dependence on agricultural products to overdependence on crude oil for its main foreign exchange earning (Latchem 1975; Commonwealth Institute 1963; Niven 1967; Aaron 2005). The fact that oil was found in this region raised the hopes of the local people that they would benefit from its sale. When this did not happen, trouble began.

Sklar and Whitaker's title 'Nigeria: Rivers of oil, trails of blood' (1995) and Obadina's book *The making of modern Africa* (2007) capture the essence of what the Niger Delta oil has done to the Nigerian nation. Obadina makes the point that ethnic nationalism has had devastating effects in Nigeria. Not only did it trigger violent activities, it also divided Nigerians. He writes: 'Since Nigeria's independence, the Ijaws increasingly have come to view themselves as belonging to a single Ijaw nation, and not as part of the country. The development of Ijaw nationalism is largely a response to the discovery and exploitation of oil on their land' (Obadina 1977: 100). In his view the Niger Delta crisis is compounded by the fact that groups and individuals make their own claims, which are not always the same.

In a nutshell, the history of oil in Nigeria falls into three phases. Phase one lasted from 1958 to 1961 and it covered the political independence period. During this time oil production was a very small industry that was almost entirely controlled by BP-Shell. This company exported oil only to Britain and Holland. The second phase started from 1962 and ended in 1969. During this time there was an attempt to diversify Nigerian oil. In Europe, sales were increasingly made to West Germany and France. Nigerian oil was also exported to Canada and the USA. In South America it was sold to Argentina. Ghana was Africa's main beneficiary. During this time the prospects for sale in Japan were already underway. The third and last phase started in 1970. This phase witnessed an unprecedented expansion of sales to Japan and the emergence of the USA as Nigeria's largest market. By 1973, Western Europe (including Britain) accounted for 51 percent of Nigerian oil. Thus, by the end of 1974, 'Nigeria had become by far the largest oil producer in Africa, bypassing Lybia which had cuta back drastically that year to a total production of 77 million tonnes while Nigeria had increased its output to 112 million tonnes' (Arnold 1977: 51). This oil boom continued until the world recession forced cutbacks in oil production.

In the middle of 1975, the Nigerian government 'was obliged to agree to the requests from oil companies such as Gulf Oil to cut down production since they simply could not find markets for their supplies of crude' (Arnold 1977:51 and appendix 5). At the same time the Nigerian government realised that unlike the main Arab oil producers, it had failed to pile up a cash reserve over the years to fall back upon. In the 1980s the GDP had negative growth rates. The growth rate of 22.8 percent recorded for 1973-1980 decreased to 14 percent during the period 1980-88 (Ekpo and Umoh: nd). Nigeria's overall economic decline since the mid-1980s, coupled with the tendency of educated Delta youths to leave the area, 'confirmed its status as an economic backwater (http://www.forgottendiaries.org/?location=Nigeria%20and%20niger%20Delta).

This dashed the hopes of the Niger Delta communities of ever reaping the fruits of oil production. Thus, during the 1980s, Delta communities started launching sporadic protests at multinational oil companies, accusing them of "brutal exploitation" (Oni and Onimode 1975: 29). During this time the incidents of violence were isolated. These protests became more organised in the 1990s (Meredith 2005). Therefore, 'the Niger Delta crisis assumed horrendous dimensions in the early 1990s with the emergence of social movements and militant youth groups', which began to challenge the Nigerian state and its policies (Ojakoroty 2008: 93). As the protests became deadly and more violent the political leadership was forced to act decisively.

The Nigerian Government's Role in the Niger Delta Crisis

Successive governments in Nigeria have dismally failed to address the Niger Delta crisis. If anything, they have wittingly and unwittingly exacerbated the problem. There is a temptation to blame the military governments for relying on the barrel of the gun as opposed to opening negotiation lines with the affected communities in an attempt to deal with the crisis. This is plausible, especially given the series of events that took place in the late 1980s and early to mid-1990s. For examples, in 1990, Ogoni leaders signed the Ogoni Bill of Rights in which they called for political control of Ogoni affairs by Ogoni people. Very little was done, such that on 10 November 1995, Ken Saro-Wiwa, a famous Nigerian activist, writer and business man and eight other activists 'were hanged by the Nigerian military government for campaigning against the devastation of their homeland, the Niger - Delta' (http://www.bvblackspin.com/2010/06/17/niger-delta-spills/).

However, the role of the military government should not be overstated. The return of civilian rule in Nigeria in 1999 did very little to address this unstable economic and sociopolitical situation. When President Olusegun Obasanjo assumed political power in 1999, he soon announced the establishment of the Human Rights Violation Investigation Commission (HRVIC), or the Oputa Panel, as it was popularly known. This brought a glimmer of hope to many Nigerians. Sadly, as the proceedings continued, it turned out that the state was implicated in most of the human rights violation issues. The Ogoni ethnic group, for example, brought before the Commission more than 10 000 petitions. As these petitions were tabled, it became clear that the state had not acted appropriately. It resorted to terror and persecution to deal with the genuine concerns of the Ogoni people and other ethnic minority groups in the Niger Delta area. Land and resources rights have always been genuine concerns in this area, but the political leadership seems either ignorant of this fact or unwilling to address it.

President Obasanjo's first term in office as a democratically elected president ended with very little change in the lives of the people of the Niger Delta. Aaron's assessment of the HRVIC led to the following conclusion: 'To the extent that genuine steps have not been taken to right these wrongs against the Niger Delta people from whose region the wealth of the nation is generated, the Oputa Panel is at best an attempt at confusing the symbolism of reconciliation with its substance' (Aaron 2005: 129).

The *Willinks commission report* of 1958 portrayed the Niger Delta as poor, backward, and neglected. More than four decades later, the situation remained the same, if not worse. There were very few roads and even fewer or no other physical infrastructure. Environmental degradation included seismic blasts and dumping of untreated waste into water and land. Gas flaring and pollution aggravated the situation. All these impacted negatively on fishing and farming-not to mention that even people's drinking water was polluted in the process (World Bank 1995; Human Rights Watch 1999). Under these circumstances health problems have become a sad reality in the Niger Delta region. Between 1976 and 1996, over 6 000 oil spills were recorded. In June 2001, a spill was reported in the rural town of Ogbodo. When this was not cleaned up three months later, 15 kilometres of soil were seriously affected. Health problems included respiratory and gastro-intestinal diseases in addition to mental distress (ERA/FoEN 2005). What has also made this situation untenable is the fact that although the Niger Delta is the economic source for Nigeria, political and economic decisions about the area are taken elsewhere in the country and imposed on the local residents. For years, local communities have had no voice whatsoever, hence these intermittent protests.

After many years of waiting since the first discovery of mineral oil in 1937, the patience of the communities of the Niger Delta ran thin. They took it upon themselves to get out of this predicament. This took different forms, including protest marches, seizure of oil company workers, vandalisation of oil equipment, killing of security personnel guarding the properties of the multinational oil companies, illegal draining and selling oil, *ad infinitum*. Local groups such as the Ijaws have consistently challenged the government to develop their region. Instead of addressing the concerns of these people, the Nigerian state has continuously sent in soldiers (mainly from the north) to quell violence. These army and police personnel have become notorious for maiming and killing people and also for destroying their property. In response, the youths resolved to organise themselves to fight government agents with the hope of controlling their priced resource, oil.

Initially, these youths used unsophisticated weapons but still managed to express their anger against the government. From the mid to the late 1990s they had access to more powerful and sophisticated weapons procured through illegal sale of oil and/or ransom money demanded from international oil companies that operate in the area. The return of multiparty democracy in the late 1990s (1998-1999) saw some of these youths taking up a rather new line of activity. They were hired and paid by politicians to disrupt campaign events for rival individual politicians and their political parties.

Some of the governors of the Niger Delta states have also been instrumental in perpetuating violence in the region. Instead of responding to the legitimate concerns of the local people they use state power to suppress them. In December 1998, for example, military authorities in Bayelsa State declared a state of emergency when members of the Ijaw ethnic group resorted to violence in their bid to seek greater local autonomy. This led to clashes with government forces. In November 1999, the army killed 2 500 and destroyed the town of Odi in Bayelsa State (Odey 2005; Vines 2005). Army officials claimed that this was a retaliation attack for the murder of 12 policemen.

Another twist of the Niger Delta crisis is that due to economic inequalities that force the locals to fend for themselves, various groups wage war against one another. The Ijaw and the Itsekiris, for example, constantly fight each other. Sometimes various groups come together to face the government. On 25 September 2004, for example, the Nigerian oil crisis took a different turn when the Niger Delta People's Volunteer Force (NDPVF) threatened to attack a number of oil facilities located in the region. The decision by Alhaji Mujahid Dokubo-Asari, the NDPVF leader, to withdraw from disarmament obligations following the Niger Delta Vigilante's (NDV) attack of the Okrika region raised a scare. On 20 September 2005, Dokubo-Asari was arrested for treason. This did not make things better in the region as more than 300 NDPVF members protested the arrest.

Developments such as these only worsened the already volatile situation in the Niger Delta. When it became clear that the government had no political will to address the Niger Delta crisis in a civilised manner, new military groups emerged and entered the fray. One of those was the Movement for the Emancipation of the Niger Delta (MEND). This group turned out to be more radical in its approach to the crisis. It was very close to the NDPVF. Soon after its establishment it immediately demanded the unconditional release of Dokubo-Asari and $1 billion compensation from Shell for polluting the area (http: // www.Globalsecurity.org/military/world/war/nigeria-2htm).These were not easy demands to meet, especially because Obasanjo's government was determined to show the militants who was in charge of the country. It is in part this power struggle between the government and the militant groups that has sustained the Niger Delta crisis. By the time President Obasanyjo established a special committee to address the Niger Delta crisis by improving education, providing employment, and developing the infrastructure, it was too little too late. At this stage the militant groups had already found their own ways and means of dealing with both the government and the international oil companies.

Most important, they had established that they could generate money out of the crisis. Thus, the Nigerian government failed to address the Niger Delta crisis. But it was not alone in this; oil companies also continued to sustain the crisis in various ways.

The Role Played by Multinational Oil Companies in the Niger Delta Crisis

From the day when the BP-Shell Company extracted the first barrel of oil in Port Harcourt, the Niger Delta region was set on a new economic and political path. From a business point of view this was indeed a great breakthrough. Although some local communities welcomed this oil extraction with a high degree of optimism, their hope for infrastructural development was soon dashed as violence irrupted (Ojakoroty 2008). When companies like Chevron Texaco (an American oil company) and Eni SPA (an Italian oil company) joined the fray, the focus further shifted from the local people in the Niger Delta region to competition among themselves-the more money the oil company wanted, the more it bribed the locals. (EPU Research Paper 2007). In the process, local communities felt dejected.

The more these companies increased oil production per day the more they ruined the local environment and the more local communities became agitated. Environmental degradation caused by the activities of oil Trans-national Corporations (TNCs) became a real ecological problem to the people of the Niger Delta region. As alluded to above, the federal government could not challenge these companies because it also benefited from their profits. One way for the oil companies to appease the local communities would have been to start development projects and improve the local infrastructure. Unfortunately, they focused more on profit making and relied on personal and state protection against the militant youths. By so doing, they declared war against the local communities.

The spate of kidnappings that have characterised the history of the Niger Delta is a desperate attempt by the local communities to demonstrate to the oil companies that they also have teeth to bite. On 15 June 2005, the Nigerian media reported that no less than six Shell workers were kidnapped by the militants. One of the militant groups calling itself the Iduwini National Movement for Peace and Development claimed responsibility for these kidnappings. Although the workers were eventually released, Shell remained vulnerable because money was not everything. As long as the Niger Delta remained undeveloped and as long as environmental degradation continued unabated, the oil companies operating in the region sat on a timed bomb.

One of the biggest mistakes made by international oil companies in the Niger Delta has been their tendency to turn local communities against one another. Together with the successive military governments they have continued to corrupt traditional leaders by giving them financial bribes so that they could have more rights to extract oil. Thus, 'the oil companies rather than involve themselves in the development of their areas of operation prefer to give financial gains to some vocal local chiefs which usually results in crisis' (EPU Research Paper 2007: 19). Moreover, they pay ransom instead of developing the area. This has made hostage-taking a lucrative business. Sometimes oil companies unwittingly turn militant groups against one another. When these groups start fighting, oil production is adversely affected. This was the case in 2003 when tribal clashes forced major international oil companies to withdraw from the Niger Delta. Subsequently, these companies shut down 40 percent of Nigeria's oil output. State governors like James Ibori of Delta State appealed to the warring factions to reach a peace deal. But such deals have failed to last because they only address the symptoms and bypass the actual ailment. The Federated Niger Delta Ijaw Communities Group vowed not to rest until there was improved political representation and better access to the Niger Delta's oil resources. Such an approach exerted pressure on the federal government to act by passing legislation to this effect (*Africa Report* 118; see Niger-Delta Development Commission, Act No. 6 of 2000). This is the crux of the matter. Unless this situation is accorded the significance it deserves, the Niger Delta crisis will remain part of the Nigerian body politic, with all its negative repercussions.

The Niger Delta Crisis: Challenges and Prospects

The Niger Delta situation poses a serious challenge to all concerned parties in Nigeria and beyond. This includes government, oil companies, and local communities that reside in the region. This, of course, does not in any way exclude the entire Nigerian population,

371

which relies on the oil profits from this region. It is clear at this juncture that political arrogance from the federal government is not the best solution to the crisis. The more the government uses force to calm the situation, the more the militants organise themselves to face the government head-on. These continued attacks and counter-attacks have a direct negative impact on the country's economy. Without oil, Nigeria's economy is bound to collapse because the government 'relies on the earnings derived from the sales of oil to be able to carry its obligation' (EPU Rescarch Paper 2007: 20). Therefore, the challenge is to keep oil production going while also avoiding clashes with the local communities. Striking the balance between the two has so far proved elusive.

The Niger Delta crisis is a national concern not only from an economic point of view but also from a political standpoint. The Niger Delta crisis tarnishes Nigeria's international political image. The crisis also creates space for the proliferation of heavy firearms that could find their way to other parts of the country and create an untenable situation that might threaten national safety. Moreover, the crisis has the potential to encourage inter- and intra-ethnic divisions. The movement established by the Ijaw group is an epitome of ethnic nationalism. Since Nigeria's political independence from 1960, the Ijaws have increasingly come to view themselves as belonging to a single Ijaw nation, and not as part of the country called Nigeria. While it is easy to blame the Ijaws for promoting ethnic nationalism, the reality is that such nationalism 'is largely a response to the discovery and exploitation of oil on their land' (Obadina 2007: 100). Ethnic nationalism has also been fuelled by justifiable feelings of injustice at the environmental damage caused by oil production by companies that operate in the Niger Delta region.

What complicates the situation (as alluded to above) is that sometimes the locals collude with these oil companies so as to reap the financial benefits that accrue from oil export. Oil companies are acutely aware of this situation and constantly use it to their advantage. For example, on 1 July 2007, violence erupted in Rivers State and it was attributed to 'sharing of booties from oil companies' (EPU Research Paper 2007: 19). The challenge is therefore not only to convince the companies to do things differently but also to convince the locals not to collude with them. Conventional economic practice dictates that as long as there is a buyer, the supplier stays in business.

Most important, one of the major challenges facing Nigeria is the fact that 'the deepening sense of alienation among the Niger Delta people poses a continuing challenge to national reconciliation' (Aaron 2005: 135). Nigeria tried to follow on South Africa's footsteps by establishing a Truth and Reconciliation Commission. However, the process was not carefully thought through. The question is: how does one reconcile in a situation where there is no justice? Marginalised groups continue to organise themselves against the state and do not see themselves as part of it. In that sense the idea of nation-building remains a farfetched and elusive dream. The fact that the youths in the Niger Delta use more sophisticated weapons means that it would be suicidal to perceive them as pushovers. The challenge facing the federal government since 1999 is to devise ways and means of bringing the people of the Niger Delta into mainstream politics in Nigeria. Failure to do so would mean that future governments will still find themselves wrestling with the same Niger Delta problem.

The situation outlined above is not impossible to address. Prospects are there. What is lacking is the political will from the side of the government and the international oil companies to listen to and address the needs of the local communities in the Niger Delta. As a point of departure, the Nigerian government must acknowledge the fact that without the Niger Delta oil, the country's economy would be in tatters. Secondly, both the oil companies and the government must admit that the concerns raised by the Niger Delta communities are real and will not dissipate. Once these two points have been addressed, both the government and the oil companies should sit down with the local communities in the Niger Delta region and discuss with them how best to address their concerns. One of the recommendations is that the Nigerian government should 'engage in negotiations with a broad-based delegation of Niger Deltians from the region's ethnic councils' (Africa Report 2006: ii). This would be both for the communities' sake and for the sake of nation-building and economic sustainability. A negotiated deal would most likely quell people's fears and make all parties want to work together to find a lasting solution.

Government-imposed solutions will be hard to implement if the locals are not happy with them. Government's decision to grant amnesty to the militants and encourage them to go to school (*Arise* 2010: 18) is a positive step forward. Sitting down with the militants, chiefs, politicians, etc. and discussing how to fund this education is a must.

Should the government implement its promise of 13 percent of the oil profits going to the Niger Delta and devise mechanisms to monitor the use of that money for infrastructure development, the crisis would gradually subside. If the government works with structures like the Niger Delta Development Corporation (NDDC) and not against them, prospects for peace look good. However, we should not be naïve to think that the Niger Delta crisis can simply disappear overnight. That would be wishful thinking. There are groups and individuals who benefit from the crisis and would want to sustain it for as long as necessary. But it is still logical to argue that negotiation is the best solution to the Niger Delta crisis. Over the years, both the police and the military forces have tried in vain to quell the violence in this region. Bringing them in again can only aggravate the already volatile situation. The blame game will not take the country forward.

Lastly, women and the local traditional leadership in the Niger Delta have a major role to play in containing the situation. The so-called militants are their children and subjects. Sitting down with them to discuss various ways of addressing the problems they are faced with other than using violence would go a long way towards minimising confrontation and avoiding bloodshed. But as mentioned above, this can only become possible if all stakeholders mentioned above have the political will to address the crisis.

Conclusion

Interterritorial conflicts are a reality in Africa. Cross-border conflicts between Nigeria and Cameroon as well as those between Kenya and Somalia are typical examples. But territorial conflicts within African countries are a serious concern. This has been the case in countries like Sudan, the DRC, Uganda, Rwanda, and Kenya-to name but a few. But whereas ethnicity and the thirst for political power have been generally credited for causing violent activities in these countries, the Niger Delta crisis has been caused and sustained almost entirely by economic inequalities and their ramifications.

The article has argued that both the Nigerian government and multinational oil companies are directly to blame for this state of affairs. They know that Niger Delta communities have a genuine case.

They also know that without oil from this region Nigeria's national economy would hit its lowest ebb but they are doing very little to redeem the situation. Instead, they resort to the use of force to silence the protesters. This has proved to be an inappropriate response. Unless government and oil companies change their modus operandi, the Niger Delta crisis will linger on indefinitely.

References

Aaron, K. K. 2005. 'Truth without reconciliation: The Niger Delta and the continuing challenge of national reconciliation'. In: *The crisis of the state and regionalism in West Africa: Identity, Citizenship and Conflict*, edited by W.A. Fawole and C. Ukeje, pp. 127-37. Dakar: CODESRIA.

Africa Report No.118, September 2006.

Arise. Country Report. 2010.

Arnold, G. 1977. *Modern Nigeria*. London: Longman.http://www.bvbl ackspin.com/2010/06/17/niger-delta-spills/ (accessed on 21/07/10).

Ekpo, A. H. and O, J. Umph. nd. 'An overview of the Nigerian Economic growth and development'.

EPU Research Paper. 2007. 'Nigeria's Niger Delta crisis: Root causes of peacelessness'.

ERA/FoEN. 2005. *The Shell report: Continuing abuses in Nigeria 10 years after Ken Saro-Wiwa*. Benin City: ERA/FoEN.

Eteng, I. 1998. 'The national question and federal restructuring in Nigeria'. In: *The challenges of African development: Tribute and essays in honour of Claude Ake*. Port Harcourt: CASS.

Fage, J. D. 1997. *A history of Africa*. Third edition. London: Routledge.

Fawole, W. A and C. Ukeje, eds. 2005. *The crisis of the state and regionalism in West Africa: citizenship, identity and conflict*, Dakar: CODSRIA. http://www.forgottendiaries.org/?location=nige ria%20and%20niger%20Delta (accessed on 21/07/10).

Human Rights Watch. 1999. *The price of oil: Corporate responsibility and human rights violations in Nigeria's oil producing communities*. New York: Human rights Watch. http://www .globalsecurity .org/military /world/ war/ Nigeria -2htm (accessed on 8/12/09).

Ikelegbe, A. 2005. 'The construction of a Leviathan: State building, identity formation and political stability in Nigeria'. In: *The crisis of the state and regionalism in West Africa: Identity, citizenship and conflict*, edited by W.A. Fawole and C. Ukeje, pp. 71-91. Dakar: CODESRIA.

Latchem, C. 1975. *Looking at Nigeria*. London: Adam and Charles Black.

Meredith, M. 2005. *The state of Africa: A history of fifty years of independence*. London: Frcc Press.

Niger-Delta Development Commission. 2000. Act No. 6.

Niven, R. 1967. *The lands and peoples of West Africa. Gambia-Sierra Leone-Ghana-Nigeria*. London: Adam and Charles Black.

Obadina, T. 2007. *The making of modern Africa*. Philadelphia: Mason Crest Publishers.

Odey, J. O. 2005. *Democracy and the ripples of executive rascality*. Enugu: Snaap Press.

Ojakorotu, V. 2008. 'The internationalisation of oil violence in the Niger Delta of Nigeria'. *Alternatives* 7 (1): 92-118.

Oliver, R. and Atmore, A. 2005. *Africa since 1800*. 5th edition. Cambridge: Cambridge University Press.

Sklar, R. and C.S. Whitaker. 1995. 'Nigeria: rivers of oil, trails of blood, prospects for unity and democracy'. *CSIS Africa Notes* 179: 1-9.

The Commonwealth Institute, 1963. *The Federation of Nigeria*. London: University of London Press.

Vines, A. 2005. Combating light weapons proliferation in West Africa. *International Affairs* 81 (2): 341-60.

World Bank. 1995. *Defining an environmental strategy for the Niger Delta*, Vol. 1. Washington, DC: The World Bank.

PART V

CULTURE, IDENTITY, AND ETHICS

CHAPTER 13

Violence, Citizenship and the Settler/Indigene Imbroglio in Nigeria

Pita Ogaba Agbese

Without doubt, there is this law [that every Nigerian is a citizen] but you should note that wherever you go in this country, you must meet those who first settled there. Therefore, the first settler is the owner of the land and the new comer becomes the settler...the first settler is the one who has the right to win and govern the land. (Alubo 2006: 231)

Everybody here can be a Nigerian citizen but you have your indigene, your indigenous area...you have your indigenous land. So there is a difference between citizenship and indigeneship, the two are not the same. When one is born in Nigeria, he is a citizen but Nigeria has been subdivided into indigenous areas where people settled before others. So when you settle before others you are indigene, those people who came [after] are settlers. (Quoted in Alubo 2006: 234)

We have waged relentless battles to correct many of the ills in our society. We have demonstrated our determination to bring about a more moral society. We see a bright and prosperous future for our country. I am particularly gratified to note how united our country is today, better than any other time in the past. In the past few months, Nigerians, from every corner of the country have amply demonstrated their yearnings for national unity, for harmony and for progress. The recent events have indicated that we are no longer divided along ethnic, tribal, religious lines or north-south divide. We have become simply Nigerians interested in the development and progress of our country. This is a great gain. Let us respect this spirit of oneness and unity in all that we do from now on. (Text of President Olusegun Obasanjo's Farewell Address to the Nation, 28 May 2007)

Introduction

The contrast between the first two quotations, on the one hand, with the third one, on the other hand, cannot be sharper. While the first two represent the inequality inherent in Nigerian citizenship, the third quotation is a denial of this political reality. It is instead, a self-glorification by President Olusegun Obasanjo in his farewell address as president in 2007 in which he extolled the imaginary successes of building a sense of national unity during the eight years of his administration. Obasanjo's optimism that his administration created an enduring national unity among all Nigerians is highly contradicted by a series of communal violence that have taken place in various parts of

379

the country since he left office in 2007. In particular, his optimism that Nigerians were no longer divided along parochial lines is belied by the mayhem in Jos and other cities in Plateau State in November 2008 and January 2010. In the course of this mayhem, thousands of Nigerians were killed by fellow Nigerians in orgies of violence.

While a *Punch* editorial in 2004 that pleaded that 'all Nigerians should be able to feel at home in any part of the country with their political and other rights fully guaranteed' (*The Punch* 23 June 2004) may be a popular sentiment, the reality on the ground is that there is no equality of citizenship in the country. Instead, Nigerians are categorised into two distinct groups: indigenes and settlers. Indigenes are those who can trace their ancestral origins to the particular geographical space in which they reside, while settlers are Nigerians who have supposedly migrated from their own ancestral lands to other parts of the country. This dichotomy limits the citizenship rights of many Nigerians. Moreover, as Philip Ostien has observed, 'indigene vs. settler fighting is endemic all over Nigeria' (Ostien 2009: 3). In fact, Obasanjo himself had, in 1993, highlighted the pernicious effect of the indigene/settler issue in Nigeria. He had said then that the 'concept of settler or non-native syndrome has of recent hardened into a theory of ethnic exclusiveness and molded and propagated to foist a pejorative meaning to advance economic and political control among competing elite groups for interests during democratic regimes' (see 'Plateau Patriots' n.d.: 13-14).

On January 17th, 2010, minor skirmishes broke out in Nasarawa Gwong, a suburb of Jos, the Plateau State capital. According to Gregory Ayanting, the Plateau State police commissioner, the trouble started when some young people in the area attacked some Christians as they were worshiping in their church.[1] soon, the orgy of violence engulfed the whole of Jos, Bukuru, and several other cities and villages in Plateau. A week later, over 500 people had been killed, thousands of people were left homeless, and hundreds of thousands of people had fled from Jos to escape the violence. Nigerians from other states of the federation who had made Jos their home began to return to their ancestral states. Andrew Agbese and Ahmad Salkida, two journalists who covered the latest violence, wrote as follows:

> In many parts of Jos and Bukuru, youths organized themselves into groups mustering whatever weapons they could; while defying the restrictions on

movements [a twenty-four curfew imposed by the state government], launched attacks on perceived enemies. There was panic during the curfew period as people fled their homes to get to areas they considered safe while others stayed back to defend their enclaves...As the security agents concentrated in quelling the fire in Jos, remote villages in local governments like Pankshin, Mangu, Barkin Ladi, and Jos South were also ignited. (See Agbese and Salkia 2010)

Many Nigerians were puzzled by the latest round of violence in Jos, coming in the wake of similar events in 2001, 2004, and 2008. Why is Jos, once reputed for its peaceful and serene nature, now virtually synonymous with mass murder, looting, brigandage, and mayhem? Why would a minor dispute between two neighbours or an armed attack on Christian worshipers in a suburb of Jos lead to a total conflagration in Plateau State itself? Why is violence the first recourse in disputes between indigenes and settlers? Why are violent conflicts between the two groups occurring with greater frequencies? What does the contestation between indigenes and settlers reveal about the nature of citizenship in Nigeria?

This chapter examines communal violence in Nigeria within the context of the indigene/settler imbroglio in the country. It contends that Nigerians do not enjoy equal citizenship within the country, as rights and privileges are apportioned on the basis of ancestry rather than residence. Thus, those Nigerians who move out of their geophysical confines of their ancestral origins to other parts of the country are considered settlers/strangers in their places of residence and they do not enjoy equal rights with those said to be indigenous to those places. The paper contends that the bifurcation of citizenship that results from the indigene/settler dichotomy is an exclusionary device that frequently leads to violent clashes. It argues that the denial of citizenship, with its associated political exclusion that is embedded in the indigene/settler distinction, provides a very persuasive context for understanding many contemporary communal conflicts in Nigeria. The paper identifies and analyses the factors that have accentuated the contestation over citizenship in Nigeria. It contends that communal violence such as that of Jos (2001, 2008, 2010), Yelwa (2002, 2004), Kafanchan (1999), Taraba State (2001), Shendam (2001), Zango-Kataf (1986, 1992), Azara (2001), Obi (2001), and many others throughout the country, will continue to pl`ague Nigeria as long as the country's citizenship remains an unsettled issue.

381

The 1999 Constitution and Citizenship in Nigeria

Requirements for Nigerian citizenship are set out in chapter 3 of the 1999 constitution. It stipulates that Nigerian citizenship can be acquired by birth, descent, registration, and naturalisation. Thus, under the constitution, Nigerian citizenship can be acquired by any person:

1) Born in Nigeria before 1 October 1960, provided one parent or one grandparent was born in Nigeria and belongs or belonged to a community indigenous to Nigeria;

2) Born in Nigeria after 1 October 1960, provided one parent or one grandparent is a Nigerian citizen;

3) Born outside Nigeria provided one parent is a Nigerian citizen.

As for Nigerian citizenship through registration, the constitution specifies that a person seeking Nigerian citizenship by this means must fulfill certain conditions: he is of good character; he has shown a clear intention of his desire to be domiciled in Nigeria; and he has taken the oath of allegiance as prescribed in the constitution. These provisions for citizenship by registration also apply to any woman who is or has been married to a Nigerian citizen and any person of full age (18 and above) and capacity born outside Nigeria of whom one of his grandparents is a Nigerian citizen.

Provisions for becoming a Nigerian citizen by naturalisation are also clearly spelled out in the constitution. A person can be a Nigerian citizen by naturalisation provided: he is of full age (18 and above); has resided in Nigeria for at least 15 years and plans to remain in Nigeria; is of good character; is acceptable to the Nigerian community where he is going to live permanently; has been assimilated into the way of life of Nigerians in that part of the Federation is a person who has made or is capable of making useful contribution to the advancement; progress and well-being of Nigeria; and has renounced any previous citizenship and has taken an oath of allegiance as prescribed in the constitution.

Several sections of the constitution provide a basket of equal rights for all citizens. For example, section 41 states as follows: a citizen of Nigeria of a particular community, ethnic group, place of origin, sex, religion, or political opinion shall not, by reason only that he is such a person:

a) be subjected either expressly by, or in the practical application of, any law in force in Nigeria or any executive or administrative action of the government, to disabilities or restrictions to which citizens of Nigeria of other communities, ethnic groups, places of origin, sex, religions, or political opinions are not made subject; or

b) Be accorded either expressly by, or in the practical application of, any law in force in Nigeria or any such executive or administrative action, any privilege or advantage that is not accorded to citizens of Nigeria of other communities, ethnic groups, and places of origin, sex, religions, or political opinions.

Similarly, section 42 proclaims as follows: No citizen of Nigeria shall be subjected to any disability or deprivation merely by reason of the circumstances of his birth. Nothing in subsection (1) of this section shall invalidate any law by reason only that the law imposes restrictions with respect to the appointment of any person to any office under the State or as a member of the armed forces of the Federation or member of the Nigeria Police Forces or to an office in the service of a body, corporate established directly by any law in force in Nigeria.

Section 43 stipulates as follows: 'Subject to the provisions of this Constitution, every citizen of Nigeria shall have the right to acquire and own immovable property anywhere in Nigeria. Every citizen of Nigeria is entitled to move freely throughout Nigeria and to reside in any part thereof, and no citizen of Nigeria shall be expelled from Nigeria or refused entry thereby or exit therefrom.' Although certain provisions of the constitution create equal citizenship for all Nigerians, there are several provisions of the constitution that equally negate the equal citizenship clauses. For example, section 14 (3) of the 1999 Constitution states as follows:

The composition of the Government of the Federation or any of its agencies and the conduct of its affairs shall be carried out in such a manner as to reflect the federal character of Nigeria and the need to promote national unity, and also to command national loyalty, thereby ensuring that there shall be no predominance of persons from a few State or from a few ethnic or other sectional groups in that Government or in any of its agencies. The same provision applies to the composition states and local governments for as the constitution stipulates: [T]he composition of the Government of a State, a local government council, or any of the agencies of such Government or council, and the conduct of the affairs of the Government or council or such agencies shall be carried out in such manner as to recognize the diversity of the people within its area of authority and the need to promote a sense of belonging and loyalty among all the people of the Federation.

These provisions were incorporated into the 1999 constitution from the defunct 1979 constitution. They were originally included in the 1979 constitution on the grounds that without such affirmative provisions, the federal government or any of its agencies would be dominated by persons from particular ethnic or regional groups. In the words of the Report of the Drafting Committee of the 1979 Constitution:

There had in the past been inter-ethnic rivalry to secure the domination of government by one ethnic group or combination of ethnic groups to the exclusion of others. It is essential to have some provisions to ensure that the predominance of persons from a few states or from a few ethnic or other sectional groups is avoided in the composition of government or the appointment or election of persons to high offices in the state. (Federal Government of Nigeria 1977: ix)

Section 143 o the 1999 constitution mandates the establishment of 'offices of Ministers of the Government f the Federation' by the president. It stipulates that when the president appoints ministers to rn the ministries, such appointments shall be made in 'conformity with the provisions of section 14(3) of this Constitution:- provided that in giving effect to the provisions aforesaid the President shall appoint at least one Minister from each State, who shall be an indigene of such State.' This requirement that appointments to federal offices and agencies must be made on the basis of state indigeneity rather than residency negates the equal citizenship provisions of the constitution. Thus, while the constitution recognises citizenship rights on the basis of residency, it greatly limits those rights through the institutionalisation of a quota system anchored on the basis of a person's ancestral state of origin. In other words, the practical effect of the constitution's federal character principle is that it privileges indigeneity above all other criteria of citizenship. As Ogoh Alubo has correctly noted:

> While the constitution acknowledges universal citizenship, it also acknowledges and indeed gives more priority to indigenes for purposes of opportunities. In the end, citizenship of Nigeria, a more vast geo-political space, is second fiddle to indigeneship. The indigenes are effectively citizens of a smaller geo-ethnic space. This practice is enforced particularly because the first only entitles one to abstract rights such as being presumed innocent until proven guilty; the second, on the other hand, has some material benefits such as employment opportunities and scholarships. This is the real basis of the contestations and conflicts: exclusion of others from available benefits and opportunities. (Alubo 2006: 245-46)

As Alubo has correctly noted, the Nigerian Constitution 'accepts indigeneity as the basis for the practice of citizenship' (237). Alubo also points out that 'denial of citizenship constantly triggers explosions of identity-based violence, usually of ethnic and religious dimensions' (239). Chris Nwodo has advanced the same argument, noting that while in theory the constitution gives every Nigerian the right to reside in any part of the country, in practice, that right is highly circumscribed 'by so many contraptionsCquota system, federal character, zoning, state of origin and the indigene/settler dichotomy among others' (Nwodo 2008).

The distinction between Nigerians who are indigenes and others who are merely settlers or strangers creates both a sense of entitlements and a sense of exclusion, respectively. The first group of Nigerians enjoys rights and privileges simply on the basis of the fact that they reside on their ancestral lands. On the other hand, the second group of Nigerians has only limited rights because those Nigerians have either moved away from their ancestral lands or are unable to trace the original homes of their ancestors. The perceived injustice inherent in the dichotomy breeds resentment and antagonism and could lead to violence even with the slightest provocation. Writing on the situation in Lagos, *Nigeria Planet* editorialized as follows: 'It is just possible that the unresolved indigene-settler question might be responsible for the state of affairs in Lagos where indigenes and their linguistic kin enjoy all the goodies while non-indigenes pay all the taxes, levies, and are compelled to make do with hand-

outs from an over bearing state government' (http://www.nigeriaplanet
.com/nig_tinubu-census-threat.html). *The Daily Sun* has also noted, in
an editorial, the pernicious effect of the indigene/settler dichotomy on
the political economy of Nigeria:

> For so long, the issue of who is an indigene and who is a settler has been a
> sore point in our relationship with one another within the states of the
> federation. Sadly, this ugly development had since the advent of the
> Nigerian Civil War and after, vitiated the common citizenship and
> statehood that our founding fathers dreamt of at independence.
> ('Indigeneship Question' 2009)

Although the federal character principle was originally designed to
guarantee fairness and equity, its application has resulted in the
creation of a dichotomy of Nigerian citizenship: indigenes and settlers.
Indigeneship has become a potent weapon through which 'settler
Nigerians' are excluded from material resources of the land. As
practised in Nigeria, proof of 'state of origin' and 'local government
origin' is required for such things as appointments, scholarship
awards, recruitment into the police and armed forces, and admission to
schools. Every Nigerian, under this practice, is required to show this
proof by ascertaining his/her ancestral origins to a particular
geophysical space in the country. Residence, alone, no matter the
duration, does not prove indigeneity. As the Taraba State Legal Team
expresses in defense of the policy of denying indigeneship to the Tiv
people who live in Taraba State:

> There is a distinction (though often ignored) between citizenship and
> indigeneship. Whereas an indigene naturally has an inherent and inalienable
> rights to his primitive and aboriginal home...in the case of a citizen he
> enjoys only residency rights outside his primitive and aboriginal domain in
> Nigeria...from evidence available before the Commission and definition
> proffered thereof, the Tiv do not qualify as indigenes of former Wukari
> Division or Taraba State of Nigeria...the Tiv in Taraba State are at best
> citizens of that State entitled to qualified enjoyment of rights by an indigene
> of Taraba State. Such qualified rights include Afull residency rights@ as
> enshrined in section 15 (3) b of the 1999 Constitution. (Quoted in Alubo
> 2006: 225-26)

The Gbong Wong Jos (traditional ruler of Jos) puts it's even more
graphically when he argues as follows: '[T]he people mixes up

citizenship and indigeneship. Citizenship is a constitutional issue. Anybody in Nigeria is a citizen of the country. Even foreigners can come in and naturalize and become citizens. But indigeneship is a different game ... (indigeneship) is that you have a virgin area, an area that is God-given and you have been there from day one...There are people who are always saying they should be given districts, and I've always been asking: Districts on whose land?' (Quoted in Ayomike 2004).

Indigeneship and settlership are more than mere categories of Nigerian citizenship. They connote privileges and exclusion, respectively. As the Taraba State Legal Team noted above, a Nigerian living outside his/her ancestral home has only limited rights. In practical terms, such persons are denied political representation, appointments to public offices, access to land, admission to schools, etc. Even if the ancestral home is putative rather than real, the settler Nigerian is expected to avail himself/herself of full citizenship rights in such fictional geophysical spaces. As Ibrahim James has pointed out, ethnic or geographical categories are frequently used as the 'basis for distributing rewards thus exacerbating the settler-host community's mutual suspicions and distrust' (James n.d.: 147). George Ehusani has noted the material disparities that exist between indigenes and settlers. As he points out:

> Whereas the so-called settlers or non-indigenes, are part of the society in every respect, worshiping with, socializing with, trading with, paying taxes with, and marrying the so-called indigenes, but when it comes to sharing resources, including ownership of land, scholarships, placement of children in colleges and universities, employment in the civil service, and political appointments, including appointment as vice-chancellors and rectors of academic institutions (hat are supposed to be supposed to be purely on merit), the indigene/settler syndrome is thrown up and the so-called settler suffers the grave injustice of discrimination and persecution. (Ehusani 2005)

Indigene/Settler Contestations: The Arenas and the Bases of the Contestations

On the surface, the indigene/settler distinction can be made on a straightforward basis. It would seem to be based on migration. The members of the group that was the first to arrive at a virgin land and subsequently remain there would be the indigenes, and other subsequent arrivals would be designated the settlers/strangers. However, the issue is not as simple as that. As Mahmoud Mamdani has noted, being a settler is not a function of the time of migration. Rather, it is a political definition framed by state power, conquest, and the law (Mamdani 1998). This creates several complexities in distinguishing between indigenes and settlers. For instance, although the Kanuri-speaking people of Lafia (Nasarawa State) trace their ancestry to Borno State in far northeastern Nigeria, and apparently arrived in Lafia at a much later time than the Tiv of the neighbouring Benue State, political power in the hands of the Kanuri in Lafia has allowed them to designate themselves indigenes of Lafia. On the other hand, the Tivs are denied the status of indigenes of Lafia or any other part of Nasarawa State. Looked at from the perspectives of the Tiv people, how would a Kanuri, whose ancestor was a recent migrant from far-away Borno, be an indigene of Nasarawa State, but a Tiv person who descended from ancestors who predated the Kanuri in arriving in Lafia be denied the same indigeneous status? In some of Nigeria's local government areas, those designated as 'settlers' are in far greater numerical majority than the indigenes themselves. The Alago/Tiv contestation in Nasarawa State is a clear illustration of this. The fear that the Tiv, in a democratic election, could use their larger number to get elected into public offices was what triggered the 2001 violent clashes in the state's Southern Senatorial District. Similar fears of the implications of Tiv numerical majority also shape the dynamics of Tiv/Jukun indigene/settler contestation

Southern Zaria in Kaduna State illustrates another dimension of the complexity of the indigene/settler issue in Nigeria. Here, the Hausa/Fulani are in numerical minority but have come to dominate the political structure of the area. Southern Zaria was historically under the suzerainty of the Emir of Zaria who appointed Hausa/Fulani district heads over the Katafs and other ethnic groups who constitute the majority of the population. Although the Hausa/Fulani hold the reins of local power, they are nonetheless designated as settlers. The people of Southern Zaria have tried to use the indigene/settler distinction to wrest political power from the Hausa/Fulani whom they accuse of exploiting them. It was the contest over political power between the two groups that led to a series of clashes in the 1980s and 1990s.

Although the Hausas of Jos are a minority vis-à-vis their Berom counterparts, the creation of Jos North Local Government in an area with a predominant Hausa population threatened to upset the balance between the two groups in the contestation over indigeneship/settlership. Control of Jos North Local Government by the Hausa would bolster their case that they are indigenes of Jos (Jasawa). Obviously, this would negate the basis (indigeneship) on which Berom political power in Jos is anchored. The Berom were therefore determined to control political power even in Jos North Local Government where Hausa's numerical superiority would have given them an advantage. It was this contestation that formed the basis of the 2008 deadly violence. Although the violence in Jos is usually presented as a religious conflict between Muslims and Christians, it is essentially a conflict resulting from the contestation between indigenes and settlers. Religion does play a role in the conflict in two significant respects. Most of the Jos Hausas are Muslims and most of their Berom counterparts are Christians. Secondly, the Beroms prefer to couch the conflict in religious terms because that bolsters their support from other Nigerian Christians living in Jos.

Indigenes and settlers have fought over land, identity, political representation, political appointments, chieftaincy institutions, and access to public institutions, including schools and recruitment into the armed forces. As Ostien correctly notes, 'the particular locations indigenes and settlers fight over are the 774 LGAs into which Nigeria is now subdivided. In the end, the fighting is about access to resources controlled by the federal, state, and local governments, through which 80% of Nigeria's GDP flows...The resources to which access is gained by control of LGAs include land, a lot of money, a lot of jobs, admissions and scholarships to schools and universities, health care, and more' (Ostien 2009: 3). For example, part of the struggle between the Hausas of Jos and the Beroms revolves around the Hausa quest for

389

identity as people of Jos (Jasawa). In the case of Tiv versus Jukun of Taraba State, the Tiv seek recognition as indigenes of Taraba to enable them have access to land and political representation and participation. Land has become an important base of capital accumulation, not just in the capital cities, but even in the rural areas. In places like Abuja, Lagos, and Port Harcourt, there is a high premium placed on land. In parts of Abuja such as Maitama and Asokoro, a plot of land may cost as much as $1 million. As more and more people lose their jobs or retire from their jobs and return to the rural areas, they put pressure on the available land. As Umar Habila Dadem Danfulani has correctly observed, 'land is central to survival, hence conflict very often occurs over access to pastoral and arable land' (Danfulani 2006: 4). Ibrahim James has shown how the struggle over land ownership has shape the dynamics of the indigene/settler relationship in the Middle-Belt of Nigeria.

> As he notes, the Structural Adjustment Program of the 1980s compelled many Nigerians to seek livelihood through farming, and Suddenly, land which used to be available to those who used or needed it became a prized possession. Both the host communities and settlers alike began to rationalize their inability to acquire and possess land to the presence of the other group, thereby undermining the imperative of their co-existence and the basis of consensus and confidence-building. These factors probably account for the preponderance of land disputes as an index in the perennial communal conflict profile of the Middle-Belt. (James, n.d. 147-48)

Several factors have shaped both the frequency and the ferocity of the conflicts between indigenes and settlers. Among the most significant of these were the series of state and local government creation exercises. At independence in 1960, Nigeria was a federation of three regions: North, East, and West. A few years later, a fourth region, Mid-west, was created. In 1967, the four regions were dismantled in favour of twelve states. In 1976, the number of states was increased by 7 to a total of 19. Today, Nigeria is a federation of 36 states. Similarly, the number of local governments has increased several-fold to a total of 774. Under the three- or four-region structure, dichotomies among Nigerians on regional basis were rather muted. To be sure, there employment discriminations against Nigerians from other regions in the regional public service but the use of ancestral origin as the basis for political representation, public service employment, access to land, and so on, was primarily a function of the state and local government creation exercises. In particular, in parts of the old Northern Region, such as Southern Zaria, where the Islamic jihad of the nineteenth century led to the imposition of Hausa/Fulani Muslim rulers on the people, the creation of states was viewed as an instrument of liberation from the Muslim rulers. According to Hassan Kukah, the creation of states and local governments resulted in 'feelings of independence' among the people of Southern Zaria. As he pointed out: '[C]oming against the background of unequal relations that have been characterized by so many years of degradation and humiliation, this *independence* was cherished' (Kukah 1993: 185).

The poor state of the Nigerian economy has also placed a higher premium on indigeneship and has accentuated the contestation between indigenes and settlers. Hassan Kukah has shown how dwindling economic opportunities have affected the dynamics of indigene/settler relationships in Southern Zaria. As he puts it:

> The people of Southern Zaria see that their oppression has not been ameliorated, as the Hausas still pose as middlemen in the minutest of business engagements, from the purchase of their seeds, the purchase of fertilizer to the sale of their crops. They see that the economic ascendancy of the Hausa settler runs in contradistinction to their own downward slope. They watch the slide of the former ace card that was attained by the acquisition of western education as their children face joblessness in the of other means economic upward mobility. (Kukah 1993: 203)

Jobs have become very scarce and in many cases, university graduates are unable to find employment several years after graduation. Since employment and other economic opportunities may depend on one's status as an indigene, the poor economy has given greater saliency to this form of identity. At the same time, the terrible economy with its concomitant high levels of unemployment among young people creates a pool of readily available manpower that can be hired to engage in looting, killing, and brigandage in the name of indigene/settler conflicts. As in the case of Jos in 2008, the police intercepted busloads of young men coming from far-off states to join the fight. This is an indication that the violence is usually well organised rather than a spontaneous response to a minor provocation.

Similarly, the use of state power as an instrument of private capital accumulation places a premium on access to public offices and it aggravates tensions between indigenes and settlers. Everybody seeks to acquire political power to use it for private enrichment. Under that context, an exclusionary device such as the indigene/settler dichotomy becomes a powerful weapon in winnowing the number of political competitors for public office. Wide availability of small arms all over Nigeria also adds ferocity and intensity to the violence between indigenes and settlers. Armed attacks against Igbos in Kano in the 1980s led to a determination on their part to arm themselves for protection. Other groups have since taken a cue from the Igbos and have similarly armed themselves. In addition, retired soldiers are frequent participants in many cases of communal violence in Nigeria.

Ineffectual government response to indigene settler violence is another major factor behind the rising number and greater lethality of indigene/settler violence. Governments hardly anticipate the violence, even though government policies themselves the substance, contours, and dynamics of the violence. Governments' responses usually consist of deploying police/soldiers to quell the violence, imposing a curfew on the city or place of violence, and establishing a commission of inquiry to investigate the violence. Sometimes when curfews are imposed, instructions are given to the military to shoot people contravening the curfew on sight, as Major-General Peter Ademokhai, the then GOC of the 1 Infantry Division of the Nigerian Army, ordered in March 1987 (*West Africa* 23 March 1987: 551). In the January 2010 violence in Jos, even the police were ordered off the streets during the curfew by the military commander!

Nigeria's notorious monumental corruption also plays a role in the indigene/settler imbroglio. People with access to governmental positions steal money with ease and in mind-boggling quantities. Farida Waziri, the chairman of the Economic and Financial Crimes Commission (EFCC), noted that the EFCC had recovered assets worth $11billion from corrupt Nigerians (see Waziri 2009). Brazen Nigerian officials now embezzle money in the billions of Naira and no longer in the millions of Naira, as was in the case in the past. The fact that those who steal or misappropriate public funds are hardly ever prosecuted or forced to return the money intensifies the competition to acquire political power and use it for private enrichment. Ethnic and religious identities and several other tools are deployed by the contestants over state power to help them succeed. They often claim to be fighting on behalf of their ethnic or religious groups, but in reality, their aim is to use state power to feather their own nests. As President Ibrahim Babangida once noted:

> An examination of the activities of those in positions of power, however, will show that in general, the benefits that accrue to ethnic groups and nationalities from having their members in elective offices are limited to a tiny minority from particular families or particular classes...These benefits never get down to the masses of the ruling ethnic groups or nationalities. For this reason, the masses of the ruling ethnic groups or nationalities are in no way better off than the others in terms of benefits from holding elective offices. (Quoted in Kukah 1993: 265)

The fact that a settler can never become an indigene exacerbates the indigene/settler imbroglio. This is particularly hard on settler groups who cannot trace their patrilocal ancestry to any particular place in Nigeria. According to the Human Rights Watch, this is one of the dilemmas of the Hausa and Jarawa ethnic groups in Plateau State. As the Human Rights Watch puts it:

> The discrimination endured by Jos's Hausa and Yelwa's Jarawa communities as non-indigenes is especially harmful because many of them cannot trace their origins back to any other place where they might be able to claim indigene status. As stateless citizens--people who are indigenes of nowhere--they face a level of disadvantage and discrimination considerably worse than that endured by other non-indigene communities, who are often able to mitigate the effects of discrimination by maintaining connections to their states of 'origin'. (Human Rights Watch 2006: 2)

Reports of commissions of inquiries on the violence are usually not made public and even if some of perpetrators of the violence are arrested, they are hardly ever prosecuted. For instance, those arrested in the 2008 Jos violence were taken to Abuja for trial but were never tried. In the past, governments have even rebuilt mosques and churches burnt during the conflagration rather than forcing the perpetrators to do so. It is the ineffectiveness of governments' response to indigene/settler violence that forced *The Guardian* to lament in a recent editorial in the following words:

> Again and again, sectarian violence erupts in Northern Nigeria. Again and again, Nigerians raise in condemnation and their governments institute commissions of inquiry to look into the remote and immediate causes of the

393

violence. In a show of political correctness, murderous rioters are corralled into police custody, but all are released without charge when the dust settles. Of the tonnes of recommendations made to avert future clashes, nothing is ever heard. Thus, the cycle of violence is perpetrated and the culture of impunity nurtured. Apart from Jos there have been deadly riots in Kano, Maiduguri, Jimeta, Gombe, Zango-Kataf, Kaduna, Kafanchan, Katsina, Funtua and Yobe. (*The Guardian* 24 January 2010)

Some married Nigerian women are doubly victimised by the indigene/settler dichotomy. If they are married to men from ancestral states different from their own, their chances of appointments into the public service or running for public offices are highly circumscribed. If they seek public employment in their states of origin, they are told do so in their husbands' states of origin. If they try to do so, they are turned down on the grounds that they should seek such employment in their states of origin. Daisy Danjuma was elected into the Senate, not from Lagos where she lived or from Taraba, the ancestral state of her husband, General Theophilus Danjuma, but from Edo State, her own ancestral state. Her case is highly unusual in being able to win an election from her ancestral state even though she is married to a man from a different state. It is possible that she was successful despite numerous odds on account of her husband's very influential position in both the government and the ruling political party (PDP).

Interestingly, naturalised Nigerians do not have to contend with the indigene/settler dichotomy. They are automatically accorded indigeneship of the state where they naturalise as Nigerians. This means that a naturalised Nigerian becomes an indigene of the state of his/her naturalisation, whereas a Nigerian who has lived much longer in that state but cannot trace ancestry to that state remains a settler!

Conclusion

As shown above, Nigeria has not been able to resolve the citizenship question. The indigene/settler imbroglio remains a major albatross on citizenship in Nigeria. Unfortunately, the dichotomy between indigenes and settlers is not likely to be bridged any time soon. Too many interests have become entrenched in this dichotomy and the fact it is used as an exclusionary device to limit access of other Nigerians to political participation, political representation, and public resources implies that it cannot be eliminated in the foreseeable future.

Note

1. There were conflicting reports on the factors that precipitated the violence. One version was that the violence broke out as a result of a dispute over land between two neighbours: a Muslim and a Christian. Yet another version was that the conflict began over a dispute in a football game among young people in Nasarawa Gwong.

References

Alubo, Ogoh. 2006. *Nigeria: Ethnic conflicts and citizenship crises in the central region.* University of Ibadan: Program on Federal and Ethnic Studies, Nigeria.

Ayomike, J.O.S. 2004. ' Of citizens and indigenes: The contradiction that is Nigeria'. *Vanguard Newspapers.*

Danfulani, Umar Habila Dadem. 2006. *The Jos Peace Conference and the indigene/settler question in Nigerian politics.* Unpublished Paper.

Ehusani, George. 2005. 'Citizenship and the indigene/settler syndrom'. *The Guardian*, 4 July.

Federal Government of Nigeria. 1977. Report of the Constitutional Drafting Committee, vol. 1. Lagos. http:www.nigeria-planet.com/nig_tinubu-census-threat.html

Human Rights Watch. 2006. Nigeria: *"They do not own this place"*Government Discrimination against 'Non-Indegenes' in Nigeria, Vol. 18, and no. 3(A): 1-68. *The Guardian* 2010. 24 January. Editorial. 'The indigeneship question'.2009. Editorial. *Daily Sun*, Monday, 27 December.

James, Ibrahim. N.d. 'Integration and delayed integration in the Middle Belt of Nigeria'. In: *The settler phenomenon in the Middle Belt and the problem of national integration in Nigeria.* Jos: Midland Press.

Agbese, Andrew and Ahmad Salkida 'Jos: When Governor Jang lost control of his domain'. *Daily Trust*, Sunday, 24 January 2010.

Kukah, Matthew Hassan. 1993. *Religion, politics and power in northern Nigeria.* Ibadan: Spectrum Books.

Mamdani, Mahmoud. 1998. 'When does a settler become a native: Reflections of the colonial roots of citizenship in Equatorial and South Africa'. Inaugural Lecture, University of Cape Town.

Nwodo, Chris. 2008. 'Beyond the Black Friday in Jos'. *Daily Sun*, Tuesday, 9 December.

Obasanjo, Olusegun. 2007. Farewell Address to the Nation, 28 May.

Ostien, Philip. 2009. 'Johan Jang and the Jasawa: Ethno-religious conflict in Jos, Nigeria'.

Muslim-Christian relations in Africa. August. Online publication of Bayruth University, Germany

'Plateau patriots'. *State of emergency: Our stand.* N.d. Vol. 1: 13-14.

The Punch 2004. 23 June. Editorial.

Waziri, Farida. 2009. "Anti-corruption fight: No sacred cow, says presidency," Lawan Hamidu http://www.voiceofnigeria.org/N igeria/Anti-corruption-fight-no-sacred-cow

CHAPTER 14

Age-Long Land Conflicts in Nigeria: A Case for Traditional Peacemaking

Joseph S. Gbenda

Introduction

Hillary Clinton, the American secretary of state, during her visit to Nigeria in 2009 declared that governance has failed in Nigeria. It is indeed a true assessment of the Nigerian leadership. Adeniran (2009: 3) describes the situation in Nigeria thus: 'Labor isn't working, health isn't working, wealth isn't working, and good breeding isn't working. Only one thing is working: corruption in high and low places with every level of governance earning good praises for being top of their games'. Leadership problems, misadministration, and the inability of the Nigerian government to handle conflicts could be seen in Niger-Delta crisis, kidnapping, political upheavals, militancy, assassinations, and religious fundamentalism. All these are struggles for scarce resources in which few people are now richer than the whole country.

Apart from the above conflicts, there are age-long land conflicts that are common currency in Nigeria. The latter is the concern of this paper. The inability of the successive regimes in Nigeria to find a long-lasting solution to the problem of ownership and usage of land mirrors the extent of governance problems in the country. As the issues connected to the conflicts are increasingly politicised, the problem is assuming more dangerous dimensions. Land is a fundamental property in traditional Nigerian societies, and is communally owned, though family or corporate ownership has existed side by side with communal ownership. It is a source of wealth and greatly valued as an indispensable factor of production. Agriculture, the oldest occupation of humankind, takes place on land. Traditional Africa in general and Nigeria in particular maintained a liberal policy of allocation of land resources. It was allocated to families and individuals while the community or clan maintained absolute ownership. The chief or the head of the lineage or clan is the custodian

397

of the land. His position is that of a trustee, holding the land for the clan or the whole community. These custodians are invested with the power to manage and administer the communal property but in the interests of members of the community. Strangers and people with problems were easily absorbed and settled without discrimination and with land to use at one's discretion. All the cultural practices and norms were carried out based on the cultural beliefs and attitudes towards life and hospitality.

Since livelihood in an agricultural economy depends on the exploitation of land and water resources, land matters and resources have become serious issues of violent conflicts in modern Nigeria (Oyeshola 2003: 125). In addition, population explosion has put pressure on land, the scarce resource. The growth in population led to increased demand for land. Today, traditional farmers, civil servants, traders, ex-servicemen, and urban workers are all involved in the fight to privatise communal lands.

If there is one problem today for which we need urgent solutions, it is that of violent conflicts in families and communities, and between ethnic groups over the uses or exploitation of land and water resources in Nigeria. These conflicts are both persistent and brutal. The persistence is seen in the perennial crises from place to place and the reoccurrence of similar problems nationwide. Most of the conflicts erupt among communities that have had strong ties that bound them together for centuries. The land use act of 1979, which provides that the governor holds all land in the state on behalf of the federal government, is not effective; the problem has continued unabated.

Theoretical Framework

This study is based on the thesis that African value systems and conflict transformation systems are viable means of resolving African conflicts today (Brock-Utne: 2001: 6). Hence, more often than not, the use of modern methods of conflict resolution has been a resounding failure. Avruch and Black (1993: 131) see 'culture as a fundamental feature of human consciousness that is constitutive of human reality'. They recommended cultural analysis, which seeks to understand the significance of an event within its own cultural context. As applied to the study, Nigeria is torn apart by extremely intense conflicts that have resulted in thousands of death and properties destroyed. It is only when potential and actual conflicts in the area are understood in religio-cultural contexts that they can be solved. Since culture is not static but changes over time and adapts to new circumstances, it is easier to combine traditional and modern approaches in peacemaking. Boege (2006: 2) rightly pointed out that traditional conflict resolution targets problems in relatively small communities in the local context, like conflict within and between families, within and between villages or clans, and between neighbours. In the case of Mbaduku-Udam, the conflict is between neighbours, while that of Ife-Modakeke is within and between communities.

The mindset of this work is that there is much to be learned from traditional ways of peacemaking, especially land matters that are deep rooted in religious culture of the various groups. A very important reason for being aware of our traditions is to draw lessons from them for the solution of current problems. It is tempting to seek innovative approaches to conflict management in Nigeria on the assumption that the failure of modern methods is in part responsible for ongoing conflict. Traditional methods may not have outlived their utility, especially when adapted to modern realities.

Some Age-Long Land Conflicts

We shall now examine the nature of some of the bitter territorial disputes (in this context land) that started before independence and that more often than not resurface with serious implications in the socioeconomic and political life of Nigeria. The northern region is religiously as well as ethnically diverse. However, religious differences in themselves do not appear to be central to conflicts as land matters. The North-Central states of Benue, Niger, Nasarawa, Kwara, Taraba, Kogi, Plateau, Southern Kaduna, and the Southern Bauchi States have witnessed the explosion of conflicts, on a scale previously unimaginable and to an extent that shook the very basis of the continued coexistence of the peoples of the region (Alubo 2006: 34). From 2000 to 2003, they had experienced more than 45 conflicts of both an interstate and intrastate character (Ayua 2006: 66). The major occupation of most of the ethnic groups who inhabit the North-Central Nigeria is farming. The need to acquire and use land for farming purposes has, therefore, been at the root of several crises in this region.

The Tiv people (Benue State), for example, are one of the major ethnic groups in the region and are found virtually in every state of the region and beyond for agriculture. Tiv land has been recognized for its superior agrarian ecology. It is an extremely fertile expanse of land with functional vegetation, alluvial soil, and mineral deposits. The area is still in the peasant agricultural state of development; food and raw materials such as rice, yams, cassava, maize, guinea-corn, beniseed, groundnut, and soya-beans, among others, are produced. There is, therefore, a huge pressure and insatiable quest for land. Most Tiv men and women struggle to have a bigger farm each year.

Violent conflicts within Tiv land and those involving their neighbours--namely, Cross-River State, Taraba, Nasarawa and Plateau States--over ownership and usage constitute the most intractable problems of Benue State government of Nigeria. There is hardly any part of Tiv land that has not experienced disputes at one time or the other.

Mbaduku-Udam Crisis

Let us pinpoint the Mbaduku-Udam crisis as one of the age-long territorial conflicts in the region. The Tiv of Mbaduku in Vandeikya Local Government Area of Benue State and Udam in the Obudu area of Cross River State have been fighting over rich patches of land in Dagba and Mbatyough areas of Mbaduku for a long time now. The Tiv people migrated from South Africa, through the Congo region and Cameroon to the Middle Benue Basin between 1715 and 1745 (Hembe 2002: 72). They met with other ethnic groups (Udam) in the region. The two groups involved in violent conflict are known to have lived peacefully for centuries. They also have a rich cultural background, close and strong ties, and historic cultural structures that are cherished, markets, and intermarriages that strengthen such ties. The interactions facilitated multilingualism, learning of each other's language, visits, and residence of members of one linguistic community in the other group. We have Tiv people living in Ogoja, Boki, Ikom, and Otukwang. On the other hand, we have the Cross River people in Vandeikya, Tsar, Korinya, Gboko, among others. The bond of friendship and mutual understanding is further strengthening by *Ityo* (palm wine), which the Vandeikya people and Konshisha get from Udam.

The close relations between the Tiv ethnic group and Cross River groups made the former absorb or assimilate a lot of traditional practices of the latter. The Tiv acquired mystical *akombo* (spiritual forces) of farming. The Tiv people in the region now produce enough yams for consumption and for local trade. A special species of yam is called *dam yo* (Udam yam). The same could be said of *mondu* (a species of yam), *ikyegh dam* (duck of Udam), and *bar dam* (salt of Udam).

In every aspect of Tiv traditional and religious life, *akombo* (mystical or spiritual forces) are involved. They are the indelible dye colouring every facet of Tiv culture, for example, in their practice of medicine, farming, and healing rituals. *Akombo a dam* is the type of magic-religious rituals that had its origin in Cross River (Udam).

Death in Tiv traditional religion is the last of the rites of passage that every man or woman has to go through on earth. Today, the Tiv people are known for elaborate burial rites lasting for many days. Tiv people borrowed the practice from their immediate neighbours in the south (Udam) who in the precolonial days and even today are known for very elaborate burial rites. The same is applicable to offering of new yams to the supernatural before eating. New yam festivals are celebrated in all areas in the Upper Cross River. The Tiv people are usually invited to participate in the ceremonies.

In another dimension, the Tiv in Kunav and Gaav areas have borrowed the *girinya* dance (war dance) from the Udam. The Tiv are very prominent and unique in the ritual dance of *girinya* to symbolize greatness. Udam, on the other hand, borrowed the art of pot making from their Tiv neighbours. The Obudu people of Cross River always invite their Tiv neighbours, especially Mbayongo, to teach them the art of fishing. In hunting expeditions, the Udam people interacted much more freely with the Mbaduku and Mbayongo of Tiv extraction. The two groups have acquired the mystical forces associated with fishing, hunting, and pot making.

It was on 27 January 1950 that a fight occurred between Tiv and Udam. Bohannan (1968: 176) narrated the incidents, saying that it was between two Tiv women and an Udam man and woman in a stream that, along one portion of its course, marks the division between Tiv and Udam. The Tiv women were fishing and had muddied the water. The Udam man and woman objected, for they drew their drinking water from this stream. The ensuing argument led to blows, and one of the two Tiv women received three relatively serious matchet wounds on her left arm. She and her companion raised the alarm by ululation and hurried back to her compound for first aid, streaming blood and shouting that the Udam had 'killed' them.

Within a short period, about 400 armed Tiv warriors came out and the Udam were equally up in arms, though no serious fighting occurred that day. The situation continued until 21 May1950, when the second Tiv-Udam misunderstanding broke out in a war (*tyav*) that lasted for five days. It is estimated that about 40 people were killed on the two sides, about 1 100 huts were burned down, and crops destroyed. From the 1950s till 2009, hardly a year passed without high tension, physical assault, cutting of heads, and general loss of lives from both sides. There are cases of full-blown wars, as both sides used sophisticated weapons and destructive cannon guns. The violent conflicts are not just over land, but also cultic emblems that make land fertile, land that the two groups shared in common in the precolonial period. In 1951, there was a peace ceremony on the boundary with colonial administrative officers present. After the independence of Nigeria in 1960, the government has always resorted to use of military force, and to police and mobile policemen to stop violence and aggression. The government has always adopted the establishment of judicial commissions of inquiry, and peace and reconciliatory meetings are held in both Obudu and Vandeikya areas to help promote peace and reconcile the parties. All these measures have not helped in the restoration of lasting peace and reconciliation.

Ife-Modakeke

It is true that the Ife-Modakeke crisis is also one of the oldest intra-ethnic conflicts not only in Yoruba land but Nigeria as a whole. The crisis started in the 1830s and has been going on for more than a century and is still claiming lives. The Modakeke people are regarded as those refugees that fled from the old Oyo Empire and settled at Ile-Ife, following the collapse of old Oyo and subsequent invasion by the

Fulani jihadists from Ilorin in the 19th century. In 1847, Ooni Abeweila created a separate settlement for those Oyo refugees who had no home to return to, and the settlement was named Modakeke. The refugees therefore maintained a separate identity and independent policy from the Ifes. According to Albert (2004: 144), the relationship between the two groups was very cordial at the initial stage. The Ooni (king) and his chiefs found them and their Oyo kinsmen back home to be good allies in movements of warfare and good hands in farm work. The Oyos provided military support to the Ifes during the Owu war of 1825 and various Ijesha invasions. These encouraged Ife chiefs to throw their doors open to more refugees as they came in greater numbers. Land was given to them and several of them worked for Ife farmers.

Most of the Modakeke people were born in Ife and might suggest that most also married Ife women. The Modakeke people have argued that they had some rights over the land, as it was bought by their forefathers. As the Ifes could no longer force the Modakeke people to their farms, among other factors, the attitude of the Ifes to strangers changed. The refugees were getting ill treated and were sold into slavery. Precolonial struggles between the Ifes and Modakeke began and the former were defeated in many battles. The treaty of peace, friendship, and trade that was signed between the British and some Yoruba traditional authorities on 4 June 1886 touched on the Ife-Modakeke conflict. The Modakeke refused to sign the treaty because it contained aspects dealing with the relocation of Modakeke to a new site.

The Ife-Modakeke crisis is basically over land ownership and usage. The Ifes wanted the Modakeke to regard them as their lord and owner of the land on which they settled. The Modakeke were also asked to pay royalties in the form of their farm yields to their Ife landowners. The colonial government in 1909 dispersed the Modakeke to Owu/Ipole, Edunabon, Ede and Odeomu. Some of the dispersed faced the problem of land scarcity and social adjustment and was later allowed to return to Ile-Ife in 1922. They were absorbed into Ife and not to be regarded as a separate town.

The Ife-Modakeke crisis resurfaced in 1946 following the commercialisation of cocoa and the huge revenues accruable to Modakeke farmers. The expected revenue from commercial cocoa made Ife land owners demand 10% of the harvested cocoa. The Modakeke lost all cases relating to the incessant demands from Ifes, even at the appeals court.

Following the 1979 commencement of party politics, the Modakeke still focused on having their own Local Government Council instead of Ife-dominated local politics. There was resumption of hostilities, as evident in 1981, 1983, 1997 violent conflicts. The colonial administrators were unable to solve the Ife-Modakeke palaver, as they sided with Ifes, who had strong supporters and dominated local politics. In the postcolonial era, the Modakeke were equally frustrated at not having their own local government council. Even the premier of Western Nigeria, Chief Obafemi Awolowo, did not recognise the Modakeke as an autonomous community. Various panels of inquiry were set up to look into the Ife-Modakeke feud, and the most popular were those set up to look into the 1981 and 1997 crisis; but none of the panels came out with a solution to the problem. More often than not, people continued to be killed on the two sides of the conflict.

The Role of the Youths, Elites, and Mystical Powers in the Crises

In both Mbaduku-Udam and Ife-Modakeke conflicts, the youths and elites have a powerful influence in fomenting trouble and in the execution of all wars as well as in the peace process. Because of the value of life and harmonious living in Tiv culture and religion, even in the event of provocation by a neighbouring community, attempts are made by elders to negotiate and resolve the problem without resorting to violence. However, it appears the elders have lost their leadership position to *Mbayev* (the youths). Gbor (2003: 33) discusses the situation:

The elders do not appear to have the last word on vital issues affecting the land as was prevalent in the past. The various clans of the Tiv, which were governed by the elders, are now being governed by the youths who, in some instances, do not only insist on what to do but also dictates to elders what has to be done in the society. In the past, in case of communal feuds involving two clans, there were some inherent control measures, which served as effective conflict resolution mechanisms. These were applied to resolve crises. Today, Tivland looks chaotic. The highly cherished cultural values inherent in Tiv religion are cast to the wind, chiefs and council of elders disregarded.

Albert (2004: 173) studied the history of the contemporary Ife-Modakeke crises and reports that most of the problems were caused by the youths. These youths also fought most of the battles on behalf of their parents. Worse still, the elites from conflict areas both outside and inside are more often than not agents of division and confusion. They donate money, arms, and ammunition to perpetrate violence. They take side with their kith and kin wrongly or rightly for selfish reasons rather than the interest of the common good of the area.

In both the Mbaduku-Udam, and Ife-Modakeke crises, several forms of mystical powers were employed in the past and even today they are invoked to give spiritual protection and achieve maximum success in war. Shishima (2005: 80-100) has uncovered the use of *Gberkpugh* (medicine against weapons and gun shuts), *Bende* (Charm belt), *Dufu* (invisibility charm), and *Tsav* (witchcraft) in Tiv wars with their neighbours and even within Tiv land. The Udam of Cross River State too has war leaders who protect themselves with charms and amulets. The Yoruba people of Ife and Modakae have a well-established culture of traditional medicine, oracles, divination, and cult groups. The Tiv people have acquired a great deal of traditional medicine from the Yoruba people. *Onisegun* is a medicine man among the Yoruba who has occupied a very important position in the social, political, religious, and economic spheres of life.

Traditional Peacemaking Mechanisms

From our reflections on conflicts in North-Central Nigeria, particularly the Tiv and their neighbours, the Ife-Modakeke, among others, it is clear that Nigeria has witnessed an unprecedented wave of various forms of conflicts over ownership and usage of land. The vigour these conflicts have assumed in contemporary Nigeria continues to threaten the continued coexistence and habitation of the different ethnic groups that make up the country. We have also uncovered that most of the bitter territorial disputes erupt among communities that have had strong ties that have bound them together for centuries.

In view of the nature of these conflicts, all efforts in the past to check or control some of these types of conflicts through administrative and bureaucratic machineries, coupled with theories and methods crafted in Euro-American institutions, have failed to yield practical results. The fields of peace studies and conflict management reflected Western intellectual traditions, worldviews, expectations, values, and rationality embedded in Western culture. The discipline has assumed that the theories and methods derived from a particularistic worldview are universally acceptable. However, this can be dangerously misleading. In the context of Nigeria, according to Oguntola-Laguda (2006: 215),

'...The processes of conflict resolution such as mediation, counseling, organizational development, conciliation, quasi-political procedures, informal tribunals, arbitration of several types and criminal and civil justice system may not achieve the desired result'.

Over the centuries, West African societies have built a wealth of experience as well as specific mechanisms and institutions to prevent conflicts, peacefully resolve conflicts once they arise, and work through reconciliation processes. The focus of this research has been on traditional processes, mechanisms, and methods used by local communities to reduce and manage and sometimes resolve conflicts at the subnational level. These range from family head, council of elders, or chiefs, religious leaders, leaders of age grades, local courts, kinship mechanisms, compensatoryprocesses, and healing ceremonies. They constitute what we may call third-party intervention in conflict resolution. In traditional thought philosophy and religion, the third party is expected to be neutral and possess the capability to diffuse tension, listen to all sides, restore peace, and put in place social mechanism for conflict resolution.

Traditional Tiv society is described as stateless, dispersed, or noncentralised in the precolonial period. There was no elaborate political, religious, or social hierarchy. We have the *ya* (compound) council in which the oldest male member of the family was the head; the next political unit was the *iye-ingyor* council, which was made up of the elders of several compounds whose membership depended on close blood relations. The *Ityo* council was made up of the representatives from different *iye-ingyor* groups. Some of the major cases tried by it include murder, organised communal labour, witchcraft, land disputes, siting of new markets, and construction of bridges. The *Tav* council was the highest decision-making body of elders in Tiv land. The council was held to deliberate on major issues affecting the people, such as warfare involving other groups, initiation into mystical forces (*akombo*), and burial ceremonies. The office of the *Tor Tiv* (paramount ruler of the Tiv people) came into existence during the colonial era. On 3 April 1947, Makir Dzekpe was officially installed as the first Tor Tiv (Luga and Tortema n.d: 27).

When any of the above institutions meets to deliberate over matters affecting them, it is called *jir*. This is an assembly of neighbours and kinsmen that decides disputes from the simplest level to the highest level. Bitter territorial disputes were handled by *jir ityo* comprising of all the segments of Tiv society, forming a court of judicature. *Jir* is held in the compound or homestead of the person who initiates it; all the elders of his lineage come as guests, to be his judges and mentors. Tiv call this sort of *jir* a "*jir* at home" or *jir* of the agnatic lineage (*jir ityo*). Lastly we have the *jir* that embraced the entire Tiv land.

In order to have influence in *jir*, an elder must have a good memory of genealogies, for most of the cases touch on genealogies in some way or other. He needs an extensive and sure knowledge of the principles and details of Tiv religion, magic, and witchcraft. He must know all the ramifications of personal relationships within his small community, for most of these important factors are not brought out in the case but are presumed to be known to all hearers. In a nutshell, Tiv elders use *jir* to *sor tar* (repair broken down relationship at interpersonal, community level and in handling cases involving other groups). In this regard, they act as peacemakers and they keep the community running smoothly.

Jir among the Tiv has two main sets of components: *lôhô jir* (convening) and *ôr jir* (discussing). The latter is done by hearing reports from diviners and reconciling them. At least one person or group should consult a diviner before *jir* is convened. The remainder of the *jir* involves discovering how the general situation revealed by the diviner is to be applied to the situation under discussion. In the course of the discussion, one's age grade, mother's lineage *pine* acts as the interlocuter to probe further into the case. *Jir* deals almost entirely in terms of *mimi*, the truth of right social relations. Since much of the suspected wrongdoing has occurred on a mystical sphere, it could be affirmed by oath. Rituals in the *jir* include *Hamber Ifan* (blowing out the curse), *Bum swem* (taking oath using *sw em* cultic emblem), and *hembe swem* (broken *swem* to dispel evil done). With the above, the elders could reach a decision accepted by all. There is *tia* (fine) in terms of tobacco, chicken, animals, or local gin shared by all. The rituals of oath-taking and declaring of innocence symbolised that the elders have discussed and reached a unanimous decision thereby *sor tar* (repairing the country). Bohannan (1957: 169-203) recorded five different cases resolved by *ijir.* However, with colonialism, Christianity weakened the traditional judicial process. Nevertheless, elements of *jir* still exist and in the new dispensation we have *jir i tamen* (supreme council of all chiefs in Tiv land) today.

The Igbo people just like the Tiv of central Nigeria had no chiefs but warrant chiefs were introduced in the colonial era. Today, the institution of kingship is well established, with Igwes or Ezes providing leadership in collaboration with kindred chiefs. Before chiefs were introduced in Tiv land and in Igbo territories that operated noncentralised forms of government, elders and council of elders were the most important peacemaking and conflict resolution mechanisms. In Yoruba land, the political head of every Yoruba kingdom was *Oba.* The Oyo and Ife kingdoms had the *Alafin* and *Ooni,* respectively. Yoruba kings had advisers. This traditional leadership is a symbol of the socioreligious beliefs of the people. Traditional rulers, councils of elders, and family heads, among others, derive their powers and authorities from custom, religion, and other conventions. In traditional matters, they remain supreme as the repository of the traditions and socio-cultural values of societies. They are expected to advise all strata of government on how best to understand and reconcile disputed lands.

There are three levels of conflict resolution approaches in traditional Yoruba court system. These are dispute resolution at the interpersonal or family level, the extended family level, and village or town level (Chief-in-Council). These levels represent the political units making up the community. The smallest political unit within Yoruba towns is the *idile,* which roughly corresponds to the nuclear family and is headed by a *bale*. This is followed by the *ebi,* the extended family headed by *mogaji*, who is usually the eldest or most influential person. Extended family includes all people who have blood ties. Lastly, we have several family compounds that are headed by a *baale* (Albert 1995: 13-31).

At the family level, minor conflicts are usually resolved immediately by scolding the troublemakers and appeasing whoever was offended. *Baale* can visit the home of the offended person to formally apologise, even after the disputes had been resolved, and to thank him for accepting a peaceful resolution to the conflict. As soon as *baale* returns from his peace mission, he calls together his household and warns them to desist from making any more trouble.

Matters or cases like land disputes that cannot be settled at the interpersonal or family level are usually taken to the *mogaji* or the *baale*. Such cases usually receive prompt attention. This is to prevent any escalation into violence that can threaten the survival of the entire lineage. Each person, starting with the plaintiff, states his or her case. Once the matter is resolved, emphasis is put on how good neighbourliness can be achieved and preserved.

The Chief-in-Council (*Igbimo ilu*) is the highest traditional institution for conflict resolution. In the past, the council had power to pass death sentence, but today the situation has changed. It can handle minor civil cases, especially those pertaining to land, chieftaincy, and inheritance. In the investigative process, after the complainant has given his evidence, the defendant, who is expected to have listened carefully, is invited to respond to the charges. It is only the chiefs who are permitted to ask questions to clarify issues, when the plaintiff or the defendant is giving evidence. The person giving the evidence is not to use offensive language, as a mark of respect to the elders that constitute the jury. After the evidence has been given, the king and his chiefs cross-examine the disputants before the judgment is given. Fines of damages are not usually awarded by the mediators in civil cases. The aim is to restore peace by settling disputes amicably. Sometimes mediators award simple fines as a deterrent to the re-occurrence of particular anti-social behaviour. This may be in form of kola nuts or local gin, both of which have ritual significance. Some of the kola nuts are broken and passed round to everyone to eat as an indirect way of celebrating the resolution of the conflict. The drink is also passed round for all to taste. If no gin or palm wine is available, ordinary water can be used. In some traditional settings, palm wine or gin is used to pour libation to the gods and ancestors of the people involved in the dispute.

On the whole, the main features of Yoruba court system include cross-examination of parties to the dispute and their witnesses. They are given sufficient time for hearing, and anyone who refuses to tell the truth will attract wrath of the gods and ancestors. Again, hearing is always speedy; it is also expected of the litigants to demonstrate robust sense of goodness towards their legal culture and to be adjudged of a well-cultured character. The verdict of the legal officials is normally accorded a greater degree of objectivity because they represent the ancestors and the soul of the Yoruba society. The legal officials endeavour to maintain social equilibrium; cases are not treated with the ultimate aim of allotting punishment, but reconciliation (Olaoba 2002: 3-4). Finally, maintenance of absolute silence and tranquility is the hallmark of judicial process in Yoruba land.

In Yoruba land, the Ifa corpus is regarded as the wisdom of *Olodumare* (God) and witness to equitable distribution of land based on justice. Idowu (1996: 106) cited the Odu corpus in which *Ela* is presented as a peacemaker. The Odu also suggests that where there is conflict, *Ela* can intervene as a third party and restore peace and harmony into the community. Religious leaders such as priests, diviners, and medicine men command much respect of their followers. The role of these religious leaders in conflict management has to do with the use of virtues of their religion to assist in investigation, analyse the conflict situation, and preach peace and harmonious coexistence among conflicting interests.

The Nigerian village or settlement usually represented a convergence of loyalties that made for a strong sense of community. Very often family ties criss-crossed the village, adding to more of the loyalties of chiefdom and ethnic group, as well as those of professional associations. Neighbours cooperated in a thousand ways, working communally on each other's farms, taking part in each other's expeditions. Neighbours borrowed tools and utensils from each other and performed innumerable services for each other. Neighbours came together not only for work and recreation, but also to solve disputes. The neighbourhood court played an invaluable role in reconciling disputants, in settling quarrels, and in imposing sanctions. The courts operated on the basis of a thorough personal knowledge of the parties involved and their families, and their interest was in maintaining peace and harmony among neighbours and villagers. A local chief might be responsible for the final decision taken, but it would have to reflect the opinions voiced in the free discussion that had preceded it.

Women, too, contribute to conflict resolution. Elderly or old women expose their nakedness or threaten to interpose themselves between the fighters in making peace. It is the gesture that signifies a curse for those who bear the responsibility for such grave acts of war. Examples include the Aba riots, and it is also a common practice in Nsukka areas of Igbo land.

The early history of relationships among Ibibio communities and between them and non-Ibibio ethnic groups were characterised by pacts (agreement or treaty or alliance or covenant or declaration made between two or moral individuals, villages, clans, or ethnic groups). Pacts had been used to form *iman* (kinship), friendship, and alliance relationships in both precolonial and contemporary Ibibio land. Bassey (2007: 149) unveiled peace pacts that were made to end intervillage, interclan, and interethnic wars or boundary disputes in Ibibio land. The process involves meeting of the two groups for negotiation, preparation of concoction by both parties into the mortar, pouring of palm wine into it, verbal pronouncements made by elders about of not fighting each other anymore, and a declaration of living like brothers and sisters forever. Lastly, the mortal pact-*Udang iman*-- was buried at the boundary agreed upon by the parties.

The pacts of Ibibio people engendered peace and positive development, promoted intergroup relations, and checked communal and interethnic conflicts. They anchored genuine and lasting reconciliation between warring communities. Pacts created obligations that contracting parties had to carry out without fail. For example, a pact guarantees each other's safety in their respective areas of jurisdiction, observation of common code of conduct, and marriages.

In Igbo land, reconciliation was conceived as the process of penitent rite, a rite of forgiveness, reacceptance, and a perfect communion with the spiritual beings. The process of rituals of reconciliation includes: confession and the ritual meal. This is based on the belief that there is power in word and that the word creates, heals, and kills. Confession is necessary for liberation. In the ritual meal, both parties, the angered and the culprit, share the drinks and meals together showing reunion. By eating together, the parties involved enter into a covenant. Propitiation by way of atonement is necessary in order that the evil committed may be removed and a right relationship restored. The ritual of oath taking is usually administered to the person who confessed his evil acts, that he would never do the evil any longer. The oath-taking helps in restoration of broken relationship and remove suspicion and fear among the parties.

The herbalists, medicine men, soothsayers, and priests equally have special roles to play in conflict management and resolution. In land matters where the village assembly of the Igbo people could not reach a decision, oracles were consulted for final adjudication. In such matters, their verdicts were final and undisputed.

Traditional Methods of Peacemaking Vis-À-Vis Modern Methods

Slave trade, colonialism, Christianity, and Westernization greatly influenced the traditional institutional mechanisms for peacemaking in Nigeria. Courts were created by the colonialists to adjudicate cases based on their legal system, which most times are not properly resolved. Many see the formal channels for justice-the police and the court-as being both expensive and corrupt. In some cases, complainants have to provide the stationery for recording their cases. It is therefore not surprising that the rich always have an advantage over the poor in the formal legal system. Lawyers hardly make the situation bearable; they really consider the economic status of their clients before fixing their professional charges (Oyeshola 2005: 47).

In traditional societies, many conflicts are resolved without calling the police. Some of the reasons for this are the intimidating size of the formal courts as contrasted with informal places used for resolving neighbourhood conflicts. Disputants, therefore, often take their cases to elders and neighbourhood mediators who can be depended upon to resolve in a local language, using familiar standards of behaviour.

The administration of justice in traditional societies was aimed at resolving conflicts rather than pronouncing judgments and punishments. Emphasis was placed on reconciliation and restoration of social harmony rather than on punishment of people involved in the conflicts. The administration was an open-air affair where all adults freely participated. The processes were held in the open with the parties in conflict being freely cross-examined. Truth was the yardstick of the delivery of justice. The 'western legal approach emphasizes establishing guilt and executing retribution and punishment without reference to the victim or the wider families or future reincorporation of the offender into the community' (Brock-Utne 2001: 3).

In traditional Africa, great emphasis was placed on peaceful resolution of disputes so as to restore social harmony to the conflicting parties. It was strongly upheld that disputes should be settled by persuasion rather than resort to force or coercion. Tiv moot, for example was made up of elders and adults as well as neighbours of the parties to a conflict. Every claim from both parties to the conflict was investigated with transparency. In very serious cases, a few people were selected to consult a diviner and they presented their findings to the group. At the end of it all, judgment was delivered and all parties shared a drink and meal. External efforts at peacemaking such as use of police, military force, conciliation commissions, and arbitration panels are often thwarted by erosion of the authority of traditional leaders, thus creating major difficulties in negotiating with legitimate community representatives who are able to implement conflict management and resolution processes. This often involves significant segments of local authority structure and often signifies community desires for stability, enhanced production, increased trade, and benefits that war often denies. Traditional authorities, women's organisations, local institutions, and professional associations have crucial roles to play in the development of grassroots peacebuilding.

Like the modern courts, from the Customary to the Supreme Court with rights of appeal, so also the resolution of conflict in the past commenced from the family court: Court of the council of elders in the compound, courts of the various societies, and the court of the Oba-in-council as the Spume Court in Yoruba land.

In trying to resolve conflicts emanating from competition for land, panels of inquiry usually do a thorough work and make a comprehensive recommendation to the government. Experience has shown that the recommendations are hardly followed. In traditional peacemaking, the decisions of elders, chiefs, and religious leaders are implemented immediately and normalcy restored.

Western forms of conflict resolution are based on negotiation and bargaining between the parties in conflict. The primary aim of negotiation and the bargaining contest is to win through the manipulation of information surrounding the conflict and the use of coercive resources to induce concession. The process of communicative interaction between the parties is determined by a motivation to gain favourable outcomes to the negotiator's own side in the dispute. In traditional peacemaking, efforts are made to avoid manipulation of facts.

Age and wealth of experience are important features of conflict management. The head of the family is usually the oldest, as are the council of elders and the chiefs. Traditionalists believe in leadership through consensus, allowing everyone to have a voice while the traditional head rules by consent. In Nigeria, just like other parts of Africa, elders are respected as trustworthy mediators because of accumulated experience and wisdom, unlike some judges in modern judicial systems.

In grassroots peacemaking, there is strong appeal to the supernatural realities in mediation, and restoration of relationships. The use of curse by elders, symbols, and interpretation of myths, drinking of herbal mixtures, and oracular consultations are effective ways of conflict management. In this regard, the guilty could repent, acknowledge responsibility, ask for forgiveness, and be reconciled with the victim's family. All these noble qualities of traditional peacemaking are lacking in modern methods of conflict transformations.

Traditional Approaches in Modern Realities

The last unit pinpoints indigenous traditional mechanisms for communication, and building shared values, consensus, and resolving conflict that were the core of earlier participatory forms of government. Studies have shown that some elements that sum up African culture have remained largely native and unchanged, despite the influence of Westernization. Adeniyi (2003: 17) captures this, saying 'it has itself remained virgin over the years'. The elements of practice have not changed significantly over centuries (Gbenda 2007: 332). In other words, very little has changed in traditional approaches to peacemaking today. Restorative and traditional practices are being proposed for use in local and national reconciliation and peacemaking processes. Indegenous practices are of diminishing importance and traditional concepts survive because they find new dimension and a new application in modern situation.

We have observed in our reflection that contemporary political developments in Nigeria have demonstrated the failure of the state to nurture the Nigerian people. The standard of administration, both the federal and state, should be improved to inspire in the minds of Nigerians, a sense of national unity, a feeling of oneness, unity in diversity, objectivity, and fairness in the redistribution of economic, social, and political benefits and opportunities. The various levels of governance should learn from the cultural heritage of accommodation and absorption of nonindigene into the society without discrimination with much land to use. We still have living examples of the Hausa and Fulani being absorbed in Kwara State, Jukun in Abinsi, Etulo and Hausa in Katsina-Ala areas of Benue State. Why then do we still call the Ifes strangers in their fatherland? Why should the Tivs in Udam, Taraba, Nasarrawa, and Plateau States is regarded as strangers.

Ethnic groups in Nigeria should be hospitable to the so-called strangers or settlers. This is because strangers were feared and accorded many privileges and opportunities in African cultural heritage. Africans believe that all humans are children of God. In some cultures, like the Tiv and Yoruba, the so-called stranger is sometimes regarded only as an unknown relative. Moreover, because people believe that divinities often take human forms to bring important messages to communities, one is careful not to harm a stranger for fear of unknowingly harming a divinity.

Today more than ever before, Nigeria is bedeviled by land problems with unending battles. Methods of conflict resolution should be drawn from the traditional culture with the guidance of traditional leaders and institutions. This includes communication styles, leadership choices, methods of negotiation, participation of parties to the conflict, and the third party, decision making structures, the system of compensation for wrongdoing, determi-nation of wrongdoing, and appropriate punishment, processes for remorse, confession, forgiveness, and reconciliation and rituals for marking closure and new relationship.

In trying to find a lasting solution for peace in the Mbaduku-Udam and Ife-Modakeke crises, and any other crises deeply rooted in religio-cultural values, the council of elders and chief's forum should be employed. Well-respected elders like those valued in precolonial Nigeria should be empowered by the federal and state governments to start peace meetings of problem solving using a nonpartisan third party. The meetings should be held outside the problem areas and emphasis should not be on who is right or wrong but on genuine reconciliation.

Fieldwork conducted in some of the warring communities revealed that the youths have poor knowledge of the history of the crises, but they use the opportunity for enrichment and politics. Chiefs and elders that are well versed in the history and culture of the areas involved in land disputes should be given the chance to review the history of cordial relationships, interconnection, and interdependence of the groups. Where they are confused, they should get the consent of their forefathers through oracle consultation and divination. Diviners in Nigeria often help the police in investigation. There is nothing wrong in referring matters of land disputes or custom matters to well-renowned oracles and diviners to get final decisions from their forefathers, since the present generation has no idea of the principles laid on land matters. These could be used in the analysis of conflict situation and for bringing about peace.

The third party should encourage the warring communities to look inward and reflect on traditional mechanisms of reconciliation of the groups and come out with suggestions. From another perspective, the Ifes and other groups involved in calling people strangers should look inward and reflect on the implications of calling a citizen of Nigeria a settler or nonindigene.

The warring communities should be encouraged by the third party to come out with a formula for healing rituals, appeasements of the gods and other spiritual agents, for the loss of lives and property and for their forgiveness. A sacred meal should be prepared and shared by all for restoration of order. The youths and elites should be encouraged to observe the resolutions. The government should address the problem of mass youth unemployment and train the youths in peace resolution mechanisms. Peace education and traditional peace management and resolutions should be taught in all levels of educational system in Nigeria. The federal government should address the indigeneship question as it features in nomination for certain appointments, ministerial positions and membership of the Federal Board, jobs, school admissions, and even differentials in school fees.

Conclusion

Conflict is indeed an inevitable aspect of human interaction. However, in the context of our reflection, the age-old animosities between the various ethnic groups to retain ownership and control of land appear to have been exacerbated by the ineffectual nature of the land use act of 1979 in the rural areas of the states. While the act provides that the governor holds all land in the state in trust for the people, the reality is that traditional forms of ownership are still more recognised among the rural populace. In trying to resolve land disputes that are rooted in the religious history, like Maduku-Udam and Ife-Modakeke among others, which are more localizsed, traditional peacemaking and conflict management is an essential ingredient in addressing the situation in Nigeria.

References

Adekanye J.B. 2007. *Linking conflict diagnosis, conflict prevention and conflict management in contemporary Africa: Selected essays.* Lagos: Ababa Press 2007.

Adeniran, E. 2009. 'Governance has failed in Nigeria says Clinton'. *The Nation*, Friday 14 August.

Adeniyi, A. 2003. 'African culture, human health and scientific enquiring: Some reflections. In: *African culture, modern science and religious thought*, edited by P. Ade Dopamu. Ilorin: Decency Printers.

Albert, I. O, T. Awe, G. Herault, and W. Omitoogun. 1995. *Informal channels for conflict resolution in Ibadan Nigeria.* Ibadan: IFRA.

Albert, I.O. 2004. 'Ife-Modakeke crisis'. In: *Community conflicts in Nigeria: Management, resolution and transformation*, edited by Onigu Otite and Isaac O. Albert. Ibadan: Spectrum Books Limited.

Alubo, O. 2006. *Nigeria ethnic conflicts and citizenship crises in the central region.* Ibadan: PEFS.

Anugwom, E.E. and P. Oji. 'Ethnic and religious crises in Nigeria: A review of past and present dimension'. In: *Religion and societal development: Contemporary Nigerian perspectives*, edited by in M. I. Okwueze. Lagos: Merit International Publications.

Avruch, K. and P.W. Black. 'Conflict resolution in intercultural settings. http://www.beyondintractability.org/articlesummary//100 33/ (accessed 30 May 2010).

Ayua, I.A. 2006. 'The historic and legal roots of conflcits in the Benue Valley'. In: *Conflicts in the Benue Valley*, edited by Timothy T. Gyuse and Oga Ajene. Makurdi: Selfers Books.

Baba, T.B. 2002. 'Population, environment and economic development in the central Nigeria area'. In: *Studies in the history of central Nigeria, Vol. I*, edited by A.A. Idrees and Y.A. Ochefu. Lagos: CSS Press.

Bassey, J.R. "African indigenous knowledge of pact-making: Its significance and relationship with the modern international treaties: A case study of pre-colonial Ibibioland'. In: *African indigenous xcience and knowledge xystems: Triumphs and tribulations*, edited by Olayemi Akinwumi. Abuja: Roots Books and Journals Ltd.

Boege, Volker. 2006. 'Traditional approaches to conflict transformation Potentials and limits'. www.berghof handbook.net Berghof Research Centre for conflict Management--First Launch, July 2006.

Bohannan, P. 1957. *Justice and judgement mong the Tiv.* London: Oxford University Pres .

———. 1968. *Tiv economy.* Evanston: Northwestern University Press.

Brock-Utne, B. 'Indigenous conflict resolution in Africa'. A draft presented to the Week-end Seminar on Indigenous Solutions to Conflicts held at the University of Oslo, Institute of Educational Research, and 23-24 February 2001.

Bur, A. 2002. 'Communal crisis and its impact on community development'. In: *Communal relations: Conflicts and crisis management strategies*, edited by Ason Bur. Makurdi: Aboko Publishers.

Gbenda, J. S. 2007. 'Time and space in Tiv traditional eschatology'. *Journal of Oriental and African Studies* 116: 319-333.

Gbor, T.W.T. 2006. *The Concept of culture and Tiv cultural values.* Makurdi: SEEYE Prints.

Hembe, G. N. 2002. 'The political and economic impact of crises in Tivland'. In: *Communal relations: Conflicts and crisis management strategies*, edited by in Ason Bur. Makurdi: Aboki Publishers.

Idowu, B. 1996. *Olodumare: God in Yoruba belief.* Lagos: Longman.

Ishola, William 2009. "Reflections on our knowledge in peace making in West Africa www.panafstrag.org/.../REFLECTIONS % 200F % 20 OUR % 20 KNOWLEDGE % ZOIN % 20PE (accessed 2 July 2009).

Luga, A. A. and J.K. Tortema. N.d. *Tor Tiv : A brief background of the institution.* Makurdi: Sato Press.

Lyam, A.A. 2006. 'Kwande crisis: A community conflict of many interests'. In: *Conflicts in the Benue Valley*, edited by Timothy T. Gyuse and Oga Ajene. Makurdi: Selfers Press,

———. 2002. 'The ecological foundations of communal crisis within Benue and its environs'. In: *Communal relations conflicts and crisis management strategies*, edited by Ason Bur. Makurdi: Aboki Publishers.

Oguntola-Laguda, D. 2006. 'The role of traditional rulers and religious leaders in conflict management in Nigeria'. In: *Issues in the practice of religion in Nigeria*, edited by M.T. Yahya. Ilorin: Decency Printers.

Olaoba, O.B. 2002. *Yoruba legal culture.* Ibadan: FOP Press.

Onah, R.C. 2004. *Experiences of tradition, custom and religion*: *Igbo example*. Enugu: Chuka Publishers.

Oyeshola, D. 2005/ *Conflict and context of conflict resolution.* Ile-Ife: Obafemi Awolowo University Press Ltd.

Shishima, S.D. 2005. '"The use of mystical powers in the 2001 Tiv-Jukun crisis in Taraba States'. In: *Causes of conflicts in the Benue Valley*, edited by Timothy T. Gyuse and Oga Ajene. Makurdi: The Centre for Peace and Development Studies.

Torkula, A.A. 2006. *The cosmology in Tiv worldview.* Makurdi: Oracle Business Ltd.

419

Utov, C.I. 2000. *The underdevelopment of Tivland.* Makurdi: The Return Press.

PART VI

INSTITUTIONS AND ORGANIZATIONS

CHAPTER 15

Constitutionalism and the territorial origins of African Civil Conflicts

John Mukum Mbaku, Esq.[1]

I. Historical Background

Colonialism was a cruel, repressive, exploitative, despotic, and extremely inhumane pact designed and agreed upon by various European countries and imposed on Africa and Africans.[2] The primary objective of this insidious pact was the maximisation of the objectives of the metropolitan economies, as well as those of Europeans resident in the colonies.[3] In order to enhance their ability to effectively exploit African resources for their benefit, the Europeans imposed on the colonies laws and institutions that disenfranchised Africans, abrogated their civil, political, and economic rights, and effectively destroyed the ability of Africans to govern themselves and allocate their resources in an equitable and efficient manner (Mbaku 2003).

As part of the effort to create an environment in each colony that was conducive to resource extraction, the European colonialists, working closely with the various mercantile companies and independent settler-entrepreneurs, brought together, through police and military force, clusters of ethnic groups to form 'a single political, economic and administrative unit' (Mbaku 2003: 103).[4] Along with new European-based institutions and judicial systems, the Europeans also imposed on each of their colonies their language and culture and other mechanisms (e.g., Christianity) designed to enhance the exploitation of the resources of the territories. In the process, traditional African values and practices were destroyed or banned, and the people exposed to, and in many instances forced to accept, a new, Eurocentric set of institutional arrangements (Mbaku 1997).

In each colony, peaceful coexistence of population groups was not made possible through voluntary and mutually beneficial social contracts but through the employment of the superior military and police force brought by the colonisers. It was common practice for the Europeans to bastardise traditional forms of governance and resource

423

allocation and replace them with European-inspired forms, all of which placed the Europeans at a comparative advantage vis-à-vis political and economic governance (see generally Fatton 1990).

Throughout colonial Africa, the various indigenous African groups found themselves unable to mount an effective campaign against European annexation of their lands. In addition to destroying traditional forms of protest, the Europeans murdered indigenous leaders, [5] banned or destroyed traditional forms of subsistence, [6] and confiscated or burned religious and social symbols.[7]

The colonial enterprise, of course, was not a democratic enterprise-the latter usually provides the governed opportunities and, in more matures democracies, facilities, to protest and hold their governors accountable (see, e.g., Mbaku 2009). Colonialism, whether considered a political, social, or economic system, effectively shut out the African peoples from participating gainfully and, in a meaningful and humane way, in governance. In fact, the colonialists foreclosed to Africans all forms and means of peaceful resistance or protest and dealt, in a most brutal and capricious way, with those who dared oppose the presence of Europeans in the colony.[8] Perhaps, more important, from the point of view of conflict in postindependence Africa, is the fact that in addition to practicing despotic rule in the colonies, the Europeans destroyed traditional African production systems, transferred Africa's wealth to Europe, and forcefully brought together under a single governance system, various population groups with distinct languages, cultures, values, and social systems. Peaceful coexistence of these groups, as mentioned earlier, was not achieved through allowing them to choose mutually beneficial economic and political governance systems, but through the employment of colonialism's enormous military and police apparatus.[9]

It is important to emphasise that colonialism's primary objective was the maximisation of European objectives in the colonies and that it was never the intention or desire of the various colonial governments in Africa to help the various ethnic groups that made up part of the population of each colony design and implement agreements that could help these groups live together peacefully. In fact, most colonial policies, which included land expropriation, establishment of plantations, mining and quarrying, and exploitation of various environmental resources, as well as the capricious and

424

arbitrary manner in which colonial policies were applied to each colony's nationality groups, actually produced an air of distrust among groups that contributed significantly to postindependence ethnic violence.[10]

The institutions brought to the colonies by the Europeans and the economic, social, and political activities of the Europeans in the colonies contributed significantly to postindependence conflicts in Africa. First, various ethnic groups, each with its own distinct language, culture, and customs, were forcefully brought together to establish a single political and economic system, which could only be kept together through the use of an extraordinary level of violence. Second, the Europeans abrogated virtually all of Africa's traditional structures for the peaceful resolution of conflict and introduced Eurocenteric conflict resolution schemes that were not locally focused (that is, they did not reflect realities in the colonies) and hence, were ill equipped to deal effectively with conflict. Third, colonialism forcefully removed Africans from their ancestral lands, alienated the lands to European entrepreneurs and mercantile companies and set the stage for a violent struggle for ethnic survival that has lasted to the present day. Fourth, colonialism either destroyed African forms of communication or created incentive systems, which forced them to adopt European languages and culture as their main forms of expression. In fact, in many colonies, the use of African languages in communication, especially in commerce, education, and government, was strictly forbidden and deliberate efforts were made by the colonial governments to destroy African cultures and traditions.[11]

Fifth, many European institutions (e.g., European-supported educational institutions) favoured some ethnic groups and disadvantaged others-this uneven approach to education produced outcomes that significantly impacted and continue to impact governance in many African countries in the postindependence era. Finally, the decolonisation process was 'reluctant, repressive, and opportunistic,' and there was no 'fundamental transformation in the economic, cultural, or bureaucratic domains' (Fatton 1990: 457). Perhaps more important is the fact that decolonisation did not offer Africans the opportunity to engage in institutional reforms to create laws and institutions, which could have allowed them to govern themselves effectively and allocate their resources in sustainable and socially equitable ways.[12] For example, had decolonisation and postindependence institutional reforms been undertaken democratically, instead of through the top-down, elite-driven manner in which they were carried out, the various ethnic groups within each country could have had the opportunity to:

1) Determine how they wanted to relate to each other; [13]
2) Resolve property rights issues related to the forceful alienation of their lands to mercantile companies during the colonial period; [14]
3) Deal with important issues, such as citizenship and what citizenship means for participation in economic and political markets; and
4) Generally secure laws and institutions that would have provided them with the tools for the peaceful resolution of conflict.

To reiterate, democratic constitution making would have provided all of the relevant stakeholder groups in each colony the opportunity to build a new, shared, and inclusive political culture, one that borrows from the best experiences of each group. Thus, despite the fact that these groups were brought together through force (i.e., not through a mutually beneficial agreement) and under less than ideal circumstances, the pre- and postindependence constitution-making process could have been used to craft and adopt laws and institutions capable of enhancing peaceful resolution of conflict, democratic governance, and the efficient and socially equitable allocation of resources in the new countries. Perhaps, more important is that democratic constitution making could have provided the various population groups within each country the opportunity to resolve important issues (e.g., citizenship and property rights, especially in land and water resources), many of which have become the basis for many violent conflicts in the postindependence period. Unfortunately, constitution making in the pre- and postindependence periods was opportunistic, top-down, elite-driven, and noninclusive. As will be examined later in this chapter, pre-independence constitutional exercises were usually undertaken in the metropolitan capitals and away from the relevant stakeholder groups. The interests of Africans were represented by urban-based elites, who were carefully selected by the colonial government to ensure that the outcomes of these "negotiations" were rules that enhanced the ability of the "departing" Europeans to have full and effective access to the resources of their former colonies.[15]

In the postindependence period, the new leaders failed to engage all relevant stakeholder groups within their territories in the type of institutional reforms that could have allowed them to reconstruct and reconstitute the postcolonial state and provide themselves with democratic governance structures. Before I take a look at the impact of opportunistic (as opposed to democratic) constitution making on postindependence conflict in Africa, I would like to further explore the impact of colonial institutions on postindependence conflict.

II. Colonial Institutions and Postindependence Conflicts in Africa

A. Introduction

One of the most important institutions brought to the colonies by the Europeans was the police force. Many scholars have studied the role played by the police in the colonisation of Africa (see, e.g., Bayley 1969). In a study of the police in colonial Nigeria, Tamuno concluded that it was the rise of crime and civil disorder that provided the impetus for the establishment of the police in the colony (see Tamuno 1970: 10ff.). He claimed that increasing levels of political and social violence, brought about by 'dynastic disputes' and 'interethnic conflicts,' contributed significantly to an increase in criminality and 'had an important bearing on the origin, development and role of [the] modern police force [in Nigeria]' (Tamuno 1970: 10). According to this characterisation, the colonial police were agents of law and order, whose job it was to help all relevant stakeholders in the colonies, which included both Europeans and Africans, live together peacefully and maximise their values.[16]

Such a characterisation of the colonial police is part of the belief by apologists for colonialism that the latter was a 'civilising' mission, 'designed to prevent African societies from degenerating in [barbaric] anarchy' (Mbaku and Kimenyi 1995: 281). According to this view, the colonial police force (and other instruments of coercion brought to the

427

colonies by the Europeans) was expected to provide the wherewithal for the colonial government to 'civilise' perpetually warring African groups and prevent them from engaging in behaviours that were destined to destroy them (Mbaku and Kimenyi 1995: 281). Looked at this way, colonialism was not the cruel, despotic and dehumanising enterprise that it actually was.

On the contrary, colonialism was not a benevolent mission, designed to enhance the ability of Africans to govern themselves and engage in productive activities for the purpose of maximizing their values. Instead, the evidence points to colonialism as a deceitful and insidious scheme designed to enrich Europeans at the expense of Africans. Specifically, colonialism had two major objectives:

1) To secure raw materials for metropolitan industries; and
2) To prepare the colonies to serve as receptacles for excess (and quite often, obsolete) output from European factories.

Lord Frederick Lugard, a British colonial officer of distinction, stated that primary commodities from tropical Africa were essential inputs for Britain's industries and that the African colonies represented important markets for the sale of British manufactures (1926: 7). Hugh E. Egerton, a well-known expert on British imperial history, noted that the 'motives which prompted the European nations upon the field of colonization were in the main two, viz. the desire to win converts for the church, and the desire to win wealth for themselves' (1966: 57).

Much of the evidence points to the maximization of European objectives as the main impetus for colonialism. As argued by the late Claude Ake (1981), colonialism evolved from or was motivated by the internal contradictions of European capitalism. He posited that

> [t]he transplanting of capitalism arises from those contradictions which reduce the rate of profit and arrest the capitalization of surplus value. Confronted with these effects, it was imperative that the capitalist, forever bent on profit maximization, would look for a new environment in which the process of accumulation could proceed apace. Capitalists turned to foreign lands attacked and subjugated them and integrated their economies to those of Western Europe (Ake 1981: 19)

Right from the beginning, colonialism never pretended to be a mutually beneficial trading arrangement between Europe and Africa. The Europeans intended to subjugate Africans, seize their lands and other resources, and re-assign the rights in these resources to themselves. Thus, the European colonialists needed 'a well-organized group possessing a comparative advantage in the efficient use of violence' (Ahire 1990: 156) to enhance their ability to bring the various population groups in each colony under control and effectively minimise the costs of resource extraction (Ahire 1990, 1991). The colonial police force, which enjoyed a comparative advantage in the employment of coercion, evolved to serve just such a function (Ahire 1990: 156-57). Of course, the police force was part of an institutional framework imposed on the colonies by the Europeans. As argued by Fatton, most colonial institutions were primarily 'structures of exploitation, despotism, and degradation' (Fatton 1990: 457).

According to Michael Crowder, 'the colonial state was conceived in violence rather than by negotiation' (1981: 11-12). The police force served effectively as the provider of the violence needed to affect land seizures, as well as compel Africans to supply the labour services needed to advance the economic interests of the Europeans. Hence, a proper examination of colonial institutions, including the police force, must be situated within a colonial political economy characterised by the forced subjugation of one group by another-because the Europeans were determined to employ state coercion as the primary tool for the allocation of resources in the colonies, the police force (and other colonial institutions, such as the courts) evolved as instruments of 'violence, used to help Europeans conquer, control, subjugate and exploit Africans' (Mbaku and Kimenyi 1995: 283; see also Danns 1982).

Some scholars view the colonial police force as a benevolent state agency, whose primary objective was 'to act impartially in the interest of the community as a whole, to preserve and re-establish the rule of law and order' (Jeffries 1952: 198-99). Ahire, however, states that any scholar who sees the colonial police force as a 'legal and constitutional imperative ignores the fact that the police in these countries were established by force, despite indigenous resistance to them' (1990: 156).

B. Sewing the Seeds of Conflict: The British Police Force in West Africa

Increased rivalry between British and other European entrepreneurs along the West African coast in the early 1800s forced the British government to consider establishing a permanent settlement in the area in order to protect the flow of raw materials to its industries. In 1851, British military forces overthrew the King of Lagos, annexed his territory, and on August 6, 1860, made the territory of Lagos a British colony (Burns 1963: 115-39; Ahire 1991: 33; Tamuno 1970: 10). The conquest of Lagos and the subsequent establishment of a permanent British presence on the Bights of Benin and Biafra resulted in an expansion of trade and plantations, as well as missionary activity. Soon, British entrepreneurs located in the region began to request that the colonial government in Lagos protect them from competition from various indigenous groups and other European merchants (e.g., the French) (Rudin 1938). The colonial police force emerged in what would later become the colony of Nigeria as a result of the 'interaction of the colonial community with the African people[s], and the attempt by the colonial government to regulate this intercourse' (Mbaku and Kimenyi 1995: 290). First, British entrepreneurs needed the police force to help them effect the forced transfer of land from the indigenous groups to them-the police were needed to effect the forced transfer of rights in land, and to enhance the ability of the owners of land, which previously had belonged to various African ethnic groups, to prevent the recapture of this land. Second, British missionaries and merchants demanded that a police force be established so that it could effectively eliminate those individuals (e.g., so-called recalcitrant chiefs and kings) whose activities were considered major obstacles to the European concept of trade and religion. As argued by Smith (1971) and Tamuno (1970), British traders and missionaries encouraged and supported the establishment of the colonial police force and, actually suggested what they believed was the appropriate role for it (see generally Smith 1971 and Tamuno 1970).

The first police force in what would become the British colony of Nigeria was established by Acting Governor of the Colony of Lagos, William McCoskry in 1861 and consisted of 25 constables. Its primary function was to guard British trading posts (Tamuno 1970: 15). The strength of the force was increased to 100 constables by Governor McCoskry's successor, Governor Freeman. The latter changed the force into an 'Armed Police Force,' arguing that such a change was needed in order to defeat warring ethnic groups, whose activities were a major constraint to British expansion into the interior of the colony, and enhance the ability of both British entrepreneurs and merchants to engage in profitable economic activities (Tamuno 1970: 16).

Analyses of the communications of British colonial officers of the period do not show that the police force was established in the colony of Lagos to fight crime and promote democratic governance. Instead, the documents reveal that the police force was established in Lagos to:

1) Help the colonial government bring more African lands under its control-that is, to expand the borders of Lagos Colony;

2) Make certain that opposing African groups did not become a major constraint to further expansion of British trade and resource extraction; and

3) Generally to protect British trade and commercial monopolies (Ahire 1990, Tamuno 1970, Ahire 1991, Anene 1966). So, in order to classify the colonial police force as a crime fighter and promoter of democratic living, one would have to reclassify resistance to exploitation, domination, and subjugation as criminal behaviour.

The police forces that emerged in West Africa and indeed in many other parts of colonial Africa had three important characteristics. First, they were intentionally staffed by people of foreign origins. In the case of the British colony of Nigeria, the police officers were mostly freed slaves from Sierra Leone, Liberia, and Lagos. Second, members of the colonial police were trained primarily in military tactics in order to enhance their ability to crush and subdue so-called 'primitive,' 'backward,' or 'heathen,' tribes (Ahire 1990: 159). Finally, the colonial police forces were not allowed to develop any institutional autonomy; instead, they were controlled directly by, and were part of, the political administration (Ahire 1990: 159). It was generally argued at the time that the pacification of Africans in order to minimise their interference with British trade and plantation interests was a political

431

issue and, as a consequence, could only be properly dealt with through the political process (Ahire 1990: 159).

After Freeman became Governor of the Colony of Lagos, London advised him to put in place a police force that could enforce sanitary and health regulations in the colony. Governor Freeman's reply to the Colonial Secretary reaffirms the connection between colonial policing and European economic activities. Freeman wrote:

> The existing wars in the interior have greatly paralyzed the trade of this place which had been increasing up till the date of their commencement. I have not a doubt that these wars could be speedily terminated if communication could be operated with some of the principal towns situated on the principal lagoons and rivers...Such communication will enable the government of this colony to use its influence to keep the various tribes of the interior at peace with one another...Once this was done, the traffic through Lagos could become active enough to render the colony self-supporting (Quoted in Ahire 1991: 35)

Governor Freeman, like other Europeans in the African colonies, attached more importance to trade than to the improvement of health and sanitary conditions in the colony. For Freeman, protection of the property rights of British merchants and planters was the most important concern of his administration. He subsequently reorganised the colonial police and raised its strength to 600 constables in 1863, most of whom were Hausa-speaking former slaves. The force's name was later changed to the Armed Hausa Police Force (AHPF). The AHPF served as a complement to the West Indian Regiment, which had been brought from The Gambia to Lagos in January 1862 (Ahire 1991: 35 and Tamuno 1970: 17-18).

The colonial police force was used effectively to eliminate African competition to British traders and planters. This is evident in the use of the AHPF to prevent the Ijebu from interfering with British trade interests along the trade route to the Lagos lagoon. The Ijebu kingdom was strategically located on the trade route from the interior to the Lagos lagoon. Ijebu's chiefs took advantage of their strategic location and 'closed all trade routes to the coast and required all produce from the interior to be sold in their frontier towns of Ejinrin and Oru at their prices' (Ahire 1991: 36). British merchants in Lagos, who were faced with higher prices as a result of Ijebu's monopolisation of trade routes from the interior of the Lagos Colony, did not seek to resolve the issue by negotiating with the Ijebu kingdom. Instead, the merchants complained to the colonial government and in 1892, Governor Denton ordered the Ijebu to stop their monopolistic practices and allow 'free and unmolested passage for all traders' (Ahire 1991: 36). The Ijebu ignored the order and Governor Denton subsequently sent a force of 500 AHPF, a detachment of the Gold Coast Hausas, the Second West Indian Regiment, and seven special service officers from Britain, which attacked Ijebu on March 18, 1892. The Ijebu were subsequently defeated and their properties seized (Ahire 1991 and Smith 1971).

Some scholars see the police and other colonial institutions as primarily instruments in aid of colonialism's so-called 'civilising' mission. This mistaken conceptualisation of colonial institutions arises from the fact that these scholars have failed to 'accurately conceptualize colonialism and its primary purpose' (Mbaku and Kimenyi 1995: 296)-forced expropriation of African resources for the benefit of the metropolitan economies. Of course, the colonial police force did deal with crime in its conventional sense; this, however, was peripheral to its more important main functions of helping the Europeans conquer Africa and forcefully extract African resources for the benefit of the Europeans and their metropolitan benefactors (see generally Tamuno 1970: 38-39).

The colonial police in West Africa, as it was in other parts of colonial Africa, were an essential part of the violence potential required by the Europeans to maintain a monopoly on power and control property rights assignments (especially in land), as well as commercial activities in the colonies. Through this process, the British and other colonial powers made violence an essential part of resource allocation. Unfortunately, such an approach to resolving economic conflicts did not die with colonialism-it survived and remains a critical part of the resource allocation systems of many African countries (Mbaku and Kimenyi 1995: 300-04).

III. The Push against the Development of Democratic Associations by Africans

The European colonial powers were aware of the fact that their domination of political economy in the colony could not be sustained if they allowed Africans to develop democratic associations. Thus, the colonial state made concerted efforts to stunt the production of creative expression among the various groups that populated each colony.[17] The European governors of the African colonies were quite aware of the critical role played by the free exchange of ideas in the development of a fully functioning democratic political and economic system. As a result, the colonial government developed and implemented political and economic policies that made it very difficult, and in some cases, impossible, for Africans to create and disseminate knowledge, undertake any meaningful type of inter-ethnic dialogue that would have enhanced the ability of each ethnic group to learn of the interests and values of the other groups that populated each colony, and hence, articulate common interests, and determine ways to resolve conflicts peacefully and develop institutions that could help them live together peacefully.[18]

Governance in colonial Africa was based on brute force (Fatton 1990: 455). The type of independent thinking that would have enhanced the ability of Africans to freely learn about their neighbours, engage in productive dialogue with their counterparts from other ethnic groups, and eventually develop ways to resolve their conflicts peacefully was banned by the colonialists. Public policy in the colonies was not developed through a participatory form of public debate and deliberation that would have produced outcomes that were favoured by each colony's relevant stakeholder groups. Instead, the Europeans forcefully imposed their will on Africans through the exercise of their comparative advantage in the employment of coercion (Fatton 1990: 455).

In postindependence Africa, governance has been based on a combination of brute force and bribery-dictators use coercion to destroy public dissent and rid themselves of political competition and bribes to co-opt political opponents who cannot be *efficiently* dealt with through force (see generally Mbaku 2007). The decolonisation project was supposed to radically transform the critical domains and render them more suitable to governance in the postindependence period. Had decolonisation been undertaken through a democratic (i.e., bottom-up, inclusive, participatory, and people-driven) process, Africans would have provided themselves with new laws and institutions, rooted in African, not European, values. Such locally focused institutional arrangements would have provided Africans with the wherewithal to allocate their resources efficiently and equitably, as well as adequately constrain civil servants and politicians and prevent them from engaging in corruption, rent seeking, and other opportunistic behaviours. At the very least, democratically constructed laws and institutions could have provided Africans with the wherewithal to live together peacefully and resolve their conflicts through peaceful means (Mbaku 1995).

The transition from colonialism to independence, as stated by Fatton (1990: 457), was both reluctant and opportunistic-not only did the departing Europeans refuse to help Africans more effectively transform the critical domains to create locally-focused institutions, capable of meeting their postindependence governance and economic needs, but in many cases, the Europeans attempted to hijack the process and create institutions that would enhance their ability to continue to monopolise political economy in the new countries (see Mbaku 2003: 109-10). In fact, in those colonies in which there were substantial populations of European settlers, the Europeans (notably, the settlers or colonists) either did not want Africans to be granted any level of political and economic autonomy or were only willing to offer Africans independence under conditions in which Europeans would continue to dominate and control government and the economy in the postindependence society.[19]

While it is true that the transition from colonial tyranny to independence and to postindependence authoritarianism was opportunistic and hence did not provide Africans with strong, locally-focused, and effective governance structures, it is critical to recognise that by the time African colonies gained independence, most of the continent 'lacked those objective criteria that have historically been associated with the rise of bourgeois forms of representation elsewhere' (Fatton 1990: 457). First, the fact that colonialism was externally imposed and designed primarily to maximise the objectives of aliens implied that there was deliberate and concerted effort by the alien invaders (i.e., the European colonialists) to minimise, and indeed stunt, the emergence of 'both a hegemonic bourgeoisie and a strong proletariat-the two classes whose conflicts and confrontations are critical in striking the political compromises and bargains necessary to the establishment of liberal democracy' (Fatton 1990: 457). Second,

European rule of Africa significantly transformed the continent's various societies, and introduced and sustained a virulent type of racism and racialism and violence that effectively precluded the development of any type of indigenous civil society within any of the colonies-this was true, whether the colonialists were British, French, Belgian, Portuguese, or Spanish. Throughout the colonial period in Africa, Africans were 'infantilized [and] stigmatized by their color' and 'denied the most basic rights' (Fatton 1990: 458). Although racial stigmatisation of Africans is today associated primarily with the southern African colonies (e.g., the South African colonies, the Rhodesias, and South West Africa), it is important to recognise that there were no colonies in Africa in which Africans were not subjected to cruel and degrading treatment by Europeans because of the colour of their skin.[20] By the time the African colonies were granted independence, most Africans, including even those who were 'beneficiaries' of the colonial system's twisted concept of 'civilisation' and had been sent to study in the metropolitan universities, were just 'powerless units of labour who had been deprived of the basic attributes of adult social beings' (Fatton 1990: 458).

The 'infantilization of Africans facilitated the imposition of the colonial dictatorship and contributed to the relative hegemony of a submissive culture of obedience and compliance to authority' and hence, delayed the emergence of an indigenous democratic civil society in most of the colonies (Fatton 1990: 458). It is important to note that the form of governance preferred by colonialism left 'no room for resistance, challenge, and revolt, and even less for democratic accountability' (Fatton 1990: 458). Throughout colonial Africa, Africans, regardless of how mature they were, were considered and treated as children, who, according to their colonial 'protectors,' were too immature to govern themselves, resolve their own conflicts, undertake any form of reasoned civic engagement, and most important, were at a stage in their development in which they certainly were not capable of effectively handling the intricacies of self-government (see Memmi 1967 and Fanon 2004).

Despite the enormous constraints imposed on the African peoples by external forces, the emancipation of the consciousness of Africans did, indeed, arrive, leading to the intense and often violent struggles for liberation that confronted colonialism in the late 1940s and early 1950s. Many scholars argue that the impetus to this emancipation 'stemmed from the opportunistic convergence of interests between the small petty-bourgeois elite and the masses' (Fatton 1990: 458). The continent's emerging elites, most of whom had been educated in Europe, recognised the fact that they could not successfully dismantle the colonial project and seize control of the apparatus of government from a heavily entrenched European political and entrepreneurial class without the help and participation of the African masses. The masses, of course, were also aware of the fact that the only viable route to liberation from colonialism's barbaric rule was 'dependent on the [indigenous] elite's capacity to articulate their grievances and organize their struggles' (Fatton 1990: 459; see also Davidson 1978). Unfortunately, the alliance between the petty-bourgeoisie and the masses that brought down colonialism failed to affect the institutional reforms needed to fully and effectively transform the critical domains and provide each new country with laws and institutions capable of supporting a robust democratic civil society. What emerged in the postindependence society were 'varied forms of personal rule that achieved varied degrees of successes with varied degrees of coercion. Where there was success, however, it was precarious, temporary, and crippled by its class and ethnic limitations; where there was failure, it was egregious, massive, and tragic. Where there remained civil liberties, they were fragile, vulnerable, and under constant threat of sudden death; where despotism prevailed, it was cruel, murderous, and incompetent' (Fatton 1990: 459).

It has been argued by some scholars that the laws and institutions that the African countries adopted at independence might have been the results of political exigency (LeVine 1964). The argument is that Africa's freedom fighters were so eager to rid themselves of colonial domination and exploitation that they were willing to forego democratic constitution making and revisit it after independence and capture and control of the apparatus of government by indigenous elites (see, e.g., LeVine 1964). Since the majority of African countries never returned to democratic state reconstruction, they have been saddled with institutional arrangements that enhance corruption and rent seeking, discourage entrepreneurs from undertaking productive activities, and perhaps more important, allow politically-dominant ethno-regional groupings to monopolise governance during most of the postindependence period. The outcome has been increased political violence as marginalised and deprived ethnic groups have resorted to violence to improve their participation levels (in economic and political markets) and minimise further marginalisation.

IV. Democratic Constitutionalism and Postindependence Conflict in Africa

A. Introduction

The solution to two of postindependence Africa's most important and intractable problems is democratic constitutionalism. What are those problems? They are:

1) The inability of each country's diverse population groups to live together peacefully; and
2) The failure of the postindependence economy to harness each country's enormous natural resource endowments and create the wealth needed to deal fully and effectively with poverty and material deprivation (Mbaku 2009: 44).

Modern constitutionalism traces its origins to the ideas of John Locke and the founders of the U.S. system of government. The practice of constitutionalism requires that the government be constitutionally limited, implying that state custodians (i.e., civil servants and politicians) are well-constrained by the law. Within such a system, conflicts between individuals and between groups (e.g., inter-ethnic conflicts) are not resolved through violent confrontation, as has been the case in most of postindependence Africa, but through constitutionally mandated procedures for conflict resolution.[21]

But is constitutionalism a universal concept? In other words, are there elements of constitutionalism that are applicable to all societies or must constitutionalism be understood only with reference to specific cultural attributes? Should African countries rely on the constitutional experience of the United States as these countries seek ways to provide themselves with effective governance structures? In recent years, the United States and other Western democracies have been engaged in a conflict with the developing countries, including those in Africa, over two international conventions-Internationals Covenant on Civil and Political Rights (ICCPR) and International Covenant on Economic, Social and Cultural Rights (ICESCR). While the developed industrial democracies, led by the United States, argue that emphasis should be placed on the constitutional guarantee of civil and political rights, especially individual rights, developing countries argue that emphasis, especially at the global level, should be placed on the guarantee and protection of economic, social, and cultural rights. Developing countries, including those in Africa, argue further that the developed countries should make available, through official development aid, resources to enhance the ability of the developing countries to realise social, economic, and cultural rights in the shortest time possible. Thus, as argued by A. E. Dick Howard, constitutionalism is 'an expression of culture' (2003).[22]

That constitutionalism is an expression of culture does not mean or imply that Africans, as they seek ways to develop governance schemes that can enhance their ability to live together peacefully, cannot benefit from the constitutional experiences of the United States and other Western democracies. In fact, when one considers the fact that the importance of the U.S. constitutional experience lies not in its formal constitution but in 'the general principles which are reflected in American constitutionalism and, further in the practical experience of making constitutional democracy work' (Howard 2003: 4), then it is clear that the American experience offers African countries very important and useful lessons on how to undertake the type of reforms that can produce institutions capable of enhancing peaceful coexistence, wealth creation, socially equitable distribution of resources, and the promotion of sustainable economic development.

It is important to note that a large number of the most basic ideas that undergird American constitutionalism reflect values and ideals that either already exist in many African cultures and are highly valued by these cultures or potentially can be employed effectively to deal with extant problems in many of these African societies (see Mbaku 2003: 44-45). Of the principles or ideas that undergird U.S. constitutionalism, three are of special importance to effective governance in Africa:

1) Federalism-a political arrangement that can be used to deal effectively with one of Africa's most intractable problems, management of ethnic diversity;

2) Separation of powers-a political principle that offers Africans the opportunity to deal with arbitrary and capricious governance; and

3) Judicial review-a process that enhances the ability of a country's judicial system to contribute effectively to peaceful resolution of conflict; this is probably the most important contribution of American constitutionalism to modern governance (see generally Howard 2003).

Here, I do not call for African countries to import, wholesale, American constitutionalism, but for these countries to recognise the values and ideals that have undergirded governance in the United States for more than 200 years and have enhanced the ability of the country to resolve its multifarious conflicts constitutionally without resort to naked violence. Some of these ideals, such as the peaceful resolution of conflict through rules agreed upon in an earlier period; do exist in many African societies, although as unwritten customs.

B. What Is A Constitution?

D. C. Mueller has defined a constitution as 'a form of *social contract* among citizens defining the rules within which society functions' (Mueller 1991: 326; emphasis added). Throughout the world, kinship networks, extended families, ethnic communities, and nationality groups serve as regulators of the behaviours of their members and seek to minimise problems arising from asymmetric information (Mueller 1991: 326 ff.). Historically, as societies have become more politically, socially, and economically complex, the effective regulation of sociopolitical interaction has mandated the adoption of more explicit and formal laws and institutions-that is, the adoption of formal social contracts. The constitution is an example of a formal social contract (see generally Mueller 1991 and Ostrom et al. 1993). Through a constitution, individuals within a society voluntarily agree to place 'restraints [or constraints] on their own behaviour in exchange for benefits to be derived from similar constraints on the activities of and behaviours of other participants in the agreement' (Mbaku 1997: 64 and Buchanan 1990).[23]

Within each country, then, a constitution plays very important roles. First and foremost, it defines and structures the limits of government power. Second, it creates legislative, executive, and judicial powers and places appropriate limits on them. Third, these limitations on the exercise of government power may come 'in the form of individual or group rights against the government and, depending on the nature of the society in question, emphasize such things as the right to liberty and security of person, or as favored by many developing societies, including those in Africa, the right of each ethnic or nationality group to its economic, social and cultural development'-that is, the right to self-determination (Mbaku 2009: 45).[24]

For the constitution to be relevant to the people whose conduct it is supposed to regulate, it must reflect those people's desires, values, aspirations, and traditions. Of course, the constitution does not have to contain every single law that is needed or required to regulate the conduct of individuals or collectivities within a country or polity. Nevertheless, the laws enacted later to deal with specific problems must reflect the overall spirit of the constitution-that is, these laws must be 'constitutional.'

What exactly are the specific functions of a constitution and why is it so critical for effective governance? A constitution:

1) Defines the competencies of government power-that is, the constitution defines the *scope* of government authority, how that power must be exercised, and the procedure for passing laws to regulate sociopolitical interaction and allow individuals to organise their lives;

2) Defines citizenship and provides procedures for the attainment of citizenship, as well as the conditions under which the individual can exercise that citizenship (e.g., which citizens can hold elective office?);

3) Defines and structures the critical domains-that is, the political, administrative, and judicial foundations of the state;

441

4) Provides the government with the power that it needs to perform its assigned functions (e.g., through the constitution, the people can grant the government the power to assess and collect taxes and use those resources to provide the people with public goods and services);

5) Provides for the separation of powers between the various branches of government; and

6) Ensures that only general principles of government are elaborated so that the constitution can have the flexibility to deal effectively with the country's changing needs and obligations. It is important to note that a well-crafted and efficient constitution is one that grants future governments with the flexibility to deal with 'unpredictable and unforeseeable challenges' (Schwartz 2003).

The efficient approach to constitution making requires that the final text provide only general political or governance principles so that future governments can have the flexibility to deal with unpredictable and unforeseeable events. However, certain critical issues must be dealt with in detail and in a specific manner during the construction of the constitution. For the African countries, an important issue that must be dealt with at the constitutional level is human rights. Virtually all the African countries failed to deal with this issue adequately at independence-they failed to provide adequate protection in their constitutions to human rights and despite the fact that many of these constitutions have been revised and amended several times during the last fifty years, the protection of human rights has been subordinated to other supposedly more important pursuits, such as regime survival. In fact, during the last five decades in the continent, many policymakers have viewed the protection of human rights as a luxury that could not be attended to until such problems as high levels of poverty and material deprivation were effectively dealt with. Ironically, many African countries have failed to realise that the effective protection of human rights actually sets up a strong and viable foundation for the rapid economic growth and wealth creation that they need to alleviate poverty and enhance development (see generally Mbaku 2009 and Takougang 2003).

Every African country has a constitution. Even one of the most brutal, exploitative, and inhumane political regimes that Africa has ever known, the apartheid regime in South Africa, had a constitution. But were these constitutions considered by the relevant stakeholders in each country as legitimate tools for governance and a means for them to organise their private lives? The unfortunate truth about the history of constitution making in Africa is that most of the constitutions that African countries adopted at independence, including the constitution of the Union of South Africa (South Africa Act, 9 Edward VII, c. 9), lacked legitimacy, which usually derives from the 'understanding and voluntary acceptance of the constitution by the people as a prescription for settling conflict within society' (Sundhaussen 1991: 108). Although these so-called constitutions were legal, they failed to clothe themselves with any form of legitimacy.[25] In virtually all cases, these constitutions were compacted without the full and effective participation of the majority of each country's relevant stakeholders and imposed on the people in an effort to enhance the ability of a small group of individuals to monopolise the supply of legislation. In the case of the Union of South Africa, the 1910 constitution was an exclusive product of deliberations undertaken by representatives of the white minority; the black majority was totally shut out of the deliberations.[26] Constitution-making in other former European colonies in Africa was not that different from the way it was undertaken in South Africa-urban elites conspired with their European benefactors to impose on the African peoples constitutional rules that did not reflect the people's interests, values, and customs and traditions. This, of course, was the result of the adoption of a top-down, elite-driven, and nonparticipatory constitution-making process, which effectively denied most of each country's relevant stakeholders the opportunity to participate fully and effectively in pre- and postindependence constitutional exercises.[27] Even after independence, the African peoples were still not consulted during any constitutional exercise. As articulated by Victor T. LeVine, '[c]onstitutional debates were only rarely conducted outside the assizes of the drafting groups, and in most cases the finished product, while often the subject of intense public discussion, remained unaltered' (LeVine 1997: 204).

Hence, while these countries had constitutions, they could hardly be said to have been practising constitutionalism. For one thing, the exercise of government agency was rarely constitutionally limited in many of these countries. In addition, the absence of constitutional limitations on the exercise of government agency implies that these governments could hardly be described as legitimate entities, especially when viewed from the perspective of the oppressed majority. Within each country, the practice of constitutionalism:

1) makes certain that the government functions in a transparent and accountable manner;

2) Enhances the full and effective participation of citizens in governance;

3) ensures an acceptable balance between the power of government on the one hand and the rights of citizens on the other-that is, the government is granted enough power to perform its functions fully, but at the same time is constrained well enough to prevent the government from becoming an instrument of plunder and exploitation;

4) provides the wherewithal for individual citizens to maximise their values without infringing on the ability of others to do the same-for example, individual entrepreneurs can engage in profit-maximising activities without preventing others from engaging in similar activities; and

5) Generally enhance the efficient and socially equitable allocation of resources, and provide structures for the peaceful resolution of conflict (Mbaku 2009: 46-47).

V. Nondemocratic Constitution Making and Conflict in Africa: A Case Study of Cameroon

A. Introduction

Cameroon is characterised by exceptional ethnic, linguistic, religious, and geographic diversity (see generally Mbaku 2005). Despite such diversity, the country was able to maintain relative stability and a significant degree of peaceful coexistence from reunification in 1961[28] until the early 1990s. Even with the additional contradictions imposed on the country first by German and then French and British colonisation, as well as the influence of Christianity, Islam, and other external factors, the country was able to remain peaceful during the first three decades after reunification. The coming together in 1961 of the former UN Trust Territory of Southern Cameroons under British administration with the République du Cameroun 'produced a polity that consisted of an extremely assertive Anglophone minority and a domineering Francophone majority with a proclivity for centralization' (Mbaku 2002: 126). Peaceful coexistence in post-reunification Cameroon was not achieved through the adoption, by the polity's relevant stakeholders, of a mutually beneficial social contract. Instead, peace between the country's diverse population groups was maintained through the government's dependence on the highly centralised and extremely repressive, exploitative, oppressive, and autocratic governance system inherited from the French (i.e., the so-called Gaullist governance system) (Mbaku 2002: 126).

It was Cameroon's Gaullist governance system, characterised by an imperial presidency, and a repressive set of institutions, which included the notorious police agencies, BMM (*Brigade Mixte Mobile*) and SEDOC (*Service d'études et de la documentation*), which enhanced the ability of Ahmadou Ahidjo, the country's first president, to maintain what appeared to be a peaceful political system from 1961 to 1982.[29]

Repressive police agencies were used effectively by the Ahidjo government to deal with political rivals. However, Ahidjo also used the enormous resources made available to him through his control of both the country's political and economic systems to 'bribe competitive elites, co-opt politically dominant and influential ethno-regional elites, neutralize them, force many of them into exile, and imprison some who challenged his repressive and authoritarian policies' (Mbaku 2002: 126).[30] Cameroon's post-reunification political stability, thus, was not achieved through the acceptance by the country's relevant stakeholder groups, of a set of laws and institutions, which they had 'selected to regulate their socio-political interaction and provide them with a peaceful means to resolve conflict' (Mbaku 2002: 126). Like the colonialists who had ruled the territory before them, both Ahidjo and later Paul Biya, used the state's competitive advantage in the employment of coercion to raise the opportunity cost of noncompliance so high that few Cameroonians dared oppose the government (Eyinga 1978).[31]

By the end of the 1980s, a combination of domestic and international events had 'conspired' to seriously undermine the ability of the extremely centralised and highly oppressive and exploitative Gaullist governance system in Cameroon to keep anti-government agitators in check. First, was the dismantling of the cruel and inhumane apartheid regime in South Africa, a development that energised pro-democracy grassroots movements throughout the continent, including those in Cameroon. Second, the cessation of superpower rivalry following the end of the Cold War, deprived many of Africa's authoritarian regimes of the financial and military support that they had received from the 'Cold Warriors'-the United States and its Western allies, on the one hand, and the Soviet Union and its Warsaw Pact comrades, on the other.[32] Finally, the global economic recession had a debilitating effect on the Cameroon economy and on the ability of Biya to secure the resources he needed to bribe his political competitors. In response to these events, Biya initiated and implemented what was basically a set of opportunistic reforms in 1990 (Mbaku 2002: 127).

It is true that Biya's reforms were reluctant, opportunistic, and designed to ensure his continued monopolisation of the apparatus of government. However, it is important to recognise that this was the first time, since reunification in 1961, that the government in Yaoundé was willing to engage in dialogue with representatives of most of the country's relevant stakeholder groups, including, especially, the Anglophones. In fact, up until this point, any Cameroonian who had attempted to criticise government policies or engage in any form of dialogue with the government about public policies, was labelled a subversive and unpatriotic element and punished severely (Eyinga 1978: 100ff.). Anyone who suggested, for example, that the government could function more efficiently and be more relevant to the lives of the people if it were decentralised, was labelled a 'separatist' and was publicly condemned, even imprisoned or forced into exile (Eyinga 1978: 100ff.)

The 1961 reunification constitution set up a federal system of government and granted the Anglophone part of the country a significant level of political and economic autonomy. Nevertheless, shortly after the so-called 'marriage of convenience' was consummated, the central government in Yaoundé moved swiftly to abrogate the agreement and establish a highly centralised, oppressive, and exploitative governance structure that came to be regarded by many Anglophones as a new form of colonialism. In fact, any Anglophones who challenged Yaoundé's centralization tendencies and called upon the central government to respect the 1961 Constitution were labelled secessionists and either imprisoned or forced into exile. By the late 1980s, many of these disaffected Cameroonians had reinvented themselves and had emerged as leaders of what was now a strong and energetic pro-democracy movement, one that was posing so serious a threat to the survival of the Biya regime that the government was now willing to engage in discourse with the movement's leaders. Hence, when the central government in Yaoundé was now willing to dialogue with the opposition, instead of resorting to the oppressive methods of yesteryear, this was considered by the pro-democracy camp as a critical turning point in the struggle to democratise governance in Cameroon (Mbaku 2002: 127).

B. Nondemocratic Constitution Making and Authoritarianism in Cameroon

What is now Cameroon is made up of two territories, which prior to independence were UN Trust Territories-the UN Trust Territory of Southern Cameroons under British administration, which gained independence in 1961, and the UN Trust Territory of Cameroons under French administration, which gained independence in 1960 (see generally Rudin 1938 and LeVine 1964). Both territories united in 1961 to form a single political entity called the Federal Republic of Cameroon. The peoples of Cameroon had two opportunities to compact a set of constitutional rules reflecting their values and one that would have allowed them to resolve their conflicts peacefully-first, when the UN Trust Territory of Cameroons under French administration was granted independence, and second, when the UN Trust Territory of Southern Cameroons under British administration gained independence and united with the now independent République du Cameroun to form the Federal Republic of Cameroon in 1961.

To select an efficient set of constitutional rules, one that would generate mutual gains for all of a polity's relevant stakeholder groups, it is absolutely required that:

447

1) All relevant stakeholders be enfranchised and provided facilities to participate fully and effectively in the process of selecting the rules-that is, constitution making should be undertaken through a democratic (bottom-up, inclusive, participatory, and people-driven) process;
2) Rules selection should be by unanimous agreement;
3) The agreement must be achieved voluntarily-force or coercion should not be used to achieve the agreement;
4) The contents of the final agreement must be accepted by all relevant stakeholders; and
5) The individual must be made the unit of analysis and the only basis from which value is derived (see Mbaku 2004a: 42).

The most important point to note here is that in order to produce a set of institutional arrangements that is locally focused and is capable of serving as an effective foundation for governance, the constitution-making process must not be restricted to or dominated by a group of elites-no matter who those elites are (Brennan and Buchanan 1985).

The process of decolonisation and preparation for independence in the UN Trust Territory of Cameroons under French administration has been examined elsewhere (see generally LeVine 1964, Joseph 1977, and Johnson 1970). In this section, I will limit the discussion to constitutional discourse in the trust territory and how it produced a constitution that was not locally focused and hence, did not reflect the values, traditions, and customs of the territory's relevant stakeholder groups. Instead, what emerged as the constitution of the new République du Cameroun, was the outcome of an opportunistic process whose main objective was to enhance the ability of a few local elites and their French benefactors to dominate and control political economy in the new country (see, e.g., Enonchong 1967).

What emerged as the constitution of the new République du Cameroun was a document produced by a Consultative Committee created by Law No. 59-56 of October 31, 1959 (Enonchong 1967: 80). Where constitution making is carried out through a democratic process, all relevant stakeholder groups elect representatives to meet in conference to draft the constitution based on political principles agreed to (through a democratic process) in an earlier period.[33] Each person serving on the constitution-making committee would be an individual who is either elected directly by the people or selected by the people's duly elected representatives. That is, membership in the committee tasked with producing a constitution for the country should be made up of representatives of the nations (or colony's) major political parties as determined by national elections.

Rules selection in the UN Trust Territory of Cameroons under French administration was not democratic. Instead, the process was top-down, elite-driven, and nonparticipatory. In fact, it was the colonial government, and not the relevant stakeholder groups, who determined who was to serve on the Consultative Committee. Perhaps more telling was the fact that the Union des Populations du Cameroun (UPC), the colony's largest and most important indigenous political organisation and the only one that represented a significant part of national political opinion, was excluded from participating in the process of selecting the political principles on which the constitution was to be based or in compacting the constitution. The decision by the French colonial government to deny the UPC participation in pre-independence constitutional discourse 'effectively eliminated a significant portion of national political opinion from the constitutional deliberations and placed the process of selecting the new rules in the hands of a group that was, for all intents and purposes, alien' (Mbaku 2004a: 43). By adopting this top-down, non-participatory approach to constitution making, the French colonial government effectively denied citizens of the trust territory the opportunity to select their own governance structures.

During the struggle for independence in the UN Trust Territory of Cameroons under French administration, the UPC was the leading opponent of continued French domination of political economy in the territory. The UPC fought an intense and often bloody war to free the territory from French exploitation and made it clear that after independence it would not allow an independent Cameroon to remain in the French Community and that French commercial and entrepreneurial interests would not be allowed to continue to dominate commerce and industry in the new country. On 13 July 1955, the colonial government proscribed the UPC and effectively drove it underground. Through proscription of the UPC, the French expected

449

to achieve several objectives. With the UPC no longer a viable political entity to capture the apparatus of government, the French would be able to manipulate the conditions for independence to put in place a puppet regime, which would enhance French access to the resources of the new country. The banning of the UPC gave France an upper hand in the decolonisation process and negatively affected political development in the country since the UPC was, at the time, the territory's 'only true nationalist party and the only one that had the organizational structure and leadership commitment to evolve into a national movement' (Mbaku 2004a: 44). Although there were several other political parties in the colony, most Cameroonians considered these other political organisations elitist and basically vehicles for the maximisation of either the objectives of the parties' leaders or the ethno-regional interests, which these parties represented. The UPC, on the other hand, was seen as representative of, and interested in, ordinary Cameroonians (of all ethnicities and classes-poor or rich), virtually all of whom had suffered tremendously and for many years under the yoke of French colonialism (Mbaku 2004a: 44; see also LeVine 1964).

The UPC, unlike many of the other political parties that operated within the trust territory, demanded immediate independence and subsequent reunification with the UN Trust Territory of Southern Cameroons under British administration. This approach to the struggle for independence attracted the sympathy of many working-class Cameroonians, many of whom were fed up with assimilationist Cameroonian elites who preached patience and the benefits of colonialism.[34] The mass of Cameroonians had become quite resentful of the privileges enjoyed by many of the colony's elites and supported the UPC's continued condemnation of the French who maintained decadent lifestyles, while ordinary Cameroonians were subjected to lives of extreme poverty and material deprivation. The trust territory's marginalised and deprived citizens were enraged by the privileges provided indigenous assimilationist elites, including traditional rulers, by the colonial government and came to believe, as did the UPC, that many of these elites were not interested in independence for the territory, especially since many of these assimilationist elites agreed with the French colonial government that the 'decolonization process be deliberately gradual and autonomy be granted only when colonial authorities were satisfied that Cameroonians could govern themselves' (Mbaku 2004a: 44-45).

The UPC, on the other hand, condemned the opportunistic indigenous elites and their French benefactors for their decadent lifestyles, all of which were made possible by the continued enslavement of the Cameroon peoples. Through its public proclamations and its many publications, the UPC betrayed its desire to rid the trust territory of French influence and presence and establish a new Cameroon-centric dispensation that would provide Cameroonians with the wherewithal to govern themselves effectively and allocate their resources in socially-optimal ways. Unlike other indigenous political organisations within the trust territory, the UPC expected independence to produce a new Cameroon nation in which the French would not be allowed to exercise the type of social, political, and economic power that they had exercised since they became 'managers' of this part of the former German colony of Kamerun in 1916 (Mbaku 2004a: 45).

The UPC's success as a popular movement and the most likely political party to rule the country after independence forced several constituencies in the territory to view it as a threat to their privileges. French entrepreneurs, especially planters, several indigenous elites, who included many traditional chiefs, and the Catholic Church, which was abhorred by the UPC's socialist leanings, viewed the UPC as a threat to their privileges within an independent Cameroon polity. The UPC's adoption of Marxism to counter what it believed to be the excesses of French capitalism in the colony was seen by the Catholic Church and French commercial and entrepreneurial interests in the colony as a direct threat. Hence, both the Church and French entrepreneurs actively supported the colonial government's efforts to rid the colony of the UPC (LeVine 1964, Joseph 1977).

After the UPC was proscribed and forced underground, French entrepreneurs, with the help of opportunistic indigenous elites, and the colonial government were able to control and manipulate the pre-independence constitutional negotiations to make certain that the outcome was a set of laws and institutions that was favourable to their continued domination of political economy in the new nation (LeVine 1964).

The 'constitution' produced by the Consultative Committee was a copy of the constitution of the Fifth French Republic (that is, the French constitution of 1958). Constitution making is supposed to be the most important part of a change from colonialism to self-governance. Through constitution making, the formerly colonised territory can choose its own laws and institutions, rid itself of the oppressor's institutional arrangements, and bring about a new dispensation, which will enhance governance and resource allocation in the new country. Such a new dispensation, unlike the colonially-imposed one, would reflect the interests, values, aspirations, traditions, and customs of the relevant stakeholders of the new country. It is only through a people-centered, inclusive, and participatory constitution-making process that a locally focused dispensation can be developed. Unfortunately, Cameroon's first constitution was not developed through such a democratic process. In fact, that constitution making was not taken seriously in the trust territory is evidenced by the fact that when the French-administered territory gained independence on 1 January 1960, it did not have a constitution. It was not until 21 February 1960, that the Consultative Committee presented the people with a draft 'constitution' for ratification (LeVine 1964: 221-24).

What the Consultative Committee presented to the people in February 1960, however, was not the product of democratic constitution making. The opposition, led by the UPC, [35] encouraged Cameroonians to reject the document. The opposition argued that the document had many defects and was not a suitable foundation for postindependence governance. First, the document was 'drafted' entirely by a group of individuals chosen and controlled by the colonial government. Second, the drafters did not make any effort to consult the people and gain their input into the process. Third, the document was a copy of the constitution of the French Fifth Republic and reflected French ideals for governance and not those of Cameroonians. Fourth, the document could not be considered a 'social contract' entered into freely by the Cameroonian peoples, since they had nothing to do with its compacting. Finally, given the fact that the constitution-making process was dominated by people with a history of oppressing Cameroonians, it was likely that these people would design rules that would enhance their ability to continue to dominate and exploit the Cameroonian peoples.

Using the enormous resources available to it, the colonial government preached adoption. The results of the ratification vote appear to support the opposition's claim that the constitution was a last-ditch effort by the French to keep an independent Cameroon under the control and domination of French interests. While 797,498 votes were cast in support of the constitution, as many as 531,000 votes were cast against adoption (LeVine 1964: 224).[36]

The 1960 constitution established a unitary state with a very strong central government and an imperial presidency, very similar to that in France. In fact, even with some adjustments to account for differences between Cameroon and France, the laws and institutions established by the Cameroon constitution of 1960 were remarkably similar to those of France's Fifth Republic (Mbaku 2004a: 46).

Some scholars have argued that the 1960 constitution in Cameroon was a product of political exigency. The argument is that Cameroonians, like most other colonised peoples, were eager to gain independence and rid themselves of continued European domination and that in order to accelerate the decolonisation process, they were willing to 'accept constitutional rules that they knew were inefficient and not very appropriate for their individual needs and values' (Mbaku 2004a: 46). The hope was that after independence and the capture and control of the apparatus of government by indigenous elites, the people would then undertake reconstruction of the postcolonial state through democratic constitution making. At this time, the country's relevant stakeholder groups would be provided the facilities (e.g., language experts and interpreters or translators) to participate fully and effectively in the process of selecting appropriate laws and institutions for the new country. Thus, despite the efforts of the opposition, what was basically a copy of the constitution of the French Fifth Republic was adopted as the foundation for establishing the new country. Some members of the Consultative Committee argued later that the decision to adopt the French constitutional model was based on Ahidjo's[37] desire to produce a constitution in the shortest time possible, without spending a lot of time on a process that involved nationwide discourse. Several indigenous opinion leaders of the time argued that gaining independence was the paramount and supreme objective and that issues of constitution making could be dealt with at a later date, and that that could be most effectively done after independence (LeVine 1964: 224 ff.)

In any polity, the constitution provides the foundation for all the rules that regulate sociopolitical interaction and hence determines how the various population groups within the country relate to each other and to the government. All institutional arrangements within the country, as well as all governance structures, must trace their origins to the constitution. Hence, the relatively strong vote against adoption of the 1960 constitution should have alerted the country's leadership to the constitution's shortcomings.[38] at the very least, national leaders should have recognised the fact that such opposition was likely to develop into a source of many problems for governance and resource allocation in the postindependence period. Most of the country's diverse population groups, virtually all of which supported the UPC, were effectively denied participation in the rules selection process since the UPC was proscribed and hence could not represent the interests of these groups.

Those Cameroonians who believed that any 'constitutional document,' no matter how it was compacted and no matter how defective it was, was adequate to enhance the ability of the trust territory to gain independence and that democratic constitution making would be pursued after statehood had been achieved, were either extremely naïve or had a lot of faith in the country's first government, which was led by Ahmadou Ahidjo. These so-called optimists did not consider the fact that Ahidjo and others, who had captured the evacuated structures of colonial hegemony and now ruled the country under a set of rules that granted them enormous powers to enrich themselves at the expense of the rest of the people, might oppose any attempt to reconstruct the postcolonial state and constrain their ability to plunder the economy for their benefit. To the dismay of the optimists, Ahidjo and his benefactors were not interested in any postindependence democratic constitution making. He used the enormous powers reposed in him by the ill-conceived 1960 constitution to crush the opposition,[39] assign additional powers to the imperial presidency, and effectively use state structures to redistribute income and wealth in his favor and that of his benefactors. By the time Ahidjo left office in 1982, corruption had become a very important part of the country's political economy and the country had eventually

454

descended into a venal society (Jua 1991, DeLancey 1989, Takougang 1993).

During his first year in office as president of the new République du Cameroun, Ahidjo refused to revisit the issue of constitution making in the country. Instead, he focused on two issues, which he considered critical to his presidency:

1) Destruction of the country's real opposition political party, the UPC; and
2) Reunification with the UN Trust Territory of Southern Cameroons under British administration.

Some of the people who had been disappointed by Ahidjo's unwillingness to return to the issue of state reconstruction through democratic constitution making in the postindependence period argued that reunification presented another opportunity for the country to undertake the type of constitution making that had eluded it in 1960. It was hoped that the Ahidjo government would use the negotiations with the UN Trust Territory of Southern Cameroons under British administration for unification to engage all of the two territories' relevant stakeholders in democratic constitution making to finally select laws and institutions capable of reflecting the values, traditions, and customs of the Cameroonian peoples. Implied in this belief was that the 1960 constitution would be abandoned in favour of a new social contract and dispensation to be created through a people-driven, inclusive, and participatory process.

C. The 1961 Constitutional Exercise: More of the Same

In an UN-supervised referendum, voters in the UN Trust Territory of Southern Cameroons voted to gain independence by merging with the République du Cameroun to form a federation.[40] this decision provided citizens of both territories with the opportunity to engage in democratic constitution making to compact and adopt rules that reflected their values, interests, aspirations, customs, and traditions. Through such a process, the federation's relevant stakeholders could produce laws and institutions, which they could claim ownership of, accept as their own, and hence, would be willing to defend against subversion by opportunistic state custodians.

Southern Cameroonians, who had voted overwhelmingly for reunification, and their leaders, believed that the federation would be a 'loose voluntary association of two political equals, with each one retaining a significant level of (constitutionally guaranteed) political and economic autonomy (that is, there would be significant devolution of power in favor of regional and local governmental units)' (Mbaku 2004a: 48). The peoples of Southern Cameroons believed that within the new political arrangement, each federated state would be guaranteed by the federal constitution the right to:

1) Keep most of its own institutions and have the authority to deal with local issues without interference from the central or federal government in Yaoundé;
2) Allocate its own resources; and
3) Maximise its values. Additionally, Southern Cameroonians believed that the federation's constitution would be designed through a democratic process, allowing them to participate fully and effectively in the choice of the new union's institutional arrangements.

They looked forward to establishing a constitutionally limited federal government whose powers would be specifically and expressly elaborated in the constitution in order to make certain that all rights not voluntarily ceded to the federal government by the federated states would be retained by the latter. Such a constitution, Southern Cameroonians believed, would 'guarantee [each federated] state's autonomy; protect the rights of its peoples and their cultures and values; and provide structures that enhanced peaceful coexistence of all of the federation's many population groups' (Mbaku 2004a: 49). Due to several constraints, the type of political arrangement envisioned by Southern Cameroonians was never established.

First, as has been argued by Stark and others (Benjamin 1972, Stark 1976), Southern Cameroons' delegation to the constitutional negotiations, which were held in the République du Cameroun town of Foumban, lacked effective legal and political support, was inexperienced, and did not have the resources needed to participate fully and effectively in constitutional negotiations. Second, the negotiations took place in the territory of the République du Cameroun, with French as the working language, despite the fact that the leader of the Southern Cameroons delegation, John Ngu Foncha, and indeed, virtually all of his team mates, could neither speak nor write French.[41]

Third, the République du Cameroun, Southern Cameroons' partner in the new federation, had already gained its independence from France and was now an established sovereign nation with its own laws and institutions. Perhaps, more important was the fact that its delegation to the constitutional negotiations was well advised by the French and had significantly more resources at its disposal than the Southern Cameroons delegation.

Fourth, most Southern Cameroonians, still resentful of their domination by Nigerians during the colonial period when the trust territory was administered by the British as part of the Nigerian colony, overwhelmingly supported reunification. Fifth, the constraints imposed on the Southern Cameroons as a condition for gaining its independence made it virtually impossible for the Southern Cameroonians to negotiate effectively at Foumban.[42]

Sixth, the République du Cameroun's leaders, as well as their benefactor, France, were quite satisfied with the governance structures established by the 1960 constitution and were not eager to abandon them in favour of a new institutional arrangement that could weaken the Gaullist system or reduce French influence in the region. Of course, not all political constituencies were satisfied with the 1960 constitution and the institutional arrangements established by it. This was evident in the fact that the new country continued to face serious political instability and the need to maintain a strong French military presence in the country, especially in traditional UPC strongholds.[43]

Finally, it has been argued by some scholars (see, e.g., Kofele-Kale 1987) and, as the evidence has since indicated, many of the elites that represented the Southern Cameroons in the constitutional negotiations were opportunists who were interested only in capturing leadership positions in an autonomous Anglophone state. Thus, they did not work hard enough to secure a federal constitution that would have produced a federal government that exhibited a significant level of transparency and was accountable to all its relevant stakeholders.

These elites were interested primarily in a political arrangement that would guarantee their control of an autonomous federated Anglophone state. Hence, they were easily duped into accepting Ahidjo's empty assurances of autonomy for the former UN Trust Territory of Southern Cameroons.[44]

In 1961, the United Nations told the Trust Territory of Southern Cameroons that it could achieve independence through one of two routes: it could gain independence by union with an independent Nigeria or with an independent République du Cameroun. As Southern Cameroonians prepared for independence, there was no indication that either Nigeria or République du Cameroun would abandon its laws and institutions and engage, with Southern Cameroons representatives, in the type of institutional reforms that would have created institutional arrangements capable of maximising the values of Southern Cameroonians. It was soon to become clear to Southern Cameroons leaders that no matter which of the two countries they chose as a partner for unification, their admission would not have any significant impact on the new federation's institutional arrangements.[45]

The UN-supervised plebiscite took place in February 1961 and Southern Cameroonians voted overwhelmingly to merge with the République du Cameroun. For Southern Cameroonians, the next stage was for them to enter into negotiations with the former French-administered territory to determine the nature of the merger. The hope, as mentioned earlier, was that the political arrangement between the two former German-controlled territories would be a loose federation that would allow each constituent state to retain significant control over its political and economic affairs. Unfortunately, as discussed earlier, the constraints imposed on the Southern Cameroons by the UN, lack of resources, and the fact that Southern Cameroons entered the negotiations as a colony, rendered the constitutional environment non-competitive and skewed it significantly in favour of the République du Cameroun. For example, due to restrictions imposed on the Southern Cameroons by the United Nations, the former's representatives could not have used the threat of exit (from the constitutional negotiations) as a weapon against Ahidjo's opportunistic and coercive tactics since the conditions for independence imposed on the territory by the United Nations precluded Southern Cameroons' existence as a sovereign political entity. While the République du

Cameroun could have exited the constitutional negotiations, retained its laws and institutions, and continued with its existence as an independent state, the Southern Cameroons did not have that option. Had the République du Cameroun exited the negotiations, Southern Cameroons would have been forced to remain a colony until Britain and the United Nations agreed on a new future for the trust territory. It was evident, even to casual observers, that Southern Cameroons would be unable to enter the constitutional negotiations either from a point of strength or as an equal partner to the independent République du Cameroun.[46]

Ahmadou Ahidjo and his République du Cameroun delegation were aware of the weaknesses of the Southern Cameroons delegation to the Foumban constitutional negotiations. For example, Ahidjo remarked that '[t]he Cameroon Republic [République du Cameroun] and the territory previously under British trusteeship [i.e., the UN Trust Territory of Southern Cameroons] constituted a single historical unit...But, on the other hand, they were two distinct political entities: on one side, an independent sovereign state possessing an international legal personality; on the other, a territory without a political international status' (Ahidjo 1964: 23). During the negotiations, Ahidjo and his ministers used this comparative advantage effectively to secure rules favourable to them and their ability to dominate and control the federation government (Benjamin 1972). Although the reunification constitution established a federation consisting of two federated states, West Cameroon (the former Southern Cameroons) and East Cameroon (the former République du Cameroun), Ahmadou Ahidjo, the new federation's first president, ruled the country as if it was a unitary state. As argued by Kofele-Kale, '[i]t was often difficult to tell in many instances where the eastern state [i.e., East Cameroon] jurisdiction left off and where that of the federal government began. The lines were quite blurred, and this only reinforced Anglophone perception of francophone domination' (Kofele-Kale 1986: 63).

Pre-unification constitutional discourse was dominated and controlled by the delegation from the République du Cameroun led by Ahidjo. Thus, it was not surprising that the outcome was a document that underscored Ahidjo's proclivity for centralisation and established for the federation, a Gaullist system of government with an imperial presidency. In fact, the only indication that the 1961 constitution was supposed to establish a federation was a list of 'Transitional and Special Dispositions,' which was inserted into the final document supposedly to make sure that each state maintained its institutions until further negotiations could be undertaken to establish a fully functioning federation.[47]

Since the 1961 constitution did not provide clear instructions on the nature and future of the new political arrangement, Southern Cameroonians were afraid that Ahidjo's proclivity towards highly centralised government with power concentrated in the presidency would move the federation into a unitary state in which West Cameroon's autonomy would be abrogated and its citizens subjected to exploitation and even recolonisation by the more economically developed and larger East Cameroon. Of greater importance is the fact that the constitution failed to make explicit the financial relationship between the Federated States and the federal government.[48] these fears were to prove quite prophetic as the central government in Yaoundé eventually turned the country into a unitary state, effectively abrogating all of West Cameroon's institutions. The laws and institutions of the former République du Cameroun became, de facto, those of the 'federation.' The relatively easy abrogation of West Cameroon's institutions could have been avoided through more effective constitutional design. For example, the parties could have entrenched in the constitution a clause to the effect that the political relationship between the two countries would automatically dissolve if the federal government attempted to behave opportunistically or engage in certain forbidden activities.[49]

In 1972, the central government in Yaoundé officially abolished what was left of the 1961 federation and turned the country into a unitary state.[50] This action was unconstitutional, since Article 47(1) of the 1961 constitution provided procedures for amending the constitution and expressly prohibited any changes that constrained or impaired the 'unity and integrity of the federation.'[51]

Today, the conflict between Cameroon's majority Francophones and the minority Anglophones continues to challenge governance in the country. Had constitution making at reunification been undertaken through a democratic process, many of the political and economic conflicts that now plague the country could have been anticipated and dealt with effectively.

VI. Conflict Resolution and Democratic Constitution Making in Africa

Many Africans, especially popular forces, have come to recognise participatory and inclusive (i.e., democratic) constitution making as the only way to provide the continent with the type of governance structures that can:

1) Enhance the peaceful resolution of conflict.
2) Promote indigenous entrepreneurship and the creation of the wealth that Africans need to confront poverty and promote sustainable development.
3) Ensure peaceful coexistence.

The full and effective participation of each country's relevant stakeholders in the design of constitutional rules is very important for producing institutional arrangements that can be considered by the people as legitimate tools for governance. Although research to acquire as much data as possible to enhance the constitution-making process is important, it is also critical that the people be enfranchised and granted the facilities (e.g., language translators) to participate fully and effectively in the process of compacting the constitution. Why? Full and effective participation of all relevant stakeholders in the rules selection process significantly improves the chances that:

1) The constitutional rules so selected will be relevant to the lives of the people whose sociopolitical interaction is to be governed or regulated by the constitution.
2) The benefits to gainers will be maximised and costs to losers will be minimized.
3) The resulting constitution will be seen by the country's population as a legitimate tool for governance, significantly improving compliance and minimising the costs of policing.
4) The people will accept the constitution and claim it as their own, effectively enhancing governance in the post-constitutional society.

461

5) Governance will be viewed by most citizens as democratic and based on their values (see generally Mbaku 2009).

Since the late 1980s, popular forces in Africa have continued to pressure their governments for institutional reforms to make government more responsive to the needs of the people. Many governments have responded by decentralising government to:

1) Bring it closer to the people.
2) To enhance the participation of heretofore excluded social and ethnic cleavages.

In some countries, various civil society groups have been empowered and provided the facilities to participate more fully and effectively in the reconstruction and reconstitution of the postcolonial state. Throughout the continent, indigenous entrepreneurs, intellectuals, students, journalists, farmers, representatives of various civil society organizations, as well as many ordinary citizens, have been granted the wherewithal to participate in the design and implementation of public policy (Robb 1999; Brinkerhoff and Crosby 2002). All these developments augur well for democratic constitution making, a process that is critical for deepening and institutionalizing democracy in Africa and providing the African peoples with effective structures for the peaceful resolution of conflict (Mbaku 2009: 53-54).

In order for there to be participatory and inclusive constitution making, there must first exist an environment, within each country, that promotes and enhances 'dialogue, public debate, accommodation, and political give-and-take. The existence of such an environment necessarily enhances peace and democracy' (Mbaku 2009: 54). Within any African country today, the decision to permit democratic institutional reforms implies that the process will be taken out of the control of a few elites and situated within popular forces, a development that can lead to significant loss of influence by the state. Within such a new institutional environment, state custodians will definitely lose their ability to engage in opportunistic behaviours (e.g., corruption and rent seeking). More important is the fact that the adoption of a participatory approach to institutional reforms, which necessarily situates reform processes within popular forces and away from the control of opportunistic and parasitic state custodians, will bring issues that are relevant and critical to the peoples' well-being to the center of the debate on reforms. Hence, vexing issues of language (e.g., what will the national language(s) be?), nationality, identity and citizenship, gender, property rights, and resource allocation, will take center stage in constitutional deliberations. These issues, which are critical to the people, have, since independence, either never been examined or have been treated only opportunistically by elites seeking ways to monopolise power. Where citizens are granted the facilities to participate fully and effectively in constitution making, they are likely to claim ownership of the constitution, view it as an outcome of their labours, and be willing to fight to defend it against subversion by opportunistic politicians and civil servants. Of course, if citizens design their own rules, they are more likely to want to comply with them, a process that can significantly minimise the costs of constitutional compliance and improve governance.

VII. Conclusion

Political economy in most of postindependence Africa has been characterised by significant bloody conflicts, some of which have resulted in the massacre of hundreds of thousands of people. Many of these violent confrontations can be traced to the failure of the decolonisation project to engage the African peoples in democratic constitution making to provide them with appropriate tools for peaceful conflict resolution in the postindependence society. Since the late 1980s, Africans have been engaged in institutional reforms to provide themselves with more effective governance structures. Unfortunately, many of the institutional reform projects that were initiated in the continent shortly after the end of the Cold War were either stillborn or have been hijacked by opportunistic individuals and groups and have produced outcomes that are not dissimilar to the oppressive governance structures that enveloped the continent during the colonial period.

One of the reasons for the failure of post-Cold War reform efforts in the continent has been due to the opportunistic nature of these reforms. Specifically, many of these countries have failed to enfranchise their citizens and provide them with the facilities to participate fully and effectively in institutional reforms. In other words, the constitution-making process in these countries, as it was during the decolonisation period, has been top-down, elite-driven, and nonparticipatory. As a consequence, many of these countries continue to live under governance structures that only serve the interests of a few elites and their foreign benefactors and governance in these countries continues to be characterised by violence, corruption, and the mass violation of the people's basic rights. Political violence, including violent ethnic mobilisation, is endemic as marginalised and deprived groups resort to violent mobilisation in order to improve participation (in economic and political markets) and minimise further marginalisation.

What is needed to arrest this cycle of violent mobilisation is democratic constitution making. Participatory institutional reforms will allow the people to produce a compact that reflects their tastes and preferences, maximises their values, and provides them with tools to engage in peaceful resolution of conflict. Perhaps more important is the fact that democratic constitution making will help Africans develop a culture of the type of constitutionalism that promotes and enhances the deepening and institutionalisation of democracy. As argued by Kanyongolo, the 'existence of a constitution which articulates democratic values and principles is not sufficient for the establishment of the political system which is democratic in practice' (1998: 2). There must be created within each country a culture of constitutionalism; participatory constitution making provides the stage within which such a culture can develop.

Notes

1. This chapter reflects only the present considerations and views of the author, which should not be attributed to either Weber State University or the Brookings Institution.
2. See generally Fatton 1990. Africans were never part of this agreement and were involuntarily and forcefully brought into what became many years of humiliation and degradation.
3. Europeans resident in the colonies consisted of three major groups:

   a. settlers or colonists-individuals who intended to remain in the colonies permanently and make them their home;

b. colonial administratorsthe various administrative and military officials who were sent to the colonies to placate Africans and enhance the ability of the mercantile companies to exploit Africa's enormous resources for the benefit of the metropolitan economies; and

c. Christian missionaries. Most colonists were plantation owners, miners, and industrialists.

The colonial enterprise never made any allowance for the maximisation of the values and/or interests of Africans. In fact, in many colonies, especially those with large populations of settlers (e.g., the four colonies, which in 1910 became the Union of South Africa, French Algeria, the Rhodesias (Northern Rhodesia, which gained independence from Britain as Zambia, and Southern Rhodesia, which became Zimbabwe at independence), the UN Trust Territory of South West Africa under South African administration (which gained independence as Namibia), and the Portuguese colonies of Mozambique and Angola), public policies were designed to minimize the interests of the African peoples. See generally Mbaku 2004b.

4. Mbaku 2003: 103. An important objective of the colonial government was to minimise the costs to the mercantile companies and the various independent European entrepreneurs resident in the colonies, of engaging in profit-generating activities. Hence, it was critical for the colonial government to bring to a minimum, the opposition of indigenous African groups to the activities of European entrepreneurs in the colonies. European institutions, including, especially, military and police forces, were used in a most brutal and effective manner to subdue African groups and minimise their opposition to European exploitation of colonial resources. Africans were incorporated into the colonial enterprise on terms that were not only favourable to the Europeans, but forced Africans to provide both their labour and other resources (e.g., land and water-use rights), without compensation, to the invading colonialists and colonists. See generally Fredrickson 1981, Rudin 1938, Brace 1964, and Burns 1963.

5. For example, in the German colony of Kamerun, King Rudolph Douala Manga Bell, the nationalist leader of the Duala ethnic group, who had read law in Germany and had developed into an astute observer of and an expert in the German legal system, was executed by the German colonial government in 1913 for, *inter alia,* his vehement opposition to German occupation of his peoples' land, abrogation of his peoples' civil, political, economic, social, and cultural rights, and producing literature that was considered treasonable or detrimental to German interests in the colony. See, e.g., Mbaku 2005.

6. The main objective of destroying traditional forms of sustenance was to force Africans to go to work for European planters, providing the cheap labour, which the Europeans needed to enhance their profit-maximizing activities. See Rudin 1938 for a rigorous examination of this practice in the German colony of Kamerun, and Fredrickson 1981 for an examination of

the efforts of Europeans to subjugate the Khoi of South Africa and force them to work as labourers in European plantations and farms.

7. Part of the effort of destroying traditional belief systems was to enhance the ability of Christian missions to carry out their so-called 'civilising' mission and the rescuing of Africans from their supposedly heathen ways. See Mbaku 2005 for an examination of efforts by French colonial authorities to destroy traditional schools and learning centres in the Kingdom of Bamoun, which was part of the U.N. Trust Territory of Cameroons under French administration. French Christian missions opposed King Njoya's educational system, which used the Bamoun language as a medium of instruction, emphasised Bamoun culture, history, and customs. The French colonial government subsequently destroyed the King's printing press, destroyed his majesty's schools, forced him into internal exile, and subsequently, through Christian missionaries, preached the supremacy of French language and culture. Also see Blier 1998 and Bjornson 1991.

8. For an examination of French brutality against Cameroonians who dared oppose the continued colonisation of their lands, see Joseph 1977. It is noteworthy that Cameroonians who supported and preached the so-called 'benefits' of colonialism, especially France's policy of assimilation (later, 'association') were rewarded handsomely-most importantly, with French citizenship. See Thompson and Adloff 1969 and Hargreaves 1967, 1969.

9. For a review of the literature on thi s critical aspect of the colonial enterprise, see Mbaku 1997. See also Fatton 1990.

10. In Cameroon, for example, the French dealt most brutally with the Bamoun Kingdom, who's King had been flirting with Islam and putting various Christian missions at risk. Some level of leniency was expressed towards the Duala and other coastal kingdoms, many of which had, even during the German era, accepted and embraced Christian missions and had, in fact, become 'disciples' or native 'missionaries' in the struggle to bring so-called 'heathen in-land tribes' into the brotherhood and sisterhood of Christ. In Cameroon, as in other African countries, postindependence governments would be dominated by individuals from ethnic groups that had been favoured by colonial policies, especially those who had benefited from Western-based educations provided by the various Christian churches. Most of these postindependence elites were schooled at church-run schools in Cameroon and then attended further training in either France or Britain. See especially Bjornson 1991.

11. In fact, in the UN Trust Territory of Cameroons under French administration, French citizenship, which came with a lot of social, economic, and political benefits, could not be achieved unless one had shown, through examination, that he or she had acquired necessary skills in French language and culture and had also given up his or her 'traditional ways' and had, in addition, accepted an occupation of a European nature, even if the latter meant subjecting oneself to exploitation as a 'domestic servant' in the household of a European. The assimilated Cameroonian,

who had aspired to and had achieved the French cultural ideal, was granted French citizenship and would now become part of the colonial project and was, of course, not expected to oppose colonialism-the latter was the assimilated individual's saviour from what would have been a life lived in debauchery, sin, and eventual descent into hell. See especially Bjornson 1991 for a discussion of French assimilationist ideology on intellectual development in colonial Cameroon.

12.   For a more detailed discussion, especially with respect to property rights and the exploitation of environmental resources, see Mbaku 2004b.

13.   The failure of the decolonisation project to provide Anglophones with the opportunity to fully articulate how they wanted to relate to other groups within the polity remains the most important gripe of the Anglophone minority in Cameroon. Many Anglophones argue that the UN and Britain, the de facto trustees of the UN Trust Territory of Southern Cameroons, breached their fiduciary duty of adequately and effectively preparing the territory for independence. For one thing, many Anglophones argue, the UN-backed referendum that resulted in the territory's absorption by the then independent République du Cameroun, did not provide the people, as it was supposed to, with the facilities to explore all available choices and options for independence and then pick the one that would have maximised their values. At the very least, the Foumban accords, which produced what was to be the constitution of the new 'reunified' country, many Anglophones argue, was a fraud perpetuated on the Southern Cameroons people, with the help of Britain, which was eager to rid itself of its trusteeship duties and France, which looked forward eagerly to capturing the former German plantations, as well as the rich oil fields on the Gulf of Guinea. In fact, that the Foumban constitutional negotiations were fraudulently carried out is evident in the fact that the resulting document was actually the 1960 constitution of the République du Cameroun. In other words, there were no negotiations at Foumban! See generally Awasom 2004 and Konings and Nyamnjoh 2004.

14.   For example, Bakweri lands around Mount Cameroon, which were seized by the German military and handed over to German mercantile companies, eventually became part of the government-owned Cameroons Development Corporation and the Bakweri have continued to argue, with a significant level of justification, that they were never compensated for the forceful alienation. A problem like this one could have been dealt with effectively during pre-independence constitutional deliberations, with the Bakweri granted the facilities to participate fully and effectively in the process. Unfortunately, this was never done and today, despite the absence of violence, the Bakweris and many such groups continue to distrust the government in all its forms. For an excellent exposition of the annexation of Bakweri lands and their subsequent alienation to German planters, see Rudin 1938. Also, the issue of what it means to be a Cameroon citizen remains a hotly debated topic in the country and has created a so-called

'eleventh' province for individuals who migrate out of their so-called ancestral lands or were born out of their homeland. For example, Bamiléké (or Bamis), whose ancestral homeland is in the West Province, but who had lived for several generations in the urban centres of Douala (considered the ancestral lands of the Duala), were suddenly asked by the Duala to return 'home' if they wanted to participate in politics. Despite the fact that these Bamis have lived in metropolitan Douala since before independence, they are still regarded by the Duala as 'strangers' or 'settlers' and hence not eligible to participate fully and effectively in the political and economic life of the city they have called home for many generations. Such issues could have been settled effectively through constitutional negotiations. See Awasom's very useful discussion, note 13 above.

15.   For a discussion of how the French manipulated the decolonisation process in the UN Trust Territory of Cameroons under French administration in order to ensure their continued access to the resources of their former 'colony,' see LeVine 1964.

16.   In this characterisation of the police, and other colonially imposed institutions of violence, no effort was made to examine the role played by colonialism in the rise of political and social violence in the colony. Colonialism was a brutal and exploitative system, designed to enhance European exploitation of Africa's resources. It was inevitable that colonialism, conceived in violence and imposed through extremely coercive strategies, would necessarily increase political and other forms of violence in the colonies. Of course, a great deal of this so-called political violence was actually African resistance to European exploitation.

17.   For a discussion of the efforts of the French colonial government to discourage the creation of knowledge in the UN Trust Territory of Cameroons under French administration, see Mbaku 2005.

18.   See Mbaku 2005: 90-93 for an examination of the French colonial administration's efforts to stunt indigenous knowledge creation in French Cameroons.

19.   This point is illustrated quite well by Ian Smith's unilateral declaration of independence in the then British colony of Southern Rhodesia, the manipulation of conditions for independence in the four colonies that became the Union of South Africa in 1910, and the long, bitter and bloody independence struggles in colonial Algeria, Mozambique and Angola. See generally Mbaku 1997, 2004b. Also Brace 1964 on Algeria; Cowen 1961 on South Africa; Judd 1997: ch. 28 (pp. 372ff.) on Southern Rhodesia; and Windrich 1975, also on Southern Rhodesia.

20.   See, e.g., Rudin 1938 for the brutal treatment of Cameroonians under German rule. This, of course, is not to minimize the brutalization of Africans for over three hundred years by various European powers in South Africa. Thus, I must recommend readers to familiarise themselves with Frederickson 1981, Doxey 1961, Hutt 1964, and Magubane 1979.

21. Note that these conflict resolution procedures would have been selected in an earlier period by the polity's relevant stakeholder groups-usually during the process of compacting the constitution. This is a very important issue for African countries, which have extremely diverse population groups and hence are faced also with diverse ways of resolving conflict. During democratic constitution making, representatives of all these groups would be able to negotiate and agree on conflict resolution processes acceptable to them and entrench them in the constitution. Full and effective participation of all relevant stakeholder groups would ensure that the outcome would be laws and institutions acceptable to them. Such a process should minimise the costs of compliance and advance and enhance the practice of constitutionalism.

22. Howard 2003. Howard is an expert on constitutionalism and American legal history.

23. As argued by Buchanan, rational individuals, faced with various uncertainties and forced to operate within a political environment characterised by conflict, will still find it mutually beneficial to be part of a social contract that imposes constraints on their behaviour (1990: 4ff.).

24. There is a very important point to make here: construction of such a social contract as represented here requires a process that calls for the enfranchisement of all relevant stakeholders within the country and the provision of facilities for them to participate fully and effectively in constitution making. The process of compacting the constitution hence must be bottom-up, inclusive, people-driven, and participatory. See, e.g., Mbaku 2003.

25. Of course, as was the case with the South African constitution of 1910, these constitutions are usually considered legitimate by a small portion of the population of the country. In the case of the Union of South Africa, the minority white population, which single-handedly put together the opportunistic document, considered it a legitimate tool of governance. Unfortunately, governance, in the case of South Africa, was preoccupied not with nation-building, but with the wretched oppression and exploitation of the black majority. In other African countries, postindependence constitutions, which were also opportunistic documents compacted by politically dominant ethno-regional groups, with the help of their foreign benefactors, served almost exclusively as instruments of plunder and oppression and hence could not be considered legitimate foundations for true governance, at least not by the majority of citizens.

26. 'Black' as used here includes all of South Africa's 'nonwhite' populations-Africans, people of mixed race ('coloureds'), Indians, Chinese, and Malays. See Mbaku 1997: 78ff.

27. See LeVine 1964 for an examination of this opportunistic approach to constitution making in the UN Trust territory of Cameroons under French administration.

28. 'Reunification' refers to the formation of a federation between the UN Trust Territory of Southern Cameroons under British administration and La République du Cameroun, the former UN Trust Territory of Cameroons under French administration, which had gained independence on 1 January 1960.

29. In November 1982, Ahidjo voluntarily relinquished power and handed the apparatus of government to his prime minister, Paul Biya, who, as of 2013, is still the president of Cameroon. See generally Eyinga 1978.

30. For a thorough analysis of the repressive Ahidjo regime, see Eyinga 1978 and for an examination of the Biya regime, see Takougang 1993, and Takougang and Krieger 1998.

31. It is important to note here that Cameroon's stability was not achieved through the practice of any form of constitutionalism, which usually makes allowance for protest and provides the citizens with the wherewithal to petition their government for redress of wrongs committed against them by the government or its agents, but instead through effective use of coercion.

32. Many of the authoritarian regimes were no longer critical elements in the global struggle for hegemony and were abandoned by their superpower benefactors.

33. Compare the process here with that which was used to choose South Africa's post-apartheid constitution.

34. Of special note is the writer Louis-Marie Pouka who regarded French colonialism in Cameroon and other parts of Africa as part of God's plan for the black people. See Bjornson 1991.

35. The UPC was now operating illegally since it had been proscribed in 1955. Despite the proscription order, the organisation remained quite popular among the mass of Cameroonians.

36. It is important to note here that while the pro-ratification forces were granted significant amounts of resources to campaign for ratification, the opposition was seriously handicapped, first, by the banning of the UPC, the opposition's most important and largest organisation, and second, by the denial of most avenues for communication then in existence (e.g., schools and churches) and the lack of access to state funding. Yet, despite these constraints, the opposition was still able to make a very significant showing.

37. Ahmadou Ahidjo was the first president of *La République du Cameroun*.

38. Of course, the ruling elites were aware of, and welcomed, the constitution's shortcomings. It was these defects that provided them with the wherewithal to monopolise governance and continue to plunder national resources for their own benefit and that of their foreign, primarily French, benefactors.

39. In fact, Ahidjo devoted a significant part of the first few years of independence, with the help of French military forces that remained in the country, to destroying any remnants of the UPC and making certain that there would be no viable opposition to his control of the apparatus of government in the new country.

40. '*République du Cameroun*' was the name taken by the UN Trust Territory of Cameroons under French administration when it gained independence on 1 January 1960.

41. Another indication of how disadvantaged the Southern Cameroonians were in regard to the constitutional negotiations is the fact that during the first several years of reunification, the federal government told Cameroonians that only the French version of the constitution of the federation adopted at Foumban was legal. The English version of the constitution, a translation from the French, was not a legal document and hence could not be cited to in any legal memoranda. Most Southern Cameroonians, all of whom had no competency in the French language, did not really know the nature of the laws that regulated their sociopolitical interaction.

42. These conditions are discussed below.

43. Many citizens of the *République du Cameroun*, as evidenced by the strong vote against the ratification of the 1960 constitution, considered that document a foreign imposition, designed to enhance the ability of a few elites and their French benefactors to continue to control political economy in the new country. See generally LeVine 1964: 224ff.

44. the most effective way that Southern Cameroons could have guaranteed its autonomy would have been to entrench such a guarantee in the constitution, and the Southern Cameroons delegation should have insisted that the constitution contain such a guarantee. Instead, the Southern Cameroons delegation depended on Ahidjo's personal assurances that the Southern Cameroons would be granted autonomy.

45. Today's Anglophones continue to question why Southern Cameroons leaders did not reject the conditions imposed on the trust territory by the United Nations and seek options that included existence as an independent entity, separate from either Nigeria or the République du Cameroun.

46. In hindsight, it appears that the Southern Cameroons delegation should have threatened to exit the negotiations and suffer a delay in independence. The cost of unification with the République du Cameroun now appears significantly higher than any costs that the territory would have suffered through a delay in its struggle for independence, especially given the fact that today, the territory is being treated by the government in Yaoundé as a colonial possession. Southern Cameroonians should not have proceeded with the negotiations, especially given their extremely weak position vis-à-vis that of the République du Cameroun.

47. In other words, the negotiations in Foumban did not establish a federation-that job was left for further negotiations, which of course never took place.

48. The Federated States were West Cameroon (the former UN Trust Territory of Southern Cameroons under British administration) and East Cameroon (the former République du Cameroun).

49. For example, in January 1962, the central government, by presidential decree, introduced the CFA franc (the currency of the République du Cameroun) into West Cameroon without consulting West Cameroon

leaders and without any effort to prepare both the people and the economy for the new currency. Although West Cameroon leaders knew that as a result of federation, the new country would eventually have to adopt uniform laws and institutions, including a common currency, they believed that harmonisation would be undertaken gradually and only after full consultation with state leaders. Through effective constitutional design, such unilateral action should have automatically invalidated the unification agreement, or at the very least, declared it unconstitutional.

50.   This was undertaken through decree No. 72-DF-270.
51.   Constitution of the Federal Republic of Cameroon, 1972, Article 47 (1).

References

Ahidjo, Ahmadou. *Contribution à la construction nationale*. Paris: Présence Africaine.

Ahire, Philip T. 1990. 'Policing and the construction of the colonial state in Nigeria, 1860-1960.' *Journal of Third World Studies* 7 (2): 151-172.

———. 1991. *Imperial policing: the emergence and role of the police in colonial Nigeria, 1860-1960*. Philadelphia, PA: Open University Press.

Ake, Claude. 1981. *A political economy of Africa*. New York: Longman.

Anene, J. C. 1966. *Southern Nigeria in transition 1885-1906: theory and practice in colonial protectorate*. Cambridge: Cambridge University Press.

Awasom, Nicodemus Fru. 2004. 'Autochthonization politics and the invention of citizenship in Cameroon.' In: *The leadership challenge in Africa: Cameroon under Paul Biya*, edited by John Mukum Mbaku and Joseph Takougang, pp. 267-98. Trenton, NJ: Africa World Press.

Bayley, David H. 1969. *The police and political development in India*. Princeton, NJ: Princeton University Press.

Benjamin, J. 1972. *Les camerounais occidentaux: la minorité dans UN état bicommunautaire*. Montréal: Les presses de l'université de Montréal.

———. 1980. 'The impact of federal institutions on West Cameroon's economic activity.' *An African experiment in nation building: the bilingual Cameroon Republic since reunification*, edited by Ndive Kofele-Kale, pp. 191-226. Boulder, CO: Westview Press.

Bjornson, Richard. 1991. *The African quest for freedom and identity: Cameroonian writing and the national experience.* Bloomington, IN: Indiana University Press.

Blier, Suzanne P. 1998. *The royal arts of Africa: the majesty of form.* New York: Harry M. Abrams.

Brace, R. M. 1964. *Morocco, Algeria, Tunisia.* Englewood Cliffs, NJ: Prentice-Hall.

Brennan, G. and James M. Buchanan. 1985. *The reason of rules: constitutional political economy.* Cambridge: Cambridge University Press.

Brinkerhoff, D. W. and B. L. Crosby. 2002. *Managing policy reform: concepts and tools for decision-makers in developing and transitioning countries.* Bloomfield, CT: Kumarian Press.

Buchanan, James M. 1990. 'The domain of constitutional economics.' *Constitutional Political Economy* 1: 1-18.

Burns, Sir A. C. 1963. *History of Nigeria.* London: George Allen.

Cowen, Denis V. 1961. *The foundations of freedom: with reference to Southern Africa.* Cape Town: Oxford University Press.

Crowder, Michael. 1981. *West Africa under colonial rule.* London: Hutchinson.

Danns, George K. 1982. *Domination and power in Guyana: a study of the police in a third world context.* New Brunswick, NJ: Transaction Books.

Davidson, Basil. 1978. *Let freedom come: Africa in modern history.* Boston, MA: Little, Brown.

DeLancey, Mark W. *Cameroon, dependence and independence.* Boulder, CO: Westview Press.

Doxey, G. V. 1961. *The industrial color bar in South Africa.* Cape Town: Oxford University Press.

Egerton, Hugh E. 1966. 'Colonies and the mercantile system.' In: *Imperialism and colonialism*, edited by George H. Nadel and Perry Curtis, pp. 57-66. New York: Macmillan.

Enonchong, H. N. A. 1967. *Cameroon constitutional law: federalism in a mixed common-law and civil-law system.* Yaoundé: CEPMAL.

Eyinga, A. 1978. 'Government by state of emergency.' In: *Gaullist Africa: Cameroon under Ahmadou Ahidjo*, edited by Richard A. Joseph, pp. 100-10. Enugu, Nigeria: Fourth Dimension.

Fanon, Frantz. 2004. *The wretched of the earth*. New York: Grove Press. Originally published by François Maspero, Paris, 1961, under the title *Les damnés de la terre*.

Fatton, R., Jr. 1990. 'Liberal Democracy in Africa.' *Political Science Quarterly* 105: 455-73.

Frederickson, George M. 1981. *White supremacy: a comparative study in American and South African history*. Oxford: Oxford University Press.

Hargreaves, John D. 1967. *West Africa: the former French states*. Englewood Cliffs, NJ: Prentice-Hall.

———. 1969. *France and West Africa: an anthology of historical documents*. London: Macmillan.

Howard, A. E. Dick. 'Toward constitutional democracy around the world: an American experience.' Remarks on*Constitutionalism, human rights, and the rule of law in Iraq*. Delivered to the United States Senate Committee on Judiciary and Foreign Relations, Washington, DC, June 25, 2003.

Hutt, H. W. 1964. *The economics of the color bar*. London: Institute of Economic Affairs.

Jeffries, C. 1952. *The colonial police*. London: Max Parrish.

Johnson, W. R. 1970. The Cameroon federation: Political integration in a fragmented society. Princeton, N.J.: Princeton University Press.

Joseph, Richard. 1977. *Radical nationalism in Cameroun: social origins of the UPC rebellion*. London: Oxford University Press.

Jua, Nantang. 1991. 'Cameroon: jump-starting an economic crisis.' *African Insight* (Pretoria) 21 (3): 162-70.

Judd, Denis. 1997. *Empire: the British imperial experience from 1765 to the present*. New York: Basic Books.

Kanyongolo, F. E. 1998. 'The constitution and the democratization process in Malawi.' In: *The state and constitutionalism in South Africa*, edited by O. Sichone, pp. 1-14. Harare, Zimbabwe: Sapes Books.

Kofele-Kale, Ndive. 1986. 'Ethnicity, regionalism, and political power: a postmortem of Ahidjo's Cameroon.' In: *The political economy of Cameroon*, edited by M. G. Schatzberg and I. W. Zartman, pp. 53-82. New York: Praeger.

Kofele-Kale, Ndive. 1987. 'Class, status, and power in post-reunification Cameroon: the rise of the Anglophone bourgeoisie, 1961-1980.' In: *Studies in power and class in Africa*, edited by Irving Leonard Markovitz, pp. 135-169. New York: Oxford University Press.

Konings, Piet and Francis B. Nyamnjoh. 2004. In: *The leadership challenge in Africa: Cameroon under Paul Biya*, edited by John Mukum Mbaku and Joseph Takougang, pp. 191-234. Trenton, NJ: Africa World Press.

LeVine, Victor T. 1964. *The Cameroons: from mandate to independence.* Stanford, CA: Hoover Institution.

———. 1971. *The Cameroon Federal Republic*. Ithaca, NY: Cornell University Press.

———. 1997. 'The fall and rise of constitutionalism in West Africa.' *The Journal of Modern African Studies* 35: 181-206.

Lugard, Lord Frederick. 1926. *The dual mandate in tropical Africa.* 3$^{rd.}$ ed. Edinburgh: William Blackwell.

Magubane, B. M. 1979. *The political economy of race and class in South Africa*. New York: Monthly Review Press.

Mbaku, John Mukum. 1995. 'Postindependence opportunism and democratization in Africa.' *The Journal of Social, Political and Economic Studies* 20 (4): 405-22.

———. 1997. *Institutions and reform in Africa: the public choice perspective*.

Westport, CT: Praeger.

———. 2002. 'Cameroon's stalled transition to democratic governance: lessons for Africa's new democrats.' *African and Asian Studies* 1 (3): 125-63.

———. 2003. 'Constitutionalism and the transition to democratic governance in

Africa.' In: *The transition to democratic governance in Africa*, edited by John Mukum Mbaku and Julius Omozuanvbo Ihonvbere, pp. 103-36. Westport, CT: Praeger.

———. 2004a. 'Decolonization, reunification, and federation in Cameroon.' In: *The leadership challenge in Africa: Cameroon*

475

under Paul Biya, edited by John Mukum Mbaku and Joseph Takougang, pp. 31-66. Trenton, NJ: Africa World Press.

———. 2004b. *Institutions and development in Africa*. Trenton, NJ: Africa World Press.

———. 2005. *Culture and customs of Cameroon.* Westport, CT: Greenwood.

———. 2007. *Corruption in Africa: causes, consequences, and cleanups*. Lanham, MD: Lexington Books.

———. 2009. 'Constitutionalism and governance in Africa.' In: *Socio-political scaffolding and the construction of change: constitutionalism and democratic governance in Africa*, edited by Kelechi A. Kalu and Peyi Soyinka-Airewele, pp. 35-57. Trenton, NJ: Africa World Press.

Mbaku, John Mukum and Mwangi S. Kimenyi. 1995. 'Rent seeking and policing in colonial Africa.' *Indian Journal of Social Science* 8 (3): 277-306.

Memmi, Albert. 1967. *The colonizer and the colonized.* Boston, MA: Beacon Press. First published by Editions Buchet/ Chastel, Corea, 1957, under the title *Portrait du colonisé précédé du portrait du colonisateur.*

Mueller, D. C. 1991. 'Choosing a constitution in East Europe: lessons from public choice.' *Journal of Comparative Economics* 15 (2): 325-48.

Ostrom, E., L. Schroeder and S. Wynne. 1993. *Institutional incentives and sustainable development: infrastructure policies in perspective*. Boulder, CO: Westview.

Robb, C. M. 1999. *Can the poor influence policy? Participatory poverty assessments in the developing world*. Washington, DC: The World Bank Directions in Development Series.

Rudin, Harry R. 1938. *Germans in the Cameroons, 1884-1914.* Princeton, NJ: Princeton University Press.

Schwartz, H. 'Building blocs for a constitution.' Remarks on *Constitutionalism, human rights, and the rule of law in Iraq*. Delivered to the United States Senate Committee on Judiciary and Foreign Relations, Washington, DC, 25 June 2003.

Smith, R. S. 1971. 'Nigeria: Ijebu.' In: *West African resistance: the military response to colonial occupation*, edited by Michael Crowder. London: Hutchinson.

Stark, Frank M. 1976. 'Federalism in Cameroon: the shadow and the reality.' *Canadian Journal of African Studies* 10: 423-43.

Sundhaussen, U. 1991. 'Democracy and the middle classes: reflections on political development.' *The Australian Journal of Politics and History* 37 (1): 100-17.

Takougang. 1993. 'The post-Ahidjo era in Cameroon: continuity and change.' *Journal of Third World Studies* 10 (2): 268-302.

Takougang, Joseph. 2003. 'Democracy, human rights, and democratization in Africa.' In: *The transition to democratic governance in Africa: the continuing struggle*, edited by John Mukum Mbaku and Julius Omozuanvbo Ihonvbere, pp. 103-36. Westport, CT: Praeger.

Takougang, Joseph and Milton Krieger. 1998. *African state and society in the 1990s: Cameroon's political crossroads*. Boulder, CO: Westview.

Tamuno, Tekena N. 1970. *The police in modern Nigeria 1861-1965: origins, development and role*. Ibadan: Ibadan University Press.

Thompson, Virginia and Richard Adloff. 1969. *French West Africa*. New York: Greenwood.

Windrich, Elaine. 1975. *The Rhodesian problem: a documentary record*, 1923-1973. London: Routledge and Kegan Paul.

CHAPTER 16

Post Conflict Reconstruction and the Resurgence of Supposedly Resolved Territorial Conflicts: Examining The DRC Peace Processes

NYUYKONGE Charles

Introduction

The conflict in the Democratic Republic of Congo (DRC) is one demonstration of the fragile nature of postconflict reconstruction in Africa. It speaks to the need to step up conflict prevention strategies to meet current challenges that have given rise to new trajectories to territorial conflicts in the region. Despite deploying a Peace Mission to the Congo (ONUC) [2] in the 1960s, and despite currently harbouring the largest and highest-funded United Nations Peace Operation (MONUC)[3] the United Nations (UN) is still finding it difficult to bring an end to the territorial conflict in what is regarded as the site for the world's worst humanitarian conflict. The conflict, therefore, seems to protract with each renewed effort to resolve it. Following field visits, extensive reading on the Congo, and interviews with conflict analysts and residents of the DRC, this paper assesses the viability of peacekeeping as a measure for preventing the resurgence of new territorial conflict. While most stakeholders are of the view that the challenges of the DRC peace process are enormous and complex, this paper interrogates the role of MONUC as a conflict-prevention mechanism, and its effectiveness in sustainable peacebuilding in the Great Lakes region. The paper enriches conceptual thinking with the view that peacekeeping as a form of external intervention has the capacity to support fragile states in their peacebuilding process, and to prevent futuristic relapse into territorial conflict. However, in its current state, peacekeeping is often deployed as an emergency interventionist force due to the fact that it is packaged with the international community's resolve to deploy only after state mechanisms have failed. This excessive protection afforded to state sovereignty often results in hasty deployments of peace operations. As a result, peacekeeping often lacks a clear vision for sustained peace. With focus often on stopping hostilities, once this is done and *perhaps* elections are organised, it is considered that the peace operation succeeded.

With the specific case of the DRC, previous studies have posited political quagmire, natural resource, and cultural underpinnings as the territorial causes of conflict. Studies also indicate that the lack of a clearly defined plan to stop hostilities in Eastern Congo can largely be accountable for the cyclical violence. The deployment of MONUC therefore, which was timelier than that of the United Mission in Rwanda (UNAMIR), was saluted across the African continent as the UN's proactive response to conflict hotspots. It equally met with speculation that the UN was taking a leading role in supporting early warning initiatives of the African Union that appealed for the deployment of a UN Special Force in the Congo. Key amongst its tasks was to maintain the ceasefire obtained in Lusaka in June 1997 and to deal with the continued conflict in Northern Kivu while containing the spreading effect of the armed FDLR-a task that MONUC relatively succeeded in fostering before proceeding to organising the first democratic elections in the Congo since its 1960 independence. The organisation of the elections in the Congo marked for the first time the UN's commitment to move peacekeeping beyond ceasefires. The new contours of peacekeepers' mandate had to be read in terms of their ability to create a stable and functional democracy. MONUC was thereby saluted in different quarters for facilitating a serene atmosphere for elections that saw Joseph Kabila emerge as the first democratically elected president of the Congo since the assassination of Patrice Lumumba in January 1961. Contrary to the expectation, therefore, that following the 2006 historic election, the fragile Congolese state had attained sovereign maturity to govern itself with limited external support, this paper posits the need for dedicated and timely funding to a new mediator who will engage a five-phased peacebuilding process that will re-orient existent theoretical and pragmatic processes of conflict prevention, and define succinctly a new direction for the prevention of territorial conflicts.[4] This new direction will focus on the role of indigenes in the different phases of durable peacebuilding.

Following this introduction, the next section will explore the causes of territorial conflicts in Africa and elsewhere. This section engages a brief differentiation between causes of conflicts and causes of conflict resurgence, with the view of demonstrating that if one cannot prima facie understand the causes of conflict, its resolution attempts will be flawed and such attempts will serve as the roots on which prospective conflicts will be erected. Section two will engage a theoretical overview of causes of conflict resurgence. This section will examine causes of conflict resurgence as propounded by two main schools of thought: Realism and Liberalism. Following this, tools of conflict resolution will reviewed with a principal focus on peacekeeping. The section will then narrow its focus to a case-specific analysis of whether peacekeeping as a tool for conflict resolution is a byproduct of intervention or mediation, and whether in the exercise of their craft, peacekeepers qualify to be called mediators or would be considered meddlers. This section argues that between 1999 to 2006, when the first democratic election in the Congo was organised, MONUC could well be considered as a mediator. However, following that period, MONUC till date (July 2006 to 2010) she is a meddler in the peace process that is largely driven by the rapprochement that was reached between the DRC and Uganda, on the one hand, and the DRC and Rwanda, on the other.

Causes of Territorial Conflicts in Africa

There are contending theories as to the causes of territorial conflicts. Conflicts seem to have a litany of literature compared to other subsidiary topics of International Affairs and African Studies. Scholars have thus far not been able to see the divide between causes of territorial conflicts and conflicts that ensue from the impotency of mechanisms tailored to resolve them. As a result, there is no dearth of literature on the causes of conflicts, but one finds hardly anyone who has contended that an ineffective resolution strategy could spark new trajectories to conflict. Existing literature on causes of conflict is sometimes limited in scope in addressing causes in particular. Adekeye Adebajo (2002) has articulated political and cultural underpinnings as responsible for conflicts. This could hold true for the Sierra Leone conflict, but in the face of global adversities, his speculations stand to be criticised because other conflicts like the Rwandan genocide emanated from imbalances in the distribution of economic, political, and social resources. Moreover, the ongoing Sudanese conflicts have religious/and or ethnic undertones with no element of cultural or political formulations, which equally go a long way to excavate the lacunae in Adekeye's speculations.

Paul Collier (2000: 9) holds the view that conflicts are fueled by economic considerations. He posits that most rebel organisations cling onto the idea of grievances in order to elicit more public support for their cause. In his hypothesis, he contemplates that a state with superfluous resources, increasing working-age population, and high unemployment rate is most likely to harbour conflict. His hypothesis, though true for many conflicts that have plagued Africa, does not explain other cases in Africa. For instance, the former British trusteeship of Cameroon fondly known as Anglophone Cameroon has been wailing for a fair share of economic, political, social, and natural resources of the country. Despite this, discontentment has not resulted in war or any from of concrete violence as has occurred in other countries. This phenomenon consequently makes Collier's assertions fluid.

Summarily, Collier and Eboe Hutchful and Kwesi Aning (2004: 199) argue that there are countries that have experienced conflict where natural resources were not articulated as the source of the conflict. They cited the examples of Chad and Ethiopia. They acknowledged that some conflicts have been fueled by purely non-resource- driven motives. This is true with the cases of Angola, Afghanistan, and Sudan. They conceded, however, that in the conflicts in Liberia, Sierra Leone, and the Democratic Republic of Congo, resources were one of the stimulants among other elements. They tried to strike a balance by postulating that the end of the Cold War culminated in the proliferation of arms, and ineffective postconflict demilitarisation, demobilisation, and reintegration of ex-combatants that culminated in an outburst of wary and distressed combatants resulting into several coup attempts (Nyuykonge, 2007) While one may agree with the grievance theory, the million-dollar question is what are people so aggrieved about as to resort to conflicts, destruction of property, murder, and assassinations? Is it about governance? Is it distribution of resources? The answer is definitely far from the propositions of the aforementioned scholars--because some countries have a resource crisis and mismanagement, repressive regimes, and poor governance, but know no conflict. That situation therefore suggests that there is yet an unknown cause of conflict, and this cause is probably one that cuts across all conflicts. The present paper contemplates that inefficacies in the mechanisms for resolving these conflicts could be the brainchild behind the cyclical resurgence of conflicts in states previously hit by territorial civil wars.

William Reno (2000) on his part contends that internal warfare is motivated by economic considerations, especially with regard to the intensification of transitional commerce. He argues that there is a relationship between corruption and politics. According to him, conflict is bound to rise where a ruler makes life uncomfortable for his citizens by encouraging allowing the degradation of minimal conditions for citizens' survival. In his postulations, Reno contemplates that the absence of good governance engenders politics as a cause of conflict. William Zartman (1995) on his part contemplates that the increase in conflict is orchestrated by the collapse of state structure. While one may agree with the collapse-of-state theory, the worrying question is: What drives the leaders to run the state aground?

Keith Somerville (1990) tries to locate the source of conflict within the geopolitical map of Africa that was bequeathed to it by the colonial powers. He contends that the colonial boundaries and state lines have led to the potpourri of people who hitherto had never before mixed as a group. This articulation is paradoxical in that it means that even if the boundaries that existed in the precolonial time were maintained, conflicts could still exist, though at different levels, and with different targets[5]

The diverse schools of thought examined above have attempted an investigation into the causes of conflict. They have posited economic underpinnings, lack of good governance, and disintegration of state institutions, religious and ethnic differences, corruption, and colonial imprints. The opinions are not quite erroneous but fail to see ultimately that conflicts emanate because the global village appears to be in consonance with the fact that peacekeeping is the first point of resort for conflict management. Moreover, the fact that the problems postulated by the above authors have engendered conflicts in some areas and not in others, despite the presence of similar factors, suggests that there is more to conflict than has been articulated by contemporary research on the subject matter. The present paper suggests that inefficacies in the dispute resolution machinery incubate further conflicts. This paper posits that if peacekeeping tools are tailored to empower stakeholders in a peace process, conflicts will be resolved before they escalate.

On the contrast between causes of conflicts and causes of conflict resurgence, it should be noted that if conflicts are not prima facie controlled, it will be difficult to tailor seamstress right solutions for them. As a result, conflicts tend to hatch new and probably even more complicated dimensions to their configuration. These new dimensions are the subsequent causes of what I dare call 'resurgent territorial conflicts'. They are largely born of improper resolution of previous conflicts-often stemming from indigenes having not been given a lead role and ownership of the peace process.

Note should also be taken of the fact that irrespective of how conflicts end, the primary aim of a conflict mediator is to restore the state to a better position than prior to the hostilities. The failure to do so or the inability to achieve this goal stands as the corner stone of future conflicts. It therefore seems that in certain postconflict states like the DRC, Somalia, and Darfur, conflicts have been protracted because of the inefficacy of the conflict resolution machinery. Whilst peacekeeping success stories have been written in Sierra Leone and Burundi, a probe into them revealed that civilian and regional participation efforts in the peacebuilding process largely account for the missions' success, thus suggesting that a lack thereof of civilian participation and indigenous involvement in peacekeeping initiatives is a pointer to future conflicts.

Following from the above, it therefore seems that in looking for territorial origins of postconflict states, one has to retrogress into previous initiatives to resolve the conflicts. Conflicts rarely escalate if the disputants' difference(s) are not allowed to rage beyond uncontrollable limits, where the parties resort to violence as a form of dialogue. Thus it is of critical importance that:

1) Peacekeeping and other mediators who appear as interventionist demonstrate some corporate responsibility of dissociating themselves if they have a stake in the conflict;
2) Mediators possess extensive knowledge of the root causes of the conflict;
3) Peacekeeping commit to empowering the indigenes to design a sustainable peace and nation-building architecture that they can jealously protect;
4) Mediators guide and not impose any measures or policies on the peace process over which they are 'privileged' custodians;
5) A support structure is established that is committed to skill transfer, empowerment of indigenes with future-oriented methods of detecting early signs of conflict and dealing with them before the deterioration of conflicts.

Against this backdrop, it therefore seems that the resurgence of conflict in postconflict states has been triggered by one or a combination of: a.) the importation of foreign peacebuilding reconstuction policies to apply to African situations-most of which do not take into account local African realities and the historical genesis of the conflict; b.) excessive emphasis on political and security reform and inadequate attention to sustainable infrastructural and social reform to attend to the needs of emanates from and victims of conflict; and c.) the demonisation of certain individuals in the community-many of whom are future potential spoilers of today's peacebuilding initiatives.

a. Conflict between Foreign and Domestic Reconstruction Policies

In the aftermath of conflict, international debate on what would be the best strategy for reconstruction and how much of the 'ever' limited resources would be apportioned to achieve this is often rife. In many instances the donors of funds propose what their money should be used for. With the case of the DRC, postconflict funds, whether in 1960 or in the 21st century (2000 till date), have never been designed to address the structural problems caused by the civil conflict. These problems have often bred new problems, ignited new strife, and entrenched identity and class differences wthat have procreated more conflicts. Some problems that have given birth to postconflict territorial conflicts include poor sanitary and living conditions to which refugee returnees have been subjected. These unsanitary conditions have given ruse to disease and instigated isolationists feelings in nationals deprived of decent shelter by a postconflict government, and this has been exacerbated by lack of quality medical facilities, hospitals, and health care. With the specific case of the DRC, many children born and abandoned by conflict-fleeing parents have never had access to formal education, and with lack of infrastructure to meet this need it is uncertain that they will ever feel integrated into the country's development agenda.

When problems ensuing from territorial conflicts such as the above are unaddressed either because of lack of resources or because of deviant usage of such resources to achieve the donor's agenda, it is unlikely that the peace process will be sustained. This is what eventually culminates in the resurgence of territorial conflicts previously resolved.

b. Excessive Focus on Security and Political Reforms Coupled with Infrastructural Development as Opposed to Social Reconstruction

Postconflict reconstruction tools used for military and political reforms sought to coax of persons in possession of illegal arms to surrender them for some monetary compensation. Security reform always takes the lion share of postconflict reconstruction budget. Second to this, resources are dedicated to the organisation of elections that some analysts consider the conception of statehood.

Often due attention is not paid to structural problems brought about by the conflicts, e.g, problems associated with refugees, like the shabby nature of camps that they occupy following the destruction of their homes. Postconflict reconstruction mechanisms are often not design to institutionalise access to education for youths disenfranchised due conflict. Often, states that are returning from conflict benefit from huge grants directed to infrastructural developments. With the case of the DRC, such grants have been used for the refurbishment of government offices and lodges to the exclusion of revamping health and educational infrastructure, which is the backbone for any society that aspires to sustainable development and a responsive system of government.

c. Reconstruction Sometimes does not Address the 'Irreconcilable Interests' of Key Actors

Civil conflicts have a plethora of beneficiaries, including rebels who illegally deal in natural resources to keep their resistance viable; peacekeepers who earn a few more dollars for outstation allowance; academics who are called periodically to analyse the conflict; and mediators, some of whom seek a name for themselves. It is therefore often difficult to ascertain whether any of these would want the conflict to stop, as their benefits would be cut back. These rather varied interests are sometimes irreconcilable and make the peacebuilding projects seem more like a disincentive for its perpetrators. In the DRC, it is on record that a rebel makes approximately $1million per annum in illicit sales of arms and resource expropriation (Snow 2005; Tamm 2002), MONUC soldiers

487

have been accused of selling arms to rebels to make more money but also to keep the conflict blazing (Thome 2008), and conferences have been organized the world over and books written from different viewpoints to address the Congolese territorial conflict.

It seems therefore like the resurgence of this conflict is orchestrated by the fact that postconflict reconstruction in the DRC has since 1960 been shrewd in a gimmick that seeks to protect the interests of different stakeholders in continued hostilities. If peace not is properly incentivised to deter conflict gains, the resurgence of territorial conflicts is more than likely inevitable.

Understanding Realist and Liberal Theoretical Perspectives of Causes of Territorial Conflicts

Realism, conceiving of international relations in terms of the struggle for power among states in an anarchic system, emphasises material, technical environments (Morgenthau 1948; Waltz 1979). From this vantage point, noncompetitive alternatives are often portrayed as utopian, and cooperative social practices appear to be impractical at best and susceptible to manipulations and abuse at worst. This theorem seems to paint of postconflict reconstruction as a futile and manipulative exercise from which further conflicts will resurge. Realists often see efforts to improve coordination and support a peace process as camouflage using humanitarian intervention and peacekeeping to exert political leverage. Postconflict reconstruction therefore adds another layer of self-interested bureaucratic actors whose viewpoints will irreconcilably clash and cause a resurge in the conflict. From this perspective, looking at MONUC as a tool for resolving the Congolese civil conflict, the description that it is a transmission mechanism of the state is somewhat founded.

According to Jackie Smith, a critical look at peacekeeping and pea cebuilding operations suggests that they are designed largely to protect, if not to promote, the interest of the peacekeeping contributing countries of the north. This skepticism generates widespread cynicism regarding Western-designed peacebuilding and conflict resolution models that in turn constrain the successful application of African traditional alternatives.

In international relations, liberalism covers a fairly broad perspective, ranging from Wilsonian Idealism to contemporary neoliberal theories and the democratic peace thesis. Here states are but one actor in world politics, and even states can cooperate together through institutional mechanisms and bargaining that undermine the propensity to base interests simply in military terms. There seems to have been a lacking factor in the relationship between the DRC and her neighbours (Uganda and Rwanda) until end of 2008 when the tides of peacebuilding changed against rebel organisation. It is strikingly true that states are interdependent and the failure to realise this potentially fuels the resurgence of conflicts. While other actors, such as transnational corporations, the IMF, and the United Nations, play a role in enhancing peace and stability and countries torn by conflicts, to do so singlehandedly without prior consultation and empowering of indigenes to drive the peacebuilding process is potentially catastrophic.

Conceptualising Mediation and Meddling Versus Intervention in Conflict Circles

The motif behind conflict mediation in Africa has recently come under the prism of strict academic attention and scholarly investigation. The struggle for independence, leading to the end of the colonial era and the attainment of independence by most African countries in the 1960s was followed by a wave of interstate and intrastate conflicts. Considering from a realist eye that conflict is a natural phenomenon in every human relationship, a ubiquitous characteristic of existence experienced at all levels of society (Jeong 2008), it thus becomes important to interrogate how these conflicts are managed, who manages, and what incentives such managers derive from a 'humanitarian' task that can be dauntingly challenging but risky as the supposed mediator saunters in conflict areas (Pruitt 2000). The DRC stands as a poignant case study for such questions because its territorial conflict has raged since 1960 when the country got its independence, and different mediators have surfaced and baptised different trajectories of the conflict by different names-First Congo War, Second Congo War, Africa's First World War, etc. How these varied nomenclatures facilitate the resolution of the conflict is as unclear as is the question of whether these mediators are interventionists or meddlers in Africa (Hart 2007). Africa has since witnessed a plethora of mediators, whether they are institutions, individuals, foreign nationals, or Africans themselves. Liddell Hart (2007) interrogates the relationship between different mediators and the effects of having several mediators on a peace process. William Zartman (1995) thinks that with several mediators or actors the task of mediation does not get any easier. The role players involved in resolving conflicts in Africa engage at different levels of intervention, including peacekeeping, peacemaking, and peacebuilding processes. These processes incorporate the general concept of mediation at all levels of conflict.

Mark Anstey (2006) defines mediation as a form of party intervention designed to assist disputing parties to reach and find a mutually acceptable settlement that can bring peace. As a technique and measure of dispute resolution, mediation is used in various dispute situations and is shaped by the issues of the dispute, the parties involved in the dispute, the dynamics of particular conflict situations, and the medium of intervention (Anstey 2006). In this light, mediators operate from a high or low power base, playing facilitative roles through the use of negotiation procedures that allow disputants to resolve their differences. Actively involved in peacekeeping operations in Africa are foreign countries and organisations such as the USA, UK, France, the UN, and the EU. However, there is the unsettled question of whether peacekeeping operations in Africa are mediation or meddling. In conflict lingo, it is often common to hear analysts saying that the US is meddling in the affairs of Russia, Yemen, or Iran, as the case maybe. From this, one can infer that meddling is an undesirable interference in the internal affairs of a sovereign state. It should also be noted that meddling may be disguised as humanitarian action. A mediator who is losing his substance and who keeps staying on may well be considered a meddler, as in the case of MONUC, over whom most Congolese civilians, rebels, and elements of the FARDC and the government have lost hope. Any mediator who participates or abets undesirable activities that culminate in loss of civilian lives or destruction of their property reduces himself or herself to a meddler.

There is the uncertainty of whether the role of peacekeepers in African is all rooted in the objectivity of intervention, and the uncertainty of whether peacekeeping operations do understand the territorial causes of African civil conflict, have a clear resolution plan, or are just in Africa for a lucrative high-paid job. Considering that Africa has become a geopolitical hot spot and a top strategic priority to the international community as a result of its rich natural resources, peacekeeping has increasingly become an issue of job security rather than an issue of humanitarian needs.

Familiarity with contradictions and historical nuances inherent in the DRC conflict and its ramifications to the Great Lakes region give MONUC leverage as a possibly better supervisor, but suffice it once again to say that mediation usually takes three phases: prenegotiation, negotiation, and postnegotiation.

In criticising the international community for meddling in the 'Darfur Tribal' conflict, Libyan President Muhammar Gadhafi said that the Darfur crisis 'does not constitute a threat to international peace and security' (*Sudan Tribune* 2010). By so doing, Gadhafi seemed to suggest that meddling is pompous or a hasty engagement in a domestic conflict that does not threaten international peace. Considering that the DRC conflict is spilling out well beyond the country's borders, and affecting neighbouring countries and other SADC member states, if one were to go by Gadhafi's contemplation, then intervention in the DRC conflict does not constitute meddling.

In other areas where the concept of meddling has been evoked, accusations have been directed against the ICC for interfering in the internal affairs of a sovereign state. The example of the MLC, Bemba's party that condemned the latter's arrest is instructive. The MLC accused the ICC of 'meddling in the internal affairs of the DRC' and said that somehow, the Court is doing Kinshasa's bidding, or attempting to try a matter that reasonably should be tried by a competent tribunal in the DRC (Musila 2007). Meddling in this case seems to point to the complicity, or rather incompetence, which is manifested by some African statesmen through the convocation of international institutions to address matters that fall within their jurisdiction. This can be contrasted with intervention where a genuine need ensuing from the perpetration of gross violations of human rights, war crimes, and crimes against humanity instigates the need for

491

'genuine', vision-driven and *humanitarian qua humanitarian intervention.* Even with this, it is still difficult to consider MONUC as an interventionist force in a strict sense, given that it was not deployed in consonance with the conditions necessary for humanitarian intervention-war crimes, crimes against humanity, genocide, and gross violations of international humanitarian law.

Bearing this in mind, it might be fitting to state that during the period between 1999 when it was first deployed into the DRC up until 2006 when the DRC successfully had its first democratic elections since independence, MONUC was a mediator. MONUC demonstrated qualities of impartiality in the implementation of the Lusaka Peace Agreement and served as *point de liaison* between the government and the rebel organisation. Trusted then as MONUC was, it reached the peak of its mediation and coordinated humanitarian activities in the Congo. It secured and distributed food from the World Food Programme and provided security to UN personnel, NGOs, and organisations in pursuit of peace. During this period, MONUC could also be seen as discharging tasks that were a prototype of an interventionist force albeit its deployment did not follow grave violations of human rights. MONUC's deployment could nonetheless be considered 'humanitarian intervention' and preventive diplomacy of the international community that feared a repeat of incidents similar to the Rwandan genocide in next-door Congo. It therefore seems from this strand of thought that in assuming the responsibility to protect (R2P) civilians, the international community has silently amended the conceptual requirements of humanitarian intervention.

In contrast to MONUC's mediation and humanitarianism above, as a tool for conflict peacebuilding, MONUC has come under sharp criticism during the periods 2006 till date (2010)-the postelection era. This has been largely because following the elections, the general assumption was that the DRC had attained sovereign maturity and needed very little or no external intervention in driving its architectural nation building plan. This (mis)conception culminated in the amendment of the mandate of MONUC, which was thereafter tasked to assist the DRC government of Joseph Kabila in governing. This task included training a new Congolese police force and serving as a support structure and military backup for the FARDC (Congolese National Army) when the need arose. This task embroiled MONUC in the affairs of the Congo even deeper and the institution lost credible ground as a mediator especially in the face of adversity when dialogue was needed between the government and rebel organisations. Its pledged allegiance to the government tainted her image when she had to be labeled by rebel organisations, including Nkunda's CNDP, as abetting government soldiers in fighting, raping, and displacing and destroying property belonging to civilians. This involvement defamed MONUC to such a level that in interrogating its vision, it was unclear that it had a vision, save for the fact that it waits up to today to be instructed by the Congolese government, which in November 2009 called for an exit plan from MONUC.

Indigenes vs. External Actors

Most of the literature on peacebuilding distinguishes between 'local', 'national', and 'international' stakeholders. These adjectives can be quite problematic and contentious in particular settings. For instance, a national actor coming from the capital city or another social group may well be considered an outsider when entering a specific community; this is why some distinguish between a 'national' and a 'local' level, but the criteria for making this distinction are unclear. Some analysts distinguish between individuals and organisations in the capital city and those living in the rest of the country; but these distinctions are generally not based on any in-depth sociopolitical analysis. Moreover, what may be true in one country may be entirely inapplicable in another.

The notions of 'indigenes'/'external actors' may be of greater utility in the success of a peace operation. Some analysts have defined insiders as 'those vulnerable to conflict, because they are from the area and living there. They are people who in some way must experience the conflict and live with its consequences personally. Outsiders are those who choose to become involved in the conflict and who have personally little to lose' (Andersonb and Olson 2003: 36). For others, this dichotomy may be more flexible as it is subjectively constructed by the actors concerned and mainly speaks to what factors an analyst chose to stress in his thesis (Culbertson and Pouligny 2007).

In all cases, it is important to understand that the relationship between indigenes and external actors is defined in a particular

493

context, according to which different parameters having to do with issues as varied as the history of the local sociopolitical configuration of the forces and the interests of designated individuals are often emphasised. Even when the distinction between 'indigenes' and 'external actors' seems to be obvious, it has to be closely considered. In many instances, external actors, especially but not only, when working with civil society, claim to work with 'indigenes', but are actually collaborating with other outsiders-in other words, with themselves (Pouligny 2005). Thus when peacekeeping initiatives fail, as is the case with Somalia, the often quick conclusion that natives are the cause of failed resolve could be misleading.

'Indigenes' and Peacekeeping: An Analysis

There are many ways to categorize indigenous peacebuilding actors. Many external actors actually interact (or think they interact) with only one particular type of actor and for one particular activity and do not need to know more about others, with the exception of potential collaborators or spoilers. This is both the most simplistic and limited way to map the local arena.

If one understands the different situations in microsociological terms, it becomes possible to identify:

i. Political actors: leaders of the main political parties, governments, legislative bodies when they exist, coordinating bodies or steering committees for the peacebuilding process, and all the agents of these entities (staff from the national administration, including the judiciary and the police, but also the political apparatus);

ii. Military actors: again, distinguishing between the leaders and others, members of constituted armies or paramilitary groups of different nature, not excluding rebel or guerrilla movements;

iii. Economic entrepreneurs (sometimes considered by outsiders as part of the local civil society, even though it rarely fits the local conception);

iv. Members of the indigenous 'civil society': formal social organisations (trade unions, NGOs, etc.) but also community and religious actors who may be less 'visible' to external actors.

    a. Several elements need to be kept in mind when considering the importance of indigenes in peacekeeping:

2. This sort of analysis makes it possible to discern variations according to different parameters, which influence indigenes' behavior and cause a future resort to civil conflicts: the nature of the ties uniting members of the societies in question and the solidarities and collaborations across different sectors, their systems of reference (or 'political culture'), the aims they pursue and their motives and circumstances for interacting with external actors on peacebuilding issues could potentially be the foundation stone of future conflicts. In other words, external actors' agenda and framing of the encounter should not be the only point of reference.

3. By their very nature-essentially taking place within states-present day African civil conflicts bring out heightened confusion among military and political actors, as well as economic and political entrepreneurs. The most resourceful individuals generally have the capacity for moving very quickly from one network to the next, changing hats very quickly, including using the general positive a priori knowledge external actors or peacekeepers have of local civil societies. When key actors in a conflict or a peace process belong to many networks at the same time, their behaviour needs to be understood in their capacity to move from one network to another, maintaining sometimes deliberate confusion as to their real status and, even more, their intentions. This confusion in part remains in the postconflict period may be the bedrock on which the seed of future territorial conflict are sowed.

4. Peace processes tend to sharpen the divergence of interests between leaders and their base, whoever they are (political actors, members of the military, and policemen, state employees, etc.). This explains why some authors distinguish

between different levels at which actors play a role, as in this graph below by John Paul Lederach.

[From John Paul Lederach's *Building Peace:* Sustainable Reconciliation in *Divided Societies* (Washington D.C.: United States Institute of Peace Press, 1997), p. 39.

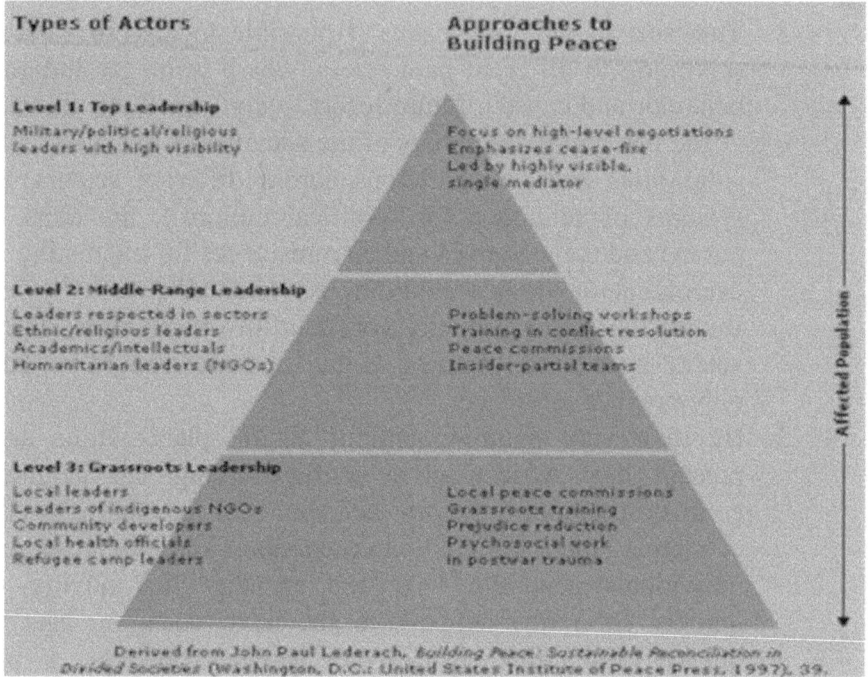

Derived from John Paul Lederach, *Building Peace: Sustainable Reconciliation in Divided Societies* (Washington, D.C.: United States Institute of Peace Press, 1997), 39.

Lederach presents a three-leadership phase-process of building peace and sustaining it. Using the triangle above, he suggests the commencement or consideration from level three, which incidentally apportions a very large space to locals, locally engineered processes, and local initiatives. The second phase is somewhat a mixture of influential indigenes whose word could in the future make or mar the peace process if excluded. Probably the best term for these persons is 'the elite'. From these is the first level of leadership, which is a conglomeration of those who are potentially crowd-and authority-pullers. As stated above, when referring to militaries, one cannot exclude the voice of the rebels, as has been repetitively done in the DRC with the demonisation of the FDLR.

This is, however, not to rule out their importance because it would be myopic to forget how fluid some local sociopolitical arenas may be, especially with the case of Somalia and parts of the DRC where indigenes see peace as a disincentive for their pre-established nefarious marine pirating and trade activities. Distinguishing between different types or levels of leadership is not always easy, and the understanding one may have at a certain time may no longer be valid a few months later. Therefore, the understanding of local contexts needs not only be as broad as possible, taking account of all social practices and daily power relations, but it must also be dynamic. External actors who go in a foreign country to work as peacebuilders do not always have that capacity. Yet, it is as important as any technical expertise they may have on a specific dimension of peace- and nation-building.

Indigenous Ownership of Peace/Nation Building

Finally, many sources distinguish peacebuilders, whether they come from the humanitarian, development, political, or security sectors, according to their main area of expertise and activity. These are organised around five pillars, which are:

- Security and Public Order
- Democracy and Good Governance
- Justice and Rule of Law
- Psycho-social Recovery
- Economic Recovery

While the thematic sections of the portal present the main underlying debates in each sector as well as the way they translate in concrete interventions, to involve locals, linking academic discussions to political vision, is a practical challenge that needs meticulous focus and attention. It is important to have indigenes in all of these sectors not just as participants and observers, but as key interveners in the design and implementation of particular activities to sustainably harness the peace process.

Not involving indigenes, involving them only to rubber-stamp the proceedings without input or involving only those with big wallets is indicative of sources of future civil conflicts. The fact that policies crafted in these set-ups are eventually handed over to the indigenes to implement is ab initio a lack of coherent and strategic obstacle to the implementation.

While the role of the UN in peacekeeping is viewed as unavoidable, it is increasingly accepted that a comprehensive assessment of the context, conflict and peace dynamics, and indigenous capacities and opportunities for peace should precede the design of peacebuilding programmes. The UN's movement towards a notion of integrated peace strategies has roots in the UN Secretary General's 2001 analysis in No Exit Without Strategy (2001) and the UNSC discussions that followed, which underscored the need for strategies to be based upon the interdependence between sustainable peace, security, and development in all dimensions (Security Council 2001) The UN's new Peacebuilding Commission (PBC) has further committed itself to advancing thinking and practice in the area of integrated peacebuilding strategies. It will support peacebuilding strategies in postconflict states as a means to prevent the future relapse to conflict. How these strategies will build and tally with other strategic policy frameworks and processes currently in existence will be fundamental to their success. It is, however, important to state that designing such policies is problematic, as no two conflicts are the same despite certain prevalent characteristic features that they may all exhibit.

Conclusion and Recommendation

All postconflict societies face a mountain of urgent needs, not all of them compatible. So to design policies in the West and want to universally apply them in every state is inordinate. Not giving regard to social needs of a people returning from conflict, or allowing them to wallow in despondency in a postconflict dispensation that inspires new hope can ignite conflict when patience for a better nation runs out.

Furthermore, debates that precede peacekeeping deployments, such as those over which country will lead the peace operation and how many contingents a country contribute; have aroused skepticism amongst certain actors of the DRC peace process. For example, Rwanda's discomfort about the intentions of increased French soldiers raised the question: Whose interests do peacekeeping mediators represent: their national interests or the interests of the deploying organisation?

Besides justice, democracy, and truth and reconciliation, there are equally daunting goals of peace, an end to impunity, healing, forgiveness, national unity, harmony, short-term relief, longer-term reconstruction, and development. And all of these are to be acted on by a new government that does not enjoy universal support and that depends on human and financial resources that are minuscule and on infrastructure that barely exists. In order to avoid conflict resurgence, postconflict reconstruction should be pioneered by locals who will own the concept, the process, and the product. However, in the event of external involvement, such involvement should come as support geared towards fostering a partnership, as opposed to prescribing stringent solutions for the peace process. Postconflict reconstruction should seek to address not only economic and political, but also emergent social challenges to the conflict.

Notes

1. MONUC is the UN Peacekeeping Mission in the Congo.
2. ONUC is the French acronym for Organisation des Nations Unies au Congo.
3. MONUC is the French acronym for Mission d'Organisation des Nations Unies au Congo.
4. See 'Indigenous ownership of peace/nation-building' in the pages that follow.
5. Equatorial Guinea and Gabon over Corisco Bay Island (1972), Malawi and Tanzania (1967), Ethiopia and Somalia (1962), Mali and Mauritania (1960), Ethiopia and Kenya over Gaduana Wells, Chad and Mali over Aouzu Strip, and Eritrea and Ethiopia over Badne, Cameroon and Nigeria over Bakassi (1994). Cited from Ikome (2004).

References

Adebajo, Adekeye. 2002. *Building peace in Africa: Sierra Leone and Guinea-Bissau.* Boulder, Colorado: Lynne Rienner, USA, 2002) pp. 79-109.

Anderson, Mary B. And Lara Olson. 2003. *Confronting war: Critical lessons for peace practitioners.* Cambridge, Massachusets: CDA.

Anstey, M. 2006. *Managing change, negotiating conflict.* 3rd Edition, Cape Town: Juta and Co.

Collier, Paul. 2000. 'Doing well out of war: An economic perspective'. In: *Greed and grievances: Economic agendas in civil wars*, edited by Mats Berdal and David Malone. Boulder, Colorado: Lynne Rienner Publishers.

Culbertson, Roberta and Beatrice Pouligny. 2007. 'Re-imagining peace after mass crime: A dialogical exchange between insider and outsider knowledge'. In: *After mass crime: Rebuilding states and communities*, edited by Beatrice Pouligny et al., pp. 271-87. Tokyo/New York/Paris: United Nations University Press.

Hart, Liddell. 2007. 'Meddlers or mediators? African interveners in civil conflicts in Eastern Africa,'. In: *Meddlers or mediators?* Edited by Gilbert Khadiagal. Boston: Martinus Nijhoff.

Hutchful, Eboe and Kwesi Aning. 2004. 'The political economy of Conflict'. In: *West African Security Challenges: Building Peace in a troubled Region,* in Adekeye Adebajo & Ismail Rashid, Eds Boulder, Colorado: Lynne Rienner Publishers, Inc.

Ikome, Francis Nguendi. 2004. *The inviolability of Africa's colonial boundaries: Lessons from the Cameroon-Nigeria border conflict.* Institute for Global Dialogue Occasional Paper No. 47. Johannesburg.

Jeong, H.W. 2008. *Understanding conflict and conflict analy*sis. Los Angeles: SAGE Publications.

Morgenthau, Hans 1948. *Politics among Nations: The Struggle for Power and Peace.* New York NY: Alfred A. Knopf.

Musila, Godfrey M. 2007. *The DRC situation: Cases before the ICC.* ISS Monograph 164.

Nyuykonge, Charles. 2007. Reformation of International Judicial Institutions as key to Global Conflict Prevention. Masters Dissertation International Relations University of the Witwatersrand. Chapter 1.

Pouligny, Beatrice. 2005. 'Civil society and post-conflict peace building: Ambiguities of international programs aimed at building "new societies"'. *Security Dialogue* 36 (4): 447-62.

Pruitt, Dean G. 2000. 'Tactics of third-party intervention'. *Orbis* 44 (2): PAGES?

Reno, William. 2000. 'Shadow states and political economy of civil wars'. In :) *Greed and grievances: Economic agendas in civil war*, edited by Mats Berdal and David Malone, pp. 43-68. Boulder, Colorado: Lynne Rienner Publishers.

Report of the Secretary-General. 2001. 'No exit without strategy: Security Council decision-making and the closure or transition of UN Peacekeeping Operations'. 20 April. S/2001/394.

'Security Council Addresses Comprehensive Approach'. 2001. *Security Council 4278th Meeting, SC*/7014, 21 Feb. 2001.

Snow, Keith Harmon. 2005. 'Rwanda's secret war: U.S backed destabilization of Central'. Africa http://zmagsite.zmag.org/Feb20 05/snow0205.html (accesses 16 July 2010).

Sommerville, Keith. 1990. *Foreign military intervention in Africa.* London: Pinter Publishers.

Sudan Tribune. 2007. 'Libyan leader says world must stop meddling in Darfur tribal conflict'. http://www.sudantribune.com/s pip.php?article24456 October 27, 2007 (last consulted on 27 Jan. 2010).

Tamm, Ingrid J. 2002. *Diamonds in peace and war: severing the conflict-diamond connection.* Cambridge, Massachusetts: World Peace Foundation.

Thome, Wolfgang H. 2008. 'More bad news from Congo, UN MUNOC forces under growing pressure'. http://www.eturbonews. com/3786/more-bad-news-congo-un-munoc-forces-under-growing-pressure (accessed on 3 Sept. 2010).

Waltz, Kenneth 1979 *Theory of International Politics.* Boston: McGraw Hill, 1979.

Zartman, William. 1995 'Dynamics and constraints in negotiations in internal conflicts'. In: *The elusive peace, negotiating an end to civil war*s, edited by William Zartman. Washington, Brookings Institution.

_____ (Ed.). 1995. *Collapsed states: Thedisintegration and restoration of legitimate authority.* Boulder, Colorado: Lynne Rienner Publishers.

CHAPTER 17

Towards An Indigenous Theory of Conflict Resolution: Reinventing Women's Roles as Traditional Peace Builders in Neo-Colonial Africa

Chris Isike and Ufo Okeke-Uzodike

Introduction

Traditionally, women have always been at the centre of peace processes-from peacemaking to peacebuilding and even sometimes preventive diplomacy-across different precolonial African societies (Amadiume 1997; Ngongo-Mbede 2003; Mohammed 2003). Women's peace agency in these societies can be located in their cultural and sociopolitical roles as well as their contributions to the overall well-being of these societies wherein these roles were reinforced by perceptions that stereotyped women as natural peacemakers, and as being more pacific than men.[1] Often, women were symbolised as paragons of morality, sacredness, goodness, and tenderness. Indeed, women's existence and power in precolonial African societies were based on an ethic of care that was rooted in their motherhood and their nature, which was tolerant of difference, collaborative, nonviolent, and as such, peaceful (see Mazuarana and McKay 1999).

However, women in neocolonial African states appear to have lost the myth/sacredness that surrounded their being and social existence in precolonial Africa. This is because apart from being marginalised socially, economically, and politically (Amadiume 1997; Nzeogwu 2000; Rehn and Johnson-Sirleaf 2001), they have become victims of assorted forms of physical abuse and sexual violence based on a warped understanding of African patriarchies,[2] which has produced negative masculinities in the continent (Isike and Okeke-Uzodike 2008). The negative impact of armed conflict and poverty on women is particularly unacceptable because not only are women disproportionate victims, they are in most cases excluded from peace processes and postconflict reconstruction in their communities. Africa arguably presents a major challenge and fertile ground for conflict and

503

peace studies because it has been more plagued by violent intrastate and interstate conflict of various kinds since the 1960s than any other continent (Patel in Maloka: 2001: 357). Recent examples (especially between 1990 and 2002) of intrastate conflicts in Africa include Rwanda, Burundi, Liberia, Sierra Leone, DRC, Sudan, and Ivory Coast. Also, within this period, there were low-intensity conflicts, so-called because despite their usually violent and perennial nature, they do not engulf the entire state in a way that leads to state collapse. These are common in some states in West, Central, and Southern Africa. Examples include Nigeria (Niger-Delta), Senegal (Casamance), Uganda (Gulu), Sudan (Darfur), and South Africa (KwaZulu-Natal).

While a multiplicity of factors are responsible for these conflicts, a number of which have territorial origins, they all reflect the failure of national political systems to prevent them *ab initio*, effectively manage their symptoms, or mediate them when they occur. It is pertinent to note that the vast majority of world leaders, governments and officials at all levels, presidents and boardrooms of transnational corporations are men (Brine 1999: 16). It is therefore not far-fetched to make two assumptions: first, that global power is gendered in favour of men, and secondly, based on this, that armed conflict has a masculine character in terms of causes since men dominate the decision-making structures and mechanisms that produce them in the first place. The question then is how and why did women transform from being active participants in precolonial peace processes to being passive observers of politics and peacebuilding in neocolonial Africa? How do they, who are the majority of the African population, fare in these conflicts? And given their precolonial peacebuilding antecedents, do they have the potential to transform politics and conflict in neocolonial Africa?

This paper argues that the positive human factor values that defined womanhood in precolonial Africa have been corrupted over time by the colonial interruption of Africa's sociocultural existence leading to the marginalisation, tokenisation, and de-feminisation of women in political and peace processes in postcolonial Africa. Excluding women from these processes is an inherent weakness of extant statist and institutional approaches to understanding and resolving conflict in the continent, as they undermine the human factor and human security basis of these conflicts. Also, even where women have been mainstreamed into politics in significant numbers, such as in Rwanda and South Africa, de-feminisation arising from the colonial corruption of gender relations makes their participation and representation in the public domain ineffective. Impliedly, the intervening sociocultural variables that impede women's political participation and make their representation ineffective must be tackled to curb the incidence of armed conflict in Africa. One way to do this is to develop an African feminist paradigm or ideology of peacebuilding that can be appropriated as a practical conflict prevention and resolution model in the continent.

In building towards an indigenous theory of conflict resolution and peacebuilding, this paper therefore contends that the feminist ethic of care that was appropriated by precolonial African women to wage peace and maintain societal harmony is still very much a part of the core of contemporary African women, and can be appropriated in resolving subnational conflicts in postcolonial Africa. Indeed, they can be developed into a model of African feminist peacebuilding that can be utilised as an ideological rallying point to transform politics and create an environment conducive for development to take place. This conclusion is aptly supported by empirical findings from a previous study of women, politics, and peacebuilding in the Niger-Delta in Nigeria and KwaZulu-Natal in South Africa (Isike, 2009).

Conceptual Framework of Analysis

This paper utilised a number of key concepts that are hereunder explicated as they were deployed within a larger *ubuntu* framework. These include conflict, peace, and peace process. A starting point of understanding *conflict* as used in this paper is that it is an inevitable phenomenon in any society. In other words, it is an inherent dimension of human relations, an undercurrent of social relations. It arises out of and shapes the challenge of how to manage economic, cultural, political, and social relations. Underlying this challenge is the problem of scarcity, which necessitates competition and requires cooperation to resolve. According to CASS (2005), although conflict structures social relations by creating intersecting channels for societal (individual/collective/group) competition and cooperation, it also has to be understood in the context of disagreement over the values/ideals to inform the socioeconomic and political organisation of state and society (CASS 2005: 6-7). These include the social relations of production and the superstructure of culture, law, and political relations, forms and systems of governance, structures and processes, including institutional ones, the distribution of and allocation of scarce resources, and the direction and emphasis of public policies (CASS 2005: 7). Viewed this way, there are different forms of conflict, such as social conflict defined by economic scarcity that manifests in poverty (human insecurity), which impairs human existence. There is also armed conflict defined by sociopolitical differences over territory and mineral resources, which manifests in political assassinations, violent confrontations, and low-intensity warfare. Another form of conflict discussed in this paper is intergender conflict, which manifests in male violence against women. All these forms of conflict are undergirded by the breakdown of social relations between individuals (i.e., men and women) and groups in societies; between communities over boundary lines and chieftaincy; and between states over territories and sovereignty. Concisely, conflict is inevitable and is rooted in relationships (see Lederach 1997; CASS 2005; Amisi 2008).

In the same vein, this paper conceptualises and utilises a relational notion of *peace*, not as the absence of violence, but as the constructive transformation and resolution of violent conflict based on gender justice, mutual respect, tolerance, and inclusion. In this light, the paper adopts a modified version of Assefa's (1993) definition of peace as involving three broad elements: the transformation of destructive conflictual interactions into cooperative and constructive relationships; reconciliation, leading to healthy, mature, ecological, social, and personal relationships of interdependence; and justice. In this way, peace involves restructuring relationships (male notions of relationships) that promote war so that they can instead advance peace. Our modification of Assefa's conceptualisation of peace is particularly pertinent in terms of the relationship between gender relations and justice. Therefore, while agreeing with Assefa that peace involves the constructive transformation of violence (see Lederach 1995), we add that it must be based on entrenching a politics of gender justice, mutual respect, tolerance, and inclusivity, which are all hallmarks of *ubuntu*. While these values are also found among men, we will argue that they are more likely to be exhibited by women.[3] In this sense, a critical mass of women in politics can bring these qualities to bear and make the difference between violent conflict and sustainable peace.

Based on our understanding of peace, the *peace process* entails a complex process of peacemaking (conflict resolution), peacekeeping, peacebuilding, and preventive diplomacy, which lead to sustainable peace. These concepts are often confused and used interchangeably. However, each represents a different stage of the whole peace process.

1) *Peacemaking,* or *conflict resolution,* is the process of mediating a cessation of violence and settlement between disputing parties to a conflict. It involves the use of varying conflict resolution techniques, such as mediation, negotiations, and representations. It can be either or both formal and informal. In formal peacemaking processes, professional negotiators/diplomats engage in direct negotiations with the main disputants with a view to agreeing on and drafting a workable peace accord. At the informal level, citizens (i.e., women) can also participate in the peacemaking process through moral suasion, prayers, peace protests, and letter writing. Informal citizenship participation in peacemaking is becoming an increasingly common way to kick-start the formal peacemaking process.

2) *Peacekeeping* involves maintaining law and order by keeping disputants from attacking each other. Peacekeeping, which is usually implemented by neutral armed forces, can take place simultaneously with peacemaking. The peacekeeping force does nothing to settle the disputant's differences or help negotiate a peace agreement. Their task is often to prevent the escalation of violence by providing a buffer between the disputants.

3) *Peace building* involves the processes and activities involved in normalising relations and reconciling the latent differences between the disputing sides in a conflict with a view to enabling sustainable peace. It is an overarching concept that includes conflict transformation, restorative justice, trauma healing, reconciliation, development, and good leadership, which all have implications for conflict prevention. Indeed, good leadership underlain by spirituality and religion is a proactive action that can prevent armed conflict and/or transform it positively when it becomes inevitable. According to Amisi (2008), because conflict is motivated by the immediacy of hatred and prejudice, transforming it requires focusing on the sociopsychological and spiritual aspects of it that are largely ignored by international diplomacy (Amisi 2008: 6; see also Mazurana and McKay 1999: 8-11). Both studies acknowledge that relationships are central to conflict transformation (peacebuilding), and that when they are well managed, human relationships can prevent future conflict. In this way, we contend that if women, for instance, are mainstreamed into politics on an equal basis with men in ways that allow them to bring their femininity into the fold, their numbers and the relational values they represent can change the character of politics. These values--cooperativeness, nonconfrontation,

tolerance, empathy, love, and care--can enthrone a more collaborative and developmental approach to politics that can prevent conflict *ab initio*. In this way, conflict prevention becomes part of holistic peacebuilding, which in itself emphasises relationships.

4) However, *conflict prevention* has developed into a distinctive sphere of peacebuilding known as preventive diplomacy, which in the context of this paper means a possible range of actions that can be taken to prevent disputes from turning into armed conflict. These are in the political, economic, and social fields, applicable especially to possible internal conflicts. According to the United Nations (1999), all the ranges/classes of preventive actions, such as preventive deployment of forces, preventive humanitarian action, and preventive peacebuilding share common characteristics. For instance, 'they all depend on early warning that the risk of conflict exists, they require information about the causes and likely nature of the potential conflict so that the appropriate preventive action can be identified, and they require the consent of the party or parties within whose jurisdiction the preventive action is to take place' (www.un.org/Docs /SG/Report99/prevent.htm). These characteristics also apply to preventing intrastate conflicts.

Theoretical Considerations for Feminising Peacebuilding

This section provides a theoretical framework for feminising politics and the peace process. The paper utilises the Human Factor theory popularised by Senyo Adjibolosoo (1995) and ties it to the Moral Imagination Model of peacebuilding theorised by John Lederach (2005). Within this human agency framework, where women's womanhood, experiences, and needs as human beings are factored into the development equation, the paper attempts to develop an African feminist model of conflict resolution and peacebuilding.

The Human Factor Theory

The main exponent of the human factor (HF) is Senyo Adjibolosoo, who states:

> Human Factor is spectrum of personality *characteristics* and other *dimensions* of human performance that *enable* social, economic and political institutions to *function* and *remain functional* over time. Such dimensions sustain the workings and application of the rule of law, political harmony, a disciplined labor force, just legal systems, respect for human dignity (rights) and the sanctity of life. (Adjibolosoo 1995: 33)

The personality traits that enhance human performance in all spheres include integrity, responsibility, trustworthiness, commitment, selflessness, truthfulness, loyalty, and discipline. Others are love, tolerance, sharing, wisdom, imagination, creativity and collegiality. Similarly, the human factor paradigm holds that there are six broad dimensions of human performance, and these include *spiritual capital* (knowledge of and connection to the laws of the universe); *moral capital* (sense of right or wrong); *aesthetic capital* (sense of beauty and ugliness); *human capital* (knowledge and skills); *human abilities* (competences); and *human potential* (dormant talents or untapped part of Being). These personality traits and dimensions of human performance are the sine qua non for the attainment of the development aspirations of any society (Adjibolosoo 1995, 1998; Owusu-Ampomah 2001). Neglecting them in any development paradigm, planning, and implementation process is a recipe for failure. As Owusu-Ampomah (2002: 66) puts it, without the human factor, the quest for sustainable human development is a wild goose chase, as the human factor represents a paradigm shift that places premium human values and positive qualities, not capital, institutions, or policies. According to Adjibolosoo (1999: 62), human factor underdevelopment and/or decay is the primary cause of the social, economic, political, and educational problems of all societies, not lack of capital, inadequate political and economic institutional arrangements, or bad policies. In other words, negative human factor traits and dimensions are a source of underdevelopment, sociopolitical disorder, and conflict, while positive human factor traits and dimensions is a necessary and sufficient condition for good governance, sustained economic growth, human-centred development, and peace.

Apart from putting emphasis on human beings as the agency and end of development, the bottom line of the human factor theory is that the quality of people who should power or enable the development process also matters. Therefore, the process of good governance must begin with human quality development,[4] that will create an environment that is conducive for good governance, which in the context of this study will go a long way in preventing conflict *ab initio*. According to Adjibolosoo, the absence of truth-telling, integrity, responsibility, accountability, trust, commitment, and transparency creates a fertile environment for serious social, economic, and political problems to thrive. This underscores the significance of good governance and political leadership in preventing and managing armed conflicts.[5]

The Human Factor, Women, and Peace Building

The human factor paradigm tells us that beyond the human security and human rights (people-centred) approaches to development, the quality of people who can make peace and development possible also matters. In other words, there is need to focus on the character traits and human dimensions of people who are more likely to make peace and development happen, and appropriate their services accordingly. For example, while according to Adjibolosoo (1995), positive human factor qualities such as integrity, accountability, selflessness, and truthfulness can create a fertile environment for good governance and development, Lederach (2005) sees relatedness, collaboration, love, empathy, and tolerance as necessary and sufficient factors for creating a fertile environment for peacebuilding. Within this context, the question is who, between men and women, is more likely to approach politics with these positive human factor traits and dimensions? Just as armed conflict takes place within a political context, there is also a political dimension of peacemaking that requires a kind of politics that is crucial for conflict transformation. This is the politics of responsibility, accountability, tolerance, empathy, accommodation, love, truth-telling, and forgiveness. Are women in Africa sufficiently disposed to both the human factor characteristics and dimensions that make development and peace possible?

The Moral Imagination Model of Peacebuilding

As John Lederach notes, the moral imagination is 'the capacity to imagine something rooted in the challenges of the real world yet capable of giving birth to that which does not yet exist; the potential to find a way to transcend, and to move beyond what exists while still living in it' (Lederach 2005: 27-29). Referring to peacebuilding, Lederach argues that the capacity to imagine and generate constructive responses and initiatives associated with the daily challenges of violence can serve to transcend and, ultimately, break the grips of those destructive patterns and cycles within which conflict is perpetuated (Lederach 2005: 29). From this perspective, the moral imagination has two qualities: transcendence and creativity. In its essence, it implies a shift from conventional wisdom and principles that governs social, political, and economic relations between people, communities, and states to a whole new paradigm (and ways of doing things) that is rooted in the capacity of humans to rise above the ordinary. In this way, the moral imagination is the capacity to perceive things beyond, and at a deeper level than, what initially meets the ordinary eye. Thus, it is a profound understanding that leads to the kind of critical turning point that has the capapcity to make the difference between violent lingering conflict and sustainable peace (Lederach 2005: 19-27). To illustrate how the moral imagination can lead to a critical turning point between conflict and peace, Lederach (2005: 7-10) employs a number of examples, such as a peace meeting in the 1990s between two mutually antagonistic communities--the Konkombas and Dagombas of northern Ghana--to drive his argument.

Basically, the highly emotional story shows how two communities locked in a historical enmity could be impelled toward an even bigger and dangerous conflict until a simple event (a peace meeting) led to a critical turning point, due to the visionary attitude of a young Konkomba man whose humility, wisdom, and kind words offered to the Dagomba monarch and people transformed the attitude of both communities and instantly melted away much of the hostility and instilled a spirit of peace between them. As Lederach noted, the moral of this story is that the marked change was neither the result of the technical expertise of the international peace mediators nor the nature and design of the peace process. As we note elsewhere, "it was not the local or national political power, exigencies, the fears of a broader war, nor the influence and pressure from the international community that created the shift" Lederach 2005: 19; Isike and Okeke-Uzodike 2010: 688). Neither was it any specific political, economic or military power. Rather, what created a turning point that was critical to breaking the age-long violence between the Dagombas and Konkombas was the appearance of the moral imagination displayed by the young spokesman of the Konkombas (Lederach 2005: 19). His attitude and tone in addressing the Dagomba Chief, calling him 'father', and kneeling before the chief and grabbing his lower leg (a deep sign of respect in Ghanaian culture) were characteristic of the moral imagination, the capacity to rise beyond violence by taking personal responsibility, acknowledging relational mutuality and, in the process, giving birth to something new (Isike and Okeke-Uzodike 2010: 688).

Indeed, Lederach (2005:10) himself sums the story thus: '[T]he possibility of change away from century-long cycles of violence began and perhaps the seeds that avoided what could have been a full-blown civil war were planted in that moment of the serendipitous appearance of the moral imagination'. Going further on the causal link between the moral imagination and peacebuilding, Lederach delineates four fundamentals--relationship, paradoxical curiosity, creativity, and risk--that require imagination separately, but which together form the moral imagination that makes peacebuilding present or practiced together, these elements make the moral imagination and peacebuilding possible as the actors work toward and improve their capacity to imagine themselves in a relationship; improve on their readiness to embrace complexity; and retreat from framing their dispute as a polarity between 'good and evil' or 'us and them', which drives the cycles of violence; develop acts of vast creativity that demonstrate new possibilities; and adopt a new willingness to step into the unknown by taking risk toward peace. It was the presence of each of these features in the story of the Konkombas and Dagombas that led to complex initiatives of peacebuilding between them that created and then sustained constructive change (Lederach 2005: 40).

Clearly then, the idea of relationships is a crucial factor in feminising the peacebuilding process. As Lederach notes, this is because it forms the bases and contexts within which succession of violence happen. It also provides the impetus for rising above those same cycles of antagonism and violence. In this way, relationships are central in providing the context for breaking violence, 'for it brings people into the pregnant moments of the moral imagination: the space of recognition that ultimately the quality of our life is dependent on the quality of life of others' (Lederach 2005: 35). Indeed, *ubuntu,* the African social ideology of communalism, which is rooted in the idea of the interconnectedness of human relationships within which people interact, reinforce, and validate each other resonates very well with the moral imagination.

It is for that reason that masculine social constructionists take the position that masculinity is a barrier to peace, given that its raison d'être is firmly anchored on the rejection of feminine ideologies that embrace and prioritise relationships, partnership, sharing, and mutual empowerment. By contrast, masculine ideologies are anchored on their preference for and promotion of independence, individualism, and aggression (Gagnon 2003: 5-9), despite the fact that masculinity actually thrives in relationships, albeit conflict nurturing and reinforcing relationships such as military camps that provide traditional masculine communities with the contexts within which brotherhood, comradeship, and a sense of connection with themselves can be nurtured. Unfortunately, such relationships serve to perpetuate violence and war because such camps are effectively instruments for socialising men to love through fear (war) and the provision of security for others, especially women. In this way, men are nurtured and socialised to be prone to aggression and war as a method of conflict resolution (Gagnon 2003: 6). Not surprisingly, men have evolved norms and cultures that regard fighting for their nations as acts of devotion, loyalty, and love. In turn, such values are embedded within a masculine worldview that valorises and prioritises aggression, power, supremacy, and zero-sum competition before, during and after conflict.

The Moral Imagination, Women and Peacebuilding

Lederach's model of the utility of the moral imagination for peacebuilding within a web of human relationships relates to this study in three significant ways. First, it means that women and men exist in an interconnected social reality where they are meant to complement each other. This means that relationships should not be perceived as a feminine but rather should be seen as human because both men and women are existentially connected, and both have need for and yearn for connection with others in the bid for survival and self-actualisation. According to Gagnon, for men, the problem is not that they reject connection; the problem is that they reject feminine forms of connection. Therefore, the challenge is for men to deconstruct and transform masculine relational ideologies, which breed conflict and war, into more inclusive foundations that would be more conducive to peacebuilding. This leads us to the second point of connection between the moral imagination model and calls for feminising peacebuilding in Africa, namely, that men can and should morally imagine and recreate a society that promotes peaceful relations within itself and with others outside it.

Therefore, because they remain critical to success of gender equality efforts, men have the challenge of transcending the orthodox wisdom and convention of patriarchy that governs gender relations in postcolonial Africa, to create new forms of relationships that are conducive to peaceful co-existence and holistic development. According to Gagnon (2003), peaceful relationships, starting from those between men and women, are necessary to negotiating mutually amicable resolution to conflicts, even though as a result of social construction of masculinity, men have learnt to reject the essential value of relationships. In Gagnon's words, '[W]hile masculine construction may be a cause for war and a deterrent to peace, it also holds the potential for transformation as the very qualities that would be necessary to pursue such ideal change are often associated with constructions of masculinity-courage, fortitude, resolution and the drive for success-and peace would not be possible without them' (Gagnon 2003: 7). Third, women generally are richly endowed with the moral capacity to embrace curiosity and complexity, as they are wont to raise above the historic traps of dualistic divisions that drive the cycles of violence, and in this way transcend orthodox gender stereotypes and the oppressive relations they spew. This is possible because women are more relational than men and thus view the same phenomenon differently; for instance, women have the capacity to imagine themselves in a web of relationships even with their enemies (see Lederach 2005: 34). And as we shall show in the next sections, African women had and still have the capacity to perceive things beyond and at a deeper level than what initially meets the ordinary eye, leading to a critical turning point that will make the difference between violent, protracted conflict and sustainable peace. For example, precolonial African women demonstrated the moral imagination that the Konkomba spokesman displayed when he chose to be humble, tolerant, and conciliatory in the face of aggression, treating the elderly enemy chief of Dagomba as his father and therefore eliciting a wiser and inherently more fatherly response from the aggressive chief to validate the relational mutuality of their (Dagomba and Konkomba) existence.

Women and Peacebuilding in Precolonial African Societies

Women in different precolonial African societies had traditional peacemaking and peacebuilding roles, as they were involved in mediating and preventing conflict within and between societies. Women's peace agency in these societies can be located in their cultural and sociopolitical roles and contributions to the overall well-being of these societies. These roles were reinforced by perceptions that stereotyped women as natural peace makers, as being more pacific than men, and they were often symbolised as paragons of morality, sacredness, goodness, and tenderness. Thus in most precolonial societies, virtues of patience, tolerance, humility, and subtle persuasiveness were seen as essentially female attributes that were reinforced through socialisation patterns that promote women primarily as child-bearers, good wives, caregivers, arbitrators of conflict, and peace promoters in the family and community (UNESCO 2003: 8). For example, according to Ntahobari and Ndayiziga (2003), in traditional Burundian society, women were considered to be bridge builders and symbols of unity between different families, clans, communities, and ethnic groups through the institution of marriage. Accordingly, girls were socialised from an early age to be open-minded, adaptable, and tolerant (Ntahobari and Ndayiziga 2003: 20). This was the case in other societies, too, such as in Nigeria, Cameroon, Namibia, Somalia, and Tanzania (Awe 1977; Ngongo-Mbede 2003; Becker 2003; Mohammed 2003; Lihamba 2003). In these societies, women were expected to embody such virtues as compassion, patience, discretion, gentleness, modesty, and self-control, which though they were considered inherent in womanhood, required reinforcement through upbringing, so that women could fulfill their role as peacemakers (Ntahobari and Ndayiziga 2003: 20). For instance, Mohammed (2003) records that in periods of conflict amongst the Somalis; there were times when a group of young, unmarried women (known as *Heerin*) from one of the warring clans paid visits to the opposing clan without the knowledge or consent of their families (2003: 103). According to him, on arrival, the *Heerin* told the people that they were unmarried women and that they wanted to be married: 'Because this was a well known tradition, the young women were welcomed, and preparations were made to ensure that they were married. This immediately stabilized the situation and set in motion a peace process that eventually resolved the conflict' (Mohammed 2003: 103). This kind of peace approach was only possible and successful because of the moral authority women were granted. They also often used these qualities and authority to mediate in disagreements between men by advising their husbands to toe the line of peace knowing full well that they (women) would bear the consequences of violent conflict to a greater degree. Such is the potency of this moral authority that women in postcolonial Africa have drawn from them to wage peace in the DRC, Sierra Leone, Liberia, Guinea, Burundi, and South Africa. For instance, in a comparative study of women and peacebuilding, Mazuarana and McKay (1999: 20) contend that women have continually drawn upon the moral authority granted to them by virtue of their being mothers, that is, creators of life, to call for peace throughout Africa.

Traditionally, women in precolonial African societies were peace agents. According to M.A.C Nwoye,[6] women engaged in peacebuilding through positive childcare, responsible mothering, and nurturing of children in ways that prepared and socialised them towards peaceful coexistence. In most precolonial societies, a culture of peace, tolerance, and an antiwar tradition are embedded in and transmitted through folktales, proverbs, poetry, songs, and dance. Traditionally, women are often seen as the transmitters of these cultural values to their progeny and to future generations through such artistic expressions. For example, Mohammed (2003) used Somali stories, poetry, songs, and proverbs to depict the important role of women as transmitters of knowledge and builders of a stable social fabric for society from the precolonial through the postcolonial era:

> Mother! Without you
> It would have been impossible to utter the alphabet
> Mother! Without you
> It would have been impossible to learn how to speak
> A child deprived of your care
> Sweet lullaby
> And soft touches
> Would not grow up.

Mother! You are the source of love
The epitome of kindness.

(Mohamed Ibrahim 'Hadrawi' in Mohammed 2003: 102)

Also, according to Mohammed (2003: 102), the following song captures the thoughts of a Somali mother describing the tyranny of the civil war in that country:

I am the foundation of the world
And I am a woman
I am the womb that gave birth to human beings
I am the pillar of life.

A very apt Somali proverb says: 'The values with which children are brought up precede their actual birth,' and Mohammed (2003) contends that they are transmitted by mothers even while the child is still in the womb. In this regard, Somalians believe that 'before becoming adults, we attend a basic school, and that school is mother' (Mohammed, 2003: 102). Indeed, in various precolonial societies, women used songs, proverbs, and poetry to transmit positive social capital values upon which peace is predicated. These values include 'patience, tolerance, honesty, respect for elders, communality and mutuality, compassion, regard for due discretion, gentleness, modesty, self-control, moderation, flexibility, and open-mindedness' (M.A.C Nwoye, 2006: NA).

Women in precolonial societies also engaged actively in peacemaking (conflict mediation). As mentioned before, age was an important social base of political power in these societies and respect was given to the elderly in general, and to elderly women in particular. For instance, M.A.C Nwoye reveals from the findings of her study on women and the peace process in six precolonial African states that 'the elderly woman' 'was respected by all, and played a key role in crisis management and conflict resolution'. This was the case amongst the Tuburs in Cameroun, for example, where the *Wog Clu* (old women) were solely responsible for conflict mediation and were consulted on problems that disturbed communal peace (Ngongo-Mbede 2003: 32). Thus, as MAC Nwoye (2006: NA) states, 'when a conflict degenerated into armed violence, an appeal would usually be made to a third party of mature years to calm the tension and reconcile the combatants. Such

517

an appeal for mediation was usually made to a woman who enjoyed the consideration and respect of all who knew her'. In the same vein, because of the sanctity attached to womanhood, women--mostly elderly women--were employed as peace envoys to facilitate peace negotiations (Mohammed 2003; Lihamba 2003). This was only possible because during war women were the only ones who could move across the zones of conflict freely and without much danger and as such were used by warring parties to study the situation, assess the prospects for peace, and facilitate contact and communication between the two warring parties.

Women in most precolonial African societies also served as intermediaries in conflicts between human beings and nature. For example, according to Ngongo-Mbede (2003), in the land of Mungo of the Cameroon, any misfortune occurring in the community brought the latter to seek the mediation of the *Kalbia* (married women). In these communities, in general, misfortune and calamities were taken to imply the existence of conflicts between the people. For instance:

> ...In the philosophy of these communities, such a succession of misfortune was not fortuitous. It was the sign that love and peace were absent from the community, and prompted the women to decide to organize an *Mbabi*. The latter was organized in a grove or on a crossroads, after consultation of the oracles. It was exclusively a meeting of women who had reached the age of the menopause. The ceremony was presided over by a woman of very advanced years whose moral integrity was usually universally acknowledged. Men could on occasion, be associated with the *Mbabi*. Even in such exceptional cases, however, it was the women who organized and presided over the ceremony of reconciling human beings with themselves, with relatives and with nature. (Ngongo-Mbede, 2003:31)

The study documents that amongst the Beti, the Mangissa, and the Eton in Cameroun, the *Mbabi* was a common purification rite aimed at restoring peace, and women frequently engaged in it both for peace, community building, and development. Ngongo-Mbede (2003: 31) contends that the *Mbabi* ritual was an exclusive preserve of women who had reached the age of the menopause, and it took place in a grove or on a crossroads, after due consultation with the oracles. And although men could be part of it, the ceremony was usually presided over by a woman of very advanced years whose moral integrity was usually universally acknowledged (Ngongo-Mbede 2003: 31). Even in such exceptional cases where men attended, 'it was the women who organized and presided over the ceremony of reconciling human beings with themselves, with relatives and with nature' (Ngongo-Mbede 2003: 31). This is also consistent with the purification rituals (*uutoni*), which women in northern Namibia performed on soldiers returning from war. The idea was to cleanse them of the guilt of and consequences of spilling blood during war, which if not done would have adverse effects for social harmony, peace and stability in their societies (see Becker 2003).

Concisely, as M.A.C Nwoye concludes, African women's roles as mothers, wives, and aunts were put to effective use in peacebuilding and conflict resolutions in precolonial African societies. Women participated firmly in inculcating the culture of peace in the children and in the practice of conflict mediation among warring factions within the family and the community (M.A.C Nwoye: 2006). They also commanded important positions in conflict resolution rituals and were significant peace activists through their roles as peace envoys in times of conflict. Though corrupted by the colonial interruption of Africa's sociocultural existence, these values are still alive and can be used for promoting peace among warring families, communities, and nations in postcolonial Africa. They can be developed into an African feminist ethic of peace that can be the cornerstone for effective conflict prevention, mediation, and peacebuilding.

Women Waging Peace in Neocolonial African States

So far, we have attempted to show that there are theoretical considerations for feminising the peace process in neocolonial Africa. To back our theoretical considerations, we have also shown that African women have a rich precolonial history of peace-waging experience based on motherhood and the ethic of care. In this section, we contend that this African feminist ethic, though corrupted by the eroding influence of Eastern and Western patriarchies that subsequently accompanied the advent of Islam and colonialism in Africa, respectively,[7] is still very much alive amongst contemporary African women. This is daily being expressed by ordinary women in the face of their marginalisation and oppression at the private and public levels of society, including in conflict situations across the continent. For example, in the heat of the bitter Tutsi and Hutu civil war in Burundi, Hutu women of Busoro near the Burundi capital of Bujumbura joined their Tutsi counterparts in the neighbouring Musanga village to march peacefully to the local government secretariat where they both demanded an end to the killing. According to Fleshman (2003), one day the women of Musanga got fed up with the chilling consequences of the war and collected what food and clothing they could for victims in Busoro and subsequently rallied their Busoro counterparts to march for peace, clasping their hands together to sing 'Give us peace. Give us peace now!' for hours before making their separate, dangerous ways back home (Fleshman 2003: 1-2). Although, as Fleshman recorded, 'the war continued, something important had changed. The road that divided them now connected them, and through their local peace group, *Twishakira amahoro* (we want to have peace), the women of the villages have worked to keep the connection strong' (Fleshman 2003: 2).

In the same vein, another example of postcolonial African women acting locally, often spontaneously, to reach across battle lines in pursuit of peace is that of the Congolese women who rallied across partisan, ethnic, and other sectional interests to organise for the broad public desire for peace in Africa's most protracted conflict state, the Democratic Republic of Congo (DRC). Ahead of the formal peace talks (Inter-Congolese Dialogue) in Sun City, South Africa, which were urged by the UN, and which included only 40 (12%) women among 340 delegates, women from across the DRC, including representatives from the warring parties and government and civil society, gathered in Nairobi to forge a common position of peace. At the end of the Nairobi debate, the women discovered that 'however deep their differences, they shared an overriding desire for peace, a broad commitment to the Lusaka peace accord and significantly, a common determination to remove constitutional and legislative obstacles to women's equality after the war' (Fleshman 2003: 15). This much was contained in a joint declaration and programme of action that offered a gender perspective to the dialogue issued by the women (Rehn and Sirleaf 2002). Specifically, the declaration and programme of action called for 'an immediate ceasefire, the inclusion of women and their concerns in all aspects of the peace process, and adoption of a 30% quota for women at all levels of government in any final settlement' (Fleshman 2003: 15).

Challenged by the lack of a critical mass of women in the actual peace negotiations in Sun City, the women selected 33 of themselves to join the official 30 women representatives to the peace talks as advisers. Excluded from the formal peace talks, the 33 women advisers functioned effectively as facilitators of the peace process as they prepared technical documents and position papers for the official delegates, lobbied the men for peace, and generally served as conduit between the masses yearning for peace back home and the peace delegates in Sun City. Of note here is that the women adopted traditional African women's instruments of drama, poetry, and appeal to motherly sacredness including, sometimes, civil disobedience to make their presence felt and tilt the negotiators towards peace. For example, reminiscent of precolonial women's power to withdraw conjugal rights from men if they refused to listen to women's appeal for peace during conflict with neighbouring communities,[8] the Congolese women's caucus subtly threatened to denounce the men back home, telling them that 'if they went back home without peace the people would beat them' (Fleshman 2003: 16). And when at the end of the peace talks, the parties could not reach an agreement, 'the women's caucus blocked the doorway and announced to reporters that delegates would have to remain in the meeting hall until peace was agreed.' However, in general, cognisant of the centrality of relationships in enabling sustainable peace and the significance of maintaining their relations with men, which was a main concern of precolonial African matriarchy, the women's caucus chose to avoid confrontation with the men, knowing that if they were to have an impact on the process from its outside position, it was necessary to establish and maintain good relations with the men. This was important because men traditionally resented actions that appeared to challenge 'traditional' gender roles and more so that the Congolese men, in the first place, reluctantly agreed to the modest increase in female delegates (Fleshman 2003: 16). The account of one of the women caucus members, Ms. Bibiane, in this regard is poignant enough to be reproduced:

At first the men were hostile because there was this group of women entering 'their' space. But we approached them in a way that made them feel secure. In African culture, the woman is your mother. The woman is your wife and your sister. If your mother or sister is talking to you, you

521

have to listen…We didn't demonize the men or try to take their place (quoted in Fleshman 2003: 16).

Clearly, this resonates well with the moral imagination as the women displayed a capacity to transcend every day conventions of human relations based on ethnic, partisan, or gender sentiments by generating constructive responses and initiatives that, while rooted in the day-to-day challenges of the DRC conflict, would ultimately break the grips of those destructive patterns and cycles within which the conflict is perpetuated and dragged on. In this way, the women laid a foundation for eventual peace as they planted the seed of a 'yes we can' mentality amongst a people who's over 50 years experience of conflict has probably blotted their capacity to imagine that peace is possible.

From Senegal, to the conflict-ridden Mano River basin countries of Liberia and Sierra Leone, to Burundi, the DRC, South Africa, and Mozambique, there are many more such examples across Africa where women are using their traditional weapons to wage peace, or in the least, ask questions of a masculinised and zero-sum politics characterised by corruption, competition, intolerance, and conflict, which underlie and perpetuate a cycle of chronic underdevelopment in the continent. The peace work of the Mano River Union Women Peace Network (MARWOPNET), a transnational women's organisation consisting of women from Liberia, Sierra Leone, and Guinea, is well known in this regard, especially in mediating the escalating conflict between Liberia and Guinea in 2001. This feat, according to Fleshman (2003: 18), demonstrated the potential of women's peacemaking efforts in Africa. Defying nationality differences and rather focusing on the things that hold them together as women, mothers, and daughters of Africa, MARWOPNET was able to get Presidents Charles Taylor of Liberia, Ahmad Tejan Kabbah of Sierra Leone, and Lansana Conte of Guinea to meet, a feat that previously proved fruitless for the then Organisation of African Unity (OAU) and the subregional Economic Community of West African States (ECOWAS) with the full complement of their diplomatic arsenal. Although the women drew the respect of President Taylor for being 'courageous' enough to meet with him to convince him to attend a regional peace summit with President Conte, it was the women's meeting that was seen as more audacious. According to Fleshman

(2003), realising that their strategy of focusing on human insecurity implications of conflict that worked with President Taylor was not working with President Conte, who remained adamant that he would not meet with Taylor, the women changed tactics. The women, through one of their representatives, told President Conte point-blank: 'You and President Taylor have to meet as men and iron out your differences, and we the women want to be present. We will lock you in this room until you come to your senses, and I will sit on the key' (Fleshman 2003: 18).

Fleshman records that when her comments were translated into French for the president, there was a long silence, and then he started laughing, after which he commented: 'What man do you think would say that to me? Only a woman could do such a thing and get by with it.' Crediting the women for changing his mind to attend the peace summit, the president said: 'Many people have tried to convince me with President Taylor, but only your commitment and your appeal have convinced' (Fleshman 2003: 18)

The point of relating these reports is to underscore the fact that the feminist ethic of care based on motherhood and women's sacredness that was appropriated by precolonial African women to wage peace and maintain societal harmony is still very much a part of the core of contemporary African women and is constantly being deployed in conflict situations such as in the Niger-Delta region of Nigeria and KwaZulu-Natal in South Africa (Isike 2009). It can be reinvented and developed into a model of African feminist peace building that women in conflict-torn African states or regions can utilise as an ideological rallying point to transform politics and conflict, and ipso facto create an environment conducive for development to thrive.

Synthesising Theory and Practice: The Plausibility of an African Feminist Ethic of Peace-Building

According to Ifi Amadiume (1997), there are two unique contributions that African women have made to world history and civilization: matriarchy and dual-sex character of African political systems, which is directly related to the matriarchal factor (Amadiume 1997: 100). She contends that African matriarchy was a fundamental social and ideological base on which African kinship and wider social and moral systems, such as *ubuntu* or *ujamaa*, rest. In her view, authentic African matriarchy had 'a very clear message about social and economic justice as it was couched in a very powerful goddess-based religion, a strong ideology of motherhood, and a general moral principle of love' (Amadiume 1997: 101). This was opposed to imperialist patriarchy, which has a basic masculinist ideology that celebrates violence, valour, conquest, and power in varying degrees, and which, according to Diop (1989), denied women their rights, subjugating and propertising them in a strict hierarchical system of family where the man (husband or father) was supreme and had power of life and death over the woman.

On the other hand, precolonial African matriarchy and patriarchy coexisted in what Diop (1989) refers to as a 'harmonious dualism' between men and women, and what Amadiume (1997:93) describes as 'fluid demarcation'. According to her, this 'embodied two oppositional or contesting systems, the balance tilting and changing all the time' (1997: 93-94). In this regard, she concluded that genders in precolonial African societies were fluid as they were a means of dividing, but also a means of integrating and co-opting in dynamic ways that enabled stability and order based on justice, equity, and fairness. This enabled a system where women's power became based on the centrality of their economic role in relation to men, and men's general belief in the sacredness of women as mothers. This was given expression in widespread goddess worship across different communities, including those that were patriarchal. According to Amadiume, 'In indigenous African religion, mystical powers and worldly prosperity are gifts inherited from our mothers. The moral ideals of this system encouraged the matriarchal family, peace and justice, goodness and optimism and social collectivism, where the shedding of human blood was abhorrent' (1997: 102).

Even in precolonial patriarchal cultures like those of the Zulus, women were traditionally able to stop fights by falling over the person being beaten. According to a study by Rakoczy (2006: 202), one of her respondents indicated that Zulu women's ability to stop fighting in this way may be due to respect for women as 'the persons who bring children', the life-givers. She contends rightly that this tradition is also commonplace amongst the Sotho people, narrating how a woman's brother was rescued by another woman who heard his cry as he was being beaten by several men. The rescuing woman 'stepped into the fray, put a blanket over her brother and probably saved his life' (Rakoczy 2006: 202). The rescuing woman did not have to know who the man being beaten was to intervene for the violence to stop. She knew instinctively as a mother who cared for her children that she had to act, more so in the understanding that she is connected to him as a human being living in the same community. The aggressors on their part knew that they could not continue beating their victim once the woman intervened in the way she did. Continuing would have meant violating the woman as well, and this they were not prepared to do as men, because of the sociocultural implications.

The crux of our argument here is that women's existence and power in precolonial African societies was based on an ethic of care that was rooted in their motherhood and their nature, which was tolerant of difference, collaborative, nonviolent and, as such, peaceful.[9] Their peace activism and agency was in itself rooted in a broader communal ideology (*ubuntu*, *ujamaa*, *negritude*, humanism, or African socialism) that operated on the basis of the mutuality of human interests through a web of relationships where everyone played their part for the good of the collective and the validation of the personal. In these societies, women never saw or placed themselves in a dichotomous relationship with men; rather, gender relations were fluid, dynamic, and complementary in difference, as Amadiume (1997) espoused. Indeed, as Gasa (2007) admonished, there is nothing wrong with Euro-American and Occidental feminist tradition, just as there is nothing wrong with or limited about Arab, Asian, or African feminisms. However, Gasa says, '[W]e must acknowledge the different historical and situational realities which may call for a different approach and an adjustment of a particular framework' (2007: 228). In her view, the connection between the detail, pattern and big picture of African feminism will assist African men and women in 'understanding our location, developing tools of analysis that are appropriate to our own situation, and applying them in a way that illustrates and illuminates rather than obscures our real and lived experiences and their multiple meanings' (Gasa 2007: 228). As mentioned before, motherhood qualities of care and nurturing and women's positive dispositions towards collaboration, interconnectedness, and peace do not imply weakness. Rather, they portray strength, as they are consistent with the affective and relational foundation of people's existence with each other. They are also consistent with Lederach's story of the Konkomba spokesman who invoked the moral imagination by transcending the conventional to turn around a protracted conflict towards sustainable peace.

According to Nodding (in Soest 1995: 166), these qualities are the foundation of a feminist perspective and ethic of peace rooted in receptivity, relatedness, and responsiveness. She contends that such a relational approach to peacebuilding may be more typical of women than men,[10] and she argues further that an approach based on law and principle is the approach of the 'detached one' (men who are detached from the experience of nurturing children and community), and therefore suggests that a feminist view, which is concerned with people, is an alternative that men can embrace as well as women (in Soest 1995: 167). Drawing from the utility of the relational ethic of care, Dorothy van Soest argues that 'a relational ethic concentrates on the moral health and vigour of relationships, not individuals, and recognises that moral judgements and decisions about how to act must take into account the relations in which moral agents live and find their identities' (Soest 1995: 167).

Supportive Empirical Evidence

Findings from a study of women and conflict, politics, and peacebuilding show that the defining features of such a feminist peace model include a caring and nurturing nature based on motherhood; empathy to community needs, which makes women less corrupt than men; tolerance of difference; sharing; and collaboration, all of which are undergirded by the notion of relational mutuality, i.e., that men and women exist in a web of relationships where their existence is intrinsically connected. From the study, women respond to conflict by embracing peace and adopting collaborative methods of engagement. The attitude of women to conflict, which underscores their response and the peace-oriented roles they play in conflict resolution, is not unconnected to the African woman's feminist ethic of care, which values interrelationships, connectedness, and empowerment rather than conflict and competition. For example, according to Mrs Iyoha,[11] while men view conflict as 'struggle or war which must be fought', women tend to see them as 'necessary evils in communities' and only give in to or endorse war after all avenues for peaceful resolution of conflict have been exhausted, and even then, they tend to hope for and pursue prospects for peace during war (Interview with Mrs Iyoha, 13 June 2007). Also, since the injured and dead in conflicts are more often their sons, husbands, and brothers, they tend to focus on the cessation of violence and the rebuilding of their homes, families, and communities (FGD with Odi women, 3 May 2007). Indeed, according to Mrs. Okolocha,[12] 'because women feel the impact of conflict more than men, they naturally advocate for peace and pursue conflict resolution'. This is corroborated by a cumulative 73% (131 out of 180 responses) of the women in the both case studies who were affected by conflict and who said they responded to the conflict in their area by 'creating alternatives for survival' (47), 'working towards peaceful resolution of the conflict' (12), 'accepted their fate and moved on' (62) or 'helping to rebuild community' (10). Another finding (lesson) from King's (1997) study in this regard is instructive:

> In performing their tasks with male colleagues, women were perceived to be more compassionate, less threatening or insistent on status, less willing to opt for force or confrontation over conciliation, even it is said less egocentric, more willing to listen and learn--though not always--and to contribute to an environment of stability which fostered the peace process. (King, 1997:4)

Concisely, women have a positive attitude and approach towards peace, as while men spoil for a fight, women toe the alternative route for peace and calm to reign. Apart from interviews responses, reasons the questionnaire respondents gave ranged from the population stake of women in the study areas, and women's interest in peace and community development, to the perception that women are less corrupt compared to men and are better suited to consensus building than men, as shown in table 1.

Table 1: Reasons Why Women in Politics Will Enhance Peacebuilding

Our survey findings reveal that women's peace agency is also rooted in their agency for good governance. An aggregation of responses on the question of women's significant contributions to good governance and development in the study areas shows that women are perceived as community developers (they installed electricity and tap water, and contributed to poverty alleviation and community building/development). They are also seen as introducing a caring and sharing approach to politics that is rooted in their femininity and motherhood (with uplifting and positive social attributes such as compassion, joy, motherliness, honesty, tolerance, and trust-worthy) and are generally peace-oriented (by working for community peace, bringing harmony, and standing against trouble). The significance of their good governance agency for peacebuilding can be understood in the light of how the frequent failure by male-dominated leadership to allocate resources equitably has fueled social and armed conflict not only in the study areas, but also in other parts of Africa.

Concluding Remarks

Studies have shown that women have the required spectrum of personality characteristics and dimensions human abilities that are necessary and sufficient for good governance and peacebuilding (see Nodding 1989; Soest 1995; King 1997; Gagnon 2003; Ngongo-Mbede 2003; Ntahobari and Ndayiziga 2003; Anderlini 2007; Isike 2009). While Lederach (2005) may not have articulated clearly the political dimensions of peacebuilding, the peace process indeed requires a kind of politics that is crucial for its success. This is the politics of responsibility, accountability, tolerance, empathy, accommodation, love, truth-telling, and forgiveness. And it is the politics that women generally represent and can bring to bear if they come into politics as women. These are the virtues that bring us to the poignant moment, the turning point that makes the difference between violent conflict and peace. Applying that perspective to the peace discourse enables us to call attention to the kind of human beings who can make peace and development possible rather than focusing on the kinds of institutions, techniques and systems that guarantee peace (Lederach, 2005). Within this human-centred framework, research into the realities and potentials of women, who constitute over half of the world's population, as instruments of a more peaceful world is a worthwhile venture.

Women's peace agency is rooted in the values of their womanhood and an ethic of care that values relationships, interconnectedness and

528

empowerment from which springs forth empathy, co-operation, tolerance, and love. These values are necessary requirements for amicable resolution of conflict and for sustaining peace. They worked very well in precolonial African societies, especially in matriarchal ones, where women had traditional roles in preventing violence, mediating conflicts, and reconciling those in conflict. In some of these traditional societies, gender was defined in flexible terms such that they allowed men and women to straddle socially constructed male and female spaces. For instance, according to Amadiume (1997), a flexible gender system in precolonial Igbo societies in Nigeria was enabled by a flexible language structure that presented 'no language or mental adjustment or confusion in references to a woman performing a typical male role' (Amadiume 1997: 17). Appropriating the utility of a flexible gender system for peacebuilding in Africa, Amisi (2008: 11) contends that the idea of a flexible gender system provides for a language that allows a formulation of a concept of peace and also of war in gendered terms that approximates the reality of a number of African societies whose gender relations are similar to those of the Ibos that Amadiume studied.[13] In other words, although the idea of flexible gender and language systems may be alien to some African societies that have a different worldview of gender relations, it offers a valuable model of understanding armed conflict and peace, and 'it can be a resource for the envisioning of peace even in societies that may not be aware of the idea' (Amisi 2008: 12). This is more so in Africa, where women are traditionally known to have the critical skills, spiritual and social capital, as well as human potential and moral imagination capacity to transform conflict from violence to peace. Indeed, African women were and continue to be an embodiment of the ethic of care and the moral imagination that are critical to changing the face and essence of politics to be more human-centred. This is expected to have some positive significance for conflict prevention, resolution, and peacebuilding in the continent if properly appropriated.

References

Adjibolosoo, S. 1995. *The human factor in developing Africa.* Wesport, Connecticut: Praeger.

Adjibolosoo, S. 1999. *Rethinking development theory and policy: A human factor critique.* Wesport, Connecticut: Praeger.

Amadiume, I. 1987. *Male daughters, female husbands: Gender and sex in an African society,* London: Zed Books.

Amadiume, I. 1997. *Re-inventing Africa: Matriarchy, religion and culture.*
London: Zed Books.

Amisi, B.K. 2008. 'Indigenous ideas of the social and conceptualising peace in Africa'. *Africa Peace and Conflict Journal* 1 (1): 1-18.

Anderlini, S. N. 2007. *Women building peace: What they do, why it matters.* Boulder, Colorado: Lynne Rienner Publishers.

Assefa, H. 1993. *Peace and reconciliation as a paradigm: A philosophy of peace and its implications on conflict, governance and economic growth in Africa.* NPI Monograph Series. Nairobi: NPI.

Brine, J. 1999. *Under-educating women: globalising inequality.* Buckingham: Open University Press.

Centre for Advanced Social Science (CASS). 2005. *Enhancing the capacity of women leaders of community organizations towards peace-building in the Niger-Delta region, Nigeria.* Port Harcourt: CASS.

Fleshman, M. 2003. 'African women struggle for a seat at the peace table'. *Africa Recovery* 16 (4): 1, 15-19.

Focus Group Discussion with 10 Women in Odi, Bayelsa State, Niger-Delta. 2007.

Gasa, N. 2007. 'Feminisms, motherisms, patriarchies and women's voices in the 1950s'. In" *Women in South African history*, edited by N. Gasa. Cape Town: HSRC Press.

Interview with Mrs E Iyoha, 2007. Oredo Local Government Area, Benin City.

Interview with Mrs H.O. Okolocha, 12 June 2007, University of Benin, Nigeria.

Isike, C. and U. Okeke-Uzodike. 2008. 'Modernizing without westernizing: redefining African patriarchies in the quest to curb HIV and AIDS in Africa'. *Journal of Constructive Theology* 14 (1): 3-20?

Isike, C. 2009. 'Feminising the peace process: a comparative analysis of women and conflict in the Niger-Delta (Nigeria) and KwaZulu-Natal (South Africa)'. PhD thesis. University of KwaZulu-Natal, South Africa

Isike, C. and U. Okeke-Uzodike. 2010. 'The moral imagination, ubuntu and African women: Towards feminizing politics and peace-building in KwaZulu-Natal (South Africa)'. *Gandhi Marg* 31 (4): 679-709.

King, A.E .1997. "Success in South Africa--impact of women in the peace process in South Africa - includes related article on women in peace missions". UN Chronicle. http:// finds articles. Com/p/ - articles /mi_m 1309/is_n3_v34/ai_20267837/ (accessed 4 September 2009).

Lederach, J. 2005. *The moral imagination: The art and soul of building peace.*
Oxford: Oxford University Press.

Lihamba, A. 2003. 'Women's peace building and conflict resolution skills, Morogoro region, Tanzania'. In: *Women and peace in Africa:Case studies on traditional conflict resolution practices.* Paris: UNESCO.

Mazurana, D.E. and S.R. McKay. 1999. *Women and peace building.* Montreal: International Centre for Human Rights and Democratic Development.

Mohammed, A.B. 2003. 'The role of Somali women in the search for peace'. In:*Women and peace in Africa: Case studies on traditional conflict resolution practices.* Paris: UNESCO.

Ngongo-Mbede, V. 2003. 'The traditional mediation of conflicts by women in Cameroon'. In: *Women and peace in Africa: Case studies on traditional conflict resolution practices.* Paris: UNESCO.

Ntahobari, J. and B. Ndayiziga. 2003. 'The role of Burundian women in the peaceful settlement of conflicts" In: *Women and peace in Africa: Case studies on traditional conflict resolution practices.* Paris: UNESCO

Nwoye, M.A.C. 'Role of women in peace building and conflict resolution in African traditional societies: A selective review'. http:// www. Afrika world. net/afrel/chinwenwoye.htm (accessed 12 February 2009).

Nzeogwu, N. 2000. 'African women and the fire dance'. http:// www .west africa review.com/vol2.1/nzegwu2 (accessed 14 August 2007).

Owusu-Ampomah, K. 2004. 'Human development paradigm and agenda: A wild goose chase'. In: *International development agenda and activities: What are we doing wrong?* Edited by S. Adjibolosoo. Bloomington: 1st Books.

Rakoczy, S. 2005. 'Religion and violence: The suffering of women'. *Sexuality in Africa Magazine* 2 (4). http:/ /www .arsrc .org /downloads /sia /dec05 /dec05 .pdf (accessed 18 September 2008).

Patel, N. 2001. 'Conflict resolution through regional organizations in Africa'. In:*A United States of Africa?* Edited by E. Maloka. Pretoria: AISA.

Rehn, E. and E. Sirleaf. 2002. *Women war peace: Progress of the world's women.* Vol.1. New York: UNIFEM

United Nations. 1999. 'Preventive diplomacy and peacemaking'. www.un.org/Docs/SG/Report99/prevent.htm (accessed 07 September 2009).

UNESCO. 2003. *Women and peace in Africa: Case studies on traditional conflict resolution practices.* Paris: UNESCO.

Vallely, P. 'from dawn to dusk: the daily struggle of Africa's women'. *The Independent*, 21 September 2006. http://www.indepe ndent.co.uk/news/world/africa/from-dawn-to-dusk-the-daily-struggle-of-africas-women-416877.html# (accessed 21 April 2013).

Van Soest, D. 1995. 'A feminist ethic for peace'. In: *Feminist Practice in the 21st* century, edited by Nan Van Den Bergh. Washington, DC: National Association of Social Workers.

Weir, J. 2007. 'Chiefly women and women's leadership in pre-colonial southern

Africa'. In *Women in South African history,* edited by N. Gasa. Cape Town: HSRC Press.

Notes

---

[1] This is even where they have been known to be actively engaged in precolonial wars of conquest, initial resistance against colonial rule, and the nationalist liberation struggles of the continent. For example, according to Becker (2003: 55-56), 'it would be erroneous to assume that women and girls played no role in the encouragement of belligerent attitudes. Nor are there any indications that mothers would have raised their children in a way that would have discouraged their inclination to battle.' However, as Nodding explained, '[W]omen's acceptance of

war does not seem to emerge from seeing striving as a virtue but rather from a desire to remain in positive relation with those who worship striving' (Noddings in Soest 1995: 168).

[2] Just as masculinities are fluid and dynamic, so we cannot speak of a single universal African patriarchy. From time, different forms of patriarchies existed in different precolonial African societies.

[3] We note that not all women have or exhibit these values, just as not all men have them. However, the social construction of gender and differentiated gender roles has generally socialised women to assume these values while men are generally socialised to assume the opposite.

[4] In a public lecture hosted by the School of Politics, University of KwaZulu-Natal, Pietermaritzburg, titled 'Human Factor and good governance in Africa', the guest speaker, Prof. Senyo Adjibolosoo argued that 'personal growth in positive human factor qualities such as integrity, accountability, responsibility, commitment, selflessness and truthfulness create a fertile environment for good governance' (10 July 2009).

[5] Conflict arises when those in political positions fail to allocate scarce resources in a manner that wins the goodwill, trust, confidence, and loyalty of citizens. Often, the resultant breakdown in relations between citizens and the state, and within citizens in the competition for access to increasingly scarce resources, manifests in violent conflict.

[6] Online publication available in http://www.afrikaworld.net/afrel/chinwenwoye.htm (accessed 12 December 2009).

[7] For example, according to Amadiume (1997: 104), 'Islamic patriarchy in Africa was followed by European imperialism and finally the present subjugation of African societies and people under European-imposed nation states. It has introduced a new gender politics, favouring men and undermining the traditional system of balance of power politics between African men and women.'

[8] See Amadiume (1987, 1997) and Nzeogwu (2000) for more details on how precolonial Nigerian women used their conjugal powers to serve as checks on the excesses of male-dominated politics. These authors contend variously that women in different communities used the threat of their nakedness to leverage policy advantages for themselves and for society in general since often their needs were communal in focus.

[9] This is not to say that all women are necessarily pacifist, as there are also records of women who have taken decisions to go to war, and where women actively participated as combatants. Even precolonial African history shows records of women regents waging war. However, as Nodding explained, 'women's acceptance of war does not seem to emerge from seeing striving as a virtue but rather from a desire to remain in positive relation with those who worship striving' (Noddings in Soest 1995: 168).

[10] This has been validated by this study as 98% percent of women in both study areas concede that women are more suited for peace building because of their natural roles as mothers who care, maintain, and nurture

[11] Mrs. F.E. Iyoha is Clerk of the Legislative arm and Chief Administrative Officer of Oredo Local Government Area of Edo state and former Head of Family Support Programme in the Local Government Area

[12] Mrs. H.O. Okolocha is a politician, writer, and lecturer of English and Literature at the University of Benin, Nigeria.

[13] See Weir (2008) and Gasa (2008), who also document evidence of women in precolonial Southern African societies (i.e. ,Zulus, Lovendus) assuming what today are strictly defined as 'male roles' by engaging in woman-to-woman marriages, owning cattle (traditional symbol of male power), and fighting wars.

PART VII

CONCLUSIONS: PRACTICAL ISSUES GOVERNANCE AND DECENTRALIZATION

CHAPTER 18:

The 'Northern Problem' and National Belonging in Zimbabwe: Finding Common Grounds in a New System of Governance

Brilliant Mhlanga

Is the colonial order being washed away with buckets of blood? Or are we witnessing the agonizing birth pangs of a genuinely postcolonial order? Is the blood in fact spilling in the maternity ward of history as a new Africa is trying to breathe? Until we know whether this is the birth of a truly decolonized Africa, we cannot celebrate. In any case, who can celebrate in the midst of all this blood and carnage? (Ali Mazrui 1995: 28)

Introduction

A discussion of a change of system of governance in Zimbabwe from a centrist perspective to either a federal project or devolved central governement is considered anathema and divisive to a nation-state whose nationalism is like a bad birthmark that continues to haunt her. Its opponents, who emotionally label it as 'disguised tribalism', have criminalised it. While this discussion remains necessary and pertinent for Zimbabwe, given the crisis spurred by lack of equitable distribution of resources, as will be shown below, it has also tended to follow ethnic fault lines between Matebeleland and Mashonaland. The latter is perceived as the region of the 'rulers', oppressors and tribalists as epitomised in the discourse of the successive state, while the region of Matebeleland is presented as the abode of the 'ruled'. The idea of narrowing this situation to an ethnic issue that exists between the Ndebele and the Shona does not hinge on the fact that devolution is a creature of ethnicity. Rather, it is because those at the forefront of purveying this discourse are people from Matebeleland region who also double as Ndebele. However, such an argument often conceals other regional cleavages that exist elsewhere in Zimbabwe, for example, among the Shona dialects; between Manicaland, Masvingo, and Mashonaland West and Central, in particular, where devolution of power as a policy project remains a viable option for them in terms of resource distribution as seen in the case of the recently discovered diamonds in Marange. While the discourse of change of system of

537

governance has the potential for riding on the shoulders of ethnicity, it also remains clearly not an ethnic issue, but a matter of resource distribution, policy formulation and implementation. But it is natural that a discourse on devolution would take a marked ethnic twist, given the history of suppressed rivalries that exist between the Shona and Ndebele in Zimbabwe.[1] However, the discourse remains extremely pertinent, especially in any constitutional discourse, and as part of democratic ideation. Its conventional interpretation as a pro-Matebeleland project makes for an unfortunate delusional engagement among pundits and scholars alike. Further, its critics who have not offered a viable option in the face of waning nationalism remotely accept the argument that it is a project that can enhance inclusivity for the future of Zimbabwe. This failure to embrace the positive effects of a change of system of governance or at least some policy projections in Zimbabwe has its roots in the nationalist liberation ethos which caricatured anything perceived to be ethnic-related as retrogressive. Hence its failure to even acknowledge ethnicity as a positive national resource that can be harnessed like any other resource in Zimbabwe's two main regions.

This attempt to caricature the discourse of a decentralised system of governance as tribally laced and inimical to progress was done in favour of a centralised system of governance that most African nationalist leaders believed conjured patriotism and oneness. Also, distrust of pluralism became a widespread tendency of postcolonial African ideologies in favour of centrist perspectives, with a top-heavy central government that conjured one-party statism. Ali Mazrui (1994: 61) observes: 'One beneficiary of this restoration of pluralism has been the democratic process, however fragile. The other has been ethnicity and politicised tribal identity. A question persists as to whether re-democratisation and re-tribalisation cancel each out'. It is my contention, therefore, that while it may be argued that democratisation, change of system of governance, and ethnicity are strange bedfellows, they can also be good bedfellows, if properly harnessed. Further, continued criminalisation of ethnicity has proven to be Africa's bane. Pluralism if properly harnessed can bring about positive notions of identity with people celebrating their peoplehood first and openly professing patriotic feelings to a nation-state without undue pressure. It is here that the African national project can post victory and its finality. Due to this need, postcolonial Africa has to be forced to take a fresh look at what was earlier considered taboo, that is, the open celebration of ethnic identity, calls for the right to self-determination and secessionist bids.

To Mazrui, all the latter had been blocked mainly due to pan-Africanism, whose underlying hymn was nationalism. This has, however, managed to help preserve inherited borders, but failed to answer the following question: How many of the state boundaries of present-day Africa will remain intact in 100 years? Mazrui (1994: 61) also adds that 'the most fundamental of all changes in the next century and half will be the boundaries of what constitutes Africa itself. Where does Africa end?' One may add: Where do colonially conjured and inherited nation-state boundaries in Africa stand, given the loud and resilient secessionist bids and calls for ethnic self-determination? It is on this note that the discourse of change of system of governance, particularly devolution of power, finds meaning.

However, its continued criminalisation and labelling as a sine-qua-non of ethnicity finds common acceptance in most of Zimbabwe's public spaces. As a result, the engagement of ethnicity following the postcolonial nationalist mindset has always been that it belongs to those 'darker' or 'backward' relics of the human past that must be quickly discarded and forgotten if common citizenship is to be forged and national unity achieved (Ndlovu-Gatsheni 2008b; Ake 2000; Young 1997; Vail 1997; Mazrui 1994; Nzongola-Ntalaja 1987). And so, devolution of power has often been bundled together with issues of ethnicity without any attempt to unpack its possible positive policy projections.

There is a need to also engage ethnicity, not as a criminalised factor in politics, but as political currency that should be understood and explained. As John Comaroff (1997: 70) says, in our attempt to grapple with ethnicity, we may want to acknowledge that it is a product of particular historical circumstances and not a mere ontological feature of human organisation. In a situation like Zimbabwe where ethnicity and the discourse of devolution of power continue to be conflated, there is need to understand ethnicity, its explanatory principle, and its currency in influencing everyday sociological relations. The imperative here is to first engage ethnicity as the conceptual fault line along which calls for change of system of governance are perceived to traverse.

This paper will offer an engagement of ethnicity followed by the discussion of the concept of devolution of power as part of the latter-day currency in Zimbabwe. Furthermore, in order to understand the ethnic imperative and its link with the discourse of change of system of governance, it is worth acknowledging that resource distribution has also tended to mirror ethnic lines. However, this crisis is not a specifically Zimbabwean problem; rather, it is an African challenge. Ken Wiwa (2000: 34) sums it by saying in Nigeria ethnicity matters more than qualifications when it comes to distributing the best jobs and scholarships. This captures the salience of ethnicity in Zimbabwe; hence the call for a change of system of governance which, it is argued tends to favour Mashonaland at the expense of other regions of the country (Mhlanga 2006). The issue of resource distribution, in particular the problem of lack of equitable distribution of resources and the discussion of devolution of power as a continuum in administrative decentralisation will be discussed. This paper contains sections that provide brief discussions of the historical and theoretical background of ethnicity and the nation and colonial antecedents, their impact on the conception of ethnicity, and ways that this later influenced the postcolonial African mindset. However, these sections do not, by any stretch of an imagination, claim to be exhaustive, but to establish a point of synapse between theory and context as witnessed in Zimbabwe.

On The 'Northern Problem'

There is no African nation-state without a 'northern problem'. As a result, a need arises for an honest engagement and assessment of the 'northern problem'. Similarly, Gerald Caplan writing in the 1960s argued that, "[F]ew of the new nations of Africa lack, as part of their colonial heritage, their potential Biafras....' (1968: 343). The metaphor of the 'northern problem', as Caplan describes it as a 'potential Biafra' of the late '60s, refers to the existence of a disgruntled group claiming a particular history and a particular identity that is different from those of the dominant ethnic groups that have tended to benefit from the state. However, the concept as stated above does not necessarily imply that these disenchanted groups and their fissures are found in the northern parts of any nation-state in Africa. Rather, as a metaphor, the implication is that most nation-states in Africa have these problems that have sought to question the state, to the extent of providing a cause in most situations for calls for a revision of systems of governance, secession, or separation. The 'northern problem' derives its main roots from residual political models inherited from departing colonial administrators, and the attendant incrementalist perspectives pursued by successive nationalist leaders seeking to ensure sustainability of the African national project. Nationalism as an ideological process[2] had a coercive wrapping effect in which all voices yearning for a different arrangement out of colonialism were drowned in the blood of the ordinary following the violent processes of state formation, thus silencing the voices that otherwise would have been audible in challenging the configurations of the nation-state, in particular, the systems of governance. Those suppressed voices that are part of the 'northern problem' also form the subaltern. Given the case of Zimbabwe, I contend that instead of vigorously refuting and dismissing the existence of such voices, it may be necessary for all political actors, social actors, intellectuals, and policy makers to openly engage them. Otherwise, their continued suppression might create fissures, as in a boiling pot that will lead to an unmanageable eruption in future.

It can be further stated that the rising challenges as evidence of the 'northern problem' in Zimbabwe have been illuminated by calls for a revision of the system of governance, with some recent calls by organisations such as; Mthwakazi People's Congress (MPC), Mthwakazi Liberation Front (MLF) calling for a total separation of the region of Matebeleland along irredentist precolonial lines. Imbovane Yamahlabezulu, another organisation from Matebeleland gave ideological impetus to the 'northern problem' by strongly advocating for a federal project. In other parts of Africa, in the 1960s, the 'northern problem' emerged through calls for federal systems of governance whose negation radicalised them to outright demands for secession in regions like the Katanga in the Republic of Congo (formerly Zaire). Lumumbist pursuing a nationalist cause perceived this as a direct indictment of the unitary state following Moise Tshombe's argument for the need for an equitable distribution of resources.[3] Many postcolonial African states have experienced violent political upheavals, as was seen in cases such as the 1967 Biafran war in Nigeria, Eritrea's secession from Ethiopia in 1993, the Caprivi crisis of 1999, the current calls for recognition of Somaliland as an independent state, the crisis in the Oromo region in Ethiopia, the case of Southern Sudan, which was concluded through a referendum in 2011 following fifty years odd years of a violent war, the Kalanga of Botswana and their calls for cultural recognition, the on-going case of the Luo in Kenya, the Lozi in Zambia and their call for the revival of the Barotse Kingdom (Caplan 1968), the case of Southern Cameroon, the Ngoni of Malawi, as witnessed in the recent government-sponsored policy aimed at limiting those from the North, the Ngoni, from occupying positions, even in tertiary institutions, and calls by the Pemba of Zanzibar for an independent state. In South Africa, the Zulus continue to manifest characteristics of 'a nation within a nation'.

In view of this African scenario and Zimbabwe's 'northern problem', it can be posited that a change of system of governance could maintain the current configurations of the nation-state. Further, one could contend that the notion of Zimbabwe being a unified nation-state has continuously been hampered by constant recriminations and contestations from within since its birth in 1980; hence the continued discourse of change of system of governance to date. The nation-state compound has often failed to blend in Africa, owing to the founding father's failure to mitigate between the object of the state and the nation as a cultural melting pot. And so the conflict between the nation as a cultural hotbed and the state continues; thus causing the state to be an antibody to society. Also, the continuous grumbling by various ethnic minorities about the current processes governing resource distribution in Zimbabwe, are a cause for concern and must not be considered mere false alarms in a situation that is pregnant with possible violent scenarios.

Of Theoretical Projections, Praxis and Locating the Setting

Africa's theoretical projections of ethnicity and nationalism have often followed European modes of engagement, thus denying it home grown practical solutions. Ethnicity, its political usage as collective consciousness continues to pepper the discourse of change of systems of governance in most African countries. However, there has been a marked shortage of critical theoretical lenses that can be used to view ethnicity's continued influence on the nationalist project vis-à-vis democratic ideation and the attendant challenges of the routinisation of policies along ethnic lines. This scarcity of theoretical locus on ethnicity in Africa has been worsened by its monumental failure to embrace studies of ethnic relations within the African context (Vail 1989; Mafeje 1971; Anderson 1983), in particular, our understanding of nationalists' instrumentalisation of ethnicity. This failure has even led to limited understanding of the fact that ethnic group boundaries, even though immutable, have a way of finding currency in conditions that would not have sparked their existence. Further, this has weakened our understanding of ethnicity as both a natural resource and an object of primordiality with a strong nativist clause. This has given impetus to its criminalisation as merely the ideology of tribalism (Mafeje 1971), thereby failing to harness it for the good of the state. This failure to understand ethnicity and to harness it as a positive natural resource is often characterised by continuous attempts to employ Marxist interpretations of rejecting various forms of ethnic-motivated conflicts in Africa. These Marxist lenses have led to the denial of the instrumentalists' positions of ethnicity on conflict (Sithole 1984: 117). Masipula Sithole (1984: 117ff.) warns against the uncritical engagement of the 'Fanonesque' adage, in particular, its 'internalized or displaced aggression', used in most Marxist interpretations of ethnic-motivated conflict scenarios. He further notes the salience of ethnicity in most conflict scenarios deserves particular attention. And ethnicity itself deserves to be explained instead of being criminalised.

The question, therefore, is: How do we define ethnicity given its bearing on resource distribution in Zimbabwe and elsewhere in Africa? Ethnicity generally follows putative commonalities that include congruities of blood, speech, and custom (Geertz 1963: 109). Similarly, Smith (1986: 15) emphasises 'myths, memories, values and symbols'. Horowitz (1985: 139) further describes its characteristics as ranging from 'birth and blood, beliefs in a common ancestry, a common history with common heroes and enemies' to a particularised territory and historical to it. Ethnicity's nativist adage shares close links with territory and indigeneity in a given space and time. Cluade

Ake (2000) says ethnicity and ethnic consciousness have to be treated as a living presence, with the potential of being produced and driven by material and innate historical forces. From this definition it can be gleaned that ethnicity is positively functional. Comaroff (1997) adds that the way in which ethnicity is experienced and expressed may vary among social groupings. However, in Africa, failure to accept the reality of its existence, its positive value and the uneven distribution of resources along ethnic lines has tended to aggravate its conflictual potential, hence its recriminations whenever it makes those regional appearances, as seen in Zimbabwe where subaltern ethnic groups are agitating for an equitable distribution of resources. The tendency has been to label as 'tribalists' those championing the cause for a change of system of governance. There is need to also accept that ethnic relations rest on how differences are understood, interpreted, represented, and sometimes decided by the cultural exigencies of history in any given context (Comaroff 1997: 73).

However, ethnicity as part of the interpellation of social differences depends on how actors are socially situated, and how they are perceived and perceive of themselves and their interests in competition for economic goods, status, and power. In such situations ethnicity works as an emblem of common interest with a shared commitment to the order of symbols and meanings offered, thus further creating a reciprocal negation of the humanity of those perceived to be part of the oppressors or those who benefit (Comaroff 1997). Power as part of resource distribution and ethnicity, given its ubiquity and complexity, is a potential cause for conflict as a human resource derived from its sociological relational 'cause and effect' usage, in particular the ambit of leadership as a major resource in a state like Zimbabwe. Power forms one major natural resource that continues to face a marked lack of equitable distribution in Zimbabwe. By implication, the ethnic group and region that holds power in a given time controls the locus of resource distribution, thus giving impetus to the need for a constitutionally defined policy of devolution of power that will translate into equitable distribution of resources.

In Zimbabwe, power has often been concentrated and centralised in Mashonaland, as was inherited from the departing colonial administrators. And so, even resource distribution tends to be skewed in favour of the regions with high concentration of power. But in a bid to maintain the status quo, the leaders embarked on a crusade of criminalising ethnicity as retrogressive and divisive. The reason for criminalising ethnicity as an ideological process is often based on the assumption of the latter's conflictual potential and the tendency to regard ethnic differences as being particularly exclusive, partly because they lack flexibility to be negotiated. Power brokers and those in power have also been at the forefront of coining such a mindset to cause a skewed retention and distribution of power as a resource in one part of the state. It is also imperative to highlight that while people prefer their own way of life and use their own standards to judge others and stress their differences from strangers, this invariably involves no denigration but implies parity even for groups regarded as hostile. Leroy Vail on the criminalisation of ethnicity says:

> African political leaders, experiencing it as destructive to their ideals of national unity, denounced it passionately. Commentators on the Left, recognising it as a block to the growth of appropriate class-consciousness, inveigh against it as a case of 'false consciousness.' [...] Development theorists, perceiving it as a check on economic growth, then deplored it. Journalists, judging it an adequate explanation for a myriad of otherwise puzzling events, deploy it mercilessly. Political scientists, intrigued by its continuing power, probe at it endlessly. If one disapproves of the phenomenon, 'it' is 'tribalism;' if one is less judgemental 'it' is 'ethnicity. (1997: 52; 1989: 01)

Having discussed ethnicity and its impact on resource distribution in a state, I now turn to the major discussion of devolution of power as a system of administrative decentralisation that may be proposed for Zimbabwe and other postcolonial states. It should be stated that given the arbitrariness of African boundaries following the cartographic mischief of the Europeans in Berlin (see, Adebajo 20120), I argue that, a federal project remains the best possible system of governance that could maintain the current inherited borders and still attend to different ethnic demands. The next section will attempt to clearly locating my line of argument with examples from Matebeleland.[4]

Matters Arising: Matebeleland and Calls for Devolution of Power

The subject of change of system of governance in Zimbabwe from a centralised system to devolution of power is often ticklish. It is a subject about which both the proponent and the critic are not at ease when engaging. As such, it is often fraught with emotions.[5] More often, the prime movers of this motion tend to passionately present their case. On the other hand, this move tends to elicit negative responses with equal vigour for fear that the prime movers are people from Matebeleland with a precolonial history[6] of having their own formidable state, the Ndebele state. In that case, the fear is that acceptance of devolution might be sowing seeds for the total separation of the region from Zimbabwe. However, this fear remains unfounded as long as certain conditions, which I shall delineate below, are met. These conditions constitute the 'northern problem'. There is need for a way of correcting the imbalances of resource distribution and closure of issues relating to gross violations of human rights, e.g., the Gukurahundi genocide.

In addition to the point above, the following examples seek to present the 'northern problem'. In 1987, at the end of the Gukurahundi genocide, which had targeted Ndebele people, the central government agreed through parliament to electrify the railway line only from Harare to Gweru, despite the fact that the National Railways of Zimbabwe was and still is headquartered in Bulawayo. This move by the government was perceived as likely to retard development of the transport network and heavy industries in the region of Matebeleland, considering that the region shares borders with countries that have viable economies, namely, Botswana, Namibia, and South Africa.

However, the biggest irony in light of the electrification the national railway line between Harare and Gweru is that the major electricity grid is generated in Matebeleland. Hwange Thermal Power station, which is located in Matebeleland, accounts for the country's 920 megawatts, with Kariba Hydro-Electricity Power station only producing 750 megawatts. Then some small electricity-generating stations, Munyati, Bulawayo, and Harare, act as back-ups to the national grid in case of a local blackout, and they only account for 300 megawatts. The sum-total of electricity consumption expectation is 2 750 megawatts, thus implying that there is a deficit of 780 megawatts (see Mhlanga 2006, Zimbabwe ICTs e-readiness survey 2005, produced by NUST, funded by UNDP). This automatically renders Zimbabwe a net importer of electricity in a bid to recoup this deficit. Then the remainder is imported, with its highest grid from South Africa through Insukamini, which is located in Matebeleland. In view of the above, a critical analysis shows that Matebeleland provides electricity for the entire country, yet it remains in darkness, and in dire need, with poor road infrastructure and poor communication networks.

Given the poor state of transport and communications infrastructure, these challenges have continued to cause a ripple effect on the economic side. For example, as stated above, the region of Matebeleland shares borders with countries (Botswana, Namibia, and South Africa) that have viable economies. Various border posts in Matebeleland are, as a result, busy in terms of foreign currency remittances, especially Beitbridge, Plumtree, and Kazungula border posts. However, due to centralisation, Zimbabwe Revenue Authority (ZIMRA), a government body that is responsible for collecting revenue for the state, has its headquarters in Harare. As a result, all data links with border posts and computer systems are first routed to Harare for processing before transactions are completed at the border posts. Given that border posts like Beitbridge and Plumtree are very busy, this creates a problem of bottlenecks, as was reported in the newspapers in the previous festive season. Also it was recently reported that ZIMRA failed to process customs and excise related duties in time and efficiently from Beitbridge due to extremely poor data links between the border post town and computer systems in Harare. This bottleneck is further compounded by both bureaucratic constipation and the need to always monitor activities in other regions from Harare--a political power game.

A critical analysis of the distance between the various border posts and Harare presents another interesting scenario. For example, the distance between Beitbridge border post and Harare is 580 kilometres, 288 kilometres between the former and Masvingo and only 230 kilometres from Bulawayo. Given these figures, it follows therefore that it is more expensive to set up and maintain communication links between the border town and the capital than to set up and maintain them from the border town to Bulawayo or Masvingo. In the case of Plumtree border post, the distance between the border post and

Bulawayo is 100 kilometres, and 539 kilometres to Harare. In view of these differences, it follows that if there is any need to enhance communication systems and to create data links, transactions could be done in Bulawayo, which is only 100km from the border post.

Further, there has been a gradual relocation of most heavy industries from Bulawayo[7] to Harare, a development that has continued to cause economic suffocation for the region and in terms of limited employment opportunities. This relocation of heavy industries has also been linked to the failure of central government to commit itself to the finalisation of water projects like the Matebeleland Zambezi Water Project (MZWP). Due to lack of water most manufacturing and heavy industries, even potential investors, such as BMW and Volkswagen, which had initially wanted to set up their industrial plants in Bulawayo, ended up settling in South Africa. Also, in terms of job opportunities that remain available, locals continue to be sidelined in favour of people from other regions, in particular Mashonaland. As one old man suggested, this development should be blamed on the fact that those in privileged positions (of being employers, managers, and directors of companies) are Shona and they tend to employ along ethnic lines.

Then in terms of human resource mobilisation, for teachers and other skilled personnel, for example, it has been noted that in teacher training colleges in the region, like the United College of Education (UCE), Hillside Teachers' College, Joshua Mqabuko Nkomo College, etc., most students are from Mashonaland. Such a development implies that of the teachers produced, most are Shona speakers, thus causing a deliberate blow to Ndebele as a language, especially for primary school children where teachers are expected to be conversant with all the subjects, including Ndebele as a language. This means that children have to be taught by teachers who cannot speak the local language. As Frantz Fanon (1967: 18) trenchantly puts it, 'a man who has a language consequently possesses the world expressed and implied by that language...Mastery of language affords remarkable power.' The same has been witnessed in other institutions of higher learning, like the National University of Science and Technology (NUST) and Bulawayo Polytechnic, which are located in Bulawayo and whose population is entirely Shona-speaking, thus prompting most social commentators to label the institutions as 'provinces of

Mashonaland in Matebeleland'. Another political activist described NUST as a 'lost development project, which was created through an act of Parliament to hoodwink the people of Matebeleland into believing that they own something.' NUST is seen as not serving Matebeleland region any purpose, in terms of nudging development. In the same vein, the prison services has been identified as one state institution that churns out more Shona prison wardens in Matebeleland that are charged with the duties of managing Ndebele prisoners. One human rights activist commented in light of this development that 'it is as if socially the role of a Ndebele is to be a criminal and to be managed by the Shona warden while you are in prison.' The latter has been observed as the state of affairs at Khami Maximum prison in Bulawayo. Various other government institutions show similar traits.

In terms of natural resource mobilisation and income-generated therefrom, a few examples would show how the centre tends to benefit. Most tourist resort centres in Matebeleland have Shona leaders holding managerial and menial jobs; these include places like Victoria Falls, Hwange National Park, Matopos, etc. Even the dominant language is Shona. In Victoria Falls, some local Ndebele youths lamented that most of 'these people' have taken all the jobs that could have been for the locals, including menial jobs. In light of these developments, it follows therefore that there is a need for a clear policy shift that would deal with employment patterns for each region in Zimbabwe. Further, these tourist resort centres as foreign currency-mobilising points have not injected most of the generated revenue into the development of local districts and the entire region of Matebeleland. Instead, all the mobilised resources are remitted to the central government in Harare. This failure to allow revenue that is generated to trickle down to the 'grassroots' has led to various grumblings within the region of Matebeleland, as most people tend to argue that revenue generated from their region tends benefit people in Mashonaland.

Challenges continue to be faced regarding the exploitation of mineral resources. Various minerals have been prospected in the region, including diamonds in Tsholotsho, methane gas and more coal deposits in Lupane and parts of Binga, gold in Insiza, and uranium in the Nyamandlovu area. Most of these have not yet been tapped. But locals have expressed fear that if these resources were to be exploited within the current system of governance, their region would not benefit. Some social actors have even blamed the central government for failing to do a detailed cost-benefit prospective analysis of these mineral deposits for fear of arousing more voices of dissent in Matebeleland. They further argue that this omission by the government further incapacitates Matebeleland and even denies the region opportunities for prospective investors.

There have been suggestions that the agriculture sector has also been suffocated as the government tends to concentrate most activities and farming inputs in Mashonaland. It was reported in the *Chronicle* newspaper of 11 January 2010 that villagers of Hwange East were complaining about being marginalised.[8] Matebeleland is generally a dry region, which is good for animal husbandry. But there are prospects for irrigation schemes if water is harnessed through the construction of dams and drilling of boreholes. However, politicians and people from Mashonaland often usurp most farming implements for dry regions. This usurping extends to the current land redistribution process. A few from Matebeleland have benefitted, while in some parts of Matebeleland, Shona people have been resettled, as reported in the *Chronicle* newspaper about the case of people from Bubi district.[9] One member of the War Veterans Association who asked the following question aptly captured this situation: 'Does that really mean people from Matebeleland do not need land? This is one major weakness of the so-called "Land re-distribution" and the government of Harare is commissioning all this by omission'.

From the above examples it follows that the people of Matebeleland have bigger challenges, hence the call for a change of centralised system of governance in favour of devolution of power. The examples presented above are only a handful; many remain to be told (Mhlanga 2009). Now with Zimbabwe in the current political and economic crisis, no detailed research has been done to assess the effects of targeted sanctions in Matebeleland region. Further, the challenge is to consider the continued scourge of HIV/AIDS in view of the crisis and the fact that Matebeleland has always been sidelined.[10] All these and many other problems will continue to haunt Zimbabwe's flagging nationalism. They many even destroy Zimbabwe in the future.[11]

Unpacking the Ticklish Subject of Devolution of Power

This section will present a critical engagement of possible ways of avoiding future conflict scenarios in Zimbabwe, given the examples constituting the 'northern problem' presented above. The concept of devolution of power as a policy model will be discussed. As suggested above, the challenge for an equitable distribution of resources hinges on the task of managing fictitious colonial boundaries. Basil Davidson (1992: 10), in support of this view, observes that Africa's crisis is deeply embedded in the institutions that were inherited upon the attainment of independence. He further explains that while we may acknowledge that the nationalism that produced nation-statism began as a genuine enterprise that looked like liberation, it changed its course. He adds that the liberation ethos that was punctuated by a state of euphoria was

> [i]n practice [...] not a restoration of Africa to Africa's own history, but the onset of a new period of indirect subjection to the history of Europe. The fifty or so states of the colonial partition, each formed and governed as though their peoples possessed no history of their own, became fifty or so nation-states formed and governed on European models, chiefly the models of Britain and France. Liberation thus produced its own denial. Liberation led to alienation. (1992: 10)

It is this failure to grapple with the differences between liberation and independence that has posed challenges for postcolonial Africa in general, and, in particular, Zimbabwe. It has led to the failure in coining feasible systems of governance. Ngwana Maseko (2008) in narrative of the war of liberation suggests that ethnic rivalries had been temporarily suspended during the liberation struggle; thereby setting a fictitious political imagination of the state they were fighting for. He adds that ethnic rivalries were only invoked upon attainment of independence. Zimbabwe as the new state became a successor state, partly following colonial administrative lines, and in a large way, the Mutapa state, since the new rulers became Shona and had lenses of the precolonial Mutapa state.[12] This led to the centralised system of governance with Harare being the focal point.

Due to these challenges, the concept of devolution of power becomes a viable solution. However, Michael Hill (2000: 61) warns, in his discussion of devolution in the United Kingdom, that such a situation involves fundamental constitutional changes. Limited devolution measures tend to open up larger matters. In order to achieve this, an honest and open engagement has to consider the extent to which Zimbabwe's regions can be reduced to a manageable number or kept as they are in order to allow for the creation of separate parliaments. Thereafter, regional structures can be set with powers to formulate and implement both social and public policy in areas like housing, employment, social welfare, health, and education, having separate taxation powers and a clear system for the election of representatives at various levels of the federal project.

Devolution of power is part of the discourse on decentralisation. It entails the transfer of authority by central governments to local-level governmental units holding corporate status granted under state legislation (Fiske 1996). Often there is a tendency to confuse a federal project with Devolution. The two are different and they do not lead to the same output. But they both remain products of institutionalised plebiscitary politics- what may be called democratic ideation. However, it must be emphasized here that federal states are by definition devolved; although the extent of legally defined and shared powers devolved by the federal government to lower-level governmental units might deserve further clarification. A Federal project remains the most suitable system of governance for managing postcolonial states, particularly, where the nation-state compound continues to falter, as is the case in Zimbabwe. It is not premised on whether the state is large or small. As a system of governance it emerges as a creature of a constitution, whereas devolution is often not. Devolution then emerges within the policy discourse as the granting of statutory powers from central government of a sovereign state by the legislature as opposed to one that is written by the republic. Even in the UK (the case of Scotland and England) where devolution is much talked about projections on devolution are informed by statutory instruments. A close assessment of the current configurations of the state, in Zimbabwe shows traditional institutions, such as, the chiefs, state universities and many more as already devolved. The major challenge for devolution in Zimbabwe has often been that the current crop of devolutionists actually does understand what devolution entails. Devolution is a policy issue whereas a federal project is a system of governance. Devolution can be carefully conflated with characteristics of a federal project to work within a given context and mode of decentralization to conjure a system of governance.

ZESN (2009) says that in a federal system of government, 'sovereignty is constitutionally divided between a central governing authority and constituent political units like states or provinces. There is self-rule and shared rule. The State resembles a miniature version of the whole in congruent federalism'.[13] In addition, ZESN offers some advantages of a federal project; although without a clear elucidation of how such a system can best function. According to ZESN, advantages would include ensuring that there is devolution of power; that government remains close to the people in tune with the daily needs and aspirations; that decentralised forms of development are encouraged; that it allows unique and innovative methods for attacking social, economic, and political problems; that it provides effective ways of linking together diverse people who happen to end up in a single political entity; and that it is a way of resolving tensions between centre and periphery.[14]

In view of the above, devolution of established regional authorities usually faces problems in most developing and revolutionary states like Zimbabwe, largely because most states are characterised by weak central governments. And so, central governments are weary of losing political control. In Zimbabwe, for example, the state functions through appointed officials, governors who represent the wishes of the central government in the provinces. The discourse of devolution has often been resisted mostly because people are worried that if the central government devolves, power regions like Matebeleland might wake up someday claiming secession or complete separation. The other reason most people might be against this form of administrative decentralisation is their ignorance of what it entails. However, another problem arises with the fact that attempts to change systems of governance at nation-state level, for most postcolonies usually happen at the point of regime change or upon the attainment of independence. Therefore, it is often difficult to transform any system of governance when the incumbent is still in control of the levers of the state as seen in Zimbabwe. However, to manage the challenge of Zimbabwe's weak central government, there is a need to institutionalise devolution of power within the state constitution by creating a federal system of governance or a lesser version of it (Hill 2000; Makumbe 1998).

There is also a need to fully grasp that devolution is part of decentralisation. Understanding decentralisation as a concept has always caused many problems for academics and has produced serious conceptual muddling (Bardhan 2002). The challenge in Zimbabwe is that it has been imbued with positive normative value, and then conflated with other concepts, thereby adding to the already existing confusion, ignoring that decentralisation, as a concept is multidimensional. Decentralisation evolves from a variety of intellectual traditions and disciplinary differences and is quite complex (Bardhan 2002). It has worked in some cases and failed in others. And so, by way of contrast, decentralisation's antonym, centralisation, has a much more precise and accepted usage, which means concentration of power, resources, and authority (power) in a single head or centre.

Decentralisation as a reform strategy is a political process because its intentions are mainly to alter the political status quo by transferring authority from one level of government and one set of actors to others. Edward Fiske (1996) observes that in this shift, officials and bureaucrats at the centre tend to be short-term political losers, while their regional counterparts and those at district and local levels, including the masses, tend to be perceived as the winners. However, failure to clearly articulate and understand its benefits on the part of officials and state bureaucrats at the centre tends to cause conflict and, sometimes, lack of political will for decentralisation to be fully implemented. Decentralisation has many advantages and limitations. Chief among them is that the outward transfer of power improves service delivery, management of resources, and policies in a given state. Further, it increases people's confidence in state structures. It also reduces unnecessary burden on the state by allowing regions to formulate, manage, and implement their own policies.

In addition, decentralisation can be further delineated into various types that is, 'administrative decentralisation', 'political decentralisation', 'spatial decentralisation', and 'market (fiscal) decentralisation'. Administrative decentralisation forms part of our preoccupation as social scientists and public administrators. The other types are not the subject of this discussion. However, in brief, political decentralisation, which is usually linked with administrative decentralization, is sometimes referred to as 'democratic decentralisation' and involves assigning power to citizens and lower levels of government to make political decisions.[15]

Administrative decentralisation, which is sometimes referred to as 'bureaucratic decentralisation', is essentially a management strategy. However, due to its versatility, political power that usually resides with state officials can be allowed to trickle down to every level of the regional structures, thus causing it to emerge as a political form of decentralisation. John Makumbe (1998: 11) suggests that it is in such cases that revolutionary regimes tend to limit political powers of a decentralised body, by limiting the allocation of local resources or simply functioning by way of appointive rather than elective government officials. This has been observed in Zimbabwe, in particular, the case of governors. However, given these differences between administrative and political decentralisation, one common factor is that authority, both political (power) and administrative, is shifted to include regions that were previously outside the system. It should be emphasised here that decentralisation is a far more complex undertaking and requires careful attention to the building of popular consensus.

Decentralisation, if properly managed, can allow for the emergence of a redistributive trend to the previously disenfranchised groups. That may even improve the potential for productive investment and innovation and human resource development of marginalised communities. This applies in the case of untapped resources like methane gas and coal deposits found in Lupane and some parts of Binga as well as to diamond deposits discovered in Tsholotsho. Even the generation of revenue in decentralisation allows income to be geographically concentrated and managed, both because of agglomeration of economies (localisation of economies) and endowments of natural resources. If properly managed, certain regions will find it much easier to raise significant tax revenue, thus limiting interregional tax competition (Bardhan 2002).

Devolution of power as part of administrative decentralisation is one of the tiers in a continuum composed of deconcentration, delegation, and devolution (Tordoff 1994, Makumbe 1998: 8). In brief, deconcentration refers to the dispersing of responsibilities by a central government--for example, a policy directed to field officers.

This form of transfer leads to spatial changes and geographical distribution of authority, but does not significantly change autonomy of the entity receiving the authority (see Hyden 1983; Rondinelli, Nellis, and Cheema 1983: 23). More important, in this form of arrangement, the central government retains authority and continues to exercise that authority through hierarchical channels of central government bureaucracy. This is the least extensive type of administrative deconcentralisation and one commonly found in most developing economies.

Delegation entails the transfer of policy responsibility to local governments or semi-autonomous organisations that are not controlled by the central government but remain accountable to it. By implication, there is transfer of government decision-making and administrative authority and responsibilities for carefully spelt-out tasks; a few examples in Zimbabwe's public institutions, public corporations, and parastatals would include institutions such as, mining boards, the Post Office and Telecommunications (PTC), Zimbabwe's electricity authority, etc. The main difference between deconcentration and delegation is that the central government continues to exercise its control by way of a contractual arrangement that ensures accountability of local government. Devolution occupies a higher level of administrative autonomy in this decentralisation continuum for local entities than under deconcentration. John Makumbe (1998; 9) and Rondinelli, Nellis, and Cheema (1983: 28) have proposed privatisation as another tier. However, this tier can still be located within fiscal (market) decentralization or fiscal federalism as Bardhan (2002) would put it, and will not be discussed in this paper.

There are various schools of thought on this discourse on decentralisation; notable among them are the French and English scholars (see Conyers 1983). Decentralisation transcends epochs in academic circles; the most common school of thought emerged in the early 1990s. Most social actionists, politicians from the left who had a soft spot for subaltern groups, the civil society, and in some cases the reactionary right, promoted it. Derivation is one major factor in decentralisation of authority, as it deals distribution of resources and revenue generated from these resources. However, it must be emphasised that power, its usage, and distance, in terms of proximity

556

and ultimately decision-making has always influenced the call for these forms of decentralisation. The school of thought that has influenced this discourse since the 1990s has focused primarily on the political aspects of decentralisation. Their interests have always been to understand whether decentralisation of any form or type can stimulate the emergence of good governance, constrain national ethnic cleavages, promote democratic practices, and facilitate the growth of civil society and increase privatisation of public sector tasks. Such concepts with their varied meanings do not necessarily present problems; rather, they require great care to avoid generating too many meanings (oversimplifications) or too few (underspecification) (see Smith 1985; Conyers 1983; Collins 1989). It is also very necessary for people to seek to understand causal relational factors that give impetus to this kind of discourse and to the groups at the forefront.

In Zimbabwe, the case of regional differences in terms of development and the failure of the central government to ascertain indices in resource allocation have given impetus to calls for devolution. Moreover, derivation as an index has failed. It is also imperative to state that our attempt to conceptualise decentralisation must be informed by an understanding of how the related state institutions receive power and resources; that is, in terms of the degree to which power and resources are taken away from central government (Zimbabwe Election Support Network (ZESN 2009).[16] However, it is my contention that contextual factors do influence individual cases, and this is supported by ZESN in their contribution on systems of governance for Zimbabwe.

Conclusion

In conclusion, an assortment of preconditions for a successful devolution and an efficient federal system must be noted. It must be stated that an initiative for such a policy must not be a product of elite reasoning (Bardhan 2002). If it grows out of the elite and their allies in the regions without taking into cognisance a broader assessment of the likely benefits and risks contained in such a policy, then doom and policy failure can be guaranteed. It must be emphasised that in some cases this policy is notoriously difficult to implement, given its often-elusive nature, and it might even be disastrous if not properly implemented. But it requires diligence, commitment, and above all political will on the part of political elites and the ordinary masses. Also sudden shifts to the region of income and welfare maintenance functions can lead to massive social and economic dislocation that is likely to leave subregional governments with the task of maintaining social safety nets and dealing with the plight of a population hit by a severe policy backlash. To avoid such a situation, regional administrators must work in tandem with all the political actors and not act like shock absorbers protecting local populations against tough indiscriminate measures of the central government.

It must be emphasized that a weak federal government or even in a devolved system in such a situation has little choice but to spend its increasingly limited fiscal and political resources to buy the loyalty of regional administrators. In the Zimbabwean situation, there is a need to guard against such situations. If that fails, then devolution or any attempted federal government will fail to perform its job as a provider of national public goods, including such fundamentals as overall law and order, social safety nets, protection of property rights, and a sound regulation of markets. Furthermore, there is a need to avoid pushing this decentralisation envelope as a way of conjuring political party loyalty. Political party loyalty tends to be preferredscouted when the central government still wants to control decentralised regions through appointive powers of political players at the centre (Makumbe 1998).

In addition to the above preconditions, the following set of factors must be considered too; first, the central government must be responsible for national public goods, guaranteeing a free market, property rights, and contract enforcements. Second, the centre has to ensure unhampered inter-regional mobility of capital and resources to enable flow in response to the incentives created by fiscal policies, regulatory regimes, and social and economic infrastructure set in the regions. Third, there must be strong political will and commitment on the part of political leaders at central government level. Fourth, those calling for devolution of power must not be taken for granted, and they must be capable of fighting for their cause in a concerted effort and be committed to this as a noble cause. It is here that ethnic issues must not be criminalised as tribalism and left unattended, as seen in Zimbabwe.

Further, this policy must by all means be a bottom-up approach and work in concert with all the other forms of decentralisation. This can be done by involving people in all the planning stages, policy formulation, and implementation stages, thus further encouraging the decentralisation of consultation as a product of harnessing available human resources and power brokering. At the least, in such an arrangement power resides with the people in the devolved regions and not with the central government. Furthermore, a reduction in remittance of resources from the regions to the centre can be managed through derivation by giving people a voice in the distribution of locally produced revenue, including the exploitation of their resources. By so doing, elite management and possible future conflict scenarios are reduced by giving locals an existentialist position of having to manage and answer for their actions without pointing fingers at the central government.

References

Adebajo, A. 2010. *The Curse of Berlin: Africa after the Cold War.* London: Hurst & Company.

Ake, C. 2000. *The feasibility of democracy in Africa.* Dakar: CODESRIA.

Anderson, B. 1983. *Imagined communities: Reflections on the origins and spread of nationalism.* London: Verso.

Bardhan, P. 2002.' Decentralisation of governance and development.' *Journal of Economic Perspectives* 16 (4): 185-205.

Becker, P. 1979. *Path of blood: The rise and conquests of Mzilikazi founder of the Matebele.* Harmondsworth: Penguin Books Ltd.

Caplan, G.L. 1968. 'Barotseland: The Secessionist Challenge to Zambia.' *The Journal of Modern African Studies* 6 (3): 343-60.

Collins, C. 1989. 'Decentralisation and the need for a political and critical analysis.' *Health Policy and Planning* 4 (2): 168-71.

Conyers, D. 1983. 'Decentralisation: The latest fashion in development administration.' *Public Administration and Development* 3 (2): 97-109.

Davidson, B. 1992. *The black man's burden: Africa and the curse of the nation-state.* Oxford: James Currey.

Fanon, F. 1967. *Black skin white masks.* New York: Grove Press.

Fiske, E.B. 1996. *Decentralisation of education: Politics and consensus.* Washington, DC: The World Bank.

Geertz, C. 1963. *Old societies and new states: The quest for modernity in Asia and Africa.* New York: Free Publishers.

Hill, M. 2000. *Understanding social policy.* 6th Edition. Oxford: Blackwell Publishers.

Horowitz, D. 1985. *Ethnic groups in conflict.* Berkley: University of California Press.

Hyden, G. 1983. *No shortcuts to progress: African development management in perspective.* London: Heinemann.

Laakso, L. and A.O. Olukoshi. 1996. 'The crisis of the post-colonial nation-state project in Africa.' In: *Challenges to the nation-state in Africa*, edited by A.O. Olukoshi and L. Laakso. Uppsala: The Nordic Africa Institute of Development Studies.

Mafeje, A. 1971. 'The ideology of 'tribalism.' *The Journal of Modern African Studies* 9 (2): 253-61.

Makumbe, J. M. 1998. *Democracy and Development in Zimbabwe: Constraints of decentralisation.* Harare: SAPES

Mazrui, A.A. 1994. 'The bondage of boundaries.' *IBRU Boundary and Security Bulletin* (April): 60-63.

Mazrui, A. A. 1995. 'The blood of experience: The failed State and political collapse in Africa'. *World Policy Journal* 12 (1): 28-34.

Mamdani, M. 1996. *Citizen and subject: Contemporary Africa and the legacy of late colonialism.* Princeton: Princeton University Press.

Mhlanga, B. 2006. 'Information and communication technologies (ICTs) policy for change and the mask for development: A critical analysis of Zimbabwe's e-Readiness Survey Report.' *The Electronic Journal on Information Systems in Developing Countries* 28 (1): 1-16.

Mudenge, S.I.G. 1990. *A political history of Munhumutapa, c.1400-1902.* London: James Currey.

Ndlovu-Gatsheni, S. J. 2008a. 'For the nation to live, the tribe must die': The politics of Ndebele identity and belonging in Zimbabwe.' In: *Society, state and African history*, edited by B. Zewde. Addis Ababa: Association of African Historians.

———. 2008b. 'Currencies of ethnicity in Zimbabwe and its implications on nation-building, democracy, land struggles and human rights'. Paper presented at the International Seminar on

560

Ethnicity, Land and Conflict, Helsinki, Finland, 25 September 2008. Unpublished.

Ndlovu-Gatsheni, S. J. 2009. *The Ndebele nation: Reflections on hegemony, memory and historiography.* Armsterdam-Pretoria: Rozenberg-UNISA Press.

Nzongola-Ntalaja. 1987. *Revolution and counter-revolution in Africa: Essays in contemporary politics.* London: Zed Books Ltd.

Rondinelli, D.A., J.R. Nellis, and G.S. Cheema. 1983. *Decentralisation in developing countries: A review of recent experience.* Washington, DC the World Bank, Working Papers.

Sithole, M. 1984. 'Class and factionalism in the Zimbabwe nationalist movement'. *African Studies Review* 27 (1): 117-25.

Smith, A.D. 1986. *The ethnic origins of nations.* Oxford: Blackwell.

Smith, B.C. 1985. *Decentralisation: The territorial dimension of the state.* London: George Allen and Unwin.

Therborn, G. 1980. *The ideology of power and the power of ideology.* London: Verso Editions.

Tordoff, W. 1994. 'Decentralisation: Comparative experience in Commonwealth Africa'. *The Journal of Modern African Studies* 32 (4): 555-80.

Touré, A.S. 1959. *Toward full re-Africanisation.* Paris: Présence Africaine.

Vail, L. 1989. *The creation of tribalism in Southern Africa.* Berkeley: University of California Press.

———. 1997. 'Ethnicity in Southern African history'. In: *Perspectives on Africa: A reader in culture, history and representation,* edited by R.R. Grinker and B.S. Christopher. Oxford: Blackwell Publishing.

Van den Berghe, P.L. 1981. *The ethnic phenomenon.* New York: Elsevier.

Wiwa, K. 2000. *In the shadow of a saint.* London: Transworld Publishers.

Young, C. 1997. 'Democracy and the ethnic question in Africa'. *Africa Insight* 27 (1): 4-14.

Zwangendaba, N. M. 2008. *ZPRA: Zimbabwe People's Revolutionary Army.* New Jersey: Xlibris Corporation.

Zimbabwe Election Support Network (ZESN). 2009. 'Systems of governance: What options for Zimbabwe.' *Standard Newspaper*, 5 December 5 2009; also at http://www.thestandard.co.zw/opinion/ 22491-systems-of-governance-what -options- for-zimbabwe.html

Notes

[1] For a detailed engagement on this aspect and on the Ndebele historiography refer to Ndlovu-Gatsheni 2009. For further reading see Ndlovu-Gatsheni 2008a.

[2] This conception of ideology as a process follows Göran Therborn's (1980: 02) position that ideology forms part of that aspect of human condition under which human beings live their lives as conscious actors in a world that makes sense, or is made to make sense to them in varying degrees. Ideology therefore becomes the medium through which this consciousness and meaningfulness operates, also as part of the unconscious psychodynamic processes. Nationalism has greatly benefited from this psychodynamic effect through various ways, by which memory is continuously reshaped, and stories are narrated and continue to be retold in the endless process of state-formation. This consciousness of everyday life and general experiences informs my conception of ideology.

[3] It is on this note that I contest, as unfortunate, the label of being a betrayer that was attributed to Moise Tshombe by most nationalists across Africa in the early '60s, thus leading to the coinage of a criminalising phrase on the 'Tshombe mentality' - reference to everyone who is perceived to be a betrayer or sell-out to the nationalist cause. Further, I argue that had nationalists, in particular, Patrice Lumumba, deeply engaged Moise Tshombe, most probably Congo would have averted the violence that has decimated millions of populations and caused more suffering.

[4] This section is influenced by the major theme *Territorial origins of African conflicts*; my argument is that conflict must not be measured by the absence of violence alone. Rather, the indices must be further expanded to encompass even continued grumblings as a result of the lack of equitable distribution of resources, and the general acrimony and hatred that exists between various ethnic groups, as seen in Zimbabwe. These acrimonious arrangements have in most cases escalated into violent upheavals in most African states. I further contend that if systems of governance are to be revisited and redrafted, we might witness a reduction in these conflicts. However, without such a radical move as to change centralised systems of governance in favour of decentralisation or a federal project, it can be further argued that the era of gunpowder remains a reality in most of Africa.

[5] For more information on this, visit my Op-ed on devolution of power, which appeared concurrently on *kubatana.net* and *newzimbabwe.com*, under the heading: 'The True Face of Devolution' (05/06/2009); http://www.newzimbabwe.com/opinio n-386The%20true%20face%20of%20devolution/opinion.aspx. As stated above, this paper also appeared on Kubatana.net on 29 May 2009 under the heading: 'Moving the centre and unpacking devolution: A ticklish subject'. http://www.kubatana.net/ht ml/archive/opin/090529bm.asp?sector=OPIN&year=2009&range_start=121 The pa-

per was further reproduced by the *Standard Newspaper* of Zimbabwe on 6 June 2009 under the heading 'Moving the centre: Unpacking devolution', and can be - accessed at: http://www.thestandard.co.zw/opinion/20521movingthe centre unpackin g-devolution.html

[6] For a detailed engagement of Ndebele precolonial history, refer to Ndlovu-Gatsheni 2009. See also Becker 1979.

[7] It is worth noting that Bulawayo, the second largest city in Zimbabwe, has often been described in the local Ndebele language as *'Kontuthu Ziyathunqa',* meaning a place of smoke. The main reason for this name and description was because for quite some time Bulawayo enjoyed being the hub of heavy industries in Zimbabwe, a situation that had been colonially inherited; however, the government then came up with various strategies for relocating all the heavy industries to Harare. This was first done through the creation of the National University of Science and Technology (NUST), this time with a unique practice-based curriculum, in which third-year students are supposed to go for an internship. The process of internship was to create a form of intelligent copying by studying how these heavy industries were managed and to devise ways of relocating them, using the same students who would have been interns upon completion of their degrees. This policy has worked. As will be discussed later in this paper, one of my respondents even labeled NUST a province of Mashonaland in Matebeleland.

[8] The story can be found in the following website: http://www.chronicle.co.zw/inside .aspx?sectid=5019&cat=1

[9] It must be emphasised that few people from Matebeleland were given land in Mashonaland. Furthermore, those from Matebeleland who got land in Mashonaland had conflicts with most local politicians; some even had their farms taken. Another story on the inequitable distribution of land in some parts of Matebeleland was published by the newzimbabwe.com. For more information on the story, follow this link: http://www.newzimbabwe.com/news 2801 War%20vets%20held%20over%20 Mat.%20land%20wars/news.aspx

[10] Even on the political side, Matebeleland has continued to be subjected to the whims of central government. An example includes the awarding of national hero status for burial in Zimbabwe-a process that is always managed by the central government, with even the National Heroes Acre being located in Harare This has prompted most social actionists and political commentators to imagine such a situation as a form of capture; one where Ndebele heroes are captured while still alive as leaders, including their bones when dead. The history of the Ndebele as a people, their myths of origin, and celebration of their heroes and memory is downplayed. That they too have their sacred places and national shrines where their heroes have to be buried has always been downplayed.

[11] It can also be argued therefore that it is natural for ordinary citizens from Matebeleland to tend to hate the imagined beneficiaries of those development projects in Mashonaland when they continuously see development and resources being taken away from their areas to other regions of the country, as presented above.

[12] For more information on the concept of a successor state refer to Mudenge 1990.

[13] Refer to the following Op-ed by the Zimbabwe Election Support Network (ZESN): 'Systems of governance: What options for Zimbabwe.' Published by the Standard Newspaper of December 5 2009, the article can be accessed here: http://www.thestan dard.co.zw/opinion/22491-systems-of-governance-what-options-for-zimbabwe.html.

[14] ZESN, 2009. Ibid.

[15] Political decentralisation also entails a situation where groups at different levels of government; central, subnational, and local are empowered to make decisions related to what affects them. Political forms of decentralisation are usually engaged by political scientists interested in democratisation and civil society seeking to identify transfer of decision-making power to lower levels of governmental units or their elected representatives. Then, 'Spatial decentralisation' is a term used mainly by planners and geographers seeking to formulate policies and programs aimed at reducing excessive urban concentration in large cities by promoting regional growth poles that have the potential to become centres of manufacturing etc. 'Market decentralisation' is generally used by economists to analyse and promote action that facilitates the creation of conditions allowing goods and services to be produced and provided by market mechanisms sensitive to the revealed preferences of individuals. It gained momentum during the era of economic liberalisation (the '80s-'90s), privatization, and the demise of command economies. Under this type of decentralization, small and large firms, community groups, cooperatives, voluntary associations, and NGOs usually provide public goods.

[16] For more information on this discussion see an Op-ed written by the Zimbabwe Election Support Network (ZESN) titled 'Systems of governance: What options for Zimbabwe.' Published by the Standard Newspaper of December 5 2009, the article can be accessed here: http://www.thestandard.co.zw/opinion/22491systemsof govern ance-what-options-for-zimbabwe.html

CHAPTER 19

Decentralization and Conflict in Africa: A Paradox?

Joseph Ayee

Introduction

Since the late 1980s, there has been a growing interest in decentralisation, which has led to several African countries implementing decentralisation policies and programs. The impetus for this movement has been the belief, by several key African policymakers, that decentralisation and the subsequent devolution of power in favor of local communities is a key element of an effective institutional reform agenda. Decentralisation, which is expected to bring government closer to the people and make it more relevant to their lives, is identified as a crucial element in the improvement of governance. As Flanders (1995) has observed, '[I]f rolling back the frontiers of the state was the policy mantra of the 1980s, then the creed of the 1990s is to roll them downward.' The World Bank has also argued that 'competent and responsive local government is central to capacity building' (1989: 58). Many of decentralisation's proponents are enthusiastic about it because it promises to contribute significantly to 'good governance', a key element of many of the strategies (such as the New Partnership for Africa's Development, or NEPAD) that have been initiated since the end of the Cold War to deal with the continent's multifarious problems. For example, advocates of good governance believe that it would reduce corruption, enhance investment in productive capacity, and generally lead to significant improvements in the quality of life of most Africans. Decentralisation, its advocates believe, is expected to reduce the ability of centre elites to engage in corruption, significantly improve transparency and accountability, and generally contribute to improved governance. Thus, decentralisation is seen as a major contributor to good governance (Turner and Hulme 1997; Manor 1999; Cheema and Rondinelli 2007).

In practice, however, decentralisation has not been very successful in many African countries. Among the reasons that have been put forth to explain the inability of many African countries to undertake effective decentralisation programs are:

1) The centralising tendencies of many postcolonial governments.
2) The lack of political commitment on the part of both politicians and bureaucrats.
3) The failure, at independence, to develop the necessary skilled workforce needed to staff the various subnational governments.
4) The failure of many postindependence African governments to fully inform their constituents of the costs and benefits of decentralization (Smith, 1985; Rondinelli et. al., 1989; Mawhood 1993; Cheema and Rondinelli 2007).

Part of the problem, of course, was the fact that many of the new leaders themselves either did not understand or appreciate the critical role played by decentralisation in governance or approached decentralisation from a purely opportunistic perspective-that is, as a tool for personal primitive accumulation. Nevertheless, it is important to recognise that decentralisation invariably involves a process through which centre elites are forced to redistribute some of their power in favor of elites at subnational political units. As a consequence, there is a tendency for centre elites to engage, only reluctantly, if at all, in any decentralisation efforts (Smith 1985; Slater 1989; Samoff 1990; Ndegwa and Levy 2004; Treisman 2007).

In addition to the transfer of power from the centre to the regional and local governmental units, decentralisation also requires changes in the political and administrative structures, as well as attention to possible conflicts arising from the fact that the process will generate, at least in the short run, gainers and losers. For example, where power is currently concentrated in the centre, the ruling elites, most of whom are urban-based ethno-regional elites, would reap most of the benefits of postindependence economic growth (Mawhood 1993; Wunsch and Olowu 1995; Wunsch 2001). Left behind and forced to operate on the political and economic periphery are the historically marginalised and deprived groups, notably, rural inhabitants. Effective decentralisation would transfer some power away from the centre to rural communities, enhancing the ability of the latter to design and implement policies more favorable to the maximisation of their own values. This process can significantly constrain the ability of centre elites to redistribute income away from the rural areas and in favour of the urban centres. Thus, while rural areas, obviously the winners of an effective decentralisation program, are likely to favor decentralisation, centre elites and their benefactors, the losers, at least in the short run, would be strictly against it and would employ all the resources, including violence, in their possession, to oppose such institutional reforms (Slater 1989; Conyers 1989; Ayee 1994; 1999; Wunsch 2001).

Against this backdrop, this chapter discusses the paradox inherent in decentralisation: on one side, decentralisation is a strategy for conflict resolution and, on the other side; it promotes and exacerbates conflicts, since it produces winners and losers, at least in the short run. Before we examine the paradox, it will be useful for us to define the concept of decentralisation, and identify its forms and strengths in order to provide the reader with a better understanding of the issues to be discussed.

Definition, Forms, and Benefits of Decentralisation

Cheema and Rondinelli (2007) define decentralisation as the transfer of power, authority, and responsibility from the central government to state, regional, and local governments, as well as the sharing of authority and resources to shape public policies and programmes designed and implemented by governments. To Smith, decentralisation means 'reversing the concentration of administration at a single center and conferring powers on local governments' (1985: 1). In this chapter, decentralisation is considered the opposite of centralisation or concentration and involves delegation of power or authority from the central government to the periphery or subnational units.

In the study of politics, decentralisation refers to the territorial distribution of power. It is concerned with the extent to which power and authority are dispersed through the geographical hierarchy of the state, and the institutions and processes through which such dispersal occurs. Decentralisation entails the division of the state's territory into smaller political jurisdictions and the creation of political and administrative institutions in those subnational units. Some of the institutions so created may themselves be further decentralized-that is, these subpolities may be further divided into smaller political jurisdictions, a process that is fact-dependent and designed to enhance governance at the local level (Smith, 1985; Crook and Manor 1998; Manor 1999; Oxhorn 2004; Cheema and Rondinelli 2007; Treisman 2007).

Social scientists have developed four typologies for the classification of decentralisation:

1) Political decentralisation: This is sometimes referred to as democratic decentralisation or devolution. It involves the creation of institutions of local governance or structures that will promote separation of powers and accountability such as federal systems of government. It also allows political space for civil society organisations (CSOs) to act as countervailing forces against the extensive power of the executive arm of government (Smith 1985; Rondinelli 1981; Cheema and Rondinelli 2007);

2) Administrative decentralisation: This is also referred to as 'deconcentration' or 'field administration'. It refers to the delegation of authority from the central government ministries, agencies, or departments in a country's capital city to its periphery institutions in the regions and districts. This arrangement is regarded as administrative in nature and does not confer discretionary powers on the peripheral units (Oxhorn 2004; Bardhan and Mookherjee 2004);

3) Fiscal decentralisation: This is the transfer of financial resources from the central government to local government units to enable them perform their responsibilities. Some of the key indicators of this type of decentralisation are the design of a revenue sharing formula, the ceding of some revenue sources to local government units by the central government, and the mobilisation and management of resources by the subnational units (Rondinelli et. al 1989; Cheema and Rondinelli 2007); and

4) Economic decentralisation: This involves moving away from "state capitalism" and opening up of the economy to competitive forces. Three key strategies which have been used in most countries to open up the economy are privatisation of parastatals, deregulation and public-private partnerships (PPPs) (Cheema and Rondinelli 2007).

It is instructive to note that these forms of decentralisation have led to some confusion over the practice of the concept in most African countries because there has been the tendency, on the part of governments, to proclaim that they are implementing decentralization, while in reality they are either engaged in implementing mainly administrative decentralisation or a mixture of political and administrative decentralisation. In the development context, scholars have linked decentralization with several benefits, such as popular - participation, equity, effectiveness, efficiency, accountability, responsiveness, equality, political education and stability, and improved governance (Rondinelli 1981; Smith 1985; Turner and Hulme 1997; Smoke 2003; Olowu and Wunsch 2004; Cheema and Rondinelli 2007). Rondinelli (1981) makes several claims regarding the economic benefits of decentralisation. According to him, 'By reducing diseconomies of scale inherent in the over-concentration of decision making in the national capital, decentralisation can increase the number of public goods and services-and the efficiency with which they are delivered-at lower cost' (Rondinelli 1981: 136).

In addition, decentralisation is believed to yield political benefits:

> Decentralisation can offset the influence or control overdevelopment activities by entrenched local elites who are often unsympathetic to national development policies and insensitive to the needs of poorer groups in rural communities.Decentralisation can increase political stability and national unity by giving groups in different sections of the country the ability to participate more directly in development decision making. (Rondinelli 1981: 136)

Conflict-Related Objectives of Decentralisation

It has been pointed out that conflict is embedded in the concept of decentralisation and its objectives (Slater 1989; Sasaoka 2008). A number of reasons have been adduced to substantiate this assertion. First, decentralisation is about the structure of power and the distribution of power, which can give rise to conflict. From this perspective, it is not surprising that ostensibly similar institutional arrangements can serve very different goals and move in very different directions. In the words of Samoff:

Decentralization has to do with power: who rules in a particular society. Who rules, however, is not uni-dimensional. Different groups may prevail in different issue arenas. Different groups may prevail in the same issue arena at different times. Claimants to power coalesce, dissolve their alliances, and construct new coalitions. In this sense, decentralization is a program for specifying who is to rule in particular settings. Therefore to make sense of its forms and consequences in particular settings we need to understand decentralization as a political initiative, as a fundamentally political process and consequently as a site for political struggle. (1990: 519)

Second, neither centralisation nor decentralisation necessarily benefits the disadvantaged (Slater 1989). As a political process, decentralisation is likely to be contested. Even when decentralized institutions and authority patterns have been established, they remain insecure. Decentralisation, therefore, is likely to be effective (to achieve the goals for which it was adopted) only when those goals and their political character are clearly specified and understood, and generally compatible with the interests of those expected to implement (and defend) it (Samoff 1990).

Third, governing elites in Africa have seen decentralisation as a way to hold on to power. By devolving responsibilities from the central state apparatus to local and regional levels, decentralisation has helped political elites to diffuse demands for greater political opening at the national level and/or increase their capacity for social control by using newly decentralised institutions to further penetrate society (Manor 1999). Examples from Ghana, Kenya, Egypt, Mozambique, Togo, Angola, and Uganda show that decentralisation policies were intended to allow greater penetration of society in order to repress political opposition and prevent the future resurgence of the opposition without opening up institutional spaces for greater citizen participation (Olowu and Wunsch 2004; Oxhorn et al. 2004; Bardhan and Mookherjee 2006; Wunsch and Ottemoeller 2004; Smoke 2004; Saito 2008).

However, it is not only ruling elites that can see decentralisation as a way to hold on to power. Friedman and Kihato (2004) have suggested that in South Africa, ethnic and racial minorities have viewed various forms of decentralisation as a way to insulate themselves from majority rule. They emphasise that 'decentralisation, particularly to provinces, either provides racial minorities with opportunities to escape majority rule or, as [former South African President] Thabo Mbeki complained in 1995, allows the divisive mobilization of ethnic identities' (2004: 180).

The local elites, on the other hand, have taken advantage of their power, knowledge and networks to use local government units for their own interest (Slater 1989). In the words of Crook, '[I]n most of the African cases, elite capture of local power structures has been facilitated by the desire of ruling elite[s] to create and sustain power bases in the countryside. Popular perceptions of the local logic of patronage politics reinforce this outcome' (2003: 86). In South Africa, for example, it has been noted that provincial and local governments create considerable scope for patronage and nepotism, and that they can provide unaccountable local elites with opportunities to use public institutions to entrench private power. Accordingly, far from providing citizens with representative vehicles, 'decentralization …diminishes democratic possibilities by entrenching local elites' (Friedman and Kihato 2004: 180).

Fourth, decentralisation in practice runs up against objections at a political level. Indeed, it is felt that decentralisation dislocates the nation, either by encouraging the appetites of certain regions for autonomy or by encouraging wealthier regions to operate as self-sufficient territories to the detriment of poorer regions. The problem of guarantees remains the issue that divides supporters and opponents of decentralisation. What guarantees are there that decentralisation will not encourage or endorse separatist or fissiparous tendencies? (Smith 1985; Wunsch and Olowu 1995; Nzouankeu 1994; Treisman 2007).

Fifth, insofar as decentralisation enhances political and fiscal autonomy of territorial subunits, it is by definition likely to exacerbate uneven development between richer and poorer areas unless balanced by central equalisation schemes (Crook 2003). Consequently, as the wealth of countries in Africa is unfairly distributed, decentralisation has accentuated the already precarious imbalance within the state because poor districts have tended to become even poorer as a result of inequitable distribution of resources. This has been exacerbated by revenue sharing formulas, which have been seen as promoting inequalities. For poor districts and regions, therefore, autonomy is void of meaning because they have continued to be dependent on the state.

Moreover, decentralisation has not always been compatible with planning policies and strategic interventions (Smith 1985; Crook 2003).

This notwithstanding, Crook (2003) has noted that in some countries in Africa, there have been positive results for decentralisation in the area of allocating new resources to poor, remote areas that previously had few or no services. For instance, in Côte d'Ivoire between 1985 and 1996, 159 small towns of the interior were given *commune* status, each receiving basic central grants and the political opportunities that accompanied the creation of an administrative and elective institution. Similarly, in Ghana, the District Assemblies Common Fund (DACF) was created to move from 'nothing' to 'something' to enable poor districts to function as decentralised units. Furthermore, Wittenberg (2006) has demonstrated that in South Africa, the decentralisation reforms brought by the 1996 Constitution have led to the distribution of resources in a more equitable and less arbitrary way according to a sharing formula, although the vertical division of resources between provincial and local levels is decided by a consultative process. The reforms are thus seen as being broadly redistributive, owing to equalisation components in the formula for horizontal allocation of unconditional grants across local governments.

Sixth, decentralisation is not necessarily linked to democracy because the devolution of power has helped to augment the dominance of those who, because of wealth or status, are already powerful at the local level. In other words:

> [I]t is conceivable, even likely in many countries, that power at the local level is more concentrated, more elitist and applied more ruthlessly against the poor than at the center. As a consequence, therefore, greater decentralisation does not necessarily imply greater democracy let alone power to the people-it all depends on the circumstances under which decentralisation occurs. (Griffin 1981: 225)

Seventh, decentralisation has resulted in corruption at the local level in most African countries resulting in inequalities and disparities among districts and regions since resources earmarked for development are squandered by some local politicians and bureaucrats. Studies have shown that decentralisation has led to the prevalence of corruption at the local level (Prud'homme, 1995; Smoke 2003; Olowu and Wunsch 2004; Cheema and Rondinelli 2007). According to the 2005 Ghana African Peer Review Mechanism (APRM) report, the modest progress made in civic participation in local governance failed to reduce corruption:

> Participants at the various stakeholders' consultations complained about the high degree of corruption in Ghana's public sphere, at both the national and regional levels. In Ho and Cape Coast, stakeholders generally felt that corruption is rampant in decentralized organs of government such as the Metropolitan, Municipal and District Assemblies. Participants at WA generally feel that unless one has contacts in Accra, the nation's capital, one will not be attended to. (2005: 172)

A number of reasons have been adduced in the literature to explain the prevalence of corruption at the local level in Africa. They include the following:

1. Relatively weak monitoring and auditing system as a result of lack of experienced staff.
2. Organisational cultures protecting influential vested interests adopting obstructionist attitudes and thereby creating a patron-client relationship.
3. The pressure of the media and civil society organisations, in as much as it exists, as a greater disincentive for corrupt practices at the national than at the local level.
4. Wide discretionary powers given to local officials.
5. Pressing demands on local politicians and bureaucrats from local interest groups (whose money and votes count) in matters such as taxation or authorization.
6. Distribution of significant resources from the centre to the subnational units without corresponding mechanisms for promoting accountability and transparency.
7. Most local bureaucrats stay very long at their duty stations and it is therefore easy for them to establish unethical relationships with local interest groups.
8. The inability of citizens to demand accountability from local politicians and bureaucrats, a problem that is largely due to illiteracy and apathy (Prud'homme, 1995; Crook and Manor 1998; Devas and Grant 2003; Olowu and Wunsch 2004; Smoke 2004; Wunsch and Ottemoeller 2004; Cheema and Rondinelli 2007; Ayee 2008).

Lastly, the implementation of decentralisation policies in several African countries has resulted in the concentration of power and resources at the local level. Consequently, there have been contestations or conflicts over these resources, with the conflicts being exacerbated by the rise of identity group politics. For example, in Uganda, the creation of local districts by the Museveni government has intensified rather than diminished local ethnic conflicts as the process has altered the majority/minority status of local ethnic groups and thereby intensified interethnic competition in such districts as Buliisa, Kabarole, Kibaale and Tororo (Green 2008). Similarly, the creation of new states and local governments in Nigeria since the 1970s has not only failed to halt ethnic and religious violence but may have even contributed to it (Ukiwo 2006).

Conflicts between the various beneficiaries and losers of decentralisation in African countries remind us yet again, that 'any hard and fast distinction between politics and administration can only be false' (Smith 1985: 201). It may be conventional to consider decentralisation as an administrative concept, and even evaluate it, and discuss change, as if these are matters to be settled by technical arguments about optimum areas, administrative efficiency, and managerial performance. Outcomes, however, in the form of regional and local government decisions, are the result of political forces in conflict. The goals of the various actors are in direct conflict with each other, and the outcomes of the conflict are determined by the strategies, resources, and power positions of each of them (Smith 1985; Slater 1989).

From the foregoing discussion, it is possible to advance one proposition: that is, that the kind of public policy being implemented will have a considerable impact on the kind of political activity stimulated by the implementation process (Lowi, 1961; 1965; Grindle, 1980). Decentralisation programs with divisible benefits, such as the sharing of power and resources and creation of states, regions or districts, exacerbate conflict and competition among those seeking to benefit from them and are therefore more difficult to execute as intended.

Decentralisation as a Conflict-Resolution Strategy

A growing number of scholars have suggested that decentralisation does not reduce ethnic conflict and secessionism, and that it even intensifies them, by reinforcing ethnic and regional identities (Hardgrave 1994; Kymlicka 1998; Dikshit 1975), producing subnational legislation that discriminates against certain groups in countries (Horowitz 1991; Lijphart et. al. 1993; Nordlinger 1972; Suberu 1994), and supplying regions with the resources to engage in ethnic conflict and secessionism, such as funds, institutions, and police forces (Bunce 1999; Kymlicka 1998; Leff 1999; Snyder 2000; Roeder 1991). These scholars have identified very important ways in which decentralisation may increase ethnic conflict and secessionism. Unfortunately, they have been unable to explain why decentralisation is more successful in reducing ethnic conflict and secessionism in some countries than in others (Crook and Manor 1998; Olowu and Wunsch 2004; Rondinelli 2007).

In their research on decentralisation, Crook and Manor (2008) and Boone (1998) have shown that the conscious use of decentralisation as a political mechanism by central governments to neutralize and contain conflicts with regional or local elites has increased substantially. As argued by Olowu and Wunsch (2004), decentralisation has proven, in the post-1990 period, to be a crucial mechanism in both international and national efforts at conflict resolution in several parts of Africa. It played a role, for instance, in the resolution of long-simmering conflicts in Ethiopia, South Africa, and Mozambique and has been useful, to some extent, for resolving conflicts in Sudan, Angola, Senegal, Congo (Brazzaville), Democratic Republic of Congo, Burundi, Rwanda, and Nigeria. However, Olowu and Wunsch want us to be cautious, and state that

> [u]nfolding events in these countries suggest that political leaders who currently are ignoring decentralisation will be compelled by the international community and the futility of the unending struggle for power to explore its potential to help manage conflict. If one assumes that the primary motivation of political leaders is to continue to hold power, one can explain both the push to centralisation in the immediate post-independence era, as well as the openness to devolution in some circumstances in the 1990s and 2000s. As the state weakened in the 1980s, and as stubborn conflicts grew worse, staying in power could be aided by careful but genuine devolution. (2004: 51)

575

Conclusion

This chapter has explored the paradoxical nature of decentralisation in Africa and shown that while decentralisation can be used as a tool to resolve and prevent conflict, it can also create conflict. Scholars who favour decentralisation also caution us about its negative impacts. Thus, Treisman (2007) has cautioned that decentralisation per se cannot be a necessary tool in conflict prevention and resolution. The African experience at decentralisation, therefore, suggests that 'a more nuanced understanding of decentralisation at the national and sub-national level is necessary to understand better how and when it may alleviate or exacerbate conflict' (Green 2008: 449).

One lesson that the chapter has conveyed is that the introduction of some sort of decentralisation reform is inevitably complex because of the many different factors and interests involved and, in particular, because of decentralisation's highly political nature. Furthermore, it is critical that the structure of government and distribution of power among the various subnational units be created through decentralization, and the impact that these distributions would have on the various stakeholders should be considered before any effort is made to undertake decentralisation. Of course, the division of power and responsibilities between various officials must be expressly spelt out in the decentralisation document, for example, the constitution (Treisman 2007: 239). If decentralisation is to work in African countries, then governments must acknowledge the need to decentralise the administrative apparatus, be aware of the power alliances within the apparatus, and correct the general tendency for those with power to receive preferential treatment at the expense of others.

References

African Peer Review Mechanism. 2005. *Country review report and programme of action for the Republic of Ghana.*
Midrand, South Africa: APRM Secretariat.
Ayee, J. 1994. *An anatomy of public policy implementation: the case of decentralization policies in Ghana.* Aldershot: Avebury.

————. 1999. *Decentralization and conflict: The case of district chief executives and Members of Parliament in Ghana.* Accra: Friedrich Ebert Foundation.

————. 2008. 'The balance sheet of decentralization in Ghana'. In: *Foundations for local governance: Decentralization in comparative perspective*, edited by F. Saito, 233-58. Leipzig: Physica-Verlag.

Bardhan, P. and D. Mookherjee (Eds.). 2006. *Decentralization and local governance in developing countries: A Comparative perspective.* Cambridge, MA: MIT Press.

Bunce, V. 1999. *Subversive institutions: The design and the destruction of socialism and the state.* New York: Cambridge University Press.

Cheema, G.S. and D.A Rondinelli. 2007. 'From government decentralization to decentralized governance'. In: *Decentralizing governance: Emerging concepts and practices*, edited by G.S. Cheema and Dennis Rondinelli, 1-20. Washington, DC: Brookings Institution Press.

Crook, R. and J. Manor. 1998. *Democracy and decentralization in South Asia and West Africa.* Cambridge: Cambridge University Press.

Crook, R. 2003. 'Decentralization and poverty reduction in Africa: The Politics of local-central relations'. *Public Administration and Development* 23: 77-88.

Devas, N. and U. Grant. 2003. 'Local government decision-making-- citizen participation and local accountability: Some evidence from Kenya and Uganda'. *Public Administration and Development* 23: 307-16.

Dikshit, R.D. 1975. *The Political geography of federalism: An Inquiry into the origins and stability.* Delhi: Macmillan Company of India.

Flanders, S. 1995. 'More power to local authorities'. *Financial Times* 6 October 1995: 5-6.

Friedman, S. and C. Kihato. 2004. 'South Africa's double reform: Decentralization and the transition from apartheid'. In: *Decentralization, democratic governance and civil society in comparative perspective: Africa, Asia and Latin America,* edited by P. Oxhorn, J.S. Tulchin, and A.D. Selee, 141-89. Baltimore: The Johns Hopkins University Press.

577

Green, E.D. 2008. 'Decentralization and conflict in Uganda'. *Conflict, Security and Development* 8 (4): 427-50.

Griffin, K. 1981. 'Economic development in a changing world'. *World Development* 9 (3): 221-26.

Grindle, M. 1980. *Politics and policy implementation in the third world.* Princeton: Princeton University Press.

Hardgrave, R., Jr. 1994. 'India: The dilemmas of diversity'. In: *Nationalism, ethnic conflict and democracy*, edited by L. Diamond and M. F. Plattner, 71-85. Baltimore: John Hopkins Press.

Horowitz, D. 1991. *A democratic South Africa? Constitutional engineering in a divided society.* Berkeley: University of California Press.

Lijphart, A., R. Rogowski, and K. Weaver. 1993. 'Separation of powers and cleavage management'. In: *Do institutions matter?* Edited by K. Weaver and B. Rockman, 146-58. Washington, DC: Brookings Institution.

Lowi, T. 1964. 'American business, public policy, case studies and political theory'. *World Politics* 16: 677-715.

———. 1965. 'Four systems of policy, politics and choice'. *Public Administration Review* 20 (3): 3-10.

Manor, J. 1999. *The political economy of democratic decentralization.* Oxford: Clarendon Press.

Mawhood, P. (ed.). 1993. *Local government in the Third World: The experience of tropical Africa*, 2nd ed., 1-12. Pretoria: Africa Institute of South Africa.

Ndegwa, S. and B. Levy. 2004. 'The politics of decentralization in Africa: A comparative analysis'. In: *Building state capacity in Africa: New approaches, emerging lessons*, edited by B. Levy and S. Kpundeh. Washington, DC: IBRD/World Bank.

Nordlinger, E. 1972. *Conflict regulation in divided societies.* Cambridge: Harvard University Center for International Affairs.

Nzouankeu, J.M. 1994. 'Decentralization and democracy in Africa'. *International Review of Administrative Sciences* 60: 213-27.

Olowu, D. 2003. 'Local institutional and political structures and processes: recent experience in Africa'. *Public Administration and Development* 23: 41-52.

Olowu, D. and J.S. Wunsch. 2004. *Local governance in Africa: The challenges of democratic decentralization*. Boulder: Lynne Rienner.

Oxhorn, P., J.S. Tulchin, and A.D. Selee (eds.). 2004. *Decentralization, democratic governance and civil society in comparative perspective: Africa, Asia and Latin America*. Baltimore: The Johns Hopkins University Press.

Oxhorn, P. 2004. 'Unravelling the puzzle of decentralization'. In: *Decentralization, democratic governance and civil society in comparative perspective: Africa, Asia and Latin America*, edited by P. Oxhorn, J.S. Tulchin, and A.D. Selee, 3-30. Baltimore: The Johns Hopkins University Press.

Prud'homme, R. 1995. 'The dangers of decentralization'. *The World Bank Research Observer* 10 (2): 201-20.

Suberu, R.T. 1994. 'The travails of federalism in Nigeria'. In: *Nationalism, ethnic conflict and democracy*, edited by L. Diamond and M.F. Plattner, 56-70. Baltimore: John Hopkins University Press.

Roeder, P.G. 1991. 'Soviet federalism and ethnic mobilization'. *World Politics* 43 (2): 196-232.

Rondinelli, D.A. 1981. 'Government decentralization in comparative perspective'. *International Review of Administrative Sciences* 47 (2): 133-45.

―――. 2007. 'Parallel and partnership approaches to decentralized governance: Experience in weak states'. In: *Decentralizing governance: Emerging concepts and practices*, edited by G.S. Cheema and D.A. Rondinelli, 21-42. Washington, DC: Brookings Institution Press.

Rondinelli, D.A., J. McCullough, and R.W. Johnson. 1989. 'Analyzing decentralization policies in developing countries: A political economy framework'. *Development and Change* 20 (1): 57-87.

Samoff, J. 1990. 'Decentralization: the politics of interventionism'. *Development and Change* 21: 513-20.

Saito, F. 2008. *Foundations for local governance: Decentralization in comparative perspective*. Leipzig: Physica-Verlag.

Sasaoka, Y. 2008. 'Decentralization and conflict'. Japan International Cooperation Agency. Paper delivered at GDN Conference, January 31.

Slater, D. 1989. 'Territorial power and the peripheral state: the issue of decentralization'. *Development and Change* 20 (2): 501-31.

Smith, B.C. 1985. *Decentralization: The territorial dimension of the state*. Allen and Unwin, London.

Smoke, P. 2003. 'Decentralization in Africa: goals, dimensions, myths and challenges'. *Public Administration and Development* 23: 7-16.

———. 2004. 'Kenya: erosion and reform from the centre'. In: *Local governance in Africa: The challenges of democratic decentralization*, edited by D. Olowu and J.S. Wunsch, 211-36. Boulder: Lynne Rienner.

Snyder, J. 2000. *From voting to violence: Democratization and nationalist conflict*. New York: Norton.

Treisman, D. 2007. *The architecture of government: Rethinking political decentralization*. Cambridge: Cambridge University Press.

Turner, M. and D. Hulme. 1997. *Governance, administration and development: Making the state work*. New York: Palgrave.

Ukiwo, U. 2006. 'The creation of local government areas and ethnic conflicts in Nigeria: The case of Warri, Delta State'. Paper presented at CRISE Conference on Federalism, Decentralization and Conflict, Department of International Development, University of Oxford.

Wittenberg, M. 2006. 'Decentralization in South Africa'. In: *Decentralization and local governance in developing countries*, edited by P. Bardhan and D. Mookherjee, 329-55. Cambridge, MA: MIT Press.

Wunsch, J.S. 2001. 'Decentralization, local governance and "recentralization" in Africa'. *Public Administration and Development* 21 (4): 277-88.

Wunsch, J.S., and D. Ottemoeller. 2004. 'Uganda: Multiple levels of local governance'. In: *Local governance in Africa: The challenges of democratic decentralization*, edited by by D. Olowu and J.S. Wunsch, 181-209. Boulder: Lynne Rienner.

Wunsch, J.S. and D. Olowu (Eds.). 1995. *The failure of the centralized state: Institutions for self-governance in Africa*, 2nd ed. San Francisco: Institute for Contemporary Studies.

CHAPTER 20

Territorial Origins of African Civil Conflicts: Consolidation and Decentralization toward Practical Solutions

Kelechi A. Kalu

Introduction: Situating the Argument

The territorial map of the continent of Africa as structured by European powers at the Berlin Conference in 1884-85 represents the highest form of corruption, exploitation, and marginalisation in the twentieth century international system. That postindependence Africa remains substantively in line with the external mapping of the continent is obvious. The resilience of colonially structured states in Africa is evidenced by the fact that most conflicts in the continent since political independence in the 1950s and 1960s are in the form of civil wars and/or political violence. For while the continent is often seen as characterised by wars, statistically, these are intrastate rather than interstate conflicts with significant cost to civilians and social relations. Empirically, except for the Somali-Ethiopian war (1977-78), Ethiopian-Eritrean war (1998-2002), and to some extent the Ugandan-Tanzanian (1978-79) conflict, the prevalence of intrastate wars in Africa suggests that these wars are mainly over verifiable political, economic, and social disharmonies that have little to do with the victims of the wars. Furthermore, and arguably, except for the civil wars in Nigeria and the violent conflict over the future of the province of Katanga during the early years of independence in the Democratic Republic of Congo, and to some extent the Angolan and Mozambican civil wars, most of the wars in the continent are not fought over state- and nation-building, but represent struggles by groups within each country for control of the apparatus of state and, by implication, the allocation of scarce resources. Consequently, at the root of cyclical civil wars and political violence in various African States is the absence of strong indigenous elites whose interests lie in cultivating existing indigenous forms of cultures, languages, and forms of conflict management in building nationalism and citizenship in support of the government and the territorial spaces referred to as 'states' in Africa. Thus, institutional reforms that:

1) Significantly improve state capacity through geographic remapping of Africa's geopolitical landscape.
2) Provide Africans with a significant level of policy autonomy and the capacity to feed themselves as the basis for industrialisation
3) Create an enabling institutional environment for more enhanced participation by all constituencies in national development.
4) Provide the facilities and the wherewithal for African States to participate fully, effectively, and gainfully in both the global economy and international affairs and perhaps, more important, enhance the ability of these countries to impact the global political economy.

These are the required necessary steps to ending the use of different aspects of territory as a basis of civil conflicts in Africa.

This chapter will begin by linking the foregoing approaches as part of the strategy to explaining the logic of the use of territory as a basis for conflict. The chapter will conclude with suggestions for practical solutions to ending such conflicts in Africa. A general overview of the issues is presented first, followed by a systematic discussion of how to reconstruct and reconstitute African States on a platform that creates internally strong, productive, and viable states in the continent that are able to discharge their international responsibilities effectively on behalf of the citizens.

Conflicts in Africa: Colonial Origins and Contemporary Legacies

Empirically, the continent of Africa has been the most conflict-prone region in the world. As argued by Richard Jackson, 'between 1980 and 1994, nearly half of the world's war-affected countries were located in Africa…and in…2000, two-thirds of the 100,000 people killed directly in armed conflicts were African' (2006: 27-28). The costs of political violence and war are enormous and mounting. For example, Jackson has determined that

584

[s]ince 1960, over eight million people have died either directly or indirectly as a result of Africa's wars, more than 5.5 million of whom were civilians. This figure does not include...over 3.5 million mostly civilians who have perished in DRC since 1998...Africa also has the highest level of internal displacement in the world and some of the largest refugees flow from conflict. In 2000, there were 14 million displaced people in Africa, 11 million of who were internally displaced...Disturbingly; Africa's wars are characterized by the large numbers of child soldiers employed by many governments and rebel groups. Of the 300,000 child soldiers...fighting in over 30 countries around the world, there are more than 120,000 in Africa. (27-28)

With so many African children involved in armed conflict, it is important to examine population changes and life expectancy in all areas. Despite economic and political uncertainties, most African nations have been experiencing increases in population. Without an effective strategy to end violent conflicts in the continent, their human and environmental costs will only continue to increase. Based on Population Reference Bureau data, [1] Africa's population in mid-2008 was estimated at 967 million with about 400 million or 42% below age 15. And based on the youthful population, Africa is projected to reach a population of 1.9 billion by the year 2050. Infant mortality is influenced significantly by the level of the mother's education. Across the board, infant mortality is highest among mothers with no education. In other words, the more education a woman has, the better the chances of her baby surviving. Education, of course, could be serving as a proxy for income, since more educated mothers are most likely to have the resources that would enable them to secure access to prenatal care, clean water, and health care, which are important determinants of infant mortality. Nevertheless, female illiteracy and income inequality remain the most important determinants of infant mortality in most of Africa.

Economically, except for Northern and Southern Africa, the percentage of the population living on less than US$2.00 per day was one-half or greater in every country except Côte d'Ivoire, where it was 49%, and 90% or higher in Nigeria and Tanzania. In terms of education, while school enrollment has generally improved, there remain problems of inequitable access beyond the primary school level. There is no country in the continent with universal access to secondary school education. At this level, parents must expend large sums of money to send their children to post-primary educational institutions that are more often than not owned and managed by non-governmental agencies, primarily religious organizations. As a consequence, children from poor families are denied the opportunities to develop the skills necessary for them to participate fully and gainfully in what is fast becoming a knowledge-based globalised economy.

Unarguably, national policies that emphasise education, especially at the primary and secondary levels, are likely to result in positive improvements in other socio-economic data. Specifically for sub-Saharan Africa, aggregate data reveal that demographically, with a total population at over 767 million, the population growth rate is 2.3%. And with a Gross National Income per capita of US$951, poverty remains high among the population. For example, the proportion of the population living below US$1.25 (PPP) a day or those classified as living in Extreme Poverty is 51%. And the proportion of the employed population living below US$1.25 (PPP) per day is 64% of the population. Overall, 36% of the population lives in urban areas. These data are relevant for understanding why civilians are likely to be vulnerable to opportunistic behaviours that result in political violence and or civil war. The point is not that poverty leads to war; rather the data should be understood as indicating that where political and economic institutions have failed or are inadequate in sustaining human security, citizens become vulnerable to physical and structural violence. Understanding how the state and the government fail to sustain human security in Africa through effective governance necessarily requires a conceptual understanding of the logical mindset of the Europeans who created the dysfunctional entities that are today the poorly managed and maladministered African States.

Conceptually, governance is at the foundation of socio-political organisation for human relations on the framework of the Westphalian state structure. Governance refers to a set of institutions and actors (Stoker 1998) whose interactions within a governmental and/or societal framework is characterised by actors' recognition of their mutual interdependence.[2] Classical political theorists and philosophers like Thomas Hobbes and Hugo Grotius argue that the state of nature is characterised by physical and material insecurity, which forces people to seek security through an organisational framework that allows some sacrifice of personal freedom for protection by the group or state. In precolonial Africa, such a search for security was confined to one's immediate ethnic and/or linguistic group and usually within a manageable territorial landmass. For Immanuel Kant, the search for company and alliance with others, which enables people to exercise their *will* and acquire honor and respect from fellow human beings, is an overriding consideration for a people's desire to escape the state of nature. In precolonial Africa, that search for honor and respect was framed around earned leadership, status, and honor. In either case, the prevailing environment evolves as a result of the choices that people have in a given socio-political and territorial location.

However, for Africans during the colonial period, except for Ethiopia, neither of the above arguments applied. European colonialist projects were based on the 'noble' assumption that non-Western societies needed to be relieved of their 'primitiveness' in order to be brought into European civilization. The strategies of that colonialist project or civilising mission-armed intervention and the institutionalisation of organised destruction-are evident in various occurrences of political violence and civil wars across Africa. Given people's desire for freedom and the role of choice, it becomes necessary to question strategies that purposefully introduce force as a route to honour and respect. In contemporary Africa, such strategies are also expected to contain the seed for planting peace in a situation where the legacy of colonial and postcolonial policies has largely undermined the status and honour of the largest number of citizens in the continent, that is, women. The failure of the colonial project to transform 'primitive' Africans into modernised Europeanized Africans has occurred largely because most colonial projects were based on an estrangement strategy that negate essential communally oriented African epistemologies that insist on harmonious co-existence between the community and the individual. Given the above discussion, it becomes possible to ask some questions: What type of socio-political arrangement is likely to ameliorate the condition of estrangement? Are there universal principles and practices that are culture neutral? To what extent are the factors of European social formation, such as religious and ethnic wars, replicable in other regions and cultures of the world? These are important questions

587

because of the conflict resolution and management cottage industry that has developed around African wars without viable rethinking or reframing of the epistemological basis of state formation that is at the root of these conflicts.

As Anthony Pagden notes, the earliest and most enduring of the European assumptions about non-Western societies is rooted in Greek civilisation. There, Plato's Eleatic Stranger complained that 'in this country, they separate the Hellenic races from the rest as one, and to all the other races, which are countless in number and have no relation in blood or language to one another, they give the single name "barbarian"' (Padgen 1998: 7-15). In a condition of severe need and scarcity, does the notion of Eleatic Stranger allow for inclusiveness on the basis of good governance and democracy alone? Responding to this question requires a closer examination of the idea of conflict as a mechanism of domination that is rooted in the colonisers' territorially based nation-states environment in which Africans find themselves.

In *Archeology of violence* (1980, trans. 1994), Pierre Clastres argues that the European encounter with non-European social formations confronted the explorers with a radically different world from their own. Clastres contends that Europeans of all persuasions in their competitive missionary projects and annexation of foreign territories had an image of the non-European as 'that of the warrior. An image dominant enough to induce a sociological observation: *primitive societies are violent societies; their social being is a being-for-war*' (1990: 140-41, emphasis added). Thus, will the new European burden developed around the conflict resolution industry be different from the earlier efforts where 'primitive peoples' and their communities were to be re-made in an image familiar to 'non-warrior' Europeans? (See Kalu 2005: 187). The civilisation of 'primitive societies' project took two forms: the Europeanisation of the primitive people and the restructuring of primitive institutions, political spaces, and economic formations to make them consistent with those of Europe. Within such frameworks, premodern non-European social groups lacking frameworks such as the state were referred to as *ethnies*. Similar social formations in Africa were referred to as *tribes*, denoting European perception of early Africans and other non-Europeans as largely nomadic. Clastres's exploration of the rationale for the 'European burden' project is insightful and deserves attention here. He asks:

> What exactly do we mean by primitive society? [P]rimitive societies are societies without a State; they are societies whose bodies do not possess separate organs of political power...*All societies with a State are divided, in their being, into the dominating and the dominated.* (87-88, emphasis added)

Clastres argues that epistemologically, from Heraclitus to Plato to Aristotle, European social thought could not conceive of a society without a king, and in societies where kings existed, it was important for the Europeans that those 'primitive' kings do things the European way. For the Europeans, a 'society is unthinkable without its division between those who command and those who obey' (1994: 88). Also, 'primitive societies are...undivided societies...classless societies-[with] no rich exploiters of the poor; [they were] societies not divided into the dominating and the dominated-no separate organ of power' (90). Further, 'the destiny of every society is to be divided, for power to be separated from society, for the State to be an organ that knows and says what is in everyone's best interest and puts itself in charge of imposing it...' (90), irrespective of the social formation or the extent to which such command-obedience structures provide security for all citizens.

Similarly, the idea of separating the society from the state is evident in the nature of land tenure laws and policies that are based on separating the individual from communal interests. It is such European-imposed divisions in colonial Africa that resulted in institutionally weak political and economic structures, which are best captured by Alexis de Tocqueville's discussion of the relationship between inheritance structure and institutionalized aristocracy.[3] Regarding the law of inheritance, Tocqueville argues that where state law is based on descent, that is, right of primogeniture, landed estates are often inherited and thus form a +--connecting point between generations without division. In such a situation, family names are tied to the landed estate, which serves as the repository of family history, memories, and a link to the future. According to Tocqueville, in contrast to state laws based on primogeniture, nations whose laws are based on equal division are apt to experience the destruction, not just of their fortunes, but also of their territory and its domains. As such, he argues that 'the law of inheritance not only makes it difficult for families to retain the same domains intact, but takes away their wish to try to do so and, in a sense, leads them to cooperate with the law in their own ruin' (1966: 46). Thus, once divided, a family estate never comes together again, which ultimately leads to a loss of *esprit de famille* that sets in motion individual selfishness to the detriment of the family and/or community. In that respect, 'the law of equal distribution progresses along two paths: by acting upon things, it affects persons; by acting on persons, it has its effect on things. By both these means it strikes at the root of landed estates and quickly breaks up both families and fortunes' (46). Thus, in situations where through primogeniture Africans remain connected to their roots, Western interference in African social formations led to social, political, communal, and cultural fragmentation. The partition of Africa for European colonial conveniences is tantamount to the sale of African lands, except that the Europeans took the land as well as the proceeds of the 'sale'. This practice continues to manifest itself in contemporary exploitation projects through transnational corporations.

By demarcating the African landmass into states, which the African nationalists at independence sustained and legitimised in their collective agreement to respect the colonial boundaries in 1964, that policy inherently continues to obstruct family and therefore communal reunion, hence the increased level of intrastate conflicts in Africa. Thus, ending or significantly reducing intrastate conflicts requires that both society and state be reunited along the lines of familiar ethno-nationalities, languages, and cultures for Africans. The first step in that process is remapping and reframing the context of socio-political organization of power and authority in Africa, which is addressed in the next section.

Remapping and Reframing the African Landmass

State formation is a result of specific historical outcomes mediated by social and political forces. Although state structure and norms may have resulted from the activities and creations of certain individuals or policy networks, its legitimacy is eventually based on the state's capacity to refract ideas and preferences of specific groups in society into a general purpose outcome. States are not necessarily autonomous from society because societal norms lead to state creation in a specific historical epoch; but they must consistently act as vectors of development and ideological underpinnings of their constituent members. States accomplish this through transparent and transformative uses of collective resources for the general purpose. The extent to which institutions of the state serve the general purpose mediates and maintains the state's legitimacy and the obedience/loyalty of citizens.

A general role of the state is to ensure the competent and effective operation of its security functions, as well as its educational purposes, and to develop the core values/ideas that lead to strong nationalism, justice, and equity. The effective state must also ensure citizens' equitable access to and use of social services. Most important, the state must provide the economic infrastructure or overhead capital (such as a fully functioning healthcare system; roads, especially farm-to-market roads; reliable sources of energy; structures for effluent disposal, especially in the urban sectors; a network of schools, especially at the primary and secondary levels; various forms of communications infrastructure; and a well-defined and enforced property rights scheme, in real and personal property, including intellectual property).

Agriculture remains the most important sector for most countries in Africa. Not only is agriculture a country's breadbasket, but it is also the foundation for further industrialisation and modernisation of the economy. Thus, an effective state's agricultural and, indeed, other economic policies must reflect the needs of both the urban and rural sectors-the needs of the urban sectors for food and those of the rural agricultural areas for markets to sell their excess output. Here, the ability of the government to provide important infrastructure to the agricultural sector, primarily farm-to-market roads, as well as other communications infrastructure (e.g., Internet services) between the urban and rural farming sectors) is critical to sustained and sustainable economic growth and development.

The notion that states are autonomous entities from society is untenable, even in Africa, but especially in European states, because states respond to demands and preferences of civil society on behalf of the citizens or risk irrelevance because they become blatantly antidemocratic and subject to challenges by non-state forces.

Therefore, the issue is the extent to which individual and group interests are managed within the context of the general-purpose function or role of the state. Equally significant for ending conflicts and political violence in a state is the extent to which the differing goals are made compatible and resolved by the same state whose vector roles necessarily lead to winners and losers in the process of policy formulation and implementation.

The foregoing leads me to argue that the existing structures of governance in Africa (that is, states) lack capacities for roles as vectors of development because they have largely been conceived as autonomous structures from society, hence, the antidemocratic behaviours of the custodians (that is, civil servants and politicians) of state power. States in Africa simply reflect the materialist preferences of illegitimate social and political forces-best described in some instances as criminal gangs-acting as if they are agents of states with general rather than patrimonial interests. Consequently, located mainly in the capital cities, these criminal gangs make no effort, except through brute force where extractive resources are located, to integrate the rural areas with the towns. In essence, the wielders of state power fail to use the instrument of governance to broadcast power across the different territories of their states. One of the unintended consequences of such neglect is that the unofficially governed territories, mainly in the non-metropolitan areas, are taken over by organized criminals who impose their own form of governance often terrorising the rural residents with impunity. The unofficially governed territories in some states, for instance, the DRC, Uganda, Nigeria, Somalia, and Sudan, often become platforms for organised challenges to state power, especially where resource extraction can serve as sources of support for this extralegal opposition. Consequently, to develop meaningful practical strategies for ending the various conflicts that continue to constrain economic growth in the continent, Africa's decision makers and citizens must think about the *structure* and set of *governance institutions* that inform domestic policies and policy implementation.

How the domestic structure works in the African context requires a clear understanding of the significant differences between the idea of state and that of governance. It requires the use of sustainable economic development policies that are based on concrete visual transformative strategies of the idea of state and governance as currently constituted to show how changing the structure of the states will bring about the prospect of ending civil and political crises. As I have argued earlier, governance is characterised by acceptable norms, institutions, and cultures of people, framed around a common language in a territorially delineated space. Structurally, governance deals with the specific functions and responsibilities of different machineries of government or institution within a given society or state (see Kalu 2005: 174). Effective and transparent governance in both public and private spheres will tend to strengthen political governance, the state, and its citizens, making it possible for each to resist the tendency toward political violence and civil war. To achieve such a level of accountability requires institutional structures that compel public officials to be good stewards of public trust across sub-Saharan African states.

Its practical realisation requires reconstruction of existing states in the continent. As I have argued elsewhere,[4] the model of the Western state, which is characterized by a set of interconnected institutions whose dynamics are often independent of the institutions of government and civil society, remains poorly specified in much scholarly discussion on Africa. For Africa, the concept of state has often been seen as coterminous with government or the ruling class. This misconception evolves from Africa's experiences with the colonialist state whose feudalistic structure maintained an absolutist and therefore all-powerful stature in its rule in Africa. The Western state as an 'organized aggregate of relatively permanent institutions of governance' (Duvall and Freeman 1981: 106) was neither entrenched as an institutionalised legal order in various African social formations nor was it deployed as a framework for unifying the different aspirations of ethnic nationalities.

The colonialist state's brutal efforts to discount primordial identities in Africa succeeded in creating artificial subjects as citizens charged with helping advance the materialist interest of the European colonists and colonialists. The outcome, a wholesale misperception of the difference between the state and government, is entrenched at various levels of education in Africa. Subsequently, with decolonisation, the new leaders saw the state in most of Africa as a material object that could be hijacked for personal, class, or group interests similar to the colonialists' projection of the state as a feudal entity with an absolutist wealth-generating structure. Essentially, colonial states in Africa were not states in the real sense of that term; rather, what the colonists institutionalised was a familiar (to them) feudalistic structure reminiscent of Europe's early experience at wealth creation through absolutist mercantilist policies like the enclosures in the United Kingdom that subordinated economic production to the interest of the monarchs. Changing the attitude of public officials in sub-Saharan Africa, therefore, requires changing the nature of the African States through building self-sustaining public institutions that will hold leaders accountable for their opportunistic stewardship of public trust. Such an understanding requires unambiguous clarification of the concepts of *state* and *government* and their mutually reinforcing capacities for advancing the individual and collective interests of citizens in each state. The process will not be easy. It will require a more proactive citizenry than is currently the case on the continent. Also, rather than the politicised identity politics that most of Africa's postindependence leaders have relied on to govern, a more nation-state-oriented politics and people-oriented-policies will have to be crafted for transformative change in Africa.

As Chazan et al. (1999) note, the concept of state is characterised by three important components. *First*, the decision-making structures, that is, the legislative, executive, political parties and parliaments, are responsible for making the decisions that advance the collective interests of the people and therefore the state. The *second* component of a state is the decision-enforcing institutions, such as bureaucracies, parastatal organisations, and security forces. The *third* and perhaps most important characteristic of the state are the decision-mediating institutions-courts, tribunals, and investigatory commissions (Chazan et al. 1999: 38-39). From this viewpoint, the state through its structures, the organisation of its people and resources, and the way its public policy agendas are set to establish policy priorities is essentially an institution of power with definite interests (38-39). But as viable as it is, the power of the state is purely conceptual and perceptual. While the broad presence of state power is institutionally and structurally effective in creating spaces for individual and group capacities for pursuing different interests, which often depends on the extent that individual or group entrepreneurial or identity politics sustain or challenge the power of the state. Such a state, with legal powers codified in a formal constitutional structure that holds its citizens and institutions accountable for their actions, has not been known across the continent of Africa either in its colonial or postcolonial existence.

As evidenced in the series of attempts in 2007 and 2008 by various African leaders (such as in Nigeria, Zimbabwe, Kenya, and Cameroon) to prolong their stay in office by manipulating the constitution to remain beyond their mandated terms of office, most leaders still see the state as private property and thus largely emphasise the vertical at the expense of horizontal nature of power and authority necessary for effective governance and economic productivity. Given that the colonial and postcolonial state structures in Africa were imposed with serious consequences to law, ethical conduct, and behaviour of government and business leaders, any efforts at transformation and change must redesign existing state boundaries and their constitutions through consultative strategies that seek the participation and input of those whose duties it is to protect and abide by the constitution. Such strategies will work if they enable citizens' participation in politics, build a strong bond on the basis of genuine nationalism, and ensure, especially at the civil society level, the vertical nature of state authority to serve as a vector to institutionalise and maintain horizontal powers and authorities in the private sector.

Clearly, if the state and its constitution result from the collective desire of the people, the exercise of state power that leads to contentious outcomes is more likely to be resolved within the state's decision-mediating institutions without resorting to civil war or coups d'état. Such legitimate outcomes are largely based on the extent to which the *government* (this refers to the specific occupants of public offices) is willing to make fair and binding decisions on national and specific issues at all times without overt and/or intentional discrimination on the basis of identifiable criteria such as religion or indigeneity.[5]

Public and symbolic demonstrations of the values of citizenship, fairness, justice, and equity by public office holders are nation-building strategies that bind different nationalities and citizens to the state and the government. In this respect, and essentially, it is not the state but the government that is responsible for nation-building; it is one of the functions of government to connect the citizens to the state.

595

Since the state is an organization of power and not a neutral concept, it is the responsibility of government to manipulate the organisation of citizens and resources to advance the national interest, which at this time for African states is nation-building. From the above, it becomes possible to see that the perceived and much debated failure of postcolonial states in Africa is a failure of government to effectively carry out its nation-building functions of providing a viable state platform for nationalism. It is the absence of viable nationalism-the connection between citizens and their government-for effective advancement of the collective good within the platform of a state that continues to inflame political violence and civil wars in many states. Therefore, a viable constitutional compact between the various ethno-nationalities in various states and/or erasure of existing state structures are likely to serve as strong platforms for ending territorial and ideological conflicts in the continent. The mechanisms are discussed below.

Mechanical Changes to State Structures in Africa

Regionally and internally, sovereign states in Africa can be either positive or negative. While the concept of sovereignty recognises every state in the world system of states as legal equals, the government of a state possesses sole legitimate right and power to use force. For African states, the influence of sovereignty can be seen in two ways. First, it may help to further the development of a constitutional democracy, and therefore good governance, in a political space characterised by differences in culture, ethnicity, class, and region. Second, in the guise of maintaining the integrity of the internal domain of a state, sovereignty may also be used to suffocate civil society and the democratic process as the experiences of many African States demonstrate.

First, although every state is now politically independent in Africa, the fear of loss of power and bad stewardship of public trust continue to constrain the use of ballot boxes to enable constructive leadership transitions. Lack of viable and acceptable institutional structures for competitive leadership transitions hinder access to power and therefore remain a major source of conflict in the continent. Thus, it is not necessarily a matter of leadership transition through elections; rather, it is whether or not other ethnic and/or religious groups should share political power and therefore national resources with dominant groups established by colonialism or through military power. Indeed, a structure that promotes equitable distribution of power and national resources and adequately constrains the exercise of government agency is likely to compel government officials to be good stewards of the public trust and reduce instances where autocrats perpetuate themselves and their cronies in power. Following recent movements for democracy, for example, former autocrats in Ghana, Kenya, Zimbabwe, Nigeria, Benin, and elsewhere have made attempts to transform themselves from autocrats to democrats, but only a few successes can be recorded in Ghana, Uganda, and Benin. Political turmoil in Central African Republic, Nigeria, Congo, and Algeria (irrespective of the election in 1999), Somalia, Angola, and Guinea Bissau continue because the autocrats transformed or not, are unwilling to preside over fair and openly competitive elections. As the cases of Nigeria (irrespective of elections), Algeria, Sudan, Mozambique, Zambia, and Kenya demonstrate, the few individuals who hold state power have unlimited influence and access to the instrument of coercion necessary to silence their opposition. Also significant is the fact that power, conceptualised as the use of force, is employed for material accumulation, corruption, and the containment of presumed radicals, violations of human rights and silencing of the media. Moreover, one of the strategies of this leadership-by-intimidation is to make it difficult for rival political groups to participate in government.

Thus, taming the existing condition of political violence and civil conflicts across the continent would take smaller steps and/or a major structural transformation of the African landmass. First, major states like Nigeria and South Africa need to lead by example and consolidate their democracies and ensure that institutions of government respect the rights of citizens irrespective of class, ethnicity, race, gender, or religion. Competitive politics and entrepreneurial energies of the citizens should be encouraged in both the traditional and formal platforms of engagement. It would require a transparent effort to embed politics at the local, regional, and national levels, where participation should be based on ideas and resources that compete for public acceptance. For example, embedding competitive political visions and practices across the state should lead the major states to serve as models of transformation for human security. In addition, terminating all relationships with African countries and/or regions that engage in undemocratic practices that often result in political violence and civil wars should minimise the tendency of individuals and groups in the continent to resort to violence for capture of the apparatus of government or to retain power through extralegal means. A second and preferred option is a strategic reconstitution of the African landmass into five super states. 6 Clearly, European states were created and organised by citizens who fought, settled their differences, and conquered the territory on which their states are built. These included decisions on what forms of government and normalised rules of behaviour and responsibilities were expected of both leaders and the led. In the case of African states, except for Ethiopia, Europeans created the states and the states in turn created the citizens in various African states. Consequently, without reforming, reframing, and restructuring the existing African states, building nationalism-the love of country and the willingness to die-and protecting the territory against political violence and civil wars will continue to rob the states of the privilege of the services of most citizens.

The strategic restructuring of states in Africa would yield five *super states* created around Algeria (North African States), Kenya (East African States), Democratic Republic of Congo (Central African States), Nigeria (West African States), and South Africa (Southern African States). The existing major states in Africa will provide the initial administrative and infrastructural support for a Constitutional Convention to harmonise economic, political, cultural, and social issues. The *consolidation* of territorial spaces as suggested here is surely a revolution in political engineering that has the capacity to transform domestic politics within the continent as well as enhance the capabilities of the various states to project external influence with effective outcome for the citizens. However, the consolidation will only be effective to the extent that it also involvestr ategic *decentralization* of governance and revenue extraction within the platform of competitive politics.

The logic of strategic *consolidation* of various states into one major state is informed by the history, capabilities, and influence of existing states in the international system. It is equally based on the assumption that capable and viable states are those that can protect the physical and human security of their citizens as well as its territory from external and internal challenges. Perhaps, among contemporary states in Africa, only South Africa potentially qualifies as a strong and viable state. Unarguably, many contemporary states in Africa are not economically viable and will remain mired in political crises because of the unsustainable and low levels of economic production and demand in the domestic markets. Some of these nations include Equatorial Guinea, Liberia, Sierra Leone, Rwanda, Burundi, Eritrea, Togo, Niger, and Chad. These and other African nations are currently unable to sustain viable export-oriented policies due to poor or non-existing comparative advantage in any product relevant to their natural and/or national resources. Also, many of these states have at one time or the other experienced convulsive political crises, violence, and outright self-negating civil wars without the capacity for internal state reconstruction. Given that the imposed colonial state structures across sub-Saharan Africa remain alien to most of the citizens, the character of the nations/societies remains unintegrated into the structures and foundations of the state to generate nationalism, goodwill, and the entrepreneurial spirit necessary for building strong viable modern states. While politics has become war for many actors in these states, the portion of the state that survives does so on the goodwill of external actors who contribute in some instances, through development aid, up to 50% of the state's annual budgets. These budgetary supports in states like Ghana, Liberia, Sierra Leone, Uganda, Chad, Kenya, and Rwanda make it possible for African states to be highly influenced by events outside their geographical borders. And some of those events are largely sanctioned by government officials based on policies aimed at continued domination and marginalisation of their peoples. Subjectively, when political, economic, social, and physical boundaries are externally influenced with the complicity of domestic leaders, those entrapped by such constraints often see the state boundaries as artificial. However, and consistent with the game of international and domestic politics, most citizens are powerless to change the rules without deadly consequences. As a result, those with the resources to leave the continent often exercise that option, thereby exacerbating the absence of viable alternative ideas and policy frameworks for change.

599

Consequently, citizens that remain often do not see the state, the government or its rules as important to their well-being. As a result, old forms of social relations-ethnic affiliations across porous boundaries, interethnic marriages, religious and language similarities, shared common experiences and economic opportunities-are used by citizens to enhance their lives out of the reach of government institutions and state mandated boundaries. Deliberate and conscious state consolidation is therefore a strategic option for enhancing the collective power of the citizens, increasing their capacity to pool their resources for effective bargaining power with external actors as well as enlarging the space for competitive politics and economic productivity without the capacity of a handful of political elites to foreclose such activities through political intimidation.

Furthermore, taking advantage of economies of scale and through pooled resources, the consolidated states will increase economic productivity and opportunities for their citizens, which will significantly reduce incidences of conflict based on the struggle to allocate scarce economic resources. Using the increased sizes and extended scopes of the new territories, the consolidated states will eliminate opportunities for military coups d'état and/or democratic transitions without transformation that have characterised leadership transitions in Africa since the 1960s. The consolidated states will have the advantage of size to constrain a handful of military cabals that often seek to hold the citizenry hostage.

With enhanced human and natural resources in each consolidated state, business interactions with transnational corporations will largely be dictated by the size of the market and the purchasing power offered by each state. Also, significantly, the consolidated states will have the tendency to eliminate the Machiavellian business strategies that continue to deprive African states of both economic profits and human resources that result in brain drain. Currently, over 40 states in the continent have signed one form or the other of concessionary agreements with the People's Republic of China. One doubts the extent to which most of these states have thought through the future consequences of these agreements, such as their effects on technology or knowledge transfer, maintenance of completed construction projects by China, employment and therefore wealth generation by citizens, including the effect of commodity price changes in the future on which the concessionary agreements are based. Where economically non-viable or institutionally weak states exist, consolidated states will be more likely to institutionalise and operate a more efficient bureaucracy with the capacity to enter into contracts that benefit the state and give it leverage to secure its future as well as the capacity to restructure local corporate and income tax collection systems, which in consolidated democracies are necessary through public works and projects for creating a sense of national identity, competitive politics, pride, and patriotism. As such, the new states, more than the existing inherited colonial institutions and states, will be more likely to effectively confront and deal with poverty, hunger and lack of educational facilities/resources as well as focus on the development of general infrastructure.

In addition, consolidated states are more likely to be effective, self-preserving, sustainable, and viable with the full participation of most of its citizens in the economic, political and social life of the state through a strategic effort that devolves power to the local and regional platforms for politics. Such *decentralisation* of power will create avenues for positive fragmentation of political elites away from existing tendencies at the national level. It will equally ensure that the nature of governance is consistent with various local options based on traditional modes of political engagement without sacrificing citizenship as the dominant identity protected and secured by the national government.

The issue of governance that is necessary for realising the foregoing suggestions is at the core of state reconstitution in Africa, which requires that existing sources of citizenship and normalised rules of law be revisited within a framework of constitutional conventions in all the consolidated states. Thus, while the identified foundational states-Algeria, Kenya, DRC, Nigeria and South Africa-will serve as the initial organising framework for state reconstitution, these states will cease to exist after a constitutional convention has resulted in the drafting and ratification of a new constitution for the consolidated states within six years-sufficient time for party formations and the conduct of elections at all levels of government. Such draft constitutions would have been translated into all major indigenous languages within each new state, gone through vigorous debates, and been amended and ratified before they become law. With

Constitutional Conventions for each state, finally, Africans will have the opportunity to determine for themselves what system of government works consistently with continental and local realities. The assumption here is that the absence of Africans at political discourse that was the Berlin Conference will be rectified by the new exercise; but more important, Africans would have given themselves their own boundaries and laws. Significantly, the process of drafting and debating new constitutions for the various states will introduce and situate politics (in its proper context)-as the redistribution of scarce economic resources on the basis of values-and result in the formation of viable interest groups whose activities will enhance existing civil institutions, traditional and modern. Furthermore, one of the consequences of such constitutional engineering exercise is ethnic consolidation, where various ethnic nationalities will tend to band together to protect their cultural practices and interests. That is a good thing because there is nothing inherently conflictual about ethnicity. It is *politicized ethnicity* that is often one of the sources of conflict in Africa. To correct that, constitutional conventions within consolidated states will enhance ethnic competitiveness, but privilege citizenship as a dominant identity-achieved through education, and private enterprise as the predominant employer of labour and the transparent implementation of public policies in the interest of the public. Thus, while helping to resolve issues of political discourse at the Constitutional Conventions, opposition groups in different parts of Africa will be able to articulate and understand the structure of power rather than how individuals acquire power. This is significant because understanding the structure of power and how it works in the contemporary political arena is likely to result in losers in a given political contest accepting their losses while preparing to compete in future games. It will also make clear the different paths through which one can be relevant in the political process without necessarily competing for public office. In the end, it is not ethnic rivalry but the perceived lack of access to power and authority and gross insufficient availability of resources within weak and non-viable state boundaries that directly explain the incidences of intrastate civil conflicts in Africa. Figure 1 is an example of multiple channels/centers of influence that are predicted to help tame civil conflicts and political violence in consolidated African states.

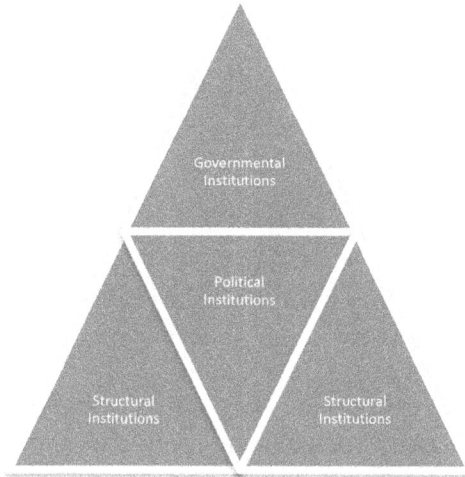

Figure 1: Institutional Structures of Consolidated States

At the governmental level are the different centers of national power-legislative, executive, judicial, and bureaucratic institutions that make and enforce national laws that affect both political and the structural institutions. The political institutions are political parties, religious institutions, labour unions, and other civil society organizations that aim to influence the decisions at the governmental institutions. The political institutional level is where the game of politics is played out, differences harmonised and conflict managed without jeopardising the state and or the citizens. The most significant aspect of the structural institutions is its composition-the citizens, local governments, the constitution, economy, and traditional/modern mode of social relations. The different levels are linked and interconnected by the citizens. The public officials at the governmental level draw support from the citizens, while political institutional actors are members of the structural institutions. Thus, every level is connected to the citizens. Therefore, in a consolidated state, citizens are the dominant actors influencing the direction of public policy by their active participation in politics at all levels. This is also the domain of territorial resources that enhance or constrain the capacity of the government and the people. It is also the platform where nationalism is

603

developed and sustained through the educational institutions, as well as sites of memories and ancestral histories of the peoples that make up the state. Consequently, to the extent that consolidated states are engaged in reframing and reforming existing state institutions to enhance citizens' capacities for full realisation of their rights and responsibilities, to that extent will the sources of political violence and civil wars be significantly reduced.

Economic Dimension of State Consolidation

The African Union (AU) and the New Partnership for Africa's Development (NEPAD) are substantive moves toward ensuring collaborative, integrated, and focused economic policies that should lead to increased economic productivity, and possibly elimination of conflicts in Africa, respect, and protection of human and peoples' rights and democratic governance on the continent. Although both the AU and NEPAD concepts are good, they lack effective pragmatic strategies for realising their stated goals of unified regional/continental development in Africa. Further, the central actors within each existing state have not proven themselves to be good stewards of the public trust. As is evident in Zimbabwe, Nigeria, Kenya, Cameroon, Guinea, and other states, public officials in many states in Africa have not shown good internal leadership as a basis for their willingness to collaborate regionally and continentally.

For example, except in regional contexts, African states require visas for interstate travel by citizens. A pragmatic follow-up to the idea of integrated efforts at economic and democratic enhancements in Africa should include an immediate implementation of the free movement of Africans within the continent restrained only by verifiable individual and/or group malfeasance. Such free movement of peoples would also be enhanced by the freedom of individuals to carry out legal business activities in any part of the continent while paying taxes to the government where such business activities are located. An immediate result of this is likely to be an enhanced knowledge, by Africans, of existing resources and opportunities in Africa that should lead to intraregional/continental trade between and amongst Africans. As a result of ease of mobility and access by Africans, such trading activities are likely to result in an economy of scale for producing exportable goods that will generate export revenue-far greater than Africa's existing share of total global trade, which is around 2%. Thus, a slight improvement in export revenue-provided political and economic institutions are strengthened to ensure stability and security-is likely to result in significant improvements in the living standards of the citizenry as well as to reduce the economic and security uncertainties that tend to make citizens vulnerable to incentives from organised criminal and oppositional groups.

Thus, the focus should be on what individual Africans can contribute to the economic and civic life of the area, region, and state in which they choose to locate themselves. Collectively, the question should be: What can individual African states and/or regions produce domestically and more competently compared to other states and regions? The answer to this question should lead to the establishment of companies and industries in identified locations on the basis of low cost of inputs for maximum outputs. Through such intracontinental-focused economic activities, products can be freely moved to continental markets and only goods that are not produced competitively in consolidated states in Africa would be imported. In the short run, and with regard to agricultural productivity, such policies should significantly increase food production, given availability of arable lands and low-cost inputs in various parts of the continent. In the long run, this strategy should result in increased capacity for domestic revenue mobilisation and the eradication of hunger on the continent. Consolidated states with enhanced labour and industrial power should increase the capacity of African states to grow wheat and other grain, which are easily produced at low cost in various states in the continent and enhance the capacity for African states to end and/or reduce food shortages caused by droughts that often are difficult to deal with because of existing state boundaries.

Although the idea of collaborative and cooperative engagement expressed by the AU and NEPAD for the resolution of African problems is good, their current strategies are not pragmatic. So far, both institutions have been tested and found wanting in Darfur and Zimbabwe where the peer review mechanism failed to ignite the engine of accountability because leaders remain self-absorbed and citizens remain fragmented along ethnic, religious, and class lines. Indeed, expecting the West to be responsible for most of the financial

605

resources needed to carry out the agenda articulated in the AU and NEPAD platforms shows African leaders' lack of seriousness to engage in their stated collaborative projects for transformative change. Transformation is simply the realisation that everything is possible and available, and therefore there are no constraints to citizens' full realisation of their civic and entrepreneurial responsibilities and interests within a state structure that provides physical and human security as a given.

Existing state structures have shown their inability to confront major state responsibilities in the international system; most have failed in their primary responsibility to citizens-protecting their physical security. Consequently, pooled resources that lead to economically effective policies will be more likely with the erasure of Africa's colonial political/territorial boundaries. Although this idea will be met with internal and external resistance, state reconstitution in Africa will be conceptually and pragmatically realized through such an exercise. When implemented, the psychological boost to the diplomatic, economic, political, and social relations of power between Africa and the rest of the world would be evident across issue areas. Reconstituting African states for more effective and competent governance will create a basis for domestic revenue mobilisation for the states and enhance their capacity to provide an enabling platform for citizens to pursue their various interests. Remapping the colonial boundaries will enable Africans to more quickly and effectively work collaboratively to deal with catastrophes like famine, conflicts, and disasters such as flooding and outbreaks of epidemics without waiting for foreign actors for citizens' basic necessities. Consolidating the states along the lines discussed above will have an added benefit of ensuring that Africa's educational institutions and infrastructures are also reformed and restructured with adequate capacities to engage in strategic and targeted education of citizens to understand and improve their environment. This will also reduce the current tendency of citizens towards economic and political emigration to the West.

Further, consolidation will also focus more attention on different aspects of African cultures. Currently, African students and scholars do not read about indigenous Africa as a matter of necessity, but rather foreign ideas, which are often transmitted through song lyrics and television programs, have become major points of reference. For example, in a discussion with some students and one of their professors at the University of the Cape Coast in Ghana in November 2009, I was quite distressed to learn that music departments' curricula in various Ghanaian-and I would suspect in many African-universities, privilege classical Western music, and that very little (if any) indigenous African music is taught. A consolidated state with pooled resources is likely to help reverse this trend, which is also evident in the departments of languages, history, and politics where theories and narratives largely reflect carryovers from the colonial states' curricula. Not emphasising indigenous languages and cultural practices among young and older scholars ensures that Africans remain alien to each other and therefore more likely to see each other as truly the 'other' who must be resisted-sometimes by violence. Thus, given the poverty of the formal educational curriculum and poor educational institutions, many Africans have no chance at transcending poverty and are thus unable to contribute ideas that could enhance their standard of living through collaborative engagement with all citizens, irrespective of their language and ethnicity. Indeed, Africans are more likely to welcome Europeans and be suspicious of other Africans as a result of fear and ignorance strategically embedded in the continent's various centres of knowledge and learning. Such fears and ignorance are evident in the ways Africans have mutilated and exterminated each other in Rwanda, Burundi, Nigeria, Sudan, Zaïre, and more recently in Kenya.

In many ways, the inattention to the life of the mind of the citizens is best characterised as a condition of elite *misology*. Leaders in many existing states have since political independence demonstrated their poor stewardship of the public trust, neglected national infrastructures, engaged in opportunistic behaviours and suffocation of civil societies, presided over decaying legal, social, and political institutions that result in wasteful spending of private and public resources, and thereby condemned the majority of Africans to the equivalent of life sentences in hell. Reversing such abysmal states of existence requires the right mixture of minds and natural resources within a new state structure that is able to develop and market quality products for both domestic use and international competitiveness that ensures human security for citizens.

The foregoing are possible when political stability, democratic governance, patriotism, and educational reforms are established as the platform for the success of Africa's development objectives and as strategies for ending violent and essentially unproductive civil conflicts. Stability, peaceful coexistence, and sustainable economic growth will be enhanced when the agenda for transformation includes reconstituting and reforming Africa's educational institutions within consolidated state platforms that will encourage African scholars in all disciplines who are currently contributing to the enhancement of the standards of education of citizens in European and American universities, as well as science and technology institutions, to return to the enhanced educational institutions to participate in relevant educational projects that will increase citizens' standard of living and help to end political crises and violence. Part of the function of the consolidated state platform and reformed educational institutions would be to train citizens to assume positions of leadership in public institutions as part of their civic responsibility rather than as an opportunity for self-enrichment through different forms of opportunism (such as corruption and rent seeking). The assumption here is that consolidated states with enhanced economic activities through emphasis on agriculture as a basis for industrialization will establish the private sector as the dominant employer of labour and human capital across the states.

Thus, as Figure 1 implies, the segmented pyramids contain several avenues for influence-various institutions and offices within the governmental level, replicated at the political and structural levels. It assumes a decentralised system of legitimate authority that brings governance closer to the people either through formal government institutions-federal, regional, state, and local levels-or through economic, religious, and traditional institutions. Such a decentralised form of authority also brings the game of politics much closer to the people. However, the most important aspect of decentralisation is the potential it has to reduce the concentration of influence and resources at the regional, state, and national levels and to bring these resources to the local level, effectively enhancing citizens' ability to participate fully and effectively in allocation. Thus, decentralisation provides for multiple political jurisdictions, making certain that resource allocation more effectively reflects local needs. The base of each of the segmented and yet interconnected pyramids is an opportunity for different ideological, economic, political, social, and religious groupings to compete for citizens' support and membership. I argue that the diffused nature of politics built on the foundation of consolidated states with viable economic and political institutions is likely to bring about an end to any form of territorially based competition that has led to violence or civil war in the past.

Another dimension of decentralisation as a strategy for ending civil and political violence in the continent is the fact that devolving power to the local levels provides opportunities for generating revenue for local development, a process that enhances the local community's contribution, not only to its own development, but also to national development through the additional tax revenues to be generated from increased economic activities. If devolution is accompanied by fiscal independence, each political jurisdiction will develop its own revenue generation institutions. Essentially, one of the first tasks of a consolidated state is to conduct a census for an accurate determination of the population of the state and of its demographics-employed and unemployed members of the various communities and towns-as a basis for policy formulation and implementation. The second task is to implement a policy that allows each regional, state, or local government to develop territorially based resources in their areas. Thus, the role of the national government is to tax revenues generated from different parts of the country as well as to ensure that all citizens' rights are protected. Fiscal decentralisation helps to decongest politics at the national level and reduce rent-seeking opportunities that are the norm in existing states across the continent. Sustainable economic development will also emerge in consolidated states when private industry is the main source of gainful employment and wealth accumulation. Also, such a state is likely to benefit significantly with the attention of local elites who will double as economic and political agents for the development of the region. Since transformational change through remapping and reframing African states, institution building, and economic growth will be made possible by people, the role of leadership in the creation of viable change will not be overlooked. This means that emphasis will be placed on the citizens as the source of governmental, political, and structural leaders in consolidated states in Africa.7

609

In Lieu of Conclusion: Leadership and Public Policy

One of the unintended consequences of Africa's decolonisation is lack of effective preparation by the nationalist leaders on how to cultivate nationalism and institutionalise sustainable processes for solving national economic and political problems. Some would argue that the problem with public policy such as ending civil conflicts in Africa remains external influences such as neocolonialism-where the emblems/logos of transnational corporations have replaced former imperial flags. They argue that these problems are evident through the intervention of institutions such as the International Monetary Fund (IMF) and the World Bank (through their collective financial impact on African states), and the irrelevance of African states in institutions such as the United Nations (which is exemplified by lack of effective stance to resolve conflicts in Rwanda, Liberia, Sudan, Somalia, Democratic Republic of Congo, and elsewhere in the continent). However, for others, the problem is internal to Africa. They cite corruption and poor management by the leaders, the apathy of the followers, ethnicity, religion, and the lack of accountable governments and institutions across the continent. While both of the above assessments of the problems of public policy in Africa are partially correct, they ignore a fundamental and perhaps dominant explanation with significant impact on mitigating political violence-the absence of *indigenous elite*.

It is the lack of productive engagement in the public policy sector by indigenous elites with viable financial, intellectual and patriotic resources that remains an obstacle to the installation and maintenance of institutional structures that are consistent with the capacity of modern states in the international system. While repugnant, what the colonialists did-first bringing the different nationalities together through an undemocratic process into one state for ease of exploitation and then exploiting their differences through autocratic strategies to keep them permanently divided-is not central to the problem of solving contemporary political violence and civil wars in much of Africa. The central problem in Africa has been the lack of a public leadership system that is nurtured by the core values of indigenous *elite* across civil society and the national landscapes.

The absence of a deep rooted, credible public leadership is directly related to the absence of national dialogue and relevant action in many African states.[8] Especially since independence, there has been no reliable vision and/or discussion on what the identity of each state and its citizens should be about and how the different nationalities that were brought together by colonialism should live and work together productively. In this respect, while European colonialists acted as *establishment and extractive elites*, postindependence African leaders, who also largely constituted themselves as *extractive elites*, had no serious thought on the structural foundation and ideas that should undergird the postcolonial states they inherited at independence. This is what remapping and reframing of territorial boundaries within the framework of consolidated states aim to correct.

Indigenous elites build legacies using ideas and institutions. Significant to the roles and functions of indigenous elites is the fact that they also nurture dreams of current generations and, for the unborn, they leave their marks in sustainable and authentic educational institutions and structures, financial and judicial infrastructural legacies with enforceable norms and stable security across the country. Most important, indigenous elites produce a self-determined citizenry with the zeal to serve their country unselfishly. Extractive elites, on the other hand, leave legacies of dug-up roads, wasted farmlands, uncompleted projects, corruption, malevolent leadership, false hopes, unfulfilled dreams, and institutional decay represented by an externally weak state that is sustained internally by force of arms, which in turn leads to organized challenge against the state.

The argument here is that despite external constraints, resourceful and committed leadership lays out a vision within a framework of ideas that galvanizes the citizens into working for the interest of the common good rather than forcing them to look for ways to thwart government efforts on the basis of their conviction that the government considers them irrelevant. The extent to which the foregoing problems can be solved will largely be a function of how the relationship between the state and civil society can be enhanced. In this respect, the colonially inherited culture of state violence and unresponsiveness to citizens must end in order to allow the state to serve the public interest within a framework of ideas that are internally generated in each consolidated state through citizens' commitment to building a society/state that they would be proud to defend with the resources at their disposal. Conditions that result in conflict as 'a process of interaction between two or more parties that seek to thwart, injure, or destroy their opponent because they perceive they have incompatible goals or interests' (Berkovitch and Jackson 1997: 2) are likely to be reduced and/or brought to an end when various African states are consolidated and are led by public officials (men and women) who are good stewards of the public trust. Precolonial conflicts in Africa afforded the losers the option of living under the norm of the larger group or movement into a different territory. Rarely did such conflicts result in one party completely exterminating the other. Indeed, most social formations in Africa were confined within manageable geographic territory occupied by the same ethnic/linguistic group with loyalty and obedience to the leaders based on the leaders' ability to provide for the group's economic needs. In most precolonial African social formations, people were not confined to specific land areas by coercion and force. In situations where force was necessary to hold the group together, individuals usually had the option to leave the group for another. Thus, the consolidated states will only be formalising an already existing practice where several ethnically related Africans move between state boundaries, especially in sub-Saharan Africa where conflicts and elite ignorance of the plight of the masses are rampart. And contrary to Jeffrey Herbst's argument that the weak nature of states in Africa is not because of the size of the states, but rather the vast geography but low population density (2000: esp. ch. 5-6), it is the small size, the existence of unofficially governed territories, poor leadership and the concentration of centers of power and authority at the center that have reduced the effectiveness of African states in discharging their responsibilities.

Consequently, to the extent that colonial boundaries are not redesigned, citizens remain trapped within the institutional structures of bygone colonial power systems that located the authority and power of governments away from the people and in capital cities. Concentration of power within the capital cities further reduced any notions of territorial integrity of the state. In this respect, most government officials are neither concerned about the welfare of the rural inhabitants of their respective states nor engaged in formulating and implementing policies that aim to integrate or link the rural areas to the capital cities. Policies that strategically integrate the rural areas into the larger political system through consolidating and enhancing state institutions and power will tend to eliminate territory as a source of conflict. In the process, they will yield a platform for solving problems of political violence and civil wars in Africa.

Notes

1. See Population Research Bureau website at http://www.prb.org. See also African Population and Health Research Center data online at http://www.aphrc.org.
2. The current chapter brings together most of my arguments on political reforms and conflict management in Africa. See the following works for references: Kalu 2001a, b, c; Kalu 2003; Kalu 2004; Kalu 2006; Kalu 2009a, b; Kalu and Kim 2009; Kalu and Soyinka-Airewele 2009.
3. Although Alexis de Tocqueville's writing was mainly on the absence of aristocratic tradition in the United States, his analysis of the impact of law on land tenure and its relationship to communal continuity and change applies to Africa. See "The Striking feature in the social condition of the Anglo-Americans is that it is essentially democratic," in Tocqueville 1966: 43-50.
4. This section draws from my earlier work on constitutionalism and management of contentious issues in Nigerian politics. See Kalu 2001a.
5. Much of the problem with governance in Africa will be resolved when individual entities are not largely categorized on the bases of indigeneity, gender, class, or religion. Such an effort has to be part of a new social and constitutional compact between all nationals so that citizenship is purposefully entrenched as the principal identity in each African state.
6. For a full discussion of the logic underlying the state reconstitution argument, see Kalu 2001c.
7. The ideas advanced so far are likely to generate questions about their viability. I do believe that it is only through imagining and giving substance to things imagined that human development is possible. The radical ideas are not so radical when one looks back in history on the bold initiatives that resulted in the formation of a United States of America out of the thirteen colonies, and the European Union, which has become a very viable player in the global economy and a strong challenger to the United States for control of the international marketplace. To those who would doubt the viability of these ideas, I ask: Why not Africans?
8. Yes, there have been many national conferences and/or truth finding and reconciliation commissions, but except for the cases of South Africa and Ghana, most of these post-Cold War national commissions in (at least from the elites' perspective) Africa (for example, Chad, Rwanda, Uganda, Zimbabwe, Benin, and Nigeria) remain highly deceptive in their intent, and therefore their outcomes are irrelevant as public policy instruments.

613

References

African Population and Health Research Center data online at http://www.aphrc.org.

Bercovitch, Jacob and Richard Jackson. 1997. *International conflict: A chronological encyclopedia of conflicts and their management 1945-1995.* Washington, DC: Congressional Quarterly.

Chazan, Naomi, Lewis Peter, Robert Mortimer, Donald Rothchild, and Stephen John Stedman. 1999. *Politics and society in contemporary Africa*, 3rd edition. Boulder, Colorado: Lynne Rienner Publishers.

Duvall, Raymond and John R. Freeman. 1981. 'The state and dependent capitalism'. *International Studies Quarterly* 25 (1): 99-118.

Herbst, Jeffrey. 2000. *States and power in Africa: Comparative lessons in authority and control.* Princeton, New Jersey: Princeton University Press.

Jackson, Richard. 2006. 'Africa's wars: Overview, causes and the challenges of conflict transformation'. In: *Ending Africa's wars: Progressing to peace*, edited by Oliver Furley and Roy May, pp. 15-29. Abingdon, Oxon: Ashgate Publishing Limited.

Kalu, Kelechi A. 2001a. 'Constitutionalism in Nigeria: A conceptual analysis of ethnicity and politics'. *The Nigerian Juridical Review* 8: 53-84.

— . 2001b. 'Ethnicity and political economy of Africa: a conceptual analysis'. In: *The issue of political ethnicity in Africa* edited by E. Ike Udogu, 35-58). Aldershot, England: Ashgate Publishers.

—. 2001c. 'The political economy of state reconstitution in Africa'. In: *Contending issues in African development: Advances, challenges, and the future,* edited by Obioma M. Iheduru, pp. 19-44. Westport, Connecticut: Greenwood Press.

—. 2003. 'An elusive quest? Structural analysis of conflicts and peace in Africa'. In: *Conflict resolution and peace education in Africa,* edited by Ernest Uwazie, pp. 19-38. Lanham, MD: Lexington Books.

—. 2004. *Agenda setting and public policy in Africa.* Burlington, Vermont, and Aldershot, England: Ashgate Publishers.

—. 2005. 'Global liberalism and indigenous governance in Africa'. In: Olufemi Vaughan, Write and Small, (eds.), *Globalization and marginalization: Essays on the paradoxes of global and local forces*, edited by Olufemi Vaughan et al., pp. 174-200. Ibadan, Nigeria: Sefer Press.

—. 2006. 'The impact of leadership on public policy in Africa: Problems and opportunities'. In: *Ethics, law and society*, edited by Jennifer Gunning and Soren Holm, Volume II , pp. 135-56. Aldershot, England: Ashgate Publishers.

—. 2009a. 'Political institutions and official development assistance in Africa'. *International Studies Review* (South Korea) 10 (2): 1-29.

—. 2009b. 'Resolving African crises: leadership role for African states and the African Union'. *African Journal of Conflict Resolution* 9 (1): 9-40.

Kalu, Kelechi A., and Jiyoung Kim. 2009. 'Political economy of development assistance: Lessons from South Korea for sub-Saharan Africa'. *International Studies Review* (South Korea) 10 (1): 29-52.

Kalu, Kelechi A., and Peyi Soyinka-Airewele, eds. 2009. *Socio-political scaffolding and the constitutionalism and democratic governance in Africa*. Trenton, New Jersey, and Asmara, Eritrea: Africa World Press.

Mbaku, John Mukum. 2004. *Institutions and development in Africa*. Trenton, New Jersey, and Asmara, Eritrea: Africa World Press.

Pagden, Anthony. 1988. 'The genesis of 'governance' and Enlightenment conceptions of the cosmopolitan world order'. *International Social Science Journal* 50 (55): 7-15.

Pierre, Clastres. 1994. *Archeology of violence*. New York: Semiotext (E).

Population Research Bureau . http://www.prb.org .

Stoker, Gerry. 1998. 'Governance as theory: Five propositions'. *International Social Science Journal* 50 (155): 17-28.

Tocqueville, Alexis de. 1966. *Democracy in America*, edited by J. P. Mayer and Max Lerner, a new translation by George Lawrence. New York: Harper and Row Publishers.

CHAPTER 21

Conclusion: Towards Territoriality, Peace Building and Conflict Transformation

Ufo Okeke-Uzodike and John Moolakkattu

There is a general belief that conflicts in Africa are often motivated by the quest for resource capture by ethnic groups who find the opportunity structure favourable to them in an environment of state incapacity. Given the relatively few border-related conflicts on the African continent, the issue of territoriality as a factor contributing to conflict causation and manifestation has been largely sidelined until recently. This volume has brought into focus not only the lingering problem of territoriality but also the need to recast or imagine it as a useful way of looking at the many civil conflicts in Africa even as it describes the different ways by which the imagining and contestation over space takes place in individual contexts. It can be seen that territoriality provides the template around which many of these conflicts over resource-access and use as well as citizenship rights are framed and challenged.

In their study on protracted internal violent conflicts between governments and insurgent groups, which they characterised as 'enduring internal rivalries' (EIR), Matthew Fuhrmann and Jaroslav Tir (2007 and 2009) enquired into whether separatist claims to territory increase the impacts of such conflicts in terms of their proclivity to evolve into a long-lasting (enduring) dispute that tends to lead to violence, its periodic recurrence, and shorter periods ('spells') of peace than other (nonterritorial) forms of conflict. The authors conclude that internal territorial conflicts do contribute to the development of enduring internal rivalries, and that EIRs involving territory are 'particularly problematic in terms of conflict recurrence and shortening of the periods of post-conflict peace' (Fuhrmann and Tir 2007: 1). They maintain that 'territorial issues dominate EIRs even though less than one-half of domestic armed conflicts are fought over territory' (Fuhrmann and Tir 2007: 2). Based on their findings, Fuhrmann and Tir conclude that territory matters significantly: conflicts without a territorial component tend to be comparatively less problematic than those with one. Reviewing previous literature, Fuhrmann and Tir found that there has been a focus on territorial aspects of the onset of internal conflict. Yet, most studies sought to reduce lingering conflicts to issues of ethnicity and identity while ignoring territory as a principal focus of research. They argue that, as a result, there is a lack of understanding of why territory is such an important contributor to conflict.

In many ways, territorial armed conflicts manifesting at intrastate and interstate levels markedly distinguish the present post-Cold War world system from older world systems. Postcolonial Africa, especially in the post-Cold War era, is characterised by a 'plethora of armed conflicts, civil wars, and brutal struggles for control over financial revenues and territories of *blood diamonds'* (Orogun (2004: 151) as well as over agricultural land, water, and oil resources (Muhammed 1997: 143-51). This has led Solomon Gomes (2004) to ask if 'Africa will ever know peace'. Africa has not known peace because territoriality as a source and characteristic of conflict has not received adequate scholarly attention or hard-nosed engagement from political leaders within and among nations. However, a number of studies have drawn attention to the territoriality dimension of conflicts. For example, Wallensteen and Sollenberg (1995: 348) observe that many wars experienced in the post-Cold War era such as those in Angola, Chechnya, Mali, Niger, Nigeria, Senegal, Sudan, and Yemen have territorial dimensions that take the form of 'challenges to the existing states'. Goertz and Diehl (1992), Vasquez (1993), Hensel (1996), and Walter (2003) have also addressed the significance of territoriality to conflicts in different regions of the world.

The authors of the individual chapters of this book carry on the scholarly effort to provide an illustration of the salience of territory to the myriad conflicts being experienced all across Africa. They show that there are a wide range of conflicts over: access to land; sea and border routes for international trade; control over natural resources; colonialism and boundary demarcation; claims over citizenship rights; and population growth and urbanisation. However, it is worth noting the position of Nsamba (chapter 8) and Mbaku (chapter 15) that elite manipulation plays a critical role in the breakout of armed conflicts over territories. No point will be served in restating the arguments presented by our various authors. This concluding note will therefore attempt to focus on what is common to the various chapters, with a view to mapping a way forward for dealing with the problem of territorial conflicts in Africa.

One common thread among the various authors is that territorial conflicts have increased and intensified because of poor governance and have resulted in failed and failing states, human insecurity, and the recourse to self-help including armed resistance to the state. This creates a vicious cycle of poor governance breeding armed conflicts, and armed conflicts further reducing the capacity of a state to govern. The breaking of this vicious circle requires human effort primarily-- especially the political will on the part of all protagonists (local, national, and international) to resolve the conflicts through unarmed and peaceful interactions and processes.

This book has attempted to describe how competing claims to citizenship, land, and authority have created a 'politics of belonging' in many African States, a phenomenon that has brought nativity and territoriality to the centre of the discourse. As Berry explains: 'Like claims to land, competing claims to citizenship frequently turned on questions of historical precedent, giving rise to debates over descent, cultural heritage and territorial origin that both reinforced the salience of these categories as sources of social and political entitlement, and challenged efforts to clarify their significance for contemporary claims to property and authority' (2009: 26). Anthony Smith talks about *ethnoscapes* and *miniscapes*. By ethnoscape he means 'a terrain invested with ethnic significance such that a particular landscape is no longer simply the sum total of fields and valleys, mountains and rivers in a given area, much less the abstractions of lines and contours on a map, but the fields where 'our ancestors' worked, the rivers which have watered 'our lands' and the hills and valleys where 'our forefathers and mothers' are laid to rest'. 'Miniscapes', in contrast, are entities that link 'a local population to a much more circumscribed terrain'. According to Smith (1999: 16-17), both of these are part of the process of 'territorialization of memory' and the 'sanctification of territory' that takes place in its wake.

State Capacity

Most of the previous chapters make references to a range of issue areas: different African States (Democratic of Congo, Nigeria, Somalia, Sudan, Uganda, and Zimbabwe) battling with the problem of state failure; the increasing incapacity of states to function within the framework of the *Weberian* state; and increasing levels of human insecurity. Though contested, the idea of state capacity refers to the ability of a government to control its territory and govern the state effectively (Wang 1995: 89). High state capacity would entail fewer opportunities for rebellion and ability to suppress rebellions as and when they arise (Raleigh 2010: 86). It is instructive that reputedly seven of the top ten failed states in the world are African and fourteen of the top twenty are African and include two of Africa's largest economies, Nigeria and Kenya (*Foreign Policy* 2011). Though countries of the Maghreb did not feature prominently among the top quarter of the world's failed states, the longstanding autocratic governments in Algeria, Egypt, Libya, and Tunisia fell in 2011 due to violent protests, and Morocco's monarchy is currently facing serious regime challenge. In essence, governments in many African countries have come under severe (sometimes violent) pressures with some struggling to maintain the capacity to govern in an environment without conflict and violence. When capricious rule is accompanied by lack of the will and capacity to address ethnic and/or resource-related grievances, a situation emerges that is conducive to the persistence-- rather than resolution or transformation--of conflict.

Human Insecurity

One consequence of this growing loss of capacity to govern is the increasing failure of the state to respond appropriately to accelerating negative global economic conditions, which have imposed increasing burdens on Africa's dependent economies that are already challenged to meet the basic needs of their citizens. Not surprisingly, many such governments are experiencing mounting difficulties with not only the maintenance of law and order and the security needs of their citizens, but also the capacity to uphold the territorial integrity of their nations. Given these circumstances, nonstate actors, including militias, have stepped in to fill the vacuum, easily mobilising aggrieved masses to agitate for primordial interests-including nascent and resuscitated territorial and border issues. As the state responds to increasing lawlessness with belligerent repression, it has also become more disconnected from the people who fall back on ethnicity and territoriality to address their needs. Once entrenched, nonstate actors-- especially the militias with access to wealth from natural resources- often adopt some of the behaviour patterns (greediness as well as nontransparent, unaccountable, and personal leadership) characteristic of the national political leadership. In Angola, for instance, it is estimated that the National Union for the Total Independence of Angola (UNITA) earned over US$ 4billion between 1992 and 1998. Similarly, in Sierra Leone, the Revolutionary United Front (RUF) received an estimated US$ 125 million from the sale of diamonds in the European market in 1999 alone (Akokpari 2007: 27-28). With such financial opportunities on offer, it is understandable why nonstate actors can become more daring and difficult to dislodge.

The persistence of horizontal inequalities also adds a new dimension to conflict in that in the absence of proactive state policies, there is a differential appropriation and distribution of resources. When the indigeneity discourse is superimposed on such inequalities, the result can be even more intransigent (Ukiwo 2009: 500).

Territorial conflicts undermine economic and social infrastructure development as they divert scarce resources away from education, healthcare, communications and transportation networks, and agriculture among others in favour of arms acquisition and troop maintenance, with the net result of increased unemployment, poverty, and insecurity for the mass of the people. In essence, rising frustration over widespread unemployment, poverty, and insecurity in most African States cannot be divorced from the cases presented in previous chapters. In this regard, Mngomezulu (chapter 12) argues from the viewpoint that economic inequality plays a critical role in the recurrent intraterritorial conflict in the Niger-Delta region of Nigeria. Similarly, working within the framework of the frustration-aggression thesis, Imbua (chapter 11) takes the position that the militancy and violence of the Movement for the Survival of the Ogoni People (MOSOP) is founded in the dissatisfaction and frustration of the peoples of Nigeria's Niger-Delta over the state's failure to respond to their demands over the years. This is also the case with the 'northern problem' in Zimbabwe, which Mhlanga (chapter 18) examines in his essay. For his part, Morris (chapter 8) also highlights how structural imbalances have contributed significantly to the northern Uganda conflicts. Sarwuan's (chapter 14) calls for a nonconventional traditional peacemaking process clearly points to the incapacity of the state to maintain peace and order within its territory.

Regional Capacity

Exacerbating the loss of capacity to govern as well as human insecurity is the lack of regional capacity to deal with intrastate conflicts, which often impose severe burdens on neighbouring and other states. Armed groups often operate from border regions and armed conflicts and violence generate not only internally displaced persons but also refugees. For example, the conflicts and violence in countries such as the Democratic Republic of Congo, Liberia, Somalia, Sudan, and Zimbabwe have had huge negative effects in many other countries in Africa, thus assuming a regional dimension. Population displacements due to conflicts and violence lead to emigration to areas away from the conflict zones, which are often relatively strong economic centres. However, such unplanned population movements create a loss of state capacity to meet the socioeconomic needs of the host communities. In turn, the breakdown in host state capacity may lead to interethnic conflicts and xenophobic attacks (for example Côte d'Ivoire, Kenya, and South Africa) and strained interstate relations between affected countries. Another aspect of the problem of lack of regional capacity to deal with armed conflicts and violence is inherited colonial boundaries that often divide people of the same ancestry, language, or culture among different states. Regional capacity is also undermined by loss of neutrality and impartiality in the affairs of neighbouring states, the existence of regional hegemons, and lack of financial means.

The Way Forward

The contributors to this volume have made appreciable efforts to propose processes that may be employed to mitigate or resolve territorial conflicts on the continent, but there seems to be no definite agreement among them on the way forward. Giving the differing sets of expert views, we will highlight a number of ways forward. These include: good governance; the development of strong states; the development of regional capacity; and peacebuilding through conflict transformation and human development. Clearly, all such strategies will require strong political will and commitment.

State capacity building is a starting point for conflict resolution in Africa. Strong states have the capacity to address the needs of their citizens and reduce their propensity for collective and organized violence, and also limit the escalation of dissensions and insurgency within the state (Sobek 2010: 267). Similarly, Braithwaite (2010) has also argued that strong state capacity insulates a state from violence given the fact that the state possesses the capability to resist any form of civil violence within its territory. Strong states are often driven by good leadership and good governance-often reflected in the form of transparent and accountable governance structures and democratic institutions. States degenerate into weak or failed ones as a result of widespread corruption, bad leadership, human rights violation, authoritarianism, and failed elections. Many states in Africa are characterised by the foregoing. In this respect, Rotberg (2003: 22) rightly argues that 'state failure is largely manmade, not accidental.' He further underscores the point:

> Wherever there has been state failure or collapse, human agency has engineered the slide from strength or weakness and willfully presided over profound and destabilizing resource shifts from the state to the ruling few. As those resource transfers accelerated and human rights abuses mounted, countervailing violence signified the extent to which states in question had broken fundamental social contracts and become hollow receptacles of personalist privilege, and national impoverishment. (Rotberg 2003: 23)

Given its human agency, the redress process of state failure, as noted by Isike and Okeke Uzodike (chapter 17), necessarily requires appropriate human intervention and positive reorientation of leadership towards the transformation of the factors that drive and shape intergroup conflicts and state failure. This, as Mngomezulu (chapter 12) argues with regard to the marginalisation of resource-bearing communities in the Niger Delta region of Nigeria, requires strong political will. Basically, in the case of the Niger Delta, the resolution of the conflict may entail: acknowledgment of the contributions of the region to the economy of the nation by the national government; acceptance by both the national government and the multinational corporations exploiting the region's natural resources that the issues raised by the communities are real and deserve to be addressed urgently; and the will and commitment by the government and the international oil companies to work with local communities in addressing the relevant issues.

Mhlanga (chapter 18), Mbaku (chapter 15) and Kalu (chapter 20) recommend institutional reforms and political and administrative restructuring in which the people, rather than the elite, will be the driving force, both for generating ideas and implementing the plan. Mhlanga calls for devolution of powers to regional and local bodies for the operation of an efficient federal system in which 'regional administrators must work in tandem with all the political actors and not act like shock absorbers protecting local populations against tough indiscriminate measures of the central government,' and 'a bottom-up approach' to policy 'involving people in all the planning stages, policy formulation and implementation stages' is adopted. Umukoro holds the view that reforming and strengthening institutions to deal with the problems of political and administrative corruption, environmental scarcity, and structural violence in the Niger Delta region with respect to air, land, and water pollution is the key to the crisis in the region.

Existing regional frameworks should be strengthened to prevent and/or resolve armed conflicts and violence in Africa. The AU, unlike the OAU, has shown some seriousness in intervening in states to restore good governance, most especially in response to crisis situations, by putting in place the Peace and Security Council (PSC), which operates in collaboration with Regional Economic Communities (RECs) in the subregions of Africa. In addition, there are other structures supported by AU that seek to emplace mechanisms that will ensure the prevention and resolution of conflicts. These include the Conference on Security, Stability, Development and Cooperation in Africa (CSSDCA) as a monitoring mechanism to make African leaders more accountable and transparent; the NEPAD's African Peer Review Mechanism (APRM) to promote democratic governance in Africa; and the Panel of the Wise to assist the Peace and Security Council on matters related to conflict prevention, management, and resolution (Alexander et al. 2003; King and Verge 2009: 2). Related to strengthening regional frameworks, Nwoko (chapter 3) suggests, following the example of Nigeria and Cameroon, that Mixed Commissions provide workable mechanisms for addressing interstate territorial disputes before they degenerate into armed conflicts. He holds that the country ceding territory may have to go an additional step of granting its former citizens dual citizenship to minimise the frustrations they will likely face in their new environment and discourage a recourse to armed struggle. Tandia (chapter 7) concludes that 'cross-border governmentalities of peacebuilding and security governance' are required to successfully 'mitigate the throes of conflictuality in the borderlands' of Casamance and in many conflicts in West Africa.

Nyuykonge (chapter 16) reaches a similar conclusion that people should not be allowed to 'wallow in despondency in a postconflict dispensation that inspires new hope [given that neglect] can ignite conflict when patience for a better nation runs out'. Nyuykonge further holds that '[i]n order to avoid conflict resurgence, postconflict reconstruction should be pioneered by locals who will own the concept, the process, and the product.' Some countries have tried to create more encompassing identities from the above. For example, in Rwanda, the discourse of Hutu as autochthon and Tutsi as foreigner has been replaced by a discourse of all Rwandan citizenship. Whether such top-down notions can really bring reconciliation and remove the weight of the past is a serious question worth pondering. Peacebuilding predicated on human development is seen as a means to meaningful conflict resolution and management on the continent. This framework presupposes that peace transcends the absence of war and violence. It emphasises a solution to the *root cause(s)* of conflicts. The root causes of war and conflicts in states are traced to the lack of access to basic human needs and absence of structures to enhance their provision. As a result, it emphasises a peace process that encompasses all aspects of the state that include institutional capacity building, promotion of good governance, and socioeconomic development (United Nations 2009: 9-10). The promotion of human security is a necessary ingredient for the prevention and resolution of conflict and entails '...the effort to promote human security in societies marked by conflict. The overarching goal of peace building is to strengthen the capacity of manage conflict without violence, as a means to achieve human security' (United Nations 2009: 11).

Building state capacity is to be founded on the promotion of good governance and democratisation. For armed conflicts, most especially the territorial ones, to be meaningfully resolved, it is imperative that people's trust in the state must be restored. Democracy should translate into meaningful development in human terms. There should also be a focus on the empowerment of the people through not only the creation of opportunities for employment but also the provision of basic needs such as education, health care, housing, and water. Horizontal inequalities can be addressed only if conscious policies aimed at achieving balanced development are adopted by a development-oriented state, a stage that most African States are yet to reach. In summary, Kofi Annan (1998) suggests the following for peace building in Africa: good governance; respect for human rights and rule of law; promotion of public accountability; enhancement of administrative capacity; strengthening democratic governance; implementation of reforms and creation of enabling environment for investment.

In essence, then, territorial conflicts (in all of its manifestations) serve to deter or retard development. In Africa, territorial conflicts not only destroy national stability and peace, but also challenge and expose the hollowness of the so-called national developmental efforts of individual governments. Quite aside from deterring new productive investments, they often destroy social infrastructure such as roads, bridges, hospitals, schools, water supply systems, and even farm lands. To exacerbate matters, many of the resources required funding developmental projects, such as education, agriculture, and health care facilities, are redirected and wasted on arms purchases and the maintenance of order, including ostensibly the mitigation of conflict. Collier et al. (2003), for instance, estimated that the Angolan war guzzled a staggering US$ 54 billion. Similarly, it was estimated that the cost of armed conflicts in Africa (most of which were territorial in origin) between 1990 and 2005 exceeded USD 300 billion--an amount that equals the overall Overseas Development Assistance in the region for the same period (UNDP 2007).

Such estimates do not account for the human costs, which are unquantifiable in terms of financial costs of wasted and lost lives and opportunities. Given such contexts and costs, there is a clear and growing need to better understand the territorial origins of African conflicts. The link of such understanding to the sustainable resolution of the region's many conflicts associated with issues of territoriality has never been more urgent. This fact is further amplified by emerging conflicts in South Sudan/Sudan, Somalia and the Horn subregion, and elsewhere. Further, more intensive and systematic research is now needed not only on the implications of territorial conflicts, but also on the best ways to stem the emergence and effects of such conflicts through the emplacement of appropriate transformation systems.

References

Akokpari, J. 2007. The political economy of human insecuirty in sub-Saharan Africa. Institute of Developing Economies, Chiba (Japan): Japan External Trade Organization VRF Series, No. 431

Alexander, L., A. Higazi, J. Mackie, J. Niño-Perez, A. and Sherriff. 2003. *Regional approaches to conflict prevention in Africa: European support to African processes*. Maastricht: ECDPM.

Annan, K. 1998. *The causes of conflict and the promotion of durable peace and sustainable development in Africa*. Report presented to the United Nations' Security Council on 16 April.

Berry S. 2009. 'Property, authority and citizenship: Land claims, politics and the dynamics of social division in West Africa'. *Development and Change* 40 (1): 23-45.

Braithwaite, A. 2010. 'Resisting infection: How state capacity conditions conflict contagion'. *Journal of Peace Research* 47 (3): 311-19.

The Foreign Policy Group. 2010. http ://www .foreign policy.com /articles/2011/06/17/2011_failed_states_index_interactive_map_an d_rankings (accessed 15 Sept. 2011).

Fuhrmann, M. and J. Tir. 2007. 'Territorial dimensions of enduring internal rivalries'. Paper prepared for the Annual Meeting of the American Political Science Association, Chicago, 31 Aug.-2 Sept...

----------. 2009. "Territorial dimensions of enduring internal rivalries'. *Conflict Management and Peace Science* 26 (4): 307-30.

Goertz, G. and P. Diehl. 1992. *Territorial changes and international conflict*. Oxford: Routledge.

Gomes, S. 2004. 'Wars and conflicts: Will Africa ever know peace?' *African Renaissance* 1 (3): 44-49.

Hensel, P. 1996. 'Charting a course to conflict: Territorial issues and interstate conflict, 1816-1992'. *Conflict Management and Peace Science* 15: 43-73.

King, M. and D. Verge. 2009. *Preventing violent conflict in Africa*. New York, Brussels, Moscow: East West Institute.

Muhammed, N.A.L. 1996. 'Environmental conflict in Africa'. In: *Conflict and the environment*, edited by N.P. Gleditsch. Dordrecht, the Netherlands: Kluwer Academic Publishers.

Orogun, P. 2004. '"Blood diamonds" and Africa's armed conflicts in the post-Cold War era'. *World Affairs* 166 (3): 151-61.

Raleigh C. 2010. 'Political marginalization, climate change, and conflict in African Sahel states'. *International Studies Review* 12 (1): 69-86.

Rotberg, R. 2003.' Failed states, collapsed states, weak states: Causes and indicators'. In: *State Failure and State Weakness in a Time of Terror*, edited by R. Robert, pp.1-26. Washington, DC: Brookings Institution Press.

Smith A.D. 1999. 'Sacred territories and national conflict'. *Israel Affairs* 5 (4): 13-31.

Sobek, D. 2010. 'Masters of their domains: The role of state capacity in civil wars'. *Journal of Peace Research* 47 (3): 267-71.

Ukiwo ,Ukoha. 2009) 'between "senior brother" and "overlord": competing versions of horizontal inequalities and ethnic conflict in Calabar and Warri, Nigeria'. *Journal of International Development* 21: 495–506.

United Nations. 2009. 'Human security and peace building in Africa: The need for an inclusive approach'http: //www. un.org/Africa/osaa/reports/human_security_peacebuilding_africa.p df (accessed 21 Sept. 2011).

Vasquez, J. 1993. 'Why do neighbors fight?' *Journal of Peace Research* 32 (3): 277-93.

Wallensteen, P. and M. Sollenberg. 1995. 'After the Cold War: Emerging patterns of armed conflict 1989-94'. *Journal of Peace Research* 32 (3): 345-60.

Walter, B.F. 2003. 'Explaining the intractability of territorial conflict'. *International Studies Review* 5 (4): 137-53.

Wang, S. 1995. 'The rise of the regions: fiscal reform and the decline of central state capacity in China'. In: The waning of the communist state, edited by Andrew G. Walder. Berkeley, USA: University of California Press.

Biographic Profiles-Territoriality, Citizenship and Peacebuilding

Pita Ogaba Agbese is Professor of Political Science and Director of the Center for International Security and Conflict Studies at the University of Northern Iowa. Professor Agbese received his PhD from Northwestern University in 1984. Previously, he served as Acting Chair of the Department of Political Science at the University of Northern Iowa. He has published extensively on issues such as civil-military relations in Africa, democratization in Africa, civil society in Africa, the environment in Africa, and civil conflicts in Africa. His most recent publication is a co-edited volume with George Klay Kieh, Jr., *The Military and Politics in Africa: From Engagement to Democratic and Constitutional Control* (2004).

Adekunle Awuwo, Professor of Political Science and International Relations, is a former Head of Politics at the University of the North (now the University of Limpopo), South Africa, former Executive Secretary of the African Association of Political Science (AAPS), and former Academic Coordinator, School of Politics, University of KwaZulu Natal (UKZN), Howard College Campus, Durban. He is currently Senior Analyst, Nigeria with the International Crisis Group West Africa Project, Dakar, Senegal. He has varied research interests and is widely published. *(From the Internet, not AA)*

Joseph R.A. Ayee is Professor and Deputy Vice Chancellor and Head, College of Humanities, University of KwaZulu-Natal, South Africa. He is the immediate past Dean, Faculty of Social Studies, University of Ghana, and Legon and also served as the Head, Department of Political Science. He has published widely in the field of public administration and policy; some of the publications have appeared in the *International Review of Administrative Sciences*, *Public Administration and Development*, *Democratization*, *Electoral Studies*, *African Studies Review*, *African Affairs* and *Development Policy Review*. He is a member of the Editorial Board of *The Journal of Modern African Studies* and a Fellow of the Ghana Academy of Arts and Sciences. He has successfully supervised 12 PhD and over 30

MPhil theses. His research interests include governance, natural resource policy, tax administration and port reform. Professor Ayee studied at the University of Ghana and The Hebrew University of Jerusalem, Israel where he obtained the MPA and PhD respectively.

Abdul Karim Bangura is professor of Research Methodology and Political Science at Howard University. He also is researcher-in-residence of Abrahamic Connections and Islamic Peace Studies at the Center for Global Peace in the School of International Service at American University. He holds a PhD in Political Science, a PhD in Development Economics, a PhD in Linguistics, a PhD in Computer Science, and a PhD in Mathematics. He is the author of 66 books and more than 550 scholarly articles. He is fluent in about a dozen African and six European languages, and studying to increase his proficiency in Arabic, Hebrew, and Hieroglyphics. He is the recipient of many teaching and other scholarly and community service awards. He also has been a member of many scholarly organizations and has served as President and then United Nations Ambassador of the Association of Third World Studies.

Joseph S. Gbenda is currently an Associate Professor in the Department of Religion & Philosophy, Benue State University Makurdi, and Nigeria. His specializes in African traditional religion and culture. His scholarship is in the areas of religion and ecology, africanization of Christianity, animal studies and local conflicts management in Africa.

David Lishilinimle hails from Begiagbai, Bendi, in the present Obanliku Local Government Area of Cross River State, Nigeria, and lectures at the Department of History and International Studies, University of Calabar. He was the overall best student in the 2001/2002 graduating class of the University of Calabar, a feat which earned him an offer of automatic employment by the University as lecturer in the Department in 2004. He obtained the Ph.D. in African Diaspora History from the University of Calabar in 2009. Dr Imbua is the author of several books, which traverse history and historical fiction, book chapters and articles in learned national and international journals. A widely travelled scholar, Dr` Imbua has permitted the translation of some of his works into French and German for the benefit of the speakers of these international languages.

Christopher Isike researches and teaches African politics at the University of Zululand, South Africa.

Laura Joseph has been has been Assistant Director with the OSU Center for African Studies since 2003. Her other professional experience includes eight years in refugee resettlement, eight years with Catholic Relief Services in various countries in Africa, and two years as a Peace Corps volunteer in Benin. She attended Georgetown University's School of Foreign Service as an undergraduate. She holds an M.A. from Johns Hopkins SAIS and an MPH from OSU.

Kelechi A. Kalu is Professor of African American and African Studies, Associate Provost for Global Strategies and International Affairs and former Director of the Center for African Studies at The Ohio State University. Prior to joining the Department of African American and African Studies at the Ohio State University, Dr. Kalu was a Professor of Political Science at The University of Northern Colorado, Greeley, and Adjunct Professor of African Politics at the Graduate School of International Studies, University of Denver. Professor Kalu is the author of Economic Development and Nigerian Foreign Policy (New York: The Edwin Mellen Press, 2000). His publications include articles in International Journal of Politics, Culture and Society, Africa Today, Journal of Nigerian Affairs, Journal of Asian and African Studies, Journal of Third World Studies, Journal of African Policy Studies, West Africa Review, The Constitution: A Journal of Constitutional Development and several book chapters on African and Third World issues. He is editor of and contributor to Agenda Setting and Public Policy in Africa (Aldershot, U.K and Burlington, VT. U.S. 2004). Dr. Kalu has served as a consultant to the World Bank on Public Sector Governance and for Asian Development Bank on Mongolia. Professor Kalu serves on the editorial board of several journals.

Fredrick Kisekka-Ntale graduated from Makerere University with a degree in Political Science, and later an MA, in international Relations and Diplomatic studies, specializing in International Humanitarian Law. For several years, Fredrick worked as a Researcher at the Makerere Institute of Social Research (MISR), Makerere University. He joined the Institute of African Studies, at the University of Leipzig, Germany, as a Doctoral Fellow and Research Scientist within the Biodiversity Transect and Analysis, and Monitoring Africa Project (BIOTA). In 2008 he received a Doctor of Philosophy (Ph.D) in Resource and Development Politics from the University of Leipzig. He has since re-Joined MISR. His research and academic work explores the relationship between people, resources, and the state in the post-colonial setting, as well as the historical and institutional process of resource management in tropical rural communities. He is currently working on the political economy of managing Uganda's oil wealth. Fredrick has published in the realm of resource politics in varied journal and several widely read publications. He has also continued to provide expert commentaries and opinions.

David Kraybill is Professor of Agricultural, Environmental, and Development Economics at Ohio State University, where his research and teaching focus on food security, climate change, and rural development in Africa. He received an M.S. in Economics from Michigan State University and a PhD in Agricultural Economics from Virginia Tech. He has served as Director of the Center for African Studies at Ohio State University, is a former Fulbright Scholar in Uganda, and currently is Co-Principal Investigator and Project Director for the Innovative Agricultural Research Initiative, a USAID Feed the Future project in Tanzania. He has been consultant with the International Food Policy Research Institute, Rockefeller Foundation, and Southeast Consortium for International Development, U.S. Department of Agriculture, World Bank, and other organizations.

John Mukum Mbaku is Presidential Distinguished Professor of Economics & Willard L. Eccles Professor of Economics and John S. Hinckley Fellow at Weber State University, Ogden, Utah, and former (1986-2007) Associate Editor (Africa), *Journal of Third World*

Studies. He is also a Nonresident Senior Fellow at The Brookings Institution, Washington, D.C. and an Attorney and Counselor at Law, licensed to practice in the Supreme Court of the State of Utah and the U.S. District Court for the District of Utah. He received the Ph.D. (economics) from the University of Georgia and the J.D. (law) and the Graduate Certificate in Natural Resources and Environmental Law from the S. J. Quinney College of Law at the University of Utah. He is a member of the American Bar Association, the Utah State Bar, Davis County (Utah) Bar Association, Utah Minority Bar Association, Southern Economic Association, Association of Third World Studies, Association of Private Enterprise Education, and a Resource Person for the Nairobi (Kenya)-based, African Economic Research Consortium. His research interests are in public choice, constitutional political economy, sustainable development, law and development, international human rights, intellectual property, rights of indigenous groups, trade integration, and institutional reforms in Africa. He has published quite prodigiously in many of the aforementioned areas in the form of books, articles and book chapters. His most recent books are *Culture and Customs of Cameroon* (Greenwood Press, 2005); *Multiparty Democracy and Political Change: Constraints to Democratization in Africa* (Africa World Press, 2006), co-edited with Julius Omozuanvbo Ihonvbere; and *Corruption in Africa: Causes, Consequences, and Cleanups* (Lexington Books, 2007).

Brilliant Mhlanga holds a PhD from the University of Westminster. His major researches are in Cultural Studies, the Dialogics of Community Radio and ethnic minority media. He is currently a Module Leader lecturing Media & Society at the University of Hertfordshire, a Researcher at Africa Media Centre, University of Westminster London and remains a Lecturer at the National University of Science and Technology (NUST), Zimbabwe. He has published in *Ecquid Novi, Critical Arts Journal* and the *Westminster Papers in Communication and Culture* among other peer-reviewed journals. He is currently working on a number of topics, among them a book titled: *Bondage of Boundaries and the 'Toxic Other' in Postcolonial Africa: The Northern Problem and the Identity Politics Today,* and another project provisionally titled: On the Banality of

Evil: Cultural Particularities and Genocide in Africa, this project examines the role of, and mediation of ethnicity, identity politics and the national question in postcolonial Africa with specific reference to Zimbabwe's Gukurahundi genocide. Dr Mhlanga is a holder of several international fellowships, chief among them being the W. K. Kellogg Foundation Fellowship for Indigenous Thought Leaders in Southern Africa and the Prestigious Arch-bishop Desmond Tutu Fellowship. His research interests include: ethnic studies, secessionist studies, nationalism and postcolonial studies, media policies and political economy of the media, and development communication, community radio, and ethnic minority media.

Bhekithemba Richard Mngomezulu is currently working as a Research Coordinator at the Durban University of Technology (DUT), and also serves on temporal basis at the School of Politics at the University of KwaZulu-Natal (UKZN). He serves as a member of Council of the Nelson Mandela Museum (NMM) and at the Council of the Economic History Society of Southern Africa (EHSSA). He has presented more than 40 papers at national and international gatherings, currently has two books under review: one on politics and higher education in East Africa, and another on the president-for-life pandemic in Africa. His research interests are in the comparative history of Africa, particularly its ethnic, religious, party and territorial conflicts.

John S Moolakkattu is Director of the School of Gandhian Thought and Development Studies, Mahatma Gandhi University, Kottayam, Kerala, India. He read at Jawaharlal Nehru University, Hyderabad Central University, University of Bradford (UK) and Mahatma Gandhi University majoring in Political Science, Peace Studies and International Relations. Between July 2008 and June 2010, he was the inaugural Gandhi-Luthuli Professorial Chair in Peace Studies at School of Politics, University of KwaZulu-Natal (UKZN), Durban, South Africa, and a Professor at IIT Madras.

John has published five books (three edited and two co-authored) and 71 research articles in rated national and international journals such as *Public Administration and Development*, *Cooperation and*

Conflict, Asian Journal of Women's Studies, Indian Journal of Gender Studies, Peace Review, Economic and Political Weekly, International Studies, and *India Quarterly*. He is the recipient of academic awards like Commonwealth Scholarship, Commonwealth Fellowship, UGC Research Award and Fulbright Visiting Professorship. He has been serving as the Editor of *Gandhi Marg* (quarterly), the premier Journal in Gandhian Studies published from New Delhi, for the last six years and is one of the founding editors of the South African Journal, *Ubuntu: Journal of Conflict Transformation.*

His areas of interest/specialisation include peace and conflict resolution studies, international relations theory, participatory planning, local governance, deliberative democracy, gender, Gandhian studies and African political economy. Address: Moolakkattu, Kidangoor P.O, Kottayam, Kerala, India - 686572. Mob: 8943688388; Email: moolakkattu@gmail.com

Nsamba Morris is a Research and Advocacy Officer with the Refugee Law Project at the School of Law, Makerere University, Uganda.

Kenneth Chukwuemeka Nwoko is a lecturer in the Department of History & International Relations Redeemer's University, Nigeria. He received his BA, MA (History) and PhD (History & Strategic Studies) from the University of Lagos, Nigeria. He researches into African history and international relations. He has published extensively in scholarly journals and contributed chapters in edited books. His publications include among others, "Folklore, Society and African Historical Reconstruction" *Journal of Black and African Arts and Civilization, (JBAAC)* Vol.5 No 1,2011,pp.193-205; "Labor Migration, Economic Practices and Cultural Identity among the Igbo in Modern Nigeria" in Apollos Nwauwa and Chima J. Korieh (eds.) *Against All Odds: The Igbo Experience in Postcolonial Nigeria* Trenton, NJ: Goldline and Jacobs Publishing, 2011, pp.239-256; "A Bleak Future, A Wasted Generation: Child Soldier in Africa" *Africana* Volume 5, No. 3, 2011, pp.68-99; "Trade Unionism and Governance in Nigeria: A Paradigm Shift from Labour Activism to Political Opposition," *Information, Society & Justice* Volume 2 No. 2, (June 2009): 139-152,

"Traditional Psychiatric Healing in Igboland, Southeastern Nigeria," *African Journal of History and Culture* Volume 1 No. 2 (June 2009): 36-43. Dr Nwoko is a laureate of CODERIA's Afro-Arab Advance Institute Rabat, Morocco. He is presently concluding research on the Afro-Arab cooperation in the era of global oil politics and new energy regime.

Charles Nyuykonge is a Doctoral Fellow at the University of the Witwatersrand, South Africa. Charles has previously worked a Policy Consultant for the African Union's African Peace and Security Program (APSP) housed at the Institute of Peace and Security Studies (IPSS), University of Addis Ababa. His research interests are broadly on mediation and conflict resolution; foreign policy and African's international relations; post-conflict peacebuilding and reconstruction in Africa; managing transitional justice and peace agreements.

Gudrun Østby (b. 1977) has a PhD in political science from the University of Oslo. She is currently senior researcher at the Peace Research Institute Oslo (PRIO) and Deputy Editor of the *Journal of Peace Research*. Her current research interests include horizontal inequalities and conflict; political institutions and conflict, education and conflict, conflict-related gender-based violence, and urban violence. Her work has appeared in journals such as *International Studies Quarterly, Journal of Conflict Resolution, Journal of Development Studies*, and *Journal of Peace Research*.

Hamilton Sipho Simelane is an Associate Professor of Economic History and Development Studies at the University of KwaZulu-Natal, Durban, South Africa. His publications include four books and over thirty articles in refereed journals regionally and internationally. He has also produced several reports for research done for different international organizations. One of his major areas of research interest is conflict arising from resource contestation. His research in this area includes contests over land resulting in conflicts, and economic security conflicts that have redefined the concept of security. He is presently researching on the present fiscal crisis in Swaziland and the attendant conflict as people's economic well-being is undermined.

Hunter Sinclair is a graduate of and former research assistant at the University of Virginia. He is now a strategic planning analyst at Southwind in Nashville, Tennessee. He is the author of several studies pertaining to strategic planning and several book reviews. He has engaged in activities initiated by the Reformed University Fellowship, Seeds of Hope Brazil, Nicaraguan Orphan Fund, and Sigma Alpha Epsilon. He also was awarded the Innovator of the Year Award by the Quorum Health Resources in 2011.

Håvard Strand (b. 1975) has his PhD in political science from the University of Oslo and is currently senior researcher at the Peace Research Institute Oslo (PRIO). His research interests include explaining onset, duration and termination of internal armed conflict; the determinants of stable political systems; the consequences of war and the collection and analysis of quantitative conflict data.

Aboubakr Tandia is a PhD candidate in Political Science at Cheikh Anta Diop University in Dakar. He worked for five years as assistant researcher in the Groupe d'Études et de Recherches sur les Migrations et Faits de Sociétés (GERM) in Gaston Berger University of Saint-Louis in Senegal. His PhD thesis is on the role of religious institutions in conflict prevention and resolution and peace building in independent Senegal (1962-2010). Mr. Tandia is also working with other colleagues on several projects on the role of religion in cross-border integration in Western Senegambia, as well as on the dynamics of peace and conflict in the borderlands of the Upper Casamance. Mr. Tandia has been a laureate of the CODESRIA governance institute in 2007 and the Governance and Development Residential School of the SOAS (London) held in Maputo in 2010 and funded by the Mo Ibrahim Foundation. Mr. Tandia has already published a paper on borderland identities and cross-border governance in Western Senegambia. Other publications on border and refugee regimes and youth politics and popular culture as well as peace, conflict and religion are forthcoming. Mr. Tandia is also co-editor of a couple of forthcoming publications on Governance and Development in Africa and African Youth and Development within the African Young

639

Researchers Network (AYRN) in which he is a founding member.

Ufo Okeke Uzodike is Dean and Head, School of Social Sciences, University of KwaZulu-Natal, South Africa. Uzodike is a Political Scientist with early educational training in Nigeria and further studies at Wake Forest University, the University of South Carolina, and the University of North Carolina, Chapel Hill, USA. His PhD is in the field of Political Science with subfield interests and specializations in International Relations and International Political Economy. Drawing from this training, his research activities straddle the linked and mutually reinforcing areas of governance, conflict and development. Specifically, his publications focus on issue-areas that have particular resonance and relevance for justice, peace, human security and development in Africa such as national foreign policies, regional integration, democratization and economic development, the roles and social rights of women, politics of religion, and conflict transformation. Ufo Okeke Uzodike serves as editor for two Journals: *Affrika: Journal of Politics, Economics and Society;* and *Ubuntu: Journal of Conflict Transformation.*

Index

C

D

644

L

M

646

647

T

U

V

W

Y

Z

www.ingramcontent.com/pod-product-compliance
Lightning Source LLC
Chambersburg PA
CBHW072058040426
42334CB00040B/1302